# Adolescence
*Development, Diversity, and Context*

Series Editor
## Richard M. Lerner
*Tufts University*

## A GARLAND SERIES

# Series Contents

We are especially grateful to Sofia T. Romero, Editor at the Boston College Center for Child, Family, and Community Partnerships, and to Imma De Stefanis, Graduate Research Assistant at the Center, for all their many contributions. Ms. Romero provided us with sage and professional editorial advice. Her wisdom, judgment, and skills enhanced the quality of our work and made it much more productive. Sr. De Stefanis collaborated extensively with us in the selection and organization of the scholarship included in the series. Her knowledge of and enthusiasm for the study of adolescence was an invaluable asset in our work.

We appreciate as well the excellent work of Carole Puccino, Editor at Garland Publishing. Her productivity and organizational skill enabled the volume to be produced with efficiency and quality. Finally, we thank Leo Balk, Vice President of Garland, for his enthusiasm for this project and for his support, encouragment, and guidance.

# Risks and Problem Behaviors in Adolescence

Edited, with an introduction by

Richard M. Lerner
*Tufts University*

Christine M. Ohannessian
*University of Connecticut*

GARLAND PUBLISHING, INC.
A MEMBER OF THE TAYLOR & FRANCIS GROUP
*New York & London*
*1999*

**Library of Congress Cataloging-in-Publication Data**

Risks and problem behaviors in adolescence / edited, with an
introduction by Richard M. Lerner and Christine M. Ohannessian.
    p.   cm. — (Adolescence : development, diversity, and context
; 5)
    Includes bibliographical references.
    ISBN 0-8153-3294-7 (alk. paper)
    1. Problem youth—United States. 2. Risk-taking (Psychology) in
adolescence—United States. 3. Health behavior in adolescence—
United States. I. Lerner, Richard M. II. Ohannessian, Christine M.
III. Series: Adolescence (New York, N.Y.) ; 5.
HV1431.R57 1999
362.74'0973—dc21                     99-33727
                                    CIP

Printed on acid-free, 250-year-life paper
Manufactured in the United States of America

# Contents

# Introduction

## Risk and Problem Behaviors in Adolescence: A View of the Issues

*Richard M. Lerner, **Christine M. Ohannessian*

Adolescent life is embedded in a complicated developmental system involving multiple features of the individual (e.g., biology, emotions, personality, and cognition) and the multiple levels of his or her social ecology (e.g., peers, family, school, the work place, and the public policy and legal systems that structure and impact behavioral opportunities for and the actions of adolescents). The articles in this volume illustrate how development is propelled by the bidirectional relations that occur between the person and all levels of the context.

The uniqueness of these person-context interactions provides a basis for individual differences in the development of risks or, in turn, in being resilient to such development. As such, they constitute as well a window of opportunity for intervening to change person-context relations in a manner that might prevent problem behaviors from occurring and/or that might serve to promote positive development (Lerner, 1986). The several models of the development of risk and resiliency that are found in this volume converge in underscoring the importance of adolescent-context relations for understanding development and for planning actions designed to prevent risk.

### Conceptualizing Adolescent Risk and Problem Behaviors

Traditionally, theoretical and empirical inquiry relating to the origin of adolescent problem behaviors has stressed either psychogenic sources that place a strong emphasis on the individual (e.g., psychoanalytic studies) or, alternatively, sociogenic sources that emphasize the individual's external environment as being the driving force of adolescent behavior (Lerner, 1986). However, contemporary theory and research are rooted in the notion that the bases for adolescent risk and problem behaviors do not lie solely within the individual or his or her environment. Rather, risks are actualized and problem behaviors arise from the dynamic, bidirectional interaction between the person and the multiple levels of his or her ecology (Bronfenbrenner and Morris, 1998; Lerner, 1998).

In essence, then, the relations within this developmental system — actions of youth on their contexts and the influence of contexts on youth — serve to decrease or increase an adolescent's risk for experiencing problem behaviors. Such a conceptualization of adolescent problem behaviors provides — as seen in the first section of this volume, in articles by Compas (1989), Fisher et al. (1996), Jessor (1992), Levitt et al. (1991), and Werner and Smith (1989) — the foundation for the research on adolescent risk and problem behaviors presented in this volume.

Together, the various concepts of the bases of risk and problem behaviors in adolescence stress that focusing on any singular domain of individual functioning (e.g., biology) yields an incomplete picture of development. Moreover, the articles in this volume stress that in order to fully understand the genesis of adolescent problem behaviors, and the individual and contextual conditions that may lead to the actualization of risks or to resilience in the face of problems, adolescent-context relations need to be assessed across time. The Werner and Smith (1989) study is a case-in-point. They note that risk and protective factors change across development; the salience of any given factor varies according to the individual's developmental stage (e.g., childhood versus adolescence).

The articles in this section of the volume have important implications for the design of interventions aimed at adolescent problem behaviors. Since adolescent problem behaviors are not caused by a single factor, and because problem behaviors tend to covary, intervention efforts must be comprehensive. They also must address the multiple levels of the adolescent and of the context. Importantly, Jessor (1992) points out that intervention programs designed to target adolescent problem behaviors should be designed to decrease risk and at the same time increase resiliency. That is, one must both prevent problems and, in turn, provide for or promote positive behaviors. Simply, prevention is not equivalent to promotion.

## Adolescent Internalizing Problems

Similar ideas about the genesis of adolescent problem behaviors are found in the next section of the volume, which focuses on internalizing problem behaviors (e.g., depression). Internalizing problems have been found to be related to characteristics of the individual (e.g., gender, coping skills) and the context (e.g., interpersonal relationships with parents and peers). Both Noam et al. (1994) and Leadbeater et al. (1995) note that a developmental perspective is required to appraise the causal antecedents of adolescent internalizing problems and other instances of developmental psychopathology. For instance, Leadbeater et al. call for a multivariate longitudinal strategy. This strategy should incorporate both individual and contextual factors as possible antecedents or predictors of adolescent internalizing problems. This approach should also take into account issues relating to diversity, given the fact that during adolescence, girls are significantly more likely to experience internalizing problems than are boys (Cohen et al., 1993; Nolen-Hoeksema, 1994; Ohannessian et al., 1996).

The papers in this section demonstrate that intervention programs need to incorporate both individual (e.g., personality) and contextual (e.g., poor family functioning) risk factors when targeting adolescent internalizing problems. Moreover, contextual factors should include both proximal contextual risks, such as those that occur in the family or school environment, along with more distal risks, such as those that occur in the broader community and cultural context in which the person is embedded. This combination is especially critical in regard to adolescent internalizing problems such as depression since many cultures have firmly embedded gender-stereotypes which appear to be closely linked to the expression of gender differences of internalizing problems.

## Problems Relating to Adolescent Sexual Behavior

Several instances of externalizing problems in adolescence are the focus of the remaining articles in the volume. Once again, the research included in these sections indicates that a system of influences, ranging from those internal to the individual to those involving multiple contexts, is involved in risk behaviors. For instance, Treboux and Busch-Rossnagel (1995) present a socialization paradigm of sexuality where the adolescent's contexts (especially parents and peers) are seen to have strong influences on adolescent sexual behavior. As articles in this section suggest, problems relating to adolescent sexual behavior may arise from relationships with peers and family, in addition to the broader community and the cultural context. Broader levels of the context are especially important in relation to adolescent sexual behavior and the prevention of problems such as adolescent pregnancy and sexually transmitted diseases.

As many of the articles in this section indicate (Ensminger, 1990; Rimberg and Lewis, 1994; Scott-Jones and White, 1990), there is a critical need to address racial, ethnic, cultural, and historical influences on adolescent sexual behavior. Thus, these articles underscore the need to address the many instances of diversity that exist within the ecology of human development. Indeed, diversity is especially relevant when examining adolescent sexual behavior, since considerable variation in sexual behaviors exists during adolescence in regard to differences in gender, race, ethnicity, and religiosity (e.g., Miller, Christopherson, and King, 1993).

Similar to preceding sections, articles in this section also emphasize the notion that problem behaviors tend to co-occur during adolescence. Unfortunately, much of the previous work examining adolescent problem behaviors has focused on a particular problem behavior (e.g., early sexual activity or substance use). As Ensminger (1990) notes, this focus is likely due to the fact that separate literatures exist for each problem behavior. In addition, in the United States, funding sources are quite distinct (e.g., within the National Institutes of Health), and thus, the separate examination of problem behaviors is virtually encouraged (Ketterlinus et al., 1994). However, since problem behaviors tend to co-occur during adolescence it is important that intervention programs avoid targeting one specific problem behavior (e.g., adolescent sexual activity). Instead, the research included in this section highlights the critical importance for programs to take a comprehensive approach, one involving risk factors that relate to problem behaviors in general.

For instance, Donavan et al. (1991) argue that prevention programs targeting adolescent problem behaviors need to focus on the lifestyle of the adolescent or the organized patterning of his or her behavior. This perspective indicates that we should not deal with parts of the pattern, but with the pattern — the system — as a whole. Accordingly, if prevention programs fail to adopt a comprehensive approach, "troubled" adolescents may simply decrease their involvement in one problem behavior while increasing their involvement in another.

## Adolescent Substance Use/Abuse

The next section of the volume focuses on adolescent substance use and abuse. Once again, we see a strong emphasis in theory, research, and intervention on the relationship between the context and the individual. For example, Bachman and Schulenberg (1993) discuss the relationship between work intensity during adolescence and involvement in problem behaviors, such as substance use. In addition, the article by Kandel and Wu (1995) demonstrates the importance of examining the broader levels of the context, such as the historical or intergenerational context. Specifically, they examine the influence of smoking by members of other generations in the family on adolescent smoking.

The papers in this section again stress the necessity of examining the underlying processes involved in adolescent problem behaviors (Turner et al., 1991). In addition, the papers illustrate the covariation of adolescent problem behaviors and the importance of examining diversity (Windle et al., 1992). Finally, these papers (Bachman and Schulenberg, 1993; Maguin et al., 1994) also provide important ideas for interventions relating to problem behaviors such as early substance use and abuse.

## Delinquency and School Drop-Out During Adolescence

In the last section of this volume, we again see that individual and contextual contributions are interactive in the genesis of adolescent problem behaviors such as delinquency and school problems. The Caspi et al.(1993) study is an excellent example of how biology and the context may interact during adolescence to place an adolescent at risk for problem behaviors (e.g., delinquency). In turn, the articles by Graham et al. (1992), Adams et al. (1985), and Brooks-Gunn et al. (1993) highlight the importance of sensitivity to various dimensions of individual (e.g., racial and ethnic) diversity and contextual (e.g., urban setting) diversity in both understanding the character of these problem behaviors and in developing ideas for their prevention.

Indeed, the studies in this final section of the volume eloquently demonstrate the need to include both person and contextual variables when designing intervention programs targeting adolescent problem behaviors. Moreover, as articles in all of the sections in this volume have shown, multiple levels of the context (e.g., parents, peers, schools, and the broader community) need to be considered when designing prevention and intervention programs.

## Conclusions

Together, the papers in this volume underscore the fact that health and resiliency and risk and problem behaviors arise from a richly textured and complex system that includes the adolescent in interaction with multiple levels of his or her context. This system may be viewed as a double-edged sword. On the one hand, it provides a set of influences (or risk factors), that, when "stacked against" the individual, place him or her at an increased risk for experiencing problem behaviors. On the other hand, the same set of influences provides targets of intervention for changing the disadvantageous relations between youth and their settings into more advantageous ones.

If the system is appropriately engaged, it can be a source of hope. It is a system characterized by plasticity, and thus by the potential for changes that may benefit youth. Indeed, the papers in this volume attest to this hope and to the fact that means can be found to create optimal developmental outcomes during adolescence.

*Richard M. Lerner holds the Bergstrom Chair in Applied Developmental Science at Tufts University. A developmental psychologist, Lerner received a Ph.D. in 1971 from the City University of New York. He has been a fellow at the Center for Advanced Study in the Behavioral Sciences and is a fellow of the American Association for the Advancement of Science, the American Psychological Association, the American Psychological Society, and the American Association of Applied and Preventive Psychology. Prior to joining Tufts University, he was on the faculty and held administrative posts at Michigan State University, Pennsylvania State University, and Boston College, where he was the Anita L. Brennan Professor of Education and the director of the Center for Child, Family, and Community Partnerships. During the 1994–95 academic year Lerner held the Tyner Eminent Scholar Chair in the Human Sciences at Florida State University. Lerner is the author or editor of 40 books and more than 275 scholarly articles and chapters, including his 1995 book, *America's Youth in Crisis: Challenges and Options for Programs and Policies.* He edited Volume 1, on "Theoretical models of human development," for the fifth edition of the *Handbook of Child Psychology.* He is known for his theory of, and research about, relations between life-span human development and contextual or ecological change. He is the founding editor of the *Journal of Research on Adolescence* and of the new journal, *Applied Developmental Science.*

** Christine Ohannessian is an assistant professor in the Department of Psychiatry at the University of Connecticut Medical School. She received her Ph.D. in Human Development and Family Studies from the Pennsylvania State University in 1992. She subsequently was a post-doctoral fellow in the Alcohol Research Center at the University of Connecticut Medical School and an assistant professor at the University of Texas in Austin. Dr. Ohannessian's research interests focus on the relationship between family functioning and adolescent problem behaviors, especially emotional problems and substance abuse. Her work focuses on resiliency and protective factors and the role that they play in protecting some individuals from developing problem behaviors. Currently, Dr. Ohannessian is examining psychosocial variables that moderate the relationship between parental alcoholism and adolescent adjustment.

## References[1]

Bronfenbrenner, U., and Morris, P.A. (1998). The ecology of developmental process. In R.M. Lerner (Ed.), *Theoretical models of human development.* Volume 1 of the *Handbook of child psychology* (5th ed., pp. 993–1028). Editor in chief: W. Damon. New York: Wiley.

Cohen, P., Cohen, J., Kasen, S., Velez, C.N., Hartmark, C., Johnson, J., Rojas, M., Brook, J., and Streuning, E.L. (1993). "An epidemiological study of disorders in late childhood and adolescence: I. Age- and gender-specific prevalence." *Journal of Child Psychology and Psychiatry, 34*(6), 851–867.

Donavan, J.E., Jessor, R., and Costa, F.M. (1991). "Adolescent health behavior and conventionality-unconventionality: An extension of problem-behavior theory." *Health Psychology, 10*(1), 52–61.

Ketterlinus, R.D., Lamb, M.E., and Nitz, K.A. (1994). Adolescent nonsexual and sex-related problem behaviors: Their prevalence, consequences, and co-occurrence. In R.D. Ketterlinus and

M.E. Lamb (Eds.), *Adolescent problem behaviors: Issues and research* (pp. 17–39). Hillsdale, NJ: Lawrence Erlbaum Associates.

Lerner, R.M. (1986). *Concepts and theories of human development.* (2nd ed.). New York: Random House.

Lerner, R.M. (1998). Theories of human development: Contemporary perspectives. In R.M. Lerner (Ed.), *Theoretical models of human development.* Volume 1 of the *Handbook of child psychology* (5th ed., pp. 1–24). Editor in chief: W. Damon. New York: Wiley.

Miller, B.C., Christopherson, C.R., and King, P.K. (1993). Sexual behavior in adolescence. In T.P. Gullotta, G.R. Adams, and R. Montemayor (Eds.), *Adolescent sexuality: Advances in adolescent development* (Vol. 5, pp. 57–76). Thousand Oaks, CA: Sage.

Nolen-Hoeksema, S. (1994). "An interactive model for the emergence of gender differences in depression in adolescence." *Journal of Research on Adolescence,* 4(4), 519–534.

Ohannessian, C.M., Lerner, R.M., Lerner, J.V., and von Eye, A. (1999). "Does self-competence predict gender differences in adolescent depression and anxiety?" *Journal of Adolescence, 2,*1999. 1–15.

## Footnote

[1]This list provides reference only to citations not included in this volume.

# Risks and Problem Behaviors in Adolescence

DEVELOPMENTAL REVIEW 12, 374–390 (1992)

# REPLY

## Risk Behavior in Adolescence: A Psychosocial Framework for Understanding and Action

RICHARD JESSOR

*Institute of Behavioral Science, University of Colorado*

A social–psychological framework for the explanation of adolescent risk behavior is presented. The framework incorporates attention to both person and situational variables, and it differentiates both sets of variables into risk factors and protective factors. Risk is then considered to be a resultant reflecting the balance of risk and protection. The framework makes clear that being "at risk" for onsetting or initiating risk behaviors is an earlier developmental stage than being "at risk" for the compromising health- and life-outcomes of actually engaging in risk behaviors. The person–situation interactionist perspective that informs the framework provides an alternative to the formulation presented by Arnett (1992) to account for "reckless" behavior in adolescence.  © 1992 Academic Press, Inc.

Contemporary explanations of complex human behavior are increasingly predicated on the interaction of personal/individual attributes with social/contextual attributes. Indeed, the ascendance of an interactionist perspective in social–developmental psychology represents a major advance in both theoretical and empirical inquiry. Such a perspective makes it possible to account not only for inter- and intra-individual differences in behavior with the same set of concepts, but also for interindividual differences in intraindividual change (see Wohlwill, 1973). The paper by Arnett (1992) illustrates a rather different perspective, one that remains largely focused on the individual, and that explanatory approach seems to reflect what Dannefer (1984) has labeled as the "ontogenetic fallacy," the idea that development is largely a process of maturational unfolding.

This paper has been modified and adapted from an earlier version that appeared in D. E. Rogers and E. Ginzberg (Eds.), Westview Press, 1992. I am indebted to Drs. John E. Donovan and Frances Costa who have been my colleagues over the past decade in the research that has shaped some of the ideas in this paper. The support of the W. T. Grant Foundation (Grant 88119488) for our most recent research on adolescent health behaviors is gratefully acknowledged. My experience on the Carnegie Council on Adolescent Development and my role in the MacArthur Foundation's Research Program on Successful Adolescent Development Among Youth in High-Risk Settings have helped me to think more deeply about some of the issues addressed here. Address correspondence and reprint requests to Richard Jessor at the Institute of Behavioral Science, University of Colorado, Boulder, CO 80309.

374

In his effort to explain "reckless" behavior in adolescence, Arnett places almost exclusive emphasis on two personal/individual attributes—sensation seeking and egocentrism—and on their emergence in adolescence and decline in adulthood. This maturational unfolding is invoked to explain the developmental changes in the prevalence of risk behavior from childhood to adulthood. A comparable emphasis on the structure, the organization, and the development of the social context across this portion of the life span is, unfortunately, lacking. Arnett's failure to elaborate an interactionist explanatory framework and to articulate and differentiate the adolescent social environment places severe limitations on the reach of his account. These limitations include at least the following: (1) the hypothesized "propensity for recklessness" in adolescence fails to account for the fact that most adolescent behavior is simply not reckless by any definition of that term; (2) the account is also unable to explain intraindividual differences in recklessness during the period of adolescence; (3) the explanation is blind to the enormous racial, ethnic, and socioeconomic differences in adolescent risk behaviors such as delinquency, sexual experience, homicide, and suicide; (4) finally, the account is unable to explain the fact that the very same behaviors occur widely in adulthood.

Further difficulties are associated with the concept of "reckless" behavior itself. The so-called recklessness is treated as a property of the behaviors since "precautions that could easily be taken are not." Thus, the so-called reckless behavior of failure to use contraception is homogenized as "reckless" whether an adolescent is simply uninformed about contraception, has limited access to it, does not feel empowered to use it, is unconcerned about the consequences of not using it, or is deliberately seeking pregnancy. Introducing the term "reckless" in this way is likely to add only conceptual confusion to research on youths at risk.

The issues I have raised thus far are meant to serve as an introduction to an alternative way of framing an explanatory approach to adolescent risk behavior. Rather than pursue further the insufficiencies of the reckless behavior perspective, or to correct the misinterpretations of Problem Behavior Theory (Jessor, 1987; Jessor, Donovan, & Costa, 1991; Jessor & Jessor, 1977) that appear in the Arnett paper, it seemed more constructive to present a different perspective on adolescent risk behavior, one that seeks deliberately to implement an interactionist orientation. In the remainder of this paper, prepared for another venue, a general social–psychological framework is developed that makes clear the complexity required of any explanation of adolescent risk behavior and, hopefully, the advantage that derives from incorporating attention to both person and context.

3

The key task for this presentation is to sketch out a conceptual framework that might facilitate both understanding and action in the arena of adolescent risk. Pursuit of that objective will involve a brief exploration of recent developments in epidemiology—particularly the emergence of behavioral epidemiology—and in social/developmental psychology—particularly its application to adolescent problem behavior.

The exploration begins with some considerations about the basic notion of *risk* itself; it then turns to an examination of the organization of adolescent risk behavior and the utility of the concept of *lifestyle;* that leads into a general conceptual framework for understanding risk behavior and an explication of its content; finally, some implications of the conceptual framework for action, that is, for prevention/intervention, will be noted. I have chosen not to review the literature in the field but, instead, to distill a perspective from several decades of theoretical and empirical work on these issues. Where useful, illustrative data will be drawn from our own research.

## A PSYCHOSOCIAL CONCEPT OF RISK

In the tradition of epidemiology, the use of the concept of risk has been essentially biomedical, reflecting a concern for adverse outcomes related to morbidity and mortality. The epidemiological search has been to locate agents or conditions that are associated with an increased probability of outcomes that compromise health, the quality of life, or life itself. Such agents or conditions are referred to as "risk factors," and the search for them has kept its focus primarily on biology and, to some extent, on the physical environment as well. Biological risk factors such as high serum cholesterol and hypertension have been linked to increased probability of cardiovascular disease, cervical dysplasia to cancer, and abnormalities in trisomy 21 to Down's syndrome. Various physical environment risk factors such as radiation, lead, or contaminated water have also been linked to adverse health outcomes and to death. The identification of risk factors has been a major achievement of epidemiology; it not only constitutes an initial step in establishing causal understanding, but often suggests a locus for effective intervention.

More recently, the epidemiological search for risk factors for disease and illness, especially for the chronic diseases, has expanded into two new domains, the social environment and behavior. With respect to the social environment, considerable attention has been given, for example, to such risk factors as stress and its implications for heart disease; the availability of and access to alcohol and tobacco, yet another aspect of the social environment, have been implicated as risk factors for cirrhosis and for lung cancer. But perhaps the most reverberating development in epidemiology has been the new awareness about *behavior* as a risk factor, and the accompanying elaboration of the subdiscipline of behavioral epidemiology. It is increasingly apparent that much of the burden of illness—heart disease and stroke, cancer, liver disease, unintended injury, and HIV infection—can be linked to patterns of human behavior. Eating behavior, sedentary behavior, drinking behavior, driving after drinking, smoking behavior, unprotected sexual intercourse, unsanitary practices, and other such actions can, it is now clear, compromise health and safety.

Insofar as behaviors constitute risk factors for morbidity and mortality, the challenge for epidemiology is to move beyond its usual biomedical focus and address a new task—the understanding of behavior and its antecedents and consequences. It is in undertaking this enterprise that epidemiology has begun to find a confluence with social/developmental psychology. For the latter, of course, the understanding of social behavior has been a traditional and important raison d'être.

The incorporation of behaviors into the rubric of risk factors entails a reformulation of thinking about the very concept of risk and about what it is that is at risk. First, it requires that the traditional restriction of the concept of risk to biomedical outcomes alone be loosened. Although behaviors do indeed have biomedical consequences, they also eventuate in social and personal or psychological outcomes. The behavior of, say, marijuana smoking by an adolescent may well involve a higher probability of pulmonary disease, but it also may involve a higher probability of legal sanctions or conflict with parents or loss of interest in school or a sense of personal guilt and anxiety. These latter are psychosocial outcomes or consequences that are linked, simultaneously, to the very same risk behavior. A *psychosocial* understanding of risk, when behaviors are risk factors, requires attention to all of their potential outcomes or consequences, not just to those that are biomedical.

Second, the reformulation requires that the restriction of the concept of risk to adverse, negative, or undesirable outcomes be loosened. Returning to the preceding example, it is clear that some of the outcomes or consequences of the behavioral risk factor of marijuana smoking can be positive, desirable, and sought after by adolescents. Smoking marijuana can lead, for example, to social acceptance by peers and to a subjective sense of autonomy and maturity. When behaviors are risk factors, the notion of risk needs to be expanded to encompass positive or desired outcomes as well as those that are adverse or negative. A psychosocial reformulation of risk calls for a thoroughgoing cost *and* benefit analysis of risk factors rather than the traditional preoccupation with only their potential costs. Behavior, including risk behavior, is clearly influenced by both.

The bankruptcy of the exhortation to "Just Say No!" is evident here— the failure to acknowledge that drug use and other risk behaviors can serve important social and personal functions for adolescents and are unlikely to be abandoned in the absence of alternatives that can provide similar satisfactions. Considerable research has shown that adolescent risk behaviors are functional, purposive, instrumental, and goal-directed and that the goals involved are often those that are central in normal adolescent development. It is not difficult to see how smoking, drinking, illicit drug use, risky driving, or early sexual activity can be instrumental in gaining peer acceptance and respect, in establishing autonomy from parents, in repudiating the norms and values of conventional authority, in coping with anxiety, frustration, and the anticipation of failure, or in affirming maturity and marking a transition out of childhood and toward a more adult status. There is nothing perverse, irrational, or psychopathological about such goals. Rather, they are characteristic of ordinary psychosocial development, and their centrality helps to explain why risk behaviors that serve such functions are so intractable to change. In failing to allocate resources to promote alternative behaviors that can serve the same goals but that are less health- and life-compromising for adolescents, the "Just Say No!" campaign revealed its moral cynicism.

The concept of psychosocial risk implicates and is concerned with the entire range of personal development and social adaptation in adolescence. Thus, *what* is at risk from engaging in risk behavior includes but far transcends physical health and physical growth. Risk behaviors can jeopardize the accomplishment of normal developmental tasks, the fulfillment of expected social roles, the acquisition of essential skills, the achievement of a sense of adequacy and competence, and the appropriate preparation for transition to the next stage in the life trajectory—young adulthood. The term "risk behavior" refers, then, to any behaviors that can compromise these psychosocial aspects of successful adolescent development. Substance abuse, withdrawal from school involvement, unprotected sexual intercourse, driving after drinking, or engaging in violence are some obvious examples.

It should be noted that I have not been using the term "risk-taking behavior." I am concerned that the latter has been responsible for a certain amount of terminological mischief in the field. Its wide currency is unfortunate because it eliminates the problematic nature of adolescent risk behavior and tends to foreclose further inquiry. When referred to as risk-taking behavior, risk behavior is already "explained." That is, it is accounted for simply by the taking of risks, the satisfaction or thrill of engaging in something risky. There is an associated unfortunate tendency as well, and that is to characterize adolescents as "risk takers." This not only results in a bit of tautological thinking that further confounds explanation but also divests the social context of any contributory role.

The concept of risk-taking behavior is certainly appropriate for that subset of risk behaviors that entail conscious awareness of the risk or danger involved and a deliberate seeking for the thrill that issues from the uncertainty of beating the odds. Playing the game of "Chicken" on the highway, taking chances on avoiding detection during certain delinquent acts, or pursuing activities like rock climbing may be exemplars. *But the larger class of adolescent risk behavior simply does not lend itself to that kind of analysis.* Few adolescents continue cigarette smoking for the thrill of seeing whether they can avoid pulmonary disease; few engage in unprotected sexual intercourse for the thrill of beating the odds of contracting an STD or becoming pregnant. Indeed, a key concern of health education is to make adolescents aware that there *are* risks associated with many of the behaviors they engage in. It seems best, then, to employ the term risk behavior rather than risk-taking behavior and to apply it to any behavior that can comprise adolescent development—whether or not the adolescent is motivated by, or even aware of, the risk involved. Such usage not only would keep the explanation of adolescent risk behavior problematic, but also would encourage the quest for a more general conceptual account.

## THE ORGANIZATION OF ADOLESCENT RISK BEHAVIOR AND THE CONCEPT OF LIFESTYLE

Another issue requires attention as we explore the way toward a general conceptual framework for adolescent risk behavior. This issue has to do with the degree to which there is structure and organization among the different risk behaviors in adolescence. Stated in other terms, the issue is whether there is intraindividual covariation among risk behaviors so that they cluster or form what might be called a risk behavior syndrome. It makes an enormous difference, for both understanding and intervention, to be dealing with separate, independent, and isolated risk behaviors or, instead, with an organized constellation of risk behaviors that are interrelated and covary. The former perspective has sustained what might be called the "problem-of-the-week" approach, in which efforts are mobilized to fight teenage pregnancy one week, drunk driving the next, illicit drug use the next, crime after that, and so on. It is also the perspective that characterizes the separate mission–orientations of the various Federal agencies, one for alcohol abuse, one for drug abuse, one for mental health, sexual behavior in yet another agency, and delinquency else-where. The latter perspective, on the other hand, suggests a more com-prehensive and simultaneous concern with the entire array of adolescent risk behaviors and promotes efforts to understand and alter the circum-stances that give rise to and that sustain such clusters or syndromes of risk behavior in adolescence.

By now, a fair amount of evidence has been accumulated on this ques-tion, and there is considerable support for the covariation perspective. The evidence for covariation is strongest for those risk behaviors that are also problem behaviors, for example, drug use, delinquency, alcohol abuse, and sexual precocity. In one of our early longitudinal studies of high school youths, for example, we found that 61% of marijuana users were sexually experienced, whereas only 18% of the nonusers were (Jes-sor & Jessor, 1977). In our later research, using maximum-likelihood factor analysis, we provided additional support for the interrelatedness of adolescent problem behaviors by showing that a single common factor accounts for their positive intercorrelations (Donovan & Jessor, 1985; Donovan, Jessor & Costa, 1988). Further support comes from latent vari-able analyses of data from our recent study of samples of junior and senior high school youths that include White, Black, and Hispanic adolescents. These analyses show, once again, the interrelatedness of adolescent prob-lem behavior; they also show that a single, second-order latent variable can account for that interrelatedness within all of the ethnic, gender, and school-level subgroups. The evidence for covariation has been less strong where nonproblem, health-risk behaviors are involved, such as eating, exercise, and safety behaviors. In the recent study just mentioned, how-ever, we have been able to show that modest interrelations do obtain among such health behaviors and that, again, a single, second-order latent variable accounts for those relations (Donovan, Jessor, & Costa, 1992). In addition, there are modest negative correlations between the problem behaviors and the health-promoting behaviors. The literature on the en-tire covariation issue has recently been reviewed in extensive detail (see Osgood, 1991, and Elliott, 1992).

Overall, the empirical evidence supports the existence of organized patterns of adolescent risk behaviors. These structures of behaviors, taken together, reflect an adolescent's way of being in the world. Their structure or organization raises interesting questions about the origin or source of the covariation and patterning. Part of the answer probably lies in the social ecology of adolescent life, an ecology that provides socially organized opportunities to learn risk behaviors together and normative expectations that they be performed together. Part of the answer probably also lies in the fact that different risk behaviors can serve the same func-

8

tions, for example, both illicit drug use and precocious sexual activity can serve as a way of affirming independence from parents.

The key import of the evidence about covariation among risk behaviors is the support it provides for the organizing concept of *lifestyle*. Unhappily drawn from the lexicon of common language, the lifestyle notion nevertheless has a core meaning denoting an organized pattern of inter-related behaviors. According to one scholar seeking to formalize the term, lifestyle consists of ". . . expressive [i.e., functional] behaviors . . . a distinctive and hence recognizable mode of living . . ." (Sobel, 1981, p. 28). The utility of the concept of lifestyle, referring as it does to the constellation or syndrome of risk behavior, is that it directs our attention to the adolescent as a whole actor rather than to each of the risk behaviors, one after another. Equally important, it raises a serious question about whether intervention efforts should remain focused, as they have been, on specific behaviors, e.g., illicit drug use, or whether they should be oriented, instead, toward influencing an adolescent's lifestyle as a whole.

## A GENERAL CONCEPTUAL FRAMEWORK FOR ADOLESCENT RISK BEHAVIOR

The discussion to this point has sought to incorporate adolescent behavior into an epidemiological perspective on risk factors. That has involved some reformulation of traditional thinking about risk and about what it is that is at risk, a reformulation hospitable to psychosocial as well as biomedical outcomes. We have argued that, as risk factors, behaviors such as illicit drug use, school dropout, unprotected sexual intercourse, encounters with the criminal justice system, or others can compromise successful adolescent development and jeopardize the life-chances of youths. The focus, thus far, has been on the psychosocial *outcomes and consequences* of risk factors when they are behaviors. It is now possible to explore behavioral risk factors in the other direction, that is, in terms of their psychosocial *antecedents and determinants*. Such exploration will lead us to a general conceptual framework for adolescent risk behavior and will illuminate, at the same time, the merging of the epidemiological perspective with that of social–developmental psychology.

The effort to conceptualize and elaborate the antecedents or determinants of risk behaviors, as established risk factors, can continue to make use of the orientation of epidemiology toward the identification of risk factors. Now the key question becomes: "What are the risk factors for the (behavioral) risk factors?" Or, in the present case, "What are the risk factors for the risk behaviors?" That epidemiological concern turns out to

9

be identical to the standard concern of social–psychological inquiry, namely, how to provide an explanatory account of complex social behavior. In both endeavors, the aim is to push back from identified risk factors to establish what one epidemiologist termed the "web of causation" (MacMahon, Pugh, & Ipsen, 1960), that is, the explanatory framework in which they are embedded and which can provide a logical account of their distribution and occurrence. Indeed, it was another epidemiologist, Milton Terris, who chastised his colleagues for their excessive preoccupation with proximal risk factors—the microorganism in infectious disease, tobacco or salt in chronic disease—while largely ignoring those that are distal, ". . . the whole complex of social and other environmental factors that create that cause, and bring it into effective contact with the host . . ." (1983, p. 16). The web of causation in epidemiology is isomorphic with explanatory theory in social psychology when behaviors are the risk factors at issue.

A comprehensive social–psychological framework for explaining behavior generally includes four major explanatory domains or sources of variance: the social environment, the perceived environment, personality, and (other) behavior. Although not traditional, more recent explanatory efforts have increasingly sought to engage a fifth domain, namely, biology/genetics. Taken together and fully articulated, these five domains would constitute the "web of causation" or the general explanatory framework for adolescent risk behavior. The schema presented in Fig. 1 represents the five domains, illustrates their content, and specifies their relationships to each other, to risk behavior, and to the potential outcomes of risk.

Before elaborating on the specific content of the various conceptual domains in the schema, I want to make some general comments about the framework as a whole. First, the framework makes apparent the complexity that is required of any responsible account of adolescent risk behavior. That account would need to engage multiple explanatory domains as well as their interactions; an explanation that confines itself to any single domain—whether genetics, the social environment, or personality—is certain to be incomplete at best and parochial at worst. Further, the widespread proclivity in the field to fasten on single-variable interventions—increasing self-esteem, say, or providing adolescents with mentors—can garner little support from such a framework, given the large array of factors and domains that must be seen to influence risk behavior.

Second, the domains that constitute the web of causation are each represented as having direct effects on adolescent risk behavior. That makes it useful to consider each domain as a separate source of risk— ocial environment risk, perceived environment risk, personality risk,

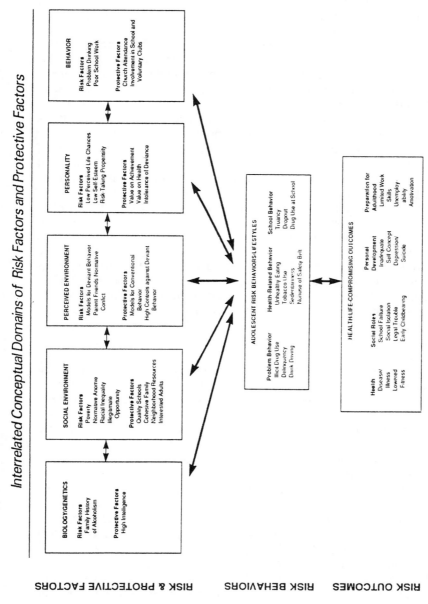

FIG. 1. A conceptual framework for adolescent risk behavior: Risk and protective factors, risk behaviors, and risk outcomes.

etc.—and to try to articulate their component variables or determinants or, in epidemiological terms, their risk factors. Third, the various risk domains are also represented as having indirect effects on adolescent risk behavior, effects that are mediated through other risk domains (for reasons of clarity, not all the interconnecting arrows have been drawn). Thus, beyond their direct effects, social environment risk factors, say, poverty and racial/ethnic discrimination, may influence the risk factor of low perceived life-chances in the personality domain and, thereby, indirectly influence risk behavior. Knowledge about direct and indirect effects ought to be of great importance to the design of intervention efforts and to decisions about the most promising loci of intervention.

Fourth, complex as the schema already is, it represents the structure of risk factors, risk behaviors, and risk outcomes only cross-sectionally, that is, at a moment in time. Of fundamental importance, and entirely missing from the figure, are the *changes* going on in each of the domains. Processes of developmental change in the adolescent and of social and historical change in the adolescent's context are, although unrepresented, clearly not meant to be ignored. Fifth, the direction of causal influence in the figure needs to be thought of as bidirectional from top-to-bottom and also from bottom-to-top. Although the primary concern of this paper has been with providing an account of risk behavior (therefore a top-to-bottom emphasis), the bidirectional arrows indicate that, of course, engaging in risk behavior can also have effects on the various domains of risk factors (a bottom-to-top influence). It is this bi- or multidirectionality of the social–psychological framework that makes the web of causation metaphor so apposite.

The particular risk factors that have been listed in each of the different risk domains are, for the most part, drawn from the research literature or implicated in various conceptual analyses of adolescent risk behavior. They are only a selected set, obviously, and meant to be illustrative. Measures of many of the variables, especially those in the perceived environment, the personality, and the behavior domains, have been employed repeatedly in our own work on Problem–Behavior Theory which is a specific variant of the general framework in Fig. 1. Multiple regression analyses, employing about a dozen or so of the measures, generally yield multiple correlations ($R$s) of about .70 when accounting for an index of multiple problem behavior among adolescents, and the $R$s range between .50 and .80 when various specific risk behaviors such as problem drinking or illicit drug use are being predicted. Thus, between 25 and 65% of the variance in adolescent risk behavior is explained, with close to 50% being modal (see Jessor & Jessor, 1977; Jessor, 1987; and Jessor et al., 1991). The measures that tend to be invariantly important across our different studies include low expectations for school achievement and low attitudinal intolerance of deviance in the personality domain; models for problem behavior among friends in the perceived environment domain; and marijuana use and poor school work in the behavior domain.

These results, ours and those of many other workers in the field, provide encouraging empirical support for the web of causation shown in Fig. 1. At the same time, however, they reveal that a large segment of the variance is left unexplained. In our own work as well as in that of others, I believe this is due at least in part to a less than satisfactory grasp on the properties of the social environment. The ultimate importance of the social environment cannot be gainsaid. The distribution of a variety of adolescent risk behaviors reflects the circumstances of poverty, racial/ ethnic marginality, and limited life-chances, as well as the presence of an underground structure of illegitimate opportunity. Such circumstances are not well-captured, however, by the usual measures of socioeconomic status, especially for adolescents, and this issue presents a crucial challenge to researchers in this field.

## THE ROLE OF PROTECTIVE FACTORS IN ADOLESCENT RISK BEHAVIOR

There is a final aspect of the framework shown in Fig. 1 that remains to be addressed, namely, the *protective factors* that are listed in each of the risk domains. The conceptual role of protective factors is to help explain a fact that is part of common awareness, namely, that many adolescents who seem to be at high risk nevertheless do not succumb to risk behavior, or get less involved in it than their peers, or, if involved, seem to abandon it more rapidly than others do. Stated otherwise, many adolescents growing up under conditions of pervasive adversity, limited resources, and intense pressures toward the transgression of conventional norms manage to overcome such circumstances and to "make it." What enables them to avoid entanglements with the criminal justice system, to remain aloof from antisocial peer groups, to avoid getting pregnant, to do well in school, to acquire the necessary skills for the transition to work and other adult roles, and to develop a sense of personal adequacy and competence?

One answer to that query would be that, appearances to the contrary notwithstanding, those who make it were, in fact, not really at high risk. For some reason, they were fortunate in not actually being exposed to or experiencing the variety of risk factors that seemed to be part of the context of their lives. In short, they were, somehow, not actually at risk or at as high risk as might have been expected. Although that is conceivable, a more likely answer is that there was indeed exposure to and

13

experience of risk, *but that it was countered by exposure to and experience of protection.* Protective factors are considered by both Garmezy (1985) and Rutter (1990) to moderate, buffer, insulate against and, thereby, to mitigate the impact of risk on adolescent behavior and development.

It is useful to think of protective factors as operating within each of the conceptual domains: in the social environment, a cohesive family, a neighborhood with informal resources, a caring adult; in the perceived environment, peer models for conventional behavior and strict social controls; in the personality domain, high value on academic achievement and on health and high *in*tolerance of deviance; and, in the behavior domain, involvement in conventional behavior, such as church attendance and school clubs. To the extent that protective factors such as these are present and operative, they should serve to attenuate, counter, or balance the impact and effects of risk factors.

There is some argumentation within the field about whether protective factors are merely the opposite or low end of risk factors or are, indeed, different factors that function actively to promote positive behavior and development and, in so doing, have a direct mitigating effect on the impact of risk factors. Heuristically, the latter position seems more useful and the various factors selected as illustrative of protection in the different risk domains in Fig. 1 were chosen to be of that sort. The mitigating role of protection is only demonstrable, logically, in the presence of risk (Rutter, 1990). In recent analyses of our own data (Jessor, Vanderryn et al., in preparation), we classified junior and senior high school males and females, on the basis of a six-component, composite risk factor score, into No Risk, Moderate Risk, and High Risk groups. We than cross-classified each risk group into High and Low Protection subgroups based on a seven-component, composite protective factor score. Analysis of variance of involvement in problem behavior showed that High vs Low Protection made no difference in the amount of problem behavior involvement for the No Risk groups; it did make a significant difference, however, for both the Moderate Risk groups and the High Risk groups. Those with High Protection had significantly lower problem behavior scores than those with Low Protection, and the interaction was significant. These findings provide support for the logic of protection, and they also illustrate the salutary role that protective factors can play in minimizing the impact of exposure to and experience with risk factors.

## ADOLESCENTS AT RISK: WHAT DOES "AT RISK" REALLY MEAN?

The conceptual framework can contribute to a more systematic understanding of what is meant when we speak of adolescents being "at risk" or, perhaps more important, being at "high risk." The issue here is how to deal with variation in the magnitude of psychosocial risk.

What is immediately apparent from the conceptual framework is that being "at risk" can have two quite different meanings. *For adolescents already involved in risk behavior*—usually those who are older—"at risk" can mean being at risk for health- and life-compromising *outcomes:* early pregnancy, school failure, trouble with the law, unemployability, and inadequate self-concept. The focus here is on the degree of risk associated with the engagement in risk behaviors—illicit drug use, problem drinking, cigarette smoking, precocious sex, or truancy. What is the risk that such engagement will compromise adolescent health, adolescent life, or successful adolescent development? This meaning of being "at risk" represents a later developmental stage in the ontogeny of risk, a stage wherein risk behaviors are already practiced and at which the concept of intervention rather than of prevention seems more appropriate.

For this stage, the assessment of the magnitude of risk would certainly include: (1) the intensity of involvement in any particular risk behavior, from a level of exploration to a level of commitment; (2) the number of different risk behaviors an adolescent is involved in, and the degree to which they constitute an organized pattern or lifestyle; (3) the earliness of age of onset of the risk behaviors (since there is evidence linking early onset to chronicity and intensity); and (4) the degree of involvement simultaneously in protective behaviors. To be "at high risk," at this stage, would imply serious and long-term involvement in an organized pattern of risk behaviors, with little involvement in protective behaviors.

*For adolescents not yet involved in risk behavior*—usually those who are younger—being "at risk" means something else, namely, the risk for *initiating, onsetting, or becoming involved in risk behaviors:* for beginning sexual intercourse, for onsetting the use of alcohol and illicit drugs, for starting to cut school, and for engaging in delinquent acts. The "at risk" focus here is the degree of risk represented in the various conceptual domains of risk in Fig. 1 and the likelihood that that risk will generate involvement in risk behaviors. This meaning of being at risk represents an earlier stage in the ontogeny of risk, a stage before risk behaviors have been engaged in and in which the term prevention, or primary prevention, seems more appropriate. For this stage, the assessment of the magnitude of risk would require consideration of the following: (1) the number and intensity of risk factors in a particular risk domain; (2) the number and intensity of protective factors in that same domain; (3) the pervasiveness of risk factors across the multiple risk domains; (4) the pervasiveness of protective factors across the multiple domains. To be "at high risk" at this stage would mean that there are multiple and serious risk factors in multiple domains and little in the way of protective factors in those same domains.

Distinguishing between the two stages of being "at risk" seems useful for both understanding and action. It should not be drawn too sharply, however. The meaning of being at risk sketched out for older adolescents, those already involved in risk behavior, would also need, of course, to consider the degree of risk and of protection in the various conceptual domains in addition to its focus on the extent of their involvement in risk behavior. Whether a risk behavior such as precocious sexual intercourse puts an adolescent at risk for life-compromising outcomes such as early pregnancy and unemployability is undoubtedly influenced by the risk factors and protective factors in that adolescent's social environment. Remaining in school or returning to school may well hinge on the avail-ability of social support, resources for child care, a caring adult, etc., in that environment. In short, risk for health- and life-compromising *out-comes* should be seen as "nested" in the conceptual framework, with the risk from risk behaviors nested in the risk from the various conceptual domains.

A final point needs to be made in considering the appraisal of variation in magnitude of risk, one that has been assumed in the discussion but not stated explicitly. Degree of risk needs to be treated conceptually as a *resultant,* an outcome of the balance of risk and protection. Two adoles-cents characterized by the same pattern of risk factors may be very dif-ferently "at risk" depending on the protective factors that affect their lives. *The logic of the conceptual framework requires arriving at a re-sultant that reflects the balance of risk and protection.* An assessment of risk that ignores protection can turn out to be severely off the mark.

## IMPLICATIONS FOR PREVENTION/INTERVENTION

A few comments about the implications of these considerations for prevention/intervention, beyond those already mentioned, may be useful. First, and perhaps of overriding importance, is the import of the com-plexity of the web of causation that has been proposed. What that com-plexity suggests is that prevention/intervention efforts that are compre-hensive promise to yield greater success than those that are more limited in scope. Programs that fail to engage multiple risk domains are unlikely to be successful or to generate lasting effects. Second, programs need to design efforts that can simultaneously reduce risk and promote protec-tion; neither strategy alone would seem optimal for effecting change. Third, programs directed at the organization and patterning of multiple risk behaviors may be more appropriate than programs focused on specific behaviors alone. Lifestyle change, while obviously a challenge, has the promise of more pervasive and more enduring impact on the repertoire of risk behaviors. Fourth, programs that acknowledge the salience of the social environment would seem especially critical. Young people growing up in adverse social environments are in double jeopardy. Not only are risk factors more intense and more prevalent in such contexts, but protective factors are less available if not, indeed, absent for many. It is in contexts such as these that risk behaviors are more likely to have irretrievable outcomes, whereas the very same behaviors in a less adverse setting often gain for the adolescent a "second chance," that is, the opportunity and support for getting back on track. Finally, the emphasis on risk behavior and on lifestyle should not be translated into making individuals alone responsible for removing the risk in their lives; such an approach would tend to "blame the victim." The present conceptual framework makes it patently clear that risk is embedded in the larger social context of adolescent life and that reduction in risk requires social change as well.

## CONCLUSION

This presentation has sought to examine how the confluence of epidemiology and social psychology can illuminate an important social problem—adolescent risk behavior. The conceptual framework that was elaborated was an effort to represent both social–psychological theory and theory in behavioral epidemiology. The epidemiologist Reuel Stallones speaks of ". . . a territory of especial beauty at the intersection of the biomedical and social sciences . . ." (1980, p. 80). It was the attractiveness of that territory for understanding complex human behavior that motivated this effort; hopefully its attractiveness will draw other scientists and practitioners to explore the same terrain.

## REFERENCES

Arnett, J. (1992). Reckless behavior in adolescence: A developmental perspective. *Developmental Review*, **12**, 339–373.

Dannefer, D. (1984). Adult development and social theory: A paradigmatic reappraisal. *American Sociological Review*, **49**, 100–116.

Donovan, J. E., & Jessor, R. (1985). Structure of problem behavior in adolescence and young adulthood. *Journal of Consulting and Clinical Psychology*, **53**(6), 890–904.

Donovan, J. E., Jessor, R., & Costa, F. M. (1988). Syndrome of problem behavior in adolescence: A replication. *Journal of Consulting and Clinical Psychology*, **56**(5), 762–765.

Donovan, J. E., Jessor, R., & Costa, F. M. (1992). *Structure of health-related behavior in adolescence: A latent-variable approach*. Manuscript under review.

Elliott, D. S. (1992). Health enhancing and health compromising lifestyles. In S. G. Millstein, A. C. Petersen, & E. O. Nightingale (Eds.), *Adolescent health promotion*, Oxford University Press (in press).

Garmezy, N. (1985). Stress resistant children: The search for protective factors. In J. Stevenson (Ed.), *Recent research in developmental psychopathology*. Oxford: Pergamon.

Jessor, R. (1987). Problem-behavior theory, psychosocial development, and adolescent problem drinking. *British Journal of Addiction*, 82(4), 435–446.

Jessor, R., Donovan, J. E., & Costa, F. (1991). *Beyond adolescence: Problem behavior and young adult development*. New York: Cambridge Univ. Press.

Jessor, R., & Jessor, S. L. (1977). *Problem behavior and psychosocial development: A longitudinal study of youth*. New York: Academic Press.

Jessor, R., Vanderryn, J., et al. (in preparation). Risk and protective factors in adolescent problem behavior: A Problem–Behavior Theory approach.

MacMahon, B., Pugh, T. F., & Ipsen, J. (1960). *Epidemiological methods*. Boston: Little, Brown.

Osgood, D. W. (1991). Covariation among health problems in adolescence. Washington D.C: Office of Technology Assessment.

Rutter, M. (1990). Psychosocial resilience and protective mechanisms. In J. Rolf, A. S. Masten, D. Cicchetti, K. H. Neuchterlein, & S. Weintraub (Eds.), *Risk and protective factors in the development of psychopathology*. Cambridge: Cambridge Univ. Press.

Sobel, M. E. (1981). *Lifestyle and social structure: Concepts, definitions, analyses*. New York: Academic Press.

Stallones, R. A. (1980). To advance epidemiology. *Annual Review of Public Health*, 1, 69–82.

Terris, M. (1983). The complex tasks of the second epidemiological revolution: The Joseph W. Mountin lecture. *Journal of Public Health Policy*, 4, 8–24.

Wohlwill, J. F. (1973). *The study of behavioral development*. New York: Academic Press.

RECEIVED March 25, 1991.

Developmental Psychology
1989, Vol. 25, No. 4, 550–559

# Parent and Child Stress and Symptoms: An Integrative Analysis

Bruce E. Compas, David C. Howell,
Vicky Phares, and Rebecca A. Williams
University of Vermont

Normand Ledoux
Northeast Kingdom Mental Health Center
Newport, Vermont

This study assessed major and daily stressful life events and psychological symptoms in a sample of young adolescents and their parents. The relation between major life events and symptoms was mediated by daily stressors for parents and their young adolescent children. Children's emotional and behavioral problems were associated with fathers' psychological symptoms but not with mothers' symptoms. Both mothers' and fathers' symptoms were associated with their sons' daily stressors, but girls' daily stressors were related only to their mothers' symptoms. Mothers' symptoms were associated with their husbands' daily hassles in families of young adolescent boys, and both parents' symptoms were associated with their spouses' hassles in families of adolescent girls. Highlights the importance of studying stress processes between individuals.

The study of stressful events during childhood and adolescence has established that major life events are related to emotional and behavioral problems in these age groups (see reviews by Compas, 1987; Johnson, 1986). Although this research has provided a strong foundation for the study of stress processes in adolescents and children, further research is needed to explore (a) the role of daily stressors in the lives of children and adolescents (i.e., clarification of stress processes *within* individuals) and (b) the relation of parents' and children's stressful events and symptoms with one another (i.e., clarification of stress processes *between* individuals).

Minor stressful events or daily hassles may play a critical role in understanding stress and symptoms within individuals. Studies have shown that daily stressors are more closely associated with symptoms than are major life events in adults (e.g., DeLongis, Coyne, Dakof, Folkman, & Lazarus, 1982; Holahan, Holahan, & Belk, 1984; Kanner, Coyne, Schaefer, & Lazarus, 1981; Monroe, 1983) and that daily stress may play a similarly important role in children and adolescents (e.g., Baer, Garmezy, McLaughlin, Pokorny, & Wernick, 1987; Compas, Davis, & Forsythe, 1985; Lewis, Siegel, & Lewis, 1984; Rowlison & Felner, 1988). Many of these studies have attempted to determine which type of stress, major or daily events, is most closely associated with symptoms. Alternatively, several authors have suggested that an integrative model of stress should include both types of events, because major events may lead to an in-

creased number of daily stressors, which in turn may lead to symptoms (e.g., Felner, Farber, & Primavera, 1983; Kanner et al., 1981; Pearlin, Lieberman, Menaghan, & Mullan, 1981). A recent prospective investigation of stress and symptoms in older adolescents during the transition from high school to college found support for this hypothesis (Wagner, Compas, & Howell, 1988). That is, major events were related to daily stressors, which in turn were associated with psychological symptoms, but there was not an independent relation between major life events and symptoms. However, this mediational process has not been examined in a wider age range of adults, adolescents, and children.

A second direction for child and adolescent stress research involves the examination of stress and symptom relations between individuals. That is, from a social ecological perspective on child development (e.g., Bronfenbrenner, 1986), one would expect youngsters' psychological functioning to affect and be affected by levels of stress and symptoms experienced by others in their family. Specifically, the possibility that stressful events experienced by mothers and fathers are related to children's distress has been examined recently by Cohen, Burt, and Bjork (1987), Holahan and Moos (1987), Thomson and Vaux (1986), and Fergusson, Horwood, Gretton, and Shannon (1985). Holahan and Moos and Fergusson and colleagues found that major life events reported by parents were significantly related to mothers' reports of children's behavior problems. In contrast, Cohen and colleagues did not find significant relations between either maternal or paternal major life events and self-reports of depression, anxiety, or self-esteem by their (young adolescent) children. Thomson and Vaux (1986) found a significant relation between paternal major life events and child "affective balance" but no relation between fathers' major events and child depression nor mothers' major events and child depression or affective balance. Furthermore, Thomson and Vaux failed to find an association between parents' reports of daily stressors and child depression or affect. In general, these studies have not found evidence for a *direct* relation between parental major or daily

This research was supported by funds from the W. T. Grant Foundation. Portions of these data were presented at the 94th Annual Convention of the American Psychological Association, Washington, DC, August 1986. We are grateful to Debbie Barr, Jill Davis, Karin Dodge, Debbie Dunlap, Terry Hanley, Beth Phillips, and Sara Thompson, for their assistance with data collection and entry, and to Tom Achenbach, Larry Cohen, Harold Leitenberg, and three anonymous reviewers for their helpful comments on an earlier version of this article.

Correspondence concerning this article should be addressed to Bruce E. Compas, Department of Psychology, University of Vermont, Burlington, Vermont 05405.

20

stressful events and child or adolescent self-reported emotional problems.

Two factors may be important in further investigation of the relations between stress and symptoms among family members. First, the relation between stress experienced by a parent and children's emotional and behavioral problems may be indirect. Cognitive models of stress and coping (e.g., Lazarus & Folkman, 1984; Moos, 1984; Taylor, 1983) predict that the effects of a stressful event, whether experienced by the self or another, are affected by the *meaning* that the event holds for the individual. Thus, a stressful event experienced by a parent should be related to a child's level of distress if the event implies a significant level of threat to the child's personal well-being or to the functioning of the family as a whole. This level of meaning may not be apparent in the mere occurrence of the event but may depend on the parent's response to the stressor. If mother or father display little or no distress in response to a stressor, a child may perceive the event as relatively benign. If a parent displays symptoms of depression, anxiety, or other signs of psychological upset in association with a stressor, however, this may convey a high degree of threat to a youngster. Thus, the relation between parental stressful events and children's emotional and behavioral problems may be mediated by parental symptoms.

A second focus for research on stress and symptoms in families involves the relation of children's stressful experiences with parents' symptoms and associations between spouses' stress and symptoms. The cues that convey the meaning of a stressful event in the life of another may be different for adults than for children. Adults may have sufficient experience with the types of stressful events typically encountered by their spouse or children for these events to hold meaning for the individual independent of the other person's response to the events. For example, when a woman reports troubles with her employer, her husband may be able to infer that this has implications for her job security and, therefore, for the economic status of the family. As a result, the husband may experience substantial distress in direct response to this event in the life of his spouse. Just as daily stressors may mediate the relation between major life events and symptoms within individuals, it is plausible that ongoing daily stressors are most salient to spouses and account for the relation between spouses' stress and symptoms. Similarly, stressors experienced by a child or adolescent that come to the attention of a parent may be distressing to the parent independent of the relation between the stressor and the psychological distress expressed by the youngster. Prior studies have not investigated these possibilities in the relation between spouses' stress and symptoms or between children's stressful events and their parents' symptoms (e.g., Billings, Cronkite, & Moos, 1983; Billings & Moos, 1984, 1985; Cronkite & Moos, 1984; Thomson & Vaux, 1986).

The present study focused on pathways among family members' stress and symptoms and tested the following hypotheses: (a) Daily stressors mediate the relation between major life events and distress at the individual level, so that major events are related to daily stressors, which in turn are related to symptoms, but a direct link between major events and symptoms was not expected. This pattern was expected for parents and children. (b) Parents' stressful events affect children through the

symptoms displayed by the parents. Thus, a direct relation between parents' major life events or daily hassles and children's emotional and behavioral problems was not expected. However, children's emotional and behavioral problems were expected to be directly associated with parental symptoms. (c) Children's stressful events were expected to be directly related to parents' psychological symptoms. (d) Husbands' and wives' psychological symptoms were expected to be related to their spouses' daily stressful events. On the basis of prior findings indicating gender differences in the occurrence of stressful events and in the association between stress and symptoms during adolescence (see Compas, 1987, for a review) as well as gender differences in parent–child relationships during adolescence (e.g., Jurkovic & Ulrici, 1985; Siegal, 1987; Silverberg & Steinberg, 1987; Steinberg, 1987), all analyses were conducted separately for males and females. Because the analyses reported here are based on cross-sectional data, they cannot be used to test true causal relationships among the variables. However, structural equation analyses were used as a first step in the identification of relations within a hypothesized model that warrant further analysis in longitudinal research (cf. Patterson, 1986).

## Method

### Subjects

Participants were 211 children and young adolescents (116 girls and 95 boys) and their parents living in the rural northeast portion of Vermont. Complete data were obtained from all 211 mothers of these children and from 162 fathers. These families represent a subset of two-parent families drawn from a sample of 309 families participating in a larger study of stress and coping in young adolescents and their parents. Only two-parent families were included because several of the hypotheses involved the relations between mothers' and fathers' stress and symptoms. The children and adolescents ranged from 10 to 14 years of age, with a mean of 12.01 years ($SD = 0.97$), and were attending the sixth through eighth grades. As is typical of the Vermont population, more than 98% of the families were White. The median family income was in the range from \$20,000 to \$24,999, ranging from less than \$3,000 to more than \$40,000. Mothers worked an average of 28.55 hr per week outside the home ($SD = 18.14$); fathers worked an average of 43.94 hr per week outside the home ($SD = 14.11$). Mothers had a mean of 13.18 years of school ($SD = 2.52$) and fathers an average of 12.80 years ($SD = 3.21$). Family socioeconomic status, as determined on the basis of education, occupation, gender, and marital status (Hollingshead, 1975), was as follows: Level I (unskilled laborer), 3%; Level II (semiskilled worker), 24%; Level III (skilled craftsperson, clerical worker), 28%; Level IV (medium business, minor professional), 34%; and Level V (major business or professional), 15%. The number of children in the families ranged from 1 to 6 with a mean of 2.65 ($SD = 1.08$).

### Procedure

All students in the sixth, seventh, and eighth grades in six rural schools were given a letter of informed consent to take home to their parents. Approximately half of the available families volunteered to take part in the study. Participation was completely voluntary, and a \$25 remuneration was given to each family for completion of the forms. Questionnaires were completed anonymously (identified only by a code number for each family).

Students completed their questionnaires at school in small groups of approximately 10 students each, with a research assistant available to explain directions and answer any questions. The measures were administered in a 50-min session, and additional measures (not reported here) were completed in a second session 1 week later. Students were given an envelope containing questionnaires for their parents and were instructed to take these materials home and return the completed parent forms in a sealed envelope the following week at the second session.

## Measures

*Adolescent stress.* The junior-high-school version of the Adolescent Perceived Events Scale (APES; Compas, Davis, Forsythe, & Wagner, 1987) was used to measure major and daily stressful events in the lives of the adolescents. The junior-high form of the APES contains a list of 164 major and daily life events representative of those experienced during early adolescence (five events related to sexuality were omitted at the request of local school officials, resulting in a measure with 159 items for the present analyses). For each event, respondents indicate whether the event has occurred within the past 3 months. If the event has occurred, subjects then rate the perceived desirability of the event on a 9-point scale ($-4$ = *extremely undesirable*, $0$ = *neutral*, $4$ = *extremely desirable*). Total weighted negative event scores were calculated by summing events rated as $-4$ through $-1$. Test–retest reliability of the junior-high-school version of the APES has been shown to be adequate over 2 weeks ($r$ = .86; Compas et al., 1987).

In order to determine specific "major life event" and "daily event" scores, the events were categorized into two groups. All items that appear on adolescent life event measures (Johnson & McCutcheon, 1980; Newcomb, Huba, & Bentler, 1981; Swearingen & Cohen, 1985) were categorized as major life events. The remaining events from the APES were independently categorized as major or daily events by three researchers familiar with this area. Categorization was based on agreement between at least two of three raters. All of the events were classified as either a major life event or a daily event, resulting in 58 major events ($\alpha$ = .73) and 106 daily events ($\alpha$ = .86). (Lists of the events are available from the authors.)

*Adolescent behavior problems.* Self-reports of adolescents' emotional and behavioral problems were obtained on the Youth Self-Report (YSR; Achenbach & Edelbrock, 1987), a checklist of 102 behavior problem items rated *not true, somewhat or sometimes true,* and *very true or often true* of the respondent. (The YSR also includes 16 socially desirable items that were excluded from the analyses.) Normative data for the Youth Self-Report Profile are based on nonreferred samples of children and adolescents. Test–retest reliability of the total behavior problem score over a 1-week period for clinically referred youngsters 11 to 18 years of age has been found to be excellent ($r$ = .87; Achenbach & Edelbrock, 1987).

*Parental stress.* Separate measures were used to assess major life events and daily hassles recently experienced by parents.[1] The Life Experiences Survey (LES; Sarason, Johnson, & Siegel, 1978) was used to measure infrequent and dramatic life changes. Subjects rated these events for occurrence during the past year and the impact that they exerted on the respondent's life (either positive or negative). The negative impact scores were summed for a total weighted negative life event score. The test–retest reliability coefficients for negative event scores reported by Sarason et al. ranged from .56 to .88. The Hassles Scale (Kanner et al., 1981) was used to measure frequent and less dramatic events. These events were rated for occurrence during the past month and for the degree of severity to which the hassle was experienced. The severity ratings were summed to create a total hassles score.

*Parental symptoms.* The Symptom Checklist-90-Revised (SCL-90-R; Derogatis, 1983) was used to assess parental psychological and somatic symptoms. The checklist is a 90-item measure designed to assess

Table 1

*Means and Standard Deviations for Parent and Child Stress and Symptom Measures*

| Measure | Boys | | Girls | |
|---|---|---|---|---|
| | M | SD | M | SD |
| **Mother** | | | | |
| Major life events | 6.33 | 7.48 | 5.18 | 7.01 |
| Daily hassles | 32.67 | 26.47 | 31.33 | 24.68 |
| Symptoms | 0.59 | 0.52 | 0.58 | 0.46 |
| **Father** | | | | |
| Major life events | 3.89 | 5.26 | 5.33 | 6.52 |
| Daily hassles | 24.12 | 20.19 | 28.69 | 24.32 |
| Symptoms | 0.37 | 0.34 | 0.39 | 0.31 |
| **Child** | | | | |
| Major life events | 10.13 | 9.09 | 16.55 | 16.23 |
| Daily events | 25.80 | 21.77 | 37.51 | 26.49 |
| Total behavior problems (*T* Score) | 50.09 | 9.54 | 50.80 | 11.04 |

a wide variety of symptoms. Respondents rate the extent to which they have been distressed by each symptom during the past week ($0$ = *not at all*, $4$ = *extremely*). Test–retest reliability, internal consistency, and concurrent validity have all been shown to be adequate (Derogatis, 1983). The Global Severity Index (GSI), which is the sum of scores on individual items divided by the total number of items, was used in all analyses. Internal consistency of the GSI for the present sample was high ($\alpha$ = .98 for mothers and .97 for fathers).

*Demographic questionnaire.* Parents completed a demographic questionnaire concerning their marital status, age, education, income, and number of children in the family.

## Results

### Descriptive Statistics

Means and standard deviations for each of the measures are presented in Table 1.[2] Mean SCL-90-R scores were calculated using the formula for the GSI (see Derogatis, 1983). Means for the present sample corresponded to a *T* score of 60 for mothers

---

[1] The three measures of stressful events used in this study were designed to assess the occurrence of events during different periods of time: 3 months for the Adolescent Perceived Events Scale, 1 year for the Life Experiences Survey, and 1 month for the Hassles Scale. These time frames have been used in other studies of major events and hassles because the time frame for each is appropriate to the nature of the events being measured (e.g., DeLongis, Coyne, Dakof, Folkman, & Lazarus, 1982; Kanner, Coyne, Schaefer, & Lazarus, 1981; Rowlison & Felner, 1988). Because these formats are used in standard administrations of these measures, they were adhered to in the present study. However, the effect of the varying time frames of these measures on the findings of this and other studies is unclear.

[2] The univariate distributions for major events and daily stressors for mothers, fathers, and children and for symptoms for mothers and fathers were all highly positively skewed. Because LISREL assumes a multivariate normal model, square-root transformations were used on these variables to achieve a closer approximation of normality. The means and standard deviations presented in Table 1, however, refer to raw data to allow comparison with findings from other studies.

Table 2
*Pearson Correlations of Parent and Child Stressful Events and Symptoms: Girls*

| Measure | 1 | 2 | 3 | 4 | 5 | 6 | 7 | 8 | 9 |
|---|---|---|---|---|---|---|---|---|---|
| **Mother** | | | | | | | | | |
| 1. Major events | — | .528 *** | .329 *** | .487 *** | .546 *** | .443 *** | .138 | −.127 | .225 *** |
| 2. Daily hassles | | — | .486 *** | .222 ** | .524 *** | .342 *** | .020 | −.128 | .198 ** |
| 3. Symptoms | | | — | .225 *ᵃ | .383 *** | .450 *** | .123 | .111 | .214 *ᵃ |
| **Father** | | | | | | | | | |
| 4. Major events | | | | — | .546 *** | .352 *** | .197 ** | .028 | .125 |
| 5. Daily hassles | | | | | — | .601 *** | .171 | −.155 | .161 |
| 6. Symptoms | | | | | | — | .026 | −.226 ** | .191 *ᵃ |
| **Child** | | | | | | | | | |
| 7. Major events | | | | | | | — | .706 *** | .436 *** |
| 8. Daily events | | | | | | | | — | .362 *** |
| 9. Behavior problems | | | | | | | | | — |

ᵃ Considered significant by chance.
* $p < .05$.  ** $p < .01$.  *** $p < .001$.

and a $T$ score of 58 for fathers when compared with the nonpatient norms on the measure (Derogatis, 1983). A multivariate analysis of variance (MANOVA) indicated that mothers reported significantly more symptoms than fathers, $F(1, 322) = 5.26, p < .001$. Univariate analyses of variance (ANOVAs) indicated that mothers reported more total symptoms as well as symptoms of interpersonal sensitivity, depression, and anxiety. Mean total behavior problems scores on the YSR Profile for this sample were in the average range (on the basis of the norms for the measure; Achenbach & Edelbrock, 1987), with a $T$ score of 50.09 ($SD = 9.54$) for boys and 50.80 ($SD = 11.04$) for girls. The families of young adolescent boys and girls did not differ on any of the parent stress and symptom measures or on demographic variables. Boys and girls differed on weighted negative major life events, with girls ($M = 16.55; SD = 16.23$) reporting more stress than boys ($M = 10.13; SD = 9.09$), $F(1, 172) = 8.46, p = .004$. They also differed on weighted negative daily events, with girls ($M = 37.51; SD = 26.49$) reporting more stress than boys ($M = 25.80; SD = 26.49$), $F(1, 172) = 9.06, p = .003$.

*Correlational Analyses*

Statistical comparison of the intercorrelation matrices for families of boys and girls (using an approach derived by Jennrich, 1970) demonstrated that the two matrices were significantly different, $\chi^2(36) = 52.32, p = .039$, providing further support for the decision to conduct all subsequent analyses for the two sexes separately. Because the analyses were in terms of correlations rather than covariances, and because there were no significant differences among the variances for boys and girls on any variables, the comparison of correlation matrices rather than covariance matrices was appropriate. Family-wise error rates were controlled for in each correlation matrix using an ordered Bonferroni procedure (Larzelere & Mulaik, 1977). As expected, for families with young adolescent girls in the home (see Table 2), major events were correlated with daily stressors, and daily stressors were correlated with symptoms for mothers, fathers, and girls.[3] Correlations between girls' emotional and behavioral problems and mothers' symptoms ($r = .214$) and fa-

thers' symptoms ($r = .191$) were not considered significant after controlling for error. Girls' daily stressors were not related to mothers' or fathers' symptoms. As hypothesized, mothers' hassles were related to fathers' symptoms ($r = .342$), and fathers' hassles were associated with mothers' symptoms ($r = .383$).[4]

[3] Correlations between self-reports of daily hassles and psychological symptoms must be examined cautiously in light of previous concerns about the possible confounds between measures of these two variables (Dohrenwend, Dohrenwend, Dodson, & Shrout, 1984; Dohrenwend & Shrout, 1985; Lazarus, DeLongis, Folkman, & Gruen, 1985). To examine the possibility of confounding in the present data, separate correlations for a subsample of mothers and fathers were run with a set of items on the Daily Hassles Scale identified as being confounded with the Symptom Checklist-90-Revised included in the analyses and excluded from the analyses (see Dohrenwend et al., 1984; Lazarus et al., 1985). The correlations were unchanged for mothers ($r = .63$ vs. $r = .65$) and for fathers ($r = .64$ vs. $r = .63$). However, the possibility still remains that these measures are confounded in that some hassles may be the result of psychological symptoms.

[4] Several items on the Adolescent Perceived Events Scale (APES) refer to events involving parents and, thus, may be confounded with parents' reports of their symptoms on the Symptom Checklist-90-Revised (SCL-90-R). A total of 24 items on the APES referring to parents were identified, and the correlation of these items with mothers' SCL-90-R Global Severity Index scores ($r = .187$) did not differ from the correlation of the nonparent-related APES items with mothers' SLC-90-R scores ($r = .143$); the correlation of APES items referring to parents with fathers' SCL-90-R scores ($r = .185$) did not differ from the correlation of items not referring to parents ($r = .076$). The possibility of a similar problem was identified in the correlations between spouses' Daily Hassles and SCL-90-R scores, because some of the items on the Daily Hassles Scale may represent stressors experienced by both spouses. Correlations between the subscales of the Hassles Scale (work, practical, setting, family, economics, and health hassles; Kanner, 1982) and spouses' SCL-90-R scores were run to test whether subscales containing items likely to be experienced by both spouses (practical, setting, family, and economics) were more highly correlated with spouses' symptoms than subscales containing items that were not likely to be experienced by both spouses (work and health). No differences were found for fathers' work or health hassles or mothers' health hassles. Only the correlation of mothers' work

Table 3

*Pearson Correlations of Parent and Child Stressful Events and Symptoms: Boys*

| Measure | 1 | 2 | 3 | 4 | 5 | 6 | 7 | 8 | 9 |
|---|---|---|---|---|---|---|---|---|---|
| **Mother** | | | | | | | | | |
| 1. Major events | — | .519*** | .375*** | .401*** | .290***[a] | .332*** | .193**[a] | .093 | .097 |
| 2. Daily hassles | | — | .587*** | .264** | .467*** | .487*** | .206**[a] | .154 | −.040 |
| 3. Symptoms | | | — | .180 | .432*** | .608*** | .167 | .316** | .157 |
| **Father** | | | | | | | | | |
| 4. Major events | | | | — | .540*** | .369*** | −.011 | −.007 | −.063 |
| 5. Daily hassles | | | | | — | .757*** | .043 | .097 | .025 |
| 6. Symptoms | | | | | | — | .087 | .262 | .305*** |
| **Child** | | | | | | | | | |
| 7. Major events | | | | | | | — | .648*** | .333*** |
| 8. Daily events | | | | | | | | — | .428*** |
| 9. Behavior problems | | | | | | | | | — |

[a] Considered significant by chance.
* $p < .05$.   ** $p < .01$.   *** $p < .001$.

With regard to the families of young adolescent boys (see Table 3), the correlations between major events and daily stressors and between daily stressors and symptoms were significant for mothers, fathers, and boys. After controlling for chance, boys' emotional and behavioral problems were significantly related to fathers' symptoms ($r = .305$) but not to mothers' symptoms. Mothers' symptoms but not fathers' symptoms were significantly related to boys' daily stressful events ($r = .316$). The correlations between mothers' daily hassles and fathers' symptoms ($r = .487$) and fathers' daily hassles and mothers' symptoms ($r = .432$) were significant.

### Causal Modeling Analyses

The hypothesized model of the relations between major events, daily events, and psychological symptoms among mothers, fathers, and their children was represented by a set of simultaneous equations.[5] Each structural equation expresses a variable as a linear function of all prior variables in the model and represents an improvement over simple bivariate correlations by accounting for relations among all of the variables in the model simultaneously. The set of simultaneous equations was solved using maximum likelihood estimation by means of the LISREL VI computer program (Jöreskog & Sörbom, 1986). We selected LISREL over multiple regression in the present analyses for three reasons. First, LISREL can take into account correlations between disturbances of two variables in a model. In this case, it was assumed that other factors (disturbances) affecting mothers' and fathers' daily hassles and symptoms (e.g., economic factors) would be correlated across parents and that this should be reflected in the model. Second, LISREL provides several indicators of the goodness of fit of the data to the hypothe-

sized model. Because we were interested in relations of stress and symptoms among mothers, fathers, and children (i.e., the family was the unit of analysis), we felt it would be important to evaluate the overall status of the hypothesized model rather than only the significance of individual paths within the model. Third, LISREL generates a set of modification indices to reflect paths that, if added to the model, could improve its overall goodness of fit. Although it is important not to modify a model solely on the basis of these indices, given the early stage of research in this area, we believed that the modification indices could be useful in identifying paths that warrant further research. On the basis of findings from prior research (Compas, 1987; Jurkovic & Ulrici, 1985; Siegal, 1987; Silverberg & Steinberg, 1987; Steinberg, 1987) and the significant difference between the correlation matrices for families of boys and girls, models were tested separately for these two groups.

We chose not to take advantage of one of the major strengths of LISREL: the ability to use latent variables that are based on multiple measures of the same construct (see Anderson, 1987, for an example of structural equation analyses with only manifest variables). To obtain multiple measures of parent and child major and daily stressors and symptoms, we would have needed

---

[5] The analyses were based on correlations computed with pairwise deletion. We chose to use pairwise deletion, rather than the more standard casewise deletion, because there were substantially less data for fathers ($n = 162$) than for mothers and children ($n = 211$). If we were to use casewise deletion, we would sacrifice the greater precision of the estimates of correlations within and between mothers and children. The disadvantages of using pairwise deletion were outweighed by the advantages of greater precision. Furthermore, although the number of subjects necessary for conducting structural equation analyses cannot be set independently of the number of variables and paths tested in the model, several authors have suggested that reliability of the findings decreases substantially with samples under approximately 100 (e.g., Tanaka, 1987). By using pairwise deletion, we were able to retain samples of 116 girls and their mothers and 95 boys and their mothers. All tests of significance in the LISREL analyses were based on the minimum sample size for the calculation of any correlation, thus keeping the tests conservative.

---

hassles with fathers' symptoms was significantly lower than the correlations of the other subscales of mothers' hassles. Thus, the association between spouses' hassles and symptoms does not appear to be attributable solely, or substantially, to hassles that were experienced by both spouses.

Table 4
*Evaluations of Models of Mothers', Fathers', and Girls' Major Events, Daily Events, and Psychological Symptoms*

| | Model tests | | | | Model comparisons $(M_0$ vs. $M_1)$ | |
|---|---|---|---|---|---|---|
| Model | $\chi^2$ | df | $R^2$ | GFI | $\chi^2$ | df |
| $M_0$ | 236.42** | 33 | | | | |
| $M_1$ | 37.40* | 19 | .717 | .895 | 199.02** | 14 |

* $p < .01$.  ** $p < .001$.

to use brief measures of each construct in order to avoid over-burdening the participants in the study (cf. Martin, 1987). We chose instead to use measures of each construct that we believe to be the most comprehensive and psychometrically sound of measures available. Each of these scales is quite long, however, prohibiting the use of multiple indicators of each construct.

The adequacy of each of the models as explanations of the data for the families of girls, as well as for comparisons between the models, is presented in Table 4. The null model, $M_0$, in which no paths are hypothesized, was not expected to fit the data and clearly does not do so: $\chi^2(33) = 236.42, p < .001$. This model serves solely as a base against which to compare a hypothesized model ($M_1$). As indicated in Table 4, $M_1$ is a significantly better fit to the data than $M_0$. The standardized structural coefficients for the hypothesized paths in $M_1$ are presented in Figure 1. Consistent with the hypotheses, the paths from major to daily events and from daily events to symptoms were significant for mothers, fathers, and girls.[6] The hypothesized relation between girls' daily stressful events and their parents' symptoms was partially supported, because the path from girls' daily stressors to mothers' symptoms was significant but the path from girls' daily stressors to fathers' symptoms was not. The hypothesis that spouses' hassles and symptoms would be related was partially supported, because the path from fathers' hassles to mothers' symptoms was significant but the path from mothers' hassles to fathers' symptoms was not. Finally, the hypothesized paths from parents' symptoms to their children's behavior problems received partial support, because fathers' but not mothers' symptoms were significantly related to girls' self-reported emotional and behavioral problems. As expected, the disturbances for parents' hassles and symptoms were significantly related.

Although $M_1$ is a significantly better fit than the null model and supports some of the hypotheses, it contains a number of nonsignificant pathways and is not a completely adequate fit to the data, $\chi^2(19) = 37.40, p = .007$ (the goodness-of-fit value was .895). The modification indices generated by LISREL suggested a modification of the model so that the direction of the path between girls' daily stressors and fathers' symptoms was from fathers' symptoms to girls' daily stressors and was negative in valence ($\beta = -.244$). The substitution of this path did reduce the chi-square value, $\chi^2 = 30.02, p = .049$, and improved the overall Goodness of Fit Index (.917). However, it is important not to give undue weight to paths that are not predicted by the

model being tested and are based only on the empirically based indices generated by LISREL (e.g., Biddle & Marlin, 1987). Thus, the adoption of a revised model including this path was not warranted. However, this path between fathers' symptoms and girls' daily stressors deserves attention in future research.

Similar analyses were conducted for the families of young adolescent boys, and the adequacy of the models to explain the data as well as comparisons between the models are presented in Table 5. The null model (in which no paths were hypothesized) did not represent the data as reflected by the highly significant chi-square, $\chi^2(33) = 226.82, p < .001$. The hypothesized model ($M_1$; see Figure 2) was a significantly better fit than the null model and did represent an adequate fit to the data as represented by the nonsignificant chi-square, $\chi^2(19) = 19.42, p = .430$ (the goodness-of-fit value was .938). The hypothesized paths from major events to daily events and from daily events to symptoms were significant for mothers, fathers, and boys. The hypothesized paths from boys' daily stressors to both mothers' and fathers' symptoms were significant. The path from fathers' symptoms to boys' emotional and behavior problems was significant, but the path from mothers' symptoms to boys' problems was not significant. Finally, the paths between fathers' daily hassles and mothers' symptoms and between mothers' daily hassles and fathers' symptoms were significant. Again, as expected, the disturbances for parents' hassles and symptoms were significantly related.

## Discussion

These findings are useful in clarifying stress–symptom relations within individual family members as well as among family members. The hypothesized model in which daily stressors mediate the relation between major life events and psychological symptoms was supported for mothers, fathers, and young adolescent children in the structural equation analyses. The paths from major events to daily hassles and from hassles to symptoms were significant in each case. The present findings extend those reported by Wagner et al. (1988) with older adolescents to young adolescents and their parents. It appears that the relation between major life events and psychological distress is mediated, to a great extent, by daily stressors. These daily stressors appear to be more psychologically salient than major events and, thus, more closely related to psychological symptoms. These findings are made more compelling because they do not appear to be the result of possibly confounded items on the Hassles Scale and the SCL-90-R such as those identified by Dohrenwend and colleagues (Dohrenwend et al., 1984; Dohrenwend & Shrout, 1985).

Consistent with previous studies by Cohen et al. (1987) and Thomson and Vaux (1986), a significant relation was not found between parents' stressful events and children's self-reports of emotional and behavioral problems. Partial support was found for the hypothesis that this relation would be mediated by the

---

[6] When direct paths from major life events to symptoms were added for parents, boys, and girls, these paths were generally not significant. These results support those reported by Wagner, Compas, and Howell (1988).

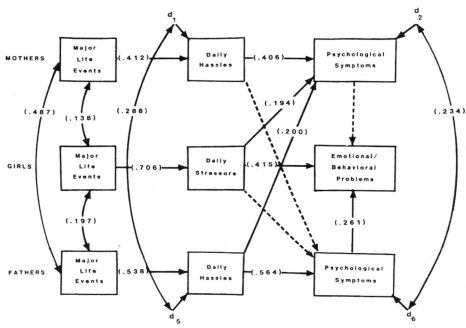

*Figure 1.* Hypothesized model of mothers', fathers', and girls' major events, daily events, and psychological symptoms. (Significant paths are represented by solid lines and nonsignificant paths by dotted lines. Values in parentheses represent standardized structural coefficients.)

level of psychological symptoms displayed by parents in association with their own self-reported stressful events, because the paths from fathers' but not mothers' symptoms to girls' and boys' emotional and behavioral problems were significant in the structural equation analyses. From the perspective of a cognitive model of stress, these findings indicate that fathers' symptoms held considerably greater emotional meaning for the present sample of young adolescent boys and girls than did symptoms of psychological distress displayed by their mothers. Given the higher base rate of a variety of symptoms reported by mothers in this sample, fathers' symptoms may be more salient and have greater impact because they occur less often. Alternatively, fathers may exert greater influence on the functioning of others in the family because of imbalances in interpersonal power dynamics. Whereas the presence of clinical depression in mothers is associated with increased disturbance in children (e.g., Beardslee, Bemporad, Keller, & Klerman, 1983; Hammen et al., 1987; Orvaschel, 1983), the present findings suggest that subclinical levels of parents' symptoms may relate to children's adjustment in a different manner. The present findings underscore the importance of obtaining data from both mothers and fathers when examining stress and symptoms in families.

With regard to the relations between children's stressful events and parents' symptoms, significant paths were found from boys' daily stressors to mothers' and fathers' symptoms and from girls' daily stressors to mothers' symptoms. These

Table 5
*Evaluations of Models of Mothers', Fathers', and Boys' Major Events, Daily Events, and Psychological Symptoms*

| Model | Model tests | | | | Model comparisons ($M_0$ vs. $M_i$) | |
|---|---|---|---|---|---|---|
| | $\chi^2$ | $df$ | $R^2$ | GFI | $\chi^2$ | $df$ |
| $M_0$ | 226.82* | 33 | | | | |
| $M_1$ | 19.42 | 19 | .648 | .938 | 207.40* | 14 |

* $p < .001$.

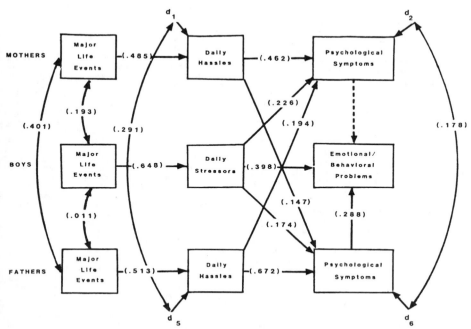

*Figure 2.* Hypothesized model of mothers', fathers', and boys' major events, daily events, and psychological symptoms. (Significant paths are represented by solid lines and nonsignificant paths by dotted lines. Values in parentheses represent standardized structural coefficients.)

paths provide support for the hypothesis that parents may be able to infer meaning from stressful events experienced by their children and, thus, are directly affected by these events. Modification indices suggested a negative path from fathers' symptoms to girls' daily stressors that was not included in the hypothesized model that we tested in the structural equation analyses. Although we chose not to develop an alternative model including this path, we believe that it is worthy of examination in future research. This pattern may reflect a tendency for young adolescent girls and boys to be affected differently by parental functioning (Siegal, 1987), a finding that would be consistent with evidence indicating that emotional autonomy and independence are encouraged at an earlier age for boys than for girls (Jurkovic & Ulrici, 1985).

The hypothesized paths between spouses' stress and symptoms were also supported in the correlational and structural equation causal modeling analyses. Correlational analyses for the entire sample corroborate earlier findings by Thomson and Vaux (1986), because spouses' daily hassles and symptoms were significantly related. In the structural equation analyses, the paths from fathers' hassles to mothers' symptoms were signifi-

cant in families of both boys and girls, whereas the path from mothers' hassles to fathers' symptoms was significant only in boys' families. These findings are generally consistent with the notion that parents' symptoms would be directly related to their spouses' stressful events separately from the symptoms displayed by their spouses. Further analyses are needed to identify possible differences between husbands and wives in their sensitivity to various subtypes of hassles. Whereas previous studies have found adult women to be more affected by stress in the lives of others than are men (e.g., Kessler & McLeod, 1984), the present findings indicate that both mothers' and fathers' psychological symptoms may be related to stressors experienced by their spouses.

Although the model for families of young adolescent girls failed to generate a completely adequate fit to the data (as reflected by the significant chi-square and a goodness-of-fit value of .895, slightly below .90), the model for boys' families did achieve an adequate fit to the data, and the models for both boys' and girls' families did explain substantial portions of the variance in stress and symptoms ($R^2 = .717$, for families of girls, and $R^2 = .648$, for families of boys). These findings provide general support for a model of stress and symptoms in families that includes both intraindividual and interindividual relations and underscore the need to examine the social context—in this case, the family—in which stress and symptoms develop. Although the general appearance of the models is approximately the same for boys and girls, given that research in this area is still at an early stage, we believe it is important to examine data such as these for possible gender differences.

Finally, several limitations of the present study must be noted. First, this investigation focused on triads within the family involving two parents and one child. Studies of stress and symptom relations including all family members will be necessary for the development of a complete model of interindividual stress and symptom processes in families. Second, it was hypothesized that the meaning of stressful events in the lives of parents is communicated to their children, at least in part, through the symptoms displayed by the parents. Direct reports of children's perceptions of the meaning of their parents' symptomatic behavior are necessary to fully validate this hypothesis. Third, because these analyses are based on cross-sectional data, they cannot be used to test true causal relationships among the variables. In fact, prospective studies of adolescents have indicated that symptoms may lead to increased stressful events (e.g., Cohen et al., 1987) or that stress and symptoms are reciprocally related (e.g., Compas, Wagner, Slavin, & Vannatta, 1986). Future studies that make use of prospective-longitudinal designs will be important in examining further this model of stress within families.

## References

Achenbach, T. M., & Edelbrock, C. (1987). *Manual for the Youth Self-Report*. Burlington, VT: University of Vermont, Department of Psychiatry.

Anderson, J. G. (1987). Structural equation models in the social and behavioral sciences: Modeling building. *Child Development, 58*, 49–64.

Baer, P. E., Garmezy, L. B., McLaughlin, R. J., Pokorny, A. D., & Wernick, M. J. (1987). Stress, coping, family conflict, and adolescent alcohol use. *Journal of Behavioral Medicine, 10*, 449–466.

Beardslee, W. R., Bemporad, J., Keller, M., & Klerman, G. L. (1983). Children of parents with major affective disorder: A review. *American Journal of Psychiatry, 140*, 825–832.

Biddle, B. J., & Marlin, M. M. (1987). Causality, confirmation, credulity, and structural equation modeling. *Child Development, 58*, 4–17.

Billings, A. G., Cronkite, R. C., & Moos, R. H. (1983). Social–environmental factors in unipolar depression: Comparisons of depressed and nondepressed controls. *Journal of Abnormal Psychology, 92*, 119–133.

Billings, A. G., & Moos, R. H. (1984). Coping, stress, and social resources among adults with unipolar depression. *Journal of Personality and Social Psychology, 46*, 877–891.

Billings, A. G., & Moos, R. H. (1985). Life stressors and social resources affect posttreatment outcomes among depressed patients. *Journal of Abnormal Psychology, 94*, 140–153.

Bronfenbrenner, U. (1986). Ecology of the family as a context for human development: Research perspectives. *Developmental Psychology, 22*, 723–742.

Cohen, L. H., Burt, C. E., & Bjork, J. P. (1987). Effects of life events experienced by young adolescents and their parents. *Developmental Psychology, 23*, 583–592.

Compas, B. E. (1987). Stress and life events during childhood and adolescence. *Clinical Psychology Review, 7*, 275–302.

Compas, B. E., Davis, G. E., & Forsythe, C. J. (1985). Characteristics of life events during adolescence. *American Journal of Community Psychology, 13*, 677–691.

Compas, B. E., Davis, G. E., Forsythe, C. J., & Wagner, B. M. (1987). Assessment of major and daily life events during adolescence: The Adolescent Perceived Events Scale. *Journal of Consulting and Clinical Psychology, 55*, 534–541.

Compas, B. E., Wagner, B. M., Slavin, L. A., & Vannatta, K. (1986). A prospective study of life events, social support, and psychological symptomatology during the transition from high school to college. *American Journal of Community Psychology, 14*, 241–257.

Cronkite, R. C., & Moos, R. H. (1984). The role of predisposing and moderating factors in the stress–illness relationship. *Journal of Health and Social Behavior, 25*, 372–393.

DeLongis, A., Coyne, J. C., Dakof, G., Folkman, S., & Lazarus, R. S. (1982). Relationship of daily hassles, uplifts, and major life events to health status. *Health Psychology, 1*, 119–136.

Derogatis, L. R. (1983). *SCL-90-R administration: Scoring and procedures manual*. Towson, MD: Clinical Psychometric Research.

Dohrenwend, B. S., Dohrenwend, B. P., Dodson, M., & Shrout, P. E. (1984). Symptoms, hassles, social supports, and life events: Problem of confounded measures. *Journal of Abnormal Psychology, 93*, 222–230.

Dohrenwend, B. P., & Shrout, P. E. (1985). "Hassles" in the conceptualization and measurement of life stress variables. *American Psychologist, 4*, 780–785.

Felner, R. D., Farber, S. S., & Primavera, J. (1983). Transitions and stressful life events: A model of primary prevention. In R. D. Felner, L. A. Jason, J. N. Moritsugu, & S. S. Farber (Eds.), *Preventive psychology: Theory, research, and practice* (pp. 191–215). New York: Pergamon.

Fergusson, D. M., Horwood, L. J., Gretton, M. E., & Shannon, F. T. (1985). Family life events, maternal depression, and maternal and teacher descriptions of child behavior. *Pediatrics, 75*, 30–35.

Hammen, C., Adrian, C., Gordon, D., Burge, D., Jaenicke, C., & Hiroto, D. (1987). Children of depressed mothers: Maternal strain and symptom predictors of dysfunction. *Journal of Abnormal Psychology, 96*, 190–198.

Holahan, C. K., Holahan, C. J., & Belk, S. S. (1984). Adjustment in aging: The roles of life stress, hassles, and self-efficacy. *Health Psychology, 3*, 315–328.

Holahan, C. J., & Moos, R. H. (1987). Risk, resistance, and psychological distress: A longitudinal analysis with adults and children. *Journal of Abnormal Psychology, 96*, 3–13.

Hollingshead, A. B. (1975). *Four factor index of social status*. New Haven, CT: Yale University, Department of Sociology.

Jennrich, R. I. (1970). An asymptotic chi-square test for the equality of two correlation matrices. *Journal of the American Statistical Association, 65*, 904–912.

Johnson, J. H. (1986). *Life events as stressors in childhood and adolescence*. Beverly Hills, CA: Sage.

Johnson, J. H., & McCutcheon, S. (1980). Assessing life events in older children and adolescents: Preliminary findings with the Life Events Checklist. In I. G. Sarason & C. D. Spielberger (Eds.), *Stress and anxiety* (Vol. 7, pp. 111–125). Washington, DC: Hemisphere.

Jöreskog, K. G., & Sörbom, D. (1986). *LISREL VI: Analysis of linear structural relationships by maximum likelihood, instrumental variables, and least squares methods* (4th ed.). Mooresville, IN: Scientific Software.

Jurkovic, G. J., & Ulrici, D. (1985). Empirical perspectives on adolescents and their families. In L. L'Abate (Ed.), *The handbook of family psychology and therapy* (Vol. 1, pp. 215–257). Homewood, IL: Dorsey Press.

Kanner, A. D. (1982, August). *Daily hassles as mediators of employment/gender differences in adaptational outcomes.* Paper presented at the 90th Annual Convention of the American Psychological Association, Washington, DC.

Kanner, A. D., Coyne, J. C., Schaefer, C., & Lazarus, R. S. (1981). Comparison of two modes of stress measurement: Daily hassles and uplifts versus major life events. *Journal of Behavioral Medicine, 4,* 1–19.

Kessler, R. C., & McLeod, J. D. (1984). Sex differences in vulnerability to undesirable life events. *American Sociological Review, 49,* 620–631.

Larzelere, R. E., & Mulaik, S. A. (1977). Single-sample tests for many correlations. *Psychological Bulletin, 84,* 557–569.

Lazarus, R. S., DeLongis, A., Folkman, S., & Gruen, R. (1985). Stress and adaptational outcomes: The problem of confounded measures. *American Psychologist, 40,* 770–779.

Lazarus, R. S., & Folkman, S. (1984). *Stress, appraisal and coping.* New York: Springer.

Lewis, C. E., Siegel, J. M., & Lewis, M. A. (1984). Feeling bad: Exploring sources of distress among pre-adolescent children. *American Journal of Public Health, 74,* 117–122.

Martin, J. A. (1987). Structural equation modeling: A guide for the perplexed. *Child Development, 58,* 33–37.

Monroe, S. M. (1983). Major and minor life events as predictors of psychological distress: Further issues and findings. *Journal of Behavioral Medicine, 6,* 189–205.

Moos, R. H. (1984). Context and coping: Toward a unifying conceptual framework. *American Journal of Community Psychology, 12,* 5–25.

Newcomb, M. D., Huba, G. J., & Bentler, P. M. (1981). A multidimensional assessment of stressful life events among adolescents. *Journal of Health and Social Behavior, 22,* 400–415.

Orvaschel, H. (1983). Maternal depression and child dysfunction: Children at risk. In B. B. Lahey & A. E. Kazdin (Eds.), *Advances in clinical child psychology* (Vol. 6, pp. 169–198). New York: Plenum.

Patterson, G. R. (1986). Performance models for antisocial boys. *American Psychologist, 41,* 432–444.

Pearlin, L. I., Lieberman, M. A., Menaghan, E. G., & Mullan, J. T. (1981). The stress process. *Journal of Health and Social Behavior, 22,* 337–356.

Rowlison, R. T., & Felner, R. D. (1988). Major life events, hassles, and adaptation in adolescence: Confounding in the conceptualization and measurement of life stress and adjustment revisited. *Journal of Personality and Social Psychology, 55,* 432–444.

Sarason, I. G., Johnson, J. H., & Siegel, J. M. (1978). Assessing the impact of life changes: Development of the Life Experiences Survey. *Journal of Consulting and Clinical Psychology, 46,* 932–946.

Siegal, M. (1987). Are sons and daughters treated more differently by fathers than by mothers? *Developmental Review, 7,* 183–209.

Silverberg, S. B., & Steinberg, L. (1987). Adolescent autonomy, parent-adolescent conflict, and parental well-being. *Journal of Youth and Adolescence, 16,* 293–312.

Steinberg, L. (1987). Recent research on the family at adolescence: The extent and nature of sex differences. *Journal of Youth and Adolescence, 16,* 191–197.

Swearingen, E. M., & Cohen, L. H. (1985). Measurement of adolescents' life events: The Junior High School Life Experiences Survey. *American Journal of Community Psychology, 13,* 69–85.

Tanaka, J. S. (1987). "How big is big enough?": Sample size and goodness of fit in structural equation models with latent variables. *Child Development, 58,* 134–146.

Taylor, S. E. (1983). Adjustment to threatening events: A theory of cognitive adaptation. *American Psychologist, 38,* 1161–1173.

Thomson, B., & Vaux, A. (1986). The importation, transmission, and moderation of stress in the family system. *American Journal of Community Psychology, 14,* 39–57.

Wagner, B. M., Compas, B. E., & Howell, D. C. (1988). Daily and major life events: A test of an integrative model of psychosocial stress. *American Journal of Community Psychology, 16,* 189–205.

Received March 22, 1988
Revision received August 26, 1988
Accepted September 13, 1988 ∎

# Referring and Reporting Research Participants at Risk: Views from Urban Adolescents

## Celia B. Fisher, Ann Higgins-D'Alessandro, Jean-Marie B. Rau, Tara L. Kuther, and Susan Belanger

*Fordham University*

FISHER, CELIA B.; HIGGINS-D'ALESSANDRO, ANN; RAU, JEAN-MARIE B.; KUTHER, TARA L.; and BE-LANGER, SUSAN. *Referring and Reporting Research Participants at Risk: Views from Urban Adolescents.* CHILD DEVELOPMENT, 1996, 67, 2086–2100. Researching developmental risks of urban youth raises ethical concerns when an investigator discovers a participant is in jeopardy. This study collected data on 147 seventh, ninth, and eleventh graders' views of 3 investigator options: (1) taking no action and maintaining confidentiality, (2) reporting the problem to a concerned parent or adult, and (3) facilitating adolescent self-referrals. Participants judged these options within the context of 5 risk domains: substance abuse, child maltreatment, life-threatening behaviors, delinquency, and shyness. Judgments of reporting options were related to grade and ratings of risk severity, but not to moral reasoning. Confidentiality was viewed favorably for risk behaviors of low perceived severity or for which the consequences of adult discovery might introduce greater risk. Confidentiality was viewed unfavorably and reporting to adults favorably for child maltreatment and threats of suicide. Self-referral was viewed favorably across all grades and risk behaviors. Implications of adolescent perspectives for research ethics are discussed.

The past 15 years have witnessed a significant shift in the way developmental scientists view their roles and responsibilities. Economic, social, political, and disciplinary factors have converged to foster increased attention to the social and applied relevance of the developmental data base (Fisher & Lerner, 1994; Fisher et al., 1993; Horowitz & O'Brien, 1989). In particular, developmental scientists are being called upon to generate knowledge about many of the societal problems jeopardizing the development of adaptive and productive life skills during the critical years of adolescence (Dougherty, 1993; Jessor, 1993; Lerner, 1993; Zaslow & Takanishi, 1993). Scholars engaged in research on developmental processes in adolescence have begun to shift the focus of their work from the laboratory to the streets in response to societal demands for knowledge and techniques that can help stem the tide of psychological risk associated with urban poverty, violence, and despair. Concern about the current risk-opportunity imbalance (Takanishi, 1993) in the lives of urban adolescents has risen with increases in the number of teenagers: living in poverty, abusing drugs and alcohol, becoming victimized by or engaged in violence, manifesting depressive symptomology, and engaging in high-risk sexual activities and other health compromising behaviors (Chase-Lansdale & Brooks-Gunn, 1994; Children's Safety Network, 1991; Cicchetti & Toth, 1993; Gans & Blyth, 1990; Jessor, 1992; Petersen et al., 1993; Richters & Martinez, 1993; Sum & Fogg, 1991; Takanishi, 1993).

## Referring and Reporting Adolescent Research Participants: An Ethical Challenge

As developmental scientists move out of the laboratory to examine developmental correlates of adolescent risk and to design and evaluate interventions that may alter such risk, participant welfare evolves from an abstract ethical issue to a concrete daily concern (Fisher & Tryon, 1990). For example, investigation of the developmental correlates of adaptive and maladaptive behaviors in hitherto underresearched urban adolescent populations has the potential to tap previously undetected problems facing individual research participants (Fisher, 1993; Fisher & Rosendahl, 1990). During the course of such data collection, adolescent participants may reveal information suggesting that they may be thinking about

Requests for reprints should be addressed to Celia B. Fisher, Fordham University, Department of Psychology, Dealy Hall, 441 East Fordham Road, Bronx, NY 10458.

30

suicide, have been or are being abused by an adult, are engaging in health-compromising behaviors, or are planning to engage in activities that might be illegal or harmful to others. This raises ethical questions concerning whether an investigator should take steps to help the participant address these problems.

## Current Ethical Guidelines on Referring and Reporting Issues

Current federal and professional guidelines offer incomplete answers about what investigators should do if during the course of experimentation they discover that an adolescent's well-being or the well-being of others may be in jeopardy. For example, Federal Regulations Part 46 Subpart D on Protections for Children Involved as Subjects in Research (Department of Health and Human Services [DHHS], 1991) does not address whether an investigator has a responsibility to report or refer adolescent research participants to parents or appropriate authorities when a problem has been discovered during the course of research. Similarly, while the American Psychological Association's (APA) *Ethical Principles of Psychologists and Code of Conduct* allows a psychologist to disclose confidential information without the consent of the individual when it is mandated by law or to protect an individual or others from harm (APA, 1992, Standard 5.05), the current terminology of the code (e.g., references to "patients" and "clients") leaves uncertain the extent to which this standard refers to research participants.

More specific guidelines appear in the Society for Research in Child Development's (SRCD) *Ethical Standards for Research with Children* (SRCD, 1993). Principle 9 of the *Ethical Standards* states that when research-derived information suggests that a child's well-being may be in jeopardy, an investigator has a responsibility to inform guardians or those expert in the field in order to arrange necessary assistance for the child (SRCD, 1993, Principle 9, p. 338). While the SRCD *Ethical Standards* raises expectations regarding investigator responsibility, it does not resolve the complex issue of deciding when it is appropriate or how to report or provide referrals for adolescent participants whose well-being is judged to be in jeopardy (Fisher, 1994).

## Referring and Reporting Options

*Taking no action.*—In the course of conducting studies with adolescent populations, researchers may utilize assessment instruments or interviewing techniques that yield previously undetected information about conditions that place an adolescent participant at developmental risk. When such facts have been uncovered, the scientific community has traditionally been reluctant to act upon such information, whether out of concern for participant confidentiality, a healthy skepticism that behaviors measured may not have "diagnostic" validity, or a commitment to scientific controls that may be jeopardized by humanitarian actions (Fisher, 1993, 1994; Fisher & Brennan, 1992; Fisher, Hoagwood, & Jensen, 1996).

The decision to take no action when such information is revealed during the course of research is supported by the importance federal and professional guidelines have placed upon the maintenance of confidentiality for research-derived information (e.g., APA, 1992, Standard 5.02; Office for Protection of Research Risks [OPRR], 1993, pp. 3-27; SRCD, 1993, Principle 11). Implicit in these guidelines is the assumption that protection of privacy is a fundamental right of those who have agreed to participate in research. Moreover, developmental scientists are aware that sharing with parents or other concerned adults research-derived information about the behaviors of individual adolescents can sometimes create stressful or harmful consequences for teenage participants, especially if adults react to such revelations with punitive measures.

The decision to take no action when confronted with information suggesting developmental risk is also supported in research situations in which assessment instruments valid for identifying group differences in the experimental setting may not have the psychometric properties sufficient to draw meaningful conclusions about individual risk (Fisher, 1993, 1994; Fisher & Brennan, 1992). For example, while adolescent alcohol use has been associated with a number of risk factors, including delinquency and unprotected sex (Kandel, Davies, Karus, & Yamaguchi, 1986), empirical information does not yet exist regarding the degree of alcohol consumption, personal characteristics, or social factors that can identify which individual adolescent might progress to alcohol abuse (Pentz, 1994). Under such circumstances, discussing the implications of specific drinking patterns with adolescents or their parents might be misleading and outside the boundaries of good ethical practice (Fisher, 1993).

31

A third factor influencing the decision to take no action when research-derived information indicates potential participant risk concerns the ways in which many investigators perceive their responsibilities and obligations to the community. Such research-derived information places investigators in what Veatch (1987) has coined the scientist-citizen dilemma: the need to reconcile the scientist's professional commitment to the implementation of well-controlled research designs with his or her humanitarian commitment to protect participant welfare (Fisher, 1993, 1994; Fisher & Rosendahl, 1990; Scarr, 1994). In such situations, investigators may be concerned that acting to assist an adolescent research participant may threaten the internal validity of an experiment (especially in longitudinal designs) or jeopardize the trust and participation of other adolescents involved in the research. This act utilitarian position (an act is morally justified if it promotes the greatest good for the greatest number of persons) has traditionally been adopted in human subjects research (e.g., Beauchamp, Faden, Wallace, & Walters, 1982). Consequently, when a conflict arises between scientific rigor and the immediate welfare of a research participant, investigators often see the production of well-controlled data that can benefit society as superseding their obligation to facilitate or procure services for individual participants (Fisher, 1994).

*Reporting risk-related information.*— In some research contexts, investigators may become aware of information suggesting delinquent behavior, the use of addictive products, or threats of harm or violence to the adolescent participant or others that appear to require immediate attention. As indicated previously, under such conditions, professional guidelines could be interpreted as encouraging an investigator to report the problem to adults who could arrange necessary assistance for the participant (e.g., APA, 1992, Standard 5.05; SRCD, 1993, Principle 9). Moreover, some investigators may take the position that under certain circumstances the immediate welfare of research participants outweighs the distal contributions to society that may be jeopardized by potential threats to the integrity of the research design created by reporting.

Investigators studying adolescent development need to also be aware that certain reporting decisions, such as the decision to report to authorities suspected child abuse, threats of violence, or certain illegal conduct, may not only be an ethical decision, but a legal requirement (Fisher, 1993, 1994; Fisher et al., 1996). Since the 1976 Child Abuse Prevention and Treatment Act, all 50 states have enacted statutes to mandate the reporting of suspected child abuse or neglect. Since states vary as to whether researchers are included in the list of individuals mandated to report child abuse (see Liss, 1994), investigators must review their own state laws to determine their personal responsibility to report child abuse and neglect as well as the responsibility of other professionals (e.g., pediatricians, school psychologists) who may be part of their research team (Fisher, 1991, 1993).

Recently, Appelbaum and Rosenbaum (1989) have raised concerns about the possibility that social science researchers may, under certain conditions, share with their practitioner colleagues the responsibility to warn third parties about suspected dangers posed by research participants (see *Tarasoff v. Regents of the University of California,* 1976). The possibility that some researchers working with violence-prone adolescents may have a duty to protect potential victims underscores the importance of considering ethical issues associated with reporting high-risk participant behaviors to adults when appropriate (Fisher, 1993; Fisher et al., 1996). There are also situations in which confidential records regarding illegal behaviors of adolescent research participants may be subject to subpoena (Melton, 1990). While researchers may obtain a Certificate of Confidentiality from the Department of Health and Human Services to protect the privacy of research participants against legally compelled disclosure of identifying information, the certificate's protection has yet to be tested in the courts (Hoagwood, 1994). Thus, investigators studying adolescent delinquency or use of illegal drugs may need to consider the extent to which reporting such behaviors to adults who can assist a participant may, in the long run, be a better form of participant protection than taking no action.

*Assisting adolescent participants to self-refer.*—There may be situations in which research-derived information suggests that an adolescent research participant would benefit from medical, social, or psychological services, but would not benefit from reporting the adolescent's risk status to concerned adults. For example, a researcher may learn that an adolescent participant has not sought medical consultation for a suspected sexually transmitted disease. While failure to receive medical attention in the era of AIDS may in fact be a life-threatening risk for the participant, informing the parent about risks associated with sexual activity may violate a teenager's privacy or even jeopardize his or her welfare. In such situations, investigators may look to the legal-medical model defining the rights of adolescents to consent to medical intervention as a guide for determining whether they should report the risk to a parent or discuss with the adolescent ways in which he or she can independently obtain services (Fisher, 1993, 1994; Fisher et al., 1996; Holder, 1981). Asher (1993) has developed and tested an innovative procedure of self-referral following research on peer rejection and loneliness in a normative sample. In his model, after completing the study, participants indicate on a form whether they would like to speak to a school social worker about "things that bother you." The adaptation of such a procedure for normative middle and high school samples may be an appropriate reporting option in studies examining individual behaviors observed to predict poor social adaptation (e.g., shyness) or delinquent behaviors judged inappropriate for formal reporting.

## Adolescents as Partners in Ethical Decision Making

When considering the implications of taking no action, reporting a suspected risk to an appropriate and concerned adult, or helping an adolescent self-refer, investigators must be wary of the potential to either overestimate or underestimate the impact of their decision on the research participant. A relatively untapped resource for assisting in such ethical decision making is the perspective of members of the population who will serve as research participants (Bok, 1978; Fisher & Fyrberg, 1994; Gergen, 1973; Levine, 1986; Melton, Levine, Koocher, Rosenthal, & Thompson, 1988; Wilson & Donnerstein, 1976). Data on adolescent perceptions of referring and reporting alternatives can help developmental scientists judge the impact that a decision to maintain confidentiality, report at-risk conditions to an appropriate adult, or assist in self-referrals may have on the research participants themselves.

Eliciting the opinions of adolescents from communities representative of prospective samples supports the moral principle of *respect for personhood* by recognizing that prospective participants are themselves moral agents, with the right to apply a moral judgment to the ethical procedures that will be used in research in which they or members of their cohort will be asked to participate (Fisher & Fyrberg, 1994). Surveying the opinions of adolescents on reporting and referring decisions can also guard against researchers either erroneously assuming that such procedures will have a devastating impact on urban youth or underestimating the potential distress associated with a particular procedure (Farr & Seaver, 1975; Fisher & Fyrberg, 1994; Veatch, 1987). Moreover, such surveys may have generalizability to the ethical decision making of investigators studying common developmental risks across a variety of settings. Finally, including members of a participant community in decision making about ethical procedures has the potential to reduce participant anxiety and increase the perceived justice of reporting decisions made during the course of research (Melton et al., 1988).

In summary, teenagers participating in research, as well as developmental scientists, stand to benefit from research investigating participant perspectives on reporting options available to investigators who discover that a research participant is in developmental jeopardy. Our goal for the present study was to provide empirical information that could assist the ethical decision making of investigators studying adolescent risk behaviors. We sought the opinions of teenagers living in a low-income urban environment since lower socioeconomic and ethnic minority youth have been the focus of recent research on adolescent risk behavior and are disproportionately vulnerable to the social problems currently facing American children and youth (Fisher, Jackson, & Villarruel, in press; Hammond & Yung, 1993; Jessor, 1992). In this investigation, we defined participant jeopardy in terms of 12 risks that have generated a significant amount of attention in the developmental literature and that might vary in perceived severity: alcohol consumption, illicit drug use, cigarette smoking, physical abuse, sexual abuse, suicide, sexually transmitted diseases (STD), truancy, vandalism, theft, violence, and shyness (Berman & Jobbs, 1991; Chase-Lansdale & Brooks-Gunn, 1994; Cicchetti & Toth, 1993; DiLalla & Gottesman, 1989; Duckworth & Dejung, 1989; Gans & Blyth, 1990; Hauck, Martens, & Wetzel, 1986; Kandel et al., 1986; Lester & Anderson, 1992; Petersen et al., 1993; Quadrel, Fischhoff, & Davis, 1993; Richters & Martinez, 1993; Stiffman & Davis, 1990; Windle, 1990). To further broaden our understanding of adolescent perspectives on these options, we sought to examine participant responses within the context of their judgments regarding the perceived severity of the risks under consideration as well as their level of moral reasoning.

## Method

### Participants

The sample consisted of 44 seventh graders (mean age = 12.7 years), 42 ninth graders (mean age = 15.1 years), and 61 eleventh graders (mean age = 17.1 years) attending a New York City public middle and high school. These two neighborhood schools served adolescents from lower- to lower-middle-class families, as indicated by an average Hollingshead (1957) score of 4 (range = 2–7) based on student reports of parents' occupations. Eighty-three percent of fathers and 62% of mothers were reported to have employment outside the home. Females comprised 66%, 43%, and 52% of seventh-, ninth-, and eleventh-grade respondents, respectively. The seventh graders primarily identified themselves as Hispanic/Latino (85.4%). In ninth and eleventh grades, self-identification was predominantly Hispanic/Latino (26.8% and 32.8%, respectively) and non-Hispanic white (29.3% and 36.2%, respectively). Students in seventh, ninth, and eleventh grades also described themselves as Asian American (2.4%, 26.8%, 19%), black (4.9%, 2.4%, 1.7%), or other (7.3%, 34.1%, 10.3%), respectively.

Approximately one-third of the students in each grade returned both parental permission and student assent forms. While this response rate can be considered moderate to low with respect to those obtained in contemporary studies on adolescent risk, our use of both active parental and child assent is a more ethically stringent participation criteria than is typically reported in the child and adolescent research literature (Fisher & Brennan, 1992).

### Procedure

Guardian permission and participant assent forms written in both English and Spanish were distributed in class for the students to take home. Students also were given the opportunity to ask for consent forms in other languages; this option was never requested, however. To encourage a joint-decision-making approach for informed consent, the guardian forms encouraged parents to discuss the study with their child prior to granting permission for the student to participate (Fisher & Rosendahl, 1990; Weithorn, 1983). The parental permission and participant assent forms informed parents and adolescents about the study's purpose and procedures, the voluntary nature of participation, and the confidential nature of the data. Information was collected anonymously: Students did not write their names on any of the response forms. After completing the questionnaires, one child approached one of the investigators and spontaneously revealed several personal problems. The investigator suggested the child see the school counselor, and, with the child's agreement, an appointment with the counselor was arranged.

### Instruments

*Reporting Options Rating Scale.*—Following a description of the purpose of the study and a brief presentation on what research psychologists do, participants were instructed as follows:

Pretend there is a research study going on in your school and the researcher finds out that you have a problem. The researcher can help you by talking to you or by telling somebody about your problem. But, you agreed to be in the study because the researcher promised not to tell anybody what you said. We want to know if you were in this pretend situation, what you think the researcher should do. Do you think the researcher should keep the promise to you and not tell anyone what you said? Do you think the researcher should talk to you first and let you get help? Or do you think the researcher should tell a parent or another concerned adult?

Participants were then asked to judge the acceptability of each of the three reporting options for each of 12 developmental risks. On the response sheets, the three reporting options (maintain confidentiality, help the adolescent self-refer, and report the problem to an adult) were listed as "Keep the promise; do not tell anyone"; "Talk to me first and let me get help"; and "Tell a parent or another concerned adult," respectively. For each reporting option, students were asked to rate what they thought a researcher should do *if you told the researcher:* "you had a drinking problem," "you had a drug problem," "you were smoking cigarettes," "you were being physically abused (hit or beaten) by an adult," "you were being sexually abused by an adult," "you were thinking about suicide," "you had a sexually transmitted disease like herpes, gonorrhea, or HIV," "you were into doing graffiti (tagging or writing on walls)," "you were cutting classes," "you were steal-

34

ing," "you were planning to hurt someone else," "you were shy." Students were asked to indicate what they "would want the researcher to do" by rating the reporting options on 4-point Likert-type scales in which 1 = "definitely yes," 2 = "probably yes," 3 = "probably no," and 4 = "definitely no."

*Risk Rating Scale.*—While many studies attempt to quantify the extent to which adolescents are exposed to developmental risks (Farrell, Danish, & Howard, 1992; Jessor, 1993; Windle, 1990), little is known of adolescents' perceptions of these problems (Dubow, Lovko, & Kausch, 1990). Immediately following completion of the Reporting Options Rating Scale, students rated the seriousness of each of the 12 risks. They were asked to "Please tell us how serious or how big of a problem the issues below are to teenagers you may know." Each risk was rated on a 4-point Likert-type scale in which 1 = "not a problem," 2 = "a small problem," 3 = "a problem," and 4 = "a big problem."

*The Sociomoral Reflection Measure— Short Form (SRM-SF).*—Since decisions concerning whether to refer or report adolescent research participants raise ethical and moral conflicts for developmental scientists, we were interested in whether adolescents would also construe the situations as calling for ethical reasoning. We hypothesized that adolescents who used higher-stage moral reasoning would be less likely to value conventional promise keeping (maintaining confidentiality) when it conflicted with participant welfare. To test this hypothesis, we used the SRM-SF (Gibbs, Basinger, & Fuller, 1992), an 11-item, group-administered, short answer questionnaire designed to assess students' sociomoral values within the context of Kohlberg's theory of moral development. Items focus on the values of contract and truth, affiliation, life, property and law, and legal justice. Respondents are asked to rate how important the value is and to give an explanation for their answer. The SRM-SF scoring manual (Gibbs et al., 1992) is organized into the Immature Level, which includes Stage 1 (unilateral and physicalistic reasoning) and Stage 2 (exchange and instrumental reasoning), and the Mature Level, which includes Stage 3 (mutual and prosocial reasoning) and Stage 4 (systematic reasoning). The total stage score is the mean of the 11 scores registered on a 10-point scale. A continuous score, the SRMS, can also be calculated. The minimally acceptable interrater reliability is 80% agreement within

one interval on the 10-point scale for the total global stage score and a difference of 0.2 on the continuous SRMS total score.

## Results

The primary purpose of this study was to gather information on how urban youth evaluate three reporting options available to investigators when a research participant tells them he or she is involved in or the victim of behaviors that present different developmental risks. To provide a context in which to interpret adolescent evaluations of reporting options, we first briefly present data on the extent to which seventh, ninth, and eleventh graders view the risks under question as serious problems for teenagers they know. Analyses of student responses to each reporting option across the various risk categories are then described. We conclude this section with a description of the relation between student levels of moral reasoning, perceived risk severity, and evaluations of different reporting options.

*Perceived Severity of Each Risk Category*

Table 1 provides the mean ratings on the extent to which adolescents viewed each risk category as a serious problem. A 3 (grade) × 2 (sex) × 12 (risk) mixed ANOVA on perceived problem severity yielded main effects of grade, $F(2, 125) = 5.05$, $p = .008$, and problem, $F(11, 115) = 21.39$, $p < .001$, and the grade × problem interaction, $F(22, 230) = 1.75$, $p = .022$. As indicated in Table 1, univariate $F$ tests yielded significant grade differences for drugs, alcohol use, child maltreatment, sexually transmitted diseases, and theft. Scheffé tests (alpha = .05) indicated that these differences reflected the fact that seventh graders perceived the problems as significantly more serious when compared to ninth and eleventh graders, with the exception of drinking, which seventh graders rated as significantly more serious than did ninth graders, but not eleventh graders.

Table 1 also illustrates the percentage of students who rated each risk problem as serious (ratings of 3 or 4). Binomial tests indicated that a significant majority of students from all grades rated shyness as either "not a problem" or a "small problem" (ps = .000). All other risks, with the exception of graffiti, were rated as serious problems by a majority of seventh graders (ps = .029–.0000). By contrast, ninth graders were more ambivalent about the extent to which the 12 developmental risks were problems

TABLE 1

MEANS, STANDARD DEVIATIONS, PERCENTAGE OF RATINGS INDICATING SERIOUS RISK, AND UNIVARIATE $F$ TESTS ON ADOLESCENT EVALUATIONS OF THE SEVERITY OF EACH RISK CATEGORY

| RISK CATEGORY | GRADE 7 ($n = 44$) | | | GRADE 9 ($n = 42$) | | | GRADE 11 ($n = 61$) | | | $F$ |
|---|---|---|---|---|---|---|---|---|---|---|
| | M | SD | % | M | SD | % | M | SD | % | |
| Substance abuse: | | | | | | | | | | |
| Drugs | 3.80 | .69 | 95 | 3.03 | 1.30 | 70 | 3.23 | 1.14 | 72 | 4.72* |
| Alcohol | 3.48 | .72 | 93 | 2.83 | 1.18 | 61 | 3.04 | 1.10 | 72 | 3.48* |
| Cigarettes | 2.95 | .88 | 71 | 2.78 | 1.07 | 65 | 2.50 | 1.16 | 46 | 2.88 |
| Child maltreatment: | | | | | | | | | | |
| Sexual abuse | 3.63 | .89 | 90 | 2.94 | 1.37 | 65 | 2.84 | 1.39 | 60 | 4.05* |
| Physical abuse | 3.65 | .66 | 95 | 2.94 | 1.29 | 67 | 2.84 | 1.32 | 63 | 4.84** |
| Life threatening: | | | | | | | | | | |
| Suicide | 3.55 | .90 | 88 | 3.00 | 1.39 | 58 | 2.96 | 1.29 | 66 | 2.55 |
| STD | 3.70 | .79 | 90 | 2.78 | 1.38 | 62 | 2.93 | 1.35 | 68 | 5.00** |
| Delinquency: | | | | | | | | | | |
| Cutting | 2.93 | .94 | 68 | 2.67 | .89 | 56 | 2.73 | .88 | 58 | .45 |
| Graffiti | 2.55 | 1.01 | 46 | 2.53 | 1.03 | 45 | 2.29 | .85 | 34 | 1.23 |
| Theft | 3.10 | .71 | 80 | 2.53 | 1.06 | 52 | 2.59 | 1.06 | 63 | 4.76** |
| Violence | 2.85 | 1.05 | 68 | 2.83 | 1.08 | 59 | 2.75 | 1.10 | 61 | .20 |
| Shyness | 1.43 | .68 | 5 | 1.53 | .81 | 8 | 1.57 | .78 | 14 | .47 |

NOTE.—Risk categories were scored on 4-point Likert-type scales, with 1 and 2 indicating the category was not perceived as a serious problem and 3 and 4 indicating it was a serious problem. Percentages indicate the proportion of adolescents rating the risk as serious with scores of 3 or 4.
* $p < .05$.
** $p < .01$.

among teenagers they knew. Only drugs and physical abuse were rated as serious by a significant majority of ninth graders, $ps = .02$ and $.04$, respectively. And, with the exception of shyness, none of the other risks yielded significant ninth grader majority opinions. Eleventh graders were somewhat more differentiating than younger students. A significant majority agreed that graffiti was not a problem ($p = .02$) and rated substance abusing behaviors (using drugs and drinking alcohol) and life-threatening behaviors (sexually transmitted diseases and suicide) as serious problems ($ps = .0001, .001, .007,$ and $.02$, respectively).

### Student Evaluations of Reporting Options

*Take no action.*—Mean ratings for an investigator's decision to take no action when informed about a participant risk and the percentage of students who gave favorable responses (ratings of 1 and 2) for this option are illustrated in Table 2. A 3 (grade) × 2 (sex) × 12 (risk) mixed ANOVA on the extent to which students agreed that an investigator should maintain confidentiality and take no action when confronted with a participant at risk yielded a significant main effect of problem, $F(11, 119) = 8.74, p < .000$, and a sex × problem interaction, $F(11, 119) = 2.76, p = .004$.

Adolescent males and females differed in their views with respect to only a few areas of risk. For example, a Tukey Multiple Comparison Test (alpha = .05) indicated that males were more likely than females to favor taking no action (indicated by lower mean scores) when risks involved the use of illegal drugs (males = 2.15, females = 2.60), alcohol use (males = 1.83, females = 2.41), delinquent violence (males = 2.24, females = 2.68), and shyness (males = 1.73, females = 2.07). While the mean ratings on suicide indicated that females were significantly more likely than males to favor no action (females = 2.53, males = 2.90), it should be noted that approximately half (52%) of both females and males disagreed with the statement that no action should be taken when suicide was a risk. Binomial tests of significance further indicated that a significant majority of males and females favored an investigator taking no action when informed about a sexually transmitted disease, cutting, graffiti, or shyness ($ps = .001-.0001$). However, a significant majority of males (73%, $p = .0004$), but not females (54%), believed investigators should take no action when risk involved drinking alcohol, and only females formed a majority opinion against acting upon information that a participant smoked (females = 81%, $p = .0000$; males

TABLE 2

MEANS, STANDARD DEVIATIONS, AND PERCENTAGE OF FAVORABLE RATINGS FOR ADOLESCENT
EVALUATIONS OF THE THREE REPORTING OPTIONS

| REPORTING OPTION AND RISK CATEGORY | GRADE 7 (n = 44) | | | GRADE 9 (n = 42) | | | GRADE 11 (n = 61) | | |
|---|---|---|---|---|---|---|---|---|---|
| | M | SD | % | M | SD | % | M | SD | % |
| Take no action: | | | | | | | | | |
| Substance abuse: | | | | | | | | | |
| Drugs | 2.54 | 1.35 | 49 | 2.54 | 1.27 | 51 | 2.33 | 1.33 | 54 |
| Alcohol | 2.07 | 1.08 | 66 | 2.21 | 1.15 | 59 | 2.26 | 1.17 | 62 |
| Cigarettes | 2.10 | 1.06 | 69 | 2.15 | 1.10 | 67 | 1.79 | .81 | 79 |
| Child maltreatment: | | | | | | | | | |
| Sexual abuse | 2.98 | 1.28 | 35 | 2.78 | 1.33 | 40 | 2.41 | 1.39 | 52 |
| Physical abuse | 2.91 | 1.25 | 40 | 2.83 | 1.20 | 35 | 2.54 | 1.25 | 48 |
| Life threatening: | | | | | | | | | |
| Suicide | 2.52 | 1.40 | 73 | 2.38 | 1.30 | 57 | 2.81 | 1.20 | 39 |
| STD | 2.48 | 1.42 | 52 | 2.03 | 1.27 | 71 | 1.85 | 1.20 | 74 |
| Delinquency: | | | | | | | | | |
| Cutting | 1.91 | 1.01 | 73 | 1.80 | 1.03 | 83 | 1.77 | 1.05 | 79 |
| Graffiti | 2.30 | 1.15 | 58 | 1.98 | 1.10 | 73 | 1.76 | .90 | 83 |
| Theft | 2.33 | 1.19 | 60 | 2.21 | 1.22 | 62 | 1.84 | 1.10 | 75 |
| Violence | 2.50 | 1.35 | 50 | 2.55 | 1.24 | 49 | 2.53 | 1.23 | 45 |
| Shyness | 2.19 | 1.31 | 62 | 2.18 | 1.14 | 62 | 1.73 | .91 | 78 |
| Tell a parent or concerned adult: | | | | | | | | | |
| Substance abuse: | | | | | | | | | |
| Drugs | 2.49 | 1.24 | 49 | 2.28 | 1.28 | 58 | 2.49 | 1.30 | 54 |
| Alcohol | 2.70 | 1.23 | 42 | 2.48 | 1.13 | 53 | 2.62 | 1.17 | 45 |
| Cigarettes | 2.74 | 1.19 | 43 | 2.85 | 1.03 | 40 | 3.21 | .89 | 24 |
| Child maltreatment: | | | | | | | | | |
| Sexual abuse | 1.72 | 1.03 | 81 | 1.78 | 1.06 | 78 | 2.12 | 1.26 | 66 |
| Physical abuse | 1.91 | 1.13 | 74 | 1.66 | .91 | 81 | 2.12 | 1.15 | 66 |
| Life threatening: | | | | | | | | | |
| Suicide | 2.02 | 1.33 | 69 | 2.10 | 1.09 | 66 | 1.84 | 1.07 | 79 |
| STD | 2.12 | 1.21 | 64 | 2.05 | 1.18 | 75 | 2.47 | 1.25 | 55 |
| Delinquency: | | | | | | | | | |
| Cutting | 3.02 | 1.17 | 58 | 3.15 | 1.04 | 72 | 3.31 | .90 | 57 |
| Graffiti | 2.58 | 1.18 | 47 | 3.10 | 1.03 | 28 | 3.29 | .88 | 14 |
| Theft | 2.63 | 1.25 | 47 | 3.00 | 1.12 | 26 | 3.18 | 1.04 | 28 |
| Violence | 2.29 | 1.15 | 60 | 2.43 | 1.13 | 53 | 2.33 | 1.07 | 57 |
| Shyness | 2.17 | 1.25 | 62 | 2.74 | 1.04 | 39 | 2.91 | .96 | 39 |
| Facilitate self-referrals: | | | | | | | | | |
| Substance abuse: | | | | | | | | | |
| Drugs | 1.51 | .84 | 88 | 1.53 | .89 | 85 | 1.36 | .75 | 90 |
| Alcohol | 1.66 | 1.06 | 86 | 1.61 | .82 | 85 | 1.35 | .62 | 97 |
| Cigarettes | 1.66 | .79 | 83 | 1.74 | .83 | 88 | 1.87 | .86 | 82 |
| Child maltreatment: | | | | | | | | | |
| Sexual abuse | 1.71 | 1.08 | 84 | 1.50 | .95 | 90 | 1.60 | .85 | 85 |
| Physical abuse | 1.93 | 1.23 | 67 | 1.53 | .89 | 85 | 1.46 | .72 | 92 |
| Life threatening: | | | | | | | | | |
| Suicide | 1.76 | 1.16 | 76 | 1.47 | .83 | 90 | 1.40 | .71 | 91 |
| STD | 1.61 | 1.07 | 83 | 1.40 | .76 | 95 | 1.38 | .65 | 95 |
| Delinquency: | | | | | | | | | |
| Cutting | 2.02 | 1.01 | 70 | 1.84 | 1.05 | 74 | 1.66 | .75 | 88 |
| Graffiti | 2.17 | 1.18 | 65 | 2.11 | 1.06 | 70 | 1.76 | .74 | 88 |
| Theft | 1.83 | 1.05 | 84 | 1.79 | .94 | 82 | 1.49 | .74 | 93 |
| Violence | 1.90 | 1.16 | 78 | 1.87 | 1.07 | 75 | 1.64 | .87 | 86 |
| Shyness | 2.15 | 1.28 | 64 | 1.90 | .92 | 77 | 1.93 | .94 | 71 |

NOTE.—Risk categories were scored on 4-point Likert-type scales, with 1 and 2 indicating favorable ratings for the reporting option and 3 and 4 indicating unfavorable ratings. Percentages indicate the proportion of adolescents giving favorable ratings of 1 or 2.

37

= 63%) or was involved in theft (females = 71%, $p$ = .0005; males = 63%).

A Newman-Keuls Multiple-Range Test (alpha = .05) on the mean scores collapsed across grades indicated that adolescent opinions formed two significantly different clusters: Students more strongly agreed with the decision to take no action when the risks involved cigarette smoking, sexually transmitted diseases, nonviolent delinquent acts, and shyness (risks that the majority of urban youth did not view as serious problems) than when the risks involved drugs, child maltreatment, suicide, and violent delinquency. Drinking fell in between these two clusters, with a mean significantly different from all risks in both categories except for drug use. Binomial tests indicated a significant majority ($ps$ = 0001 − .0000) of students believed that no action should be taken when research participants revealed they were smoking cigarettes, had a sexually transmitted disease, were engaged in nonviolent delinquency (cutting, graffiti, theft), or were shy.

*Telling a parent or concerned adult.*— Mean ratings for this reporting option and the percentage of adolescent participants viewing this option favorably (ratings of 1 and 2) are provided in Table 2. A 3 (grade) × 2 (sex) × 12 (risk) mixed ANOVA on the extent to which students agreed that an investigator should inform a parent or adult when confronted with a participant at risk yielded significant main effects of grade, $F(2, 128)$ = 3.57, $p$ = .031, and problem, $F(11, 118)$ = 18.35, $p$ = .000.

On average, seventh graders' ratings were more in agreement with telling a parent or adult ($M$ = 2.31) than were ninth graders' ($M$ = 2.48) or eleventh graders' ($M$ = 2.74). However, individual univariate tests for grade effects for each of the 12 risk categories yielded significance only for graffiti, $F(2, 144)$ = 6.16, $p$ = .003, and shyness, $F(2, 144)$ = 5.99, $p$ = .003. Scheffé tests (alpha = .05) further indicated that for these two categories seventh graders were significantly more in favor of reporting these behaviors to adults than were the older students, although binomial tests did not yield significant seventh-grade majority opinions for these two risks. Binomial tests of significance did demonstrate that a significant majority of ninth and eleventh graders strongly disagreed with the decision to report graffiti to a parent or adult ($ps$ = .007 and .001, respectively).

A Newman-Keuls Multiple-Range Test (alpha = .05) on the mean scores collapsed across grade indicated that ratings for child maltreatment (physical and sexual abuse) and suicide were significantly more favorable toward telling a concerned adult than ratings for other risks. By contrast, mean ratings for cigarette smoking and nonviolent delinquency were significantly more unfavorable toward the decision to tell another concerned adult than mean ratings for other risks. Newman-Keuls Multiple-Range Tests did indicate that, as a group, the urban youth surveyed in this study rated telling a concerned adult about participant risks related to child maltreatment (sexual abuse and physical abuse) and suicide significantly more favorably than telling an adult about cigarette smoking and nonviolent delinquency. Binomial tests further confirmed this pattern, demonstrating that a significant majority of students were in favor of reporting information about child maltreatment (physical and sexual abuse) and life-threatening risks (suicide and STD) and were not in favor of reporting cigarette smoking, graffiti, or theft ($ps$ < .0003).

When responses were evaluated by grade, a majority of seventh, ninth, and eleventh graders thought an investigator should tell a parent or adult if he or she was told by a participant that they had been physically or sexually abused ($ps$ = .02–.0001). A significant majority of ninth graders thought an adult should be informed if students told an investigator they had a sexually transmitted disease ($p$ = .0027), while a significant majority of eleventh graders thought threats of suicide should be reported ($p$ = .0000). In contrast, the majority of ninth and eleventh graders strongly believed that adults should not be told if an investigator discovered that a research participant was stealing or writing graffiti ($ps$ ranged .004–.0000). In addition, most ninth graders disagreed with the decision to tell an adult if cutting was involved ($p$ = .03), and most eleventh graders disagreed with reporting to an adult if cigarette smoking was involved ($p$ = .0001). An overview of the means in Table 2 indicates that the urban youth surveyed clearly differentiated among risk categories when judging the appropriateness of an investigator's decision to either take no action or tell an adult when the investigator learned a participant was at risk. For example, for each of the 12 risk categories, judgments favoring reporting the information to an adult were negatively correlated with judgments favoring keeping the information confidential ($rs$ = .27–.66, $p$ < .01 – .001).

*Facilitating self-referrals.*—As indicated by the mean ratings and percentage of adolescents viewing this option favorably (see Table 2), across all grades and risk categories, the majority of students thought favorably about an investigator's decision to talk about a problem with the research participant and let the participant seek help. A 3 (grade) × 2 (sex) × 12 (risk) mixed ANOVA on student responses to this reporting option yielded a main effect for problem, $F(11, 118)$ = 4.90, $p$ = .000. No other significant main or interaction effects emerged.

A Newman-Keuls analysis (alpha = .05) indicated few significant differences across risk categories. With grade collapsed, responses regarding self-referrals for graffiti and shyness were significantly higher than responses to speaking to the participant about drugs, drinking, child maltreatment, and life-threatening risks. Additionally, ratings for cutting were significantly higher than for drugs and sexually transmitted diseases. No meaningful significant patterns emerged when risk ratings were analyzed by grade. This is not surprising since binomial tests of probability indicated that this rating option was viewed favorably by a significant majority of the urban youth surveyed for all 12 risk categories ($ps$ = .0000). Similar patterns emerged when binomials were conducted by grade, with two exceptions: (1) a significant ninth-grade majority favoring self-referrals did not emerge for graffiti, signaling more ambivalence, and (2) a significant seventh-grade majority did not emerge for physical abuse, cutting, graffiti, or shyness, perhaps reflecting the seventh graders' preference for the more definitive solutions of either taking no action or reporting to an adult.

## Levels of Moral Reasoning

Interrater reliability for scoring student responses to the Sociomoral Reflection Measure—Short Form (SRM-SF) was calculated as percent agreement within one interval and as the difference between raters on the continuous SRMS total score for three pairs of raters. Percent agreement for the three rater pairs on half the sample protocols was 90%, 86%, and 100%. The difference on the SRMS continuous scores between pairs ranged from .07 to .18; all were below the allowed scoring difference of .20.

*Moral reasoning as a developmental variable.*—The range of global stage scores

for this sample was from Stage 1(2) to Stage 3(4). One protocol was scored as Stage 1(2), identified as an outlier, and dropped from all analyses. In addition, 14 seventh-grade, 4 ninth-grade, and 5 eleventh-grade protocols were unscorable, leaving 123 cases for analyses. The global stage scores for these cases ranged across 9 points on Gibbs et al.'s (1992) 10-point interval scale; they were thus grouped into three levels corresponding to preconventional reasoning (Stages 2[1] and 2), transition to conventional reasoning (Stages 2[3] and 3[2]), and solid conventional reasoning (Stages 3 and 3[4]).

A 3 (grade) × 2 (sex) ANOVA yielded a main effect for grade only, $F(2, 117)$ = 16.21, $p$ < .0001. A Scheffé contrast showed that eleventh graders reasoned significantly higher than both seventh and ninth graders, and that seventh and ninth graders were not different from each other. As expected, the majority (70%) of seventh graders reasoned at Level 1, the majority (73%) of ninth graders reasoned at Level 2, and 57% and 37% of eleventh graders reasoned at Level 2 and Level 3, respectively. The urban youth sampled in this study demonstrated developmental trends in moral reasoning consistent with those reported in previous studies of similar populations (Black, Paz, & DeBlassie, 1991; Gregg, Gibbs, & Basinger, in press). Neither sex nor the sex × grade interaction were significant.

*Moral level, perceived severity of risks, and student evaluation of reporting options.*—A 3 (grade) × 3 (moral level) × 12 (risk) mixed ANOVA revealed no significant main effects or interactions on level of perceived risk. Contingency coefficients calculated between moral level and perceived severity for each of the 12 risks also failed to yield significant alpha levels. A 3 (moral level) × 2 (sex) × 12 (risk) mixed MANOVA with each of the three reporting options as a dependent variable also failed to reveal any significant main or interaction effects. The lack of relationship between level of moral reasoning and perceived risk severity is congruent with previous findings suggesting that, when faced with situations that could affect their peers or themselves, adolescents who score at the preconventional (Stage 2) or beginning conventional level (Stages 2/ 3, 3/2, and 3) on hypothetical tests of moral reasoning do not consistently apply these reasoning strategies to real-life situations (Kohlberg, 1984; Power, Higgins, & Kohlberg, 1989).

## Discussion

Research methodologies aimed at describing and understanding the developmental strengths and vulnerabilities of adolescence have the potential to tap previously undetected problems facing individual participants. Investigators who learn of potential participant risks need to consider whether they should take no action, alert an adult who can help the adolescent, or assist participants in making self-referrals. Current ethical guidelines offer incomplete answers as to what investigators should do if during the course of experimentation they discover that an adolescent's well-being may be in jeopardy. As a consequence, developmental scientists have relied on their individual ethical perspectives, advice from colleagues, and evaluations from institutional review boards and funding agencies. An equally important but untapped resource for ethical decision making is empirical data on how adolescents prospectively evaluate the reporting options available to investigators.

In the past, developmental scientists have shown a healthy skepticism toward the ethical benefits of facilitating services for research participants perceived to be at risk out of concern for the validity of such risk estimates, participant autonomy, and the maintenance of essential experimental controls. In recent years, researchers working with vulnerable and disenfranchised populations of urban youth have struggled with decisions that can allow them to meet dual obligations of scientific responsibility and participant care (Fisher, 1993, 1994; Fisher et al., 1996). Until now, these struggles have gone on in the absence of data on how adolescents themselves view investigator responsibilities. Perhaps the most important contribution of the present study to research ethics is the finding that urban youth do not view the maintenance of confidentiality favorably in situations in which an investigator learns that a research participant is a victim of or engaged in behaviors adolescents perceive to be serious problems.

The extent to which reporting a problem to a concerned adult was viewed favorably by the urban youth in our sample was influenced by both perceived risk severity and developmental level. Across grade, the majority of adolescents favored reporting child maltreatment and threats of suicide to a concerned adult. Younger adolescents were more likely to see other risks as serious and were also more in favor of reporting these risks to adults. Ninth graders were more ambivalent in their perceptions of risk severity and reporting, while eleventh graders were more likely to differentiate among severity of risks and all reporting options. Favorable responses for reporting certain risk behaviors were paralleled by unfavorable responses to taking no action, even when the investigator had promised confidentiality. These findings raise the disconcerting possibility that even under traditional informed consent procedures, in which participant confidentiality is assured, adolescents, especially middle schoolers, may expect to be helped when they tell an adult investigator that they are a victim of abuse or involved in high-risk behaviors. An investigator's failure to help a teenager who has disclosed such problems may unintentionally send messages that the problem is unimportant, that no services are available, or that knowledgeable adults can not be depended upon to help children in need.

Perhaps not surprisingly, facilitating self-referrals (Asher, 1993) was viewed favorably by a majority of seventh, ninth, and eleventh graders across risk contexts that drew mixed or strongly negative views for no action or reporting to an adult. While allowing for self-referral protects adolescent autonomy, it runs the risk of compromising participant welfare and parental responsibility (Fisher, 1993; Scarr, 1994). The increasing rise in health-endangering behaviors and life-threatening experiences of urban youth have raised ethical questions regarding the conditions under which adolescents can participate in research without guardian consent (Fisher, 1993; Fisher et al., 1996; Holder, 1981). Researchers and ethicists have raised concerns about situations in which guardian consent is in the best interests of the child or may violate an adolescent's privacy or jeopardize his or her welfare (Brooks-Gunn & Rotheram-Borus, 1994; Gaylin & Macklin, 1982). Facilitating self-referrals for adolescents at risk raises similar issues. For example, across grades, students favored no action concerning sexually transmitted diseases, and female students strongly believed that a researcher should keep information regarding cigarette smoking and theft confidential, while males favored no action if drinking behaviors were revealed. While these risks were more likely to have been judged as serious problems in some grades, students may have thought that the consequences of others finding out about these activities (e.g., law enforcement officials finding out about theft or parents learning of sexual activity, smoking, or drinking behaviors) outweigh any gain that might occur if the investigator sought intervention.

One way to address this problem is to determine the adequacy of school and community services for urban youth as well as whether or not adolescent participants have the maturity to utilize and benefit from these services independent of parental guidance. That adolescents in our sample appeared to view reporting options within the practical context of problem severity rather than the hypothetical context of moral reasoning underscores the need for researchers to familiarize themselves with the practical aspects of providing self-referrals or reporting behaviors to parents or adults in the community. This would include becoming familiar with local mental health and social service resources for urban adolescents and their families as well as the personal and legal consequences of reporting abusive or life-threatening behaviors. Once an investigator has determined these issues to her or his satisfaction, information clarifying how risks will be identified, and if and to whom (parents or adolescents) referrals will be made, should be included in both parental consent and participant assent forms (Fisher, 1993, 1994; Fisher et al., 1996). Along similar lines, both parents and adolescents need to be informed of the limitations of confidentiality, including statutory obligations to report suspicions of child abuse, at the outset of a research project.

Investigators considering reporting options for urban adolescent research participants must also be sensitive to the possibility of overreporting or overreferring minority or low-income youth. At present there is a paucity of information on developmental patterns in various urban cultural groups, a lack of culturally appropriate assessment instruments and services, and among urban youth a disproportionate amount of exposure to and participation in abusive or delinquent behaviors (Edelbrock, 1994; Richters & Martinez, 1993). Accordingly, investigators may find that service options for self-referrals are inadequate or that reports to concerned adults create an unjust burden on poor and minority youth (Fisher, 1993; Jackson, 1993; Scarr, 1994; Scott-Jones, 1994).

In conclusion, empirical investigation of adolescent expectations regarding the reporting responsibilities of developmental

scientists can inform ethical decisions and enhance the investigator-participant relationship through mutual respect (Fisher & Fyrberg, 1994; Melton et al., 1988). This research is the first of which we are aware that explicitly assessed both adolescents' views of risk-taking behaviors and what they would want investigators to do if they were to reveal those behaviors during the course of a research study. Since this study was a fact-finding mission to begin to determine whether there is a context of legitimation for breaking confidentiality within the culture of urban adolescents, we chose to recruit a normative sample and use hypothetical situations, rather than target adolescents whom we could identify as specifically engaged in the risk behaviors. Conclusions drawn from these findings are by their very nature limited to students' responses to hypothetical problems as well as to the specific community surveyed. We hope that our efforts will encourage other investigators to empirically examine the implications of their ethical practices for participant development and well-being and to consider designing methodological and statistical procedures that include reporting and referring actions as factors in research designed for adolescents with identified risks.

Maintaining a balance between scientific responsibility and participant welfare will continue to be a difficult ethical challenge for scientists engaged in expanding our knowledge of the developmental strengths and vulnerabilities of urban youth. Incorporating participant perspectives into our ethical decision making has the potential to contribute to both the continued development of our science and the individuals whose participation make this science possible.

## References

American Psychological Association. (1992). Ethical principles of psychologists and code of conduct. *American Psychologist, 47,* 1597–1611.

Appelbaum, P. D., & Rosenbaum, A. (1989). Tarasoff and the researcher: Does the duty to protect apply in the research setting? *American Psychologist, 44,* 885–894.

Asher, S. R. (1993, March). *Inviting children to self-refer.* Paper presented as part of the invited symposium on "Ethical issues in the reporting and referring of research participants" at the biennial meeting of the Society for Research in Child Development, New Orleans.

Beauchamp, T. L., Faden, R. R., Wallace, R. J. Jr.,

& Walters, L. (1982). *Ethical issues in social science research*. Baltimore, MD: Johns Hopkins University Press.

Berman, A. L., & Jobbs, D. A. (1991). *Adolescent suicide assessment and intervention*. Washington, DC: American Psychological Association.

Black, C., Paz, H., & DeBlassie, R. R. (1991). Counseling the Hispanic male adolescent. *Adolescence*, 26, 223–232.

Bok, S. (1978). *Secrets: On the ethics of concealment and revelation*. New York: Pantheon.

Brooks-Gunn, J., & Rotheram-Borus, M. J. (1994). Rights to privacy in research: Adolescents versus parents. *Ethics & Behavior*, 4, 109–123.

Chase-Lansdale, P. L., & Brooks-Gunn, J. (1994). Correlates of adolescent pregnancy and parenthood. In C. B. Fisher & R. M. Lerner (Eds.), *Applied developmental psychology* (pp. 207–236). New York: McGraw-Hill.

Children's Safety Network. (1991). *A data book of child and adolescent injury*. Washington, DC: National Center for Education in Maternal and Child Health.

Cicchetti, D., & Toth, S. L. (1993). *Child abuse, child development, and social policy*. Norwood, NJ: Ablex.

Department of Health and Human Services. (1991, August). *Code of federal regulations, protection of human subjects* (DHHS Title 45 Public Welfare, Part 46). Washington, DC: Government Printing Office.

DiLalla, L. F., & Gottesman, I. I. (1989). Heterogeneity of causes for delinquency and criminality: Lifespan perspectives. *Development and Psychopathology*, 1, 339–349.

Dougherty, D. M. (1993). Adolescent health: Reflections on a report to the U.S. Congress. *American Psychologist*, 48, 193–201.

Dubow, E. F., Lovko, K. R., & Kausch, D. F. (1990). Demographic differences in adolescents' health concerns and perceptions of helping agents. *Journal of Clinical Child Psychology*, 19,, 44–54.

Duckworth, K., & Dejung, J. (1989). Inhibiting class cutting among high school students. *High School Journal*, 72.

Edelbrock, C. (1994). Assessment of child psychopathology. In C. B. Fisher & R. M. Lerner (Eds.), *Applied developmental psychology* (pp. 294–315). New York: McGraw-Hill.

Farr, J. L., & Seaver, W. B. (1975). Stress and discomfort in psychological research: Subject perceptions of experimental procedures. *American Psychologist*, 30, 770–773.

Farrell, A. D., Danish, S. J., & Howard, C. W. (1992). Relationship between drug use and other problem behaviors in urban adolescents. *Journal of Consulting and Clinical Psychology*, 60, 705–712.

Fisher, C. B. (1991). Ethical considerations for research on psychosocial interventions for high-risk infants and children. *Register Report*, 17, 9–12.

Fisher, C. B. (1993). Integrating science and ethics in research with high-risk children and youth. *SRCD Social Policy Report*, 7(4), 1–27.

Fisher, C. B. (1994). Reporting and referring research participants: Ethical challenges for investigators studying children and youth. *Ethics & Behavior*, 4, 87–95.

Fisher, C. B., & Brennan, M. (1992). Application and ethics in developmental psychology. In D. L. Featherman, R. M. Lerner, & M. Perlmutter (Eds.), *Life-span development and behavior* (pp. 189–219). Hillsdale, NJ: Erlbaum.

Fisher, C. B., & Fyrberg, D. (1994). Participant partners: College students weigh the costs and benefits of deceptive research. *American Psychologist*, 49, 417–427.

Fisher, C. B., Hoagwood, K., & Jensen, P. (1996). Casebook on ethical issues in research with children and adolescents with mental disorders. In K. Hoagwood, P. Jensen, & C. B. Fisher (Eds.), *Ethical issues in research with children and adolescents with mental disorders* (pp. 135–238). Hillsdale, NJ: Erlbaum.

Fisher, C. B., Jackson, J. F. , & Villarruel, F. (in press). The study of ethnic minority children and youth in the United States. In R. M. Lerner (Ed.), W. Damon (Series Ed.), *Handbook of child psychology: Vol. 1. Theoretical models of human development* (5th ed.). New York: Wiley.

Fisher, C. B., & Lerner, R. M. (1994). Foundations of applied developmental psychology. In C. B. Fisher & R. M. Lerner (Eds.), *Applied developmental psychology* (pp. 3–20). New York: McGraw-Hill.

Fisher, C. B., Murray, J. P., Dill, J. R., Hagen, J. W., Hogan, M. J., Lerner, R. M., Rebok, G. W., Sigel, I. E., Sostek, A. M., Smyer, M. A., Spencer, M. B., & Wilcox, B. (1993). The national conference on graduate education in the applications of developmental science across the lifespan. *Journal of Applied Developmental Psychology*, 14, 1–10.

Fisher, C. B., & Rosendahl, S. A. (1990). Risks and remedies of research participation. In C. B. Fisher & W. W. Tryon (Eds.), *Ethics in applied developmental psychology: Emerging issues in an emerging field* (pp. 43–60). Norwood, NJ: Ablex.

Fisher, C. B., & Tryon. W. W. (1990). Emerging ethical issues in an emerging field. In C. B. Fisher & W. W. Tryon (Eds.), *Ethics in applied developmental psychology: Emerging Issues in an emerging field* (pp. 1–14). Norwood, NJ: Ablex.

Gans, J. E., & Blyth, D. A. (1990). *America's adolescents: How healthy are they?* (AMA Profiles of Adolescent Health series). Chicago: American Medical Association.

Gaylin, W., & Macklin, R. (1982). *Who speaks for the child: The problems of proxy consent.* New York: Plenum.

Gergen, K. J. (1973). The codification of research ethics: Views of a doubting Thomas. *American Psychologist, 8,* 907–912.

Gibbs, J. C., Basinger, K. S., & Fuller, D. (1992). *Moral maturity: Measuring the development of sociomoral reflection.* Hillsdale, NJ: Erlbaum.

Gregg, V., Gibbs, J. C., & Basinger, K. S. (in press). Patterns of delay in male and female delinquents' moral judgment. *Merrill-Palmer Quarterly.*

Hammond, W. R., & Yung, B. (1993). Psychology's role in the public health response to assaultive violence among young African-American men. *American Psychologist, 48,* 142–154.

Hauck, W. E., Martens, M., & Wetzel, M. (1986). Shyness, group dependence, and self-concept: Attributes of the imaginary audience. *Adolescence, 21*(83), 529–534.

Hoagwood, K. (1994). The Certificate of Confidentiality at the National Institute of Mental Health: Discretionary considerations in its applicability in research on child and adolescent mental disorders. *Ethics & Behavior, 4,* 123–131.

Holder, A. R. (1981). Can teenagers participate in research without parental consent? *IRB: Review of Human Subjects Research, 3,* 5–7.

Hollingshead, A. B. (1957). *Two-Factor Index of Social Position.* Unpublished manuscript, Yale University.

Horowitz, F. D., & O'Brien, M. (1989). In the interest of the nation: A reflective essay on the state of our knowledge and challenges before us. *American Psychologist, 44,* 441–445.

Jackson, J. F. (1993). Multiple caregiving among African Americans and infant attachment: The need for an emic approach. *Human Development, 36,* 87–102.

Jessor, R. (1992). Risk behavior in adolescence: A psychosocial framework for understanding and action. In D. E. Rogers & E. Ginzburg (Eds.), *Adolescents at risk: Medical and social perspectives* (pp. 19–34). Boulder, CO: Westview.

Jessor, R. (1993). Successful adolescent development among youth in high-risk settings. *American Psychologist, 48,* 117–116.

Kandel, D., Davies, M., Karus, D., & Yamaguchi, K. (1986). The consequences in young adulthood of adolescent drug involvement. *Archives of General Psychiatry, 43,* 746–754.

Kohlberg, L. (1984). *Essays on moral development: Vol. 2. The psychology of moral development.* San Francisco: Harper & Row.

Lerner, R. M. (1993). Early adolescence: Toward an agenda for the integration of research, policy, and intervention. In R. M. Lerner (Ed.), *Early adolescence: Perspectives on research, policy, and intervention* (pp. 1–16). Hillsdale, NJ: Erlbaum.

Lester, D., & Anderson, D. (1992). Depression and suicidal ideation in African American and Hispanic American high school students. *Psychological Reports, 71,* 618.

Levine, R. J. (1986). *Ethics and regulation of clinical research.* Baltimore and Munich: Urban & Schwarzenberg.

Liss, M. B. (1994). Child abuse: Is there a mandate for researchers to report? *Ethics & Behavior, 4,* 133–146.

Melton, G. B. (1990). Certificates of confidentiality under the public health service act: Strong protection but not enough. *Violence and Victims, 5,* 67–71.

Melton, G. B., Levine, R. J., Koocher, G. P., Rosenthal, R., & Thompson, W. C. (1988). Community consultation in socially sensitive research: Lessons from clinical trials of treatments for AIDS. *American Psychologist, 43,* 573–581.

Office for Protection of Research Risks (OPRR), Department of Health and Human Services, National Institutes of Health. (1993). *Protecting human research subjects: Institutional review board guidebook.* Washington, DC: Government Printing Office.

Pentz, M. A. (1994). Primary prevention of adolescent drug abuse. In C. B. Fisher & R. M. Lerner (Eds.), *Applied developmental psychology* (pp. 435–474). New York: McGraw-Hill.

Petersen, A. C., Compas, B. E., Brooks-Gunn, J., Stemmler, M., Ey, S., & Grant, K. E. (1993). Depression in adolescence. *American Psychologist, 48,* 155–168.

Power, F. C., Higgins, A., & Kohlberg, L. (1989). *Lawrence Kohlberg's approach to moral education.* New York: Columbia University.

Quadrel, M. J., Fischhoff, B., & Davis, W. (1993). Adolescent (in)vulnerability. *American Psychologist, 48,* 102–116.

Richters, J. E., & Martinez, P. (1993). Children as victims of and witnesses to violence in a Washington, D.C. neighborhood. In L. A. Leavitt & N. A. Fox (Eds.), *The psychological effects of war and violence on children* (pp. 243–280). Hillsdale, NJ: Erlbaum.

Scarr, S. (1994). Ethical problems in research on risky behaviors and risky populations. *Ethics & Behavior, 4,* 147–156.

Scott-Jones, D. (1994). Ethical issues in reporting and referring in research with low-income minority children. *Ethics & Behavior, 4,* 97–198.

Society for Research in Child Development. (1993?). Ethical standards for research with children. In *Directory of members* (pp. 337–339). Ann Arbor, MI: SRCD.

Sum, A. M., & Fogg, W. N. (1991). The adolescent poor and the transition to early adulthood. In P. B. Edelman & J. Ladner (Eds.), *Adolescence and poverty: Challenge for the 1990s* (pp. 37–109). Washington, DC: Center for National Policy Press.

Takanishi, R. (1993). The opportunities of adolescence—research, interventions, and policy: Introduction to the special issue. *American Psychologist*, **48**, 85–86.

*Tarasoff v. Regents of the University of California* (CA 1976), 131 Cal. Rptr. 14, 551 P.2d 334.

Veatch, R. M. (1987). *The patient as partner.* Bloomington: Indiana University Press.

Weithorn, L. A. (1983). Children's capacities to decide about participation in research. *IRB: A Review of Human Subjects Research*, **5**, 1–5.

Wilson, D. W., & Donnerstein, W. (1976). Legal and ethical aspects of nonreactive social psychological research: An excursion into the public mind. *American Psychologist*, **31**, 765–773.

Windle, M. (1990). A longitudinal study of antisocial behaviors in early adolescence as predictors of late adolescent substance use: Gender and ethnic group differences. *Journal of Abnormal Psychology*, **99**, 86–91.

Zaslow, M. J., & Takanishi, R. (1993). Priorities for research in adolescent development. *American Psychologist*, **48**, 185–192.

JOURNAL OF RESEARCH ON ADOLESCENCE, 1(4), 349–378

# The Psychosocial Foundations of Early Adolescents' High-Risk Behavior: Implications for Research and Practice

Mira Zamansky Levitt, Robert L. Selman,
and Julius B. Richmond
*Harvard University and the Judge Baker Children's Center*

Recent research indicates that adolescents' own risk-taking behavior is one of the greatest threats to their social, physical, and emotional development. A conceptual developmental model is proposed to help explain why factual knowledge of health and educational risks alone, or even in conjunction with social skills competence, does not appear to protect adequately adolescents from certain high-risk behavior. The goal of the proposed model is to help us to understand better the role temperament/ biological, socio-cultural, and psychosocial factors play over time in the developmental process by which some early adolescents become habituated to certain health/educational risks, and others do not. A specific emphasis is placed on the need for research incorporating in-depth analyses of basic developmental capacities and culturally embedded personal meaning systems that early adolescents construct as they attempt to integrate their experiences of exposure to high-risk behavior. The model provides a framework for programs of research and prevention geared toward raising the affectively based awareness of health and education risks in order to close the identified knowledge–action gap.

## INTRODUCTION

Some of the biggest risks faced by today's children and adolescents involve choices that they themselves make. Confronted with easy access to highly addictive substances (e.g., crack) and lethal weapons, potentially lethal consequences of unprotected sexual activity (AIDS), and pressures for school absence or drop out in the face of increasingly

---

Requests for reprints should be sent to Mira Zamansky Levitt, Judge Baker Children's Center, 295 Longwood Avenue, Boston, MA 02115.

competitive job markets that often require higher education as a means to get a decent paying job, young people's decisions can have serious impact on their present and future physical, psychological, and economic well-being.

In the interest of preventing adolescents from taking high-risk paths that threaten their futures, numerous first generation psycho-educational programs have been designed to teach (or preach to) adolescents about the potential harmful effects of specific habituations (e.g., cigarette smoking, alcohol usage, etc., cf. Hamburg, 1990). Such programs assumed that ignorance about consequences accounts for children's willingness to take dangerous risks. Unfortunately, these programs have not promoted the low-risk behavior patterns as anticipated. The relatively high incidence of teenage smoking, for example, despite the Surgeon General's warnings about its links to cancer (e.g., Richmond, 1979), and declines in other segments of the population demonstrates that factual knowledge about a subject is not translated directly and predictably into action. Clearly, the complexity of the causal relationship between knowledge about risks and behavior in the sense of specific actions and patterns of habituation must not be underestimated (C. E. Lewis & M. A. Lewis, 1983; Rash & Pigg, 1979; Richmond & Kotelchuck, 1984; Willgoose, 1979).

In response to the failure of programs, largely classroom based, that merely provide factual information about risks, a second generation of preventive approaches that acknowledge the social context in which risk-taking behaviors occur has concentrated on equipping youngsters with the social know-how to avoid risky actions. Through approaches based on Bandura's (1977) social learning theory and Jessor and Jessor's (1977) problem behavior theory, adolescents are taught the personal and social management skills by which to resist risk-prone social influences (e.g., G. J. Botvin, Baker, Renick, Filazzola, & E. M. Botvin, 1984; G. J. Botvin & Eng, 1982; Schinke & Gilchrist, 1984). These approaches to inoculating children and adolescents against risk have been found to provide some protection against social pressures, for example, to moderate drinking and smoking behaviors (e.g., G. J. Botvin & Dusenbury, 1989). In our view, however, they are potentially limited because they advocate that children automatically internalize externally derived values and skills characteristic of adults. Little attention is paid to understanding the developmental processes of childhood and adolescence that underlie risk-taking behavior, and to integrating these processes with the skills and values being imparted. The ongoing, if somewhat decreasing, prevalence of the drug problem is unfortunate evidence that programs devoid of grounding in the developmental antecedents of risk-taking behavior are ultimately inadequate.

Clearly, factual knowledge and social management skills are prerequisites for mature decision making about risk-taking behavior. Nevertheless, before more effective models of prevention can be developed, the gap between both knowledge and management skills, and action in different domains of risk-taking behavior must be better understood. To this end, prospective investigations are needed to clarify the developmental antecedents of different habituation patterns of risk-taking behavior, both risk-prone and risk-resilient (J. Block, J. H. Block, & Keyes, 1988; Brook, Whiteman, & Gordon, 1986; R. Jessor & S. L. Jessor, 1977, 1978; Kandel, Kessler, & Margulies, 1978; Kellem, Brown, Rubin, & Ensminger, 1983; Smith & Fogg, 1978). If high risk habituations can be likened to a disease process, we are interested in understanding the natural history of the illness. In other words, what conditions exist premorbidly to predispose individuals or groups to begin experimentation with risky behavior? What leads some from experimentation to frequent/regular usage/abuse, and what makes it possible for some to revert back to lower frequencies of the activity, or abstinence?

As a first step, this article represents an effort to develop a conceptual model of the processes by which the psychosocial foundations for dangerous risk-taking and risk-resilient patterns are adopted and shaped in childhood and early adolescence. This model does not seek to replace current views of risk-taking behavior. Instead, our goal is to complement existing formulations as well as the intervention approaches described above with a way of understanding habituation pathways, and to highlight potentially critical features of the developmental process for purposes of more effective prevention.

Prevention programs among the early adolescent age groups are particularly important because research shows that the longer an individual waits before engaging in the kinds of risk-taking behaviors that often begin at this age, such as smoking or drinking, the less likely he is to begin or more likely he is to quit if he does begin (Donovan, R. Jessor, & S. L. Jessor, 1983). In the case of some activities for which experimentation can be dangerous (e.g., use of crack, unprotected sexual activity), non-use is clearly the most desirable state. In the case of other activities for which the most dire consequences are delayed (e.g., smoking cigarettes, alcohol consumption, cutting class), the optimum experimentation process/habituation state is less obvious. Recent longitudinal evidence suggests, for example, that it is less important to prevent use than misuse and abuse of drugs, and that some degree of experimentation may correlate with better overall adjustment (Shedler & J. Block, 1990). In keeping with this, our interest in the processes that underlie different habituation patterns is less on measuring absolute frequencies of risk-taking behaviors than on articulating the way in which risk-taking behaviors are managed in intrapersonal and interpersonal contexts.

As described in detail in the following, the goals for the model are: (a) to articulate the developmental psychological factors that mediate between the knowledge about risks and actual habituation patterns of risk-taking behavior, (b) to understand how the development of these factors varies as a function of the individual's biological make-up and socio-cultural context, and (c) to consider briefly the model's implications for programs of research and prevention efforts.

Our article primarily addresses two common classes of dangerous risk-taking behaviors. One includes risks that primarily threaten the physical health of the individual, such as smoking, drinking alcohol, drug abuse, and unprotected sexual activity. The second includes educational risks such as cutting class, failing in or dropping out of school, where socioeconomic status stands to be most jeopardized. Both classes of risk pose serious threat to emotional functioning. We assume, based on large scale sociological studies of multiple risk-taking behaviors, that there may be some interdependency between the two sets of risk activities, and that some broad, pervasive influences underlie both sets of problem behaviors (J. Block et al., 1988; Cox & Vale, 1985; Gorsuch & Butler, 1976; R. Jessor & S. L. Jessor, 1977; Kandel, 1980).

Our discussion may or may not be relevant to other kinds of risky activities that may be viewed positively, such as athletic risks (e.g., trying out for a physically dangerous team sport), or academic challenges (e.g., striving to do well in school against the pressure and risk of peer rejection). However, these are not our focus because they are usually undertaken with group or self-enhancing goals in mind. We do not deny the positive value of risk taking in certain contexts, and necessarily espouse low risk over high risk only when the costs are paid in terms of damage to health and distress to the self and to those who care about the person.

## Primary Forces on Risk-Taking Behavior

One set of forces that may move children and adolescents to take high risks consists of constitutional predispositions such as biologically based personality traits. For example, according to Zuckerman (1979, 1983), a high level of sensation seeking is a personality trait with a strong biological substratum involving neurotransmitters in the limbic region of the brain. Defined in terms of "the need for varied, novel, and complex sensations and experiences and the willingness to take physical and social risks for the sake of such experience" (Zuckerman, 1979, p. 10), sensation seeking has been correlated with substance abuse among adolescents (Andrucci, Archer, Pancoast, & Gordon, 1989; Teichman, Barnea, & Ravav, 1989).

Associations have also been made between substance abuse and central nervous system impairment, although it is not clear which is primary. That is, excessive drinking may cause neurological impairment. Alternatively, cognitive deficits in problem solving, judgment, and neurological impairment of behavioral control may predispose to substance abuse (Elliott, 1989; Løhrberg, 1986). Unfortunately, there are virtually no data available by which to evaluate the relationship among neurological status, personality traits, and substance abuse.

More generally, temperament refers to physiologically based proclivities toward or away from impulsivity and/or requirements for high levels of stimulation. Recent lines of research (e.g., Farley, Strelow, & Gale, 1985; Kagan, 1988; Lerner et al., 1986) document that some individuals are more likely to engage in risky behavior because, from birth, they seem to thrive on thrilling experiences, whereas others appear to be more naturally shy and inhibited youngsters who strive to avoid excitement or perceived risks like drinking and smoking.

A second set of forces that place some individuals at greater risk include the familial, environmental, and socio-cultural contexts in which they grow up. Whereas biology is important in understanding the risk-taking behavior of an individual adolescent, socio-cultural and environmental forces have a more broadly based impact. Other things being equal, when a behavior is observed as commonplace and socially sanctioned within a given milieu (home, neighborhood, community), fewer perceived risks come to be associated with it for the populations of children and adolescents in question.

Socio-cultural influences are particularly critical in the domain of risk-taking behavior since the decisions about whether or not to engage in such behaviors are always made in relation to a social context. For example, knowledge about the ill effects of smoking appears to have had differential impact on various segments of society, least influencing the smoking behavior of the poor and the young (Evans, 1976). But just what about environments is risky or risk-preventing, and how this gets translated into risk-taking behavior has yet to be understood fully.

What is known is that the peer culture is a strong influence affecting whether and when youth begin using drugs (Newcomb & Bentler, 1989; Robinson, Killen, Taylor, Telch, & Bryson, 1987). It is peers who model and encourage the use of drugs, as well as provide substances. Early adolescence in particular is a period of experimentation with adult behaviors during which the influence of peers to engage in behaviors

49

such as sex, smoking, and drinking, helps to promote autonomy from parents.

Notwithstanding adolescent strivings for independence from parents in favor of the peer culture, influential adults, particularly parents and teachers (Williams, 1971) also exert considerable influence, in either a positive or negative direction on youngsters' risk-taking behavior. In other words, adult figures may be able to increase or decrease the likelihood of an adolescent's initiation into substance abuse (Halebsky, 1987). Parental factors associated with substance abuse include harsh, distant ties with children (Barnes, 1984; Reese & Willborn, 1983; Shedler & Block, 1990), authoritarian disciplinary styles (A. Jurich, Polson, J. Jurich, & Bates, 1985), permissive attitudes toward drug use (Kandel, 1980; McDermott, 1984), and the management of stress through the use of drugs in the absence of alternative coping strategies (Brook, 1984; Jurich et al., 1985).

The powerful influences of biology and socio-cultural environment helps explain why information-giving psychoeducational prevention programs do not always have their anticipated effect on adolescent risk-taking behavior. Education may be relatively ineffective in countering the risk-taking habits (behavior) of the child with a strong temperamental predisposition to engage in risk-taking behavior. Similarly, education about the harmful effects of unprotected sexual activity is likely to fall on deaf ears for the youth in high-risk environments. In describing work with street youth, for example, Hersch (1987) wrote:

> Not one [educator] I interviewed believes they are making a substantial change in the behavior of this population. Why? The teens won't remember; they will reason it is OK to have sex with friends; some girls want to get pregnant; their johns give them more money if they don't use a condom. Mostly, though, there are so many ways to die everyday on the street that they cannot focus on something that may kill them years from now. (p. 37)

However, the insufficiency of information alone to effect risk-taking behavior is characteristic not only of extreme biological make-up or socio-cultural environments but also of children and adolescents who live in average-risk environments and are not characteristically thrill-seekers (Fantini & Weinstein, 1983). Furthermore, the fact that some resilient children in high-risk environments resist risky behavior whereas some children in low-risk environments engage in risk-taking behavior emphasizes that environmental influences alone do not determine risk-taking behavior. Neither, we would argue, do biological predispositions by themselves dictate outcomes.

One way in which socio-cultural and biological factors bring to bear their influence on patterns of risk-taking behavior is through the phenomenological experience of stress, boredom, and sensation seeking. Etiological findings indicate that whereas some benign or nonproblem use of drugs in adolescence occurs in social or peer settings, abuse or problem use of drugs is often generated by internal stress, limited life opportunities, and unhappiness (Newcomb & Bentler, 1989). Social class may dictate the nature of the stress (e.g., poverty, pressure to achieve, anxiety over pubertal changes), and biological factors may regulate the threshold of boredom (e.g., sensation seekers are likely to experience more situations as boring and have less tolerance for it than non-sensation seekers), but we suggest that both experiences exist to one degree and in one form or another for most adolescents. Accordingly, our model incorporates stress and boredom, and sensation seeking as two primary pervasive experiences that, in most instances, are at the root of risk-taking behavior.

The same risk-taking behavior may serve the function of relieving either stress or boredom. For example, an adolescent may cut a math class because of the stress associated with academic pressures; alternatively, cutting a class may be undertaken in hope of stirring up some excitement in an otherwise mundane existence. In fact, during interviews we undertook with a group of adolescent girls in an urban school setting, one adolescent told us that she would not cut if she did not know she'd be at risk for getting caught, and if there were no punishment associated with it; "being a little scared is what makes it fun." We believe that a similar function operates for health-related risk-taking behaviors such as substance abuse and sexual activity.

Although biological and socio-cultural factors each operate on their own to determine risk-taking behavior, their interactive force on the maturing organism results in a third source of influence. This third factor is a process of psychosocial development that is critical to our understanding of the antecedents of risk-prone versus risk-resistant courses. In contrast to the relatively static psychological factors that have heretofore been implicated in risk-taking behavior, for example, outcome expectations, self-cognitions, and perceptions of the environment (see Abellah & Heslin, 1984; Bandura, 1977; Dielman, Leech, Lorenger, & Horvath, 1984; Dweck & Elliott, 1983; Gochman, 1971; R. Jessor & S. L. Jessor, 1977; Kristiansen, 1985), psychosocial development is by definition, inherently plastic.

There is disagreement as to what fuels psychosocial change, focussed mainly around the relative contribution of biological maturation and environmental experience. In contrast, the concept of what constitutes change in psychological processing as a function of development, although not universally agreed on is more widely accepted (Harris, 1957; Lerner, 1979). According to the organismic developmental perspective taken in this article (Werner, 1948), all development proceeds from states of global fusion to more differentiated, and hierarchically integrated states. With regard to psychosocial development in particular, previous research has described a continuum of qualitative levels, ranging from the undifferentiated, egocentric, and physicalistic at the less developed end of the scale, to the differentiated and integrated, perspectival, and psychological, at the more mature end (Damon & Hart, 1988; Schorin & Hart, 1988; Selman, 1980).

It is important to emphasize that the concept of development should not be equated with time, or even with chronological age (Werner, 1948). Developmental aspects of organization can show regression as well as progression with time, and children of the same chronological age can show very different levels of development in any domain in different contexts.

Assuming that risk-taking behavior represents dangerous responses to stress and boredom, we are interested in how the relationship between knowledge of risks and actual risk-taking behavior is mediated by developmental processes to effect the ultimate habituation course (non-use, experimentation, heavy use) taken by the developing adolescent.

### A Closer Look at the Psychosocial Processes That May Impact on Risk-Taking Behavior

Though derived from the interaction of biological and socio-cultural forces, psychosocial development is considered distinct from either force as it influences risk-taking behavior. We propose that, in the context of risk-taking behavior, psychosocial development can be analyzed into three basic components. Two of these components, knowledge and social management skills, have been studied in previous research, although not necessarily from a development perspective. As already discussed, these components also have been the focus of previous preventive intervention efforts. However, knowledge programs have focussed more on providing information, often of negative consequences of risks, rather than emphasizing quality of understanding, and social skills programs have focussed more on specific skills ("Look him in the eye, just say no!") than on helping to foster developmentally more adequate social strategies for dealing with stress and boredom. In order to understand further why these cognitive and interpersonal factors have not sufficiently explained risk-taking behavior, we introduce a third, developmentally grounded component in our model, the personal meaning of risk-taking behavior.

As indicated in the cross-sectional view of Figure 1, through the psychosocial lens (leaving aside, temporarily, the influences of biological and social contexts), risk-taking behavior is at the heart of a network that incorporates knowledge about health and educational risks, personal/ interpersonal skills to manage conflict around risk, and the personal meaning of risk-taking behavior.

According to this model, all three components of risk-related psychosocial development: knowledge about the risk, management skills to deal with the risk, and the personal meaning of the risk, are assumed to undergo developmental transformations. The cylindrical shape of the figure represents the transformation in conceptual structure across developmental levels of the three components that occurs for children and adolescents over time as a function of their biologically based dispositions and interaction with their socio-cultural environment. From this developmental framework, the following section describes how we conceptualize and operationalize the nature of the knowledge, management skills and personal meaning that growing children use to make decisions about risk-taking behavior, and what it means to say that there are different developmental levels of knowledge, management skills, and personal meaning.

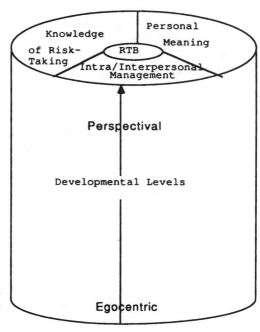

FIGURE 1 Components and developmental levels of risk-taking behavior (RTB).

53

*Knowledge as the growth of understanding.* Prevention programs that aim to protect youth by increasing their knowledge of the consequences of risk-taking behavior furnish information and facts. In contrast, knowledge, in our model, does not merely refer to a repertoire of information or facts about risks. Our developmental orientation demands that we attend also to the sophistication of understanding of the risks themselves. In other words, one can have knowledge about a given risk-taking behavior at different developmental levels of conceptual organization, as contrasted with differences in absolute amount of acquired information. For example, awareness that cigarette advertising is not allowed on television or that Marlboro is the brand of cigarettes that uses cowboys in their commercials are aspects of informational or factual knowledge readily learned by children as well as adolescents. In contrast, to understand that Marlboro advertisements typically depict a cowboy in order to suggest the appealing personal characteristics of people who choose this brand (a relatively high developmental level of understanding) rather than to think the ad simply implies that cowboys like Marlboros, or if one wants to be a cowboy, one should smoke Marlboros (a relatively low developmental level of understanding) is an example of developmental differences in understanding or knowledge. Recent research suggests the growth from the lower to the higher level of understanding occurs across the middle childhood and preadolescent years (Glynn, Leventhal, & Hirschman, 1985).

Considerable attention has already been given to articulating more specifically how activities associated directly with risks such as smoking (Bibace & Walsh, 1981), or indirectly with risk prevention such as knowledge about body functioning (Crider, 1981; Gellert, 1962; Nagy, 1953), health and illness (Bibace & Walsh, 1980; Natapoff, 1978; Perrin & Gerrity, 1981; E. C. Perrin & J. M. Perrin, 1983) and eating (Bibace & Walsh, 1981), can be conceptualized at different levels of cognitive development. What cuts across all of these developmental hierarchies of knowledge related to risk taking are general cognitive transformations from immature, concrete, global, undifferentiated conceptualizations to more mature conceptualizations characterized by flexibility, reversibility, greater differentiation of concepts, and the capacity to think hypothetically. For example, the use of addictive substances such as cocaine may be understood accurately—but incompletely—by a 6 year old as globally life threatening to the self in a physical way. Later on, at age 12 or 13, cocaine addiction will probably be more differentially understood as both physically and psychologically harmful (as well as pleasurable, or at least a way to relieve stress or boredom). With age, experience, and further development, the older adolescent has an even more differentiated understanding of the subtle differences as well as a more integrated understanding of the relation between these two aspects of addiction.

*Management as developing an expanded repertoire of interpersonal negotiation and intrapsychic coping strategies.*  As described earlier, the state of the art in psychoeducationally focussed risk-taking prevention programs has moved beyond prohibitions and informational scare tactics. These programs have forged links between cognition and behavior by providing both information and social management skills that focus children's attention on recognizing and guarding against the influences of peer pressure and advertising campaigns (e.g., G. J. Botvin et al., 1984; Weissberg, Caplan, & Sivo, 1989). Our model, however, maintains a more developmental emphasis than other social competence constructs. The interest here is not only on what specific skills the adolescent uses in different situations, but also on the developmental level at which he or she actually uses intra- and interpersonal negotiation strategies in peer and authority relationships and can coordinate social perspectives, which contributes to the capacity to manage social influences on risk-taking behavior.

Specifically, within our model, the management skills component focuses on the way the individual copes with conflict within the self and negotiates conflict with others that are aroused in the broad context of social interactions associated with risk-taking behavior. How people actually manage and resolve the conflict aroused in risky social contexts plays a major role in whether or not they actually take risks. More developmentally mature solutions require individuals to differentiate between self and others, and recognize the importance of their own perspective as well as perspectives other than one's own.

In a complementary way, decision making regarding risk-taking behavior occurs on an intrapsychic level when the child or adolescent attempts to reconcile competing forces within the self about how to behave, such as a wish to adhere to parental values versus a need to assert one's autonomy. The evaluation of intrapersonal conflict resolution is typically approached from a psychoanalytic perspective, which assumes the influences on the personality of anxiety-provoking unconscious wishes and motivations that provoke conflict as they strive for expression (A. Freud, 1965).

Although seldom studied within the context of adolescent risk-taking behavior, developmental analysis of these modes of intrapersonal conflict resolution has received some attention. G. E. Vaillant (1977; McCullough, C. O. Vaillant, & G. E. Vaillant, 1986), for example, formulated a developmental hierarchy of the intrapsychic defense mechanisms which are thought to represent internal processes of coping with conflict within the self. His four developmental levels (psychotic, immature, neurotic, and mature defenses) is a useful framework by which to assess the maturity of how adolescents manage intrapsychic aspects of risk-taking behavior.

In addition to this individual internal struggle, decision making about risk taking also emerges interpersonally. Defined subjectively, interpersonal conflicts place the individual in the position of reconciling his own interest with those of others. From a developmental perspective, the quality of the decisions about risk-taking behavior that are made in conflictual situations will presumably be related to the maturity of the repertoire of negotiation strategies available to the child. Developmental analysis of emerging repertoires of interpersonal negotiation strategies according to levels of maturity has been the focus of our own work for the last ten years (e.g., Selman, Beardslee, Schultz, Krupa, & Podorefsky, 1986; Selman & Schultz, 1990). Briefly, according to this categorization scheme, developmental levels range from impulsive, unreflective, non-psychological, and egocentric styles of interaction to more mature collaborative, reflective styles that differentiate and respect the needs and concerns of both the interpersonal relationship and the individuals involved. The research extensively studied both the developmental emergence of this repertoire and the factors, both intrapsychic and interpersonal, that lead to the selection of strategies from the repertoire. This helps us to understand from a developmental point of view, the reasons for the gaps between thought and action (Selman, Yeates, & Schultz, in press).

*Developmental aspects of personal meaning.* Although helping adolescents to understand the nature of the relation of risks to self development and to practice decision-making management skills in the social context is likely to be more effective than giving information about risks alone, we suggest that future (third generation) psychoeducational programs, as well as programs of research, will need to consider the inner, subjective life of the adolescent, a focus that has been sorely missing in previous research on adolescent problem behavior (Feldman & Elliott, 1990). In order to understand how information and management skills are integrated and applied in actual risk-taking contexts, we must address what a given risk-behavior means for a given adolescent with a personalized set of passions, aspirations, frustrations, and anxieties. Accordingly, the third component depicted in the figure reflects a motivational, subjectively defined process at the interface of knowledge and management which we have labelled *personal meaning.*

Personal meaning is conceptualized in our model as the primary filter through which specific new skills, experiences, and information related to risk-taking behavior pass. Failure to address the personal significance given to information about risks and to the strategies that can be used for dealing with risk may be one reason why programs designed to teach children management skills and information do not necessarily promote risk-resilient behavior. One cannot assume, according to the personal meaning component, that a given piece of information will necessarily evoke the same emotional response (e.g., fear, hope, determination) in all children.

The significance of the personal meaning component is as follows. A child may have information about the physical health hazards of behavior such as smoking or alcohol consumption, or may have learned a range of interpersonal skills for responding to the opportunity to smoke or offers to take drugs. However, this child may not be able to make use of the information or skills to protect himself if he merely understands in the abstract the effects of a given risky behavior and response strategies. The personal meaning component implies that in addition to this conceptual understanding of the behavior in question, the child must also be interested or invested in issues related to the behavior and be able to anticipate the personalized impact of these consequences on himself in real-life situations, consequences that are likely to be affectively charged. In other words, the child's personal meaning-making activity synthesizes the information and management techniques to determine the emotional significance associated with engaging in a risky behavior or not. No matter how much children are taught information about risk-taking behavior or strategies to deal with risky situations, the impact of the risk must be catalysed by the meaning associated with the behavior for a given child. Even if adolescents can be shown to have a capacity for taking a long-term perspective on such latent health risks as smoking, this understanding will have little impact on that subset of adolescents who themselves do not have a long-term perspective on their own lives and opportunities. Adolescents, by and large, know that smoking is unhealthy. But when do they begin to believe it is unhealthy for themselves?

Against what yardstick does one analyze the personal meaning associated with risk-taking behavior? The personal meaning of any kind of behavior includes the values, attitudes, and beliefs held by the individual about the behavior in question. Because one's values, attitudes, and beliefs are central to an individual's self-concept and way of relating to others, we agree with those such as Baumrind (1987), who suggested that the personal meaning of risk-taking behavior should be examined in terms of its implications for the individual's efforts to achieve both a sense of personal autonomy and a capacity for meaningful intimacy in ongoing interpersonal relationships. Based on this, we operationalize the personal meaning of a risk-taking behavior as a function of its meaning for the individual's self-concept and interpersonal relationships. As described in the following, when an individual acts in a particular context of risk, personal meaning coordinates the influence of knowledge about risks and management strategies with other powerful socio-cultural and biological influences.

Like knowledge and social management, the personal meaning of high risk behavior is considered to have a developmental component. The developmental aspect of personal meaning refers to the formal structure of the understanding behind explanations for behavior, structures which transform qualitatively with increasing maturity. For example, consider the case of the young adolescent male who defends his beer drinking by saying, "Drinking isn't dangerous; it's just what I do at parties. Everybody does it except the nerds," as contrasted with the adolescent boy who drinks in moderation at parties, "Because I'm shy and it helps me feel less nervous when girls are around. I'm concerned about some of the risks, but overall, I think it's worth taking a few drinks." How does the integrative role of personal meaning differentiate these two boys? Looking superficially at behavior, both boys are engaging in the same risk-taking action of drinking alcohol. Yet their different justifications suggest that drinking alcohol means something very different for the two boys, and these differences can be characterized in part in developmental (as well as socio-cultural and temperamental) terms. For the first boy, this meaning, if taken at face value, includes an immature interpersonal conception of peers, who are lumped into two gross categories (the nerds who do not drink and the non-nerds who do), thereby showing minimal capacity for differentiating points of view. His self-awareness is also immature, characterized by a denial of potential risk, and an inability to conceptualize alcohol as an entity apart from his own action of drinking. For the other boy, a relatively more mature stance, involving evidence of both mature self-reflection and social affiliation, appears to underlie his actions. We suspect that the relative hazards for self or others of the risk-taking behavior would also be different for each of them.

The developmental component of personal meaning must be distinguished from, but related to, the socio-cultural foundations of that meaning. For example, in certain cultural contexts, adolescents' increasing loyalty to family is very important, whereas in others, independence from parents is more greatly valued. But personal meaning can also vary within a given cultural context because the developmental status of the individual, as well as biological factors, interact with the socio-culturally defined meaning. When an adolescent says she engages in risky behavior (e.g., cutting classes) because she's bored, it is necessary to sort out peer cultural meaning of the term, boredom, from its developmental meaning. For example, in pilot interviews with diverse groups of adolescents, one girl told us she starts mock fights with other kids (physical, but reportedly not serious or hostile) in school because "I'm bored." One possible conclusion from this statement is that within the peer culture, play fighting is a socially accepted way for this girl to relieve boredom and seek excitement in her school culture. Another possibility, however, is that this girl describes her inner experience in undifferentiated fashion. That is, she uses the term bored in a global, non-specific sense, to imply any source of discomfort or disequilibrium, such as anger at her parents for keeping her in the house ("they're boring"), or frustration about challenging schoolwork ("the teacher's boring"). Such fusion of her perceived experience into a single term would translate into a lower developmental level of meaning making. In contrast to knowledge and management components, the special research challenge of assessing personal meaning lies in the design of a dialogue that is itself relevant and meaningful to adolescents, and which facilitates differentiation of socio-cultural and developmental aspects of the meaning of specified high-risk behaviors.

A final point about personal meaning is its implications for the stimulus value of particular risks. Some risks are inherently more difficult to resist than others, regardless of the fortitude afforded by developmental maturity, relative risk-free socio-cultural environment and risk-averse biological constitution. For example, the stimulus value of having sexual relations with a willing partner to whom one is attracted, even in the absence of adequate protection, might put a vulnerable individual at more risk than a similar offer from a partner unattractive to the self. The former opportunity might be particularly irresistible for an adolescent who is relatively unhabituated to dealing with his or her sexual feelings. Nevertheless, the significance of the personal meaning component is that the attractiveness of the stimulus is embodied not only in the stimulus itself but in the perceiver of the stimulus, whose likes, fantasies, age, life history, and so on, combine to ascribe a particular value to that stimulus. Stimulus value, then, becomes a transactional construct.

The developmentally changing nature of the three psychosocial components has been emphasized. However, the other two important sources of influence on the risk-taking behavior of the adolescent, socio-cultural and biological, should also not be regarded as static. Both the individual's socio-cultural and biological environments are subject to change, particularly during the adolescent years. If socio-economic status has not changed at least once in absolute sense by the time adolescence is reached, then it may change in relative standing as the adolescent moves from primary to secondary school. Similarly, although (in the absence of psychopharmacological manipulation) biologically based temperamental proclivities are relatively fixed, the hormonal surges in adolescence bring about changes in mind and body of a most dramatic nature. Indeed, it has been argued that the unprecedented number and kinds of changes that characterize adolescence themselves predispose adolescents to greater risk. Nevertheless, neither socio-cultural factors nor biological ones can be considered as inherently plastic as the psychosocial development to which they, through their interaction, give rise.

**The Conceptual Model**

We are now ready to describe our conceptual model formally. As indicated earlier in Figure 1, we conceptualize an individual's risk-taking behavior as being at the core of influence of three developmentally defined components, namely knowledge, management skills, and personal meaning. We suggested that, with development, each component becomes a moving target that is constantly evolving to effect risk-prone or risk-resistant courses. Figure 2 integrates the three psychosocial components of Figure 1 with biological and socio-cultural forces, also assumed to be at work as major factors in their own right. The figure reflects the primary direction and magnitude of influence among the components and forces as described throughout the article.

The model asserts a conceptual dependence among the growth of knowledge, risk-management skills, and personal meaning. That is, when neither temperament nor environment is extreme, the three psychosocial components (knowledge, management, and personal meaning) are presumed to be synchronous in developmental level and reciprocal in their mutual influence as in Figure 1. Higher levels of any one component are enabled or anticipated when the remaining two components are themselves in developmental balance. In contrast, low levels of any one component would be expected if both of the other two components were conceptualized at a low level.

For example, developmentally speaking, an average 6 year old is not likely, nor expected, to distinguish clearly the physical and psychological addictive qualities of alcohol because children of this age have neither the experience nor the necessary cognitive differentiating power. This child's understanding of persons is likely to focus on physical features, and he or she naturally views the value of relationships in a fairly (concrete) utilitarian, "what does the other do for me?" manner. In this sense this child's knowledge is, relatively speaking,

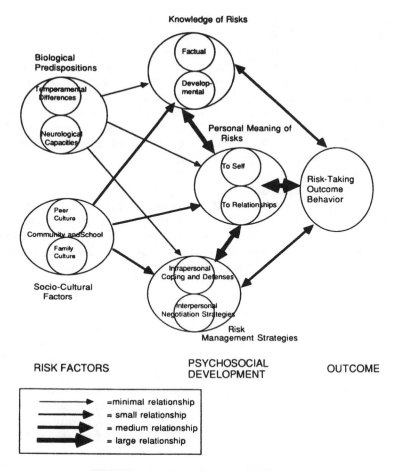

FIGURE 2    Model of risk-taking behavior.

developmentally immature but age appropriate and not pathological. When this knowledge acquires personalized meaning by being applied to the self's own actions, the child might be expected to be vehemently, but somewhat naively, opposed to drinking ("it tastes bad and makes you sick"), particularly on the part of parents whose relationship to him or her is defined, from a dependent stance, as taking care of him or her, particularly in a physical sense (immature, but age appropriate self-understanding). Similarly, we would expect relative immaturity in his or her management strategies for resolving conflict. The child's strategy for negotiating with others to stop drinking may be to demand uniliterally or plead (an age appropriate but still developmentally

61

immature level of interpersonal negotiation). With regard to intrapersonal conflict, his or her approach may be to deny (also a developmentally immature, but age appropriate defense mechanism) that he will ever be even tempted to experiment. Although his psychosocial schemes are relatively immature, offering him or her little flexibility, perspective-taking ability, and so on, average-risk environments (e.g.,a stable middle-class family in a safe suburban community) do not pose significant challenges, in that the expectations for a boy this age are largely externally defined (e.g., go to school, eat your meals, be in bed by 8:00 p.m.). Thus, development here is in accord with functional adaptation.

By age 14, according to our model, things have changed all around. If normal development has occurred, knowledge will be more sophisticated. At this higher level of development the teenager is more aware of the complexities of the risks of drinking, the tradeoffs, and the short-term versus long-term effects. He or she will be more aware of persons as social as well as physical beings. The personal meaning of drinking also will be expected to be at a higher level. With a shift in reliance on parents for physical survival to peers for social validation, the adolescent now reconciles the physical risks of drinking with its implications for self-esteem and personal status. In this sense we would also predict the adolescent to be less absolute, unilateral, and impulsive in his or her conflict management skills than the 6 year old. Instead of only having one approach, commanding, the 14 year old may be able to draw from a repertoire that now allows for a collaborative approach, or at least reciprocity ("I won't start drinking if you will try to quit"). Similarly, the psychologically healthy early adolescent will use more mature defensive strategies to manage internal conflict, perhaps intellectualizing the issue of whether or not to drink, or putting it on hold for consideration at another time when the context presents relatively less stress. At this age, even average-risk environments require that the adolescent contend with more complex information (from a variety of sources besides parents), needs (e.g., sexual, academic), and options (e.g., for more for experimenting behavior). Although specific behaviors or choices are more difficult to predict, we would nevertheless expect that this maturation would fortify the adolescent against this heightened challenge, so that an individual capable of mature developmental levels of functioning in all three domains is more likely to act in ways that minimize risk.

Although the three components are assumed to be conceptually dependent on one another, the personal meaning component is afforded a somewhat special status. As the component that carries the emotional charge of the risk-taking behavior in question, personal meaning is thought to breathe life into the individual's knowledge and management skills, activating them, as described in Figure 2, so that they make a difference in the individual's risk-taking behavior. Without such activation by personal meaning, the effects of knowledge and management presumably remain latent, as observed in the relatively disappointing results of educational programs that address only knowledge and management skills. As such, personal meaning is ascribed a mediating role between knowledge and management, and interfacing with actual risk-taking behavior.

In addition to the conceptual dependence among the three components of knowledge, management, and personal meaning, the model posits an influence of the core behavior (e.g., quality and quantity of drinking or smoking) on the three components. In other words, once a risk-taking action is taken, it impacts back onto knowledge, management skills, and personal meaning for the future. The capacity of actual experience to influence the developmental components that surround it conceptually reflects the essential role that life experience plays in our model. The bi-directionality of this influence suggests that our model is regulatory over time, rather than causal. For example, suppose heavy drinking with peers is the behavior at the core of influence of relatively low level knowledge about drinking and an undifferentiated passive, follow the leader approach to managing peer pressure and conflict. If the consequences of the behavior include an unpleasant hangover and observation that others in the crowd managed to abstain, then an additional piece of knowledge and new management options may well be fed through the system when the opportunity to drink arises again. The actual impact on personal meaning will depend on what motivated the behavior (whether it was rooted in expectation of physical pleasure, need for peer acceptance, or some other value), on how the modifications in knowledge are processed, and on which new management skills are put into practice.

It should be stressed that what is proposed by our model as preventing high risk is not the absolute developmental level of the knowledge, management, and personal meaning components, but the age-appropriate relative balance among the three. Moreover, we are not proposing that individuals at higher levels of development are necessarily or automatically less at risk than those at lower developmental levels, but that as the nature of the risks an individual confronts changes with age, more differentiated and integrated developmental levels are needed to deal with these challenges. Reciprocally, a higher developmental level of competence may generate new contexts for risk (R. M. Lerner, 1979, 1984). In one sense, youngsters of different ages may not experience the same type of risk. For example, 6 year olds do not usually face the pressures of managing the kind of sexual activity confronted by pubertal adolescents. In another sense, the same risk may present itself differently, as in the aforementioned example, where drinking alcoholic beverages was considered for youngsters at two different ages, each of whose developmental level effected a unique experience of the risk at hand.

In sum, the advantage for individuals at higher levels of development is not that risks are abolished but that these individuals are better equipped to confront safely the more serious kinds of risks that are encountered in adolescence. If any one of the three components falls developmentally short of the others, then the individual lacks the resources for optimal coping, becoming more vulnerable to the risk.

Thus, there is a risk factor for children in developmental transition to ₊dolescence, whose psychosocial maturation may not necessarily occur uniformly across components at a rate commensurate with the increasing challenges being posed by the environment. We know strong temperamental proclivities and extreme environmental conditions such as poverty, easy access to risk-taking behaviors, many peers engaging in risk-taking behavior, and lack of family or social support can put children and adolescents at greater risk regardless of their level of developmental maturity across domains (Schorr, 1988). Indeed, environments may exercise their high-risk or low-risk effects, in part, through their contribution to or interference with the synchronous development of the three components.

**Implications for Research**

It is not the aim of this article to resolve the arguments of the relative influences of nature and nurture on risk-taking behavior, but rather to understand better how temperament and environment interact with the developmentally based psychosocial factors that mediate between risk-related knowledge and patterns of risk-taking behavior. At any given point in time or in any given situation (represented by a cross-sectional slice of the cylinder in Figure 1), special actions (located at the core) will be a function of the developmental balance of the three components (knowledge, personal meaning, and management skills) as they are influenced by biological predispositions (conceptualized as variations in temperament or neuropsychological processes) and environmental factors (conceptualized as socio-cultural variations and the degree of support or risk in the social environment).

An alternative way to conceptualize the relationship between the developmental status among the three components and risk-taking behavior is that a high enough developmental level of one or more of the three psychosocial components protects against risk, even if there is imbalance among the developmental levels of the three components. In other words, instead of an association between high risk-resistance and age appropriate symmetry among the developmental levels of the three components, it could also be that risk-resistance is associated with an overall averaged maturity level to which each of the components contributes, so that higher levels of any one or more components would compensate for lower levels of the remaining components. In this case, the magnitude or developmental absolute value of the components, regardless of which were mature and which were immature, would be critical to an understanding of variations in risk-taking behavior.

Our support for the salience of synchrony among the components derives in part from our developmental framework, in which stability is commonly associated with equilibration among component parts. Piaget (1970), for example, maintained that new cognitive schemes could be consolidated and accessed only when a balance occurred between the dialectical processes of assimilation and accommodation. We also argue against the stance that any one of the three components can function in compensatory fashion for the others because, by making all three components interchangeable, the mediating or executive role of the personal meaning component is de-emphasized. If in fact very high levels of knowledge and/or management skills could make up for immaturity of personal meaning, then it is indeed surprising that existing educational prevention programs (which focus on these two components) have not been successful in altering risk-taking behavior. Nevertheless, whether risk-resilience is actually associated with overall magnitude of developmental level among the three components, or whether the balance in developmental level among the components must be considered, remains a question for empirical determination.

Figure 2 offers the comprehensive view of the conceptual model. The three psychosocial components, and socio-cultural and biological influences are included, as well as outcome behavior. The path analysis, illustrated by the arrows, indicates directions of influence. As a guide for in-depth research into the model, the thickness of the arrows reflects hypotheses about the relative strength of some factors as predictors of others. For example, a central hypothesis of the model which encompasses the discussion above is that comprehensive maturity of psychosocial development can provide protection against risky environments and dispositions.

This general hypothesis can be further broken down into four specific hypotheses generated from the model, all of which are testable empirically with appropriate methodology:

1. We expect all components of our conceptual model (i.e., the psychosocial components of developmental knowledge, management strategies, personal meaning, biological predispositions, and socio-cultural factors) to be related to high-risk behavior, but because personal meaning is hypothesized to be the central organizer of risk-taking behavior, particularly at the adolescent period of transition, we expect the personal meaning variable to be more highly related to actual behavior than the other components at any one point in time.

2. We expect the strong influence of socio-cultural factors and biological predispositions on risk-taking behavior to be integrated by psychosocial development. This suggests they will not predict risk-taking behavior after the three psychosocial components are taken into account.

3. As stated earlier, we expect maturity of psychosocial development can provide protection against risky environments (e.g., socio-cultural or socioeconomic stress) and extreme dispositions (e.g., temperament).

4. We expect that there will be a systematic relationship between the adolescents' psychosocial growth and changes in their risk-taking behavior over time. Specifically, the relationship between changes in dangerous risk-taking behavior and psychosocial growth is hypothesized to be negative; large increases in such behaviors as habitual or excessive drinking and smoking or school failure are likely to be associated with little growth in psychosocial abilities, whereas decreases in these behaviors (reformed experimenters) are expected to be associated with large increases in psychosocial development.

Although empirical testing of these and other hypotheses is clearly critical to the validation of the conceptual model, a more primary focus, one on which the testing of all these hypotheses depends, is the development of procedures by which the three psychosocial components can be assessed. In particular, the design of in-depth, structured, yet probing interviews by which to tap into youngsters' developmental variation in personal meaning reflects, perhaps, the greatest challenge for a program of research posed by the model. The importance of the assessment of personal meaning is a function of its role as a unique ingredient in the as yet unsolved mystery of adolescent risk-taking behavior. A program of research focussed on personal meaning may well pick up where approaches concentrating on knowledge and management skills left off in helping us to understand the developmental antecedents of risk-taking behavior and design effective prevention strategies.

The difficulty of the assessment of personal meaning rests with the fact that it is, by definition, a construct that eludes evaluation by traditional measurement techniques such as survey questionnaires or self reports. Indeed, a research program based on the conceptual model is distinguished from previous lines of investigation into risk-taking behavior by the fact that it seeks to gather qualitative information of personal meaning to the individual. As a result, it requires a commitment to the process of in-depth individual data collection as well as to the individuals from whom data are collected. Individuals are not likely to reveal personally meaningful perspectives in brief, intermittent or superficial research relationships characteristic of currently utilized methods. A developmental analysis of personal meaning needs to rely more on the skills and ongoing nature of clinical interviewing while still maintaining high empirical standards of consistency, reliability, and focus.

**Implications for Intervention:**
**Prevention and Health Promotion**

The premise of this article has been that the developmental antecedents of adolescent risk-taking behavior are not well understood, and that without such a knowledge base to guide them, it is unlikely that risk-prevention programs will succeed. Thus, although the primary aim of the article has been to describe a model by which risk-taking behaviors may be conceptualized in terms of their underlying processes, we shall say a few words about the model's translation into intervention efforts. However, a meaningful discussion of the implications for intervention deserves a forum in its own right.

According to our model, risk-resistent behavior is fostered through synchronous development (higher level functioning) across all three sectors of the cylinder: domain-specific knowledge, management skills, and personal meaning. The question of prevention shifts, then, from how do we promote specific risk-resistent behavior (e.g., smoking cessation), to how do we promote higher levels of knowledge, management skills, and personal meaning? Previous research confirms that general knowledge and management skills can indeed be fostered in the classroom. In contrast, despite its crucial mediating role, personal meaning is not a feasible target for explicit pedagogical intervention. As it embodies values, attitudes, and feelings, personal meaning is not amenable to direct developmental training in the way that knowledge and management strategies may be. How, then, can synchronous development across the three components be achieved?

In the effort to promote resistance to high-risk behavior, personal meaning has a central role with respect to the medium through which the other two components, knowledge and management, are acquired.

The model suggests that knowledge and management skills must be learned in a context that is personally meaningful if they are to have an impact on actual risk-taking behavior. Thus, whereas the focus of direct intervention needs to be on the development of knowledge and management, the process of acquiring knowledge and management skills in a personally meaningful context is presumed to facilitate developmental change indirectly in the personal meaning system. This maturation makes it possible for the individual to utilize the higher levels of knowledge and management that have been learned.

The main criterion for the design of a personally meaningful context in which to learn knowledge and management skills is that the adolescent must be able to feel the implications of taking health or educational risks in some powerful but not overwhelming way. This process can occur only through real-life action that confronts the adolescent with real-life consequences as opposed to reading, being lectured to, or even role-playing hypothetical situations about risk-taking.

From the perspective of the model, the growth-promoting function of the social context occurs in intrapersonal and interpersonal processes through active confrontation with risky experience as it stimulates, within the peer context, and with adult guidance, real-life concern for the interests of the self and interpersonal relationships. In particular, some of our own past research (Selman & Schultz, 1990) suggests that a triadic unit of an adult working with children in pairs may be a very powerful format through which to promote psychological development.

Because of the personal nature of the experiences being discussed, through the parameters of peer interaction and affective connections, participants become more aware of their feelings and the meaning that is made of them. According to the model, this will enable them to try out more mature conceptions of the meaning of a risky behavior, and, perhaps, to construct new systems of meaning as a function of the triadic interaction. Operationally, this translates into a more developmentally advanced manner of relating the significance of risk-taking behavior to the self-concept and the conception of interpersonal relationships in a way that maximizes utilization of knowledge and management skills, and in a way that bolsters resiliency. In this way, all three components of risk-taking behavior are promoted, and the likelihood of negative or too high risk-taking behavior should be minimized. The objective is not to instill specific values or impose particular meaning on risk-taking behavior beyond the advocacy of decisions that balance the concerns of the self and relationships in a mature, collaborative manner.

## CONCLUDING COMMENTS

For purposes of illustrating the conceptual model, we have concentrated mainly on its application to health and educational risks. The question arises, then, as to how generalizable is the utility of the model to other risk-taking behaviors, especially those that might be considered more serious. One way to address the question of the model's applicability to other, more serious behaviors is to consider whether there is reason to believe that the developmental processes underlying risk taking in other domains is sufficiently different from those underlying smoking, drinking, cutting of classes, and so on, to render the model irrelevant. Along these lines, it is true that each risk-taking behavior may be unique in some ways. For example, alcohol and cigarette use play different roles in an individual's health course. Although early use is highly correlated with later habituation for both drugs, the association is stronger for smoking than drinking; adolescent drinking is not necessarily predictive of adult alcohol abuse (Donovan et al., 1983). Nevertheless, there are a number of reasons why our discussion of the model with respect to these specific behaviors is likely to apply to other behaviors which may be considered more serious (e.g., AIDS, violence with handguns).

First, domains of risk-taking behavior are not mutually exclusive. As stressed by R. Jessor (1982), co-morbidity of risk-taking behaviors is common. Deadly forms of risk-taking may simultaneously go hand-in-hand with others that seem more superficially benign. For instance, most deaths and serious injuries among youth are the results of accidents and violence typically involving alcohol, and heavy or frequent drinking may affect physical maturation and inhibit social skill development (Richmond, 1979). In other cases, different risks occur sequentially, with more serious behaviors following on the heels of the less serious. Substance use, for example, almost always occurs in a predictable progression of stages, with alcohol and cigarettes often serving as gateway drugs leading to involvement with more serious, illicit drugs (Kandel et al., 1978).

Second, as just described, we assume that, along with smoking, drinking, and cutting/dropping out, other risk behaviors that may be considered more serious may all be related to the same core experiences of stress and boredom/adventure. The task for the model, then, would be to clarify how these experiences come to be translated or expressed into the developmental antecedents of one risk-taking behavior versus another.

In contrast to focussing on the adequacy of the model itself to account for the developmental antecedents of more serious behaviors, there is another way to approach the question of the model's parameters of utility. Throughout this article we have stressed that our conceptual model expands on previous approaches to understanding risk-taking behavior by introducing both the new developmental aspect of personal meaning into the formulation and the associated method of assessing this factor through qualitative, personalized data collection techniques. From this vantage point, the model might be limited to the extent that it would be more difficult for youngsters to share their views on personal experience with more serious kinds of behaviors. Of course, it is worth carefully considering how some risk-taking behaviors come to be associated with greater morbidity than others. For example, alcohol and tobacco are the most abused drugs within the adult world with regard to both numbers involved and magnitude of the consequences, though society attends more to the problems caused by higher profile illicit drugs (Newcomb & Bentler, 1989). In the spirit of personal meaning, perhaps evaluation of morbidity must itself rest to a certain degree with the individual.

Despite our generalized focus on intrapersonal and interpersonal maturity, we do not ignore the importance of the bottom line, namely whether the child or adolescent is engaging in activities that threaten its health (e.g., degree of alcoholic drinking) or education. If indeed our conceptual model were put to the empirical test, a major criterion of validity or success would be whether specific behavioral changes (e.g., decrease in cigarette smoking, graduation from school) were associated with developmental maturity of the knowledge, management skills, and personal meaning systems.

Such objective goals and evaluative benchmarks are not, we believe, incompatible with the perspective that we hope this article has emphasized for future efforts geared toward understanding and promoting healthy behavior among today's youth. Ours is a perspective that views outcome not simply in quantitative terms, asking, for example, whether the number of alcoholic drinks consumed in a week has decreased. More importantly, our assessment of outcome would focus as well in qualitative terms on how the child or adolescent was able to utilize his knowledge, life skills, and personal meaning to manage both the intrapersonal and interpersonal concerns that arose whenever he was faced with the opportunity to drink. The adolescent who drives after drinking is managing the intra- and interpersonal concerns in a much more risky manner than the adolescent who drinks, but has the good sense and character to ask someone else to get behind the wheel. Our developmental model offers a way of qualifying the differences between these two adolescents in a way that might offer some leverage for helping both of them to be better agents of responsibility for their own well-being. If in the study of psychosocial aspects of high-risk behavior and its development, knowing and know-how are half the battle, then making developmentally more adequate meaning out of that knowledge is, we hypothesize, the missing ingredient.

## ACKNOWLEDGMENT

We acknowledge the William T. Grant Foundation, the Smith-Richardson Foundation, and the Spencer Foundation for their support of the work reported here.

## REFERENCES

Abellah, R., & Heslin, R. (1984). Health, locus of control, values and the behavior of family and friends: An integrated approach to understanding preventive health behavior. *Basic and Applied Social Psychology, 5,* 283–293.

Andrucci, G. L., Archer, R. P., Pancoast, D. L., & Gordon, R. A. (1989). The relationship of MMPI and Sensation Seeking Scales to adolescent drug use. *Journal of Personality Assessment, 53,* 253–266.

Bandura, A. (1977). Self-efficacy: Toward a unifying theory of behavioral change. *Psychological Review, 84,* 191–215.

Barnes, G. (1984). Adolescent alcohol abuse and other problem behaviors: Their relationships and common parental influences. *Journal of Youth and Adolescence, 13,* 329–347.

Baumrind, D. (1987). A developmental perspective on adolescent risk taking in contemporary America. In C. E. Irwin, Jr. (Ed.), *New directions for child development: Adolescent social behavior and health* (Vol. 37, pp. 93–125). San Francisco: Jossey-Bass.

Bibace, R., & Walsh, M. E. (1980). Development of children's concepts of illness. *Pediatrics, 66,* 912–917.

Bibace, R., & Walsh, M. E. (1981). Children's conceptions of illness. In R. Bibace & M. Walsh (Eds.), *New directions for child development: Children's conceptions of health, illness, and bodily functions* (Vol. 14, pp. 13–48). San Francisco: Jossey-Bass.

Block, J., Block, J. H., & Keyes, S. (1988). Longitudinally foretelling drug usage in adolescence: Early childhood personality and environmental precursors. *Child Development, 59,* 336–366.

Botvin, G. J., Baker, E., Renick, N . L., Filazzola, A. D., & Botvin, E. M. (1984). A cognitive-behavioral approach to substance abuse prevention. *Addictive Behaviors, 9,* 137–147.

Botvin, G. J., & Dusenbury, L. (1989). Substance abuse prevention and the promotion of competence. In L. A. Bond & B. E. Compas (Eds.), *Primary prevention and promotion in the schools* (pp. 146–178). Newbury Park, CA: Sage.

Botvin, G. J., & Eng, A. (1982). The efficacy of a multicomponent approach to the prevention of cigarette smoking. *Preventive Medicine, 11,* 199–211.

Brook, J. S. (1984). Identification with paternal attributes and its relationship to the son's personality and drug use. *Developmental Psychology, 20,* 1111–1119.

Brook, J. S., Whiteman, M., & Gordon, A. S. (1986). Dynamics of childhood and adolescent personality traits and adolescent drug use. *Developmental Psychology, 22,* 403–414.

Cox, B., & Vale, J. (1985). *Drugs and the eye.* Boston: Buttersworth.

Crider, C. (1981). Children's conceptions of the body interior. In R. Bibace & M. Walsh

(Eds.), *New directions for child development: Children's conceptions of health, illness, and bodily functions* (Vol. 14, pp. 49–65). San Francisco: Jossey-Bass.

Damon, W., & Hart, D. (1988). *The development of self understanding.* New York: Cambridge University Press.

Dielman, T. E., Leech, S. L., Lorenger, A. T., & Horvath, W. J. (1984). Health, locus of control and self esteem as related to adolescent health behavior and intentions. *Adolescence, 19,* 76.

Donovan, J. E., Jessor, R., & Jessor, S. L. (1983). Problem drinking in adolescence and young adulthood: A follow-up study. *Journal of Studies on Alcohol, 44,* 109–137.

Dweck, C. S., & Elliott, E. S. (1983). Achievement motivation. In P. H. Mussen (Ed.), *Handbook of child psychology: Vol. 4. Socialization, personality, and social development* (4th ed., pp. 643–691). New York: Wiley.

Elliott, R. W. (1989). Neuropsychological sequelae of substance abuse by youths. In C. R. Reynolds & E. Fletcher-Janzen (Eds.), *Handbook of clinical child neuropsychology* (pp. 311–334). New York: Plenum.

Evans, R. I. (1976). Smoking in children: Developing a social psychological strategy for deterrence. *Preventive Medicine, 5,* 122–127.

Fantini, M. D., & Weinstein, G. (1983). Reducing the behavior gap. *National Education Association Journal, 57,* 22–35.

Farley, F., Strelow, J. F., & Gale, A. (1985). *The biological bases of personality and behavior.* Washington, DC: Hemisphere.

Feldman, S. S., & Elliott, G. R. (1990). *At the threshold: The developing adolescent.* Cambridge, MA: Harvard University Press.

Freud, A. (1965). *Normality and pathology in childhood.* New York: International University Press.

Gellert, E. (1962). Children's conceptions of the content and functions of the human body. *Genetic Psychology Monographs, 65,* 293–405.

Glynn, K., Leventhal, H., & Hirschman, R. (1985). A cognitive developmental approach to smoking prevention. In C. S. Bell & R. Battjes (Eds.), *Prevention research: Deterring drug abuse among children and adolescents.* Washington, DC: National Institute on Drug Abuse, Division of Clinical Research.

Gochman, D. S. (1971). Some correlates of children's health beliefs and potential health behavior. *Journal of Health and Social Behavior, 12,* 148–154.

Gorsuch, R. L., & Butler, M. C. (1976). Initial drug abuse: A review of psychological factors. *Psychological Bulletin, 83,* 120–137.

Halebsky, M. (1987). Adolescent alcohol and substance abuse: Parent and peer effects. *Adolescence, 22,* 961–967.

Hamburg, B. (1990). *Life skills training: Preventive interventions for young adolescents.* (Report of the Life Skills Training Working Group). Washington, DC: Carnegie Council on Adolescent Development.

Harris, D. B. (Ed.). (1957). *The concept of development.* Minneapolis: University of Minnesota Press.

Hersch, P. (1987, January). Coming of age on city streets. *Psychology Today,* pp. 28–37.

Jessor, R. (1982). Critical issues in research on adolescent health promotion. In T. Coates, A. Petersen, & C. Perry (Eds.), *Promoting adolescent health: A dialogue on research and practice* (pp. 447–465). New York: Academic.

Jessor, R., & Jessor, S. L. (1977). *Problem behavior and psychosocial development: A longitudinal study of youth.* New York: Academic.

Jessor, R., & Jessor, S. L. (1978). Theory testing in longitudinal research on marijuana use. In D. B. Kandel (Ed.), *Longitudinal research on drug use* (pp. 41–71). New York: Wiley.

Jurich, A., Polson, C., Jurish, J., & Bates, R. (1985). Family factors in the lives of drug users and abusers. *Adolescence, 20,* 143–159.

Kagan, J. (1988). *Rational choice in an uncertain world*. San Diego, CA: Harcourt Brace Jovanovich.

Kandel, D. B. (1980). Drug and drinking behavior among youth. *Annual Review of Sociology, 6*, 235–285.

Kandel, D. B., Kessler, R. C., & Margulies, R. Z. (1978). Antecedents of adolescent initiation in stages of drug use: A developmental analysis. In D. B. Kandel (Ed.), *Longitudinal research on drug use* (pp. 73–99). New York: Wiley.

Kellem, S. G., Brown, C. H., Rubin, B. R., & Ensminger, M. E. (1983). Paths leading to teenage psychiatric symptoms and substance use: Developmental epidemiological studies in Woodlawn. In S. B. Guze, F. J. Earls, & J. E. Barrett (Eds.), *Childhood psychopathology and development* (pp. 17–47). New York: Raven.

Kristiansen, C. M. (1985). Value correlates of preventive health behavior. *Journal of Personality and Social Psychology, 49*, 748–758.

Lerner, R. M. (1979). A dynamic interactional concept of individual and social relationship development. In R. L. Burgess & T. L. Huston (Eds.), *Social exchange in developing relationships* (pp. 271–305). New York: Academic.

Lerner, R. M. (1984). *On the nature of human plasticity*. New York: Cambridge University Press.

Lerner, R. M., Lerner, J. V., Windle, M., Hooker, K., Lenerz, K., & East, P. L. (1986). Children and adolescents in their contexts: Tests of a goodness of fit model. In R. Plomin & J. Dunn (Eds.), *The study of temperament: Changes, continuities and challenges* (pp. 99–114). Hillsdale, NJ: Lawrence Erlbaum Associates, Inc.

Lewis, C. E., & Lewis, M. A. (1983). Improving the health of children: Must the children be involved? *Annual Review of Public Health, 4*, 259–283.

Løhrberg, T. (1986). Neuropsychological findings in the early and middle phases of alcoholism. In I. Grant & K. M. Adams (Eds.), *Neuropsychological assessment of neuropsychiatric disorders* (pp. 415–440). New York: Oxford University Press.

McCullogh, L., Vaillant, C. O., & Vaillant, G. E. (1986). Toward reliability in identifying ego defenses through verbal behavior. In G. E. Vaillant (Ed.), *Empirical studies of ego mechanisms of defense* (pp. 61–72). Washington, DC: American Psychiatric Press.

McDermott, J. (1984). The relationship of parental drug use and parents' attitudes concerning adolescent drug use to adolescent drug use. *Adolescence, 19*, 89–97.

Nagy, M. H. (1953). Children's conceptions of some bodily functions. *The Journal of Genetic Psychology, 83*, 199–216.

Natapoff, J. N. (1978). Children's view of health: A developmental study. *American Journal of Public Health, 68*, 995–1000.

Newcomb, M. D., & Bentler, P. M. (1989). Substance use and abuse among children and teenagers. *American Psychologist, 44*, 242–248.

Perrin, E. C., & Gerrity, P. S. (1981). There's a demon in your belly: Children's understanding of illness. *Pediatrics, 67*(6), 841–849.

Perrin, E. C., & Perrin, J. M. (1983). Clinician's assessments of children's understanding of illness. *American Journal of Diseases of Children, 137*, 874–878.

Piaget, J. (1970). Piaget's theory. In P. Mussen (Ed.), *Carmichael's manual of child psychology* (3rd ed., pp. 703–773). New York: Wiley.

Rash, J., & Pigg, R., Jr. (1979). *The health education curriculum*. New York: Wiley.

Reese, C. D., & Willborn, B. L. (1983). Correlates of drug abuse in adolescents: A comparison of families of drug abusers with families of non-drug abusers. *Journal of Youth and Adolescence, 12*, 55–64.

Richmond, J. B. (1979). *Healthy people*. (The Surgeon-General's Report on Health Promotion and Disease Prevention; DHEW [PHS] 79-55071). Washington, DC: Health, Education and Welfare.

Richmond, J. B., & Kotelchuck, M. (1984). Personal health maintenance for children. *The*

*Western Journal of Medicine, 141,* 816–823.

Robinson, T., Killen, J. D., Taylor, C. B., Telch, M. J., & Bryson, S. W. (1987). Perspectives on adolescent substance use: A defined population study. *Journal of the American Medical Association, 258,* 2072–2076.

Schinke, S. P., & Gilchrist, L. D. (1984). *Life skills counseling with adolescents.* Austin, TX: Pro-Ed.

Schorin, M. Z., & Hart, D. (1988). Psychotherapeutic implications of the development of self-understanding. In S. Shirk (Ed.), *Cognitive development and child psychotherapy* (pp. 161–186). New York: Plenum.

Schorr, L. (1988). *Within our reach: Breaking the cycle of disadvantagement.* New York: Anchor Press/Doubleday.

Selman, R. L. (1980). *The growth of interpersonal understanding.* Orlando, FL: Academic.

Selman, R. L., Beardslee, W. R., Schultz, L. H., Krupa, M., & Podorefsky, D. (1986). Assessing adolescent interpersonal negotiation strategies: Toward the integration of structural and functional models. *Developmental Psychology, 22,* 450–459.

Selman, R. L., & Schultz, L. H. (1990). *Making a friend in youth: Developmental theory and pair therapy.* Chicago: University of Chicago Press.

Selman, R. L., Yeates, K. O., & Schultz, L. H. (in press). Interpersonal understanding and action: A development and psychopathology perspective on research and intervention. In D. Cicchetti & S. Toth (Eds.), *Rochester Symposium on Developmental Psychopathology* (Vol. 3). Hillsdale, NJ: Lawrence Erlbaum Associates, Inc.

Shedler, J., & Block, J. (1990). Adolescent drug use and psychological health: A longitudinal inquiry. *American Psychologist, 45,* 612–630.

Smith, G. M., & Fogg, C. P. (1978). Psychological predictors of early use, late use, and non-use of marijuana among teenage students. In D. B. Kandel (Ed.), *Longitudinal research on drug use* (pp. 101–113). New York: Wiley.

Teichman, M., Barnea, Z., & Ravav, G. (1989). Personality and substance abuse among adolescents: A longitudinal study. *British Journal of Addiction, 84,* 181–190.

Vaillant, G. E. (1977). *Adaptation to life.* Boston: Little, Brown.

Weissberg, R., Caplan, E., & Sivo, R. (1989). A new conceptual framework for establishing school-based social competence promotion programs. In L. A. Bond & B. E. Compas (Eds.), *Primary prevention and promotion in the schools* (pp. 255–298). Newbury Park, CA: Sage.

Werner, H. (1948). *The comparative psychology of mental development.* New York: International Universities Press.

Willgoose, C. E. (1979). *Health education in the elementary school.* Philadelphia: Saunders.

Williams, T. M. (1971). *Summary and implications of review of literature related to adolescent smoking* (Contract No. HSM 110-71-145). Washington, DC: U.S. Department of Health, Education, and Welfare, Health Services and Mental Health Administration, Center for Disease Control, National Clearinghouse for Smoking and Health.

Zuckerman, M. (1979). *Sensation seeking: Beyond the optimal level of arousal.* Hillsdale, NJ: Lawrence Erlbaum Associates, Inc.

Zuckerman, M. (1983). A biological theory of sensation seeking. In M. Zuckerman (Ed.), *Biological bases of sensation seeking, impulsivity, and anxiety* (pp. 37–76). Hillsdale, NJ: Lawrence Erlbaum Associates, Inc.

Received July 9, 1990
Revision received February 1, 1991
Accepted April 22, 1991

Amer. J. Orthopsychiat. 59(1), January 1989

# HIGH-RISK CHILDREN IN YOUNG ADULTHOOD:
## A Longitudinal Study from Birth to 32 Years

Emmy E. Werner, Ph.D.

*The developmental courses of high-risk and resilient children were analyzed in a follow-up study of members of a 1955 birth cohort on the island of Kauai, Hawaii. Relative impact of risk and protective factors changed at various life phases, with males displaying greater vulnerability than females in their first decade and less during their second; another shift appears under way at the beginning of their fourth decade. Certain protective factors seem to have a more general effect on adaptation than do specific risk factors.*

Even in the most discordant and impoverished homes, and beset by physical handicaps, some children appear to develop stable and healthy personalities, and display a remarkable degree of resilience in the face of life's adversities. Such youngsters have recently become the focus of attention of a handful of researchers who have asked what the protective factors are in these children and in their caregiving environment that ameliorate, or buffer, their responses to stressful life events. But, in contrast to the well-established track record of mental health studies of individuals who develop serious disorders, research on protective factors and individual resilience is still in its infancy, "a new scientific region to explore" *(Anthony, 1978, p. 3).*

### KAUAI LONGITUDINAL STUDY

One of the largest interdisciplinary investigations of the roots of resiliency in vulnerable children is a prospective longitudinal study of a multiracial cohort of 698 infants born in 1955 on the island of Kauai, Hawaii. Beginning in the prenatal period, the Kauai Longitudinal Study has monitored the impact on development of a variety of biological and psychosocial risk factors, stressful life events, and protective factors in early and middle childhood, late adolescence, and, now, young adulthood *(Werner, 1986; Werner, Bierman, & French, 1971; Werner & Smith, 1977, 1982).* The principal goals of the Kauai Longitudinal Study were *a)* to document, in naturalistic fashion, the course of all pregnancies and their outcomes in an entire community from the prenatal period until the offspring reached adulthood, and *b)* to assess the long-term consequences of perinatal complications and adverse early rearing conditions on the individuals' physical, cognitive, and psychosocial development.

Along the way, we learned that *both* vulnerability (susceptibility to negative developmental outcomes under high risk conditions) and resiliency (successful adaption following exposure to stressful life events)

Based on a paper presented at the 1988 annual meeting of the American Orthopsychiatric Association in San Francisco. The author is at the University of California, Davis.

are relativistic concepts that do not preclude change over time.

From its inception, this has been a multidisciplinary study. Public health nurses recorded the reproductive histories of the women, and interviewed them in each trimester of pregnancy, noting any exposure to physical or emotional trauma. Physicians monitored any complications that occurred during the prenatal, labor, delivery, and neonatal periods. Nurses and social workers interviewed the mothers in the postpartum period and when the children were one and ten years old. They also observed the interaction of parents and offspring in the home. Pediatricians and psychologists independently examined the children at ages two and ten. They assessed their physical, intellectual, and social development, and noted any physical handicaps, and learning or behavior problems.

From the beginning of the study we also recorded information on the material, intellectual, and emotional aspects of the family environment, including stressful life events that brought discord or disruption to the family unit.

When the children reached school age, their teachers evaluated their academic progress and classroom behavior. In addition, the children were given a wide range of aptitude, achievement, and personality tests in the elementary grades and in high school. We also, with permission of the parents, had access to the records of the public health, educational, and social service agencies in the community, and to the files of the local police and family court. Last, but not least, we gained the individual perspectives of the members of the birth cohort when we interviewed them at ages 18 and at ages 30–32.

*High-Risk Children*

It should be emphasized that most of the infants in this cohort were born without complications after uneventful pregnancies, and grew up in supportive home environments. But one third of the infants could be considered "at risk" because they had experienced moderate to severe degrees of perinatal stress, were born into poverty, were reared by mothers with little formal education, and lived in a family environment troubled by discord, desertion, or divorce, or marred by parental alcoholism or mental illness. Two out of three of these at-risk children, all of whom encountered four or more such cumulative risk factors before the age of two, developed serious learning or behavior problems by the age of ten, or had delinquency records, mental health problems, or teenage pregnancies by the age of 18. Surprisingly, however, one out of every three of them (30 males, 42 females) — some 10% of the total cohort — developed instead into competent, confident, and caring young adults.

Looking back over the lives of these 72 resilient individuals, we contrasted their behavioral characteristics and caregiving environment with those of the high-risk youth of the same age and sex who had developed serious coping problems at ages ten or 18. We found a number of characteristics within the individuals, within their families, and outside the family circle that contributed to their resilience.

Even as infants, the temperamental characteristics of the resilient subjects elicited positive attention from family members as well as from strangers. By the age of one, both boys and girls were more frequently described by their caregivers as "very active;" the girls as "affectionate" and "cuddly," the boys as "good-natured" and "easy to deal with." The resilient infants had fewer eating and sleeping habits that distressed their parents than did the high-risk infants who later developed serious learning or behavior problems.

As toddlers, the resilient boys and girls already tended to meet the world on their own terms. The pediatricians and psychologists who examined them at age 20 months noted their alertness and autonomy, their tendency to seek out novel experiences, and their positive social orientation, especially among the girls. They were more advanced in communication, locomotion, and self-help skills than the children who later developed serious learning and behavior problems.

In elementary school, teachers reported that the resilient children got along well with their classmates. They had better reasoning and reading skills than high-risk children who developed problems, especially the girls. Though not especially gifted, these children used whatever skills they had effectively. Both parents and teachers noted that they had many interests and engaged in activities and hobbies that were not narrowly sex-typed. Such activities provided solace in adversity and a reason for pride.

By the time they graduated from high school, the resilient youth had developed a positive self-concept and an internal locus of control. On the California Psychological Inventory (CPI), they displayed a more nurturant, responsible, and achievement-oriented attitude toward life than their high-risk peers who developed coping problems. The resilient girls were also more assertive, achievement-oriented, and independent.

The resilient boys and girls tended to grow up in families with four or fewer children, with a space of two years or more between themselves and their next sibling. Few had experienced prolonged separations from their primary caretaker during the first year of life. All had the opportunity to establish a close bond with at least one caregiver from whom they received plenty of positive attention when they were infants.

Some of this nurturing came from substitute parents, such as grandparents or older siblings, or from the ranks of neighbors and regular baby-sitters. Such substitute parents played an important role as positive models of identification. Maternal employment and the need to take care of younger siblings contributed to the pronounced autonomy and sense of responsibility noted among the resilient girls, especially in households where the father was absent.

Resilient boys were often first-born sons

who did not have to share their parents' attention with many additional children. There were some males in the family who could serve as a role model (if not the father, then a grandfather, older cousin, or uncle). Structure, rules, and assigned chores were part of their daily routine in adolescence.

The resilient boys and girls also found emotional support outside their own families. They tended to have at least one, and usually several, close friends, especially the girls. They relied on an informal network of kin and neighbors, peers and elders, for counsel and support in times of crisis. Some had a favorite teacher who became a role model, friend, and confidant for them.

Participation in extracurricular activities played an important part in the lives of the resilient youth, especially activities that were cooperative enterprises. For still others, emotional support came from a youth leader, or from a minister or church group. With their help the resilient children acquired a faith that their lives had meaning and that they had control over their fate.

We noted in our analyses that as disadvantage and the number of stressful life events accumulated, more such protective factors were needed as counterbalance in the lives of these high-risk individuals, to ensure a positive developmental outcome.

**THE 30-YEAR FOLLOW-UP**

When we had last interviewed the members of the 1955 birth cohort, at age 18, we were aware that the maximum period for mental breakdown was still ahead of the high-risk youth *(Werner & Smith, 1982)*. We did not yet know how well they would adapt to the demands of the adult world of work, marriage, and parenthood.

Since 1985, we have been involved in a follow-up of these resilient youth and of comparison groups of high-risk subjects from the 1955 birth cohort who had previously developed problems. Our follow-up has had two general objectives: *1)* to trace the long-term effects of stressful life events in childhood and adolescence on the adult adaptation of men and women who were exposed to poverty, perinatal stress, and parental psychopathology; and 2) to examine the long-term effects of protective factors (personal competencies, sources of support) in childhood and adolescence on their adult coping.

The present follow-up finds our cohort at a stage which provides an opportunity to reappraise and modify the initial mode of adult living established in the previous decade. The transition period at age 30 is biologically the peak of adulthood, a time of great energy, but also among the most stressful points in the adult life cycle (Levinson, 1986). We believe, as did Lowenthal and her colleagues (1977), that such a transitional life stage a) maximizes individuals' awareness of their life circumstances, b) yields insights into the ways in which individuals adapt to stressful life situations, and c) increases their readiness to discuss these matters.

**METHOD**

During 1985–86, we located some 80% (N = 545) of the survivors of the 1955 birth cohort. The majority still live on Kauai and among them are most of the former "problem" children. Some 10% have moved to other Hawaiian islands (Oahu, Maui, and Hawaii), most to Honolulu. Another 10% live on the U.S. mainland, some 2% live abroad. Among those who moved away from Kauai are many of the resilient individuals.

The instruments administered in individual sessions with the subjects are: a checklist of stressful life events, Rotter's Locus of Control scale, the EAS Temperament Survey for Adults (Buss & Plomin, 1984), and a structured interview. The interview assesses the subjects' perception of major stressors and support in their adult lives: in school, at work, and in their relationships with their spouses or mates, their children, parents, in-laws, siblings, and friends. It concludes with an assessment of the indi-

vidual's state of health, satisfaction, and well-being at the present stage of life.

In addition, we have access to the records of the District and Circuit courts in Kauai, in Honolulu, and on the other outer islands. They contain civil, criminal, and family court files which are open to the public and cover the period since our last follow-up at age 18. These files contain not only records of major violations of the law, but also information on such domestic problems as desertion, divorce, delinquent child support payments, and spouse and child abuse.

We also have access to the state-wide mental health registry which records diagnoses and treatment outcomes for all members of the 1955 birth cohort (and their parents) who have received in- or out-patient mental health services since the last follow-up, and to the records of the State Department of Health which registers marriage licenses, and birth and death certificates.

So far, we have follow-up data in adulthood on every member of the 1955 cohort who has been a defendant in a criminal or civil law suit, or whose marriage ended in divorce by age 30. We also have follow-up data on 86% of the resilients subjects, 90% of the teenage parents, 75% of the offspring of alcoholics, 75% of the delinquents, and 80% of the individuals who had developed mental health problems by the age of 18.

**RESULTS**

*Stressful Life Events*

More than half of the stressful life events that significantly increased the likelihood of having a criminal record or an "irrevocably broken marriage" by age 30 for members of this cohort took place in infancy and early childhood. Among the events with negative effects on the quality of adult coping for both men and women were: 1) the closely spaced birth of a younger sibling in infancy (less than two years after birth of the index child); 2) being raised by a mother who was not married at the time of the child's birth; 3) having a father who was permanently absent during infancy or early childhood; 4) prolonged disruptions of the family life and separations from the mother during the first year of life (these included unemployment of the major breadwinner, illness of the parent, and major moves); and 5) having a mother who worked outside the home without stable substitute child care during the first year of the child's life.

A significantly higher proportion of males with a criminal record (including promotion of harmful drugs, theft and burglary, assault and battery, rape, and attempted murder) experienced such disruptions of their family unit in their early years, as did the men and women whose marriages had ended in divorce by age 30.*

For the females, teenage pregnancies, teenage marriages, marital conflict, problems in their relationships with their fathers, and financial problems in their teens also significantly increased the likelihood of divorce by age 30; for the males, it was the absence of the father, as well as the death of the mother, or of a grandparent or close friend before age 10. Such events occurred in significantly greater frequency among children in this birth cohort who had been born and raised in chronic poverty.

## Resilient Individuals

Now let us examine some of the competencies and sources of support that characterized those members of the cohort who had been resilient children. So far, we have follow-up data in adulthood on 62 (26 males, 36 females), of whom one third are of Japanese descent, one third Philippino, and one third part-Hawaiian mixtures. All had grown up in poverty and had previously coped successfully with the effects of perinatal stress, parental psychopathology, or discord and disruption in their family units. They had graduated from high school during the height of the energy crisis and joined the workforce during the worst recession since the

Great Depression. In spite of these economic constraints, these young men and women are coping well with the demands of one of the most stressful periods in the adult life cycle.

*Education and vocation.* Both men and women in this group are highly achievement-oriented. With few exceptions, they have pursued education beyond high school (three out of four have some college education) and are satisfied with their performance in school. With the exception of one male and three females, they are currently in full-time employment; the women predominantly in semiprofessional and managerial positions, the men in the professions or in skilled trades and technical jobs. Three out of four are satisfied with their current work. In terms of both educational and vocational accomplishments, these high-risk individuals from economically poor backgrounds have fared as well or better than low-risk comparison groups of the same sex and age. The majority of the resilient men and women list career or job success as their primary objective at this stage of life, followed by self-fulfillment; fewer choose such traditional objectives as a happy marriage or children.

*Marriage.* The resilient women have made more transitions into multiple life trajectories than the resilient men. Eighty-five percent are married and work, among them the 75% who have young children. In contrast, only 40% of the resilient men are currently married, and only 35% have children.

The significant gender difference in life trajectories observed in this group may be, in part, a consequence of the recent women's liberation movement, but it may also represent realistic adaptations to economic circumstances, similar to those reported by Elder *(1974)* for the *Children of the Great Depression.* Whatever the reasons, there seems to be a greater reluctance among the resilient males than among the resilient fe-

---

* Tables and figure summarizing these and other findings in this section may be obtained directly from the author.

males to make commitments to marriage, or to remarry if their first marriage ends in divorce.

A significantly higher proportion of males than females in this group report that the break-up of a long-term relationship between the ages of 18 and 30 has been a source of great stress to them (53% males vs 31% females). The expectations from such a long-term relationship also differ significantly by gender. The majority of both males and females want permanency and security from marriage, but a significantly higher proportion of females expect intimacy and sharing from such a relationship (69.2% female vs 38.5% male)

*Children.* For those among the resilient adults who are parents, the primary goal for their children is acquisition of personal competencies and skills. A significantly higher proportion of resilient women than men expects high achievement from their offspring, and stress early independence in their sons and daughters. In contrast, a significantly higher proportion of resilient men than women considers the "opportunity to care for others" as the most positive aspect of being a parent (71.4% males vs 20.8% females), and tolerates dependence in their young children (71.4% vs 19.0%). These are the same individuals who were rated as more "androgynous" in their interests and activities by their parents and teachers in childhood and adolescence.

*Sources of worry.* The greatest source of worry among the resilient men and women at this stage in their lives appears to be problems of family members, especially the health of parents or in-laws, or divorces among parents or siblings. Work conditions are reported as major worries by a higher proportion of men; a significantly higher proportion of women tend to worry about their children.

At age 30, the proportion of self-reported health problems is significantly higher among these high-risk resilient individuals than among low-risk comparison groups (46% vs 15%). Some 55.6% of the resilient

men report health problems that appear related to stress, such as back problems, dizziness and fainting spells, problems with overweight, and ulcers. Most of the health problems reported by 40% of the resilient women are related to pregnancy and childbirth (emergency D & C, miscarriages, C-sections, toxemia of pregnancy, and premenstrual migraine headaches).

*Sources of support.* The overwhelming majority of the resilient men and women at age 30 consider personal competence and determination to be their most effective resources in coping with stressful life events. On Rotter's Locus of Control Scale, both sexes scored significantly (more than 2 $SD$) below the standardization group in the *internal* direction (as they did on the Fear subscale on the EAS Adult Temperament Scale).

Both sexes also value the support of a spouse or mate, and faith and prayer. In fact, faith and prayer were significantly more often reported as sources of support by resilient high-risk individuals than by their low-risk peers of the same age (33% vs 15%). But the resilient women draw on a significantly larger number of sources of support (including friends, older relatives, siblings, co-workers, mental health professionals, and self-help groups) than do the resilient men. In contrast, the resilient males seem to rely more exclusively on their own resources, with some additional support from spouses or parents. They less frequently derive emotional support from friends and co-workers.

*Life satisfaction.* Despite some continuing financial worries and the stress of multiple transitions into work, marriage, and parenthood, three out of four among the resilient men and women in their early thirties consider themselves "happy" or "satisfied" with their current status in life. Indeed, a significantly higher proportion of the high-risk resilient individuals than their low-risk peers rate themselves as "happy" and "delighted" with their current life circumstances (44% vs 10%).

It appears from this preliminary analysis of our 30-year interview data that most resilient individuals who had coped successfully with adversity in childhood and adolescence are also competent in coping with their adult responsibilities. But, as at age 18, more resilient women tend to weather stressful life events with less impairment to their health; they also rely on more sources of support than do resilient men.

A relatively high proportion of the men in this group appears to be reluctant to commit themselves to sustained intimate relationships. Success in these individuals may have been attained at the cost of spontaneous enjoyment of life *(see Cohler, 1987, p. 406)*. One such individual, recently divorced, summed up his attitude when queried about the most important thing that happened in his life so far:

The realization of how harsh life really is—how relationships can leave deep, within, hurts that don't seem to go away. With understanding and care, much can be accomplished—with sincere motivation and determination. Believe in yourself, and accomplish the best you can do, and know it is your own achievement that brings you along. Enjoy life and respect it.

Cohler *(1987)*, in an excellent review chapter, pointed out that there are still relatively few studies of the manner in which people use reflection upon their own past experiences as a resource to promote later resilience. Looking back at their lives, many of the resilient men and women in our study commented, with some surprise, on their own strength and accomplishments:

F1: I feel good about myself—actually going through a lot of hurdles and having survived it, I know now I can make it on my own . . .
F2: I like myself . . . I surprise myself a lot with the knowledge I gained from all the jobs and the people I've met in the jobs. Lots of opportunities came my way . . .
M1: The struggle to succeed strengthened me—gave me confidence.

Others look forward to the challenges ahead in their lives:

M2: I've accomplished a lot—some of my goals I wanted to reach, but I am always setting new goals.

M3: I thank God that he gave me the power and strength to be where I am. I just think I am 30 years young—I have so much more to do in my life—I cannot believe I've gone through 30 years. I can't possibly do all I want to do in 60 –70 years . . .
F3: I feel good—I feel that things are really rolling, moving along. It's neat to be married, to get to know a person better, to build a relationship . . . I feel young to be 30 . . .

A few sense a time clock ticking away, and feel that they have fallen short of the mark, in spite of considerable attainment:

F4: 30? I feel that every day of my life I am starting from new. 30 scares me—I am not young any more. Well—I do feel 30. I look in the mirror and see the first white hair.
M4: Ten years go by in a snap, sitting in my living room, on my easy chair—and now I am 30 . . . I am still trying to figure out what I am supposed to accomplish, I haven't done the best I could. I can do more.

Thus, not all of the resilient individuals are happy and satisfied with their life situation in their early thirties. One male and two females rated themselves as either "unhappy" or "mostly dissatisfied." While no one in the resilient group has had periods of sustained unemployment or run afoul of the law, 20% of the resilient men and women who married were divorced by the time they reached age 30. Two of the resilient women (one the daughter of a mentally ill mother) have had to seek help from mental health professionals since graduating from high school. Two males and one female had problems with substance abuse in their early twenties, but are now rehabilitated.

*Positive Change*

By the same token, we may ask if positive changes have taken place among the high-risk children who had developed problems during their teens. Have protective factors operated in their lives to turn the balance toward resiliency? Preliminary follow-up data suggest some answers for two high-risk groups: *1)* teenage mothers whose status *a)* deteriorated or *b)* improved in the third decade of life; *2)* delinquents *a)* with and *b)* without a criminal record by age 30.

*Teenage mothers.* So far we have obtained follow-up information in adulthood on 24 of the 28 teenage mothers in this birth cohort (one had died of cancer). Ten had established stable relationships with a spouse or mate by the time they reached their late twenties, and had also improved their financial lot. The others were either divorced or separated, and had serious financial worries, They either lived in chronic poverty or were supported by welfare agencies.

Teenage mothers whose lot improved had less anxious, insecure relationships with their caregivers as infants, and a stronger feeling of security as part of their family in adolescence than teenage mothers whose lot deteriorated. A higher proportion of "successful" teenage mothers modeled themselves after mothers who had held a steady job when the teenagers were children, and a smaller proportion had problems in their relationship with their fathers in adolescence.

A sociable disposition, an internal locus of control, and more nurturant, responsible and flexible attitudes characterized the teenage mothers whose lot improved in their twenties and early thirties. The unimproved group tended to consist of women who were more anxious, dependent, and inhibited and believed that events happened to them as a result of factors beyond their control.

A significant proportion of improved teenage mothers had sought additional education beyond high school and prepared themselves for skilled, semiprofessional or managerial positions. While they went to school, their sources of child-care differed from those of the teenage mothers who did not seek further education and who are now found mostly in unskilled positions as adults. A higher proportion of improved teenage mothers relied on help by siblings, friends, or in-laws; among the unimproved, care was mostly extended by the young women's parents, possibly increasing their dependency.

Those who improved in status reported the following balance of protective factors: their own determination, high social support, and a moderate amount of stressful life events. Our numbers are small, but we note that our findings are similar to those reported by Furstenberg and his associates in his follow-up of black teenage mothers in the Baltimore area *(Furstenberg, Brooks-Gunn, & Morgan, 1987).*

*Delinquent youth.* Thirty-one individuals (26 males, 5 females) from the 1955 birth cohort had a criminal record by age 30. While most had been delinquents in adolescence (involved in burglary, car theft, and larceny), it must be kept in mind that they constituted a minority of all delinquents — about one third ($N = 27/89$). Identifying prospective criminals at an early age is of greater practical importance than identifying potential juvenile delinquents, most of whom turn out to be only temporary nuisances *(Werner, 1987).*

As in the Cambridge Study in Delinquent Development, conducted among London working youth *(Farrington, Gallagher, Morley, St. Ledger, & West, 1988; West, 1982),* we found among the "crime resistant" delinquents a much smaller proportion considered to be troublesome by their classroom teachers and their parents during middle childhood. Among those who entered an adult criminal career, a significantly higher proportion had been considered dishonest by both teachers and parents, and had exhibited temper tantrums, uncontrolled emotions, and extreme irritability, aggression, and bullying behavior in the classrooms at age ten.

Delinquents who did not commit any adult crimes also had significantly higher scores in early childhood on developmental examinations that assessed their sensory-motor and social competence. In addition, they were less frequently considered to be in need of mental health services by age ten than those who went on to commit adult crimes.

Last, but not least, the presence of an intact family unit in childhood, and especially in adolescence, was a major protective factor in the lives of delinquent youth who turned out to be only temporary or minor offenders. Five out of six of the delinquents with an adult criminal record came from families where either the mother or the father was absent during their adolescence because of separation or divorce. Only one out of four among the delinquents without an adult crime record grew up in a home where either the mother or the father was permanently absent in their teens. Delinquents without a later crime record also had a lower divorce rate by age 30 than did those with a criminal record.

DISCUSSION

Three types of protective factors emerge from our analyses of the developmental course of high-risk children from infancy to adulthood: *1)* dispositional attributes of the individual, such as activity level and sociability, at least average intelligence, competence in communication skills (language, reading), and an internal locus of control; *2)* affectional ties within the family that provide emotional support in times of stress, whether from a parent, sibling, spouse, or mate; and *3)* external support systems, whether in school, at work, or church, that reward the individual's competencies and determination, and provide a belief system by which to live.

The preliminary findings reviewed here also suggest that such protective factors may have a more generalized effect on adaption in childhood, adolescence, or adulthood than do specific risk factors or stressful life events such as poverty, perinatal stress, parental alcoholism or psychopathology, and teenage pregnancy.

The qualities that define individual resilience have been demonstrated in children from different ethnic groups, different socioeconomic strata, and different cultural contexts; among the multiracial children of Kauai, as well as among black children on the U.S. mainland, and Caucasian children in the U.S. and in Europe *(Garmezy, 1985;*

*Rutter, 1985; Werner, in press).* Rutter has summed them up succinctly:

Resilience . . . seems to involve several related elements. Firstly, a sense of self-esteem and self-confidence; secondly, a belief in one's own self-efficacy and ability to deal with change and adaptation; and thirdly, a repertoire of social problem solving approaches. *(Rutter, 1985, p. 607)*

The influence of protective factors that enhance resilience in high-risk children appears to operate both directly and indirectly as chain reactions over time. A major challenge ahead of us is the examination of each of the individual links in such longitudinal chains.

Our longitudinal data indicate that the relative impact of risk and protective factors changed from infancy through early and middle childhood to late adolescence and young adulthood. At each developmental stage there was a shifting balance between stressful life events that heightened individual vulnerability, and protective factors that enhanced resilience. This balance changed, not only with the stages of the life cycle, but also with the gender of the individual.

Both our own and other American and European studies have shown repeatedly that boys are more vulnerable than girls when exposed to biological insults and caregiving deficits in the first decade of life, but that this trend is reversed when females become more vulnerable in late adolescence, especially with the onset of early childbearing. Judging from our follow-up data, by the age of 30 the balance appears to be shifting back in favor of the women.

An individual is able to cope so long as the balance among risks, stressful life events, and protective factors is manageable. But when risk factors and stressful life events outweigh the protective factors, even the most resilient individual can develop problems. They may be serious coping problems, or of the less visible type whose symptoms are internalized, as with the stress-related health problems we noted among some of the resilient males in their early thirties, and their difficulties in establishing intimate, committed relationships.

For the clinician, intervention may be conceived as an attempt to shift the balance for the client from vulnerability to resilience, either by decreasing exposure to stress-related health risks or life events (such as the impact of parental alcoholism, psychopathology, or divorce), or by increasing the number of protective factors (communication and problem-solving skills, or sources of emotional support) available. For the researcher, the challenge of the future is to discover how the chain of direct and indirect linkages between protective factors is established over time so as to foster escape from adversity for vulnerable children.

## REFERENCES

Anthony, E.J. (1978). A new scientific region to explore. In E.J. Anthony, C. Koupernik, & C. Chiland (Eds.), *The child and his family: Vol. 4, Vulnerable children,* New York: Wiley.

Buss, A.H., & Plomin, R. (1984). *Temperament: Early developing personality traits.* Hillsdale, NJ: Erlbaum.

Cohler, B.J. (1987). Adversity, resilience and the study of lives. In E.J. Anthony & B.J. Cohler (Eds.), *The invulnerable child.* New York: Guilford.

Elder, G.H. (1974). *Children of the Great Depression: Social change in life experience.* Chicago: University of Chicago Press.

Farrington, D.P., Gallagher, B., Morley, L., St. Ledger, R.J., & West, D. (1988). Are there any successful men from criminogenic backgrounds? *Psychiatry, 51,* 116–130.

Furstenberg, F., Brooks-Gunn, J., & Morgan, S.P. (1987). *Adolescent mothers in later life.* New York: Cambridge University Press.

Garmezy, N. (1985). Stress-resistant children: The search for protective factors. In *Recent research in developmental psychopathology* (Journal of Child Psychology and Psychiatry, Book Suppl. vol. 4). Oxford: Pergamon Press.

Levinson, D.J. (1986). A conception of adult development. *American Psychologist, 41,* 3–13.

Lowenthal, M., Thurnher, M., & Chiriboga, D. (1977). *Four stages of life.* San Francisco: Jossey-Bass.

Rutter, M. (1985). Resilience in the face of adversity: Protective factors and resistance to psychiatric disorder. *British Journal of Psychiatry, 147,* 598–611.

Werner, E.E. (1986). Resilient offspring of alcoholics: A longitudinal study for birth to age 18. *Journal of Studies on Alcohol, 47,* 34–40.

Werner, E.E. (1987). Vulnerability and resiliency in children at risk for delinquency: A longitudinal study from birth to young adulthood. In J.D. Burchard & S.N. Burchard (Eds.), *The prevention of delinquent behavior.* Beverly Hills: Sage.

Werner, E.E. (in press). Protective factors and individual resilience. In S.J. Meisels & J.P. Shonkoff (Eds.), *Handbook of early intervention: Theory, practice and analysis.* Cambridge, England: Cambridge University Press.

Werner, E.E., Bierman, J., & French, F. (1971). *The children of Kauai.* Honolulu: University of Hawaii Press.

Werner, E.E., & Smith, R.S. (1977). *Kauai's children come of age.* Honolulu: University of Hawaii Press.

Werner, E.E., & Smith, R.S. (1982). *Vulnerable but invincible: A longitudinal study of resilient children and youth.* New York: McGraw-Hill.

West, D.J. (1982). *Delinquency: Its roots, careers and prospects.* London: Heinemann.

For reprints: Emmy E. Werner. Ph.D., Dept. of Applied Behavioral Sciences, 123 AOB IV, University of California, Davis, CA 95616

*Development and Psychopathology*, 6 (1994), 519–532
Copyright © 1994 Cambridge University Press
Printed in the United States of America

# Conduct and affective disorders in developmental perspective: A systematic study of adolescent psychopathology

GIL G. NOAM, KATHERINE PAGET, GAYLE VALIANT,
SOPHIE BORST, AND JOHN BARTOK
*Laboratory of Developmental Psychology and Developmental Psychopathology,
Harvard Medical School and McLean Hospital*

**Abstract**

This study examined the relationship of psychiatric diagnoses to gender, IQ, and ego development level in an inpatient sample of 269 adolescents. It was found that adolescents with an affective disorder diagnosis, in contrast to those with a diagnosis of conduct or mixed affective–conduct disorder, were more likely to (a) be female, (b) have higher IQ scores, and (c) have higher ego development levels. No significant age differences were found between groups. Comparisons between the single diagnosis and mixed disorder groups indicated that the mixed disorder group is characterized by the most severe symptoms found in each of the pure affective and conduct disordered groups. A relationship between type of DSM-III diagnosis and ego development level in adolescence was demonstrated after controlling for the effects of age, gender, and IQ. These results are offered as an explication of the developmental dimensions inherent in DSM-III psychiatric diagnoses.

Until recently, psychiatric diagnoses reflected a strong developmental orientation. This orientation was based on the psychoanalytic assumption that psychopathology could be understood in the developmental terms of early childhood. But despite a wealth of implicit and explicit developmental ideas, most psychoanalytic principles lacked a systematic empirical and statistical base. The goal of achieving greater

reliability and validity in diagnosis went hand-in-hand with the elimination of these psychodynamic-developmental principles from clinical diagnoses. As a consequence, developmental thinking remains peripheral to DSM-III and DSM-IIIR systems (American Psychiatric Association [APA], 1980, 1987). Especially within child and adolescent psychiatry, a growing recognition has emerged that future diagnostic systems will have to take into account the reality that childhood and adolescent disorders occur in the context of changing developmental tasks and fundamental transformations of cognition, emotion, and social adaptation (Kazdin, 1989; Vaillant & Drake, 1985). This step can be taken with greater theoretical sophistication and empirical precision than in the past because basic developmental research in psychopathology has be-

We would like to acknowledge generous support from the Alden Trust, the American Suicide Foundation, the Hall-Mercer Foundation and the Simches Family Fund. Thanks are also due to John Houlihan, Shoshanna Liptzin, and Barbara Panza for manuscript preparation.

Address correspondence and reprint requests to: Dr. Gil Noam, Laboratory of Developmental Psychology and Developmental Psychopathology, McLean Hospital, Harvard Medical School, 115 Mill Street, Belmont, MA 02178.

gun to bear fruit (e.g., Cicchetti, 1984; Cicchetti & Toth, 1991; Noam, 1988; Rutter & Garmezy, 1983). For example, epidemiological and longitudinal studies have documented differential prevalence rates of symptomatology and diagnoses at different ages (e.g., Achenbach & Edelbrock, 1987; Angold & Costello, 1991; Institute of Medicine, 1989), providing important normative base rates. However, as developmental psychopathology research has expanded and become more complex, the use of chronological age as the critical indicator has been found to be deficient for reasons not unlike those posited by Wohlwill (1973) two decades ago. Psychological processes, such as cognition, self-awareness, as well as defense and coping styles are usually defined independently of age and undergo important transformations in ways not following neat age transitions (e.g., Noam, 1988; Noam & Valiant, 1994). Many of these developmental dimensions have now been studied in greater depth, including cognitive development (e.g., Fischer, 1980; Piaget, 1981), moral maturity (Kohlberg, 1969), perspective-taking (e.g., Chandler, 1976; Flavell, Botken, Fry, Wright, & Jarvis, 1968), the working model of attachment (e.g., Bowlby, 1980; Bretherton, 1990; Crittenden, 1990), and defenses (e.g., Vaillant, 1993). Until recently, only a handful of empirical studies have begun to specify the psychiatric conditions and psychological dysfunctions along these various developmental lines (Chandler, in press; Masten, Best, & Garmezy, 1990; Sroufe, 1989). This study takes the step of systematically relating adolescent diagnostic nosology to ego development (Loevinger, 1976), one important way of addressing the evolution of underlying social cognitive processes.

For Loevinger, the ego is the master trait around which personality is constructed. The assumption is that each person has a customary orientation to self and world and that there are stages and transitions around which these "frames of reference" may be grouped. While accumulating evidence indicates that different developmental domains follow their own developmental paths (e.g., Damon & Hart, 1982; Fischer, 1980), and that people do not perform at their most mature levels under all conditions, theorists from a variety of traditions have observed a continuous attempt in humans to bring into meaningful relationships the variety of experiences in the cognitive, emotional, and social domains (e.g., Bowlby, 1952; Erikson, 1950; Vaillant, 1977; Werner, 1948). Erikson, who built his identity theory most explicitly around the concept of ego synthesis and integration, specified this cross-domain integration in a way that made possible the work of other developmental researchers, such as Loevinger. Loevinger shares in the focus on overarching self-processes while creating a method for systematic empirical investigation. Our own use of the theory and method of ego development is based on the strength of its constructivist focus, that subjects at all ages organize their experiences through the filter of their understanding about self and world. That these ways of systematically framing social meanings are related to typical forms of symptomatology and psychopathology has been an important organizing hypothesis of our line of research. Of course, specific forms of psychopathology have to be related to subdomains of development, and the discrepancies of different developmental processes can serve as indicators of dysfunction (e.g., Noam, 1993), but it is equally important to gain insight into the broader domain of ego and self-development to create necessary bridges between development and psychopathology.

Specifically, we investigated the developmental aspects of conduct and affective disorders in hospitalized adolescents, and we hypothesized that conduct problems are associated with delays in ego development whereas affective disorders are in part associated with developmentally more mature, "internalizing" stages of ego development. In addition, we explored the complex issue of whether adolescents who have both conduct and affective disorders bear a closer resemblance to one of the single diagnosis groups.

These hypotheses stem from the recognition that some items that comprise the conduct disorder diagnosis can be reconstructed as developmental deficits. For example, the lack of guilt and concern for others' feelings and property corresponds to typical descriptions of early levels of social and ego development (e.g., Loevinger, 1976; Selman, Jaquette, & Bruss-Saunders, 1979). On the other hand, certain dimensions of affective disorder, especially the more typical internalized guilt feelings and the concern with the loss of others, correspond with more mature ego developmental descriptions. It was our hypothesis that these diagnostic differences are not solely related to ego development but are related as well to such variables as gender and IQ. We will discuss the rationale for these hypotheses after introducing in greater depth the concept of ego development and the important relationships among psychiatric diagnoses, ego development, age, gender, and IQ.

### Ego development

Each of the Loevinger stages of ego development differs along dimensions of impulse control, conscious concerns, and interpersonal and cognitive styles. In Loevinger's scheme, individuals whose ego functioning is least mature use a needs-gratification frame of reference. They tend to act impulsively with little capacity for delay, think in concrete dichotomous concepts, and have little awareness of their inner states. They tend to feel helpless and their interpersonal relations are dependent and exploitative. The three stages that share these characteristics, the Impulsive stage (I-2), the Self-Protective stage (Delta), and the transitional stage (Delta/3) between Self-Protective and the next level are referred to as *preconformist*. The average U.S. adult man and woman and many adolescents function at one of two *conformist* stages, the Conformist stage (I-3) or the Self-Aware stage (I-3/4). Individuals at these stages use an interpersonal-acceptance frame of reference and tend to refer to others' expectations in their behavior, thoughts, and emotions. They

have achieved a capacity for delay and some self-awareness. Inner states are usually expressed in terms of the stereotypes popular within their reference group. Their interpersonal relations tend to be oriented toward acceptance and being accepted. Individuals who function at the most mature ego stages use a self-actualizing frame of reference. They can adapt flexibly to situational demands, think in complex terms, and cope with inner conflict with a high degree of self-awareness. Their interpersonal relationships emphasize mutuality and respect for individual differences. The four stages that share these characteristics are the Conscientious stage (I-4), the Individualistic stage (I-4/5), the Autonomous stage (I-5), and the Integrated stage (I-6); they are referred to as *postconformist*.

Our research attempts to explicate the important relationships among diagnoses, gender, and ego development. Specifically, we hypothesize that adolescent girls functioning at a mature level of ego development are more prone to affective problems than conduct problems, whereas adolescent boys delayed in ego development are more likely to suffer from conduct problems than affective problems.

The literature on ego development and its relationship to age, gender, IQ, and psychopathology to be reviewed in the following sections suggests it to be a highly relevant social-cognitive index for exploring psychopathology in adolescence. This index is broad-based in that ego development incorporates a variety of developmental processes. While there is evidence that the different domains that constitute ego development may have to be studied separately, in this phase of research, when we know so little about the general relationships between development and psychopathology, it is important to investigate inclusive patterns, such as self, ego, and identity as well as subprocesses (e.g., impulse regulation, moral judgement, self-reflection).

### Age

Age has been the major predictor of ego development in cross-sectional studies of normative samples of adolescents (Gfellner, 1986; Sullivan, McCullough, & Stager, 1970) and in eight longitudinal studies (see Redmore & Loevinger, 1979, for a review). This means that even though ego development is defined and coded by means of a logic in development, the progression in ego development is empirically related to chronological age, at least up to adulthood. The findings from these studies of normal adolescents indicate that the shift from preconformist to conformist ego levels normally occurs during middle adolescence. Despite these empirical associations, the study of ego development provides an important tool, in that different ages in the lifespan, such as adolescence, have a wide range of levels of ego organizations embedded in them. Clinical samples of adolescents, for example, display pervasive delays in ego development, with most adolescents at preconformist rather than conformist levels (see Noam, 1984; Noam, Hauser, Santostefano, Garrison, Jacobson, Powers, & Mead, 1984; for a review).

## Gender

Gender differences have been found in levels of ego development during adolescence. In nonclinical samples of adolescents (Gfellner, 1986; Redmore & Loevinger, 1979), girls are typically one half-stage ahead of boys; a similar finding has been noted in clinical samples (Gold, 1980). Gender also appears to be related to type of disorder. With females tending to display affective symptomatology more frequently than males (Angold & Rutter, 1992; Rutter & Garmezy, 1983); conduct disorders are typically more frequent in boys than girls from age 5 through adulthood (Graham & Rutter, 1973; Kastrup, 1977; Lavik, 1977; Remschmidt, Hohner, & Merschmann, 1977; Rutter, Cox, Tupling, Berger, & Yule, 1975; Rutter, Tizard, & Whitmore, 1970/1981; Shepard, Oppenheim, & Mitchell, 1971; Werry & Quay, 1971; Zoccolillo, 1993).

## IQ

IQ and ego development level relationships have been found in normal populations (Redmore & Loevinger, 1979), but only a small handful of studies have measured both ego development level and IQ in a clinical population (Browning & Quinlan, 1985; Frank & Quinlan, 1976; Rozsnafszky, 1981; Wilber, Rounsaville, Sugarman, Casey, & Kleber, 1982). Although a closer look at subtest variation in a clinical sample has been undertaken (Browning & Quinlan, 1985), the relationship of IQ to psychiatric diagnosis has yet to be explored.

## Psychopathology

In a group of empirical studies that have examined the relationship of ego development to psychopathology in adolescents, ego development has emerged as a relevant lens. Delinquency, aggression, and other externalizing behaviors and a greater degree of maladjustment and psychiatric impairment have been found to be associated with preconformist levels of ego development (Browning, 1986; Frank & Quinlan, 1976; Noam, 1984; Noam et al., 1984; Noam & Houlihan, 1990; Noam, Recklitis, & Paget, 1991; Recklitis & Noam, 1990). Some adolescent work suggests an association between ego maturity and the presence of emotional disorders (Gold, 1990; Noam, Kilburn, & Ammen-Elkins, 1989), but the need for detailed studies is great. Two recent studies report that relatively advanced ego development (conformist level) predicts greater vulnerability to suicidal behavior among adolescent girls (Borst & Noam, 1989; Borst, Noam, & Bartok, 1991). The relationship between ego level and psychopathology emerges not only when behavioral indices are used, but also when standardized tests of psychopathology are utilized. For example, ego level was related to the total number of symptoms, the broad band externalizing and internalizing factors and certain behavioral subscales from the Child Behavior Checklist (Achenbach & Edelbrock, 1987) in a sample of inpatients in a psychiatric hospital (Noam et al., 1984). Over 80% of psychiatric inpatients were delayed in ego development in contrast to a nonclinical control group, where 90% functioned at age-appropriate levels (Noam,

1984). In an MMPI study, Gold (1980) found that high school students' ego level scores were related to symptomatology type and adjustment. The findings of these investigations suggest that psychopathology in adolescents is, in part, related to delayed ego development. These results also suggest that an inverse relationship between ego development and externalizing disorders exists and that ego maturity in psychiatric populations heightens the risk of internalizing disorders and suicidality. But this line of research needs to be extended so that developmental relationships between conduct disorders and affective disorders can be explored in greater detail.

Our inpatient sample is most frequently characterized by some type of conduct disorder or affective (mood) disorder. Moreover, when adolescents experience depression, it is often accompanied by conduct disorders and behavioral problems such as delinquency, substance abuse, and truancy (e.g., Garber, 1984). This co-morbidity is a frequent presenting diagnosis in inpatient facilities. The psychological profiles of these adolescents needs to be examined in contrast to same-aged counterparts who exhibit purely affective or purely behavioral disorders.

## Method

### Subjects

Two hundred sixty-nine child and adolescent patients (120 boys and 149 girls) took part in this study. This sample comprised admissions to a child and adolescent inpatient unit in a psychiatric hospital between 1983 and 1988. Patients who were between 11 and 17 years old at the time of admission were included ($M$ age = 13.9, $SD$ = 1.20). The second selection criterion was DSM-III diagnosis based on the Diagnostic Interview Schedule for Children (DISC; A. J. Costello, Edelbrock, Dulcan, Kalas, & Klaric, 1984). Patients with diagnoses of conduct disorder, affective disorder, or mixed conduct-affective disorder were included. Exclusions were due to premature discharge,

poor reading ability, or inability or refusal to complete the testing. The mean Wechsler Full Scale IQ of the sample was 102.2 ($SD$ = 13.91). Based on Hollingshead's (1957) two-factor index of social position, 75% of the families fell in the middle range (Social classes 2, 3, or 4) with the remainder of families occupying the highest and lowest ends of the distribution.

### Measures and procedures

*Diagnoses.* The Diagnostic Interview Schedule for Children – Child Version (DISC-C) is a standardized diagnostic interview developed for the National Institute of Mental Health by A. J. Costello et al. (1984) for use in epidemiological studies of children and adolescents aged 6–18 years. The DISC-C contains 264 items that inquire about behaviors and emotions both past and current. These symptoms correspond to DSM-III diagnostic criteria for childhood and adolescent disorders and generate a DSM-III Axis I diagnosis. Trained child psychologists and child psychiatrists interviewed all adolescents within the first 3 weeks of admission. The DISC's reliability and validity have been found to be as good or better than that of other established structured interviews (E. J. Costello et al., 1988). On the basis of the DISC-C, patients were selected with an affective or conduct disorder because they represent the major psychiatric disturbances of childhood and adolescence in inpatient settings. A number of studies have found that depression and conduct disorder show a considerable overlap (Carlson & Cantwell, 1980; Chiles, Miller, & Cox, 1980; Edelbrock & Achenbach, 1980). This overlap was found in our inpatient facility, as well; therefore, we also included a group of patients with both conduct and affective disorder. This resulted in the following diagnostic distribution: 39% conduct disorder, 20% affective disorder, and 41% in the mixed category of both conduct and affective disorder.

*Ego development.* The Washington University Sentence Completion Test (SCT) measure of ego development was introduced by Loevinger and her colleagues (Loevinger, 1976; Loevinger, Wessler, & Redmore, 1970). The measure consists of 36 incomplete sentence stems, with slightly different versions used for males and females. Patients are asked to complete sentence stems such as "When I am with a man . . . " and "The thing I like about myself is . . . ." The responses to the SCT were scored by experienced raters according to a standardized scoring protocol (Loevinger, 1979). An ego stage score (Total Protocol Rating [TPR]) and a numerical score (Item Sum Score [ISS]) were derived for each protocol. The scoring of protocols was carried out by trained raters whose reliabilities were greater than $r = .85$. The SCT has proven validity and reliability as well as sensitivity to changes over time (see Hauser, 1976; Loevinger, 1979; for reviews).

*Design.* In our research design, ego development was first used in its discontinuous stage form in order to examine ego level's association with psychiatric diagnoses. Patients who obtained a TPR score of Stage 3 and above were grouped in the conformist category (12% of the sample); the remaining 88%, obtaining TPRs of 2, Delta and Delta/3, were grouped as preconformist. After the univariate relationships between variables had been examined, the relative contribution of ego development in conjunction with the other variables in predicting psychiatric diagnosis was explored. To this end, the continuous score of ego development (ISS) was used in the subsequent hierarchical discriminant analyses.

## Results

The univariate relationships between psychiatric diagnosis and dimensions of gender, ego development level, IQ, and age are displayed in Table 1 for the 269 adolescents. Examination of Table 1 indicates a trend for more females than males in the affective disorder diagnostic group. The affective disorder group scored significantly higher on the Wechsler Intelligence Scale for Children—Revised than the conduct or mixed

disorder groups. While there were no significant differences between diagnostic group ages, there were significant differences between ego levels, with the affective disorders group having the highest proportion of conformist youths and the mixed and conduct disorders groups having a higher proportion of preconformist youths.

As age has been shown by previous researchers (e.g., Rutter & Garmezy, 1983) to bear some relationship to diagnostic prevalence, additional analyses were undertaken to further explore the interaction of these variables. Diagnostic groups were considered separately and the relationship between age and ego development plotted for each group. The relationship between age and ego level demonstrated by group indicates a more linear trend ($r = .40$, $p < .01$) among affective disordered youths and a significant, though weaker, relationship among the mixed disordered youths ($r = 24$, $p \leq .01$) and conduct disordered youths ($r = 24$, $p \leq .01$). The differences between these correlations were not statistically significant, however.

While the background variables of gender, IQ, and age were relevant with regard to their association with psychiatric diagnosis, of critical importance for our research was the association of ego development level with psychiatric diagnosis. To examine the relationship of these variables in predicting diagnoses, a hierarchical discriminant analysis (Tabachnick & Fidell, 1983) was performed using diagnostic group (i.e., mixed disorders, pure affective disorders, pure conduct disorders) as the grouping variable and gender, ego development (ISS), age, and IQ as the predictor variables. Gender, age, and IQ were all given equal weight and entered into the analysis prior to ego development. Results of this analysis are provided in Table 2. It can be seen that both ego development and IQ provide the best predictor variables of diagnostic group with the mixed and pure conduct disordered groups bearing greater similarity to each other than to the affective disorder group. While the discriminant function derived from this analysis provided a reason-

**Table 1.** *Characteristics of the sample (n = 269)*

| Characteristic | Conduct Disorder ($n = 104$) | Mixed Conduct/ Affective ($n = 111$) | Affective Disorder ($n = 54$) | Significance |
|---|---|---|---|---|
| Gender (%) | | | | |
| Male | 51 | 45 | 32 | $\chi^2 = 5.47, p < .06$ |
| Female | 49 | 55 | 68 | |
| Ego level (%) | | | | |
| Preconformist | 93 | 89 | 76 | |
| Conformist | 7 | 11 | 24 | $\chi^2 = 10.41, p < .01$ |
| IQ[a] | 101.8 (13.4) | 100.0 (13.7) | 107.4 (14.4) | $F = 5.26, p < .006$ |
| Age (in years)[a] | 14.0  (1.0) | 13.9  (1.2) | 13.8  (1.4) | $F = .63$, ns |

[a]Mean followed by standard deviation in parentheses.

**Table 2.** *Discriminant function analysis of diagnostic groups*

| Variable | Wilks's Lambda | F | p |
|---|---|---|---|
| Gender | .97 | 2.76 | .07 |
| Ego development | .94 | 7.87 | < .001 |
| Age | 1.00 | .63 | ns |
| IQ | .96 | 5.26 | < .01 |

Discriminant Function Coefficients

| Variable | Function 1 | Function 2 |
|---|---|---|
| Gender | .25 | − .66 |
| Ego development | .71 | − .06 |
| Age | − .43 | .49 |
| IQ | .34 | .70 |

Diagnostic Group Discriminant Functions

| Group | Function 1 | Function 2 |
|---|---|---|
| Mixed disorder | − .45 | − .10 |
| Conduct disorder | − .15 | .10 |
| Affective disorder | .59 | .00 |

Classification Results

| | No. of Cases | Predicted Group | | |
|---|---|---|---|---|
| | | Mixed | Conduct | Affective |
| Mixed disorder | | | | |
| n | 111 | 65 | 34 | 12 |
| % | | (58.6) | (30.6) | (10.8) |
| Conduct disorder | | | | |
| n | 104 | 54 | 44 | 6 |
| % | | (51.9) | (42.3) | (5.8) |
| Affective disorder | | | | |
| n | 54 | 27 | 12 | 15 |
| % | | (50) | (22.2) | (27.8) |

*Note:* 46.10% of cases correctly classified.

93

**Table 3.** *Diagnostic characteristics of the sample (n = 269)*

| Characteristic | Conduct Disorder (*n* = 104) | Mixed Conduct/ Affective (*n* = 111) | Affective Disorder (*n* = 54) | Chi-Square Value | *p* Significance |
|---|---|---|---|---|---|
| | | Diagnosis (%) | | | |
| Alcohol abuse or dependence | | | | | |
| Not present | 79 | 70 | 93 | 10.63 | < .005 |
| Present | 21 | 30 | 7 | | |
| Cannabis abuse or dependence | | | | | |
| Not present | 92 | 85 | 100 | 10.63 | < .005 |
| Present | 8 | 15 | | | |
| Other substance abuse or dependence | | | | | |
| Not present | 97 | 93 | 98 | 3.43 | ns |
| Present | 3 | 7 | 2 | | |
| Affective disorder dx | | | | | |
| Level 1 | | 68.5 | 70 | .06 | ns |
| Level 2 | | 31.5 | 30 | | |
| Suicidal ideation | | | | | |
| None | 85 | 40.5 | 39 | 53.21 | < .0001 |
| Level 1 | 3 | 4.5 | 4 | | |
| Level 2 | 13 | 55 | 57 | | |
| Suicide attempts | | | | | |
| None | 86 | 52 | 59 | 35.23 | < .0001 |
| Level 1 | | 7 | | | |
| Level 2 | 14 | 41 | 41 | | |
| Conduct disorder dx (conduct disorder and mixed groups only) | | | | | |
| Level 1 | 68 | 56 | | 3.51 | .06 |
| Level 2 | 32 | 44 | | | |
| Conduct disorder dx (conduct disorder and mixed groups only) | | | | | |
| Aggressive | 13.5 | 25 | | 7.74 | .02 |
| Nonaggressive | 50 | 33 | | | |
| Both aggressive and nonaggressive | 36.5 | 41 | | | |
| Conduct disorder dx (conduct disorder and mixed groups only) | | | | | |
| Socialized | 90 | 91.5 | | .01 | ns |
| Unsocialized | 10 | 8.5 | | | |

able prediction of mixed disordered adolescents (58.6%), and a slightly less good classification of conduct disordered patients (42.3%), the classification of affective disordered youths was fairly poor (27.8%).

To further explore the distinguishing features of these groups, diagnostic patterns for the mixed, pure conduct, and pure affective groups were compared in a series of chi-square analyses based on DISC diagnoses. Table 3 presents the results of comparisons among the three groups on alcohol and substance abuse and types and levels of diagnoses. These comparisons indicate that the mixed disorder group shares the most severe symptoms that *each* of the pure affective and conduct disordered groups exhibit independently, presenting a profile of youths who typically are both more symptomatic and demonstrate higher levels of pathology. Among the mixed diagnosis group the types of conduct disorders and their severity tend to be more attenuated compared to the pure conduct disorder group. The mixed diagnosis group tends to have more persistent and pronounced (i.e., Level 2) conduct diagnoses (44% vs. 32%) as well as significantly more aggressive conduct disorder diagnoses (66% vs. 50%). At the same time, the mixed diagnosis group is shown to have a similar proportion of mild (i.e., Level 1) and persistent (i.e., Level 2) affective disorders to the pure affective disorder group. Similar levels of suicidal ideation and attempts are also found among the mixed and pure affective groups, whereas these are much less present among the pure conduct disorder group. Similarly, cannabis and alcohol abuse and dependence are more prevalent among the mixed diagnosis and pure conduct disorder groups but largely absent among affective disordered youths.

## Discussion

The results of this study demonstrate the existence of a relationship between type of DSM-III psychiatric diagnosis and ego development level in adolescence after controlling for the effects of IQ, age, and gender. Such a finding suggests that Loevinger's method is more sensitive to issues of psychopathology than had earlier been hypothesized (Loevinger, 1968). Our previous findings concerning the relationships between ego development level achieved and treatment requests (Dill & Noam, 1990), symptomatology (Noam & Dill, 1991; Noam et al., 1984), diagnoses (Noam & Houlihan, 1990), and defense and coping styles (Noam et al., 1991) all pointed to its relevance to clinical research use. The standardized DSM-III and DSM-III-R diagnostic nosology (APA, 1980, 1987) appears to, at least in part, be amenable to a developmental analysis and extension.

These results also suggest that the course of psychiatric disorders needs to be understood in developmental terms. The adolescents who were diagnosed with an affective disorder were not only more likely to be female, but were also developmentally more like nonhospitalized adolescents in their ego development levels than were their counterpart groups of conduct disordered or mixed disordered patients. This is in line with other studies in which investigators have defined internalizing behaviors, of which affective or mood problems are a subset, as developmentally more mature (Cowan, 1982), as more psychologically complex, (Phillips & Zigler, 1964), and occurring at later ages in childhood than externalizing behaviors (Edelbrock & Achenbach, 1980).

The research on childhood depression (Digdon & Gotlieb, 1985; Kazdin, 1990) and epidemiological studies (Kashani et al., 1987; Rutter & Garmezy, 1983; Ryan, 1989) suggest a substantial increase in depressive disorders in adolescence compared to childhood. Often these findings are interpreted to suggest causality between maturational growth and the emergence of affective disorders. For example, this greater incidence might relate to hormonal changes and the higher incidence of depression in girls may be due to their earlier entrance into puberty (Brooks-Gunn & Peterson, 1984; Lerner & Foch, 1987). A social-cognitive explanation of the greater incidence of depression in adolescence suggests that the reorganization that generally occurs in adolescence, with the emerging capacity for formal operational thought and more mature perspective-taking and self-reflection (Elkind, 1967; Flavell, 1963; Noam, 1986; Selman et al., 1979), can bring with it a reattribution to internal sources of the unhappiness formerly seen as stemming from external sources. Such a transformation would likely lead to more self-blame, guilt, and other depressive symptomatology. With the development of these capacities, a biographical framing of self (Noam, 1993) emerges and can heighten a sense of hopelessness. Of course, these processes often occur in concert with other risk factors, such as biological predisposition, attachment history, pubertal timing, and family dysfunction. It has been far more common, however, to focus on these latter dimensions than on the continued developmental path in cognitive and social cognitive capacities. This is not surprising, since development is usually framed in terms of progressive acquisition of skills and increasing adaptive capacities, and it requires a shift in perspective to view these advances as simultaneously creating new risks.

One study that has received a great deal of attention in the literature (Kovacs & Paulauskas, 1984) also tested such a social-cognitive hypothesis with regard to depressive symptomatology. At first, Kovacs and Paulauskas used a seldomly applied measure of Piagetian formal operations as their yardstick (Goodnow, 1962), but when this instrument failed to distribute their 8–13-year-old depressed subjects across pre-operational, concrete operational, and formal operational stages, a social-cognitive task was given more weight (Selman et al., 1979). Nonetheless, no support was found for their hypothesized relationship between developmental level and depressive symptomatology. These results may be more an artifact of the research design and instrumentation than a statement about the development of aspects of symptomatology. In their careful study, a restricted range of symptomatology was examined, and within this range of depression, certain symptoms, such as hopelessness, self-deprecation, and inability to experience pleasure were tested for their relationship to developmental level. The specificity of such hypotheses, coupled with an age range of subjects that spanned childhood through adolescence (with great potential variation in cognitive level) may be, in part, responsible for the lack of significant findings. Our study, by contrast, restricts the age range to adolescence and expands the range of symptomatology. A first step has also been taken to include other predictive variables from previous studies, such as gender and IQ. The support we found for our hypotheses may reflect these design variations. The excellent longitudinal research of Kovacs and associates, with its multiple follow-up studies, has heightened interest across a variety of depression research projects, facilitating more conclusive answers to the question of how

affective disorders and social cognition relate.

Our findings concerning the association between early ego development and conduct disorder diagnoses are in line with several other studies of adolescents' symptomatology. As detailed earlier, a greater degree of externalizing and more severe behavioral problems exist in adolescents with delayed ego development (Browning, 1986; Frank & Quinlan, 1976; Noam et al., 1984; Noam & Houlihan, 1990). The resemblance of the dual-diagnosis group to the pure conduct disorder group in terms of delays in ego development level, gender, and IQ coupled with their diagnostic symptomatology (which reflects the most severe symptoms from among both the pure affective and conduct disordered groups) requires further study.

In general, the relationship between conduct and affective disorders is poorly understood. Studies investigating childhood affective disorders report the simultaneous presence of conduct disorder in 7–37% of the probands (Carlson & Cantwell, 1980; Kovacs, Feinberg, Crouse-Novak, Paulauskas, & Finkelstein, 1984; Puig-Antich, 1982; Ryan et al., 1987). Samples of juvenile delinquents showed comparable prevalence rates (13–44%) of lifetime affective disorder (Alessi, McManus, Grapentine, & Brickman, 1983; Chiles et al., 1980; Kashani et al., 1980; McManus, Alessi, Grapentine, & Brickman, 1984).

Precisely how conduct and affective disorders are associated is the subject of much research and debate in the literature (Harrington, Fudge, Rutter, Pickler, & Hill, 1991; Kovacs & Goldstone, 1991). For example, Puig-Antich (1982) found an episodic depressive course in prepubertal boys, in which conduct problems followed the recovery and relapse of depression. Yet in other studies, conduct disorder preceded the onset of emotional disturbance or major depressive disorder (Graham & Rutter, 1973; Kovacs et al., 1984). These studies indicate the difficulties in drawing firm conclusions about the association between conduct and affective disorders. Whatever the course of association, however, the present findings suggest that the mixed-diagnoses group, presenting with the more marked symptoms of both the affective and conduct disordered groups, yet displaying none of their ameliorating characteristics (e.g., the higher IQ or higher ego-levels found among the affective disorder group, or lower levels of suicidality seen among the pure conduct disorder group) merit particular attention.

Co-morbidity of psychiatric diagnosis has been found to enhance suicide risk (Brent et al., 1988; Kreitman, 1986). Shafii, Steltz-Lenarsky, Derrick, Beckner, and Whittinghill (1988) found 81% of adolescent suicide completers were most often characterized by depression with substance abuse, conduct disorder, or other mental disorder. Similar findings by Shaffer (1974), Pfeffer, Plutchick, and Mizruchi (1983), and Brent (1987) led to the postulation of two suicidal profiles for depressed and impulsive/conduct disordered youth. Work by Borst et al. (1991), Borst and Noam (1993), and Noam and Borst (in press) suggests that distinct ego development levels may further characterize these profiles, with the depressed youths having higher ego levels than the impulsive/conduct disordered youths.

From an ego development perspective, we expected the mixed diagnosis group to be more like the pure conduct than the pure affective disorder group because we have found in earlier studies a clearer trend between early ego developmental levels and

externalizing symptoms than between more mature levels and internalizing symptoms. However, the specific pathways of disorders and their causation require a great deal of further longitudinal research. The relationship between age and ego development found in the present analyses demonstrates that while absolute level of ego development is related to psychological dysfunction, with youths in the pure affective group demonstrating higher mean ego levels than either the pure conduct or mixed diagnosis groups, the interaction of age with developmental level merits further study (Valiant & Noam, manuscript in preparation).

Longitudinal study will shed additional light on the developmental trajectories of these pure or mixed diagnosis disorders. For example, does an adolescent who, upon admission for treatment, is diagnosed with a conduct disorder or mixed disorder and is developmentally delayed, then progresses in ego development during the treatment interval become more depressed and less "externalizing" in his/her psychopathology? A follow-up study of patients after 9-months of treatment (Noam et al., 1991) suggests that ego development maturity even in this short period results in (a) more mature defensive styles, (b) more adaptive coping strategies, and (c) less externalizing symptomatology than does no change in ego development. It now becomes essential to further integrate developmental psychopathology research with detailed clinical nosology of conduct and affective disorders in children.

## References

Achenbach, T. M., & Edelbrock, C. (1987). *Manual for the youth self report and profile*. Burlington: University of Vermont, Department of Psychiatry.

Alessi, N. E., McManus, M., Grapentine, W. L., & Brickman, A. (1983). The characterization of depressive disorders in serious juvenile offenders. *Journal of Affective Disorders, 6,* 9–17.

American Psychiatric Association. (1980). *Diagnostic and statistical manual of mental disorders* (3rd ed.). Washington, DC: Author.

American Psychiatric Association. (1987). *Diagnostic and statistical manual of mental disorders* (3rd ed., rev.). Washington, DC: Author.

Angold, A., & Costello, E. G. (1991). Developing a developmental epidemiology. In D. Cicchetti & S. L. Toth (Eds.), *Rochester Symposium on Developmental Psychopathology: Vol. 3. Models and integrations* (pp. 75–96). Rochester, NY: Rochester University Press.

Angold, A., & Rutter, M. (1992). Effects of age and pubertal status on depression in a large clinical sample. *Development and Psychopathology, 4*(1), 5–28.

Borst, S., & Noam, G. G. (1989). Suicidality and psychopathology in hospitalized children and adolescents. *Acta Psychologica, 52,* 165–175.

Borst, S. R., & Noam, G. G. (1993). Developmental psychopathology in suicidal and nonsuicidal adolescent girls. *Journal of the American Academy of Child and Adolescent Psychiatry, 32*(3), 501–508.

Borst, S. R., Noam, G. G., & Bartok, J. (1991). Adolescent suicidality: A clinical-developmental approach. *Journal of the American Academy of Child and Adolescent Psychiatry, 30*(5), 796–803.

Bowlby, J. (1952). *Maternal care and mental health.* Geneva: World Health Organization.

Bowlby, J. (1980). *Attachment and loss: Loss, sadness, and depression.* New York: Basic Books.

Brent, D. A. (1987). Correlates of medical lethality of suicide attempts in children and adolescents. *Journal of the American Academy of Child and Adolescent Psychiatry, 26*, 87–89.

Brent, D. A., Perper, J. A., Goldstein, C. E., Kolko, D. J., Allan, M. J., Allman, C. J., & Zelenak, J. P. (1988). Risk factors for adolescent suicide. A comparison of adolescent suicide with suicidal inpatients. *Archives of General Psychiatry, 45*(6), 581–588.

Bretherton, I. (1990). Open communication and internal working models: Their role in the development of attachment relationships. In R. Thompson (Ed.), *Nebraska Symposium on Motivation: Vol. 36. Socioemotional development* (pp. 57–114). Lincoln: University of Nebraska Press.

Brooks-Gunn, J., & Peterson, A. C. (1984). Problems in studying and defining pubertal events. *Journal of Youth and Adolescence, 13*(3), 181–196.

Browning, D. L. (1986). Psychiatric ward behavior and length of stay in adolescent and young adult inpatients: A developmental approach to prediction. *Journal of Consulting and Clinical Psychology, 54*, 227–230.

Browning, D. L., & Quinlan, D. (1985). Ego development and intelligence in a psychiatric population: Wechsler subtest scores. *Journal of Personality Assessment, 49*(3), 260–263.

Carlson, G. A., & Cantwell, D. P. (1980). Unmasking masked depression in children and adolescents. *American Journal of Psychiatry, 137*, 445–449.

Chandler, M. J. (1976). Social cognition: A selective review of current research. In W. Overton & J. Gallagher (Eds.), *Knowledge and development* (Vol. 1). New York: Plenum Press.

Chandler, M. J. (in press). Self continuity in suicidal and non-suicidal adolescents. In G. Noam & S. Borst (Eds.), *Children, Youth and Suicide: Developmental Perspectives. New directions in child development.* San Francisco: Jossey-Bass.

Chiles, J. A., Miller, M. L., & Cox, G. B. (1980). Depression in an adolescent delinquent population. *Archives of General Psychiatry, 37*, 1179–1184.

Cicchetti, D. (1984). The emergence of developmental psychopathology. *Child Development, 55*(1), 1–7.

Cicchetti, D., & Toth, S. L. (Eds.). (1991). *Rochester Symposium on Developmental Psychopathology: Vol. 2. Internalizing and externalizing expressions of dysfunction.* Hillsdale, NJ: Erlbaum.

Costello, A. J., Edelbrock, C. S., Dulcan, M. K., Kalas, R., & Klaric, S. H. (1984). *Development and testing of the NIMH diagnostic interview schedule for children on a clinical population: Final report* (Contract No. RFP-DB-81-0027). Rockville, MD: Center for Epidemiologic Studies, National Institute for Mental Health.

Costello, E. J., Costello, A. J., Edelbrock, C., Burns, B. J., Dulcan, M. K., Kalas, R., Brent, D., & Janiszewski, S. (1988). Psychiatric disorders in pediatric primary care. *Archives of General Psychiatry, 45*, 1104–1116.

Cowan, P. (1982). The relationship between emotional and cognitive development. *New Directions for Child Development, 16*, 49–82.

Crittenden, P. M., & Craig, S. E. (1990). Developmental trends in the nature of child homicide. *Journal of Interpersonal Violence, 5*(2), 202–216.

Damon, W., & Hart, W. (1982). The development of self-understanding from infancy through adolescence. *Child Development, 53*, 841–864.

Digdon, N., & Gotlieb, I. H. (1985). Developmental considerations in the study of childhood depression. *Developmental Review, 5*, 162–199.

Dill, D. L., & Noam, G. G. (1990). Ego development and treatment requests. *Psychiatry, 53*, 85–91.

Edelbrock, C. S., & Achenbach, T. M. (1980). A typology of child behavior profile patterns: Distribution and correlates for disturbed children aged 6–16. *Journal of Abnormal Child Psychology, 8*, 441–470.

Elkind, D. (1967). Egocentrism in adolescence. *Child Development, 38*, 1025–1034.

Erikson, E. (1950). *Childhood and society.* New York: Norton.

Fischer, K. (1980). A theory of cognitive development: The control and construction of hierarchies of skills. *Psychological Review, 87*, 477–531.

Flavell, J. H. (1963). *The developmental psychology of Jean Piaget.* New York: Van Nostrand.

Flavell, J. H., Botken, P., Fry, C., Wright, J., & Jarvis, P. (1968). *The development of role taking and communication skills in children.* New York: Wiley.

Frank, S., & Quinlan, D. (1976). Ego development and adjustment patterns in adolescence. *Journal of Abnormal Psychology, 85*, 505–510.

Garber, J. (1984). The developmental progression of depression in female children. *New Directions for Child Development, 26*, 29–58.

Gfellner, B. (1986). Ego changes in moral development in adolescents: A longitudinal study. *Journal of Adolescence, 9*, 281–302.

Gold, S. N. (1980). Relations between level of ego development and adjustment patterns in adolescents. *Journal of Personality Assessment, 44*(6), 630–638.

Goodnow, J. J. (1962). A test of milieu effects with some of Piaget's tasks. *Psychological Monographs, 76*, 1–21.

Graham, P., & Rutter, M. (1973). Psychiatric disorder in the young adolescent: A follow-up study. *Proceedings of the Royal Society of Medicine, 66*, 1226–1229.

Harrington, R., Fudge, H., Rutter, M., Pickler, A., & Hill, J. (1991). Adult outcome of childhood and adolescent depression: II. Links with antisocial disorders. *Journal of the American Academy of Child and Adolescent Psychiatry, 30*(3), 434–439.

Hauser, S. T. (1976). Loevinger's model and measure of ego development: A critical review. *Psychological Bulletin, 83*, 928–955.

Hollingshead, A. B. (1957). *Two factor index of social position.* Unpublished report, New Haven, CT.

Institute of Medicine. (1989). *Research on children and adolescents with mental, behavioral and devel-*

opmental disorders. Washington, DC: National Academic Press.

Kashani, J. H., Carlson, G. A., Beck, N. C., Hoeper, E. W., Corcoran, C. M., McAllister, J. A., Fallahi, C., Rosenberg, T. K., & Reid, J. C. (1987). Depression, depressive symptoms, and depressed mood among a community sample of adolescents. *American Journal of Psychiatry, 144*, 931–934.

Kashani, J. H., Manning, G. W., McKnew, D. H., Cytryn, L., Simonds, J. F., & Wooderson, P. C. (1980). Depression among incarcerated delinquents. *Psychiatry Research, 3*, 185–191.

Kastrup, M. (1977). Urban-rural differences in 6 year olds. In P. J. Graham (Ed.), *Epidemiological approaches in child psychiatry* (pp. 181–194). London: Academic Press.

Kazdin, A. E. (1989). Developmental psychopathology. *American Psychologist, 44*, 180–187.

Kazdin, A. E. (1990). Childhood depression. *Journal of Child Psychology and Psychiatry, 31*(1), 121–160.

Kohlberg, L. (1969). Stage and sequence: The cognitive developmental approach to socialization. In D. Goslin (Ed.), *Handbook of socialization, theory and research* (pp. 347–480). New York: Rand McNally.

Kovacs, M., Feinberg, T. L., Crouse-Novak, M. A., Paulauskas, S. L., & Finkelstein, R. (1984). Depressive disorders in children. *Archives of General Psychiatry, 41*, 229–237.

Kovacs, M., & Goldstone, D. (1991). Cognitive development of depressed children and adolescents. *Journal of the American Academy of Child and Adolescent Psychiatry, 30*(3), 388–392.

Kovacs, M., & Paulauskas, S. L. (1984). Developmental stage and the expression of depressive disorders in children: An empirical analysis. *New Directions for Child Development, 26*, 59–80.

Kreitman, N. (1986). The clinical assessment and management of the suicidal patient. In A. Roy (Ed.), *Suicide* (pp. 181–195). Baltimore, MD: Williams & Wilkins.

Lavik, N. J. (1977). Urban-rural differences in rates of disorders. A comparative psychiatric population study of Norwegian adolescents. In P. J. Graham (Ed.), *Epidemiological approaches in child psychiatry* (pp. 223–251). London: Academic Press.

Lerner, R., & Foch, T. T. (Eds.). (1987). *Biological-psychosocial interactions in early adolescence.* Hillsdale, NJ: Erlbaum.

Loevinger, J. (1968). The relation of adjustment to ego development. In S. S. Sells (Ed.), *The definition and measurement of mental health* (pp. 161–180). Washington, DC: Government Printing Office.

Loevinger, J. (1976). *Ego development.* San Francisco: Jossey-Bass.

Loevinger, J. (1979). Construct validity of the Sentence Completion Test of ego development. *Applied Psychological Measurement, 3*, 281–311.

Loevinger, J., Wessler, R., & Redmore, C. (1970). *Measuring ego development: Vol. 2. Scoring manual for women and girls.* San Francisco: Jossey-Bass.

Masten, A., Best, K., & Garmezy, N. (1990). Resilience and development: Contributions from the study of children who overcome adversity. *Development and Psychopathology, 2*, 425–444.

McManus, M., Alessi, N. E., Grapentine, W. L., & Brickman, A. (1984). Psychiatric disturbances in serious delinquents. *Journal of the American Academy of Child Psychiatry, 23*, 602–615.

Noam, G. G. (1984). *Self, morality and biography: Studies in clinical-developmental psychology.* Unpublished doctoral dissertation. Harvard University, Cambridge.

Noam, G. G. (1986). The theory of biography and transformation and the borderline personality disorders (Part II): A developmental typology. *McLean Hospital Journal, XI*, 2.

Noam, G. G. (1988). A constructivist approach to developmental psychopathology. *Developmental psychopathology and its treatment. New Directions for Child Development, 39*, 91–121.

Noam, G. G. (1993a). Ego development, true or false? *Psychological Inquiry, 4*(1), 43–48.

Noam, G. G. (1993b). "Normative Vulnerabilities" of the self. In G. G. Noam and T. Wren (Eds.), *The moral self* (pp. 209–238). Cambridge, MA: MIT Press.

Noam, G. G., & Dill, D. L. (1991). Adult development and symptomatology. *Psychiatry, 54*, 208–217.

Noam, G. G., Hauser, S., Santostefano, S., Garrison, W., Jacobson, A., Powers, S., & Mead, M. (1984). Ego development and psychopathology: A study of hospitalized adolescents. *Child Development, 55*, 184–194.

Noam, G. G., & Houlihan, J. (1990). Developmental dimensions of DSM-III diagnoses in adolescent psychiatric patients. *American Journal of Orthopsychiatry, 60*(3), 371–378.

Noam, G. G., Kilburn, D., & Ammen-Elkins, G. (1989). *Adolescent development and psychiatric symptomatology.* Unpublished McLean Hospital Report, Belmont, MA.

Noam, G. G., Recklitis, C., & Paget, K. (1991). Pathways of ego development: Contributions to maladaptation and adjustment. *Development and Psychopathology, 3*(3), 311–328.

Noam, G. G., & Valiant, G. (1994). Clinical-developmental psychology in developmental psychopathology: Theory and research of an emerging perspective. In D. Cicchetti & S. Toth (Eds.) *Rochester Symposium on Developmental Psychopathology: Vol. 5. Disorders and dysfunctions of the self.* Rochester, NY: Rochester University Press.

Noam, G. G., & Borst S. (in press). Developing meaning – Losing meaning: Understanding suicidal behavior in the young. In G. G. Noam and S. Borst (Eds.) *Children, Youth and Suicide: Developmental Perspectives.* New Directions in Child Development. San Francisco: Jossey Bass.

Pfeffer, C. R., Plutchik, R., & Mizruchi, M. S. (1983). Suicidal and assaultive behavior in children: Classification, measurement and interrelations. *American Journal of Psychiatry, 140*, 154–157.

Phillips, L., & Zigler, E. (1964). Role orientation, the action-thought dimension, and outcome in psychiatric disorder. *Journal of Abnormal and Social Psychology, 68*, 381–389.

Piaget, J. (1981). Intelligence and affectivity: Their relationship during child development. Palo Alto, CA: Annual Reviews.

Puig-Antich, J. (1982). Major depression and conduct disorder in prepuberty. *Journal of the American Academy of Child Psychiatry, 21*, 118–128.

Recklitis, C. J., & Noam, G. G. (August, 1990). *Aggression in adolescent psychopathology: Develop-*

*ment of personality dimensions.* Paper presented at the annual meeting of the American Psychological Association, Boston, MA.

Redmore, C., & Loevinger, J. (1979). Ego development in adolescence: Longitudinal studies. *Journal of Youth and Adolescence, 8,* 1–20.

Remschmidt, H., Hohner, G., & Merschmann, W. (1977). Epidemiology of delinquent behavior in children. In P. J. Graham (Ed.), *Epidemiological approaches in child psychiatry.* London: Academic Press.

Rosznafsky, J. (1981). The relationship of level of ego development to Q-sort personality ratings. *Journal of Personality and Social Psychology, 41,* 99–120.

Rutter, M., Cox, A., Tupling, C., Berger, M., & Yule, W. (1975). Attainment and adjustment in two geographical areas: I, The prevalence of psychiatric disorder. *British Journal of Psychiatry, 126,* 493–509.

Rutter, M., & Garmezy, N. (1983). Development psychopathology. In E. M. Hetherington (Ed.), *Mussen's handbook of child psychology. Socialization, personality, and social development* (Vol. 4, pp. 775–911). New York: Wiley.

Rutter, M., Tizard, J., & Whitmore, K. (1970/1981). *Education, health and behavior.* Huntington, NY: Krieger. (Original work published 1970, London: Longmans)

Ryan, N. D. (1989). Major depression. In C. Last & M. Hershon (Eds.), *Handbook of child psychiatric diagnosis* (pp. 317–329). New York: Wiley.

Ryan, N. D., Puig-Antich, J., Ambrosini, P., Rabinovich, H., Robinson, D., Nelson, B., Iyengar, S., & Twomney, J. (1987). The clinical picture of major depression in children and adolescents. *Archives of General Psychiatry, 44,* 854–861.

Selman, R. L., Jaquette, D., & Bruss-Saunders, E. (1979). *Assessing interpersonal understanding: An interview and scoring manual in five parts.* Unpublished manuscript, Cambridge, MA.

Shaffer, D. (1974). Suicide in childhood and early adolescence. *Journal of Child Psychology and Psychiatry, 15,* 275–291.

Shafii, M., Steltz-Lenarsky, J., Derrick, A. M., Beckner, C., & Whittinghill, J. R. (1988). Comorbidity of mental disorders in the post-mortem diagnosis of completed suicide in children and adolescents. *Journal of Affective Disorders, 15*(3), 227–233.

Shepard, M., Oppenheim, B., & Mitchell, S. (Eds.). (1971). *Childhood behavior and mental health.* London: University of London Press.

Sroufe, A. (1989). Pathways to adaptation and maladaptation: Psychopathology as developmental deviation. In D. Cicchetti (Ed.), *Rochester Symposium on Developmental Psychopathology: Vol. 1. The emergence of a discipline* (pp. 13–40). Hillsdale, NJ: Erlbaum.

Sullivan, E. V., McCullough, G., & Stager, H. A. (1970). A developmental study of the relationship between conceptual, ego and moral development. *Child Development, 41,* 399–411.

Tabachnik, B. G., & Fidell, L. S. (1983). *Using multivariate statistics.* New York: Harper & Row.

Valiant, G. L., & Noam, G. G. (manuscript in preparation). *Age/stage dysynchrony in adolescent development and psychiatric diagnoses.* Unpublished manuscript.

Vaillant, G. E., & Drake, R. E. (1985). Maturity of ego defenses in relation to DSM-III axis II personality disorder. *Archives of General Psychiatry, 42,* 597–601.

Vaillant, G. (1993). *The wisdom of the ego.* Cambridge, MA: Harvard University Press.

Werner, H. (1948). *Comparative psychology of mental development.* New York: International University Press.

Werry, J. S., & Quay, H. C. (1971). The prevalence of behavior symptoms in younger elementary school children. *American Journal of Orthopsychiatry, 41,* 136–143.

Wilber, C. H., Rounsaville, B., Sugarman, A., Casey, J., & Kleber, H. (1982). Ego development in opiate addicts. An application of Loevinger's stage model. *Journal of Nervous and Mental Disease, 170,* 202–208.

Wohlwill, J. F. (1973). The concept of experience: S or R? *Human Development, 16*(1–2), 90–107.

Zoccolillo, M. (1993). Gender and the development of conduct disorder. *Development and Psychopathology, 5*(1–2), 65–78.

JOURNAL OF RESEARCH ON ADOLESCENCE, 5(1), 1–29

# Gender-Linked Vulnerabilities to Depressive Symptoms, Stress, and Problem Behaviors in Adolescents

Bonnie J. Leadbeater, Sidney J. Blatt, and Donald M. Quinlan
*Yale University*

Ample research has shown that female adolescents endorse more internalizing and fewer externalizing symptoms than do male adolescents, but explanations for these gender differences have not been forthcoming. In this review, we integrated research findings of gender differences in subtypes of depressive vulnerabilities and in reactivity to stressful life events involving the self or others in order to suggest possible explanations of gender differences in adolescent psychopathology. Adolescent girls show greater interpersonal depressive vulnerability and greater reactivity to stressful events involving others. In contrast, gender differences have not been found in adolescents' self-critical depressive vulnerability and in their reactivity to stressful events involving issues of self-worth. We argue that adolescents with heightened interpersonal depressive vulnerability (who fear abandonment and seek attention and nurturing) are more reactive to stressful events involving others and are more likely to exhibit internalizing than externalizing syndromes. On the other hand, adolescents with heightened self-critical depressive vulnerability (who experience guilt and self-blame and avoid interpersonal intimacy) are more reactive to stressful events involving threats to the self and are more likely to exhibit externalizing, in addition to internalizing, syndromes.

Recent theories of developmental psychopathology emphasize the transaction of antecedent conditions, individual vulnerabilities, and potentiating and protective environmental factors in determining risks

Requests for reprints should be sent to Bonnie J. Leadbeater, Department of Psychology, Yale University, Post Office Box 208205, New Haven, CT 06520.

101

for negative outcomes (Cicchetti & Rizley, 1981; Cummings & Cicchetti, 1990; Garmezy, Masten & Tellegen, 1984; Gottlieb, 1991; Rutter & Rutter, 1993). Considerable research has addressed individual, family, and social factors that potentiate or protect against internalizing and externalizing syndromes in adolescents. Until recently, however, this research has tended to overlook both the causal role of depressed affect (Cole & Zahn-Waxler, 1992) and the moderating role of gender in the differential expression of adolescent psychopathology.

The research evidence that we reviewed shows that girls exhibit higher levels of internalizing disorders and are more likely to endorse depressive symptoms that express somatic problems, sad affect, and loneliness. Boys, on the other hand, are more likely to exhibit externalizing disorders and to endorse depressive symptoms that express antagonism, aggression, and an inability to work. Research also shows gender differences in subtypes of depression (i.e., interpersonal and self-critical depressive vulnerabilities). Adolescent girls are more likely to suffer from interpersonal depressive preoccupations (feelings of loss or loneliness) than are boys, but girls also are equally likely to experience self-critical depressive preoccupations (feelings of failure and lack of self-worth). Similar gender differences have been observed in adolescents' reactivity to stressful life events that involve or affect others (e.g., illness in a family member), rather than to events that directly affect self-esteem (e.g., academic failures; Gore, Aseltine, & Colten, 1993; Wagner & Compas, 1990). Girls are reactive to both types of stress, whereas boys react primarily to stressful events that directly affect them. Using a transactional model of development to integrate these findings, we posit that differential vulnerabilities to interpersonal or self-critical depressive experiences, when potentiated by stressful life events involving the self and/or others, differentially predict higher levels of internalizing or externalizing problem behaviors in girls and boys. Directions for future research and implications of gender differences for understanding the onset, prevention, and treatment of adolescent psychopathology are highlighted in our conclusion.

## GENDER-LINKED VULNERABILIES TO DEPRESSION

### Distinguishing Depression , Depressive Symptoms, and Internalizing and Externalizing Syndromes

The term *depression* refers to a continuum of affective disturbances that includes dysphoric mood or feelings of sadness, a syndrome or cluster of symptoms, and a psychiatric disorder (Blatt, 1974; Cantwell & Baker, 1991). Criteria for dysthymia or major depression—psychiatric disorders defined by the *Diagnostic and Statistical Manual of Mental Disorders* (DSM–III–R; American Psychiatric Association, 1987)—comprise a specific cluster of affective and somatic symptoms that have a minimum duration and impact on adaptive functioning. Although research indicates that these criteria may be applied independently of age, the organization of symptoms may differ across age and gender (see Blatt, 1991; Cantwell & Baker, 1991; Kazdin, 1989; Radloff, 1991). In addition epidemiological investigations have shown significant increases in depressive symptoms reported by recent cohorts of adolescents and young adults, especially for women (Kandel & Davies, 1982, 1986; Klerman & Weissman, 1989; Petersen, Sarigiani, & Kennedy, 1991; Rutter, 1986). Although not equivalent to clinical depression, self-reported symptoms may indicate risk for depression as a psychiatric disorder (Barrera & Garrison-Jones, 1988; Roberts, Lewinsohn, & Seeley, 1991).

Many other distinct clinical disturbances (e.g., conduct disorders) have been found to co-occur with clinical depression in children and adolescents (Carlson & Cantwell, 1980; Cole & Carpentieri, 1990; Craighead, 1991; Rohde, Lewinsohn, & Seeley, 1991). Self-reported depressive symptoms are also associated with other adolescent mental health and behavioral problems in studies involving community-based samples of adolescents (Achenbach & Edelbrock, 1987; Blatt, Hart, Quinlan, Leadbeater, & Auerbach, 1993; Colten, Gore, & Aseltine, 1991; Horwitz & White, 1987; Reinherz et al., 1989, 1990; Reinherz, Frost, & Pakiz, 1991). Together, these research findings suggest that factors that create vulnerabilities to depression or depressive symptoms may also create risks for the development of other problem behaviors in adolescents. However, the possible process that explains these links remains relatively unexplored.

Adolescent problem behaviors are frequently dichotomized into internalizing disturbances (e.g., depression, anxiety, suicidality, and eating disorders) and externalizing disturbances (e.g., oppositional disorders, delinquency, and school problems; Achenbach, 1991; Achenbach & Edelbrock, 1978). Nevertheless, although some adolescents' problems are primarily internalizing or externalizing, these categories are not mutually exclusive (Achenbach, 1991; Cohen, Gotlieb, Kershner, & Wehrspann, 1985; Colten et al., 1991). Achenbach (1991) reported moderate correlations between internalizing and externalizing syndromes in large samples of community-based and clinic-referred adolescents on the Youth Self Report (YSR; mean $rs$ = .64 and .52, respectively). In partial explanation of this overlap, Achenbach reported that depressed/anxious mood was significantly correlated not only with internalizing symptoms for nonreferred and clinic-referred boys (rs = .80 and .85, respectively) and girls (rs = .81 and .89, respectively) but also with externalizing symptoms in nonreferred and referred boys (rs = .50 to .47, respectively) and girls (rs = .57 to .47, respectively). Several other studies of community-based samples of adolescents showed moderate associations between self-reported depressive symptoms and broad assessments of internalizing and externalizing disorders (Blatt et al., 1993; Colten et al., 1991; Horwitz & White, 1987; Reinherz et al., 1989, 1990, 1991).

The co-occurrence of depression or depressive symptoms and other problem behaviors in adolescents, together with the shared variance observed in internalizing and externalizing syndromes, suggests that some common causal factors may create risks for both types of disturbances. On the other hand, both the distinctiveness of diagnostic categories that may be applied to adolescents and the clustering of some adolescents' problems as primarily internalizing or primarily externalizing, necessitate questioning further what factors uniquely predict or moderate the differences in expressions of different types of problem behaviors (Allen, Leadbeater, & Aber, 1994). This review highlights how depressive vulnerabilities may result in differential adolescent responsiveness to particular types of stressful life events and in different expressions of psychopathology.

## Gender Differences in Internalizing and Externalizing Disorders

Researchers have consistently shown that women endorse more internalizing symptoms, whereas men endorse more externalizing symptoms (Achenbach and Edelbrock, 1987; Achenbach, Howell, Quay, & Conners, 1991; Ostrov, Offer, & Howard, 1988). Although the percentage of variance accounted for by gender is typically small (1% to 4%), differences in the items differentially endorsed by boys or girls on the YSR (Achenbach, 1991) are notable. All 22 internalizing items were endorsed more frequently by girls. These included somatic problems (e.g., headaches, nausea, skin problems, weight problems, overtiredness, dizziness, and eating problems), depressed mood (e.g., sad, cries a lot, worries, feels lonely, feels unloved, is self-conscious), and aggression against the self (e.g., has suicidal thoughts, feels persecuted, harms self). In contrast, boys more frequently endorsed problem behaviors for 12 of the 19 items related to externalized aggression (e.g., destroys things, mean to others, threatens others, swears, brags, teases a lot, thinks about sex too much) and delinquent acts (e.g., destroys things, disobeys at school, fights, bad friends, sets fires, steals outside of home). In a community-based sample, Colten et al. (1991) also found more internalizing problems (anxiety, depression, and somatic problems) among girls and more externalizing behaviors (delinquency, problem behaviors at school, and poor grades) among boys.

The prevalence of discrete problems in adolescents also reflects these gender differences (e.g., Horwitz & White, 1987; Rohde et al., 1991). Men in the United States are three times more likely to die from violent causes (accidental death, suicides involving guns or hanging, and homicide) than are women (Kandel, Raveis, & Davies, 1991; U.S. Bureau of the Census, 1990; Wetzel, 1989). Antisocial behaviors are also approximately three times more frequent among men than among women (Graham, 1979) and generally begin at an earlier age for boys (median age 10) than for girls (median age 13; Kazdin, 1987). On the other hand, girls make more suicide attempts (Wetzel, 1989), and 90% to 95% of anorexics and bulimics are female (McGrath, Keita, Strickland, & Russo, 1990). Postpubescent girls are more likely than postpubescent boys to show depression (Nolen-Hoeksema, 1990).

## Gender Differences in the Prevalence and Expression of Depressive Symptoms

Because of historical beliefs that adolescents could not experience the affective quality of depression exhibited by adults (e.g., Mahler, 1963; Weiner, 1982), few systematic investigations of the prevalence of depressive symptoms in community-based samples of adolescents existed prior to 1980. Since that time, however, at least 20 studies have been published in which depressive symptoms were directly assessed in samples with a minimum of 99 adolescents (see Table 1). All were cross-sectional and used self-report measures (i.e., the Beck Depression Inventory, [BDI] Beck, Steer, & Garbin, 1988; the Center for Epidemiological Studies Depression Scale, Radloff, 1977 and Weissman, Orvaschel, & Padian, 1980; the Children's Depression Inventory (CDI), Kovacs, 1982; or a 5-item assessment of depressed mood, Kandel & Davies, 1982). One study used diagnostic interviews (Kashani et al., 1987). The proportions of adolescents reporting at least moderate levels of symptoms ranged from 13.5% to 34%. There was more consistency in the proportions reporting severe levels of symptoms (5% to 8.6%). These proportions correspond to rates of clinically diagnosed major depression and dysthymia in community-based samples of adolescents (Kashani et al.).

TABLE 1

Sex Differences in Depressive Symptoms in Community-Based Samples of Adolescents

| Study | N | Age (years)/ Grade | SES/Race | Depression Assessed By | Findings | Effect Size |
|---|---|---|---|---|---|---|
| Kandel and Davies, 1982 | 8,206 | 14–18 | diverse/diverse | Kandel scale | F > M | .52 |
| Teri, 1982 | 645 | 9th–12th | middle/white | BDI | F = M, totals | .10 |
| | | | | | F > M, severe | |
| Siegel and Griffin, 1984 | 99 | 13–18 | upper–middle/ white | BDI | F = M, totals | NA |
| | | | | | F = M, severe | |
| Kaplan et al., 1984 | 389 | 11–18 | diverse/diverse | BDI | F > M* | NA |
| Baron and Ferron, 1986 | 291 (Canadians) | 13–17 | lower–middle/ white | BDI | F > M | .55 |
| Sullivan and Engin, 1986 | 103 | 10th–11th | middle/white | BDI (short) | F = M | .32 |
| Kashani et al., (1987) | 150 | 14–16 | diverse/white | Diagnostic interviews | F > M, major depression and dysthymia | NA |
| Worchel et al., 1987 | 304 | 3rd–12th | diverse/diverse | CDI | F > M, totals | NA |
| | | | | | F > M, severe | |
| Friedreich et al., 1988 | 269 | 13–16 | upper–middle/ white | BDI | F = M | .06[a] |
| Allgood-Merten et al., 1990 | 802 | 9th–12th | middle–upper/ white | CES-D | F > M, totals | .27[a] |
| | | | | | F > M, severe | |

106

| Larson et al., 1990 | 406 | 10-15 | diverse/diverse | CDI | F > working class M | -.04 |
| Larsson and Melin, 1990 | 547 (Swedish) | 13-17 | not reported | BDI | F > M | .68[a] |
| Reinherz et al., 1990 | 377 | 15 yrs | lower-middle/white | CDI | F > M | .33 |
| Worchel et al., 1990 | 752 | 13-18 | diverse/diverse | CDI | F > M | .26 |
| Baron and Peixoto, 1991 | 134 | 11th-12th | middle/white | BDI | F > M | .48 |
| Block and Gjerde, 1990 | 106 | 18 | diverse/diverse | CES-D | F = M | .25 |
| Colten et al., 1991 | 1,033 | 15-18 | middle/NA | CES-D | F > M | .41 |
| Luthar and Blatt, 1991 | 142 | 14-17 | lower/diverse | CDI | F = M | .18 |
| Petersen et al., 1991 | 169 | 12th | middle-upper/white | Kandel scale | F > M | .54 |
| Reinherz et al., 1991 | 385 | 18 | middle-lower/white | CDI | F > M | .17 |
| Blatt et al., 1993 | 610 | 9th-12th | middle-upper/white | CES-D | F > M | .75 |

*Note.* BDI = Beck Depression Inventory. CDI = Children's Depression Inventory. CES-D = Center for Epidemiological Studies Depression Scale. F = Female. M = Male.

[a]Estimation based on $F$ or $t$ statistics, assuming equal variances, not included in calculation of mean effect size.

*p = .06.

Although studies of depressive symptoms in prepubescent children have resulted in reports of equivalent levels across gender or somewhat higher levels in boys, gender differences begin to emerge shortly after puberty, with girls scoring higher than boys (Nolen-Hoeksema, 1990; Nolen-Hoeksema, Girgus, & Seligman, 1991; Petersen et al., 1991). Studies of clinic-referred adolescents also have resulted in reports of more clinically diagnosed depression in women (Kashani, Sherman, Parker, & Reid, 1990). Findings from all but one of the studies reviewed were that women reported more depressive symptoms than did men (Table 1). The average effect size (weighted for sample size) was moderate (.46).[1]

Several authors have recently conjectured that differences in socialization lead to gender differences in the expression of psychological distress, with girls showing an internalizing pattern of symptom expression and boys a more externalizing pattern (Gjerde, Block, & Block, 1988; Gjerde & Block, 1991; Horwitz & White, 1987; Kandel & Davies, 1982; Kaplan, 1986; Nolen-Hoeksema, 1987; Radloff & Rae, 1979; Weissman & Klerman, 1977). Early support for this view was suggested by Kandel and Davies (1982), who found that the total distribution of delinquent and/or depressed adolescents is the same for boys and girls, but that delinquency is higher for boys (68% compared to 57%) and depressed mood is higher for girls (56% compared to 36%). Subsequently, with a clinic-based sample of 13- to 18-year-old adolescents, Kashani et al. (1990) found that girls reported more affective blunting (e.g., sadness, hopelessness, etc.), more concerns about appearance, and more vegetative symptoms than boys. In an item analysis of the BDI, Kaplan and Arbuthnot (1985) found that girls endorsed bodily concerns more often than boys, such as feeling unattractive and trying to lose weight. With 3rd- to 12th-grade students, Worchel, Nolan & Wilson (1987) found that girls endorsed more internalizing items (e g., sadness, loneliness, fatigue, worry about doing things wrong or having bad things happen, not liking themselves, and wanting more friends), whereas boys endorsed more externalizing items (e.g., getting into fights and having to be pushed to do homework). Using psychologists' ratings on the California Adult Q-Sort (Block, 1978),

---

[1]Inspection of the findings of all these studies suggests that socioeconomic status may interact with observed gender differences. Kaplan, Hong, and Weinhold (1984) reported a trend toward more depressive symptoms, $p = .06$, in girls in their sample of adolescents with diverse ethnic and socioeconomic status, but this did not hold when age and socioeconomic status were controlled. Larson, Raffaelli, Richard, Ham, and Jewell, (1990) found that working-class men reported higher symptom levels than did working- and middle-class women and middle-class men.

Gjerde et al. (1988) reported that dysphoric men were seen as more disagreeable, aggressive, and antagonistic than nondysphoric men and dysphoric women were seen as more ego-brittle, unconventional, and ruminating than nondysphoric women. Allgood-Merten, Lewinsohn, and Hops (1990) found that depressive symptoms on the Community Epidemiological Survey of Depression (CES–D) were significantly correlated with assessments of low self-esteem, negative body image, low number of masculine attributes, and self-consciousness. Girls scored higher than boys on each of these variables. Craighead (1991) found that more female adolescents scored high on both depression and anxiety, whereas more boys scored high on both depression and sociopathy. Nolen-Hoeksema (1990) argued that women's more ruminative (internalizing) coping styles predispose them to longer and more frequent bouts of depression, whereas men's more performance-oriented (externalizing) efforts to distract themselves from depressive feelings lead to shorter, less frequent experiences of depression, but also to more externalizing disorders and drug use.[2]

## Depressive Vulnerability

Researchers from several theoretical perspectives have differentiated two personality styles that leave individuals at risk for depression or depressive symptoms and that may be relevant to the development of other problem behaviors, as well. Cognitive developmental and psychoanalytic theories (e.g., Blatt, 1974; Blatt, D'Afflitti, & Quinlan, 1976; Blatt, Quinlan, Chevron, McDonald, & Zuroff, 1982), cognitive–behavioral theories (e.g., Beck, 1983; Robins & Luten, 1991), ethological and attachment theories (Bowlby, 1980), and interpersonal orientations (Arieti & Bemporad, 1978, 1980) all stress the importance of differentiating persons preoccupied with interpersonal or sociotropic concerns from those preoccupied with concerns about self-definition, competence, or worth. The former are prone to see themselves as helpless, to

---

[2]Gender differences have generally not been found in studies of college students (Hammen & Padesky, 1977; Whiffen & Sasserville, 1991). Nolen-Hoeksema (1987) suggested that college women may self-select for positive mental health, although higher levels of eating disorders and suicides in college students (Wetzel, 1989) speak against this interpretation. However, studies of depression and gender stereotypes have reported that higher rates of psychological distress are related to a lack of identification with masculine traits (Allgood-Merten et al., 1990; Craighead, 1991; Horwitz & White, 1987; Landrine, 1988; Whitley, 1984), and it is possible that college women in general see themselves as more efficacious than their noncollege peers.

fear abandonment by others, and to have extreme desires for closeness and nurturing by others. Depression occurs in these individuals in response to disruptions of satisfying interpersonal relations. On the other hand, individuals preoccupied with issues of self-definition are prone to see themselves as failing, incompetent, and guilty in relation to personal expectations or goals. They express anger or ambivalence in relationships with others, whom they experience as disapproving and rejecting. Depression in these individuals focuses on events that disrupt self-esteem.

Theoretical and empirical work with college students and clinical populations (Blatt & Homann, 1992; Blatt & Zuroff, 1992), as well as with adolescents (Batgos & Leadbeater, 1994; Fichman, Koestner, & Zuroff, 1992; Zuroff, 1993; Zuroff, Koestner, Franz & Powers, 1992), have also begun to address possible associations among the depressive subtypes and the quality of interpersonal relationships or attachments to others. Community-based samples of individuals with high interpersonal depressive vulnerability have anxious/preoccupied attachments characterized by an intense valuing of emotional closeness. These people strive for acceptance from valued others in order to maintain a sense of self-acceptance. In clinical samples, high interpersonal vulnerability is associated with extreme anxieties about loss, neglect, deprivation, and abandonment in relationships. On the other hand, self-critical vulnerability in both nonclinical and clinical populations is characterized by negative perceptions of both self and others and a fearful/avoidant attachment pattern. Others are distanced by highly self-critical individuals. Despite the craving for others' approval, self-critical individuals anticipate that others will be critical and untrustworthy. They avoid close involvement as protection against anticipated rejection. Among college women, self-criticism is associated with lower levels of trust, less self-disclosure, and unsuccessful conflict resolution (Blatt & Zuroff, 1992). Self-criticism in school-age adolescents is associated with impaired attachments to both parents and peers (Batgos & Leadbeater, 1994; Fichman et al., 1992). Differential attributions to self and others that stem from the two types of depressive vulnerabilities may well create differences in perceived interpersonal contexts that affect both available social supports and types of interpersonal events that can be perceived as stressful (Blatt & Zuroff, 1992). We argue later that these differences may also set the stage for differences in expressions of psychopathology as internalizing or externalizing symptoms.

Four major instruments have been developed to assess these two depressive styles in adults: the Depressive Experiences Questionnaire (DEQ; Blatt et al., 1976, 1982; Zuroff, Quinlan, & Blatt, 1990), the

Sociotropy–Autonomy Scale (SAS; Beck, 1983; Beck, Epstein, Harrison, & Emery, 1983; Robins, 1985), the Dysfunctional Attitude Scale (DAS; Cane, Olinger, Gotlib, & Kuiper, 1986; Oliver & Baumgart, 1985; Weissman & Beck, 1978), and the Personal Style Inventory (Robins & Ladd, 1991). Multiple assessments of the psychometric properties of these measures have confirmed the distinctiveness of interpersonal and self-critical depressive styles in adults and college students (Blaney & Kutcher, 1991; Blatt & Zuroff, 1992; Riley & McCranie, 1990; Zuroff et al., 1990; Zuroff, Moskowitz, Wielgus, Powers, & Franko, 1983). Individuals usually show a predominance of one or the other subtype, but some show a mix of the two (Beck, 1983; Blatt & Zuroff, 1992).

Although past research on these depressive vulnerabilities has focused on adults and college students, the factor structure of the recently developed adolescent version of the Depressive Experiences Questionnaire (DEQ–A; Blatt, Schaffer, Bers, & Quinlan, 1992) suggests that interpersonal and self-critical depressive vulnerabilities may also characterize adolescents' depressive attributions. Construction of the DEQ–A involved revising 43 of the original 66 items of the adult DEQ to make the scale more appropriate for adolescents. The remainder of the adult DEQ items were retained in their original form. The DEQ–A was administered to two groups of high school students from lower- or middle- and upper-socioeconomic backgrounds. Factor analysis of the responses yielded three factors (Dependency, Self-Criticism, and Efficacy) that are highly similar to factors identified on the adult DEQ. For both dependent and self-critical styles, internal consistency and test–retest reliability were substantial. For college students completing both forms, correlations between parallel factor scores on the adolescent and the adult DEQs exceeded .75 for all factors. As for the adult DEQ, both the Dependency and Self-Criticism factors were correlated with, but distinct from, measures of depressive symptoms. Focusing on an inner-city sample of adolescents, Luthar and Blatt (in press) reported stronger associations for Dependency than for Self-Criticism with assessments of diffuse tension, worry, and sensitivity to others' behavior. Associations with Self-Criticism were stronger for depressive symptoms and concerns about losing others' approval. The term *interpersonal vulnerability* is used throughout this article rather than *dependency* in order to reflect the broader interpersonal preoccupations of individuals who are high on this dimension (i.e., fears of loss, abandonment) and to eschew the misleading and negative connotations associated with the term *dependency* in relation to women's and girls' functioning.

Gender differences in interpersonal and self-critical depressive styles have also been reported. On a variety of measures, adult men endorsed more self-critical items, whereas adult women endorsed more interpersonal items (Chevron, Quinlan, & Blatt, 1978; Riley & McCranie, 1990; Whiffen & Sasserville, 1991; Zuroff et al., 1990). An exception to this pattern was found by Robins and Luten (1991), who reported no gender differences using Beck's SAS. In contrast to the research with adults, in studies involving both suburban and inner-city adolescents who filled out the DEQ–A or SAS, girls scored significantly higher than boys for interpersonal vulnerability, but gender differences for self-critical vulnerability were not significant (Baron & Peixoto, 1991; Blatt et al., 1993; Luthar & Blatt, in press).

## Depressive Vulnerabilities and Sensitivities to Stressful Life Events

Recent reviews of research with adults and college students suggest that different types of depressive vulnerability correspond to different reactivity to stressful life events involving relationships or affecting the self (Blatt & Zuroff, 1992; Nietzel & Harris, 1990, Smith, O'Keefe, & Jenkins, 1988). Individuals with an interpersonal depressive style are especially vulnerable to negative interpersonal events, including threats to intimacy and closeness in relationships. On the other hand, individuals with a self-critical depressive style are reactive to a wider range of events that are less specifically congruent with their personality style.

In reviewing the literature on stress in adolescents, Compas (1987) pointed to the need for investigations of the pathways from individual vulnerabilities to stressful life events and for delineation of factors that make some individuals more vulnerable than others to particular stressors. He specifically suggested that"individuals with a self-critical schema may be vulnerable to negative achievement events, while others with a dependent (or interpersonal) self-schema may be vulnerable to interpersonal loss events"(p. 298). In other words, depressive vulnerabilities may influence appraisals of the significance of negative life events and coping responses. For example, disruptions in a romantic relationship can be perceived as threats to being loved and taken care of, to personal competence in romantic relationships, to approval in the eyes of peers, or to all three. Similarly, failing a test may be interpreted as a threat to one's ability to please a teacher or one's parents or as a threat to one's ability to meet one's own expectations for success. Further study is needed to assess possible differences in the attributions of meaning to stressful events by adolescents with high levels of interpersonal and self-critical vulnerabilities.

## Gender Differences in Adolescent Vulnerability to Stressful Events

Considerable research with adolescents has demonstrated that women are more reactive to stressful life events involving others than are men and that they are equally reactive to stressful life events affecting themselves. These findings parallel observations mentioned previously that adolescent girls have greater interpersonal depressive vulnerability (focused on concerns about relationships) but do not differ from boys in self-critical vulnerability (focused on concerns about competence). These gender links suggest that subtypes of depressive vulnerabilities may also be related to differences in boys' and girls' reactivity to stressful life events involving the self or others.

Studies of the effects of stress and developmental outcomes in children and adolescents typically focus on several nonexclusive sources of stress. These include (a) environmental conditions of deprivation and disadvantage, often operationalized as low socioeconomic status; (b) major, acute stressful life events (e.g., illness, divorce, death of a parent); (c) minor hassles that characterize daily living (e.g., failing tests, arguments with friends or family); and (d) specific normative events or life transitions (e.g., onset of puberty, birth of a sibling, or change of schools). Chronic stressors and daily hassles appear to be better predictors of maladjustment in children and adolescents than major life events (Compas, 1987). Reviews of this literature (Colten & Gore, 1991; Compas, 1987; Luthar, 1991) also indicated that stressful life events are associated with adolescent problems such as depression and anxiety, delinquent behavior, suicide attempts, somatic distress, and oppositional behaviors. However, the proportion of variance accounted for by stressful life events is typically small (less than 15%), suggesting that other factors may influence this association.

As both adults (Belle, 1987; Wethington, McLeod, & Kessler, 1987) and adolescents, women are more likely than men to report stress from negative events involving important people in their social networks. However, women do not differ from men in reporting stress from events happening to themselves (e.g., academic failures). In two large-scale studies of high school students (Newcomb, Huba, & Bentler, 1981; Siddique & D'Arcy, 1984) associations between psychological symptoms and stressful events happening to others were higher for women than for men, but associations between stressful life events happening to the self and psychological symptoms were similar for both. Reinherz et al. (1989) found that girls who experienced the loss of a parent were over nine times more likely to report serious depression on the CDI than were girls who had not experienced such a loss. This difference was not significant for boys. Allgood-Merten et al. (1990) found that female adolescents reported more major negative events and daily hassles and rated them as more stressful than boys; girls also reported higher levels of depressive symptoms. Colten et al. (1991) found stronger associations for teenage girls than for teenage boys between stressful events within their relationships, families, or friends and the presence of somatic, substance abuse, and behavioral problems. Roos and Cohen (1987) found that a masculine gender–role orientation functioned as a buffer to stressful life events in college undergraduates. Gore et al. (1993) found that boys in Grades 9 to 11 reported more exposure to recent personal stresses than did girls in these grades, but the girls reported more stress in events happening to family and friends and in their own relationship problems with family and friends. Similarly, Larson and Ham (1993) reported that fifth- to ninth-grade boys reported more negative life events overall; but girls reported more negative events with friends, and boys reported more negative school events. Both parent- and self-reports of negative events were also associated with negative affect and depressive symptoms, grade point average, teacher-rated classroom adjustment, and parent reports of child problem behaviors in the older adolescents.

Exceptions to this pattern of findings showing greater reactivity to interpersonal stressors in girls include a study by Daniels and Moos (1990), who found that girls reported more physical health-related stressors than did boys, but they did not differ from boys in reporting social network stress or negative life events. Compas and Wagner (1991) found that junior-high- and high-school girls reported more interpersonal stressful life events (i.e., more negative network, intimacy, peer, and family events) than did boys. However, they found no significant interactions between gender and type of stressful events in predicting psychological symptoms.

Researchers have argued that girls' greater vulnerability to stresses involving others reflects their socialization to be responsive to the needs of others and the centrality of mutual concerns in their self-definitions (Gilligan, 1988). It is possible, as Gore et al. (1993) argued, that the additive effects of girls' greater exposure to stresses involving others, when accompanied by difficulties in mobilizing social support and a strong interpersonal caring orientation, heighten their reactivity to the problems of others. This description of girls who are most likely to be highly reactive to stresses involving others is remarkably similar to the description of adolescents with heightened interpersonal depressive vulnerability.

It is possible that there are also gender differences in reactivity to different types of stresses involving the self. Girls appeared to be more concerned than boys about relatively unchangeable aspects of their body shape and appearance (Rodin, 1992) but showed similar or less concern than boys did with stresses involving more mutable, performance demands or competencies related to the self.

## Depressive Vulnerabilities and Gender Differences in Internalizing and Externalizing Syndromes

Empirical research has only begun to explore the relationships among depressive vulnerabilities and differential involvement in problem behaviors. A recent study by Blatt et al. (1993) investigated the relations among the subtypes of depressive vulnerabilities and adolescents' engagement in internalizing and externalizing disorders. A predominantly White sample of 278 girls and 259 boys attending ninth to twelfth grade in a suburban high school completed the CES–D (Radloff, 1977), the DEQ–A, and the YSR (Achenbach & Edelbrock, 1987). After level of depressive symptoms on the CES–D was partialed out, interpersonal and self-critical vulnerabilities added differentially to the explained variance of internalizing and externalizing disorders. As anticipated, interpersonal vulnerability explained significant additional variance in internalizing, but not externalizing, disorders. Self-critical vulnerabilities added significantly to the explained variance in both internalizing and externalizing disorders. Gender differences were not found in the patterns of these relations.

In subsequent analyses of these data, however, gender differences were found in the likelihood of being classified as high (i.e., one standard deviation above the group means calculated separately for men and women) in both interpersonal vulnerability and the internalizing syndrome, on the one hand, or in both self-criticism and the externalizing syndrome, on the other. As Table 2 shows, girls were five times more likely (10.3% of girls) than boys (2.7% of boys) to be categorized as high in both interpersonal vulnerability and the internalizing syn-

TABLE 2
Percentages of Males and Females With Scores Falling at One Standard Deviation
Above the Means for Both Depressive Vulnerability and Internalizing
or Externalizing Syndromes

| Classification | Females[a] | Males[b] |
|---|---|---|
| Interpersonal/Internalizing | 10.3 | 2.7 |
| Interpersonal/Externalizing | 7.0 | 2.3 |
| Self-critical/Internalizing | 6.6 | 5.8 |
| Self-critical/Externalizing | 3.3 | 6.9 |

[a]$n = 278.$ [b]$n = 246.$

drome. Girls were also more likely to be high in both interpersonal vulnerability and the externalizing syndrome (7% of girls and 2.3% of boys). In contrast boys were twice as likely (6.9%) as girls (3.3%) to be categorized as high in both self-criticism and the externalizing syndrome. Gender differences for the frequency of co-occurrence of high levels of self-criticism and the internalizing syndrome were slight. Thus, although the relationships among the subtypes of depressive vulnerability and problem behaviors did not differ by gender, the frequency of co-occurrence of severe interpersonal vulnerability and internalizing disorders was substantially greater in the girls, and the frequency of co-occurrence of severe self-criticism and externalizing disorders was greater in the boys.

## Models of the Relations Among Depressive Vulnerabilities, Stress, and the Development of Internalizing and Externalizing Disorders

Longitudinal research on problem behaviors in adolescents has confirmed the relationships among environmental stress and dysfunctional interpersonal relationships in the development and persistence of internalizing and externalizing disorders (Compas, 1987; Compas, Slavin, Wagner, & Vannatta, 1986; Elliott, Huizinga, & Menard, 1989; Jessor & Jessor, 1978; Loeber, 1988, 1990; Luthar, 1991; Robins & Rutter, 1990). Positive interpersonal relations and personal competence in several domains (e.g., academics, sports, and community involvement) have also been shown to protect against the development of psychopathology (e.g., Achenbach, 1991; Dishion, Patterson, Stoolmiller, & Skinner, 1991; Leadbeater, Hellner, Allen, & Aber, 1989; Luthar, 1991; Masten et al., 1988; Rutter, 1979). The interaction of competence and depression in children has been described as a positive-feedback loop in which performance difficulties contribute to depression that in turn augments feelings of incompetence (Cicchetti & Aber, 1986; Cicchetti & Schneider-Rosen, 1984; Cicchetti, Toth, & Bush, 1988; Cole, 1991; Cole & Zahn-Waxler, 1992; Cummings & Cicchetti, 1990). Longitudinal research also has suggested that relationships between depressive symptoms and stressful life events may be reciprocal in adolescents, with symptoms not only resulting from but also predicting the occurrence of stressful events (Compas, 1987; Leadbeater & Linares, 1992; Swearingen & Cohen, 1985). Advances in understanding causal directions of the multivariate relationships among individual vulnerabilities, potentiating factors, and psychopathology depend on the clear specification of theoretical models of anticipated relationships among these variables.

We posit two transactional models specifying the relationships among self-critical or interpersonal depressive vulnerabilities, heightened sensitivities to stressful life events involving others or the self, and the occurrence of internalizing or externalizing disorders in adolescents.

The first model involves individuals with heightened interpersonal vulnerability who, as has been said, are preoccupied with the affection of others, feelings of loneliness and helplessness, fears of abandonment, desires for intense closeness, and difficulty in expressing anger overtly. Stressful events involving others (e.g., arguments or fights with parents or peers, breaking up with boyfriends or girlfriends, family conflicts) potentiate these feelings, especially in the absence of protective sources of social support (i.e., peers, siblings, parents, other adults). Subsequent psychopathology should involve internalizing behaviors that have the desired effect of maintaining the concern and involvement of significant others (e.g., somatic complaints, eating disorders, pregnancy, suicidal ideation and gestures). Because individuals with interpersonal vulnerability are concerned with protecting or maintaining relationships, they are less likely to engage in aggressive, destructive, or violent delinquent behaviors (Blatt, 1974, 1991). The literature on interpersonal depressive styles, reactivity to stresses involving others, and internalizing disorders concurs in suggesting that this pathway to the development of psychopathology may be more likely for girls than boys.

The second model involves individuals with high levels of self-critical vulnerability. With their particular sensitivity to negative evaluations, they experience excessive feelings of guilt, hopelessness, worthlessness, and inadequacy. Adults and peers are perceived as critical, and intimate relationships are avoided or reacted to with anger and hostility. Stressful life events that negatively affect perceptions of self-worth potentiate these feelings. Subsequent psychopathology should involve externalizing behaviors that demonstrate personal powers or deflect self-criticism, such as defiance of authority, delinquency, aggression towards others, school disciplinary problems, and high-risk sexual activity, as well as internalizing behaviors related to perceptions of low self-worth. In contrast, perceived competence in some domain of activity may help to protect against the likelihood of psychopathology. No gender differences in the occurrence of heightened self-critical depressive vulnerability or in reactivity to stressful life events involving the self have been found. Nevertheless, externalizing disorders are more frequent in boys. It may be that more self-critical girls concurrently experience heightened interpersonal depressive vulnerability or that their socialization for reactivity to others de-

117

creases the likelihood of their expressing externalizing behaviors. Socialization practices that involve greater tolerance for the expression of aggression in men may also heighten the likelihood of their expression of externalizing symptoms. Thus, it is anticipated that the pathways specified by this model will be more likely to occur in boys.

## RESEARCH IMPLICATIONS

No multivariate longitudinal research has yet tested the causal relationships specified by the two transactional models. Although the proposed models posit pathways for the development of psychopathology in adolescence, the literature reviewed also includes studies of adults and college students. This suggests that research using this model may also advance our understanding of the development and maintenance of mental health problems or psychiatric disorders in older samples, but it also limits the generalizability of some findings for adolescent samples. Nevertheless, the predominantly cross-sectional studies reviewed give support to many of the bivariate associations proposed. These are as follows:

1. The co-occurrence of internalizing behaviors and depressive symptoms are more frequent in adolescent women, whereas the co-occurrence of externalizing behaviors and depressive symptoms are more frequently observed in men.
2. Female adolescents are more likely than male adolescents to show interpersonal depressive vulnerabilities and are more reactive to stressful life events involving others but do not differ from boys in vulnerability to self-criticism and sensitivity to stressful events involving themselves.
3. The occurrence of high levels of both interpersonal depressive vulnerability and internalizing disorders is more likely in adolescent women, whereas the occurrence of high levels of both self-critical vulnerability and externalizing disorders is more likely in men.

Despite the evidence for these bivariate relationships, longitudinal studies of the multivariate relationships specified in these models are clearly needed. The study of causal relationships in multivariate models of the development of psychopathology has become more possible with the increased accessibility to psychologists of multivariate statistical techniques, such as structural equation modeling (Connell, 1987). With clear specification of the anticipated pathways for the development of psychopathology, multivariate methods offer a significant advancement in our ability to explore complex, long-term associations among multiple variables. A multivariate longitudinal strategy is essential to an investigation of the role of depressive vulnerabilities as causal antecedents to problem behaviors in adolescents. Possible reciprocal effects among depressive vulnerabilities, life stress, and existing problem behaviors in predicting increased behavioral problems (and the effects of protective factors in decreasing them) should also be tested. Given the salience of the issues of dependence and autonomy and of relatedness and self-definition in adolescent development and the particular gaps in our understanding of female adolescent development, research involving interpersonal and self-critical dimensions of depressive vulnerability is of particular importance.

This research must also take into account the apparent greater sensitivity of adolescents to chronic stress and daily hassles than to major life events. It must also examine the meaning and importance of stressful life events for the individual adolescent (Compas & Wagner, 1991). Whether adolescents with high levels of interpersonal or self-critical vulnerability have heightened reactivity to stresses involving others or themselves or, alternately, whether they are more likely to differentially attribute interpersonal or self-definitional concerns to any stressful life events has not been studied. The differential reactivity to different types of stressful events across different ethnic or racial groups has also not been studied. Individuals from racial or ethnic groups that emphasize greater collective responsibility for group members may have greater sensitivity to stressful life events involving significant others.

## GENDER AND PSYCHOPATHOLOGY

Observed relationships between gender and personality dimensions or between gender and problem behaviors cannot themselves be thought of as explanations of problematic outcomes (McGrath et al., 1990; Nolen-Hoeksema, 1990). Gender differences can only point to the need to investigate the factors that cause them. The psychological processes that make each gender uniquely vulnerable to specific negative events and specific negative outcomes are poorly understood. However, the influence of gender stereotyping on the development and maintenance of psychopathology in adolescents can be clearly inferred from the literature that we have reviewed. Research showing that women are more concerned with relationships and appearance should not be taken as inevitable, normative, or as the biologically-based attributes of women. In this case, *what is* is clearly not *what ought to be*. The unfortunate trend of reinforcing stereotypical visions of women as self-disclosing, empathic, relational, and caring and of men as guarded, assertive, independent, separate, and rational (Chodorow, 1989; Gilligan, Ward & Taylor, 1989) serves to normalize, rather than challenge, gender differences that may create vulnerabilities to psychopathology. These stereotypes fail to acknowledge that not only interpersonal but also self-definitional concerns are significant for girls. The interpretation of symptoms of interpersonal vulnerability as a sign of excessive dependency or weakness that should be countered with efforts to increase autonomy and independence may also miss the real protective effects of sensitivity to interpersonal attachments in both women and men. Similarly, socialization of boys that underemphasizes interpersonal sensitivities may reinforce feelings of detachment that allow expression of aggression against others.

Successful treatment approaches to adolescent depression have advocated either an interpersonal (Mufson, Moreau, Weissman, & Klerman, 1993) or a cognitive (Beck, 1976) focus. From the perspective of the models that we are advancing, both treatment approaches may be important for intervening in or even preventing internalizing or externalizing syndromes in adolescents. Interventions, like normal development, should ultimately lead to the integration of relational and self-definitional issues, with the individual progressing to more mature expressions in both developmental lines (Blatt & Behrends, 1987; Blatt & Blass, 1990, in press). Excessive concerns about relatedness in the absence of a sense of autonomy and agency may be what creates a sense of urgent dependency on others, just as autonomy outside the context of supportive relationships can be experienced as alienation (Benjamin, 1988). A secure sense of personal competence (e.g., being good at academics, sports, dance, art, or work) in the context of supportive, reliable relationships may be the real protector of adolescent mental health. Prevention of problem behaviors in adolescents must be directed at the promotion of experiences of self-efficacy that include interpersonal attachments and at the formation of attachments that permit experiences of self-efficacy (Allen, Aber, & Leadbeater, 1990; Batgos & Leadbeater, in press; Blatt & Blass, 1990).

Differences in the expression of psychopathology may also have implications for whether adolescents seek help and for what types of interventions they receive. Given what Winnicott (1975) called the *nuisance value* of externalizing behaviors, adolescents engaged in such activities may be more likely than those with internalizing problems to come to the attention of school or community disciplinary authorities. The less socially disruptive behaviors of adolescents with internalizing disorders are more likely to go unnoticed (Garland, 1993). Declines in academic achievement, frequent short absences from school, multiple somatic complaints, and social withdrawal may well be among early internalizing expressions of distress.

School-based prevention programs have focused primarily on cognitive approaches to social-skill deficits and on the prevention of externalizing behaviors (Conduct Problems Prevention Research Group, 1992; Dishion et al., 1991; Weissberg, Caplan, & Harwood, 1991). These programs have only recently begun to address affective vulnerabilities and the prevention of internalizing syndromes (Beardslee, 1990; Clarke, Hawkins, Murphy & Sheeber, 1993; Cole & Zahn-Waxler, 1992; Petersen et al., 1993). We anticipate that better knowledge of the role of different types of depressed affect in the development of problem behavior syndromes will have direct implications for improving intervention and prevention programs. Prevention efforts also need to look beyond existing differences in individual personality dimensions to the sociocultural causes of gender-linked psychopathology. Gender stereotyping is culturally based and pervasive. Recent research has suggested that implicit stereotyped attitudes and values are often not conscious (Banaji & Greenwald, 1994). Nevertheless, they are entrenched in cultural values and appear in advertising, on television, in child rearing practices, and in strongly held beliefs about what "real men" do and how "good girls" look or behave.

## ACKNOWLEDGMENT

We are grateful for the editorial assistance of John Auerbach.

## REFERENCES

Achenbach, T. M. (1991). *Manual for the Youth Self-Report and 1991 Profile*. Burlington: University of Vermont Department of Psychiatry.

Achenbach, T. M., & Edelbrock, C. (1978). The classification of child psychopathology: A review and analysis of empirical efforts. *Psychological Bulletin, 85*, 1275–1301.

Achenbach, T. M., & Edelbrock, C. (1987). *Manual for the Youth Self-Report and Profile*. Burlington: University of Vermont Department of Psychiatry.

Achenbach, T. M., Howell, C. T., Quay, H. C., & Conners, C. K. (1991). National survey of problems and competencies among four- to sixteen-year-olds. *Monograph of the Society for Research in Child Development, 56*(3, Serial No. 225).

Allen, J. P., Aber, J. L., & Leadbeater, B. J. (1990). Adolescent problem behaviors: The influence of attachment and autonomy. *Psychiatric Clinics of North America, 13*, 455–467.

Allen, J. P., Leadbeater, B. J., & Aber, J. L. (1994). The development of problem behavior syndromes in at-risk adolescents. *Development and Psychopathology, 6*, 323–342.

Allgood-Merten, B., Lewinsohn, P. M., & Hops, H. (1990). Sex differences and adolescent depression. *Journal of Abnormal Psychology, 99,* 55–63.

American Psychiatric Association. (1987). *Diagnostic and statistical manual of mental disorders: DSM–III–R* (3rd ed.). Washington, DC: Author.

Arieti, S., & Bemporad, J. R. (1978). *Severe and mild depression: The therapeutic approach.* New York: Basic.

Arieti, S., & Bemporad, J. R. (1980). The psychological organization of depression. *American Journal of Psychiatry, 136,* 1365–1369.

Banaji, M. R., & Greenwald, A. G. (1994). Implicit stereotyping and prejudice. In M. P. Zanna & J. M. Olson (Eds.), *The psychology of prejudice: The Ontario Symposium.* (Vol. 7, pp. 55–76). Hillsdale, NJ: Lawrence Erlbaum Associates, Inc.

Baron, P., & Perron, L. M. (1986). Sex differences in the Beck Depression Inventory scores of adolescents. *Journal of Youth and Adolescents, 15,* 165–171.

Baron, P., & Peixoto, N. (1991). Depressive symptoms in adolescents as a function of personality factors. *Journal of Youth and Adolescence, 20,* 493–500.

Barrera, M., & Garrison–Jones, C. (1988). Properties of the Beck Depression Inventory as a screening instrument for adolescent depression. *Journal of Abnormal Child Psychology, 16,* 263–273.

Batgos, J., & Leadbeater, B. J. (1994). Attachments to mothers, vulnerability to interpersonal or self-critical subtypes of dysphoria and quality of peer relationships in adolescence. In M. B. Sperling & W. H. Berman (Eds.), *Attachment in adults: Clinical Development and Perspectives* (pp. 155–178). New York: Guilford.

Beardslee, W. (1990). Development of a clinician-based preventive intervention for families with affective disorders. *Journal of Preventive Psychiatry and Allied Disciplines, 4,* 39–61.

Beck, A. T. (1976). *Cognitive therapy and the emotional disorders.* New York: International Universities Press.

Beck, A. T. (1983). Cognitive therapy of depression: New perspectives. In P. J. Clayton & J. E. Barrett (Eds.), *Treatment of depression: Old controversies and new approaches* (pp. 265–290). New York: Raven.

Beck, A. T., Epstein, N., Harrison, R. P., & Emery, G. (1983). *Development of the sociotropy–autonomy scale: A measure of personality factors in psychopathology.* Unpublished manuscript, University of Pennsylvania, Philadelphia.

Beck, A. T., Steer, R. A., & Garbin, M. G. (1988). Psychometric properties of the Beck Depression Inventory: Twenty–five years of evaluation. *Clinical Psychology Review, 8,* 77–100.

Belle, D. (1987). Gender differences in moderators of stress. In R. D. Barnett, L. Biener, & G. K. Baruch (Eds.), *Gender and stress.* New York: Free Press.

Benjamin, J. (1988). *The bonds of love: Psychoanalysis, feminism, and the problem of domination.* New York: Pantheon.

Blaney, P. H., & Kutcher, G. S. (1991). Measures of depressive dimensions: Are they interchangeable? *Journal of Personality Assessment, 56,* 502–512.

Blatt, S. J. (1974). Levels of object representation in anaclitic and introjective depression. *Psychoanalytic Study of the Child, 24,* 107–157.

Blatt, S. J. (1991). Depression and destructive risk-taking behavior in adolescence. In L. P. Lipsitt & L. L. Mitnick (Eds.), *Self-regulatory behavior and risk-taking: Causes and consequences* (pp. 285–309). Norwood, NJ: Ablex.

Blatt, S. J., & Behrends, R. S. (1987). Separation–individuation, internalization and the nature of therapeutic action. *International Journal of Psychoanalysis, 68,* 279–297.

Blatt, S. J., & Blass, R. (1990). Attachment and separateness: A dialectic model of the products and processes of psychological development. *The Psychoanalytic Study of the*

*Child, 45,* 107–127.

Blatt, S. J., & Blass, R. (in press). Relatedness and self definition: A dialectic model of personality development. In G. G. Noam & K. W. Fischer (Eds.), *Development and vulnerability in relationships.* Hillsdale, NJ: Lawrence Erlbaum Associates, Inc.

Blatt, S. J., D'Afflitti, J. P., & Quinlan, D. M. (1976). Experiences of depression in normal young adults. *Journal of Abnormal Psychology, 85,* 383–389.

Blatt, S. J., Hart, B., Quinlan, D. M., Leadbeater, B. J., & Auerbach, J. (1993). The relationship between dependent and self-critical depression and problem behavior in adolescents. *Journal of Youth and Adolescence, 22,* 253–269.

Blatt, S. J., & Homann, E. (1992). Parent–child interaction in the etiology of depression. *Clinical Psychology Review, 12,* 47–91.

Blatt, S. J., Quinlan, D. M., Chevron, E. S., McDonald, C., & Zuroff, D. (1982). Dependency and self-criticism: Psychological dimensions of depression. *Journal of Consulting and Clinical Psychology, 50,* 113–124.

Blatt, S. J., Schaffer, C. E., Bers, S., & Quinlan, D. M. (1992). Psychometric properties of the Depressive Experiences Questionnaire for adolescents. *Journal of Personality Assessment, 59,* 82–98.

Blatt, S. J., & Zuroff, D. (1992). Interpersonal relatedness and self- definition: Two prototypes for depression. *Clinical Psychology Review, 12,* 527–562.

Block, J. (1978). *The Q-sort method in personality assessment and psychiatry restored.* Palo Alto, CA: Consulting Psychologists Press.

Block, J., & Gjerde, P. E. (1990). Depressive symptoms in late adolescents: A longitudinal perspective on personality antecedents. In J. E. Rolf, A. Masten, D. Cicchetti, K. Neuchterlein, & S. Weintrab (Eds.), *Risk and protective factors in the development of psychopathology* (pp. 334–360). New York: Cambridge University Press.

Bowlby, J. (1980). *Attachment and loss: Vol. 3. Loss, sadness, and depression.* New York: Basic Books.

Cane, D. B., Olinger, L. J., Gotlib, I. H., & Kuiper, N. A. (1986). Factor structure of the Dysfunctional Attitude Scale in a student population. *Journal of Clinical Psychology, 42,* 307–309.

Cantwell, D. P., & Baker, L. (1991). Manifestations of depressive affect in adolescence. *Journal of Youth and Adolescence, 20,* 121–134.

Carlson, G. A., & Cantwell, D. P. (1980). Unmasking masked depression in children and adolescents. *American Journal of Psychiatry, 137,* 445–449.

Chevron, E. S., Quinlan, D. M., & Blatt, S. J. (1978). Sex roles and gender differences in the experience of depression. *Journal of Abnormal Psychology, 87,* 680–683.

Chodorow, N. (1989). *Feminism and psychoanalytic theory.* New Haven, CT: Yale University Press.

Cicchetti, D., & Aber, L. J. (1986). Early precursors of later depression: An organizational perspective. In L. Lipsett & C. Rovee-Collier (Eds.), *Advances in infancy* (Vol. 4, pp. 87–137). Norwood, NJ: Ablex.

Cicchetti, D., & Rizley, (1981). Developmental perspectives on the etiology and intergenerational transmission and sequelae of child maltreatment. *New Directions for Child Development, 11,* 31–56.

Cicchetti, D., & Schneider-Rosen, K. (1984). Toward a transactional model of childhood depression. In D. Cicchetti & K. Schneider-Rosen (Eds.), *Childhood depression: New directions for child development* (pp. 5–28). San Francisco: Jossey-Bass.

Cicchetti, D., Toth, S., & Bush, M. (1988). Developmental psychopathology and incompetence in childhood: Suggestions for intervention. In B. B. Lahey & A. E. Kazdin (Eds.), *Advances in Clinical Child Psychology* (Vol. 11, pp. 1–71). New York: Plenum.

Clarke, G. N., Hawkins, W., Murphy, M., & Sheeber, L. (1993). School–based primary prevention of depressive symptomatology in adolescents: Findings from two studies. *Journal of Adolescent Research, 8,* 183–204.

Cohen, N. J., Gotlieb, H., Kershner, J., & Wehrspann, W. (1985). Concurrent validity of the internalizing and externalizing profile patterns of the Achenbach Child Behaviors Checklist. *Journal of Consulting and Clinical Psychology, 53,* 724–728.

Cole, D. A. (1991). Preliminary support for a competence-based model of depression in children. *Journal of Abnormal Psychology, 100,* 181–190.

Cole, D. A., & Carpentieri, S. (1990). Social status and the comorbidity of child depression and conduct disorder. *Journal of Consulting and Clinical Psychology, 58,* 748–757.

Cole, P.M., & Zahn-Waxler, C. (1992). Emotional dysregulation in disruptive behavior disorders. In D. Cicchetti & S. L. Toth (Eds.), *Rochester Symposium on Developmental Psychopathology: Vol. 4. Developmental perspectives on depression* (pp. 173–209). Rochester, NY: University of Rochester Press.

Colten, M. E., & Gore, S. (1991). *Adolescent stress: Causes and consequences.* New York: Aldine de Gruyter.

Colten, M. E., Gore, S., & Aseltine, R. H. (1991). The patterning of distress and disorder in a community sample of high school aged youth. In M. E. Colten & S. Gore (Eds.), *Adolescent stress: Causes and consequences* (pp. 157–181). New York: Aldine de Gruyter.

Compas, B. E. (1987). Stress and life events during childhood and adolescence. *Clinical Psychology Review, 7,* 275–302.

Compas, B. E., Slavin, L. A., Wagner, B. M., & Vannatta, K. (1986). Relationship of life events and social support with psychological dysfunction among adolescents. *Journal of Youth and Adolescence, 15,* 205–221.

Compas, B. E., & Wagner, B. M. (1991). Psychosocial stress during adolescence: Intraper-sonal and interpersonal processes. In M. E. Colten & S. Gore, (Eds.) *Adolescent stress: Causes and consequences* (pp.67–85). New York: Aldine de Gruyter.

Conduct Problems Prevention Research Group. (1992). A developmental and clinical model for the prevention of conduct disorder: The Fast Track Program. *Development and Psychopathology, 4,* 509–528.

Connell, J. (1987). Structural equation modeling and the study of child development: A question of goodness of fit. *Child Development, 58,* 167–175.

Craighead, W. E. (1991). Cognitive factors and classification issues in adolescent depres-sion. *Journal of Youth and Adolescence, 20,* 311–315.

Cummings, E. M., & Cicchetti, D. (1990). Toward a transactional model of relations between attachment and depression. In M. T. Greenberg, D. Cicchetti, & E. M. Cum-mings (Eds). Attachment in the preschool years: Theory, research, and intervention (pp. 339–372). Chicago: University of Chicago Press.

Daniels, D., & Moos, R. H. (1990). Assessing life stressors and social supports among adolescents: Applications to depressed youth. *Journal of Adolescent Research, 5,* 268–289.

Dishion, T. L., Patterson, G. R., Stoolmiller, M., & Skinner, M. L. (1991). Family, school, and behavioral antecedents to early adolescent involvement with antisocial peers. *Developmental Psychology, 27,* 172–180.

Elliott, D. S., Huizinga, D., & Menard, S. (1989). *Multiple problem youth: Delinquency, substance use, and mental health problems.* New York: Springer-Verlag.

Fichman, L., Koestner, R., & Zuroff, D. C. (1992). *Depressive styles in adolescence.* Manu-script submitted for publication.

Friedreich, W. N., Reams, R., & Jacobs, J. H. (1988). Sex differences in depression in early adolescents. *Psychological Reports, 62,* 475–481.

Garland, A. (1993). *Pathways to adolescent mental health services: Adolescent help-seeking and teacher identification and referral.* Unpublished doctoral dissertation, Yale University, New Haven, CT.

Garmezy, N., Masten, A. S., & Tellegen, A. (1984). The study of stress and competence in children: A building for developmental psychopathology. *Child Development, 55,* 97–111.

Gilligan, C., Ward, J., & Taylor, J. M. (1989). *Mapping the moral domain.* Cambridge, MA: Harvard University Press.

Gjerde, P. F., & Block, J. H. (1991). The preschool family context of 18 year olds with depressive symptoms: A prospective study. *Journal of Research on Adolescence, 1,* 63–91.

Gjerde, P. F., Block, J., & Block, J. H. (1988). Depressive symptoms and personality during late adolescence: Gender differences in the externalization—internalization of symptom expression. *Journal of Abnormal Psychology, 97,* 475–486.

Gore, S., Aseltine, Jr., R. H., & Colten, M. E. (1993). Gender, social–relational involvement and depression. *Journal of Research on Adolescents, 3,* 101–125.

Gottlieb, B. H. (1991). Social support in adolescence. In M. E. Colten & S. Gore (Eds.), *Adolescent stress: Causes and consequences* (pp. 281–306). New York: Aldine de Gruyter.

Hammen, C. L., & Padesky, C. A. (1977). Sex differences in the expression of depressive responses on the Beck Depression Inventory. *Journal of Abnormal Psychology, 86,* 609–614.

Horwitz, A. V., & White, H. R., (1987). Gender role orientations and styles of pathology among adolescents. *Journal of Health and Social Behavior, 28,* 259–271.

Jessor, R., & Jessor, S. (1978). *Problem behavior and psychosocial development: A longitudinal study of youth.* New York: Academic.

Kandel, D. B., & Davies, M. (1982). Epidemiology of depressive modes in adolescence. *Archives of General Psychiatry, 39,* 1205–1212.

Kandel, D. B., & Davies, M. (1986). Adult sequelae of adolescent depressive symptoms. *Archives of General Psychiatry, 43,* 255–262.

Kandel, D. B., Raveis, V. H., & Davies, M. (1991). Suicidal ideation in adolescence: Depression, substance use, and other risk factors. *Journal of Youth and Adolescence, 20,* 289–319.

Kaplan, A. (1986). The "self-in-relation": Implications for depression in women. *Psychotherapy, 23,* 234–242.

Kaplan, J., & Arbuthnot, J. (1985). Affective empathy and cognitive role-taking in delinquent and nondelinquent youth. *Adolescence, 20,* 323–333.

Kaplan, S. L., Hong, G. K., & Weinhold, C. (1984). Epidemiology of depressive symptomatology in adolescents. *Journal of the American Academy of Child Psychiatry, 33,* 91–98.

Kashani, J. H., Carlson, G. A., Beck, N. L., Hoeper, E. W., Corcoran, C. M., McAllister, J. A., Fallahi, C., Rosenberg, T. K., & Reid, J. C. (1987). Depression, depressive symptoms, and depressed mood among a community sample of adolescents. *American Journal of Psychiatry, 144,* 931–934.

Kashani, J. H., Sherman, D. D., Parker, D. R., & Reid, J. C. (1990). Utility of the Beck Depression Inventory with clinic-referred adolescents. *Journal of the American Academy of Child and Adolescent Psychiatry, 29,* 278–282.

Kazdin, A. E. (1987). *Conduct disorders in childhood and adolescence.* Newbury Park, CA: Sage.

Kazdin, A. E. (1989). Developmental differences in depression. In B. B. Lahey & A. E. Kazdin (Eds.), *Advances in Clinical Child Psychology* (Vol. 12, pp. 193–219). New York: Plenum.

Klerman, G. L., & Weissman, M. M. (1989). Increasing rates of depression. *Journal of the American Medical Association, 261,* 2229–2235.

Kovacs, M. (1982). *The Children's Depression Inventory: A self–rated depression scale for school-aged youngsters.* Unpublished manuscript. University of Pittsburgh, Pittsburgh, PA.

Landrine, H. (1988). Depression and stereotypes of women: Preliminary empirical analyses of the gender role hypothesis. *Sex Roles, 19*, 527–541.

Larson, R., & Ham, M. (1993). Stress and "storm and stress" in early adolescence: The relationship of negative events with dysphoric affect. *Developmental Psychology, 29*, 130–140.

Larson, R. W., Raffaelli, M., Richard, M. H., Ham, M., & Jewell, L. (1990). Ecology of depression in late childhood and early adolescence: A profile of daily states and activities. *Journal of Abnormal Psychology, 99*, 92–102.

Larsson, B., & Melin, L. (1990). Depressive symptoms in Swedish adolescents. *Journal of Abnormal Child Psychology, 18*, 91–103.

Leadbeater, B. J., Hellner, I., Allen, J. P., & Aber, L. (1989). Assessment of interpersonal negotiation strategies in youth engaged in problem behaviors. *Developmental Psychology, 25*, 465–472.

Leadbeater, B. J., & Linares, L. O. (1992). Depressive symptoms in Black and Puerto Rican adolescent mothers in the first 3 years postpartum. *Development and Psychopathology, 4*, 449–466.

Loeber, R. (1988). The natural histories of conduct problems, delinquency, and associated substance abuse: Evidence for developmental progressions. In B. B. Lahey & A. E. Kazdin (Eds.), *Advances in clinical child psychology* (Vol. 11, pp. 73–124). New York: Plenum.

Loeber, R. (1990). Development and risk factors of juvenile antisocial behavior and delinquency. *Clinical Psychology Review, 10*, 1–41.

Luthar, S. (1991). Vulnerability and resilience: A study of high–risk adolescents. *Child Development, 62*, 600–616.

Luthar, S. S., & Blatt, S. (1993). Dependent and self-critical depressive experiences among inner-city adolescents. *Journal of Personality, 61*, 365–386.

Luthar, S. S., & Blatt, S. J. (in press). Dependent and self-critical depressive experiences among inner-city adolescents. *Journal of Personality Assessment.*

Mahler, M. S. (1963). Thoughts about development and individuation. *Psychoanalytic Study of the Child, 18*, 307–324.

Masten, A. S., Garmezy, N., Tellegen, A., Pellegrini, D. S., Larkin, K., & Larsen, A. (1988). Competence and stress in school children: The moderating effects of individual and family qualities. *Journal of Child Psychology and Psychiatry, 29*, 745–764.

McGrath, E., Keita, G. P., Strickland, B. R., & Russo, N. F. (1990). *Women and depression.* Washington, DC: American Psychological Association.

Mufson, L., Moreau, D., Weissman, M. M., & Klerman, G. L. (1993). *Interpersonal psychotherapy for depressed adolescents.* New York: Guilford.

Newcomb, M. D., & Bentler, M. D. (1988). *Consequences of adolescent drug use: Impact on the lives of young adults.* Newbury Park, CA: Sage.

Newcomb, M. D., Huba, G. J., & Bentler, P. M. (1981). A multidimensional assessment of stressful life events among adolescents: Derivation and correlates. *Journal of Health and Social Behavior, 22*, 400–415.

Nietzel, M. T., & Harris, M. J. (1990). Relationship of dependency and achievement/autonomy to depression. *Clinical Psychology Review, 10*, 279–297.

Nolen-Hoeksema, S. (1987). Sex differences in unipolar depression: Evidence and theory. *Psychological Bulletin, 101*, 259–282.

Nolen-Hoeksema, S. (1990). *Sex differences in depression.* Stanford, CA: Stanford University Press.

Nolen-Hoeksema, S., Girgus, J. S., & Seligman, M. E. P. (1991). Sex differences in depression and explanatory style in children. *Journal of Youth and Adolescence, 20*, 233–246.

Oliver, J. M., & Baumgart, B. P. (1985). The Dysfunctional Attitude Scale: Psychometric properties in an unselected adult population. *Cognitive Theory and Research, 9*, 161–169.

Ostrov, E., Offer, D., & Howard, K. H. (1988). Gender differences in adolescent symptomatology: A normative study. *Journal of the American Academy of Child and Adolescent Psychiatry, 28*, 394–398.

Petersen, A. C., Compas, B., Brooks-Gunn, J., Stemmler, M., Ey, S., & Grant, K. E. (1993). Depression in adolescents. *American Psychologist, 48*, 155–168.

Petersen, A. C., Sarigiani, P. A., & Kennedy, R. E. (1991). Adolescent depression: Why more girls? *Journal of Youth and Adolescence, 20*, 247–272.

Radloff, L. S. (1977). The CES–D Scale: A self-report depression scale for research in the general population. *Applied Psychological Measurement, 3*, 385–401.

Radloff, L. S. (1991). The use of the Center for Epidemiologic Studies Depression Scale in adolescents and young adults. *Journal of Youth and Adolescence, 20*, 149–166.

Radloff, L. S., & Rae, D. S. (1979). Susceptibility and precipitating factors in depression: Sex differences and similarities. *Journal of Abnormal Psychology, 88*, 174–181.

Reinherz, H. Z., Frost, A. K., & Pakiz, B. (1991). Changing faces: Correlates of depressive symptoms in late adolescence. *Family and Community Health, 14*, 52–63.

Reinherz, H. Z., Frost, A. K., Stewart-Berghauer, G., Pakiz, B., Kennedy, K., & Schille, C. (1990). The many faces of correlates of depressive symptoms in adolescents. *Journal of Early Adolescence, 10*, 455–471.

Reinherz, H. Z., Stewart-Berghauer, G., Pakiz, B., Frost A. K., Moeykens, B. A., & Holmes, W. M. (1989). The relationship of early risk and current mediators to depressive symptomatology in adolescence. *Journal of the American Academy of Child and Adolescent Psychiatry, 28*, 942–947.

Riley, W. T., & McCranie, E. W. (1990). The Depressive Experiences Questionnaire: Validity and psychological correlates in clinical sample. *Journal of Personality Assessment, 54*, 523–533.

Roberts, R. E., Lewinsohn, P. M., & Seeley, J. R. (1991). Screening for adolescent depression: A comparison of depression scales. *Journal of the American Academy of Child and Adolescent Psychiatry, 30*, 58–66.

Robins, C. J. (1985). *Effects of simulated social reflection and achievement failure on mood as function of sociotropy and autonomous personality characteristics.* Unpublished manuscript, Duke University, Durham, NC.

Robins, C. J., & Ladd, J. (1991). *Personal Style Inventory, Version II.* Unpublished manuscript, Duke University, Durham, NC.

Robins, C. J., & Luten, A. G. (1991). Sociotropy and autonomy: Differential patterns of clinical presentation in unipolar depression. *Journal of Abnormal Psychology, 100*, 74–77.

Robins, L. N., & Rutter, M. (1990). *Straight and devious pathways from childhood to adulthood.* Cambridge, MA: Cambridge University Press.

Rodin, J. (1992). *Body Traps.* New York: Morrow.

Rohde, P., Lewinsohn, P. M., & Seeley, J. R. (1991). Comorbidity of unipolar depression: II. Comorbidity with other mental disorders in adolescents and adults. *Journal of Abnormal Psychology, 100*, 214–222.

Roos, P. E., & Cohen, L. H. (1987). Sex roles and social support as moderators of life stress adjustment. *Journal of Social Psychology, 52*, 576–585.

Rutter, M. (1979). Protective factors in children's responses to stress and disadvantage. In M. W. Kent & J. E. Rolfe (Eds.), *Primary prevention of psychopathology: Vol. 3: Social competence in children* (pp. 49–74). Hanover, NH: University Press of New England.

Rutter, M. (1986). The developmental psychopathology of depression: Issues and perspective. In M. Rutter, C. Izard, & P. Read (Eds.), *Depression in young people: Development and clinical perspectives* (pp. 3–30). New York: Guilford.

Rutter, M., & Rutter, M. (1993). *Developing minds: Challenge and continuity across the life span.* New York: Basic Books.

Siddique, C. M., & D'Arcy, C. (1984). Adolescence, stress, and psychological well-being. *Journal of Youth and Adolescence, 13,* 459–473.

Siegel, L. J., & Griffin, N. J. (1984). Correlates of depressive symptoms in adolescents. *Journal of Youth and Adolescents, 13,* 475–487.

Smith, T. W., O'Keefe, J. C., & Jenkins, M. (1988). Dependency and self-criticism: Correlates of depression or moderators of the effects of stressful events? *Journal of Personality Disorders, 2,* 160–169.

Sullivan, W. O., & Engin, A. W. (1986). Adolescent depression: Its prevalence in high school students. *Journal of School Psychology, 24,* 103–109.

Swearingen, E. M., & Cohen, L. H. (1985). Life events and psychological distress: A prospective study of young adolescents. *Developmental Psychology, 21,* 1045–1054.

Teri, L. (1982). Depression in adolescence: Its relationship to assertion and various aspects of self-image. *Journal of Clinical Child Psychology, 11,* 101–106.

U.S. Bureau of the Census. (1990). *Statistical Abstracts of the United States, 1990* (110th ed.). Washington, DC: Author.

Wagner, B. M., & Compas, B. E. (1990). Gender, instrumentality, and expressivity: Moderators of the relation between stress and psychological symptoms during adolescence. *American Journal of Community Psychology, 18,* 383–406.

Weiner, I. B. (1982). *Child and adolescent psychopathology.* New York: Wiley.

Weissberg, R., Caplan, M., & Harwood, R. (1991). Promoting competent young people in competence-enhancing environments: A systems-based perspective on primary prevention. *Journal of Consulting and Clinical Psychology, 59,* 830–841.

Weissman, A. N., & Beck, A. T. (1978). *Development and validation of the Dysfunctional Attitude Scale: A preliminary investigation.* Paper presented at the meeting of the American Psychological Association, Toronto, Canada.

Weissman, M. M., & Klerman, G. L. (1977). Sex differences and the epidemiology of depression. *Archives of General Psychiatry, 34,* 98–111.

Weissman, M. M., & Klerman, G. (1991). Depression in adolescence: Gender differences. In R. M. Lerner, A. C. Petersen, & J. Brooks-Gunn (Eds.), *Encyclopedia of adolescence.* New York: Garland.

Weissman, A. N., Orvaschel, H., & Padian, N. (1980). Children's symptoms and social functioning on self report scales. *Journal of Nervous and Mental Disorders, 168,* 736–740.

Wethington, E., McLeod, J. D., & Kessler, R. C. (1987). The importance of life events for explaining sex differences in psychological distress. In R. C. Barnett, L. Biener, & G. K. Baruch (Eds.), *Gender and stress* (pp. 144–156). New York: Free Press.

Wetzel, J. R. (1989). *American youth: A statistical snapshot.* Washington, DC: The William T. Grant Commission on Work, Family, and Citizenship.

Whiffen, V. E., & Sasserville, T. M. (1991). Dependency, self-criticism, and recollections of parenting: Sex differences and the role of depressive affect. *Journal of Social and Clinical Psychology, 10,* 121–133.

Whitley, B. E., Jr. (1984). Sex-role orientation and psychological well-being: Two meta-analyses. *Sex Roles, 12,* 207–225.

Winnicott, D. W. (1975). *Through pediatrics to psychoanalysis.* New York: Basic Books.

Worchel, F. F., Hughes, J. N., Hall, B. M., Stanton, S. B., Stanton, H., & Little, V. Z. (1990).

Evaluation of subclinical depression in children using self-, peer-, and teacher-report measures. *Journal of Abnormal Child Psychology, 18*, 271–282.

Worchel, F. F., Nolan, B., & Wilson, V. (1987). New perspectives on child and adolescent depression. *Journal of School Psychology, 25*, 411–414.

Zuroff, D. C. (1993). *Adult attachment styles of individuals vulnerable to depression.* Unpublished manuscript, McGill University, Montreal.

Zuroff, D. C., Koestner, R., Franz, C. E., & Powers, T. A., (1992). Self-criticism at age 12: A longitudinal study of interpersonal relationships, achievement, and adjustment. Manuscript submitted for publication.

Zuroff, D. C., Moskowitz, D. S., Wielgus, M. S., Powers, T. A., & Franko, D. L. (1983). Construct validation of the Dependency and Self-Criticism Scales of the Depressive Experiences Questionnaire. *Journal of Research in Personality, 17*, 226–241.

Zuroff, D. C., Quinlan, D. M., & Blatt, S. J. (1990). Psychometric properties of the Depressive Experiences Questionnaire. *Journal of Personality Assessment, 55*, 65–72.

Received November 23, 1992
Revision received June 4, 1993
Accepted October 6, 1993

# Correlates of Sexual Activity in Early Adolescence

Diane Scott-Jones
*University of Illinois, Urbana-Champaign*
Anne B. White
*North Carolina State University*

*Demographic, social, and social-cognitive variables associated with beginning sexual activity were assessed in 114 Black and White males and females in early adolescence (X age = 13.95 years), recruited from public schools and community agencies. Of the sample, 28% reported having sexual intercourse at least once. There were no significant race or gender differences in sexual activity or age at first intercourse. Mother's education, having a boyfriend/girlfriend, educational expectations, and age were significant predictors of sexual activity. For nonsexually active adolescents, boyfriend/ girlfriend and age were significant predictors of noncoital sexual interactions. Among sexually active adolescents, Whites were more likely than Blacks to use contraception regularly and to use effective methods. In future research and practice, more attention needs to be given to (a) the development of cross-gender relationships; (b) the use of withdrawal as a contraceptive method, especially among Blacks; and (c) the educational expectations and related life options of adolescents.*

Beginning sexual activity is a normal and important aspect of development, marking in part the transition to adulthood. Although the average age for the onset of puberty has declined in the twentieth century (Roche, 1979; Warren, 1983), the general cultural expectation is that young biologically mature adolescents will delay sexual activity. The cultural requirement of a chaste

This research was supported by grants to the first author from the National Institutes of Health Biomedical Research Fund and from the National Science Foundation. Portions of this work were presented at the annual meeting of the American Psychological Association, New York, August 1987, and portions were submitted by the second author in partial fulfillment of the requirements for the master's degree. The authors wish to thank Darrell Cooke and Sylvia Biddle for research assistance, and three anonymous reviewers for their helpful critiques. The authors also wish to acknowledge the Wake County Public Schools and other community organizations for their assistance in recruiting participants. Special thanks are extended to the participating students and their parents.

*Journal of Early Adolescence,* Vol. 10 No. 2, May 1990 221-238
© 1990 Sage Publications, Inc.

adolescence is not borne out in adolescents' behavior, however. Adolescents are becoming sexually active at earlier ages (Hofferth, Kahn, & Baldwin, 1987; Zelnik, Kantner, & Ford, 1981). By the end of the adolescent years, more than 80% of males and more than 70% of females are sexually active (Hayes, 1987).

The timing in the life course of first sexual intercourse is of great import for adolescents' development. Young sexually active adolescents are at high risk for unintended pregnancy because they are less likely than older adolescents to use contraception (Morrison, 1985). In addition, the period of subfertility following menarche, during which the likelihood of pregnancy is relatively low, may be shorter now than in the past (Lancaster, 1986). Only 2% of all births to adolescents are to those less than 15 years of age (Children's Defense Fund, 1988), but that proportion is slightly greater today than was true in the past (Baldwin, 1984; Vinovskis, 1981). Further, the problems associated with unplanned pregnancy are especially pronounced in early adolescence. The younger the adolescent when the pregnancy occurs, the greater the negative effect on educational attainment (Card & Wise, 1978; Furstenberg, 1976; Mott & Maxwell, 1981). Adolescents who are 18 and 19 years of age and have completed their schooling may experience pregnancy and childbirth without marked impairment of their life plans. In contrast, young school-age adolescents' life options are likely to be substantially diminished as a consequence of unplanned pregnancy.

Young adolescents may be biologically ready to initiate sexual activity but must function in a social milieu in which early sexual activity is likely to have negative consequences for later development. Therefore, it is important to understand the developmental contexts associated with the early initiation of sexual activity. Young adolescents have been understudied, however, and research on adolescent sexuality in general has focused on demographic factors, female subjects, and a limited range of racial and social class groups (Weddle, McKenry, & Leigh, 1988). The present study examined correlates of sexual activity among young adolescent males and females, including both Blacks and Whites with a similar range of socioeconomic backgrounds. A model including demographic, social, and social-cognitive variables was used to predict sexual activity in young adolescents.

Demographic variables associated with beginning sexual activity include age, single-parent household, gender, and race. Older adolescents are more likely than younger adolescents to be sexually active (Hofferth et al., 1987). Adolescents from single-parent homes are more likely than those from two-parent families to be sexually active (Chilman, 1986). Single parenting may be related to less control and monitoring of adolescents' behavior. In general, male adolescents are more likely than female adolescents, and Black adolescents more likely than White adolescents, to report being sexually active. Gender and race differences are somewhat complex, however.

Existing data regarding first sexual activity of males and females have not formed an entirely consistent picture. Finkel and Finkel (1981) reported a mean age of 12.8 years for males, including Blacks, Whites, and Hispanics. Cvetkovich and Grote (1980) reported that the mean age of first intercourse was 11.75 years for Black males, compared to 15 years for Black females and White males and females. In contrast, a prospective longitudinal study of middle-class White adolescents (Jessor, Costa, Jessor, & Donovan, 1983; Jessor & Jessor, 1975) indicated that in high school, females were more likely to be sexually active than were their male classmates. Females' earlier age of reaching biological maturity might lead them to be sexually active at an earlier age than males. The societal double standard regarding male and female sexual behavior would, however, contribute to earlier sexual activity for males. The double standard might lead also to a differential bias in self-reported sexual activity, with males more likely and females less likely to report the actual incidence of sexual activity.

National surveys have indicated that Black adolescents are more likely than White adolescents to be sexually active. In these large-scale surveys, however, race was confounded with socioeconomic status. Hofferth et al. (1987) controlled for mother's education and other variables and still found that Black adolescents were more likely than Whites to be sexually active. Other research has found that with poverty and basic skills controlled, differences in sexual activity between Blacks and Whites are not significant (Children's Defense Fund, 1986). Pleck (1987) also found few differences in sexual activity of Black and White adolescents in studies that did not have race and socioeconomic status confounding. The inclusion of males makes a difference in racial comparisons. In a study of adolescent females, differences in sexual activity between Blacks and Whites were greater for older than for younger adolescents (Hofferth et al., 1987). In contrast, Hayes (1987) concluded that racial differences in sexual activity are especially pronounced among young adolescents. These data included males; young Black males reported very high rates of sexual activity. Although Blacks overall have higher rates of sexual activity than do Whites, the recent increases in sexual activity and pregnancy have occurred among White adolescents (Hofferth et al., 1987; Zelnik & Kantner, 1980).

In addition to demographic variables, social and social-cognitive variables may be related to beginning sexual activity. Among these variables are adolescents' cross-gender relationships, their beliefs about male and female roles, and their perceptions of the future in the areas of education and marriage.

133

Early dating and a steady relationship have been related to sexual activity (Furstenberg, 1976; Zelnik et al., 1981). Initial sexual experiences tend to be with one partner. Adolescents may want to retain their steady relationship and may become sexually active for that reason. In a study of middle-class White adolescents, Jessor et al. (1983) found that the most frequent context reported for first intercourse was a steady dating relationship. Having a girlfriend or boyfriend may provide opportunity for and pressure toward sexual activity.

Young adolescents' sexual behaviors both influence and are influenced by adolescents' conceptions of masculinity and femininity (Chilman, 1986). Although conceptions of gender roles have changed in the recent past, males appear to be more traditional than females (Canter & Ageton, 1984; Osmond & Martin, 1975; Roper & Labeff, 1977). Early adolescents' conceptions of gender roles appear to be more traditional and stereotyped than are those of younger children (Streitmatter, Santa Cruz, & Ellis-Schwab, 1984) or older adolescents (Chandler, Sawicki, & Stryffeler, 1981). Gender-role norms regarding power in male-female relationships appear to be related to adolescents' developing sexual conduct. If adolescents view males as dominant and aggressive and females as passive and submissive, adolescents are more likely to become sexually active and to fail to use contraceptives than if gender roles are more egalitarian (Cvetkovich, Grote, Lieberman, & Miller, 1978; Ireson, 1984; Jorgensen & Alexander, 1983; Jorgensen, King, & Torrey, 1980; MacCorquodale, 1984; Rosen, Martindale, & Griselda, 1976). Adolescents holding stereotyped views of gender roles may view sexual relations as male conquests. Females frequently cite persuasion from males as a reason for beginning sexual activity; the younger adolescent female appears to have more difficulty resisting male persuasiveness than does the older adolescent female (Furstenberg, 1976; Rogel, Zuehlke, Petersen, Tobin-Richards, & Shelton, 1980).

Beginning sexual activity is likely to be related to adolescents' perceptions of the transition to adulthood. Thinking about the future and related decision-making processes (Rogel et al., 1980) are important components of adolescents' sexual behavior. Adolescents' expectations for two key events in their future lives as adults, completing formal education and becoming married, may be related to beginning sexual activity.

Adolescents who have high expectations for school success may be likely to delay sexual activity and to use contraception when sexually active. Rivara, Sweeney, and Henderson (1985) found that adolescent fathers were less likely than same-age nonfathers to view pregnancy as disruptive of future educational and career plans; the two groups were similar on other variables, such as frequency of intercourse and contraceptive knowledge. Many adolescents who become pregnant or father a child have poor basic skills and low educational expectations before the pregnancy occurs (Rindfuss, St. John, & Bumpass, 1984). Adolescent pregnancy is frequently viewed as a cause of poor educational outcomes, given that adolescent mothers and fathers complete fewer years of school than do their agemates (Card & Wise, 1978; Furstenberg, 1976; Mott & Maxwell, 1981). The developmental trajectory that leads to low educational attainment for adolescent mothers and fathers may begin prior to the pregnancy, with low educational expectations and achievement in early adolescence.

The age at which adolescents expect to get married might be related to sexual activity. A striking feature of the contemporary pattern of family formation is the delay in the age of first marriage (Ventura, 1985). Furstenberg, Brooks-Gunn, and Morgan (1987) pointed out that the deferral of marriage interferes with the traditional pattern of courtship, in which sexual activity occurs in the context of probable marriage. Adolescents may not be motivated to postpone sexual activity until marriage if marriage is perceived as a distant and uncertain future event. Consequently, the timing of the transition into mature sexual behavior and the responsible expression of sexuality may be difficult issues for some adolescents.

To summarize, sexual activity in early adolescence may be associated with demographic, social, and social-cognitive variables. Demographic variables include gender, race, age, family structure, and socioeconomic status. Social and social-cognitive variables include having a girl- or boyfriend, gender role attitudes, perceptions of power in cross-gender dyads, educational expectations, and marriage expectations. The purpose of the present study was to assess the relationship of these variables to the beginning of sexual activity in young adolescents.

## METHOD

### Participants

Participants were 28 Black female, 28 White female, 28 Black male, and 30 White male early adolescents who were recruited from the public schools, community organizations, and public housing authority of a southeastern city. Parents of participants gave written, informed consent. Each participant received two free movie tickets after completing the procedure.

Demographic characteristics of the sample are presented in Table 1. Mean age of participants was 13.95 years, with a range of 12.5 to 15.5 years. Parental educational level, which was used as an index of socioeconomic

TABLE 1:    Sample Characteristics

| | X̄ Age in years | X̄ Mother Education[a] | X̄ Father Education[a] | One-parent families (%) |
|---|---|---|---|---|
| Black females (n = 28) | 14.1 | 2.85 | 3.28 | 50 |
| White females (n = 28) | 13.8 | 3.14 | 3.08 | 36 |
| Black males (n = 28) | 13.9 | 2.65 | 3.15 | 36 |
| White males (n = 30) | 14.3 | 2.86 | 3.17 | 23 |
| Total sample | 13.95 | 2.88 | 3.16 | 36 |

a. Assessed on a 4-point scale: 1 = *less than high school*, 2 = *high school degree*, 3 = *some college*, and 4 = *college degree or more*.

status, was assessed on a 4-point scale (1 = *less than high school*, 2 = *high school degree*, 3 = *some college*, and 4 = *college degree or more*). Mean educational level was 2.88 for mothers and 3.16 for fathers, with a range from 1 to 4 for both variables. Of the participants, 36% lived in single-parent families.

### Interview Schedule

A structured interview was developed to assess the variables included in this study. Adolescents were asked whether they lived with two parents or with one parent, whether they had a girlfriend or boyfriend, the age at which they expected to get married, and how far they expected to go in school. The assessment of gender roles, sexual activity, and contraceptive use will be described in more detail. The interviewer noted the birthdate, race, and gender of participants. For ease of administration and scoring, separate forms were used for males and females.

The variable, gender-role, was operationalized as specific behaviors and attitudes of the adolescent rather than as the global personality traits used in some assessments (e.g., Bem, 1974; Spence & Helmreich, 1978). Two measures of gender-role were developed. The first measure, gender-role attitudes, included questions about male-female roles in four subsets: family, employment and education, social institutions, and personal behaviors (adapted from Brogan & Kutner, 1976; Osmond & Martin, 1975). Each subset contained six items requiring responses on a five-point Likert-type scale. To safeguard against response bias, half of the questions were phrased

136

so that affirmative responses represented traditional gender roles and the other half were phrased so that affirmative responses represented nontraditional gender roles. Examples of items were "Women are as reliable in emergencies as men are" and "The husband should take primary responsibility for major decisions, such as buying a car." Responses were scored so that high scores represented traditional gender roles. Scores for each subset and total score were computed. Because a repeated measures analysis of variance indicated no significant difference among the four subsets, the total score was used in the present report.

The second measure of gender role focused on the adolescent's own self-reported behavior related to power and decision-making in male-female dyadic relationships (adapted from Jorgensen et al., 1980). This measure contained five items requiring responses on a 5-point Likert-type scale. Examples of items were "When you and your boy(girl) friend go to movies, who decides which movie you will see?" and "When you and your boy(girl) friend disagree on something, who usually wins out?" Responses were scored so that high scores represented male power. For adolescents who reported not having a boyfriend or girlfriend, a second set of questions was used, in which each item was presented as a hypothetical situation. Examples of items were "When a boyfriend and a girlfriend go to the movies, who should decide which movie to see?" and "When a boyfriend and a girlfriend disagree on something, who should win out?"

Questions to assess the dependent variables, sexual activity and contraceptive use, were similar to those in previous studies. The language of the questions was appropriate for the age of the participants. Adolescents were asked if they had ever had sexual intercourse ("had sex" or "gone all the way"). For those responding yes, additional questions were asked regarding age at first sexual intercourse and frequency of sexual intercourse.

Contraceptive use was assessed by asking sexually active adolescents to select from a list which method(s) they used. Regularity of contraception was assessed on a 4-point Likert-type scale, ranging from *never* to *always* using contraception. The contraceptive method that sexually active early adolescents reported using most frequently was judged to be effective or ineffective on the basis of statistics on failure rates of contraceptive methods as they are typically used (Hatcher, Guest, Stewart, Trussell, & Frank, 1984). Methods with failure rates of less than 10% were considered effective; thus the pill, the IUD, and the condom were considered effective. Contraceptive knowledge was assessed by asking all adolescents, including those sexually active and those not sexually active, to indicate from the list which contraceptive method(s) they believed to be effective and which method they believed to be best.

137

For adolescents who indicated they had not become sexually active, questions were asked about the extent of their noncoital sexual behavior (none, kissing, touching from the neck up, touching from the waist up, touching from the waist down), the age at which they expected to have first sexual intercourse, and whether they expected to have first sexual intercourse before marriage.

### Procedure

Trained interviewers, matched to the gender of the respondent, administered structured, individual interviews at public schools and at community centers. Although matching the race of interviewer to subject would have been desirable, that match was not possible because schools and other agencies chose not to identify the race of the participant in advance of the scheduled interview. All interviewers were Black. Each interviewer presented a mature but youthful demeanor, which facilitated the establishment of rapport with the adolescents.

Interviewers engaged the respondents in a brief conversation to help respondents feel at ease before beginning the interview. Respondents were told that the interview focused on adolescents' ideas and experiences, particularly regarding relationships between males and females, sexual activity, and contraceptive use, and were assured that all responses would be kept confidential. A standard form was used by the interviewers to record each adolescent's responses to the interview questions, with the exception of questions regarding the respondent's own sexual behavior. For these questions, the adolescent wrote responses on a separate form, which was sealed in an envelope until data were entered into the computer.

The procedure, which was approved by the appropriate university ethics committee, appeared to elicit open and honest responses from the adolescents. Most of the adolescents appeared eager to talk with the interviewers. Only one adolescent appeared to be uncomfortable during the interview and was allowed to discontinue participation.

## RESULTS

Results are presented in four sections. The first section presents some preliminary analyses of demographic characteristics of the sample. Analyses of sexual activity are presented in the second section. In the third section, findings are given on noncoital sexual activity among adolescents who had not had sexual intercourse. The fourth section reports data on contraceptive use among the sexually active adolescents and the contraceptive knowledge of all respondents. Major data analyses employed stepwise logistic regression (for dichotomous dependent variables) and stepwise ordinary least-squares (OLS) regression techniques. Intercorrelations among the major variables used in the regression analyses are presented in Table 2. An examination of the matrix of correlations indicated no correlations greater than .38 among the predictor variables; thus multicollinearity was not a problem.

## Preliminary Analyses

To provide additional information about the sample characteristics presented in Table 1, analyses were conducted to test for race and gender differences. Analysis of variance indicated no significant race or gender differences nor interaction in mother's or father's education in this sample. The finding regarding father's education should be interpreted with caution; father's education was not reported by 23% of the sample, including 10 Black females, 2 White females, 8 Black males, and 6 White males. Although single-parent families occurred more frequently among Blacks and females than among Whites and males, chi-square analyses indicated no significant race or gender differences. Thus race was not significantly confounded with parental education and family structure in this sample. Although the race/gender groups differed in mean age by only a few months, analysis of variance indicated a significant interaction of race and gender, $F(1, 110) = 9.05, p < .003$. Pairwise comparisons indicated that White males ($\overline{X} = 14.3$ years) were significantly older than Black males ($\overline{X} = 13.9$ years) and White females ($\overline{X} = 13.8$ years) in this sample; Black females ($\overline{X} = 14.1$ years) were not significantly different from any other group. Because of this unexpected interaction, age was entered as a predictor variable in regression analyses predicting sexual activity and contraceptive use and as a covariate in the analyses of variance testing for race and gender differences.

## Sexual Activity

For the entire sample, 28% reported having intercourse at least once. There were no race or gender differences in the numbers of adolescents who reported having become sexually active. Similarly, there were no race or gender differences in age at first intercourse ($\overline{X} = 12.16$ years). For the majority of sexually active adolescents, sexual activity occurred infrequently; 22% reported having sex once, 47% reported not very often (every 4 to 6 months), 25% reported often (every 4 to 6 weeks), and 6% reported very often (once a week or more).

139

**TABLE 2:** Intercorrelations Among Demographic Variables, Social and Social-Cognitive Variables, and Sexual Activity

| | 1 | 2 | 3 | 4 | 5 | 6 | 7 | 8 | 9 | 10 | 11 | 12 |
|---|---|---|---|---|---|---|---|---|---|---|---|---|
| 1. Mother's education | 1.00 | | | | | | | | | | | |
| 2. Age | -.17 | 1.00 | | | | | | | | | | |
| 3. Gender | -.12 | .10 | 1.00 | | | | | | | | | |
| 4. Race | .13 | .04 | .02 | 1.00 | | | | | | | | |
| 5. Family structure | .03 | .00 | .17 | -.03 | 1.00 | | | | | | | |
| 6. Girlfriend, boyfriend | .26** | .20* | .14 | -.07 | -.02 | 1.00 | | | | | | |
| 7. Gender role attitudes | -.37*** | .20* | .35*** | -.07 | -.05 | .17 | 1.00 | | | | | |
| 8. Male/female power | .02 | -.07 | .33*** | .20* | .03 | -.14 | .11 | 1.00 | | | | |
| 9. Educational expectations | .36*** | -.20* | -.29** | .10 | .02 | -.09 | -.38*** | .12 | 1.00 | | | |
| 10. Marriage expectations | -.07 | .05 | .05 | -.16 | .07 | -.18 | .06 | .11 | -.03 | 1.00 | | |
| 11. Sexual activity | -.39*** | .32*** | .07 | -.13 | -.06 | .40*** | .23* | -.11 | -.31*** | .06 | 1.00 | |
| 12.[a] Noncoital sexual interactions | .14 | .25* | .16 | .08 | -.07 | .40*** | -.01 | -.12 | .00 | -.08 | — | 1.00 |

*$p < .05$; **$p < .01$; ***$p < .001$.
a. Excludes sexually active subjects, $n = 82$.

140

Because the dependent variable of interest, whether the adolescent is sexually active or inactive, is dichotomous, logistic regression analysis was used instead of ordinary least-squares regression. Predictor variables were age, sex, race, single-/two-parent family, gender roles (traditional gender roles and power in male/female dyads), having a boyfriend/girlfriend, educational expectations, and expected age of marriage.

Results of the stepwise logistic regression analysis are presented in Table 3. Significance level for entry into the model was .05; model $\chi^2$ (4) = 34.03, $p <$ .0001; model $R^2$ = .24. Variables significantly related to sexual activity were mother's education, having a boyfriend/girlfriend, educational expectations, and age. The higher the mother's educational level, the less likely the adolescent was to be sexually active. Adolescents who reported having a girlfriend or boyfriend were more likely to be sexually active than those who did not have such a relationship. Of the entire sample ($N$ = 114), 46.5% (53) reported having a girlfriend or boyfriend; 53.5% (61) said they did not. The older the adolescents, the more likely they were to be sexually active. The higher adolescents' educational expectations, the less likely they were to be sexually active. No students had expectations lower than high school graduation. Of those students who did not have definite expectations for college attendance, 50% were sexually active. Of those who expected to go to college, 29% were sexually active. Only 13% of those considering graduate school were sexually active.

## Noncoital Sexual Activity

Adolescents who had not had sexual intercourse were asked about the extent of their sexual interactions that did not involve intercourse, with answers including none, kissing, touching above the neck, touching above the waist, and touching below the waist. A stepwise OLS regression, using the same set of independent variables that were used to predict sexual activity/inactivity, indicated that having a girlfriend or boyfriend and age were significant predictors of noncoital sexual interactions. Significance level for entry into the model was .05; model $F(1, 80)$ = 11.93, $p <$ .0001. Results of the regression analysis are presented in Table 3.

Adolescents who had not had sexual intercourse expected to have first intercourse at a mean age of 20.3 years. There were no significant race or gender differences in the age at which these young adolescents expected to become sexually active.

Adolescents who had not had sexual intercourse were asked if they expected to have first intercourse before marriage. Regression analysis indicated that gender was the only significant predictor of expecting sexual

TABLE 3: Stepwise Regression of Sexual Intercourse and Noncoital Sexual Interactions on Social and Demographic Variables

| Variable entered | Beta | Standard error | $\chi^2$ |
|---|---|---|---|
| | | Sexual Intercourse | |
| Mother's education | –.68 | .29 | 5.52* |
| Friend | 1.50 | .55 | 7.34** |
| Age | .07 | .03 | 5.19* |
| Educational expectations | –.62 | .31 | 3.92* |
| Model $\chi^2(4) = 34.03, p < .0001$ | | | |
| Model $R^2 = .24$ | | | |

| | Beta | Standard error | F |
|---|---|---|---|
| | | Noncoital Sexual Interactions | |
| Boyfriend, Girlfriend | 1.06 | .26 | 16.07*** |
| Age | .04 | .01 | 6.87** |
| Model $F(1, 80) = 11.93, p < .0001$ | | | |
| Model $R^2 = .25$ | | | |

*$p < .05$; **$p < .01$; ***$p < .001$.

intercourse before marriage, $F(1, 80) = 5.74$, $p < .02$. More males (73%) expected to have sexual intercourse before marriage than did females (40%). Interestingly, among all respondents, the mean age expected for marriage was 25.5 years, which is greater than the mean age expected for first intercourse.

### Contraceptive Use and Contraceptive Knowledge

Regularity of contraceptive use was reported on a 4-point scale, ranging from 1 = *never* to 4 = *always*. The majority of sexually active adolescents did not use contraceptives regularly. Of all sexually active adolescents, 16% reported never using contraceptives, 63% reported sometimes, 13% reported often, and 9% reported always. Analysis of variance indicated significant race and gender differences and no significant interaction. Sexually active White adolescents ($\overline{X} = 2.54$) reported more regular contraceptive use than did sexually active Black adolescents ($\overline{X} = 1.89$), $F(1, 30) = 5.20$, $p < .03$.

Sexually active males ($\overline{X}$ = 2.39) reported more regular contraceptive use than did sexually active females ($\overline{X}$ = 1.86), $F(1, 30)$ = 4.19, $p < .05$.

The most frequently used contraceptive methods were male-controlled methods: condoms (44%), an effective method, and withdrawal (31%), an ineffective method. Blacks were more likely than Whites to report using withdrawal; Whites were more likely than Blacks to report using condoms. A chi-square analysis indicated that Whites (77%) were more likely than Blacks (26%) to use effective methods. $\chi^2(1)$ = 7.94, p < .005.

All adolescents, including those sexually active and those not sexually active, were asked to indicate, from a list of eight contraceptive methods, the methods they believed to be effective and the method they believed to be best. Data for the contraceptive pill, condom, and withdrawal are presented in Table 4. Adolescents most frequently indicated that contraceptive pills are effective (88%). Chi-square analyses for the sexually active and inactive adolescents combined indicated no race or gender differences in adolescents indicating pills as effective and no race differences in adolescents indicating condoms or withdrawal as effective. Males were more likely than females to believe that condoms are effective, $\chi^2(1)$ = 11.51, $p < .001$, and that withdrawal is effective, $\chi^2(1)$ = 11.30, $p$ .001. Inspection of the percentages in Table 4 suggests that sexually active adolescents are more likely than those not sexually active to indicate that condoms and withdrawal are effective methods.

When asked which is the best method, no sexually active adolescent and only 2% of those not sexually active chose withdrawal. Adolescents most frequently chose the contraceptive pill as the best method. Females more frequently chose the contraceptive pill than did males, $\chi^2(1)$ = 6.14, $p < .01$. Males chose condoms more frequently than did females, $\chi^2(1)$ = 15.24, $p < .001$. Chi-square analyses indicated no race differences in adolescents' choice of the contraceptive pill or the condom as the best contraceptive method. Sexually active adolescents, especially White males, appeared to be more likely than those not sexually active to report condoms as the best method.

## DISCUSSION

The majority of the young adolescents in this sample were not sexually active. A sizable minority, however, had experienced sexual intercourse at least once. More than one-fourth (28.1%) of the adolescents in this study reported that they had become sexually active. For the adolescents who had become sexually active, the average age of first sexual activity was approx-

143

TABLE 4:   Percentage of Sexually Active and Not Active Adolescents Reporting the Pill, Condom, and Withdrawal as Effective and as Best Methods

| | Total | Black | White | Male | Female |
|---|---|---|---|---|---|
| Effective methods[a] | | | | | |
| Pill | | | | | |
| Sexually active | 88 | 89 | 85 | 89 | 86 |
| Not active | 80 | 73 | 87 | 78 | 83 |
| Condom | | | | | |
| Sexually active | 69 | 58 | 85 | 83 | 50 |
| Not active | 55 | 51 | 58 | 70 | 40 |
| Withdrawal | | | | | |
| Sexually active | 28 | 32 | 23 | 44 | 7 |
| Not active | 13 | 11 | 16 | 23 | 5 |
| Best method | | | | | |
| Pill | | | | | |
| Sexually active | 56 | 63 | 46 | 33 | 86 |
| Not active | 56 | 43 | 67 | 50 | 62 |
| Condom | | | | | |
| Sexually active | 34 | 21 | 54 | 56 | 7 |
| Not active | 18 | 21 | 16 | 30 | 7 |
| Withdrawal | | | | | |
| Sexually active | 0 | 0 | 0 | 0 | 0 |
| Not active | 2 | 3 | 2 | 3 | 2 |

a. Each respondent could have indicated more than one response as effective.

imately 12 years. An accurate assessment of the sexual experience of young adolescents is very difficult. The sporadic nature of early sexual activity adds to the difficulty in accurately assessing its occurrence. More than two-thirds of the sexually active adolescents in this sample reported having had sexual intercourse only once or only once every 4 to 6 months. Hofferth et al. (1987) pointed out that interpreting data on the sexual experience of young adolescents is difficult because an unknown but possible substantial percentage of early experiences are actually sexual abuse.

Although adolescents are sometimes treated as a homogeneous age group, many developmental changes occur during the adolescent years: Older adolescents are more likely to be sexually active, even within the narrow age range of the present study. This finding suggests the need to focus on narrow ages within the adolescent years, rather than to treat adolescence as one developmental period.

Adolescent sexuality needs to be understood in the context of other developing behaviors of adolescents. The development of close personal relationships with the opposite gender and the development of academic achievement expectations are two areas identified as important in the present study. Adolescents who report having a girlfriend or boyfriend are more likely to be sexually active. A girlfriend or boyfriend relationship may provide the opportunity for and pressure toward sexual activity.

The development of close relationships with members of the opposite gender occurs outside the context of probable marriage. Consistent with the current societal norm of delaying marriage, the mean expected age for first marriage in this sample was 25.5 years. Unlike educational expectations, expectations for age at marriage were not related to beginning sexual activity in this sample. These data suggest that the adolescents did not associate first sexual activity with marriage. For those not sexually active, the mean expected age for first sexual activity was slightly over 20 years.

The large gap in expected ages for first sexual intercourse and for marriage suggested that these adolescents will have sexual intercourse outside the context of probable marriage. Yet many of these adolescents, especially females, appeared to hold on the cultural value of delaying sexual intercourse until marriage. When asked directly whether they expected to have sexual intercourse before marriage, 60% of the females and 27% of the males answered no. These data suggested that many adolescents, particularly females, had conflicting values that may interfere with a planned and responsible approach to their early sexual behavior.

Adolescents who expected to remain in school for long periods of time were less likely to be sexually active. If adolescents expect to continue their formal education, they may be motivated to avoid placing themselves at risk for unplanned pregnancy. The level of educational expectations that appeared to make a difference was college attendance. None of the adolescents in this sample had expectations lower than high school graduation. Of those students who did not have definite expectations for college attendance, 50% were sexually active. Of those who expected to go to college and those considering graduate school, 29% and 13%, respectively, had become sexually active.

Results of this study have implications for future research and for programs aimed at preventing unplanned adolescent pregnancy. Because of the volunteer sample of Black and White young adolescents, the results may not generalize to all adolescents, particularly those from other racial/ethnic groups or of different ages. The finding regarding the use of withdrawal as a contraceptive technique among Black adolescents suggests the need for more explicit information on contraception. Males in particular may need to be the focus of prevention, given that the most used techniques, withdrawal and condoms, are methods controlled by the male. Because adolescents tend not to use the methods they themselves believe to be most effective, problems may exist in accessibility of effective contraception. In her extensive review of the literature on adolescent contraceptive behavior, Morrison (1985) concluded that adolescents dislike using contraceptives and have a generalized negative attitude toward contraception. Information on contraception needs to be provided in a manner that facilitates effective use. More research is needed on adolescents' decision to use contraception and their choice among various methods.

The finding that having a girlfriend or boyfriend is a significant predictor of sexual activity suggests that adolescents also need guidance in developing close personal relationships with opposite-gender friends. In some sex education programs, the information provided about sexuality is technical and ignores the emotional and personal context in which sexual activity usually occurs. Adolescents need help in developing appropriate and responsible expressions of varying degrees of intimacy. The study of sexual behavior has not typically been connected to the study of dating and other adolescent social behavior. The integration of sexual intimacy into developing cross-gender relationships is an important area for future research.

Finally, the role of high educational expectations in delaying sexual activity suggests a third major need in the prevention of unplanned adolescent pregnancy. Adolescents need a reason, as well as the capacity, to delay parenthood. Programs that help adolescents to increase their educational expectations and enhance their life options should indirectly help to prevent unplanned pregnancy. Adolescents whose future holds only poverty and the most menial work may see little gain in delaying sexual activity and childbearing. Future research needs to examine the parallel development of behaviors and attitudes in the areas of sexuality and education.

## REFERENCES

Baldwin, W. (1984). *Adolescent pregnancy and childbearing—Rates, trends, and research findings from the CPR, NICHD*. Bethesda, MD: Demographic and Behavioral Sciences Branch, Center for Population Research.

Bem, S. L. (1974). The measurement of psychological androgyny. *Journal of Consulting and Clinical Psychology, 42,* 155-162.

Brogan, D., & Kutner, N. G. (1976). Measuring sexrole orientation: A normative approach. *Journal of Marriage and the Family, 38,* 3140.

Canter, R. J., & Ageton, S. S. (1984). The epidemiology of adolescent sex-role attitudes. *Sex Roles, 11* 657-676.

Card, J., & Wise, L. (1978). Teenage mothers and teenage fathers: The impact of early childbearing on the parents' personal and professional lives. *Family Planning Perspectives, 10,* 199-205.

Chandler, T. A., Sawicki. R. F., & Stryffeler, J. M. (1981). Relationship between adolescent sexual stereotypes and working mothers. *Journal of Early Adolescence, 1,* 72-83.

Children's Defense Fund. (1986). *Preventing adolescent pregnancy: What schools can do.* Washington, DC: Author.

Children's Defense Fund. (1988). *Teenage pregnancy: An advocate's guide to the numbers.* Washington, DC: Author.

Chilman, C. S. (1986). Some psychosocial aspects of adolescent sexual and contraceptive behaviors in a changing American society. In J. B. Lancaster & B. A. Hamburg (Eds.), *Schoolage pregnancy and parenthood: Biosocial dimensions* (pp. 191-218). New York: Aldine de Gruyter.

Cvetkovich, G., & Grote, B. (1980). Psychosocial development and the social problem of illegitimacy. In C. S. Chilman (Ed.), *Adolescent pregnancy and childbearing: Findings from research* (pp. 15-41). Washington, DC: U.S. Department of Health and Human Services.

Cvetkovich, G., Grote, B., Lieberman, E. J., & Miller, W. (1978). Sex role development and teenage fertility-related behavior. *Adolescence, 13,* 231-236.

Finkel, M. L., & Finkel, D. J. (1981). Sexual and contraceptive knowledge, attitudes, and behavior of male adolescents. In F. Furstenberg, R. Lincoln, & J. Menken (Eds.), *Teenage sexuality, pregnancy, and childbearing* (pp. 327-335). Philadelphia: Temple University Press.

Furstenberg, F. F. (1976). *Unplanned parenthood: The social consequences of teenage childbearing.* New York: Free Press.

Furstenberg, F. F., Brooks-Gunn, J., & Morgan, S. P. (1987). *Adolescent mothers in later life.* New York: Cambridge University Press.

Hatcher, R., Guest, F., Stewart, G., Trussell, J., & Frank, E. (1984). *Contraceptive technology.* New York: Irvington.

Hayes, C. D. (1987). *Risking the future: Adolescent sexuality, pregnancy, and childbearing,* Vol. 1. Washington, DC: National Academy Press.

Hofferth, S. L., Kahn, J. R., & Baldwin, W. (1987). Premarital sexual activity among U.S. teenage women over the past three decades. *Family Planning Perspectives, 19,* 46-53.

Ireson, C. J. (1984). Adolescent pregnancy and sex roles. *Sex Roles, 11,* 189-201.

Jessor, R., Costa, F., Jessor, L., & Donovan, J. E. (1983). Time of first intercourse: A prospective study. *Journal of Personality and Social Psychology, 44,* 608-626.

Jessor, S. L., & Jessor, R. (1975). Transition from virginity to nonvirginity among youth: A social-psychological study over time. *Developmental Psychology, 11,* 473-484.

Jorgensen, S. R., & Alexander, S. J. (1983). Research on adolescent pregnancy-risk: Implications for sex education programs. *Theory into Practice, 22,* 125-133.

Jorgensen, S. R., King, S. L., & Torrey, B. A. (1980). Dyadic and social network influences on adolescent exposure to pregnancy risk. *Journal of Marriage and the Family, 42,* 141-155.

Lancaster, J. B. (1986). Human adolescence and reproduction: An evolutionary perspective. In J. B. Lancaster & B. A. Hamburg (Eds.), *School-age pregnancy and parenthood: Biosocial dimensions* (pp. 17-38). New York: Aldine de Gruyter.

MacCorquodale, P. L. (1984). Gender roles and premarital contraception. *Journal of Marriage and the Family, 46,* 57-63.

Morrison, D. M. (1985). Adolescent contraceptive behavior: A review. *Psychological Bulletin, 98,* 538-568.

Mott, F. L., & Maxwell, N. L. (1981). Schoolage mothers: 1968 and 1979. *Family Planning Perspectives, 13,* 287-292.

Osmond, M. W., & Martin, P. Y. (1975). Sex and sexism: A comparison of male and female sexrole attitudes. *Journal of Marriage and the Family, 37,* 744-758.

Pleck, J. H. (1987). Sexuality and contraception. In Consortium for Research on Black Adolescence (Ed.), *Black adolescence: Topical summaries and annotated bibliographies of research* (pp. 64-72). Storrs, CT: Consortium for Research on Black Adolescence.

Rindfuss, R. R., St. John, C., & Bumpass, L. L. (1984). Education and the timing of motherhood: Disentangling causation. *Journal of Marriage and the Family, 46,* 981-984.

Rivara, F., Sweeney, P., & Henderson, B. (1985). A study of low socioeconomic status Black teenage fathers and their nonfather peers. *Pediatrics, 75,* 648-656.

Roche, A. F. (1979). Secular trends in human growth, maturation, and development. *Monographs of the Society for Research in Child Development, 44,* (Whole No. 179).

Rogel, M. J., Zuehlke, M., Petersen, A., Tobin-Richards, M., & Shelton, M. (1980). Contraceptive behavior in adolescence: A decision making perspective. *Journal of Youth and Adolescence, 9,* 491-506.

Roper, B. S., & Labeff, E. (1977). Sex roles and feminism revisited: An intergenerational attitude comparison. *Journal of Marriage and the Family, 39,* 113-119.

Rosen, R. A., Martindale, L., & Griselda, M. (1976). *Pregnancy study report.* Detroit, MI: Wayne State University.

Spence, J. T., & Helmreich, R. L. (1978). *Masculinity and femininity: Their psychological dimensions, correlates, and antecedents.* Austin: University of Texas Press.

Streitmatter, J. L., Santa Cruz, R. M., & Ellis-Schwab, M. (1984). Early adolescent attitudes toward sex roles. *Journal of Early Adolescence, 4,* 231-238.

Ventura, S. (1985, April). *Recent trends and variations in births to unmarried women.* Paper presented at the biennial meeting of the Society for Research in Child Development, Toronto, Canada.

Vinovskis, M. A. (1981). An epidemic of adolescent pregnancy? Some historical considerations. *Journal of Family History, 6,* 205-230.

Warren, M. P. (1983). Physical and biological aspects of puberty. In J. Brooks-Gunn & A. Petersen (Eds.), *Girls at puberty: Biological and psychosocial perspectives* (pp. 3-28). New York: Plenum.

Weddle, K. D., McKenry, P. C., & Leigh, G. K. (1988). Adolescent sexual behavior: Trends and issues in research. *Journal of Adolescent Research, 3,* 245-257.

Zelnik, M., & Kantner, J. F. (1980). Sexual activity, contraceptive use, and pregnancy among metropolitan-area teenagers, 1971-1979. *Family Planning Perspectives, 12,* 230-237.

Zelnik, M., Kantner, J. F., & Ford, K. (1981). *Sex and pregnancy in adolescence.* Beverly Hills, CA: Sage.

Requests for reprints should be addressed to Diane Scott-Jones, Department of Educational Psychology, University of Illinois, 1310 S. 6th Street, Champaign, IL 61820.

# Sexual Activity and Problem Behaviors among Black, Urban Adolescents

## Margaret E. Ensminger

*Johns Hopkins University*

ENSMINGER, MARGARET E. *Sexual Activity and Problem Behaviors among Black, Urban Adolescents.* CHILD DEVELOPMENT, 1990, **61**, 2032–2046. This article focuses on whether sexual activity is best considered in the same paradigm as adolescent substance use and assault or separately. Among black, inner-city adolescents ($N$ = 705), followed longitudinally since first grade, 3 questions were examined: (1) how these 3 behaviors co-occur, (2) their early family and school precursors, and (3) their relations with adolescent school behavior and parental supervision. The 3 most frequent patterns were compared: no problem behaviors, only sexual activity, and the combination of sexual activity, heavy substance use, and/or assault. In general, the multiproblem adolescents differed from the other adolescents in their behavior and parental supervision. While sex-only males were similar to the no-problem males, sex-only females differed from the no-problem girls in their family origins. These results suggest that by examining adolescent behaviors in their co-occurring combinations in epidemiologically defined populations, variations in pathways to deviance can be better understood.

Although sexual activity, substance use, and physical assault in excess are considered deviant behavior among adolescents of any segment of the U.S. population, these behaviors may have different precursors, as well as different outcomes, across subpopulations. It is the purpose of this article to describe the frequency and co-occurrence of sexual activity, substance use, and physical assault among adolescents in a black, urban community, and the possible precursors to these behaviors. I am particularly concerned with (1) the frequency that sexual activity co-occurs with these other problem behaviors in a black, urban population of adolescents and (2) whether the precursors and correlates of sexual activity are the same when it occurs without other problem behaviors as when it co-occurs with them. Sexual activity of adolescents may be better understood if considered in the context of other behaviors such as drug use and delinquency than if considered in isolation from these variables.

Adolescent sexual intercourse, delinquency, and substance use have most often been examined separately, possibly as the result of separate literatures and sources of research funding. However, they do co-occur, but with unknown frequency, across segments of the U.S. population (Donovan & Jessor, 1985; Ensminger, 1987; Jessor & Jessor, 1977; Miller & Simon, 1974; Mott & Haurin, 1988; Osgood, Johnston, O'Malley, & Bachman, 1988; Robins & Wish, 1977; and Zabin, Hardy, Smith, & Hirsch, 1986). Jessor and Jessor (1977) have suggested that alcohol use, marijuana use, delinquent behavior, and sexual intercourse constitute a "problem behavior syndrome" in adolescence. They maintain that these adolescent behaviors are preceded by a concurrence of psychological, environmental, and behavioral factors that facilitate and predispose the individual toward these behaviors. Theories of deviance such as social control theory (Hirschi, 1969), social learning theory (Akers, 1977), or self-derogation theory (Kaplan, 1975) also emphasize the generality of deviance and do not differentiate those factors that might explain one type of adolescent behavior compared to another. One explanation for why problem behaviors co-occur is

The author wishes to acknowledge the contributions of the Woodlawn community, its families, and children who have provided support and guidance for this research over many years. Sheppard G. Kellam and Jeannette Branch have been critically important to the design and implementation of this research and service program since its inception. The author is grateful to Cheryl S. Alexander, David D. Celentano, George Bohrnstedt, Gary A. Chase, Joy G. Dryfoos, William Eaton, Craig K. Ewart, Laurie Kane, Ann C. Klassen, Jane Pearson, Carol Weisman, and Renata Wilson for their comments and suggestions on earlier drafts of the manuscript. Anonymous reviewers of this paper also suggested improvements. These analyses were supported by National Institute of Mental Health 1 RO1-MH/AA 39500-01 and the Alcoholic Beverage Medical Research Foundation. The collection of the adolescent data was funded by National Institute of Drug Abuse. Reprint requests should be sent to Margaret E. Ensminger, Department of Health Policy and Management, The Johns Hopkins School of Hygiene and Public Health, 624 North Broadway, Baltimore, MD 21205.

that one behavior may be a stepping stone to another, and that participation in these behaviors follows a sequential pattern (Kandel, 1975; Robins & Wish, 1977; Yamaguchi & Kandel, 1984). For example, alcohol use leads to marijuana use or drug use leads to crime. A second explanation is that these behaviors share common influences. For example, feeling alienated from school may lead to both early sexual activity and marijuana use.

These behaviors may contribute to adolescent difficulties. Early sexuality can lead to early childbearing, affecting the adolescent mother's economic, social, and psychological well-being (Hofferth & Moore, 1979; Kellam, Adams, Brown, & Ensminger, 1982). The problems with substance use include health hazards, increased risk taking, their illegality, the association of early use with later abuse, and the possible negative effects on physical performance, including driving, and performance in social roles, especially school. Aggression, specifically assault behaviors, may result in harm to others or oneself.

Several investigators have examined the question of whether there is a single underlying tendency toward deviance among adolescents (Huba, Wingard, & Bentler, 1981; Mott & Haurin, 1988; Osgood et al., 1988; Windle, Barnes, & Welte, 1989). These studies have examined the question of how well relations among observed (manifest) variables, such as marijuana use or sexual activity, are explained by unobserved (latent) variables, often labeled as deviance. They have demonstrated that there seems to be a latent variable factor that explains a significant proportion of the variance in these behaviors (Huba et al., 1981; Osgood et al., 1988; Windle et al., 1989). However, they have also shown, in varying degrees, that the separate behaviors have unique aspects not accounted for by the latent variable. Osgood et al. (1988), in a longitudinal study of high school seniors, found that among the behaviors they studied, criminal behavior was most closely linked to the general tendency, while dangerous driving was the least linked. Some behaviors such as alcohol use and illicit drug use (other than marijuana) varied over time in their relations with general deviance. Mott and Haurin (1988) found in the National Longitudinal Survey of Youth that the patterns of linkage varied by racial and ethnic groups as well. Among minority teenagers, substance use and sexual activity were not as highly linked as they were for white youth. (The Mott and Haurin study was unique in including sexual activity as one of the behaviors examined.)

Clearly, these studies suggest that examination of the developmental pathways should consider each behavior within the context of the others. Specifically, in this article I examine whether the pathways leading to adolescent sexual behavior within a specific population subgroup are similar for those adolescents who are sexually active as well as engaging in other problem behaviors compared to those who are sexually active but not involved in frequent substance use or assault behaviors. I compare the early origins in the family, early behavioral responses in first grade, later adolescent school attachment, and family supervision of those who are only sexually active to those who are sexually active as well as heavy substance users and/or physically assaultive. The frequencies with which these patterns occur among the study population are also presented. The adolescents included in the study were all first graders in a black inner-city community on the south side of Chicago.

Other researchers have distinguished among the factors related to these separate behaviors in various populations. Kandel, Kessler, and Margulies (1978) found specific antecedents for use of liquor, marijuana, and other illicit drugs within a population of New York State high school students. McCord (1981) also found specific antecedents for alcoholism and criminality. In a longitudinal study of 224 boys followed into their thirties, noncriminal alcoholics were more similar in their background characteristics to the noncriminal, nonalcoholic group than to criminals, either with an alcohol problem or without.

Explanations for these adolescent problem behaviors have been suggested both in the general deviance literature as well as in the literature that focuses on single behaviors. I examine some of the psychosocial influences that are frequently described as leading to adolescent deviance or problem behaviors: family origins influencing opportunities, early behavioral responses in school, adolescent school behavior and attachment, and parental supervision.

*Family origins.*—A number of theories about deviance emphasize the lack of family educational and economic resources for those who engage in deviant behaviors. The lack of opportunities leads to frustration and the search for alternative sources of rewards and fulfillment (Cloward & Ohlin, 1960). Being from a low socioeconomic family background related to increased sexual behavior among teenage girls (Hogan & Kitagawa, 1985; Moore, Wenk, Hofferth, & Hayes, 1987). Yet the relation of parental social class to adolescent substance use and delinquency has not been strong (Bachman, Johnston, & O'Malley, 1981; Kandel, 1980). Parents' own past behavior may influence their children as well. Mother's early or current sexual behavior was related to her children's increased sexual activity in several studies (Fox, 1981; Newcomer & Udry, 1984). However, it does not necessarily predict other problem behaviors. Data from the National Survey of Children showed that while adolescents of teenage mothers reported a higher percentage of ever having engaged in sexual intercourse and a higher percentage of stealing, they reported about the same percentage of experience with substance use compared to adolescents of older mothers (Furstenberg, Brooks-Gunn, & Morgan, 1987).

Family structure may affect family interaction patterns or family resources, which then affect the child's behavior. Children or adolescents from mother-alone families and mother-absent families show poorer social adaptation to school, more delinquent behavior, and earlier sexual activity than those from mother/father or mother/other adult families (Dornbusch et al., 1985; Ensminger, Kellam, & Rubin, 1983; Inazu & Fox, 1980; Kellam, Ensminger, & Turner, 1977; Zelnik, Kantner, & Ford, 1981). Differences in family background may also influence children because of different expectations that parents have regarding their children's future.

*Early behavioral responses.*—One of the most replicated findings in the longitudinal delinquency and drug literature is that early aggressive behavior predicts later delinquency and drug use (Anthony, 1985; Conger & Miller, 1966; Lefkowitz, Eron, Walden, & Huesman, 1977; McCord, 1983; Mitchell & Rosa, 1981; Robins, 1978). In the Woodlawn study, males who were rated aggressive in first grade by their teachers were more likely to use substances and be delinquent as adolescents; those who were rated as shy were less likely to use substances and to be delinquent than other males; those males who were both shy and aggressive were the most likely category to report later substance use and delinquency (Ensminger et al., 1983; Kellam, Brown, Rubin, & Ensminger, 1983). No such relations were found for females. However, the effect on adolescent sexual behavior of early aggressive behavior has not been reported. If adolescent sexual behavior has similar pathways as substance use and delin-

quency, we would expect early aggressive behavior to increase the likelihood of sexual behavior and early shyness to inhibit it.

*Adolescent school behavior and attachment.*—A problem behavior (Donovan & Jessor, 1985; Jessor, 1987; Jessor & Jessor, 1977) or a social control framework (Hirschi, 1969) emphasize the nonconforming or deviant aspects of early sexual experience, substance use, and delinquency. From these perspectives, low expectations for academic goals, problems in school, low attachment to school, as well as weak supervision by parents contribute to increased levels of problem behavior.

*Parental supervision.*—Much of the literature on how family characteristics influence teenage behaviors has been concerned with parental discipline and monitoring; the extent of parental supervision, the clarity of parental expectations, and the consistency of parental responses are the aspects thought to be important (Patterson, 1982; Wilson, 1980). W. J. Wilson (1982; cited in Hogan & Kitagawa, 1985) has suggested that parental supervision is an especially salient characteristic in low-income black neighborhoods. The importance of parental supervision has been supported in empirical findings. Weak parental supervision has been related to delinquency (Farrington, 1978; Loeber & Loeber, 1986; McCord, 1981; Patterson, 1982; Wilson, 1980), to teenage sexual activity (Abrahamse, Morrison, & Waite, 1988; Hogan & Kitagawa, 1985), and to drug use (Ensminger, Brown, & Kellam, 1982; Miller & Simon, 1974).

## Method

### Study Design and Population

The data for this study were gathered prospectively on consecutive cohorts of first-grade children in the poor, black Chicago community of Woodlawn in the 1960s. The focus here is on the 1966–1967 cohort of first graders ($N = 1,242$), who were assessed three times in first grade, once in third grade, and again 10 years later when they were age 16 or 17. Data were also gathered from the mothers or mother surrogates of this cohort when the children were in first grade and again at the 10-year follow-up.

In 1975–1976, 939 (75%) of the mothers or mother surrogates out of the total 1,242 families were interviewed. The mothers' refusal rate was 5.9%; 11.6% of the families could not be located; 6.5% of the families had moved from Chicago, and 0.3% ($n = 4$) of the children from the study population were deceased. Of the 939 teenagers of the reinterviewed mothers, 75% ($n = 705$) of the teenagers participated in the reassessments, 9.5% refused to participate, 5% who agreed to participate were not reassessed because data collection funding ended prematurely, 1.5% had moved out of Chicago, 2.2% were unavailable to be interviewed because they were in an institution, and 6.7% could not be located. The study population for this article consists of the 705 teenagers who were reassessed.

In order to assess possible bias resulting from sample attrition, the mothers who were reinterviewed were compared with those who were not, using the first-grade information that was available on both. The mothers not reinterviewed were more likely to have started childbearing in adolescence, had been more mobile before and during the child's first-grade year, and had children who were more likely to have been in parochial schools in first grade. (Parochial schools did not maintain centralized school records, as did the public school system.) They did not differ in their 1966–1967 psychological well-being, early family income, welfare status, or the number or types of adults at home. There were no differences in the social adaptational status or the psychological well-being between the children of the reinterviewed mothers and the children of those not reinterviewed (Kellam, Ensminger, & Simon, 1980).

Among teenagers whose mothers were interviewed, those who did not participate in the teenage assessments did not differ from those who were assessed according to mothers' reports of their teenagers' delinquency, alcohol and drug use, social contact, acceptance of authority, cognitive achievement, concentration, and seriousness about school. Maternal ratings of the teenagers' self-esteem and psychiatric distress did not differentiate those who were reinterviewed from those who were not. Mothers of teenagers who were not reassessed, however, rated their children as less mature and reported that their families were more likely to express anger than interviewed mothers whose teenagers were not reassessed. The reports of family background characteristics showed that families of teenagers who were not reassessed did not differ from their peers in terms of family structure, income, or in most aspects of family interaction.

### Description of Teenage Problem Behavior

The information on teenage sexual behavior, alcohol and drug use, and assault comes from adolescent self-reports in the

What's Happening? instrument (Petersen & Kellam, 1977), administered by black college students to about five to eight adolescents in a standardized process that emphasized listening to the concerns of the teenagers, building trust, and assuring confidentiality. The questions were presented on slides and audiotape to control for differences in reading ability and to standardize the pace and the general administration of the questions.

Teenagers were asked about the frequency of experience ever in sexual intercourse. Response categories were (1) never, (2) one or two times, or (3) three or more times. The teenagers also indicated their frequency of drinking beer or wine, drinking liquor, and of using marijuana during the past 2 months and during their lifetime. The reports of lifetime prevalence of these substances are used here.

Teenagers were asked how frequently (on a five-point scale) in the last 3 years they had performed each of 23 delinquent acts (Gold, 1970; Johnston, 1973; Lefkowitz et al., 1977). Six of these referred to physical assault behaviors: carrying a weapon, having a serious fight at school, being in a gang fight, getting something by threatening, hurting someone badly, and hitting a teacher (Cronbach's alpha = 0.76 for males and 0.68 for females). The six items were summed together (possible range of 6 to 30) to make an assault scale.

### Description of Independent Variables

*Family origins.*—Family structure in first grade and during adolescence, whether the mother was a teenager when she started childbearing, maternal education, and the mother's expectations regarding the child's future education are examined here. These were all reported by the mothers (or mother surrogates) in first grade, at adolescence, or both. The family types include mother-father families, mother-alone families, and mother-other adult families. While the proportion of adolescents with these adolescent behaviors was greater in mother-absent families than in other family types, there were too few to be included in multiple variable analyses (19 families in first grade and 34 in the adolescent follow-up). Since first-grade and adolescent family structure were highly correlated, only first-grade family structure is included in the analyses.

Adolescents whose mothers were teenagers when they began childbearing were compared to those with older mothers. Maternal education was examined by whether the mother reported at least a high school education or not. Mothers were asked in both interviews how far they expected their child to go in school. Those children whose mothers expected they would attend college were compared to those whose mothers did not.

*Early behavioral responses in school.*—Woodlawn first-grade teachers rated each child as adapting, mildly maladapting, moderately maladapting, or severely maladapting in their classroom on shyness, aggressiveness, and learning problems. The conceptual basis, reliability, and validity of these data are described elsewhere (Kellam, Branch, Agrawal, & Ensminger, 1975; Kellam & Ensminger, 1980). Children rated as adapting on shyness, aggressiveness, or learning problems were compared with those rated maladapting.

*Adolescent school behavior and attachment.*—Five items were selected to reflect a measure of school attachment (Hirschi, 1969): How important is doing well in school to you? How far would you like to go in school? How far do you think you will go? How do your teachers think you are doing? How satisfied are you with your teachers' opinion? (Cronbach's alpha = 0.68). Adolescents with low school bonds were compared with those who had medium or high school bonds. An important indicator of school behavior among adolescents is how frequently they skip a day of school without an excuse. Teenagers who reported they skipped school five or more times were compared with those who had skipped fewer times or no times.

*Parental supervision.*—Parental supervision was measured by two items asking the teenagers what rules their parents had about the time they were expected home on weeknights and what rules their family had regarding school, such as homework. They indicate whether the teenager perceived rules and parental monitoring. Those whose parents had rules regarding schooling and those whose parents expected them home before 10:00 on school nights were categorized as having strong supervision. Others were categorized as having weak supervision.

## Results

### Patterns of Co-occurrence of Adolescent Problem Behaviors

The frequency of Woodlawn adolescents' involvement in these behaviors is shown in Table 1. (While the later analyses use a physical assault scale, the frequencies for each of the six assault scale items are shown because the scale frequency itself has little meaning.) The frequency of sexual intercourse reported

is similar to that reported in other studies with black adolescents. Fifty-six percent of the Woodlawn females and 93.3% of the males reported that they had engaged in sexual intercourse one or more times; this frequency for the females is similar to the 55.1% reported by black 16-year-old females living in metropolitan areas who took part in a 1976 national survey of 15–19-year-old females (Zelnik et al., 1981). Among a nationally representative cohort of males and females who were 14–22 years of age in 1979, 78.6% of black males and 45.7% of black females had sexual intercourse prior to age 17 (Mott & Haurin, 1988).

A detailed comparison of the substance use patterns of Woodlawn teenagers with other samples has been made elsewhere (Kellam et al., 1980); in general, Woodlawn teenagers reported more marijuana use but less hard liquor use than teenagers in other studies; many studies of drug and alcohol use among adolescents do not ask separately about beer or wine and other alcohol.

The frequencies of 23 delinquent acts reported by the Woodlawn teenagers were compared with those in two other community delinquency studies that used similar items and were conducted during the same year as the Woodlawn follow-up (Cernkovich & Giordano, 1979; Ensminger et al., 1983; Hindelang, Hirschi, & Weis, 1981). The frequencies reported in the three studies were similar for most of the items. However, Woodlawn teenagers reported more assault behaviors than teenagers in the other two studies.

Sexual intercourse is significantly correlated (at $p < .001$) with the three substance use variables and assault. The lowest correlation is with assault—.19 for females and .20 for males; the highest is with marijuana use—.47 for females and .42 for males. Table 2 shows these correlations (among uncategorized variables) separately for males and females. While the frequency of involvement in the problem behaviors differs for males and females, the correlations among the problem behaviors are virtually identical for the two sexes.

In order to examine further how these behaviors co-occur, the adolescents were combined according to the behaviors in which they were involved. When to classify an adolescent as "sexually experienced," a "beer drinker," a "marijuana user," and so on becomes an issue at this point and for this specific population. One option is to count any teenager who has ever initiated any of

TABLE 1

PERCENTAGE OF ADOLESCENTS WHO PARTICIPATED IN SPECIFIC ADOLESCENT
ACTIVITIES EVER IN LIFETIME

| | SEXUAL INTERCOURSE | | |
| --- | --- | --- | --- |
| | Never | 1–2 Times | 3+ |
| Males (n = 340) ..................... | 6.8 | 21.5 | 71.8 |
| Females (n = 356) .................. | 44.1 | 24.4 | 31.5 |

| | SUBSTANCE USE | | |
| --- | --- | --- | --- |
| | Never | 1–19 Times | 20+ |
| Males: | | | |
| Beer ............................. | 14.6 | 50.4 | 35.0 |
| Marijuana ........................ | 28.4 | 35.1 | 36.5 |
| Hard liquor ...................... | 53.4 | 32.6 | 14.1 |
| Females: | | | |
| Beer ............................. | 25.8 | 56.7 | 17.5 |
| Marijuana ........................ | 48.8 | 34.6 | 16.6 |
| Hard liquor ...................... | 61.8 | 32.6 | 5.6 |

| | ASSAULT ACTIVITIES | | | |
| --- | --- | --- | --- | --- |
| | Never | 1–2 Times | 3–4 Times | 5+ |
| Males: | | | | |
| Carried a weapon ............... | 40.5 | 29.3 | 8.8 | 17.3 |
| Got into a serious fight at school .. | 48.1 | 33.8 | 8.7 | 9.3 |
| Been in a gang fight ............. | 58.5 | 24.3 | 6.7 | 10.5 |
| Got something by threatening .... | 64.6 | 23.9 | 5.6 | 5.9 |
| Hurt someone badly ............. | 60.1 | 28.5 | 5.0 | 6.5 |
| Hit a teacher ................... | 70.6 | 22.3 | 3.2 | 3.8 |
| Females: | | | | |
| Carried a weapon ............... | 73.6 | 15.6 | 3.6 | 7.2 |
| Got into a serious fight at school .. | 68.2 | 25.6 | 3.1 | 3.1 |
| Been in a gang fight ............. | 81.3 | 16.4 | 1.7 | .6 |
| Got something by threatening .... | 85.8 | 9.8 | 1.9 | 2.5 |
| Hurt someone badly ............. | 83.6 | 14.2 | 1.1 | 1.1 |
| Hit a teacher ................... | 81.1 | 15.0 | 1.4 | 2.5 |

TABLE 2

CORRELATIONS AMONG PROBLEM BEHAVIORS

| | Sexual Activity | Beer/Wine | Marijuana | Assault |
| --- | --- | --- | --- | --- |
| Beer/wine: | | | | |
| F ............ | .32 | | | |
| M ............ | .31 | | | |
| Marijuana: | | | | |
| F ............ | .47 | .60 | | |
| M ............ | .42 | .60 | | |
| Assault: | | | | |
| F ............ | .19 | .27 | .27 | |
| M ............ | .20 | .33 | .30 | |
| Hard liquor: | | | | |
| F ............ | .23 | .67 | .52 | .32 |
| M ............ | .23 | .62 | .52 | .35 |

NOTE.—All coefficients are significant beyond the $p < .000$ level. F = female ($N = 350$); M = male ($N = 327$).

these behaviors as involved in that activity. Among some adolescents, however, occasional experimentation leads to regular participation, whereas in others it does not. The results of studies that have examined the consequences of adolescent drug use in early adulthood suggest that it may be useful to separate "occasional" from "regular" involvement (Kandel, Davies, Karus, & Yamaguchi, 1986; Newcomb & Bentler, 1988). One way to do this is to include only those adolescents who reported more frequent involvement. Adolescents who reported they had used beer or wine, marijuana, or liquor 20 times or more were categorized as a beer or wine user, a marijuana user, and/or a liquor user; those who had sexual intercourse at least three times or more were categorized as sexually involved;[1] those who had a score on the assault scale of 16 (top 25%) or more were counted as involved in assault. These categories were derived somewhat arbitrarily, but they indicate more frequent involvement in each of the activities than that indicated by a one-time-ever initiation, and frequent involvement seems to have consequences later.

By these criteria, over half (57%) of the females were not frequently involved in any of the behaviors (see Table 3). About 16% of the females were only sexually active. About 11% were using beer, marijuana, and were possibly involved with hard liquor and/or assault but were not sexually active, while about 17% were involved with these behaviors and were also sexually active.

Almost half of the males were not involved in substance use or assault, according to the criteria for the study—about 22% of the males were in the "no-problem" category and about 27% were in the "sex-only" category. For those males who were involved with substance use or assault, most were sexually active; only 5% of the males were involved in substance use or assault and were not sexually active. About 20% of the males were sexually active and used beer and/or marijuana, while about 26% used hard liquor and/or were high on assault as well as using beer/marijuana and were sexually active (see Table 3). These data show considerable variation in how these behaviors co-occur; while there is considerable overlap among these behaviors, there is little evidence supporting a single syndrome involving all three behaviors.

*Early and Adolescent Family and School Characteristics*

In order to better understand the precursors to these problem behaviors, a number of comparisons were made. The family background, early behavioral responses to school, adolescent school attachment, and parental supervision of teenagers only involved in sexual intercourse (sex only $n = 85$ males; $n = 53$ females) were first compared to those of teenagers involved in the problem behaviors of substance use and assault as well as sexual intercourse (multiproblem $n = 147$ males and $n = 57$ females). This assesses whether precursors of frequent sexual activity are different compared to precursors of multiple problem behaviors. Teenagers who were only sexually active were also compared to those who reported no frequent problem behaviors (no problem $n = 70$ males; $n = 197$ females)

[1] Including those who have had sex one or two times with those who have never had sex categorizes virgins with nonvirgins. There are several reasons why this was done. First, within this population, most males and many of the females had initiated sexual activity, and sexual activity as a frequent activity is better captured by the higher category. Second, the "no-sex" category and the "little-sex" category were similar on an important consequent status—high school graduation—while they differed from the "more-frequent" sex category. Both males and females who reported "no sex" or "little sex" were more likely to graduate from high school (by school record report) than those who reported "frequent sex" (see below).

| | MALES | | FEMALES | |
|---|---|---|---|---|
| | High School Grad | Drop-Out | High School Grad | Drop-Out |
| No .......... | 9 | 8 | 99 | 36 |
| | (7.4%) | (5.1%) | (50.5%) | (33.0%) |
| Little ........ | 36 | 25 | 52 | 23 |
| | (29.8%) | (16.0%) | (26.5%) | (21.1%) |
| Frequent ..... | 76 | 123 | 45 | 50 |
| | (62.8%) | (78.8%) | (23.0%) | (45.9%) |

School drop-out information was obtained from the Chicago School Board in 1982. If students progressed through the school system at an expected rate, they would have graduated in 1978, 2 years after the reports of problem behaviors were obtained.

TABLE 3

PATTERNS OF INVOLVEMENT OF WOODLAWN ADOLESCENTS
IN PROBLEM BEHAVIORS

| | Females | Males |
|---|---|---|
| No problem | 197 | 70 |
| | (57.4) | (21.9) |
| Sex only | 53 | 85 |
| | (15.5) | (26.6) |
| Substance use/assault only: | | |
| Beer/marijuana only | 27 | 9 |
| | (7.9) | (2.8) |
| Beer/marijuana, hard liquor/assault | 9 | 8 |
| | (2.6) | (2.5) |
| Sex and substance use/assault: | | |
| Sex, beer/marijuana only | 39 | 65 |
| | (11.4) | (20.4) |
| Sex, beer/marijuana, assault | 8 | 40 |
| | (2.3) | (12.5) |
| Sex, beer/marijuana, hard liquor | 9 | 21 |
| | (2.6) | (6.6) |
| Sex, beer/marijuana, assault/hard liquor | 1 | 21 |
| | (0.3) | (6.6) |
| N | 343 | 319 |

NOTE.—Numbers in parentheses are column percents.

to determine if sex-only teenagers are distinguishable from no-problem teenagers in terms of precursors. Finally, the no-problem adolescents were compared to the multiproblem adolescents. Too few adolescents ($n = 17$ males; $n = 36$ females) were only involved with substance use or assault (and not sexual intercourse) to form a separate category, and they are excluded from the comparisons.

These analyses employ multiple logistic regression to evaluate the effects of several sets of independent variables on the adolescent behaviors. The dependent measure is the log odds of being in the sex-only category compared to (a) the no-problem category and (b) the multiproblem category, or (c) being in the multiproblem category compared to the no-problem category. Since logistic regression allows a limited number of independent variables, a two-step process is used to identify significant independent variables. First, separate regressions are performed with variables from the following: early family, adolescent family, first-grade behavioral response, adolescent school attachment, and truancy and parental supervision. Regressions are run separately for males and females. In the second step, those early and adolescent family and school factors that significantly differentiated (at the $p < .10$ value) the three problem behavior categories are included together in the same logistic regression analysis. (The

significance level of .10 was chosen rather than the traditional .05 level because the first step was intended only as an initial selection process.) Table 4 summarizes the results of this initial step in terms of the variables included in each regression and the variables retained for the second step for both males and females.

*Males*

The sex-only and the no-problem males did not differ from each other on any of these variables. Table 5 includes logistic regression effect parameters and standard errors for the final regression models. Compared both to the sex-only and the no-problem males, the multiproblem males were more likely to have been rated aggressive in first grade, to have been frequently truant, and to have weaker curfew rules. In addition, the multiproblem males were more likely to have had a mother who began childbearing as a teenager than the no-problem males.

Any comparison of results across the three logistic regressions needs to take into account statistical power considerations. Those regressions that include larger numbers of adolescents are more likely to show a "significant" result with the same effect size because they have more statistical power. The effect parameters (regression coefficients) are included in Tables 5 and 6 so that

157

## TABLE 4

### SUMMARY TABLE OF FOUR LOGISTIC REGRESSIONS

|  | Males | Females |
|---|---|---|
| **Family conditions:** | | |
| Teenage motherhood | * | * |
| Mother's education | – | * |
| Family structure | * | – |
| **Mother's expectations:** | | |
| re: child's future education | – | – |
| re: adolescent's future education | – | * |
| **First-grade behavioral responses:** | | |
| Aggression | * | * |
| Shyness | * | – |
| Underachievement | – | * |
| **Adolescent school and family attachment:** | | |
| School bonds | * | * |
| **Parental supervision:** | | |
| re: schoolwork | – | – |
| re: time home on school nights | * | * |
| Truancy | * | * |

NOTE.—Logistic regressions of (1) family, first grade; (2) family, adolescence; (3) first-grade social adaptation status; (4) adolescent school and family attachment on adolescent behavior, males and females. Asterisk indicates variables distinguished at least two of the behavior categories (no problem, sex only, multiproblem) at the $p \leq .10$ level.

## TABLE 5

### LOGISTIC REGRESSION OF EARLY AND ADOLESCENT FAMILY ORIGINS, FIRST-GRADE SOCIAL ADAPTATIONAL STATUS (SAS), ADOLESCENT SCHOOL AND FAMILY ATTACHMENTS ON TEENAGE BEHAVIORS, MALES

|  | No Problem (0) vs. Sex Only (1) ($n$ = 143) | No Problem (0) vs. Multiproblem (1) ($n$ = 198) | Sex Only (0) vs. Multiproblem (1) ($n$ = 209) |
|---|---|---|---|
| **Family origins:** | | | |
| Mother-father (0) | .046 | – .096 | .257 |
| Mother alone (1) | (.20) | (.19) | (.17) |
| Mother-father (0) | – .420 | .110 | .741 |
| Mother other (1) | (.29) | (.25) | (.25) |
| Teenage mother (0 = no, 1 = yes) | .684[+] | .814* | .139 |
|  | (.18) | (.17) | (.161) |
| **First-grade SAS:** | | | |
| Aggression (0 = adapting, 1 = maladapting) | – .122 | .781* | 1.018** |
|  | (.21) | (.19) | (.18) |
| Shy (0 = adapting, 1 = maladapting) | – .694[+] | – .392 | .104 |
|  | (.19) | (.18) | (.18) |
| **Adolescent school and family attachment:** | | | |
| School attachment (0 = high, 1 = low) | – .023 | .480 | .653[+] |
|  | (.18) | (.19) | (.17) |
| School truancy (0 = low, 1 = high) | – .300 | .991* | 1.204*** |
|  | (.22) | (.19) | (.18) |
| Rules: curfew (0 = strong, 1 = weak) | .233 | 1.444*** | 1.396*** |
|  | (.18) | (.20) | (.191) |

NOTE.—Regression coefficients are listed above and standard errors are below in parentheses.
[+] $p < .10$.
* $p < .05$.
** $p < .01$.
*** $p < .001$.

## TABLE 6

### LOGISTIC REGRESSION OF FAMILY ORIGINS, FIRST-GRADE SOCIAL ADAPTATIONAL STATUS (SAS), ADOLESCENT SCHOOL AND FAMILY ATTACHMENT ON TEENAGE BEHAVIORS, FEMALES

| | No Problem (0) vs. Sex Only (1) (n = 231) | No Problem (0) vs. Multiproblem (1) (n = 233) | Sex Only (0) vs. Multiproblem (1) (n = 100) |
|---|---|---|---|
| Family origins: | | | |
| Mother's education (0 = high school grad, 1 = <high school) | .870* | .013 | −.800 |
| | (.20) | (.19) | (.26) |
| Teenager mother (0 = no, 1 = yes) | .868* | .331 | −.671 |
| | (.18) | (.19) | (.24) |
| First-grade SAS: | | | |
| Underachievement (0 = adapting, 1 = maladapting) | −.034 | −.844+ | 1.085+ |
| | (.20) | (.22) | (.30) |
| Aggression (0 = adapting, 1 = maladapting) | .396 | .218 | .432 |
| | (.22) | (.23) | (.31) |
| Mother's expectation: adolescence (0 = some college, 1 = high school or less) | .608 | .647+ | −.021 |
| | (.19) | (.19) | (.23) |
| Adolescent school bonds: | | | |
| School attachment (0 = high, 1 = low) | −.066 | .801* | 1.075* |
| | (.19) | (.20) | (.24) |
| School truancy (0 = low, 1 = high) | .478 | .975* | .527 |
| | (.22) | (.20) | (.26) |
| Parental supervision rules: curfew (0 = strong, 1 = weak) | .784* | .937* | .383 |
| | (.18) | (.19) | (.25) |

NOTE.—Regression coefficients are listed above and standard errors are below in parentheses.

+ $p < .10$.
* $p < .05$.
** $p < .01$.
*** $p < .001$.

effect sizes as well as statistically significant effects may be compared across the three models. For males, none of the nonsignificant effect parameters seem to be of a magnitude to suggest the results differ because of differences in the number of males in each group.

*Females*

The sex-only females were more likely than the no-problem girls to have mothers who began childbearing as a teenager, to have mothers who did not finish high school, and to report permissive family rules about the time they were expected home on school nights (see Table 6). They did not differ on any variables that were related to their own early or adolescent school behavior. In contrast, the multiproblem girls report fewer strong school bonds and more truancy than the no-problem girls. They are also over twice as likely as the no-problem girls to report permissive rules about their curfew on school nights.

The sex-only girls also reported stronger school bonds than the multiproblem females. Otherwise, they did not differ. In terms of power considerations, the comparison of the sex-only females with the multiproblem females has less statistical power to detect differences than the other two regressions. The parameter indicating the difference in mothers' education between sex-only and multiproblem girls ( − .800) is similar in size to that effect (.870) for the comparison of the no-problem to the sex-only females; yet one is statistically significant and the other is not. This nonsignificant effect parameter suggests that the sex-only females have different family origins, not only in comparison to the no-problem females but possibly in comparison to the multiproblem females as well.

## Discussion

Two questions have guided this article: first, whether we can best understand sexual activity in the same paradigm as adolescent substance use or physical assault or whether it needs to be considered separately, and, second, whether adolescent sexual activity when it occurs in the absence of substance use or physical assault has similar antecedents and correlates as sexual activity that occurs with substance use or physical assault. Three patterns were defined based on the teenagers' repeated involvement in sexual activity, physical assault, and substance use.

For both males and females, these behaviors were intercorrelated. Frequent substance use or assault without sexual activity did not even occur frequently enough to be able to examine as a separate category. However, those who were sexually active but were not frequently involved with substance use or physical assault seemed to be an important subgroup.

The sex-only males were hardly distinguishable from the no-problem males (except for their sexual activity), while the multiproblem males were quite distinct in both their early and adolescent school behavior. While early aggression in males seems to lead to later substance use and delinquency, it does not seem to lead to later sexual activity, at least when sexual activity does not co-occur with these other behaviors. Aggression, as indicated by ratings by first-grade teachers 10 years prior to measurement of adolescent behaviors, distinguished those males involved in substance use, assault, and sexual activity from those males involved only in sexual activity.

According to a peer influence explanation, differences in these behaviors may be partially accounted for by peer associations and peer behaviors. The findings reported here, however, suggest that certain males identified as early as first grade are at higher risk for involvement in later adolescent multiple behaviors. Early tracking, or ability grouping, in school may provide a link between these findings and those that find that adolescent peer associations are related to adolescent behaviors. That is, males rated as aggressive by their teachers in first grade may be placed in the same classrooms with each other (Kellam, 1990). They may subsequently be more likely to engage in problem behaviors both because of their behavioral response patterns and because of their peer contact with others who may have similar responses.

In contrast to the results for the sex-only males, there are distinct developmental antecedents for the sex-only females. They come from families characterized by teenage motherhood and low maternal education. Their backgrounds seem circumscribed in the opportunities that may provide alternatives to early childbearing. The multiproblem females differed in their adolescent school attachment and truancy; they did not differ in those family origins. The distinct family origins of the sex-only girls may put them at higher risk than the multiproblem girls for becoming teenage mothers themselves, while the lack of adolescent attachment to school may lead to school dropout among the multiproblem females.

The results for the multiproblem males and females seem to conform to what is suggested in the literature regarding deviant adolescents. Compared to the no-problem adolescents, they were more likely to be truant from school, they were less supervised by their parents, they reported less school attachment, and the males had a history of aggressive behavior. In contrast, sexual activity when it does not co-occur with other problem behaviors seems to have a different meaning for males and females. The sex-only females had distinct family origins from the no-problem females, while the sex-only males did not differ from the no-problem males.

The greater frequency and the greater acceptance of sexual intercourse for adolescent males in this population as well as in U.S. society may help explain these gender differences. The social constructions of these behaviors as acceptable or unacceptable, desirable or to be avoided may be an additional factor that determines whether the influences on these behaviors are shared. As suggested by both Mott and Haurin (1988) and Osgood et al. (1988), the "common origin" model may be more applicable if the behaviors under study are all considered deviant. In contexts where both teenage sexual activity and substance use are considered deviant or unconventional, the developmental origins of these behaviors may be more similar than in social contexts where one behavior is normative and the other is not. These norms may vary by the community being studied, by gender, by age, or by historical period.

Parental supervision was the only common influence examined here for problem behavior categories. The importance of parental supervision and monitoring has been emphasized in most theories of adolescent deviant behavior such as social control theory and problem behavior theory. Adolescents' perception of stricter rules was consistently associated with all patterns of problem behaviors. Whether this indicates fewer opportunities for these behaviors to occur, more parental awareness of children's behavior, more parental control over the adolescents' behavior, or more parental concern for their adolescents is not clear from these findings but needs further investigation.

The influence of teenage motherhood on the future lives of the children is underscored in this study. The sex-only females and the multiproblem males were both more likely to have mothers who started childbearing as a teenager than those in the no-problem category. Since maternal education and family structure (including mother being the only adult) were both included in the analyses, the impact of teenage mothering cannot be explained by the greater likelihood of single parenting in these families or the lower educational attainment of teenage mothers. Modeling, different family interaction patterns, or the greater social isolation of these families may each play a role in these results.

These analyses differ in several important ways from those of other investigators examining the linkage among various adolescent deviant behaviors. First, past studies have utilized broad nationally representative populations or diverse populations not representative of any particular community. The population for this article consists of a well-defined community population of inner-city black adolescents. Poverty, urban crowding, and being black are held constant, and variations in developmental antecedents and outcomes are the focus (Kellam & Ensminger, 1980; Kellam, 1990). These results and those from several other studies have shown that sexual behavior as well as substance use and assault vary among black adolescents by early behavioral responses, family origins and supervision, and neighborhood and school characteristics (Furstenberg et al., 1987; Hogan & Kitagawa, 1985). Community-specific studies such as the one reported here are necessary complements to studies based on national probability samples. Because community epidemiological studies include defined populations and hold constant the macroscopic characteristics of the environment, they may focus more closely and carefully on the effects of family and personal circumstances than is possible using survey data from national samples.

Second, problem behaviors were defined by frequent involvement in an activity rather than initiation. This seems consistent with several longitudinal studies suggesting that negative consequences of adolescent problem behaviors are more likely to result from frequent involvement rather than experimentation (Kandel et al., 1986; Newcomb & Bentler, 1988).

Third, co-occurring patterns rather than single behaviors or those based on a latent trait factor were examined. Replication in other populations is needed to understand the patterns of co-occurrence and the origins in other adolescent populations both similar and dissimilar to that of Woodlawn. These results, based on a defined population of inner-city adolescents, indicate enough variation in the patterns of co-occurrence to examine sex only compared to sex and substance use/assault. In other populations, the patterns of co-occurrence may well differ. For example, among other adolescents the "substance use/assault only" category may occur more frequently.

By examining a profile of behaviors, both common and unique pathways to adolescent behaviors may be identified. A comparison of adolescents involved in a specific behavior such as sexual activity, substance use, or delinquency with those not involved in that specific behavior may miss important distinctions if the other behaviors are not included in the analysis. Since sexual intercourse frequently co-occurs with other adolescent behaviors such as substance use, a comparison of those who are sexually active with those not sexually active, ignoring their involvement in other behaviors, may produce findings that pertain as much to substance use as to sexual intercourse. Further, any distinct characteristics of the sex-only adolescents would not be observed.

# References

Abrahamse, A. F., Morrison, P. A., & Waite, L. J. (1988). *Beyond stereotypes: Who becomes a single teenage mother?* Santa Monica, CA: Rand.

Akers, R. L. (1977). *Deviant behavior: A social learning perspective*. Belmont, CA: Wadsworth.

Anthony, J. (1985). Young adult marijuana in relation to antecedent misbehaviors. In L. Harris (Ed.), *Problems of drug dependence 1984* (pp. 238–244). NIDA Research Monograph No. 55. Washington, DC: U.S. Superintendent of Documents.

Bachman, J. G., Johnston, L. D., & O'Malley, P. M. (1981). Smoking, drinking and drug use among American high school students: Correlates and trends. *American Journal of Public Health, 71*, 59–68.

Cernkovich, A., & Giordano, C. (1979). A comparative analysis of male and female delinquency. *Sociological Quarterly, 20*, 131–145.

Cloward, R. A., & Ohlin, L. E. (1960). *Delinquency and opportunity*. New York: Free Press.

Conger, J. J., & Miller, N. C. (1966). *Personality, social class and delinquency*. New York: Wiley.

Donovan, J. E., & Jessor, R. (1985). Structure of problem behavior in adolescence and young adulthood. *Journal of Consulting and Clinical Psychology, 53*, 890–904.

Dornbusch, S. M., Carlsmith, J.M., Bushwall, S. J.,

Ritter, P.L., Leiderman, H., Hastorf, A. H., & Gross, R. T. (1985). Single parents, extended households, and the control of adolescents. *Child Development, 56*, 326–341.

Ensminger, M. E. (1987). Adolescent sexual behavior as it relates to other transition behaviors in youth. In S. L. Hofferth & C. D. Hayes (Eds.), *Risking the future* (Vol. 2, pp. 36–55). Washington, DC: National Academy Press.

Ensminger, M. E., Brown, C. H., & Kellam, S. G. (1982). Sex differences in antecedents of substance use among adolescents. *Journal of Social Issues, 38*, 25–42.

Ensminger, M. E., Kellam, S. G., & Rubin, B. R. (1983). School and family origins of delinquency: Comparisons by sex. In K. T. Van Dusen & S. Mednick (Eds.), *Prospective studies of crime and delinquency* (pp. 73–97). Boston: Kluwer Nijhoff.

Farrington, D. P. (1978). The family backgrounds of aggressive youths. In L. A. Hessor, M. Berger, & D. Shaffer (Eds.), *Aggression and antisocial behavior in childhood and adolescence* (pp. 73–93). Oxford: Pergamon.

Fox, G. L. (1981). The family's role in adolescent sexual behavior. In T. Ooms (Ed.), *Teenage pregnancy in a family context* (pp. 73–130). Philadelphia: Temple University Press.

Furstenberg, F. F., Jr., Brooks-Gunn, J., & Morgan, S. P. (1987). *Adolescent mothers and their children in later life*. New York: Cambridge University Press.

Gold, M. (1970). *Delinquent behavior in an American city*. Belmont, CA: Brooks/Cole.

Hindelang, M. J., Hirschi, T. N., & Weis, J. G. (1981). *Measuring delinquency*. Beverly Hills, CA: Sage.

Hirschi, T. (1969). *Causes of delinquency*. Berkeley: University of California.

Hofferth, S. L., & Moore, K. A. (1979). Early childbearing and later economic well-being. *American Sociological Review, 44*, 784–815.

Hogan, D. P., & Kitagawa, E. (1985). The impact of social status, family structure, and neighborhood on the fertility of black adolescents. *American Journal of Sociology, 90*, 825–855.

Huba, G. J., Wingard, J. A., & Bentler, P. M. (1981). A comparison of two latent variable causal models for adolescent drug use. *Journal of Personality and Social Psychology, 40*, 180–193.

Inazu, J. K., & Fox, G. L. (1980). Maternal influence on the sexual behavior of teenage daughters. *Journal of Family Issues, 1*, 81–102.

Jessor, R. L. (1987). Problem-behavior theory, psychosocial development, and adolescent problem drinking. *British Journal of Addiction, 82*, 331–342.

Jessor, R. L., & Jessor, S. L. (1977). *Problem behavior and psychological development: A longitu-*

*dinal study of youth*. New York: Academic Press.

Johnston, L. (1973). *Drugs and American youth*. Ann Arbor, MI: Institute for Social Research.

Kandel, D. B. (1975). Stages in adolescent involvement in drug use. *Science*, 190, 912–914.

Kandel, D. B. (1980). Drug and drinking behavior among youth. *Annual Review of Sociology*, 6, 235–285.

Kandel, D. B., Davies, M., Karus, D., & Yamaguchi, K. (1986). The consequences in young adulthood of adolescent drug involvement. *Archives of General Psychiatry*, 43, 746–754.

Kandel, D. B., Kessler, R. C., & Margulies, R. Z. (1978). Antecedents of adolescent initiation into stages of drug use: A developmental analysis. In D. B. Kandel (Ed.), *Longitudinal research on drug use* (pp. 73–99). New York: Wiley.

Kaplan, H. B. (1975). *Self-attitudes and deviant behavior*. Pacific Palisades, CA: Goodyear.

Kellam, S. G. (1990). Developmental epidemiological framework for family research on depression and aggression. In G. R. Patterson (Ed.), *Depression and aggression in family interaction.* (pp. 11–48). Hillsdale, NJ: Erlbaum.

Kellam, S. G., Adams, R. G., Brown, C. H., & Ensminger, M. E. (1982). The long-term evolution of the family structure of teenage and older mothers. *Journal of Marriage and the Family*, 44, 539–554.

Kellam, S. G., Branch, J. D., Agrawal, K. C., & Ensminger, M. E. (1975). *Mental health and going to school: The Woodlawn program of assessment, early intervention, and evaluation*. Chicago: University of Chicago Press.

Kellam, S. G., Brown, C. H., Rubin, B. R., & Ensminger, M. E. (1983). Paths leading to teenage psychiatric symptoms and substance use: Developmental epidemiological studies in Woodlawn. In S. B. Guze, F. J. Earls, & J. E. Barrett (Eds.), *Childhood psychopathology and development* (pp. 17–51). New York: Raven.

Kellam, S. G., & Ensminger, M. E. (1980). Theory and method in child psychiatric epidemiology. In F. Earls (Ed.), *Studying children epidemiologically* (Vol. 1, pp. 145–180). International Monograph Series in Psychosocial Epidemiology. New York: Neal Watson Academic Publishers.

Kellam, S. G., Ensminger, M. E., & Simon, M. B. (1980). Mental health in first grade and teenage drug, alcohol, and cigarette use. *Drug and Alcohol Dependence*, 5, 273–304.

Kellam, S. G., Ensminger, M. E., & Turner, R. J. (1977). Family structure and the mental health of children: Concurrent and longitudinal community wide studies. *Archives of General Psychiatry*, 34, 1012–1022.

Lefkowitz, M. M., Eron, L. D., Walden, L. O., & Huesman, R. R. (1977). *Growing up to be violent: A longitudinal study of the development of aggression*. New York: Pergamon.

Loeber, R., & Loeber, M. S. (1986). Family factors as correlates and predictors of juvenile conduct problems and delinquency. In M. Tonry & N. Morris (Eds.), *Crime and justice* (Vol. 7, pp. 29–149). Chicago: University of Chicago Press.

McCord, J. (1981). Alcoholism and criminality: Confounding and differentiating factors. *Journal of Studies on Alcohol*, 42, 739–749.

McCord, J. (1983). A longitudinal study of aggression and antisocial behavior. In K. T. Van Dusen & S. A. Mednick (Eds.), *Prospective studies of crime and delinquency* (pp. 269–275). Boston: Kluwer-Nijhoff.

Miller, P. Y., & Simon, W. (1974). Adolescent sexual behavior: Context and change. *Social Problems*, 22, 58–76.

Mitchell, S., & Rosa, P. (1981). Boyhood behaviour problems as precursors of criminality: A fifteen-year follow-up study. *Journal of Child Psychology and Psychiatry*, 22, 19–33.

Moore, K. A., Wenk, D., Hofferth, S. L., & Hayes, C. D. (1987). Trends in adolescent sexual and fertility behavior. In S. L. Hofferth & C. D. Hayes (Eds.), *Risking the future* (Vol. 2, pp. 353–503). Washington, DC: National Academy Press.

Mott, F. L., & Haurin, R. J. (1988). Linkages between sexual activity, and alcohol and drug use among American adolescents. *Family Planning Perspectives*, 20, 128–136.

Newcomb, M. D., & Bentler, M. D. (1988). *Consequences of adolescent drug use*. Beverly Hills, CA: Sage.

Newcomer, S. F., & Udry, J. R. (1984). Mothers' influence on the sexual behavior of their teenage children. *Journal of Marriage and the Family*, 46, 477–485.

Osgood, D. W., Johnston, L. D., O'Malley, P. M., & Bachman, J. G. (1988). The generality of deviance in late adolescence and early adulthood. *American Sociological Review*, 53, 81–93.

Patterson, G. R. (1982). *Coercive family processes*. Eugene, OR: Castalia.

Petersen, A. C., & Kellam, S. G. (1977). Measurement of the psychological well-being of adolescents: The psychometric properties and assessment procedures of the How I Feel. *Journal of Youth and Adolescence*, 6, 229–247.

Robins, L. N. (1978). Sturdy childhood predictors of adult antisocial behavior: Replications from longitudinal studies. *Psychological Medicine*, 8, 611–622.

Robins, L. N., & Wish, E. (1977). Childhood deviance as a developmental process: A study of 223 urban black men from birth to 18. *Social Forces*, **56**, 448–471.

Wilson, H. (1980). Parental supervision: A neglected aspect of delinquency. *British Journal of Criminology*, **20**, 203–235.

Wilson, W. J. (1982). *Urban poverty, social dislocations, and public policy.* Paper presented at the Conference on the Future of Our City, University of Chicago.

Windle, M., Barnes, G. M., & Welte, J. (1989). Causal models of adolescent substance use: An examination of gender differences using distribution-free estimators. *Journal of Personality and Social Psychology*, **56**, 132–142.

Yamaguchi, K., & Kandel, D. B. (1984). Patterns of drug use from adolescence to young adulthood: II. Sequence of progression. *American Journal of Public Health*, **74**, 688–672.

Zabin, L. S., Hardy, J. B., Smith, E. A., & Hirsch, M. B. (1986). Substance use and its relation to sexual activity among inner-city adolescents. *Journal of Adolescent Health Care*, **7**, 320–331.

Zelnick, M., Kantner, J. F., & Ford, K. (1981). *Sex and pregnancy in adolescence.* Beverly Hills, CA: Sage.

JOURNAL OF RESEARCH ON ADOLESCENCE, 5(4), 469–487
Copyright © 1995, Lawrence Erlbaum Associates, Inc.

# Age Differences in Parent and Peer Influences on Female Sexual Behavior

Dominique Treboux
*State University of New York at Stony Brook*

Nancy A. Busch-Rossnagel
*Fordham University*

The aim of this study was to develop and test a model of the influence of parents and friends on adolescent female sexual behavior that would integrate age-related changes in these influences. Self-report measures assessing discussion of sexual topics with parents and friends, perceived approval of sexual behavior, sexual attitudes, and sexual behavior were administered to 267 high-school and college-aged female subjects. As expected, results suggested that the influence of friends and parents varied as a function of the age of the adolescent. The effects of discussion with mother and parental approval on sexual behavior operated indirectly through sexual attitudes, with the effect of discussion with mother being the strongest in the 9th and 10th grade. The indirect influence of friends' approval on sexual behavior via sexual attitudes varied across the three age groups, peaking in 11th–12th grades; the direct effect of friends' approval on sexual behavior peaked in the college sample.

Many disciplines, such as family sociology, demography, and social psychology, have studied adolescent sexuality and identified parents and peers as important influences on sexual behavior. However, there has been a dearth of models that integrate these findings with knowl-

Requests for reprints should be sent to Dominique Treboux, Department of Psychology, State University of New York, Stony Brook, NY 11794–2500.

165

edge of age-related changes in the social network of adolescents. Yet, identification of age or of developmental differences has implications for the creation or implementation of developmentally appropriate sexuality programs (e.g., adolescent pregnancy prevention programs, sex education) as well as the understanding of adolescent sexuality (Crockett & Chopak, 1993; Koch, 1993; Treboux & Busch-Rossnagel, 1991).

The primary purpose of this study was to apply a developmental orientation (with its emphasis on age-related changes) to the research literature on adolescent sexual behavior. As such, we first present a theoretical basis for understanding developmental changes in parent and peer influences on adolescent behavior. Second, we propose a model of parent and peer influences on adolescent sexual behavior that provides the context for testing age-related questions regarding those influences. Finally, we identify the age differences that we expect in the paths of influence.

## THEORETICAL BASIS FOR AGE-RELATED CHANGES IN PARENT AND PEER INFLUENCES ON ADOLESCENT BEHAVIOR

During the adolescent period the emergence of sexuality does not occur within a void; rather, it develops in the context of other developmental tasks of adolescence, such as the establishment of identity, the development of autonomy, and the formation of intimate relationships (Havighurst, 1972). In dealing with these tasks, adolescents tend to rely on their parents and peers at different times and to different extents. Douvan and Adelson (1966) argued that the influence of parents and peers on behavior will differ as a function of the age of the adolescent. According to these researchers, young adolescents are still emotionally dependent on their parents and conform to parental values, whereas middle adolescents substitute a dependency on peers for their emotional dependency on parents and tend to conform to their peers' attitudes and behaviors. By late adolescence, individuals are less dependent on both parents and peers to guide their attitudes and behaviors and are more self-directed.

Empirical research has supported the theoretical formulations postulated by Douvan and Adelson (1966): Conformity to peers tends to peak between 9th and 10th grades and autonomy from parents tends to increase during the adolescent years (Berndt, 1979; Steinberg & Silverberg, 1986). Perceived controlling behavior (e.g., degree of strictness) of parents tends to decrease during the high school years (Jessor

& Jessor, 1977), whereas perceived controlling behavior of friends seems to peak during the middle of the high school years and to decrease thereafter (Hunter & Youniss, 1982).

The findings from Jessor and Jessor's (1975, 1977) longitudinal study of adolescent problem behavior suggested that the developmental formulations proposed by Douvan and Adelson (1966) can be applied to adolescent sexual behavior. Adolescents perceived more approval for engaging in sexual behavior from their parents and their peers as they got older. In turn, virgins were more likely than nonvirgins to perceive their parents and friends as disapproving of sexual behavior. Nonvirgins, as well as virgins who became sexually active in the year following initial assessment, stressed the importance of independence and loosened their ties to the family in favor of a greater dependency on friends. However, Jessor and Jessor (1975, 1977) did not identify the paths of influence among variables such as attitudes (e.g., perceived attitudes of parents and friends) and behaviors (e.g., sexual behavior). Causal models allow researchers to test hypothesized models of both direct and indirect effects among dependent, intervening, and independent variables (Biddle & Marlin, 1987), thereby facilitating a greater understanding of the processes involved in development. We sought to enhance such understanding by testing such a model in this study.

## SPECIFICATION OF THE MODEL USED TO TEST FOR AGE DIFFERENCES IN PARENT AND PEER INFLUENCES ON ADOLESCENT SEXUAL BEHAVIOR

To examine age differences in parent and peer influences, we first developed a general model of the paths of influence, one which allowed us to test for age differences in the paths. The model is based on a socialization paradigm of sexuality, one that views sexual behavior as learned rather than internally driven (Miller & Fox, 1987), identifies parents and peers as significant socialization agents, and emphasizes the role of communication and perceived attitudes of others. Specifically, the model proposes that discussion with parents and peers about sexual topics and perceived parental and peer approval of sexual behavior influence sexual behaviors directly and indirectly through the sexual attitudes of the adolescent; this model is presented in Figure 1.

In support of the direct effects of parent and peer influences (communication and approval), several studies have found that the amount of parental communication about sex tends to delay or prevent an adolescent's sexual activity (Fox, 1981; Lewis, 1973). When friends are

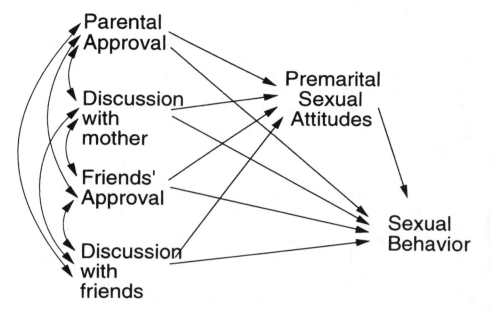

FIGURE 1 Hypothesized model of the relationships among parent and peer variables, sexual attitudes, and sexual behavior.

the primary source of sexual information, adolescents tend to report higher levels of sexual involvement (DeLamater & MacCorquodale, 1979; Lewis, 1973; Spanier, 1977). Given that communication with parents is unrelated to parental sexual attitudes (Fisher, 1986a, 1986b), we did not expect our exogenous variables to be related.

Previous studies also indicated that attitudes of others have a direct effect on adolescent sexual behavior. Adolescents who perceive less disapproval for engaging in premarital sexual behavior from parents or peers are more likely to engage in premarital intercourse (Jessor & Jessor, 1977; Thomson, 1982) and female adolescents are more likely to make the transition to nonvirginity if their best friends are sexually active than if their best friends are not active (Billy & Udry, 1985).

A substantial body of literature supports a strong association between sexual attitudes—conceptualized as the acceptability of certain sexual behaviors (Reiss, 1967)—and sexual behavior in both high school and college samples (DeLamater & MacCorquodale, 1979; Jorgensen & Sonstegard, 1984; McCormick, Izzo, & Folcik, 1985; Reiss, 1967); this literature lends support to the path between attitudes and behavior.

Finally, the paths between parent and peer variables and attitudes are supported by studies that have found a strong association between sexual attitudes and parental attitudes (DeLamater & MacCorquodale, 1979; Shah & Zelnik, 1981) and, similarly, between sexual attitudes and attitudes of friends (Reiss, 1967; Shah & Zelnik, 1981). Fisher (1986a) found that similarity between parent and child sexual attitudes was high in early adolescence and low in middle adolescence. Similarity to parental views is associated with less permissive sexual attitudes and behavior (Shah & Zelnik, 1981) and similarity to friends' attitudes is associated with more permissive attitudes (Reiss, 1967; Shah & Zelnik, 1981) as well as with more frequent sexual intercourse (Shah & Zelnik, 1981).

## AGE DIFFERENCES IN PARENT–PEER INFLUENCES ON ADOLESCENT SEXUAL BEHAVIOR

We believe that the utility of this model is that it serves as a tool for testing age differences in the paths of influence on sexual behavior. Within the model, the influence of parents and peers on adolescent sexual behavior was hypothesized to vary as a function of the age of the adolescent.[1] Specifically, parents' influence was expected to decline over the adolescent years, whereas friends' influence was expected to increase. In other words, we expected that discussions with parents and parental approval would have their greatest impact on the sexual behavior of young adolescents, exerting influence either directly on sexual behavior or indirectly through their impact on sexual attitudes. Conversely, effects of discussion with friends and friends' approval on sexual behavior (direct or indirect effects) were expected to be the strongest in middle adolescence. The influence of both parents and peers was expected to decline in late adolescence.

## METHOD

### Sample

Participants were part of a larger sample recruited for a project on adolescent sexuality (Treboux, 1989). Participants were recruited from two high schools in New Jersey and from two colleges in New York.

---

[1]There are no conventions for showing the expected age differences in the magnitude of the paths of influence, so these are not visually portrayed in the figure.

Given that research and theory have suggested that there is a differential influence of friends on male and female behavior (Billy & Udry, 1985; Billy, Rodgers, & Udry, 1984; Douvan & Adelson, 1966; Treboux & Busch-Rossnagel, 1990) and that our male sample size was too small to test for sex differences in the model, only female subjects were included in the study. Only participants with complete data were included in the analyses.

The sample was composed of 55 ninth and tenth graders (mean age = 15.2 years, $SD$ = .6), 120 eleventh and twelfth graders (mean age = 17.3 years , $SD$ = .7), and 88 college students (mean age = 19.8 years, $SD$ = 1.4). Eighty-five percent of the participants were White, and 73% were living with both parents. Using Hollingshead's (1975) ratings, the median occupational status of the parents was 6 (i.e., technician, semi-professional, or small business owner) for mothers and 7 (i.e., manager, minor professional, entertainer, or artist) for fathers. In terms of religious affiliation, 49% of the high school students and 82% of the college students identified themselves as Catholic. Approximately 75% of the high school students were planning to attend college following graduation.

Fifty-three percent of the girls in this sample were nonvirgins, a figure consistent with the 1988 National Surveys of Family Growth, which reported that 53.2% of girls between the ages of 15 and 19 are nonvirgins (Forrest & Singh, 1990). The percentage of nonvirgins at each grade was: 19% of 9th and 10th graders; 59% of 11th and 12th graders; and 66% of college students. The overall mean for age at first intercourse was 16 years ($SD$ = 1.7) and the average number of times sexually active female subjects engaged in sexual intercourse in the preceding month was 3.4 times ($SD$ = 3.1).

**Measures**

To operationalize the constructs in the model, minor changes were made to existing measures. Internal consistencies are reported for the total female sample. To obtain estimates of test–retest reliabilities on the scales, 58 college students completed the questionnaires two weeks after the initial testing.

The Parental Approval of Sexual Behavior Scale (PASB) and the Friends' Approval of Sexual Behavior Scale (FrASB) measure adolescents' perceptions of their parents' and friends' approval of respondents engaging in four behaviors (kissing, light petting, heavy petting, and sexual intercourse) at four levels of relationship involvement (someone with whom they had gone out once or twice, someone with whom they were going steady, someone with whom they were in love, and someone whom they were planning to marry). A sample item of the PASB and FrASB is "If you engaged in heavy petting with someone you're in love with, what reaction would you expect from the following if they knew about it?" The wording of the scale, including responses, was based on the Parental Approval of Problem Behavior Scale (Jessor & Jessor, 1977), whereas the levels of relationship involvement were based on the Premarital Permissiveness Scale (Thomson, 1982).

Below each of the 16 questions, each referent (mother, father, and friends) was listed and responses were reported on a 4-point Likert scale ranging from 1 (would strongly disapprove) to 4 (would approve). Scores were given separately for mothers, fathers, and friends. A summary parental approval score was used, given the high correlation between mothers' approval scores and fathers' approval scores, $r(249)$ = .84.[2] Total Parental Approval scores ranged from 32 (strong disapproval) to 128 (approval). Of the 27% of the participants who did not live with both parents, 22% (mother absence, $n = 3$; father absence, $n = 13$) had missing data for one parent, indicating that they did not know how the absent parent would feel about their sexual behavior. For these participants, the total scale score for the present parent was doubled. The PASB yielded a coefficient alpha of .95 and a test–retest reliability coefficient of .82.

FrASB scores ranged from 16 to 64. The FrASB had a coefficient alpha of .90 and a test–retest reliability coefficient of .81.

The Discussion of Sexual Topics Checklist was used to measure the number of sexual topics adolescents discussed with their mothers. Adapted from the Sex Education Inventory (Bennett & Dickinson, 1980), the checklist differed in terms of the number of topics listed; instead of the general topic of birth control, specific methods of birth control were listed (e.g., condoms, birth control pill). The checklist required respondents to indicate which of the 17 topics listed (e.g., pregnancy, "how far to go" on a date) had been discussed with their parents. Three categories were included: topics discussed with mother, topics discussed with father, and topics discussed with both parents. To score discussion with mother, any topic that indicated discussion with mother or with both parents was given a score of 1. Discussion of sexual topics with mother scores (DST-Mother) ranged from 0 to 17. The DST-Mother coefficient alpha was .91 and the test–retest reliability coefficient was .82.

---

[2] There were mean differences between perceived mother ($M$ = 39.57, $SD$ = 8.85) and father ($M$ = 37.28, $SD$ = 9.05) approval scores, $t(262)$ = 7.19, $p < .001$.

The Discussion of Sexual Topics with Friends (DSTFR) Checklist assessed the number of sexual topics adolescents discussed with their friends. Identical to the DST-Mother, the DSTFR required respondents to indicate which of the 17 topics listed had been discussed with their friends. The coefficient alpha for the DSTFR was .90 in this sample, and the test–retest reliability coefficient was .88.

The Premarital Sexual Attitudes Scale (PSAS), a 16-item scale, measured adolescents' personal acceptance of four sexual behaviors (kissing, light petting, heavy petting, and sexual intercourse) at four levels of relationship involvement (someone with whom they had gone out with once or twice, someone with whom they were going steady, someone with whom they were in love, and someone whom they were planning to marry). Based on Reiss's (1967) Premarital Sexual Permissiveness Scale, the PSAS was modified by increasing the number of sexual behaviors and by changing the referent to the self, a method used by Herold (1981) to measure premarital sexual attitudes. Scoring of the PSAS was based on a 5-point Likert-type scale ranging from 1 (*strongly disagree*) to 5 (*strongly agree*). Responses were summed to provide the total sexual permissiveness score, which ranged from 16 (less permissive sexual attitudes) to 80 (highly permissive sexual attitudes). The PSAS yielded a coefficient alpha of .89; the test–retest reliability coefficient was .68.

The Sexual Behavior Inventory (SBI) measured heterosexual involvement in the past two years. Respondents indicated the frequency of each of four types of sexual behavior (tongue kissing, light petting, heavy petting, and sexual intercourse) on a 4-point Likert-type scale ranging from 1 (*never*) to 4 (*frequently*). The SBI was based on the Sexual Experience Inventory developed by Bennett (1984). At the request of the schools, changes from the original scale included the omission of explanations that accompanied light and heavy petting.[3]

The original scoring procedure was modified so that responses could be weighted. First, a score of zero was given to all never responses. To assign more weight to light petting than to kissing, to heavy petting than to light petting, and to intercourse than to heavy petting, the following scores were assigned: kissing was scored as 1, 2, and 3 for once or twice, sometimes, and frequently, respectively; light petting was scored as 4, 5 and 6; heavy petting as 7, 8, and 9; and sexual intercourse as 19, 20, and 21. The scores of the four items were summed to yield the total sexual behavior score. Thus, a respondent who en-

---

[3]"Going all the way" was included as a descriptor of sexual intercourse. Consistent with the original measure, the SBI was intended to measure sexual behaviors that were voluntary and heterosexual; however, this intent was not made explicit.

gaged frequently in kissing, light petting, and heavy petting—but never in sexual intercourse—received a score of 18, whereas the non-virgin respondent received a minimum score of 19. Total sexual behavior scores ranged from 0 to 39 and yielded a test–retest reliability coefficient of .91.

## Procedure

Participating high schools assumed responsibility for obtaining informed consent from both parents and students. Eighty-seven percent of the high school students enrolled in the health classes in which the questionnaires were administered participated in the study. Sixty-two percent of the college students were recruited through the subject pool of one college; the remaining participants were recruited through psychology classes. All adolescents were told that they were participating in a study of adolescent and young adult sexuality and would be answering a number of questions about their sexual behaviors and attitudes. The types of questions to be asked were explained (e.g., "a number of questions ask about how your parents and friends would react if you engaged in certain behaviors"). Questionnaires were administered in small groups. To insure confidentiality of responses and to control for order effects, the order of the scales was counterbalanced in a Latin square design.

## RESULTS

The focus of the analyses was on determining age differences in the paths of influence from parents and peers to sexual behavior. However, in Appendix A, we present means and standard deviations of scores on parent and peer scales and on behavior scales and results from analyses of variance (ANOVAs) to provide information regarding age differences in the level of parent and peer approval of sexual behavior and in discussion of sexual topics. In turn, to test our age-related hypothesis, we used structural equation modeling; this procedure affords tests of whether a set of variables show a different pattern of interrelations at different ages or across different groups (Green, 1992). As such, the proposed model was tested separately for the three age groups to examine age differences in the influence of parents and peers throughout the adolescent years.

## Assessing the Goodness-of-Fit of the Model

The LISREL VII program (Jöreskog & Sörbom, 1989) was used to ana-lyze the goodness-of-fit of the model. LISREL estimates the unknown parameters (e.g., path coefficients) in the model. In this model, the number of parameters to be estimated equated the number of known parameters (e.g., covariance between variables); in other words, the model was just identified, so a model with fewer direct effects was tested. Given that, theoretically, a change in the influence of parents is expected to occur in early adolescence, fewer age differences in the direct effects of parent influences from midadolescence to late adoles-cence were expected; as such, the direct paths from parental approval and from discussion with mother to sexual behavior were eliminated from the model at all ages. Conversely, given that the influence of friends was hypothesized to be different across the age groups, the direct effects of friends' approval and of discussion with friends on sexual behavior were maintained in the model.

A multisample analysis was conducted to compare the goodness-of-fit of the reduced model at each age level: early (9th and 10th grades), midadolescence (11th and 12th grades), and late adolescence (college). This model was accepted in the multisample analysis, $\chi^2(6, N = 263) = 6.88, p = .33$. For 9th and 10th grade girls, the goodness-of-fit index was .98; for 11th and 12th grade girls, the goodness-of-fit index was .99; and for college women, the goodness-of-fit index was .99. These results suggest that the model provides a good fit to the data.[4]

## Assessing Age Differences in the Paths of Influence

To assess age differences, we first tested the most restrictive model, which equated the magnitude of the paths (i.e., the path coefficients in the beta and gamma matrices) across the three age groups. This model did not fit the data, $\chi^2(20, N = 263) = 37.87, p < .01$. The beta matrix reflects path coefficients between attitudes and behavior, whereas the gamma matrix reflects the path coefficients between parent and peer variables to attitudes and behavior. Because we expected age differ-ences in the gamma matrix, we tested the model that equated the path coefficients from the attitudes to sexual behavior (beta matrix) but

---

[4]The intercorrelations among variables for each age group are presented in Appendix B. To insure the appropriate use of LISREL, we tested an additional model in which the effects of the exogenous variables on sexual behavior were mediated through sexual attitudes. We conducted a multisample analysis to compare the goodness-of-fit of this model for each grade level. The results were significant, $\chi^2(12, N = 263) = 40.09, p < .001$, indicating that the indirect effects model either did not fit the data or the existence of age

allowed age differences in the path coefficients from parent and peer variables to attitudes and behavior (gamma matrix); this model was accepted, $\chi^2(8, N = 263) = 8.16$, $p = .42$. Hence, subsequent analyses fixed this path coefficient across age groups.

To examine age differences in the influence of parent and peer variables (gamma matrix), the path coefficients were equated across age groups, except for those that were expected to show age differences on an a priori basis; that is, the direct and indirect path coefficients from friends' approval to sexual behavior and from discussion with friends to sexual behavior. When the path coefficients from discussion with friends were allowed to vary, both models were rejected: for the model with the direct path coefficient from discussion with friends to sexual behavior, when allowed to vary, $\chi^2(18, N = 263) = 35.77$, $p < .01$; and for the model with the path coefficient from discussion with friends to sexual attitudes, when allowed to vary, $\chi^2(18, N = 263) = 32.64$, $p = .02$. The model with the direct path coefficient from friends' approval to sexual behavior, when allowed to vary, was rejected, $\chi^2(18, N = 263) = 32.53$, $p < .02$. Only the model with the path coefficient from friends' approval to sexual attitudes, when allowed to vary, was accepted, $\chi^2(18, N = 263) = 28.02$, $p = .06$.

These results suggest that the most appropriate model for these data include age differences in the indirect path coefficient from friends' approval through attitudes to sexual behavior. The goodness-of-fit indices were .95, .98, and .95 for the three age groups, respectively. Although these results indicate that the model provides an acceptable fit to the data, modification indices showed that the path coefficient between mother discussion and premarital sexual attitudes should be allowed to vary in the 9th- and 10th-grade group. Given that this modification was consistent with a priori expectations derived from the previously mentioned literature, a model allowing age differences in the path coefficients from friends' approval to attitudes and from discussion with mother to attitudes was tested and accepted, $\chi^2(17, N = 263) = 20.96$, $p = .23$. However, this model had a large root mean square residual for the college sample ($RMR = 41.77$) suggesting that the fit of the model could be improved. Modification indices provided a useful means for assessing what changes in the model would improve its fit to the data. The largest modification index was for the path coefficient between friends' approval and sexual behavior in the college sample; because age differences in this influence were consistent with our a priori expectations, we decided to free it. Thus, a final model was tested and accepted, $\chi^2(16, N = 263) = 16.00$, $p = .45$, in which the path coefficient from (a) friends' approval to sexual attitudes was allowed to vary in all three age groups, (b) discussion with mother to sexual attitudes was allowed to vary in the 9th and 10th age group, and (c) friends' approval to sexual behavior was allowed to vary in the college sample. (See Figure 2.)

## Solutions for the Model for Each Grade Level

This model fixed the following path coefficients that were significant across the three age groups: premarital sexual attitudes that had a positive effect on sexual behavior, $\beta = .17$, $z = 4.44$, $p < .001$; parental approval of sexual behavior and discussion with friends that had positive effects on premarital sexual attitudes, $\beta = .16$, $z = 3.39$, $p < .001$ and $\beta = .18$, $z = 3.56$, $p < .001$, respectively; and discussion with friends that had a positive direct effect on sexual behavior, $\beta = .08$, $z = 3.45$, $p < .001$.

The results for the three age groups, when the path coefficients were allowed to vary, are presented separately. First, for 9th and 10th grade girls, the goodness-of-fit index was .98; the root mean square residual was 5.63. All three of the path coefficients allowed to show age differences were significant: Discussion with mother was negatively related to participant's acceptance of premarital sex, $\beta = -.25$, $z = 2.81$, $p < .01$; friends' approval of sexual behavior was positively associated with sexual attitudes, $\beta = .44$, $z = 5.61$, $p < .001$; and friends' approval had a positive effect on sexual behavior, $\beta = .07$, $z = 2.50$, $p < .01$. The last path coefficient was equated in the 9th and 10th and in the 11th and 12th grade samples. The total coefficient of determination (an index of the total variance predicted by all the equations jointly) for the 9th and 10th grade sample was .63. The squared multiple correlations for the individual equations were $R^2 = .60$ for sexual attitudes and $R^2 = .17$ for sexual behavior, indicating that the model explained more of the variance in sexual attitudes than in sexual behavior.

For 11th and 12th grade girls, results indicated that the model provided an even better fit to the data: the goodness-of-fit index was .99 and the root mean square residual was 4.00. Friends' approval had a positive direct effect on sexual attitudes, $\beta = .64$, $z = 8.16$, $p < .001$, and in the path coefficient that was fixed for 9th and 10th and for 11th and 12th grades, friends' approval had a positive effect on sexual behavior, $\beta = .07$, $z = 2.50$, $p < .01$. The path coefficient between discussion with mother and sexual attitudes that was fixed for 11th and 12th graders and the college sample was not significant. The total coefficient of determination for the 11th and 12th grade sample was .54. The squared multiple correlations for the individual equations were $R^2 = .52$ for sexual attitudes and $R^2 = .10$ for sexual behavior.

For college women, the goodness-of-fit index for the model was .97 and the root mean square residual was 22.74. Friends' approval of

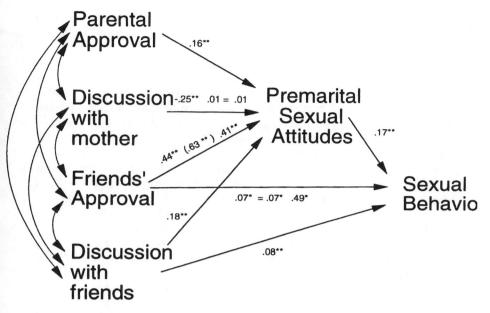

FIGURE 2  Solutions for the model for all three grade levels. Paths with significant age differ-ences have three coefficients, which refer to the 9th and 10th grade, 11th and 12th grade, and college age samples respectively. Path coefficients that were fixed across the age groups are indicated by an equal sign. *p < .01. ** p < .001.

sexual behavior had both a direct positive effect on sexual behavior, $\beta$ = .49, z = 2.61, p < .01, and an indirect effect on sexual behavior via sexual attitudes, $\beta$ = .41, z = 4.27, p < .001. The total coefficient of determination for the college sample was .41. The squared multiple correlations for the individual equations were $R^2$ = .51 for sexual attitudes and $R^2$ = .08 for sexual behavior.

## DISCUSSION

The aim of this study was to develop and test a model of the influence of parents and friends on adolescent sexual behavior that would inte-grate age-related changes in these influences. As expected, results sug-gested that the influence of friends and parents varied as a function of the age of the adolescent. The effects of discussion with parents and parental approval on sexual behavior operated indirectly through sex-ual attitudes with the effect of discussion with mother being the strongest in the 9th and 10th grades. The indirect influence of friends' approval on sexual behavior via sexual attitudes varied across the three age groups, apparently peaking in 11th and 12th grades, whereas the direct effect of friends' approval on sexual behavior seemed to peak in the college sample.

Consistent with the expectation that parents would exert most of their influence in early adolescence, we found that the importance of discussing sexual topics with mothers appears to peak in 9th and 10th grades, at which time it has a negative effect on sexual attitudes. These findings indicate that young adolescent girls are using their mothers as sources of information; whether these discussions are initiated by mother or daughter is unclear. However, the information conveyed is important for this age group because it affects their views on engaging in premarital sex. In a similar vein, Fisher (1986a) found that the sexual attitudes of young adolescents and parents were highly correlated when parent–child communication was high; but the attitudes were not related when the parent–child communication was low.

However, the influence of mothers does not remain stable across adolescence. In our study, the amount of discussion with mother had no effect on sexual attitudes in the later age groups. Similarly, Fisher (1986b) found that, regardless of the amount of discussion taking place, middle adolescents' attitudes bore no similarity to mothers' attitudes. Conversations with mothers tend to center around issues of reproduction (Fox, 1980; Thornburg, 1981); mothers' attitudes tend not to favor premarital intercourse, which may not be consistent with the needs of middle adolescents who are presumably thinking about engaging in or actually engaging in sexual intercourse.

Why do mothers lose their influence in the later age groups? Douvan and Adelson (1966) suggested that friends replace mothers in this area; our findings support this hypothesis. The influence of friends operated in two ways: Indirectly through its effect on sexual attitudes and directly on sexual behavior. The indirect effect of perceptions of friends' approval seemed to peak in 11th and 12th grades. We had also expected that, by late adolescence, individuals would be less susceptible to peer influence; but our findings suggest that the direct influence of peers is actually stronger in college than in the younger age groups.

Presumably, there are two ways in which adolescents appraise their friends' approval of their sexual behavior. One avenue is through asking their friends' opinions and advice regarding their behaviors or relationships (e.g., discussing "how far to go" on a date). Evidence for this avenue of peer influence comes from our finding of differences in mean level of discussion with friends from early to late adolescence (see Appendix A). The significant increase suggests that friends are replacing mothers in middle to late adolescence. Another avenue for friends' influence is through observing friends' behavior. Thus, if one's friends are engaging in sexual intercourse, one may assume that they would approve of one engaging in similar behavior. Most of the college students in our sample were living in dormitories, making their friends' behaviors easily observable; this situation may explain why the direct effect of friends' attitudes on behavior seemed to peak in college. Moreover, in the college years, late adolescents are forming new friendships and are possibly choosing friends whose behaviors or attitudes are consistent with their own; this could result in a greater effect of friends' influence.

The power of the model in explaining sexual behavior was considerably less than was the case for sexual attitudes. Over 50% of the variance in sexual attitudes was explained at each grade level. The amount of variance in sexual behavior that was accounted for ranged from 17% in the youngest sample to 8% in the college-age sample, findings consistent with the results of Jorgenson and Sonstegard (1984). The relation between sexual attitudes and behavior may be weak in all three groups because adolescents may not have had the opportunity to engage in sexual behaviors (e.g., never being in a serious relationship). Moreover, endorsing attitudes without engaging in behaviors consistent with those attitudes may provide the adolescent with an arena for exploring one's sexuality without dealing with the consequences of those behaviors. For example, a young girl may see herself as a "free spirit" and endorse "free love" attitudes but not engage in premarital sex. As such, she can test the reactions of parents and peers and see what being permissive entails without having to deal with the more negative potential consequences of engaging in the behaviors (e.g., pregnancy, a "bad" reputation, or AIDS). In fact, just solely on her age, she may expect to encounter different reactions regarding appropriate sexual behavior (Spreecher, McKinney, Walsh, & Anderson, 1988).

Our findings also suggest that other variables may be operating to influence sexual behavior. Hence, future research with the model should include additional influences on sexual behavior, such as characteristics of the dyadic relationship in terms of time in the relationship, commitment to the relationship, and relationship satisfaction (Christopher'& Cate, 1985; Herold & McNamee, 1982; Jorgensen, King, & Torrey, 1980). Other variables of interest include partner's sexual attitudes and parental and peer approval of partner's behaviors. Within a developmental context, a study is needed that examines couples throughout the adolescent years in order to disentangle effects from parent, peer, and partner influences. One might expect that, over time, a couple takes on an identity of its own, one that overrides the pressures associated with parent and peer approval.

In addition to including the influences from the partner, research should examine whether it is appropriate to select a college sample as representative of late adolescents. In this study, 75% of the high school sample were expecting to attend college, suggesting a continuity in sample characteristics between the high school and the college samples. However, the question remains whether these findings are generalizable to noncollege late adolescents.

Another limitation of this study is that the religious backgrounds of the high school and the college samples differed, with the college samples reporting a greater proportion of Catholics. Affiliation to Catholicism in itself is not an accurate predictor of sexual behavior. One study of sexual behavior with adolescents conducted by Devaney and Hubley (Hayes, 1987) found no differences between Catholics and those from other denominations in the likelihood of reporting sexual activity. It should be noted, however, that religiosity in terms of strength of beliefs and practice has been found to have a restraining effect on sexual activity (DeLamater & MacCorquodale, 1979; Hayes, 1987; Zelnik, Kantner, & Ford, 1981). Thus, if the college students were more religious, age differences in attitudes and behavior may have been masked because participants tend to endorse more conservative sexual attitudes and behavior.

Our findings suggest the utility of a developmental approach to understanding adolescent sexual behavior, an approach recently advocated by others (Crockett & Chopak, 1993; Koch, 1993). Future research should take into account the possibility of differences in the meaning of sexuality to adolescents of various ages as well as in the predictors of sexual behavior for the different ages within adolescence. There is a paramount need for longitudinal research in this area if we are to understand fully the development of sexual behavior and sexual decision-making.

## ACKNOWLEDGMENTS

These data were collected as part of Dominique Treboux's dissertation submitted to Fordham University and were presented at the Society for Research on Adolescence conference, Atlanta, GA, in March, 1990.

We thank Richard Lerner and anonymous reviewers for their insightful and provocative comments and suggestions. We gratefully acknowledge the assistance of Larry DeCarlo in the LISREL analyses. We also thank the principals, parents, and students who agreed to participate in this study.

# REFERENCES

Bennett, S. M. (1984). Family environment for sexual learning as a function of father's involvement in family, work and discipline. *Adolescence, 19*, 609–627.

Bennett, S. M., & Dickinson, W. B. (1980). Student–parent rapport and parent involvement in sex, birth control and venereal disease education. *Journal of Sex Research, 16*, 114–130.

Berndt, T. J. (1979). Developmental changes in conformity to peers and parents. *Developmental Psychology, 15*, 608–616.

Biddle, B. J., & Marlin, M. M. (1987). Causality, confirmation, credulity, and structural equation modeling. *Child Development, 58*, 4–17.

Billy, J. O. G., Rodgers J. L., & Udry, R. J. (1984). Adolescent sexual behavior and friendship choice. *Social Forces, 62*, 653–678.

Billy, J. O. G., & Udry, J. R. (1985). The influence of male and female best friends on adolescent sexual behavior. *Adolescence, 20*, 21–32.

Christopher, S. F., & Cate, R. M. (1985). Anticipated influences on sexual decision-making for first intercourse. *Family Relations, 34*, 265–270.

Crockett, L. J., & Chopak, J. S. (1993). Pregnancy prevention in early adolescence: A developmental perspective. In R. M. Lerner (Ed.), *Early adolescence: Perspectives on research, policy and intervention* (pp. 315–333). Hillsdale, NJ: Lawrence Erlbaum Associates, Inc.

DeLamater, J., & MacCorquodale, P. (1979). *Premarital sexuality*. Madison: University of Wisconsin Press.

Douvan, E., & Adelson, J. (1966). *The adolescent experience*. New York: Wiley.

Fisher, T. D. (1986a). An exploratory study of parent–child communication about sex and the sexual attitudes of early, middle, and late adolescents. *Journal of Genetic Psychology, 147*, 543–557.

Fisher, T. D. (1986b). Parent–child communication about sex and young adolescents' sexual knowledge and attitudes. *Adolescence, 21*, 517–527.

Forrest, D. J., & Singh, S. (1990). The sexual and reproductive behavior of American women, 1982–1988. *Family Planning Perspectives, 22*, 206–214.

Fox, G. L. (1980). The mother–adolescent daughter relationship as a sexual socialization structure: A research review. *Family Relations, 29*, 21–28.

Fox, G. L. (1981). The family's role in adolescent sexual behavior. In T. Ooms (Ed.), *Teenage pregnancy in a family context* (pp. 73–130). Philadelphia: Temple University Press.

Green, J. A. (1992). Testing whether correlations matrices are different from each other. *Developmental Psychology, 28*, 215–224.

Havighurst, R. J. (1972). *Developmental tasks and education* (3rd ed.). New York: David McKay.

Hayes, C. D. (Ed.). (1987). *Risking the future: Adolescent sexuality, pregnancy and childbearing*. Washington, DC: National Academy Press.

Herold, E. S. (1981). Measurement issues involved in examining contraceptive use among young single women. *Population and Environment, 4*, 128–144.

Herold, E. S., & McNamee, J. E. (1982). An explanatory model of contraceptive use among young single women. *Journal of Sex Research, 18*, 289–304.

Hollingshead, A. B. (1975). *Four factor index of social status*. (Available from A B. Hollingshead, P.O. Box 1965, Yale Station, New Haven, Connecticut 06520)

Hunter, F. T., & Youniss, J. (1982). Changes in functions of three relations during adolescence. *Developmental Psychology, 18*, 806–811.

Jessor, R., & Jessor, S. L. (1975). Transition from virginity to non-virginity among youth: A social–psychological study over time. *Developmental Psychology, 11,* 473–484.

Jessor, R., & Jessor, S. L. (1977). *Problem behavior and psychological development.* New York: Academic.

Jöreskog, K. G., & Sörbom, D. (1989). *LISREL VII: A guide to the program and its applications.* Chicago, IL: SPSS, Inc.

Jorgensen, S. R., King, S. L., & Torrey, B. A. (1980). Dyadic and social network influences on adolescent exposure to pregnancy risk. *Journal of Marriage and the Family, 42,* 141–155.

Jorgensen, S. R., & Sonstegard, J. S. (1984). Predicting adolescent sexual and contraceptive behavior: An application of the Fishbein model. *Journal of Marriage and the Family, 46,* 43–55.

Koch, B. P. (1993). Promoting healthy sexual development during early adolescence. In R. M. Lerner (Ed.), *Early adolescence: Perspectives on research, policy and intervention* (pp. 293–307). Hillsdale, NJ: Lawrence Erlbaum Associates, Inc.

Lewis, R. A. (1973). Parents and peers: Socialization agents in the coital behavior of young adults. *Journal of Sex Research, 9,* 156–170.

McCormick, N., Izzo, A., & Folcik, J. (1985). Adolescents' values, sexuality and contraception in rural New York County. *Adolescence, 20,* 385–395.

Miller, B. C., & Fox, G. L. (1987). Theories of adolescent sexual behavior. *Journal of Adolescent Research, 2,* 269–282.

Reiss, I. L. (1967). *The social context of premarital sexual permissiveness.* New York: Holt, Rinehart & Winston.

Shah, F., & Zelnik, M. (1981). Parent and peer influence on sexual behavior, contraceptive use and pregnancy experience. *Journal of Marriage and the Family, 43,* 339–348.

Spanier, G. B. (1977). Sources of sex information and premarital sexual behavior. *Journal of Sex Research, 13,* 73–88.

Spreecher, S., McKinney, K., Walsh, R., & Anderson, C. (1988). A revision of the Reiss Premarital Permissiveness Scale. *Journal of Marriage and the Family, 50,* 821–828.

Steinberg, L., & Silverberg, S. B. (1986). The vicissitudes of autonomy in early adolescence. *Child Development, 57,* 841–851.

Thomson, E. (1982). Socialization for sexual and contraceptive behavior: Moral absolutes versus relative consequences. *Youth and Society, 14,* 103–128.

Thornburg, H. D. (1981). Adolescent sources of information on sex. *Journal of School Health, 51,* 274–277.

Treboux, D. (1989). The relative influence of parents and peers on adolescent sexual behavior and contraceptive use as a function of age in adolescence. Unpublished doctoral dissertation, Fordham University, Bronx, New York.

Treboux, D., & Busch-Rossnagel, N. A. (1990). Social network influences on adolescent sexual attitudes and behaviors. *Journal of Adolescent Research, 5,* 175–189.

Treboux, D., & Busch-Rossnagel, N. A. (1991). Sexual behavior, sexual attitudes, and contraceptive use: Age differences in adolescence. In R. M. Lerner, A. C. Petersen, & J. Brooks-Gunn (Eds.), *Encyclopedia of adolescence* (pp. 1018–1021). New York: Garland.

Zelnik, M., Kantner, J., & Ford K. (1981). *Sex and pregnancy in adolescence.* Beverly Hills, CA: Sage.

Received January 22, 1991
Revision received July 29, 1994
Accepted August 5, 1994

APPENDIX A

Means and Standard Deviations of Scores on Parent and
Peer Scales and on Behavior Scales

| | Grade Level | | | | | |
| | 9th–10th [a] | | 11th–12th [b] | | College [c] | |
| Variable | M | SD | M | SD | M | SD |
|---|---|---|---|---|---|---|
| Discussion with mother | 8.3 | 4.0 | 7.6 | 4.3 | 7.3 | 4.2 |
| Parental approval | 74.9 | 16.4 | 77.3 | 17.3 | 77.5 | 16.7 |
| Discussion with friends | 9.3 | 4.4 | 10.0 | 4.0 | 12.3 | 2.9 |
| Friends' approval | 51.9 | 8.0 | 52.6 | 7.9 | 53.1 | 7.0 |
| Sexual attitudes | 58.1 | 8.2 | 59.9 | 11.1 | 59.4 | 7.6 |
| Sexual behavior | 13.8 | 12.9 | 26.9 | 13.8 | 27.8 | 13.6 |

*Note.* Results of 3 group, one-way ANOVAs indicated that both sexual behavior and discussion with friends differed significantly as a function of grade, $F(260) = 22.02$, $p < .001$, and $F(260) = 12.98$, $p < .001$, respectively.

[a] $n = 55$. [b] $n = 120$. [c] $n = 88$.


APPENDIX B

Intercorrelations Between Scales for 9th–10th Grade, 11th–12th Grade, and
College Students

| Variable | Discussion With Mother | Friends' Approval | Discussion With Friends | Sexual Attitudes | Sexual Behavior |
|---|---|---|---|---|---|
| 9th–10th grade students[a] | | | | | |
| Parental approval | .03 | .51*** | .08 | .47*** | .14 |
| Discussion with mother | — | −.16 | .53*** | −.22 | .13 |
| Friends' approval | | — | .18 | .73*** | .28* |
| Discussion with friends | | | — | .22 | .35** |
| Sexual attitudes | | | | — | .28* |
| Sexual behavior | | | | | — |
| 11th–12th grade students[b] | | | | | |
| Parental approval | .19** | .46*** | .10 | .42*** | .10 |
| Discussion with mother | — | .12 | .36*** | .16 | .10 |
| Friends' approval | | — | .34*** | .69*** | .24*** |
| Discussion with friends | | | — | .38*** | .28*** |
| Sexual attitudes | | | | — | .25*** |
| Sexual behavior | | | | | — |
| College students[c] | | | | | |
| Parental approval | −.02 | .46*** | .02 | .41*** | .12 |
| Discussion with mother | — | −.14 | .36*** | .02 | −.02 |
| Friends' approval | | — | .26** | .59*** | .28** |
| Discussion with friends | | | — | .31*** | .11 |
| Sexual attitudes | | | | — | .49*** |
| Sexual behavior | | | | | — |

[a] $n = 55$. [b] $n = 120$. [c] $n = 88$.

*$p < .05$. **$p < .01$. ***$p < .005$.

JOURNAL OF RESEARCH ON ADOLESCENCE, 4(3), 453–464
Copyright © 1994, Lawrence Erlbaum Associates, Inc.

# Older Adolescents and AIDS: Correlates of Self-Reported Safer Sex Practices

Helene M. Rimberg
*Virginia Consortium for Professional Psychology*

Robin J. Lewis
*Old Dominion University*

The relationship among knowledge about AIDS, sex guilt, components of the Health Belief Model (perceived barriers, benefits, severity, and susceptibility), and self-reported safer sex practices was examined in 18- and 19-year-old college students. Knowledge about AIDS was not related to self-reported safer sex practices, but self-reported safer sex practices were positively related to sex guilt. In addition, safer sex practices were inversely related to perceived barriers to practicing safe sex. Results further indicated that although the overall level of AIDS-related knowledge was adequate, some participants displayed misconceptions about the efficacy of preventive measures. Females reported more behavior change in the direction of safer sex than did males. Implications of these findings for future research and preventive programs are also discussed.

High-risk sexual behaviors and failure to use safe sex practices seem to be prevalent in the young population. Researchers (Baldwin & Baldwin, 1988; Hingson, Strunin, Berlin, & Heeven, 1990) found that adolescents engage in a number of sexual behaviors that increase the risk of contracting AIDS: multiple sexual partners, failure to use condoms, and anal intercourse. Furthermore, previous studies (Goodman &

Requests for reprints should be sent to Robin J. Lewis, Department of Psychology, Old Dominion University, Norfolk, VA 23529–0267.

Cohall, 1989; Hingson et al., 1990; Strunin & Hingson, 1987) reported that only 15% to 39% of their adolescent samples said they changed their sexual behavior due to concern about contracting AIDS. Research conducted in university settings has also failed to show encouraging results about changes in sexual behaviors (e.g., Hirschorn, 1987; Katzman, Mulholland, & Sutherland, 1988; Simkins & Eberhage, 1984; Simkins & Kushner, 1986; Thurman & Franklin, 1990).

In general, older adolescents and college students appear to be knowledgeable about AIDS (cf. Burnette, Redmon, & Poling, 1990; Edgar, Freimuth, & Hammond, 1988; Loos & Bowd, 1989; Turner, Anderson, Fitzpatrick, Fowler, & Mayon-White, 1988). However, this knowledge does not seem to be associated with safer sex behavior (Goodman & Cohall, 1989; Gray & Saracino, 1989). Gray and Saracino reported that 83% of their college sample believed they were either at no, or low risk to contract AIDS. Thus, it seems that most young people do not feel particularly vulnerable to AIDS, which reduces the chance of altering their sexual behaviors.

The Health Belief Model (HBM; Janz & Becker, 1984) may provide a useful framework to understand this lack of behavior change. This model consists of four dimensions that are thought to be important considerations in why individuals may or may not adopt certain behaviors related to disease prevention. These dimensions are: perceived susceptibility to the disease/condition, perceived severity of the disease, perceived benefits of adopting certain behaviors, and perceived barriers to adopting new behaviors. Behavior change is thought to be more likely when one's perceived susceptibility is high, when perceived severity is greater, when benefits are expected, and when barriers are few. When the HBM has been examined specifically with regard to AIDS, perceived susceptibility (a belief in one's own likelihood of developing AIDS), perceived severity, and perceived barriers were associated with safe sex behavior change (Allard, 1989; Hingson et al., 1990).

Personality characteristics may also play a role in the lack of behavior change toward safer sex practices. One such variable is sex guilt, defined by Mosher and Cross (1971) as a "generalized expectancy to self-mediated punishment for violating, or anticipating violating standards of proper sexual conduct" (p. 27). Researchers found that sex guilt is consistently related to less sexual activity (D'Augelli & Cross, 1975; Gerrard, 1982; Gerrard & Gibbons, 1982; Langston, 1973; Mosher, 1979; Mosher & Cross, 1971). However, those who are sexually active, despite exhibiting high sex guilt, tend to be less effective contraceptors (Geis & Gerrard, 1984; Gerrard, 1982, 1987). Because some contraceptive devices also lower the risk of HIV transmission, it seemed worthwhile to examine the potential relationship of sex guilt and self-reported safer sex practices.

In our study, we examine the relations among knowledge about AIDS, other psychosocial factors, and self-reported safer sex practices. The dimensions of the HBM, the personality characteristic of sex guilt, and knowledge about AIDS were used as predictors to examine the outcome variable of sexual behavior change. It was hypothesized that perceived susceptibility, perceived barriers to safer sex practices, and sex guilt would be stronger predictors of behavior than would be perceived severity, perceived benefits to safer sex, or knowledge. It was expected that susceptibility, benefits, and severity would all be positively related to self-reported behavior, whereas barriers and sex guilt would be inversely related to behavior.

## METHOD

### Participants

Eighty-seven women and 40 men from Old Dominion University volunteered for this study in exchange for course credit. Only students who were 18 to 19 years old were permitted to participate.[1] No students declined to participate at the outset of the study and none withdrew from the study. Participants were asked to indicate their number of lifetime sexual partners. Twenty participants (16%) reported they had never had sexual intercourse. Because the focus of this research was on changes in sexual behavior, data from these 20 virgins were not analyzed.[2] Of the remaining 107 nonvirgins included in the final sample, 28 were male and 79 were female. Twenty-six percent of participants reported having one sexual partner, 21% reported two or three partners, 21% reported four or five partners, and 32% reported more than five partners.

---

[1]Although no data were gathered on participants' socioeconomic status or race, it can be assumed that these students are representative of the student body at our medium-sized urban university in the Southeast. The percentage of minority students on our campus is approximately 17% and in the absence of specific data addressing this issue, one can assume that this would be the approximate percentage of minority students in our sample.

[2]Although important information could be obtained from our subsample of virgins, we decided to eliminate them from the analyses in order to create a somewhat more homogeneous sample of students who had all had sexual intercourse at least once. Because the focus of our research was on safer sex behavior change, we were concerned that safer sex behavior change might be very different for virgins compared to nonvirgins.

## Measures

*AIDS Knowledge Scale (AKS).*   The AKS consists of slight modifications of two previously established measures—the Knowledge Scale of AIDS and the Casual Contagion Scale (DiClemente, Zorn, & Temoshok, 1986). These scales were developed to assess knowledge about the transmission, cause, and treatment of AIDS. Internal consistency for the original measure was adequate ($\alpha$s = .72 and .75). The original version of this measure was modified slightly for this study in order to reflect more accurately current developments in AIDS research and treatment. For example, an original item stated, "A new vaccine has recently been developed for the treatment of AIDS." It was felt that this item was confusing because there are treatments available for the symptoms of AIDS (e.g., AZT), but there is not a vaccine for the prevention of AIDS. Thus, this original item was changed to two new statements: "A new vaccine has recently been developed for the prevention of AIDS," and "Drugs are available for the treatment of AIDS-related symptoms."

*HBM items.*   Forty-six items were developed specifically for this study to assess dimensions of the HBM. These items comprised four subscales based on the theoretical dimensions of the HBM. Many items were adapted from previous investigations of the HBM and AIDS, and from the AIDS literature (e.g., DiClemente et al., 1986; Goodman & Cohall, 1989; Manning, Balson, Barenberg, & Moore, 1989; Manning, Barenberg, Gallese, & Rice, 1989; Siegel & Gibson, 1988; Strunin & Hingson, 1987). Sample items included "There's no chance that I will eventually get AIDS" (susceptibility); "I don't like to prepare for sex, it decreases the spontaneity" (barriers); "How effective do you think condoms are in preventing the spread of AIDS?" (benefits); and "I'd rather get any disease other than AIDS" (severity). Participants responded to items using either a 3- or 5-point Likert-type scale. A mean score was generated for each subscale.[3]

*Behavior Change Questionnaire (BCQ).*   Participants indicated how their behavior changed, if at all, because of AIDS for 11 individual items, such as: selection of partner, use of condoms, engaging in sexual intercourse, involvement in a monogamous relationship, engaging in oral sex, carefulness in sexual relations, length of time dating prior to engaging in sexual intercourse, engaging in anal sex, reducing the

---

[3]The individual items for these scales are available upon request from Robin J. Lewis.

types of sexual practices, asking one's partner about his or her sexual history, and multiple sexual partners. Participants used a 5-point scale ranging from *much less likely to* ... (1) to *much more likely to* ... (5). Some items were reverse worded to avoid response set. A mean score was generated such that higher scores reflected behavior change in the direction of safer sex practices. The BCQ had a coefficient alpha of .79, indicating good internal consistency.

*Marlowe–Crowne Social Desirability Scale—Short Form (SDS).*
This 13-item scale, a shortened version of the original 33-item Marlowe–Crowne Social Desirability Scale, measures socially conforming behaviors in normal participants (Reynolds, 1982). The M–CSDS has sound psychometric properties (Reynolds, 1982; Zook & Sipps, 1985) and was used in this study to determine if participants utilized a socially desirable response set that might raise questions about their responses to items regarding sensitive sexual matters.

*Mosher Forced Choice Sex Guilt Inventory (MFCSGI).* The MFCSGI is a well-researched measure of sex guilt with established validity and reliability (see Mosher, 1979, for a review of psychometric information). The 28-item modified version of the MFCSGI (Langston, 1973) was used in this study. Respondents chose between two responses regarding a variety of sexual activities (e.g., "If in the future I committed adultery ... (a) I wouldn't feel bad about it"[low guilt] or "(b) it would be sinful" [high guilt]). An index of sex guilt was obtained by adding the number of responses indicative of high guilt. Higher scores on this measure indicated higher sex guilt.

*Sexual Behavior Scale (SBS).* A 20-item scale was developed to assess participants' safe and risky sexual practices during the past 6 months. Current research findings and reports on the transmission of HIV were used as guidelines in identifying and discriminating between risky and safe behaviors. Only the risky behaviors were relevant to this study because they were utilized to describe the risky behaviors of this older adolescent population.

## Procedure

All participants were invited to complete a variety of measures in a study examining college students' sexual behaviors. Potential participants were assured of anonymity and complete confidentiality due to the sensitive nature of the subject matter. Participants were tested in small groups and completed the measures in random order.

## RESULTS

### Reliability of Measures

Internal consistency for each measure was established by computing alpha coefficients. These alphas ranged from .60 to .80 with one exception—the 4-item Perceived Severity Scale ($\alpha = .24$). Closer examination of the scale revealed that none of the items was strongly correlated with any other. Because each item appeared to be measuring something different, the decision was made to be consistent with previous research (cf. DiClemente, Zorn, & Temoshok, 1987) by using the single item that seemed, in terms of face validity, to best measure the dimension of perceived severity as put forth by the HBM. The item chosen was "I'd rather get any other disease than AIDS."

Because of concerns that respondents might use a socially desirable response set as they answered the personal questions on these measures, all measures were correlated with social desirability. It did not appear that participants' utilized such a response set ($rs$ ranged from .03 to .26). The only variable that was significantly correlated with social desirability was barriers, $r = -.26$.

### Sexual Practices of the Sample

When participants were asked about their sexual behavior practices in the past 6 months, the following percentages for risky sexual practices were obtained: 21% had intercourse without a condom, 26% had sexual relations with a person whose sexual history was unknown to them, 13% had sex with someone they had just met (a "pick-up"), 41% had oral sex, 5% had anal sex without a condom, .9% had sex with a homosexual man. None, however, reported having sex with a bisexual man, an IV drug user, a person with AIDS or a positive HIV test, or a female prostitute.

### Health Belief Model, Knowledge, Sex Guilt, and Behavior Change

The relationship of the components of the HBM, AIDS knowledge, and sex guilt with self-reported sexual behavior change was examined using a multiple-regression analysis with self-reported sexual behavior change as the criterion variable. Predictor variables were: AIDS

190

TABLE 1
Multiple Regression for Self-Reported Safer Sex Behavior for Predictor Variables

| Variable | r | Beta | t | sig t |
|---|---|---|---|---|
| Barriers | −.24 | −.25 | 2.60 | .01 |
| Sex Guilt | .24 | .21 | 2.17 | .03 |
| Susceptibility | .11 | .18 | 1.90 | .06 |
| Benefits | .10 | .18 | 1.79 | .08 |
| Gender | .21 | .17 | 1.73 | .09 |
| Severity | < .01 | .02 | 0.20 | .84 |
| Knowledge | .03 | .01 | 0.13 | .90 |

*Note.* Overall regression equation, multiple $R = .42$, $F(7, 99) = 3.14$, $p < .01$.

knowledge (total score on the AKS), perceived susceptibility, perceived benefits, perceived barriers, the one-item perceived severity measure, sex guilt, and gender of participant. It should be noted that multicollinearity among predictors was not a problem, with the magnitude of correlations ranging from $r = .03$ to $r = .32$.

When safer sex behavior change was regressed simultaneously on these predictors, a significant equation was obtained, $F(7, 99) = 3.14$, $p < .01$, accounting for approximately 18% of the variance in behavior change (see Table 1). Barriers and sex guilt accounted for significant proportions of unique variance in sexual behavior change. Benefits, susceptibility, and gender of the participant accounted for marginally significant variance in behavior change. Safer sex behavior change was associated with higher levels of sex guilt and fewer perceived barriers, and it was marginally associated with more perceived susceptibility and more perceived benefits. Finally, women reported more safer sex behavior change than men, $t(53.51) = 2.30$, $p < .05$ ($Ms = 4.00$ vs. 3.76, respectively).

To examine whether gender of the participant interacted with any of the predictors to affect behavior change, interaction terms were created and entered after the main effect terms just described were entered. None of these interaction terms was significant.

## Level of Knowledge

On the AKS, the mean score for correct responses was 85.9% ($SD = 9.6$). However, some participants had misconceptions about what are, and are not, effective means of protection against the HIV virus that causes AIDS. Specifically, 31% and 39% of the participants erroneously believed that oral contraceptives and diaphragms, respectively, could reduce the risk of AIDS.

## DISCUSSION

This study expanded previous research by assessing psychosocial variables that might clarify the relationship among knowledge about AIDS and associated sexual behavior change. As expected, knowledge about AIDS was unrelated to safer sexual behavior, suggesting that current methods of presenting information about AIDS may not be effective in reducing risky behaviors.

Results indicate that self-reported safer sex practices appear most likely when one tends to feel guilty about sexual matters, perceives few barriers to practicing safer sex, and to a lesser degree if one perceives benefits to practicing safer sex and feels personally susceptible to AIDS. Finally, safer sex behaviors appear more likely to occur in females than in males.

Based on previous studies that examined the relationship between sex guilt and contraception (cf. Gerrard, 1982), it was predicted that sex guilt would be inversely related to safer sex behavior. That is, consistent with research that high-sex-guilt individuals are less likely to use contraception, we expected these individuals to report fewer safer sex practices. However, the finding that sex guilt was positively related to safer sex behaviors suggests that sex guilt may promote safer sex behavior. Correlational designs, however, preclude determination of such a sequential relationship.

It is also possible that this relationship between sex guilt and self-reported safer sex behaviors may be mediated by sexual activity. In response to the fear of AIDS, high-guilt individuals may be even more likely to avoid sexual activity. Self-reported safer sex behavior may then simply reflect avoidance of any sexual behavior rather than safer sex practices. This explanation would be consistent with results of previous research suggesting that high-sex-guilt individuals are generally less sexually active, but when sexually active, are less likely to initiate contraceptive behaviors. Further research that separates avoidant from preventive behavior is needed before the relationship of sex guilt and safer sex behavior in the age of AIDS can be understood.

Perceived severity was unrelated to self-reported safer sex practices. It is possible that the measurement problems of the perceived severity subscale are responsible for this finding. It seems possible that respondents might endorse the 1-item, "I'd rather get any other disease than AIDS," for reasons having nothing to do with the perceived severity of AIDS. For example, a homophobic individual, who believed that AIDS is primarily a "homosexual disorder," may not fear the deadly nature of AIDS nearly as much as the stigma associated with AIDS. Therefore, it is imperative that future researchers create items regarding the perceived severity of AIDS that more clearly tap into the degree to which one believes AIDS is a severe, deadly disease. When the meaning of the perceived severity item (or items) is clarified, the nature of the relationship between severity and safer sex practice can be examined further.

## Level of AIDS-Related Knowledge

Results indicate that within an older adolescent population, students get approximately 80% of the questions correct when asked about how HIV is transmitted and how AIDS is treated. Although these results seem to suggest that younger college students know a lot about AIDS and know what to do to protect themselves, additional findings raise some questions. Although more students seem to be aware that AIDS is transmitted through sexual intercourse and view condoms and abstinence as being effective preventative measures, a remarkable proportion of them maintain erroneous beliefs about the AIDS-preventative characteristics of oral contraceptives and the diaphragm. It may well be that younger college students are confusing effectiveness for contraception with effectiveness for AIDS prevention. This suggests that in the absence of more specific information about AIDS prevention, students are relying on what they know about already, namely contraception.

## Conclusions

Although older adolescents appear to have adequate levels of AIDS-related knowledge, they seem to be less clear about what they can do to protect themselves from infection by HIV. In general, young college students are not practicing safer sex practices even though their knowledge about AIDS is adequate. Rather, it appears that the barriers they perceive to practicing safer sex (e.g., difficulty or discomfort about using condoms, talking with partners or others about sexual issues), and their feelings of guilt about sexual matters are the strongest predictors of safer sex behavior.

In addition to the affective dimension of sex guilt, another factor that seems to be important with regard to safer sex practices involves the interpersonal nature of sexual relations. Due to the interactional nature of sexual relations, it may be useful in future research to include measures of communication abilities as well as assessing alcohol and drug use, self-esteem, and interpersonal comfort or skill.

Additionally, there are implications for prevention and education programs. It seems that knowledge about AIDS is not enough to promote safer sex behavior. Rather, approaches that combine cognitive, affective, behavioral, and environmental components are needed. Specifically, particular attention should be paid to addressing perceived barriers to safe sex and affective experiences such as guilt.

Finally, we acknowledge that this research was conducted using a sample of older adolescents who are not in the same general risk category such as IV drug users, homosexual men, or those individuals living in our inner cities. However, these adolescents are engaging in risky sexual practices such as unprotected sex, not talking with their partners about their sexual history, and having "one-night stands." Therefore, understanding what is associated with safer sex behaviors for these young people is, indeed, important.

## ACKNOWLEDGMENTS

This research is based on Helene Rimberg's doctoral dissertation at the Virginia Consortium for Professional Psychology, under the direction of Robin J. Lewis.

Helene Rimberg is now at the Morrison Center in Portland, Oregon.

## REFERENCES

Allard, R. A. (1989). Beliefs about AIDS as determinants of preventive practices and of support for coercive measures. *American Journal of Public Health, 79,* 448–452.

Baldwin, J. D., & Baldwin, J. I. (1988). AIDS information and sexual behavior on a university campus. *Journal of Sex Education and Therapy, 14,* 24–28.

Burnette, M. M., Redmon, W. K., & Poling, A. (1990). Knowledge, attitudes, and behavior of college undergraduates regarding Acquired Immune Deficiency Syndrome. *College Student Journal, 24,* 27–38.

D'Augelli, J. F., & Cross, H. J. (1975). Relationship of sex guilt and moral reasoning to premarital sex in college women and in couples. *Journal of Consulting and Clinical Psychology, 43,* 40–47.

DiClemente, R. J., Zorn, J., & Temoshok, L. (1986). Adolescents and AIDS: A survey of knowledge, attitudes and beliefs about AIDS in San Francisco. *American Journal of Public Health, 76,* 1443–1445.

DiClemente, R. J., Zorn, J., & Temoshok, L. (1987). The association of gender, ethnicity, and length of residence in the Bay area to adolescents' knowledge and attitudes about acquired immunodeficiency syndrome. *Journal of Applied Social Psychology, 17,* 216–230.

Edgar, T., Freimuth, V. S., & Hammond, S. L. (1988). Communicating the AIDS risk to college students: The problem of motivating change. *Health Education Research, 3,* 59–73.

Geis, B. D., & Gerrard, M. (1984). Predicting male and female contraceptive behavior: A discriminant analysis of groups high, moderate, and low in contraceptive effectiveness. *Journal of Personality and Social Psychology, 46,* 669–680.

Gerrard, M. (1982). Sex, sex guilt, and contraceptive use. *Journal of Personality and Social Psychology, 42,* 153–158.

Gerrard, M. (1987). Sex, sex guilt, and contraceptive use revisited. The 1980's. *Journal of Personality and Social Psychology, 52,* 975–980.

Gerrard, M., & Gibbons, F. X. (1982). Sexual experience, sex guilt, and sexual moral reasoning. *Journal of Personality, 50,* 345–359.

Goodman, E., & Cohall, A. T. (1989). Acquired immunodeficiency syndrome and adolescents: Knowledge, attitudes, beliefs, and behaviors in a New York adolescent minority population. *Pediatrics, 84,* 36–42.

Gray, L. A., & Saracino, M. (1989). AIDS on campus: A preliminary study of college students' knowledge and behaviors. *Journal of Counseling and Development, 68,* 199–202.

Hingson, R. W., Strunin, L., Berlin, B. M., & Heeven, T. (1990). Beliefs about AIDS, use of alcohol and drugs, and unprotected sex among Massachusetts adolescents. *American Journal of Public Health, 80,* 295–299.

Hirschorn, M. W. (1987). AIDS is not seen as a major threat by many heterosexuals on campuses. *The Chronicle of Higher Education, 28,* 32–33.

Janz, N. K., & Becker, M. H. (1984). The Health Belief Model: A decade later. *Health Education Quarterly, 11,* 1–47.

Katzman, E. M., Mulholland, M., & Sutherland, E. M. (1988). College students and AIDS: A preliminary survey of knowledge, attitudes, and behavior. *Journal of American College Health, 37,* 127–130.

Langston, R. D. (1973). Sex guilt and sex behavior in college students. *Journal of Personality Assessment, 37,* 467–472.

Loos, C., & Bowd, A. (1989). AIDS related behavior change, knowledge, and opinions among first year university students. *Canadian Journal of Counselling, 23,* 288–295.

Manning, D. T., Balson, P. M., Barenberg, N., & Moore, T. M. (1989). Susceptibility to AIDS: What college students do and don't believe. *Journal of American College Health, 38,* 67–73.

Manning, D. T., Barenberg, N., Gallese, L., & Rice, J. C. (1989). College students' knowledge and health beliefs about AIDS: Implications for education and prevention. *Journal of American College Health, 37,* 254–259.

Mosher, D. L. (1979). The meaning and measurement of guilt. In C. E. Izard, (Ed.), *Emotions in personality and psychopathology* (pp. 105–130). New York: Plenum.

Mosher, D. L., & Cross, H. J. (1971). Sex guilt and premarital sexual experiences in college students. *Journal of Consulting and Clinical Psychology, 36,* 27–32.

Reynolds, W. M. (1982). Development of reliable and valid short forms of the Marlowe–Crowne Social Desirability Scale. *Journal of Clinical Psychology, 38,* 119–125.

Siegel, K., & Gibson, W. C. (1988). Barriers to the modification of sexual behavior among heterosexuals at risk for acquired immunodeficiency syndrome. *New York State Journal of Medicine, 88,* 66–70.

Simkins, L., & Eberhage, M. G. (1984). Attitudes toward AIDS, herpes II, and toxic shock syndrome. *Psychological Reports, 55,* 779–786.

Simkins, L., & Kushner, A. (1986). Attitudes toward AIDS, herpes II, and toxic shock syndrome: Two years later. *Psychological Reports, 59,* 883–891.

Strunin, L., & Hingson, R. (1987). Acquired immunodeficiency syndrome and adolescents: Knowledge, beliefs, attitudes, and behaviors. *Pediatrics, 79,* 825–828.

Thurman, Q. C., & Franklin, K. M. (1990). AIDS and college health: Knowledge, threat, and prevention at a northeastern university. *Journal of American College Health, 38,* 179–184.

Turner, C., Anderson, P., Fitzpatrick, R., Fowler, G., & Mayon-White, R. (1988). Sexual behavior, contraceptive practice, and knowledge of AIDS in Oxford University students. *Journal of Biosocial Sciences, 20,* 445–451.

Zook, A., & Sipps, G. J. (1985). Cross–validation of a short form of the Marlowe–Crowne Social Desirability Scale. *Journal of Clinical Psychology, 41,* 236–238.

Received October 30, 1991
Revision received August 25, 1992
Accepted August 23, 1993

Developmental Psychology
1993. Vol. 29, No. 2. 220–235

# How Part-Time Work Intensity Relates to Drug Use, Problem Behavior, Time Use, and Satisfaction Among High School Seniors: Are These Consequences or Merely Correlates?

Jerald G. Bachman and John Schulenberg

This study related *work intensity* (hours worked per week) to indicators of psychosocial functioning and adjustment by using nationally representative samples of high school seniors, totalling over 70,000 respondents, from the classes of 1985–1989. Consistent with previous research, bivariate correlations were positive between work intensity and problem behaviors; these associations were diminished (but not eliminated) once background and educational success indicators were controlled, thus suggesting that selection factors contribute to the correlations. Work intensity appears to reduce the likelihood of getting sufficient sleep, eating breakfast, exercising, and having a satisfactory amount of leisure time. Conceptual and policy implications are discussed, including the possibility that long hours of part-time work may be both a symptom and a facilitator of psychosocial difficulties.

In recent decades, it has been assumed that there are several benefits attributable to the part-time employment of adolescents; these include easing the transition from school to work and dealing with the limitations of formal schooling (e.g., overlong protection from the "real world," narrow age segregation, and lack of contact with adults). According to this point of view, a job gives the adolescent an opportunity to demonstrate responsibility, achieve autonomy, and gain real-world experience. In some cases, the adolescent may be able to gain some work experience that is directly relevant to his or her future career. Another very obvious benefit is that the working adolescent typically earns money, although most of that is used as disposable income (Bachman, 1983a). At the societal level, adolescent part-time work can be viewed as a means for transferring work attitudes and competencies to tomorrow's adult workers. And, of course, it also provides employers with a source of relatively inexpensive, unskilled labor.

Jerald G. Bachman and John Schulenberg, Institute for Social Research, University of Michigan.

Portions of this article were presented at the 1991 Biennial Meetings of the Society for Research on Child Development, Seattle, Washington. This research was supported by grants from the National Institute on Drug Abuse (R01DA01411), the National Institute on Alcohol Abuse and Alcoholism (T32AA07477), and the University of Michigan Substance Abuse Center.

We wish to thank Sharon Leech for her assistance with data management and analyses; Joyce Buchanan for her assistance with text management and editing; and Lloyd Johnston, Jeylan Mortimer, Patrick O'Malley, and John Wallace for their helpful comments on an early draft of the article. We are grateful also to Ellen Greenberger and Laurence Steinberg for their careful reviews and comments on later drafts. Of course, we remain solely responsible for the interpretations of the findings.

Correspondence concerning this article should be addressed to Jerald G. Bachman, Survey Research Center, Institute for Social Research, University of Michigan, Ann Arbor, Michigan 48106-1248.

Many of the assumptions just listed apparently served as a foundation for government legislation aimed at improving the future employment prospects of disadvantaged youth during the 1960s and 1970s (e.g., the 1964 Economic Opportunity Act and the Comprehensive Employment and Training Act of 1973). Likewise, the 1970s witnessed a strong push toward a generalized integration of school and work. Various government panels (e.g., National Commission on Youth, 1980; President's Science Advisory Committee, Panel on Youth, 1974; Work-Education Consortium, 1978) stressed the virtues of work for young people and recommended that efforts be made to combine education and work experiences. For example, the National Commission on Youth (1980) suggested that part-time work could be the "single most important factor" in the socialization of youth to adulthood, fostering such attributes as independence and responsibility, realistic career decisions, and good work attitudes and habits. Unfortunately, these panels typically relied little on empirical evidence (Hamilton & Crouter, 1980). Nevertheless, it appears that the prescription that young people take on part-time work during their high school years has been widely followed for more than a decade now; the majority of high school students are employed during the school year, and many put in long hours on the job.

In recent years, the assumptions regarding the benefits of part-time work during adolescence have been challenged by social scientists, and much concern has been raised about the possible costs of typical part-time work experiences. Most notably, in a series of studies based on both cross-sectional and longitudinal investigations of adolescents from Orange County, California, Greenberger and Steinberg and their colleagues (e.g., Greenberger & Steinberg, 1986; Greenberger, Steinberg, & Vaux, 1981; Greenberger, Steinberg, Vaux, & McAuliffe, 1980; Steinberg, Greenberger, Garduque, & McAuliffe, 1982; Steinberg, Greenberger, Garduque, Ruggerio, & Vaux, 1982; Steinberg, Greenberger, Garduque, Vaux, & Ruggiero, 1981) have suggested that what adolescents do and what they learn in the

198

workplace may not always be beneficial to their psychosocial development and health and that working long hours may detract from other experiences that are important for the adolescent. In particular, their evidence indicates that the number of hours worked per week, or *work intensity*, is positively related to a variety of problem behaviors (e.g., drug and alcohol use and delinquency; see also, e.g., Bachman, Bare, & Frankie, 1986; Mortimer, Finch, Shanahan, & Ryu, 1992a) and negatively related to school performance (see also, e.g., Bachman et al., 1986; Charner & Fraser, 1987; Lillydahl, 1990; Mortimer & Finch, 1986; Mortimer et al., 1992a; Yasuda, 1990; but see, e.g., D'Amico, 1984; Hotchkiss, 1986; Mortimer, Finch, Shanahan, & Ryu, 1992b). In a recent cross-sectional study, Steinberg and Dornbusch (1991) provided cross-validation of many of these relations with work intensity using a large and heterogenous sample of high school students. In accord with much of the previous literature, they concluded that "the correlates of school-year employment are generally negative" (p. 309).

Nevertheless, the debate over the costs and benefits of part-time work is likely to continue. In our view, at least three critical issues regarding work intensity remain unresolved. One such issue is the trade-off between the costs and benefits of part-time work. As Mortimer and her colleagues (e.g., Mortimer et al., 1992a, 1992b; Yamoor & Mortimer, 1990; see also Steel, 1991) have indicated, much of the relevant research has focused on the negative correlates of part-time work, while failing to consider the possible positive correlates. There is evidence indicating that there are indeed some possible benefits of part-time work, including increased personal responsibility and orientation toward the future (e.g., Steinberg et al., 1981; Steinberg, Greenberger, Garduque, Ruggerio, & Vaux, 1982; Stevens, Puchtell, Ryu, & Mortimer, 1992). If work intensity does contribute to both positive and negative psychosocial outcomes, it is important for both theoretical and policy considerations to understand these trade-offs.

The second critical issue pertains to the shape (i.e., linear or nonlinear) of the relationships between work intensity and the given correlates. The practical question underlying this issue is, "How much part-time work is too much?"—a question that reflects several statements in the literature indicating that the negative effects of part-time work are particularly strong for those working more than 15 or 20 hr per week (e.g., Charner & Fraser, 1987; Greenberger & Steinberg, 1986). An auxiliary issue here is whether working zero hours is best treated as a simple end point to the continuum of work intensity.

The third critical issue, and in many ways the most important, involves the causal direction underlying correlations with work intensity. Much of the relevant literature apparently assumes that work intensity causes the various positive and negative correlates, particularly given the typical analytic strategies (cf. Lillydahl, 1990). Nevertheless, there is agreement among several researchers that this issue has not been fully addressed (e.g., Bachman et al., 1986; Greenberger & Steinberg, 1986; Mortimer & Finch, 1986; Mortimer et al., 1992a, 1992b; Steinberg & Dornbusch, 1991), leaving open the possibility that the correlations reflect primarily self-selection, specifically, (a) work intensity may be the result, rather than the cause, of the correlates, or (b) both work intensity and the correlates may be the result of more fundamental or causally prior "third variables."

For example, longitudinal evidence from Mortimer and her colleagues (e.g., Mortimer, Finch, Ryu, & Shanahan, 1991) indicates that the relationship between work intensity and substance use is partly due to preexisting differences in substance use, suggesting that those factors that contribute to higher levels of substance use also contribute to longer hours of part-time work. A likely third variable here would be earlier educational commitment and success (Schulenberg, Bachman, O'Malley, & Johnston, 1992). Indeed, in considering the negative correlates of work intensity (e.g., poor school performance, delinquency, and drug use), the sheer consistency of previous findings suggests the possibility that long hours of work reflect one component of a syndrome of *problem behavior* (Jessor & Jessor, 1977) or *precocious development* (Newcomb & Bentler, 1988) that is manifest before entry into part-time work. In any event, this issue regarding third variables must be more fully addressed before reaching firm conclusions about the costs and benefits of part-time work.

In the present investigation, we address the three critical issues just discussed, using nationally representative data drawn from recent cohorts of high school seniors. In an attempt to provide a more complete picture of both the positive and negative correlates of part-time work, we focus our attention on four broad psychosocial domains: (a) substance use (including cigarette, alcohol, marijuana, and cocaine use); (b) other problem behaviors (including interpersonal aggression, victimization, and trouble with police); (c) time use (including time spent on sleep, exercise, and dating); and (d) general and specific life satisfaction and self-esteem. In an effort to discern any optimal level of work intensity, we examine the shape of the relation between work intensity and each outcome variable. Finally, in an attempt to consider possible third-variable explanations, we conduct multivariate analyses that control background characteristics, as well as educational success and commitment. In particular, we contrast the impact of various indexes of educational commitment and success with the impact of work intensity.

## Method

The data were drawn from the Monitoring the Future project, an ongoing study of high school seniors conducted by the Institute for Social Research at the University of Michigan. The study design has been described extensively elsewhere (Bachman & Johnston, 1978; Bachman, Johnston, & O'Malley, 1987; Johnston, O'Malley, & Bachman, 1991). Briefly, it includes nationally representative surveys of each high school senior class beginning in 1975, plus follow-up surveys mailed each year to a subset of each senior class sample. The senior year data from the classes of 1985–1989 were used in the present analyses.

### Samples and Procedure

A three-stage probability sample (Kish, 1965) is used each year to select approximately 135 public and private high schools representative of the 48 coterminous states. Questionnaires are administered during school hours each spring, usually in a regularly scheduled class period. Special procedures are used to ensure confidentiality; these procedures are explained carefully in the questionnaire instructions and reiterated by the interviewers. Student response rates were 83% to 84% for each of the survey years included in this report.

Five different questionnaire forms were used each year, each administered to a random one fifth of the sample (except that a sixth form was added in 1989). Key items concerning part-time work, as well as demographic measures and self-reports of drug use, appear on all forms. Some other items of interest appear on only one form; accordingly, analyses involving such items were based on only about one fifth of the total sample.

Because there are some gender differences in hours worked, in pay, in other key measures such as grade point averages (GPAs), and especially in many of the drug-use measures, all analyses were conducted separately for male and female students (see also Mortimer et al., 1992a, 1992b; Mortimer, Finch, Owens, & Shanahan, 1990; Steinberg, Greenberger, Garduque, Ruggiero, & Vaux, 1982; Yamoor & Mortimer, 1990). The numbers of cases providing employment data were 34,575 male seniors and 37,288 female seniors. Numbers of cases for specific analyses were somewhat smaller because of missing data on other variables.

## Measures

The predictors in the present analyses consisted of background characteristics, indexes of educational commitment and success, and work status and intensity. The outcome variables consisted of indexes of substance use, problem behavior, time use, and satisfaction.

*Predictors.* Background characteristics included cohort, region, urbanicity, parent education, and race. Five senior-year cohorts were included, ranging from 1985 to 1989. Region consisted of four categories, including the South, Northeast, North Central, and West. Urbanicity consisted of five categories, ranging from farm to large urban area. Parent education was based on the average of mother's and father's educational level, and possible responses ranged from at least one parent not graduating from high school (coded as 1) to at least one parent attending graduate or professional school after college (coded as 5). Four race categories were distinguished: White (77.1%); Black (10.9%); Hispanic, including Mexican American and Latin American (5.7%); and "other," including American Indian, Asian American, and other (6.2%).

Three indexes of educational success and commitment were used, including high school GPA, 4-year college plans, and high school curriculum. High school GPA was based on a single item concerning typical grades over the high school years, and possible responses ranged from C– or lower (coded as 1) to A (coded as 5). College plans were measured with a single item, and possible responses ranged from "definitely won't graduate from a 4-year college" (coded as 1) to "definitely will graduate from a 4-year college" (coded as 4). High school curriculum was measured with a single item, and responses were grouped into three categories: college preparatory, general, and vocational–technical.

The measure of hours of part-time work was based on responses to the question, "On the average over the school year, how many hours per week do you work in a paid or unpaid job?" Response categories included none, 5 hr or less, 6–10, 11–15, 16–20, 21–25, 26–30, and more than 30 hr. The fact that some of the jobs were unpaid complicated some preliminary analyses and blurred potentially important distinctions. Accordingly, any respondent who reported working but indicated zero earnings was placed in a separate category, *working but not for pay.* The result is a nine-category variable distinguishing those who were not working at all, those working but not for pay, and those working various numbers of hours (six 5-hr increments, plus those working more than 30 hr).[1] The distribution of respondents across these categories is shown in Table 1. As is evident, nearly three fourths of the seniors were employed (working for pay), and over one third of the male students and over one fourth of the female students were working more than 20 hr per week.

Table 1

*Part-Time Work Status and Work Intensity by Gender*

| Variable | Male seniors | | Female seniors | |
|---|---|---|---|---|
| | N | % | N | % |
| Work status | | | | |
| Not working | 6,487 | 18.8 | 7,680 | 20.6 |
| Working for pay | 25,898 | 74.9 | 27,120 | 72.7 |
| Working, not for pay | 2,190 | 6.3 | 2,488 | 6.7 |
| Total | 34,575 | 100.0 | 37,288 | 100.0 |
| Hours worked per week[a] | | | | |
| 5 or less | 2,347 | 9.1 | 2,348 | 8.7 |
| 6–10 | 2,801 | 10.8 | 3,186 | 11.7 |
| 11–15 | 3,321 | 12.8 | 4,458 | 16.4 |
| 16–20 | 5,390 | 20.8 | 6,721 | 24.8 |
| 21–25 | 4,747 | 18.3 | 4,994 | 18.4 |
| 26–30 | 3,365 | 13.0 | 2,903 | 10.7 |
| 31 or more | 3,927 | 15.2 | 2,510 | 9.3 |
| Total | 25,898 | 100.0 | 27,120 | 100.0 |

[a] Includes only those working for pay.

*Outcome variables.* The four categories of outcome variables are summarized in Table 2, including means and standard deviations by gender. The indexes of current substance use included cigarette use, heavy drinking, marijuana use, and cocaine use. As indicated in Table 2, dichotomous codings were used to facilitate interpretation (i.e., means represent percentages of users). The focus was on consumption levels beyond what some may consider "casual use." The Monitoring the Future substance use indexes have been found to possess good psychometric properties (in-depth considerations of reliability and validity of the indexes are provided in O'Malley, Bachman, and Johnston, 1983, and Johnston and O'Malley, 1985).

Four indexes of other problem behaviors over the past year included interpersonal aggression (measured with a 5-item scale), general victimization (measured with a 4-item scale), trouble with police (coded as a dichotomy), and arguments with parent(s). Each of these indexes was based on items that were included in one of the five questionnaire forms; thus the corresponding analyses were based on approximately one fifth of the sample. There were four variables concerning how the students spent their time, three of which were health-related activities, including how often the individual gets at least 7 hr of sleep per night, eats breakfast, and exercises vigorously. All three were based on one fifth of the sample. The fourth time-use variable was the average frequency of dating (based on the total sample). Finally, there were three indexes of general and specific life satisfaction (including satisfaction

[1] The possibility exists that some of those working for pay were also doing some additional not-for-pay work and that the hours of work per week reported by such individuals reflected both types of work. As a check against that possibility, we examined an additional question, which was asked of only one fifth of the seniors, concerning paid jobs held currently or during the past 3 months. For all respondents who completed both questions, we were able to examine similarities and differences in their reports of hours worked. In spite of the difference in time intervals covered, about three quarters of all responses were identical for the two items, most such "mismatches" were small (i.e., about 5 hr), and the mismatches were about equally divided between those reporting more and those reporting fewer hours for the current or recent job (compared with their work "on average over the school year"). We thus conclude the hours of work measure, as operationalized here, was not appreciably inflated by unpaid work.

Table 2

*Description of Outcome Variables and Means and Standard Deviations by Gender*

| Outcome variable | Description and coding | Male seniors | | Female seniors | |
|---|---|---|---|---|---|
| | | M | SD | M | SD |
| **Substance use** | | | | | |
| Cigarette[a] | ≤ half-pack a day during past month = 100; if not = 0 | 10.71 | 30.93 | 10.98 | 31.26 |
| Alcohol[a] | Five or more drinks in a row at least once in past 2 weeks = 100; if not = 0 | 44.21 | 49.66 | 27.58 | 44.69 |
| Marijuana[a] | Used at least once in past month = 100; if not = 0 | 23.10 | 42.15 | 17.83 | 38.28 |
| Cocaine[a] | Used at least once in past month = 100; if not = 0 | 5.30 | 22.41 | 3.65 | 18.76 |
| **Problem behavior** | | | | | |
| Interpersonal aggression | Average of five items concerning frequency of aggression toward others in past year ($\alpha$ = .72), ranging from 1 = *none* to 5 = *5 or more times* | 1.26 | 0.50 | 1.10 | 0.24 |
| Victimization | Average of four items concerning frequency of personal and property violations in past year ($\alpha$ = .56), ranging from 1 = *none* to 5 = *5 or more times* | 1.34 | 0.49 | 1.20 | 0.34 |
| Trouble with police[a] | Any trouble in past year = 100; if not = 0 | 32.61 | 46.88 | 13.17 | 33.82 |
| Arguments with parents | Arguments during past year, ranging from 1 = *none* to 5 = *5 or more times* | 3.74 | 1.39 | 4.08 | 1.23 |
| **Time use** | | | | | |
| Sleep | Average frequency of getting ≥ 7 hr/night, ranging from 1 = *never* to 6 = *every day* | 4.14 | 1.41 | 3.92 | 1.38 |
| Breakfast | Average frequency of eating breakfast, ranging from 1 = *never* to 6 = *every day* | 3.75 | 1.79 | 3.24 | 1.68 |
| Exercise | Average frequency of exercising vigorously, ranging from 1 = *never* to 6 = *every day* | 4.15 | 1.51 | 3.45 | 1.46 |
| Dating | Average frequency of dating, ranging from 1 = *never* to 6 = *over 3 times per week* | 3.41 | 1.55 | 3.62 | 1.64 |
| **Satisfaction** | | | | | |
| Life | Satisfaction with life as a whole, ranging from 1 = *completely dissatisfied* to 7 = *completely satisfied* | 5.23 | 1.44 | 5.05 | 1.54 |
| Leisure | Satisfaction with how leisure time is spent, ranging from 1 = *completely dissatisfied* to 7 = completely satisfied | 4.38 | 1.88 | 4.14 | 1.90 |
| Job | Satisfaction with job (if employed), ranging from 1 = *completely dissatisfied* to 7 = *completely satisfied* | 4.81 | 1.70 | 4.75 | 1.74 |
| Self-esteem | Average of eight items based on Rosenberg (1965) ($\alpha$ = .84), with responses ranging from 1 = *low* to 5 = *high* | 4.11 | 0.68 | 4.00 | 0.76 |

*Note.* Means and standard deviations are drawn from the multiple classification analyses.

Responses are coded as a dichotomy (0 or 100), and corresponding means represent percentages of those engaged in given behavior.

with life as a whole, with the way leisure time is spent, and with the job) and a self-esteem scale based on Rosenberg (1965). All four indexes were based on one fifth of the sample. Additional information concerning each of the indexes, including reliability information for the scales, is provided in Table 2 (*N*s are provided in Table 3).

## Analysis Strategy

A basic question addressed in this article is whether there is some optimal number of hours for part-time work by high school seniors. Put differently, the question is whether any problems associated with work seem to mount more rapidly once a certain number of hours is exceeded. Any such relationships are, by definition, not strictly linear. Thus our analysis required a technique that could reveal nonlinear (as well as linear) relations. We also needed a technique that could accommodate multiple predictors, some of which (e.g., region) were categorical rather than continuous. Multiple classification analysis (MCA), a form of dummy-variable simultaneous-entry multiple regression analysis, is ideally suited to such analysis tasks. It uses categorical predictors and is thus sensitive to nonlinear as well as linear relationships (Andrews, Morgan, Sonquist, & Klem, 1973).

An extensive series of analyses was carried out using MCA. Hours of part-time work, along with background factors and measures of educational success, were used as joint "predictors" of each of the "outcome" variables.[2] The full MCA findings are available elsewhere (Bachman & Schulenberg, 1992); we present here a distillation of the findings.

## Results

### Background Characteristics and Educational Success Linked to Work Status and Intensity

The first step in the analysis examined how the background and educational success measures were linked to part-time work status (working, not working, or working but not for pay).

[2] We use terms such as those in quotation marks as a matter of convenience, although we recognize that cross-sectional survey data used in this analysis—and in most other studies of the correlates of student work—often cannot be classified unambiguously as either "independent" or "dependent" variables.

The strongest predictor of working (as opposed to not working or working but not for pay) was race; employment was most frequent among White seniors (75% of male students and 74% of female students), least frequent among Black seniors (60% of male students and 55% of female students), and intermediate among Hispanic seniors (67% of male students and 60% of female students) and all others (65% of male students and 61% of female students). Among male students, the likelihood of working was somewhat lower among those planning for college, those with GPAs of "A," and those in the college prep curriculum, whereas those in the vocational–technical curriculum were more likely than average to be working. Among female students, such differences appeared only weakly or not at all. For both male and female students, likelihood of employment was greater among those living in large urban areas and lower among those living in smaller towns or in the country. The next step focused on just those respondents who held part-time jobs (for pay) and examined how the background and educational success measures were linked to variations in work intensity (i.e., the numbers of hours they worked). There was very little difference in average hours worked according to race; although Black seniors were less likely than White seniors to hold any part-time job, among those who were employed, the numbers of hours were slightly (but trivially) higher for the Black seniors. The most important correlates of amount of hours worked were the measures of educational success; work hours correlated negatively with plans for college graduation, GPA, and being in the college prep curriculum. (Hours of work also correlated negatively with parental education.) The several measures of educational success (as well as parental education) all overlapped in their negative relationships with work intensity, with the result that the multivariate relationships were weaker than the bivariate ones; nevertheless, none of the indicators of educational success was reduced to a zero or trivial relationship in MCAs predicting work intensity, and thus all were retained in the subsequent analyses.

### Employment and Hours of Work Linked to Use of Drugs

Earlier analyses of Monitoring the Future data showed some positive association between hours of work and use of drugs (Bachman, Johnston, & O'Malley, 1981; Bachman et al., 1986). We now present a more detailed examination of the shapes of such relationships, both bivariately and with controls for background and educational success.

The results of these and subsequent analyses using MCA are presented in two complementary forms: Figures 1–4 present the shapes of relationships between hours worked and the dependent variable.[3] Table 3 displays summary statistics from the MCAs showing strength of bivariate and multivariate relationships between each of the education and employment predictors and the dependent variable. The *bivariate* relationships are indicated by the *eta* coefficients, which can be interpreted as similar to zero-order product-moment correlations, except that the eta coefficients capture nonlinear as well as linear relationships. The *beta* coefficients indicate strength of multivariate relationships (again, both linear and nonlinear) when all predictors (i.e., background, educational success indicators, and work status/intensity) are simultaneously included in the equa-

tion. Although the coefficients capture both linear and nonlinear relationships, we should note that in fact the patterns involving college plans and grades are mostly linear.

The drug data are presented as dichotomies indicating prevalence of use (i.e., percentages of seniors who used a drug or who used it at a particular level). Converting these dependent variables to dichotomies reduced the variance to be explained and thus lowered coefficients indicating strength of relationship; however, because the majority of seniors fell into the single category of nonuse along each of the drug-use dimensions, the reduction in variance was modest (see Bachman & Schulenberg, 1992).

*Cigarette use.* Most high school seniors have tried cigarettes sometime in their lifetime, but most have not used them within the past year. Among the few who reported any use in the past year, most smoked on a daily basis and many smoked a half-pack or more a day. Figure 1, Part A, and also the first rows of Table 3, present key results from MCAs using hours of work, plus background and educational success measures, to predict prevalence of half-pack or more smoking. The figure displays a strong bivariate association between hours of work and half-pack smoking (solid lines), which remains fairly strong after controls for background and educational success (dashed lines). Particularly clear in the figure is the fact that the pattern is almost entirely linear. With each increment in hours of work, the prevalence of half-pack smoking rises, starting at about 5%–6% among those who worked 5 hr or less per week and rising to about 19% among those who worked more than 30 hr—a ratio of 3 to 1. After controlling background and educational success, this ratio is reduced to about 2 to 1. Also evident in the figure is the finding that those with no job had below-average smoking prevalences (more so for male seniors than for female seniors), but not quite as low as those working 5 hr or less.

Educationally successful students were far less likely than average to become regular smokers. Table 3 shows, for both male and female seniors, relatively strong negative relationships between the indicators of educational success and the use of cigarettes. Each of the three educational success indicators showed a stronger bivariate association with smoking than did the part-time work measure, and the multivariate beta coefficients also tended to be stronger (which is impressive when one considers that the education indicators overlap extensively). These controls for educational success and background characteristics accounted for about one third of the relationship between hours of work and cigarette use. Specifically, for male students, the bivariate eta coefficient of .141 is reduced to a multivariate beta coefficient of .091, that is, a 35% reduction; for female students, the reduction is 31% (from .118 to .082).

*Alcohol use.* The majority of high school seniors were current users of alcohol; indeed, fully two thirds of the male seniors and nearly as many of the female seniors reported using

---

[3] We treated the small proportion who reported working but not for pay as another separate category in the MCAs in order to be able to include all respondents. The findings for this group are unremarkable, thus we opted not to include them in Figures 1–4, although full results for them are included in our more detailed report.

Table 3

*Bivariate and Multivariate Multiple Classification Analysis Coefficients Relating Educational Success Indicators and Work Intensity to Outcome Variables for Male and Female High School Seniors*

| | | | Educational success indicators | | | | | | | |
| | | | College plans | | Curriculum | | Grade point average | | Work intensity | |
| Outcome variable | Gender | N | Eta | Beta | Eta | Beta | Eta | Beta | Eta | Beta |
|---|---|---|---|---|---|---|---|---|---|---|
| **Substance use** | | | | | | | | | | |
| Cigarettes | M | 32,792 | −.214 | −.127 | −.176 | −.017 | −.176 | −.118 | +.141 | +.091 |
| | F | 35,813 | −.189 | −.105 | −.160 | −.085 | −.168 | −.117 | +.118 | +.082 |
| Heavy alcohol | M | 31,698 | −.100 | .035 | −.093 | .039 | −.144 | −.130 | +.102 | +.066 |
| | F | 34,855 | −.062 | .015 | −.057 | .032 | −.118 | −.120 | +.094 | +.065 |
| Marijuana | M | 32,567 | −.100 | −.051 | −.086 | .031 | −.153 | −.132 | +.065 | .037 |
| | F | 35,602 | −.084 | .033 | −.075 | .039 | −.143 | −.128 | +.092 | +.068 |
| Cocaine | M | 32,873 | −.073 | .036 | −.070 | .039 | −.084 | −.060 | +.069 | +.050 |
| | F | 35,870 | −.061 | .027 | −.068 | .049 | −.083 | −.062 | +.069 | +.056 |
| **Problem behavior** | | | | | | | | | | |
| Interpersonal aggression | M | 6,530 | −.130 | .047 | −.134 | −.059 | −.145 | −.100 | +.132 | +.096 |
| | F | 7,039 | −.115 | .044 | −.114 | −.064 | −.150 | −.121 | +.107 | +.082 |
| Victimization | M | 6,520 | −.071 | .013 | −.093 | −.053 | −.115 | −.084 | +.113 | +.102 |
| | F | 7,033 | .048 | .034 | −.087 | −.050 | −.100 | −.073 | +.102 | +.092 |
| Trouble with police | M | 6,524 | −.076 | .019 | −.075 | .031 | −.146 | −.144 | +.102 | +.076 |
| | F | 7,034 | .066 | .052 | .044 | .031 | −.083 | −.081 | .047 | .045 |
| Arguments with parents | M | 6,513 | .046 | .035 | .048 | .028 | .038 | −.079 | +.096 | +.078 |
| | F | 7,032 | .042 | .020 | +.084 | +.071 | .013 | −.074 | +.123 | +.083 |
| **Time use** | | | | | | | | | | |
| Sleep | M | 5,651 | +.087 | +.079 | +.052 | .018 | +.076 | .066 | −.189 | −.186 |
| | F | 6,397 | .042 | .049 | .004 | .026 | .052 | −.059 | −.181 | −.182 |
| Breakfast | M | 5,681 | +.126 | .041 | +.140 | +.063 | +.151 | +.092 | −.142 | −.120 |
| | F | 6,425 | +.117 | .024 | +.132 | .043 | +.187 | +.140 | −.141 | −.113 |
| Exercise | M | 5,655 | +.214 | +.143 | +.172 | .053 | +.130 | +.055 | −.162 | −.130 |
| | F | 6,405 | +.168 | +.114 | +.145 | +.052 | +.085 | .049 | −.134 | −.127 |
| Dating | M | 32,759 | .045 | .029 | .049 | .031 | .058 | .047 | +.146 | +.132 |
| | F | 35,820 | −.112 | −.086 | −.072 | .034 | −.061 | .038 | +.137 | +.110 |
| **Satisfaction** | | | | | | | | | | |
| Life | M | 6,147 | +.090 | +.054 | +.068 | .023 | +.116 | +.093 | .053 | .043 |
| | F | 6,787 | +.070 | .050 | +.072 | .032 | +.131 | +.115 | −.076 | −.069 |
| Leisure | M | 6,162 | .018 | .014 | .025 | .015 | .060 | .076 | −.167 | −.177 |
| | F | 6,793 | .011 | .012 | .004 | .024 | .033 | .039 | −.171 | −.181 |
| Job | M | 3,639 | .012 | .017 | .022 | .007 | .046 | .047 | .081 | .082 |
| | F | 4,227 | .056 | .058 | +.057 | +.050 | +.053 | .031 | .044 | .050 |
| Self-esteem | M | 6,295 | +.186 | +.140 | +.132 | .029 | +.193 | +.149 | .049 | .028 |
| | F | 6,833 | +.161 | +.077 | +.132 | .046 | +.187 | +.151 | .050 | .041 |

*Note.* Eta coefficients express the bivariate correlation (both linear and nonlinear) between each predictor and each outcome variable. Beta coefficients express the multivariate association when other factors are controlled (see text). M = male; F = female. A plus sign indicates a predominantly positive association; a minus sign indicates a predominantly negative association; no sign indicates that relationship is either nonlinear or trivial. Significance levels and confidence intervals for these coefficients vary according to $N$; however, any coefficient in this table ≥ .040 is significantly different from zero ($p ≤ .01$).

alcohol during the past 30 days. Current alcohol use was positively related to number of hours worked, and controlling for background and educational success reduced these relationships by 26% for male seniors and 27% for female seniors. Unlike the findings for cigarette use, current alcohol-use prevalence rates were lowest for those without jobs. (See Bachman & Schulenberg, 1992, for full details on this measure of alcohol use.)

A more worrisome measure of alcohol use involves occasional heavy drinking; nearly half of the male seniors and more than a quarter of the female seniors had five or more drinks in a row at least once during the 2 weeks preceding the survey. This dimension of alcohol use also was positively related to hours

worked, and the pattern is fairly linear among both male and female seniors, as shown in Figure 1, Part B. Here again prevalence rates were lowest among those not working. Controls for background and educational success reduced these relationships by about one third (35% for male seniors and 31% for female seniors), as indicated in Table 3.

*Marijuana use.* Marijuana use declined steadily throughout the 1980s, but it remains the most widely used illicit drug among young people (Johnston et al., 1991). Figure 1, Part C, shows that marijuana use was positively related to hours of part-time work, although the patterns are weak and differ slightly between male and female seniors (see also Table 3). Among male seniors, the bivariate relationship is quite small but fairly

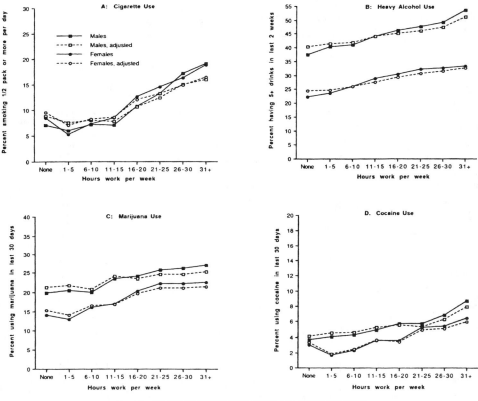

*Figure 1.* Use of drugs related to hours of work, with and without controls
for background and educational success.

linear; however, controls for background and educational success (which accounted for 43% of the relationship) left only a minor distinction between those working 10 hr or less (21%–22% estimated monthly marijuana users) and those working more hours (about 24% estimated users). Among female seniors, the bivariate relationship is slightly larger (and reduced by about 26% by the controls); but here there is little or no differentiation in marijuana prevalence related to variations in working time above 15 hr (20%–21% estimated users, after controls).

*Cocaine use.* Cocaine use declined sharply after 1986, and monthly prevalence among high school seniors was quite low by 1989; however, we found that the secular trend in use of this drug (as was true also for marijuana) was unrelated to the other variables that are the focus of this article. Figure 1, Part D,

shows that monthly prevalence of cocaine use is positively correlated with hours of work; indeed, among male students, the prevalence among those working over 30 hr was more than double that of those working 5 hr or less, whereas among female students, the contrast between these two groups is even greater. The pattern is fairly linear and reduced by 28% for male students and 19% for female students after background and educational success were controlled.

We also found that amphetamine use was positively related to hours of work; patterns for both male and female students are very similar to the cocaine data for male students shown in Figure 1, Part D (see Bachman & Schulenberg, 1992, for details).

*Summary.* Although the drugs reviewed here differed greatly in prevalence rates among high school seniors, they showed important similarities in their association with work intensity. First, consistent with our earlier findings and with other studies cited earlier, there were positive bivariate relationships between hours of work and use of each drug. Second, the patterns of relationship between hours of work and each dimension of drug use were in most respects fairly close to linear, both before and after controlling for background and educational success. The most general interpretation of the drug use findings in this section would have to be that part-time work is related to drug use, and the more hours worked, the greater the likelihood of use. These mostly linear relationships are consistent with our own earlier analyses of drug use (Bachman et al., 1986), but they contrast somewhat with the findings of Steinberg and Dornbusch (1991); their overall index of drug use rose sharply between 1–10 hr and 11–15 hr but showed little further change at 16–20 hr or 21 hr or more. Third, the introduction of controls for background and educational success reduced the strength of those relationships typically by a factor of about one quarter to one third; we note that these reductions represent lower bound estimates, both because we used a simultaneous entry analysis procedure and because the controls certainly were less than perfect.

## Employment and Hours of Work Linked to Other Deviant Behaviors

Drug use has been a focus of great concern in recent years, but there are a variety of other deviant or problem behaviors that for many years have been studied by those interested in youth and in social problems. We turn now to a set of measures in which seniors report their own misbehaviors and also their victimization by the misbehaviors of others.

*Interpersonal aggression.* Figure 2, Part A, shows that interpersonal aggression is positively correlated with work intensity, and the relationships were reduced by about one quarter (27% for male seniors and 23% for female seniors) when background and educational success were controlled. Male students working more than 30 hr per week reported twice as much aggressive behavior as those working 15 hr or less; the results were similar for female students, although their rates of aggression were far lower than those of male students. (Note that the scaling of this index is such that the lowest possible score is 1.0, indicating zero aggressive behavior; thus, even among male seniors working over 30 hr per week, aggression was not very extensive.) Among both male and female students, the pattern of association departs somewhat from linearity; there was little variation in aggression until hours of work were fairly long—indeed, the real increases involved only the longest hours worked (i.e., over 30 hr per week). These findings offer some support for the argument (cf. Greenberger & Steinberg, 1986) that working very long hours (in addition to attending school) can leave seniors irritable and aggressive.

A separate index of theft also was found to be positively related to work intensity, with relatively little change (reduction of 15% for male students and 21% for female students) after inclusion of the control measures (see Bachman & Schulenberg, 1992, for details). The pattern is roughly linear among male students; among female students, theft rose for those who worked more than 10 hr but changed little thereafter.

*Victimization.* We reported earlier that those working

longer hours were generally more likely to be perpetrators of aggression and theft; now we consider whether they are also more likely to be on the receiving end of such behaviors. Our earlier analysis examined a number of items separately, and nearly all showed "a clear tendency for higher rates of victimization among those working the longest hours" (Bachman et al., 1986, p. 92). For present purposes we used a single index of victimization. Figure 2, Part B, shows somewhat "bumpy" but predominantly positive associations between hours of work and victimization. At the extremes, rates of victimization were at least half again as high among those working more than 30 hr compared with those working 5 hr or less or those with no job. Controlling for background and educational success reduced the relationship by only about 10% for male and female seniors.

Does this suggest that a good deal of such victimization occurs in or near the work environment itself, with longer hours on the job thus placing an adolescent in increased danger? The evidence is not consistent with this interpretation; the majority of all victimization reported by seniors takes place in or near the schools, regardless of part-time work situation (see Bachman et al., 1986).

*Trouble with police.* A single item asked seniors how often in the last 12 months they had gotten into trouble with police because of something they did; most said not at all, and most of the rest reported that it happened only once. We thus chose to analyze a simple dichotomy, as we did for the drug-use measures, and report the percentages of seniors who had any trouble with police. The results in Figure 2, Part C, show somewhat positive correlations with hours of work. Including the controls reduced this relationship by 25% for male students but only 4% for female students. Among male students, those not employed showed the lowest prevalence of trouble with police; however, that was not the case for female students. On the whole, and especially in the case of male seniors, these findings do little to support the notion that having students actively involved in part-time jobs will keep them "out of trouble." (Of course, this leaves open the question of whether some of those students who choose to work long hours might encounter more trouble if they were not kept so busy on their jobs.)

*Arguing or fighting with parent(s).* Another single item asked seniors how often in the last 12 months they had argued or had a fight with either parent. About half of the female students and nearly as many male students chose the top response category (five or more times), and the overall means show that the typical senior recalled having three or four such encounters.[4] Figure 2, Part D, shows that as hours worked increased from 5 hr or less up to the 16–20 hr category, arguments and fights with parents tended to increase; however, beyond 20 hr the pattern for male seniors is bumpy and difficult to interpret, whereas for female seniors the confrontations with parents seemed to decline somewhat as hours of work increased beyond 20 hr (although the latter finding was damped down after controlling for background and educational success). The lowest rates of arguments and fights occurred among those not work-

---

[4] We suspect that the majority of such encounters are more aptly described as "arguments" than as "fights." Certainly the sex difference here, which contrasts sharply with sex differences in the aggression items, is consistent with that suspicion.

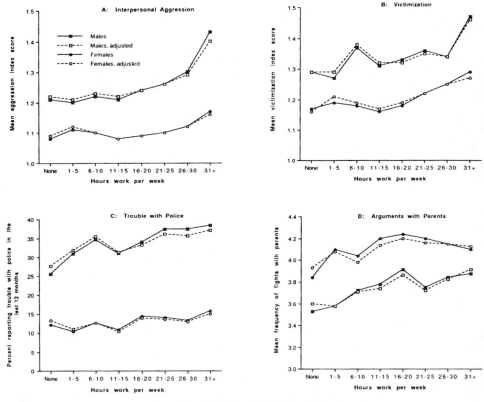

*Figure 2.* Other deviant behaviors related to hours of work, with and without controls for background and educational success.

ing. The inclusion of the controls caused the relationship to decrease by 19% for male students and 33% for female students.

*Summary.* Like the measures of drug use examined in the preceding section, these several measures of other deviant behaviors showed generally positive linkages with hours of work. Although some of the patterns departed from linearity in various ways, there is little to suggest any optimal number of hours that high school students could work before generating some increase in problem behavior. Rather, it appears that each increment in number of hours worked is associated with an increase in one or more of the problems.

### Employment and Hours of Work Linked to Time Use: Health-Related Behaviors and Dating

One of the criticisms of part-time work among high school students, especially when it involves long hours, is that it may steal time from other important activities. Here, we are concerned with how work intensity might interfere with taking time to eat breakfast, getting enough sleep, periodically exercising, and dating.

*Getting enough sleep.* To the question, "How often do you get at least 7 hours of sleep?" the median response among high school seniors was *most days* (which is the fourth category on a 6-point scale ranging from *never* to *everyday*). Figure 3, Part A, shows relatively strong negative correlations between hours of work and getting 7 hr of sleep. The relationships were equally strong among male and female seniors, almost perfectly linear, and utterly unaffected by controls for background and educational success.

*Eating breakfast.* Responses to a question about eating breakfast were bimodal: More than a third of the male students, and even more female students, reported that they sel-

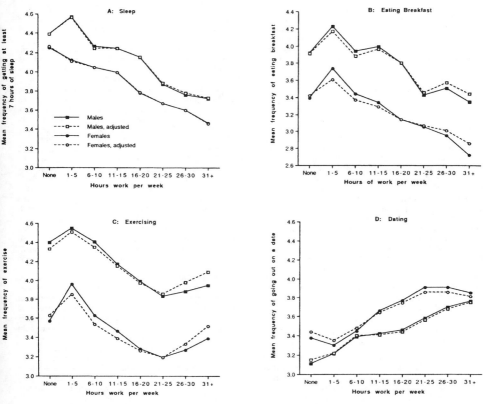

*Figure 3.* Time use related to hours of work, with and without controls for background and educational success.

dom or never eat breakfast; more than a third of the male students, but only half as many female students, reported doing so every day or nearly every day. Figure 3, Part B, shows fairly strong negative correlations with hours of work and patterns that are nearly linear. Here, however, there was a modest reduction in strength of association when other factors were controlled (15% for male seniors and 20% for female seniors). Those with no job were more likely to eat breakfast than average, but not quite as likely as those working 1–5 hr.

*Exercising vigorously.* A question about exercise referred to jogging, swimming, calisthenics, or any other active sports. We suspect that some respondents were unlikely to include vigorous work activity within this category, and thus any on-the-job exercise may have been underestimated. Figure 3, Part C, shows results for this measure that are somewhat similar to those for the other health-related behaviors. As work intensity

increased up to the category of 21–25 hr of work, the likelihood of exercise decreased. Beyond 25 hr, however, further increases in work intensity were associated with increased reports of exercise; this was true for both male and female students, and the pattern became more pronounced when background and educational success were controlled. It may be that working long hours often includes enough vigorous activity to be reported in this question (in spite of the wording bias in favor of sports). It is much less plausible that increasing the hours committed to part-time work by another 5 or 10 hr or more would free up more time for sports. Here again, those without jobs exercised more than average, but not quite as much as those working just a few hours.

*Dating.* Does time competition mean that those seniors who work long hours on a part-time job spend less time in dating? The answer is clearly negative, as shown in Figure 3,

Part D. Among male students, the positive association between hours worked and frequency of dating was linear, and the relationship was reduced by only 10% with the inclusion of controls for background and educational success. Among working female students, the relationship was linear up to the 21–25 hr category, but higher hours were not associated with any increase in dating. Female seniors not working showed rates of dating just above those for female seniors working 5 hr or less. The strength of relationship for female seniors was reduced by 20% by the controls.

In accord with previous research (e.g., Greenberger et al., 1980; Mortimer & Shanahan, 1991), a separate measure assessing total evenings out for fun and recreation showed only weak and nonlinear associations with hours of work, with male students averaging slightly less than 3 evenings out per week and female students averaging slightly more than 2. It thus appears that in spite of whatever time restrictions their jobs imposed, those who worked long hours were more likely than average to devote a portion of their leisure time to dating (although even these individuals averaged no more than one date per week).

*Summary.* The relationships involving hours of sleep provide the strongest and least ambiguous evidence of a cost that seems directly attributable to long hours of student employment: Students who spend more hours on the job simply have less time for sleep. To a considerable extent, they also short change themselves with respect to other health-relevant behaviors, such as eating breakfast and exercising vigorously. On the other hand, these findings also show that, in general, those seniors who worked 10 hr or less per week were no worse off than those with no job, and those who worked just 5 hr or less per week actually seemed somewhat better off.

### Employment and Hours of Work Linked to Satisfaction and Self-Esteem

Most of the outcomes considered thus far have been rather objective indexes of psychosocial functioning. But any verdict on the costs and benefits of work status and intensity during adolescence also should take account of adolescents' happiness and well-being. In this section we consider subjective indexes related to satisfaction with life overall, to satisfaction with specific aspects of adolescents' lives, and to self-esteem.

*Satisfaction with life.* Results regarding satisfaction with life are presented in Figure 4, Part A. For male seniors, the association between work intensity and satisfaction with life was weak and nonlinear, especially after adjustments for background and educational success. The association was fairly weak and nonlinear for female seniors as well; however, satisfaction was lower among female seniors working more than 25 hr per week and was especially low among those working more than 30 hr.

*Satisfaction with leisure time.* One might suspect, given the apparent costs of work in terms of time for sleep and other health-relevant behaviors, that satisfaction with leisure time would be negatively related to work intensity. Such was the case for both male and female seniors; the relationship was strong and nearly linear, as shown in Figure 4, Part B. Controls for background and education did not reduce the association (actually, it was slightly enhanced). It is interesting to note in Table 3 that satisfaction with the way leisure time was spent was unre-

lated to college plans and curriculum and showed only a weak curvilinear association with GPA (B level students reported slightly greater satisfaction than those with either higher or lower grades).

*Satisfaction with job.* One might suppose that seniors working long hours would be less satisfied with their jobs because of the time pressures. Conversely, one could imagine that only those particularly satisfied with their jobs would be willing to work such long hours. In fact, neither such pattern appears to dominate, as shown in Figure 4, Part C. Job satisfaction showed only weak and inconsistent relationships with hours of work (and with each of the educational success indexes). Clearly, those working the longest hours are not below average in job satisfaction, but neither are they very much above average.

*Self-esteem.* Whereas satisfaction with leisure time is much more influenced by work intensity than by educational success, the opposite is clearly the case for self-esteem. The coefficients in Table 3 show that self-esteem was strongly and positively linked with grades and with planning for college, whereas the association with hours of work was small and further reduced by controls for background and educational success. Figure 4, Part D, shows that those working long hours averaged slightly lower self-esteem than those working few hours; however, the figure also shows that after controlling for the lower grades and college plans of those working long hours, their (adjusted) self-esteem scores were indistinguishable from those working few hours.

*Summary.* The satisfaction measures provide important information regarding the impact of work status and intensity. Detailed inspection of Figure 4, Parts A–C, shows that those working 6–10 hr per week (both female and male students) were among the most satisfied. It is interesting that for female students, working only 1–5 hr per week did not appear to yield high levels of satisfaction, a finding that may be due less to the number of hours, per se, than to the type of work that female students working less than 5 hr per week are likely to hold (e.g., babysitting). Overall, and particularly for male students, those who worked the longest hours (i.e., over 30 hr per week) reported both the highest job satisfaction and the lowest satisfaction with the way their leisure time is spent. As noted in previous studies (e.g., Steinberg & Dornbusch, 1991), self-esteem showed little relationship with number of hours worked per week.

### Discussion

We set out in these analyses to address three critical issues regarding work intensity: (a) What are the trade-offs between possible costs and benefits of part-time work intensity? (b) Do the patterns of findings suggest any optimal level of part-time work? (c) To what extent should the correlates of part-time work intensity be viewed as *consequences*?

Within the array of constructs that we considered, our findings show the correlates of part-time work intensity to be largely undesirable. Most notably, work intensity was positively correlated with smoking cigarettes, drinking alcohol, using illicit drugs, interpersonal aggression, theft, victimization, trouble with police, arguments with parents, lack of sleep, and lack of exercise. Work intensity was negatively correlated with seniors'

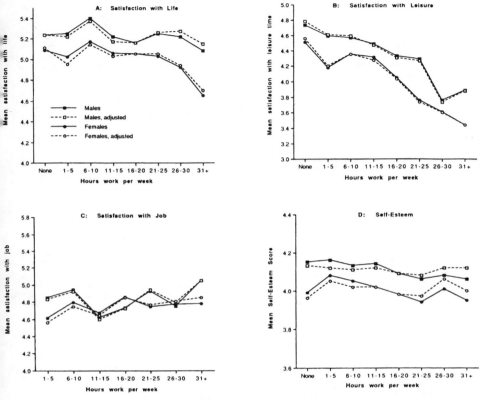

*Figure 4.* Satisfaction and self-esteem related to hours of work, with and without controls for background and educational success.

satisfaction with the way their leisure time is spent. And, of course, our initial analyses showed that work intensity was negatively correlated with various indicators of educational success. These bivariate relationships are generally consistent with the findings of Greenberger and Steinberg and colleagues (e.g., Greenberger & Steinberg, 1986; Steinberg & Dornbusch, 1991) and the findings of Mortimer and colleagues (e.g., Mortimer et al., 1991; Mortimer et al., 1992b), all noted earlier. The present work provides the additional advantages of nationally representative samples and numbers of cases large enough to permit fairly fine-grained analyses. Furthermore, our findings regarding health-related behaviors (perhaps reflecting time constraints) add important new information to the growing body of literature on the possible impacts of part-time work on psychosocial development during adolescence.

The large samples permitted detailed examination of the shapes of relationships with hours of work. Whereas Steinberg and Dornbusch (1991) used four categories, we used a seven-category scale with essentially equal intervals; this enabled us to check carefully for linearity and to observe important differences at the upper levels of hours worked. Although we did find some patterns that departed from linearity, such departures were not consistent across variables and were often not even consistent between male and female seniors on the same variable. By far the most dominant finding was that with each increase in number of hours worked, the associated problems also increased. It is also the case that no work at all is not necessarily better than 1–5 hr of work per week.

Now we confront the third and most difficult issue: To what extent are these mostly undesirable correlates properly interpreted as the consequences—the direct or indirect results—of part-time work intensity? Let us focus on what we consider to be the most important set of correlates, those having to do with educational success.

Like Steinberg and Dornbusch (1991), we found that students who did less well in school than their peers tended to work long hours in part-time jobs. More specifically, we found that students who had poor grades throughout high school, those who did not plan to complete college, and those who had been held back one or more grades at some point during their primary or secondary schooling all were more likely to work long hours in part-time jobs by the time they reached the end of their senior year in high school.[5] Although we are citing only correlational findings obtained from cross-sectional data, we view this evidence as strongly suggesting that prior educational successes, failures, and adjustments have a lot to do with adolescents' willingness to commit long hours to employment while still enrolled in school. In other words, although work intensity may make some additional contributions to poor school performance, we think the predominant causal process underlying these correlations is that students with a history of poorer performance and less interest in schooling are, as a consequence, more willing to spend long hours in a part-time job (cf. Lillydahl, 1990).

### Work Intensity as Part of a Syndrome

The bivariate data on drug use and other problem behaviors clearly show positive correlations with work intensity, but we have seen that these correlations are at least partly attributable to prior differences in background characteristics and educational success; such findings are also consistent with recent longitudinal evidence from Mortimer and her colleagues concerning selection effects (e.g., Mortimer et al., 1991). We think it may be useful to interpret this set of findings as reflecting a syndrome of behaviors that are interrelated and at least to some extent mutually reinforcing. Working long hours is not the first of such behaviors to emerge, by any means. An early indicator in some cases is that a student is held back a grade in school. Poor grades in general can also be an early indicator. Early initial use of cigarettes and alcohol, as well as marijuana and other illicit drugs, are yet other factors in the syndrome. In many (but not all) cases, it seems appropriate to treat long hours of part-time work as a part of such a syndrome of problem behaviors (Jessor & Jessor, 1977) or precocious development (Newcomb & Bentler, 1988). Thus construed, heavy time commitment to employment can be seen as an important symptom of a potentially wide range of psychosocial difficulties.

According to Jessor and Jessor (1977), an important component of the problem behavior syndrome is transition proneness, a form of "pseudomaturity" in which individuals engage in adultlike behaviors before they have the requisite perspectives and responsibilities that typically come with adulthood. This is in accord with Greenberger and Steinberg's (1986) concern that long hours of work move one toward a "pseudoadulthood." But rather than viewing work intensity as part of an exclusively negative syndrome, we prefer the somewhat broader concept of precocious development as described by Newcomb and Bentler (1988): "The syndrome of behaviors underlying precocious de-

velopment may be both positively and negatively valued and are not uniformly seen as problems or deviant" (p. 39). Thus, those students working long hours may be anticipating and experiencing a quicker transition to young adulthood than their agemates working fewer hours. In particular, those not anticipating college attendance are likely to work long hours, suggesting that for many of them the worker role is already more dominant than the student role and long hours on the job may be viewed as quite functional (cf. Stern & Nakata, 1989).

None of this suggests to us that precocious development, as a syndrome, is developmentally optimal. Indeed, as Newcomb and Bentler (1988) indicated, an underlying theme of precocious development is the inability to delay gratification. Consistent with Jessor and Jessor's (1977) notion of transition proneness, Newcomb and Bentler (1988, pp. 37–38) stated that "there may be a strong drive and need to grow up quickly and enjoy the positive aspects of adulthood, without waiting until this would naturally occur. As a result, the rewarding aspects of adulthood are sought and coveted (i.e., drug use, autonomy, sexual involvement), while avoiding the more difficult tasks of adulthood that would be gained with experience and maturity (e.g., responsibility, forethought)." Clearly, the notion of premature affluence (Bachman, 1983a) could also be seen as reflecting this inability to delay gratification; accordingly, to the extent that working long hours exacerbates this tendency by providing an easy means to conspicuous consumption, work intensity might contribute further to the precocious development syndrome. Nevertheless, it seems to us that part-time work, and especially high work intensity, occur relatively late in the syndrome, thus suggesting that work intensity is perhaps more a symptom than a cause of various psychosocial difficulties.[6]

### Social Policy Issues and Implications

There has been a good deal of controversy concerning the possible advantages and disadvantages of part-time work among adolescents (see, e.g., Greenberger & Steinberg, 1986; Mortimer et al., 1992a, 1992b; Steinberg & Dornbusch, 1991; Stern & Nakata, 1989). The controversy centers less on the correlational findings themselves and more on interpretations and policy recommendations. But even with respect to policy

---

[5] The 1991 Monitoring the Future survey of seniors, carried out after virtually all of the present analyses were completed, included for the first time a question specifically asking about grade failure (i.e., whether the respondent had ever been held back at any point during elementary or secondary school). It is noteworthy that among the 1991 seniors, those who had been held back were about one and one-half times more likely to be working long hours (26 hr or more per week) compared with those who never held back. Because most such grade failures occur before high school and any commitment of long hours to part-time jobs, this relationship would seem to reflect primarily a causal pattern of poor school performance contributing to long hours of work.

[6] The desire to work long hours and earn a lot of money may emerge earlier, but laws constrain younger adolescents from being employed long hours in the formal work sector. One effect of such laws is to limit most causal impacts of part-time work to later adolescence.

implications, there may be large areas of agreement. We begin by stressing those.

First, given the typical work experiences of high school seniors, we think that most observers would agree that those students who do not choose to work long hours are generally better off than those who do.[7] Given the evidence suggesting that educational success predisposes students to avoid excessive involvement in part-time work, we feel confident that most observers would support early academic development and intervention efforts as an action step. (Of course, there are already many other important reasons for supporting such efforts to strengthen early academic success.)

Second, it also seems safe to say that most observers would support efforts toward making the present array of part-time jobs more educationally useful, particularly in terms of preparation for future employment experiences. Greenberger and Steinberg (1986, pp. 227–230) offered a number of practical suggestions as to how employers might "optimize adolescents' work environments"; in addition to limiting hours of employment, they suggested greater variety in activities (e.g., job rotation) and greater amounts of cross-age contact (e.g., older adults as mentors or role models). They also encouraged schools to "integrate adolescents' work experience into school activities" (pp. 230–233), including the idea of schools developing standard checklists for supervisors to use in rating their student employees, and then maintaining files of such ratings that could be used by the students as an additional "credential" even after they graduate (see also Bachman, 1983b; Hamilton, 1990). Hamilton (1990) called for more comprehensive changes in at least some youth jobs; his proposed Americanized version of the German apprenticeship system would result in worthwhile work experiences during adolescence, as well as smoother transitions into adult employment.

But job improvement will take time and effort, and increasing early educational successes will take even more; in the meantime, the question remains as to how society should deal with those students who, for good reasons or poor, want to be employed—often for long hours. Steinberg and Dornbusch (1991) suggested that "parents, educational practitioners, and policymakers should continue to monitor the number of weekly hours that adolescents work during the school year" (p. 313). But the question remains, what should follow from the monitoring? Specifically, if some students wish to commit themselves more heavily to part-time work, should parents and policymakers treat such employment opportunities as troublesome distractors or as potentially valuable alternatives?

We think there may be more than one correct answer to this question. On the one hand, there may be many students who are neither profoundly alienated from school nor strongly committed to the delays in gratification that educational success requires; they are thus vulnerable to the seductions of quick earnings and "premature affluence"—the typical teenage pattern of "earn and spend" rather than "earn and save/invest in the future." For such individuals, the best prescription may be for parents and counselors to urge limitations in working hours so that schooling can remain the primary area of involvement. On the other hand, we suspect there are at least some individuals who reach high school carrying a much heavier burden of frustrations with the schooling process. Under current condi-

tions, if effective educational remediation is not available for such students, increased involvement in part-time work may actually help to prevent a complete disengagement (i.e., dropping out of school), and employment may also provide an alternative basis for feelings of self-worth. Such a compensatory phenomenon may underlie our findings (see also Bachman et al., 1986) and those of others (e.g., Steinberg & Dornbusch, 1991) that self-esteem is practically unrelated to hours of work.

In the long run, however, we continue to believe that the best approach is to address basic needs for early scholastic intervention, positive school climates, high expectations, thorough development of basic skills, and the like (Goertz, Ekstrom, & Rock, 1991; see also Bachman, O'Malley, & Johnston, 1978). A parallel argument would be that the best way to avoid students working long hours in part-time jobs would be to improve their interest in and commitment to school, so that they would not wish to overinvest in work at the possible expense of their schooling. In other words, our preference is to focus primarily on a *demand reduction* strategy that seeks ways to reduce students' desires for long hours of work, in contrast to a *supply reduction* strategy that would simply place additional legal or quasi-legal constraints on the hours students can work.

## Conclusion

We agree with Greenberger, Steinberg, and others that for quite some time there has been a large discrepancy between the idealized notions about employment being good for adolescents and the job experiences actually available. We are also convinced that work intensity among contemporary high school students is correlated with many potentially detrimental behaviors. Indeed, our own analyses reported here clearly indicate that most of the correlates of work intensity are undesirable. Our own interpretation is that work intensity can be closely linked to a more general syndrome of precocious development, much of which predates extensive part-time employment during the school year.

In addition to that general conclusion, we also draw several finer grained distinctions. One such distinction is that different correlates of work intensity may involve different causal patterns. Another distinction is that not all teenage jobs are as limited and limiting as are the typical teenage jobs. Finally, we stress that the mix of job experiences presently available to adolescents is something that could be changed, given concerted action by parents, educators, enlightened employers, and policymakers.

We believe that there currently exists enough variability along several important dimensions to assume that some part-

---

[7] Most seniors work in jobs that they describe as not being acceptable work "for most of their lives"—rather, they characterize their jobs as the sort of thing people do "just for the money" (Bachman, Bare, & Frankie, 1986). Important exceptions are many work-study jobs, which generally involve school programs designed to integrate school and work to improve the later transition from school to work. Students working long hours in such jobs may be doing so for somewhat different reasons than students with long hours in the more typical part-time job, and the impacts of such employment experiences are likely also to be different.

time work experiences are, in balance, developmentally beneficial for certain adolescents. What characterizes these jobs, these young people, and the interaction between the two? We see such questions as particularly promising for future research, especially given the likelihood that school-year employment is likely to remain an important part in the life of many, if not most, adolescents.

## References

Andrews, F. M., Morgan, J. N., Sonquist, J. A., & Klem, L. (1973). *Multiple classification analysis* (2nd ed.). Ann Arbor, MI: University of Michigan, Institute for Social Research.

Bachman, J. G. (1983a). Premature affluence: Do high school students earn too much money? *Economic Outlook USA, 10,* 64–67.

Bachman, J. G. (1983b). Schooling as a credential: Some suggestions for change. *International Review of Applied Psychology, 32,* 347–360.

Bachman, J. G., Bare, D. E., & Frankie, E. I. (1986). *Correlates of employment among high school seniors* (Monitoring the Future Occasional Paper No. 20). Ann Arbor, MI: University of Michigan, Institute for Social Research.

Bachman, J. G., & Johnston, L. D. (1978). *The Monitoring the Future project: Design and procedures* (Monitoring the Future Occasional Paper No. 1). Ann Arbor, MI: University of Michigan, Institute for Social Research.

Bachman, J. G., Johnston, L. D. & O'Malley, P. M. (1981). Smoking, drinking, and drug use among American high school students: Correlates and trends, 1975–1979. *American Journal of Public Health, 58,* 147–166.

Bachman, J. G., Johnston, L. D., & O'Malley, P. M. (1987). *Monitoring the future: Questionnaire responses from the nation's high school seniors, 1986.* Ann Arbor, MI: University of Michigan, Institute for Social Research.

Bachman, J. G., O'Malley, P. M., & Johnston, J. (1978). *Youth in transition: Vol. VI. Change and stability in the lives of young men.* Ann Arbor, MI: University of Michigan, Institute for Social Research.

Bachman, J. G., & Schulenberg, J. (1992). *Part-time work by high school seniors: Sorting out correlates and possible consequences* (Monitoring the Future Occasional Paper No. 32). Ann Arbor, MI: University of Michigan, Institute for Social Research.

Charner, I., & Fraser, B. (1987). *Youth and work: What we know, what we don't know, and what we need to know.* Washington, DC: W. T. Grant Foundation, Commission on Work, Family, and Citizenship.

D'Amico, R. (1984). Does employment in high school impair academic progress? *Sociology of Education, 57,* 152–164.

Goertz, M. E., Ekstrom, R. B., & Rock, D. (1991). High school dropouts: Issues of race and sex. In R. M. Lerner, A. C. Petersen, & J. Brooks-Gunn (Eds.), *Encyclopedia of adolescence* (pp. 250–253). New York: Garland.

Greenberger, E., & Steinberg, L. (1986). *When teenagers work: The psychological and social costs of adolescent employment.* New York: Basic Books.

Greenberger, E., Steinberg, L., & Vaux, A. (1981). Adolescents who work: Health and behavioral consequences of job stress. *Developmental Psychology, 17,* 691–703.

Greenberger, E., Steinberg, L. D., Vaux, A., & McAuliffe, S. (1980). Adolescents who work: Effects of part-time employment on family and peer relations. *Journal of Youth and Adolescence, 9,* 189–202.

Hamilton, S. F. (1990). *Apprenticeship for adulthood: Preparing youth for the future.* New York: Free Press.

Hamilton, S. F., & Crouter, A. C. (1980). Work and growth: A review of research on the impact of work experience on adolescent development. *Journal of Youth and Adolescence, 9,* 323–338.

Hotchkiss, L. (1986). Work and schools: Complements and competitors? In K. Borman & J. Reisman (Eds.), *Becoming a worker* (pp. 90–115). Norwood, NJ: Ablex.

Jessor, R., & Jessor, S. L. (1977). *Problem behavior and psychological development: A longitudinal study of youth.* San Diego, CA: Academic Press.

Johnston, L. D., & O'Malley, P. M. (1985). Issues of validity and population coverage in student surveys of drug use. In B. A. Rouse, N. J. Kozel, & L. G. Richards (Eds.), *Self-report methods of estimating drug use: Meeting current challenges to validity* (NIDA Research Monograph No. 57; ADM 85–1402). Washington, DC: U.S. Government Printing Office.

Johnston, L. D., O'Malley, P. M., & Bachman, J. G. (1991). *Drug use among American high school seniors, college students and young adults, 1975–1990* (DHHS Publication No. ADM 91–1813). Washington, DC: U.S. Government Printing Office.

Kish, L. (1965). *Survey sampling.* New York: Wiley.

Lillydahl, J. (1990). Academic achievement and part-time employment of high school students. *Journal of Economic Education, 21,* 307–316.

Mortimer, J. T., & Finch, M. D. (1986). The effects of part-time work on adolescents' self-concept and achievement. In K. Borman & J. Reisman (Eds.), *Becoming a worker* (pp. 66–89). Norwood, NJ: Ablex.

Mortimer, J. T., Finch, M., Owens, T. J., & Shanahan, M. (1990). Gender and work in adolescence. *Youth and Society, 22,* 201–224.

Mortimer, J. T., Finch, M. D., Ryu, S., & Shanahan, M. (1991, April). Evidence from a prospective longitudinal study of work experience and adolescent development. In J. T. Mortimer (Chair), *New evidence on the benefits and costs of employment, work intensity, and work quality for adolescent development.* Symposium conducted at the 1991 biennial meetings of the Society for Research on Child Development, Seattle, WA.

Mortimer, J. T., Finch, M. D., Shanahan, M., & Ryu, S. (1992a). Adolescent work history and behavioral adjustment. *Journal of Research on Adolescence, 2,* 59–80.

Mortimer, J. T., Finch, M. D., Shanahan, M., & Ryu, S. (1992b). Work experience, mental health, and behavioral adjustment in adolescence. *Journal of Research on Adolescence, 2,* 25–58.

Mortimer, J. T., & Shanahan, M. (1991, June). *Adolescent work experience and relationship with peers.* Paper presented at the 1991 American Sociological Association Meeting, Cincinnati, OH.

National Commission on Youth (1980). *The transition to adulthood: A bridge too long.* New York: Westview Press.

Newcomb, M. D., & Bentler, P. M. (1988). *Consequences of adolescent drug use: Impact on the lives of young adults.* Newbury Park, CA: Sage.

O'Malley, P. M., Bachman, J. G., & Johnston, L. D. (1983). Reliability and consistency in self-reports of drug use. *International Journal of the Addictions, 18,* 805–824.

President's Science Advisory Committee, Panel on Youth (1974). *Youth: Transition to adulthood.* Chicago: University of Chicago Press.

Rosenberg, M. (1965). *Society and the adolescent self-image.* Princeton, NJ: Princeton University Press.

Schulenberg, J., Bachman, J. G., O'Malley, P. M., & Johnston, L. D. (1992). *High school educational success and subsequent substance use: A panel analysis following adolescents into young adulthood.* Unpublished manuscript, University of Michigan, Institute for Social Research.

Steel, L. (1991). Early work experience among white and non-white youths: Implications for subsequent enrollment and employment. *Youth and Society, 22,* 419–447.

Steinberg, L. D., & Dornbusch, S. M. (1991). Negative correlates of part-time employment during adolescence: Replication and elaboration. *Developmental Psychology, 27,* 304–313.

Steinberg, L. D., Greenberger, E., Garduque, L., & McAuliffe, S. (1982). High school students in the labor force: Some costs and benefits to schooling and learning. *Educational Evaluation and Policy Analysis, 4,* 363–372.

Steinberg, L. D., Greenberger, E., Garduque, L., Ruggiero, M., & Vaux, A. (1982). Effects of working on adolescent development. *Developmental Psychology, 18,* 385–395.

Steinberg, L. D., Greenberger, E., Garduque, L., Vaux, A., & Ruggiero, M. (1981). Early work experience: Effects on adolescent occupational socialization. *Youth and Society, 12,* 403–422.

Stern, D., & Nakata, Y.-F. (1989). Characteristics of high school students' paid jobs, and employment experience after graduation. In D. Stern & D. Eichorn (Eds.), *Adolescence and work: Influences of social structure, labor markets, and culture* (pp. 189–233). Hillsdale, NJ: Erlbaum.

Stevens, C. J., Puchtell, L. A., Ryu, S., & Mortimer, J. T. (1992). Adoles-

cent work and boys' and girls' orientations to the future. *Sociological Quarterly, 33,* 153–169.

Work-Education Consortium (1978). *Work and service experience for youth.* Washington, DC: Manpower Institute.

Yamoor, C., & Mortimer, J. T. (1990). Age and gender differences in the effects of employment on adolescent achievement and well-being. *Youth and Society, 22,* 225–240.

Yasuda, K. E. (1990). *Working and schooling decisions: A study of New Hampshire teenage labor market behavior and the level of educational attainment* (First and Second Interim Reports). Concord, NH: Department of Employment Security, Economic and Labor Market Information Bureau.

Received July 1, 1991
Revision received May 11, 1992
Accepted June 9, 1992 ∎

JOURNAL OF RESEARCH ON ADOLESCENCE, 2(4), 317–330
Copyright © 1992, Lawrence Erlbaum Associates, Inc.

# Alcohol Use, Suicidal Behavior, and Risky Activities Among Adolescents

Michael Windle, Carol Miller-Tutzauer, and
Donna Domenico
*Research Institute on Addictions*

Secondary-data analyses were conducted with the National Adolescent Student Health Survey to investigate relations between alcohol use, suicidal ideation and attempts, and risky (dangerous) activities among early (8th graders) and mid-adolescents (10th graders). Higher levels of alcohol use were associated with increases in the frequency of suicidal ideation and attempts across grade levels and for sex. Similarly, higher levels of alcohol use were associated with more frequent involvement in risky activities (e.g., swimming alone, taking someone else's medication) across grade levels and for sex. Logistic-regression models indicated that sex, alcohol use, and risky behaviors were significant predictors of suicidal ideation and attempts. Particularly salient were findings for heavy alcohol-using, high risk-taking female adolescents who had attempted suicide. For 8th graders, the probability of having attempted suicide for this subgroup was 0.52 and for 10th graders this subgroup was 0.47.

Suicide was the fifth-leading cause of death among teenagers and young adults in 1960; in 1985 it was the second-leading cause of death among teenagers (Centers for Disease Control, 1985). Research regarding suicidal behavior has indicated that the peak age of attempted suicide, or parasuicide, is during the 15 to 19 age range (Hawton & Goldacre, 1982; Rutter, 1986). Furthermore, whereas completed suicides are more frequent among males, suicide attempts are more frequent among females. In addition to sex differences in attempted and completed suicides, numerous studies have been conducted to identify factors that distinguish adolescents with suicidal ideation from adolescent

---

Requests for reprints should be sent to Michael Windle, Research Institute on Addictions, 1021 Main Street, Buffalo, NY 14203.

attempters and completers (see reviews of Hawton, 1986; Spirito, Brown, Overholser, & Fritz, 1989). That is, rather than conceptualizing these suicidal behaviors along a continuum with a common etiology, different factors are posed to contribute to the specified behaviors. For example, Kosky, Silburn, and Zubrick (1990) used an outpatient sample of children/adolescents and reported that those who had attempted suicide (relative to those who had had suicidal thoughts but no attempt) had higher levels of chronic family discord and substance abuse. Rutter (1986) reported that overt depressive disorders were more highly associated with suicide attempts than with suicidal ideation among adolescents. Shaffer (1986) studied differences between adolescent suicide attempters and completers and indicated that the groups did not differ with regard to depression; however, suicide attempters and completers manifested higher levels of antisocial behavior and interpersonal aggression than nonsuicidal depressives.

Whereas most studies of adolescent suicide have been conducted with clinical samples, several studies of suicidal behaviors have been conducted with nonclinical adolescent samples. The rates of suicidal ideation and attempts have been markedly high for those nonclinical sample studies that have been reported (e.g., Albert & Beck, 1975; Garrison, 1989; Smith & Crawford, 1986). For example, Smith and Crawford (1986) reported that 63% of a high school sample indicated prior suicidal ideation and 11% had attempted suicide on one or more occasions. Research reviewed by Hawton (1986) and Spirito et al. (1989) has suggested that alcohol or substance abuse is often associated with adolescent suicide attempts, though the magnitude of the association varies across studies. Garfinkel, Froese, and Hood (1982) reported that the rate of substance abuse at the time of the suicide attempt for a sample of children and adolescents seen in an emergency room was 11.3%.

The generalizability of relations between adolescent suicidal behaviors and alcohol use among clinical and emergency room samples to national adolescent samples is largely unknown. As such, using data from a nationally representative adolescent sample, the first objective of this study was to investigate the interrelations between adolescent alcohol use and suicidal ideation and attempts. The second objective was to study interrelations between alcohol use and nonsuicidal, but risky, activities that may result in accidental serious injury or death (e.g., unsupervised swimming, taking someone else's prescribed medicine). Suicidal behavior and risky activities are viewed as distinct conceptual domains that are associated with risk for adolescent health and mortality. Alcohol use during adolescence is proposed as a correlate of both suicidal behaviors and risky activities, though the function(s) served by alcohol (e.g., self-medication vs. enhancement) may differ. Associations have been reported between adolescent suicidal behavior and substance use (e.g., Hawton, 1986; Shaffer, 1986). In addition, Zuckerman (1972) reported that higher sensation seeking is associated with higher levels of substance use among adolescents. Although the measure of risk-taking behavior used in this study has not been compared with standardized measures of sensation seeking, we view it as containing ratings of items that yield scores consistent with the domain of risk-taking behaviors.

The third objective was to investigate the combined associations of alcohol use and risky activities on suicidal behaviors. That is, for instance, was the combination of lowered inhibitions, influenced by alcohol use and a risk-taking propensity, associated with a higher probability of suicidal behavior among adolescents? Clark, Sommerfeldt, Schwarz, Hedeker, and Watel (1990) suggested that at least a portion of adolescent high risk takers had a history of suicide attempts. In addition, R. Jessor and S. L. Jessor's (1977) research has suggested that problematic behaviors tend to covary during adolescence.

The data used in this study are from the National Adolescent Student Health Survey (NASHS; 1989), which was administered to more than 11,000 8th- and 10th-grade students nationwide in the fall of 1987. The large, nationally representative sample of early and mid-adolescents provided a unique data source for investigating the three primary objectives stated previously, and for studying possible sex differences in interrelations between alcohol use, suicidal behavior, and risky activities.

## METHOD

The NASHS was initiated in 1985 by the American Health Association, the Association for the Advancement of Health Education, and the Society for Public Health Education. All three organizations worked in conjunction with the American Alliance for Health, Physical Education, Recreation, and Dance. Other Federal agencies that participated in the planning and development of the survey were the National Institute on Drug Abuse, the Center for Disease Control, and the U.S. Department of Education.

The NASHS is the first major national study of adolescent health issues in more than 20 years. The goal of the survey was to assess adolescents' knowledge of health issues and to use this information to plan new health objectives in the future. Eight health areas were addressed in this survey including drug and alcohol use, suicide, violence, acquired immune deficiency syndrome, sexually transmitted diseases, nutrition, consumer skills, and injury prevention. These eight health areas were selected through committees created by governmental agencies and co-sponsoring health organizations. Survey questions for each health area were developed by a panel of nationally known experts from that area.

## Subjects

The NASHS data were drawn from a representative sample of 224 public and private schools in 20 states randomly selected by Macro Systems, Inc. of Silver Springs, MD. Of the 224 schools, 190 were public and 34 were private. Three mandatory classes (e.g., English) were randomly selected for 8th and 10th graders from each school. Standard informed-consent forms describing the purpose of the study and the content areas to be surveyed were distributed by teachers to students to take home. Those parents who preferred that their child not participate in the study were requested to sign and return the form to the teacher and their child would then be excluded from participation in the study. Approximately 89% of eligible 8th graders and 86% of eligible 10th graders participated in the study; 7% of 8th graders and 11% of 10th graders were absent on the day of the survey assessment; and 3% of 8th graders and 3% of 10th graders were excluded due to lack of parental or adolescent consent. There was no make-up day to survey those students who were absent on the regularly scheduled survey day. The participation rate of adolescents in the NASHS is equivalent to or exceeds the rate of participation among adolescents in other large-scale high school surveys.

The sample consisted of approximately 11,400 8th- and 10th-grade students ranging from 11 to 17 years of age ($M = 13.44$, $SD = 0.76$, for 8th graders; $M = 15.33$, $SD = 0.72$, for 10th graders). Eighth-grade students were selected as representative of the junior high school population because the 8th grade represents the middle level of junior high/middle school; 10th-grade students were chosen as representative of the high school population based on the higher dropout rate of 11th- and 12th-grade students.

The students' racial and ethnic backgrounds were as follows: White = 72.7%, Black = 12.6%, Hispanic = 8.6%, Asian = 2.6%, Native American = 1.1%, other = 2.4%. The number of females nearly equaled the number of males for each grade level: Females comprised 50.2% of the 8th graders and 50.7% of the 10th graders; males comprised 49.8% of the 8th graders and 49.3% of the 10th graders. Data were pooled across racial and ethnic groups because comparisons for the three most highly represented groups (Whites, Blacks, and Hispanics) indicated minor differences in suicidal ideation and attempts. Specifically, the percentages of affirmative responses to suicidal ideation for Whites, Blacks, and Hispanics were 33.5%, 28.5%, and 36.1%, respectively. The percentages of affirmative responses to suicidal attempts for Whites, Blacks, and Hispanics were 13.3%, 12.7%, and 16.8%, respectively.

**Measures**

In order to sample a wide range of issues relating to adolescent health, three separate survey forms were developed. All three forms contained a "seed" set of 11 questions pertaining to demographics (age, sex, ethnicity) and substance use (alcohol, cigarettes, and drugs). In addition to the identical set items across the three forms, each form included a specialized set of items related to various aspects of adolescent health. The data from the survey form used in this study included questions about suicide, alcohol use, and adolescents' risky behaviors.

Our assessment of adolescents' suicidal behaviors involved two questions — one related to suicidal ideation and the other related to suicide attempts. The suicidal ideation item asked, "Have you ever seriously thought about trying to hurt yourself in a way that might result in your death?" Suicide attempts were evaluated through the question, "Have you ever actually tried to hurt yourself in a way that might have resulted in your death?" Both questions utilized a dichotomous (yes–no) response format.

The alcohol consumption measure involved asking students "On how many occasions, if any, have you had alcoholic beverages to drink such as wine, wine coolers, beer, mixed drinks, or hard liquor during the last 30 days?" Response options included 0 occasions, 1 to 2 occasions, 3 to 5 occasions, 6 to 9 occasions, 10 to 19 occasions, 20 to 39 occasions, and 40 or more occasions. We formed three drinking groups on the basis of responses to this question — abstainers (0 occasions), light drinkers (1 to 5 occasions), and moderate/heavy drinkers (6 or more occasions). We recognize the limitations inherent in assessing alcohol involvement solely on the basis of number of occasions of drinking due to the absence of information on the amount (quantity) consumed per occasion. Unfortunately, data on the amount consumed per occasion were not available as part of the NASHS. Nevertheless, correlation of the frequency of alcohol use with an index of number of occasions of heavy drinking (i.e., number of occasions of drinking five or more drinks) resulted in a Pearson correlation coefficient of 0.70 ($p < .001$), thus lending some support to our use of frequency of drinking as an indicator of level of alcohol involvement.

Our assessment of risk-taking behaviors centered around nine specific risky activities adolescents may or may not have engaged in: taking another person's medication; swimming alone; diving in water of unknown depth; taking alcohol/drugs while playing sports; driving an all terrain vehicle; using a gun for any reason; riding with a driver who is under the influence of alcohol/drugs; skating in an unsupervised area; and surfing or swimming in an unsupervised area. By risk taking, we are referring to an individual difference variable in which some individuals selectively engage in activities that increase the probability of serious injury or death, whereas other individuals either engage in these activities at a much lower rate or not at all. Each of the nine items was phrased "During the past year how many times have you participated in each of these behaviors?" A 6-point scale response format was utilized: *0 times* (1), *1 to 3 times* (2), *4 to 6 times* (3), *7 to 10 times* (4), *11 to 20 times* (5), and *more than 20 times* (6). We constructed a measure of adolescent risk taking by recoding responses for the nine risky behaviors to the midpoints of the response categories. The items were then summed to form a single index of risky behavior. The internal consistency estimates for the risk measure were 0.67 for 8th graders and 0.71 for 10th graders. We then formed three risk groups on the basis of the summed risk index: low risk takers (4 or fewer instances of engaging in risky behaviors), moderate risk takers (greater than 4 risky incidences up to 30 incidences), and high risk takers (more than 30 incidences). Each of the three risk groups contained approximately one third of the total sample.

**Procedure**

Parental consent forms were distributed to students in each grade level in the selected schools approximately 2 to 3 weeks prior to testing. Prior to the test date, teachers and administrators met with the students to describe the survey and the procedures to be used, including the anonymity of the students. Data were collected during the fall 1987 semester. On the test date the survey was administered to a representative cross section of students in each grade level (i.e. 8th and 10th) in a standardized data form that allowed for easy entry and subsequent data analysis. Three classes from each grade level were chosen from the sampled schools, and each of the three forms of the survey was distributed to each class. To ensure privacy and confidentiality among the students, the survey was administered and collected by individuals who were not employees of the school, and teachers were present only for disciplinary reasons. Students were given approximately 30 to 40 min to complete the survey. After this time the surveys (both completed and uncompleted) were collected, placed in a manila envelope, and sealed in the students' presence. Upon completion of this procedure, one student from each class was assigned to deliver the sealed envelope to a designated administrative office. The students were then thanked for their participation and dismissed from the survey.

## RESULTS

Examination of the frequency distribution of adolescents' suicidal behaviors across the three alcohol consumption categories confirmed our expectations. As shown in Table 1, the incidence of both suicidal ideation and attempts increased with increasing levels of alcohol use. Furthermore, this pattern remained consistent with boys and girls as well as across grade levels. Of particular interest are the extremely high levels of suicidal ideation among girls in the heavy alcohol-consumption group. Among 8th-grade girls, 60% of the heavy drinkers thought about committing suicide and 37% reported attempting suicide, while among 10th-grade girls 63% of those in the heavy drinking category contemplated suicide with 39% reporting carrying through with an attempt. There was also a linear trend between level of alcohol involvement and the percentage of respondents who answered affirmatively to knowing someone who had attempted suicide. To the extent that the person known to have attempted suicide serves as a role model, suicidal risk among adolescents may be increased.

TABLE 1
Percentage of Adolescents Reporting Various Suicidal Behaviors

| Grade | Sex | Alcohol Group | Thought About Committing Suicide | Attempted Suicide | Knew Someone Who Attempted Suicide | N |
|-------|-----|---------------|----------------------------------|-------------------|------------------------------------|-----|
| 8 | Female | Abstain | 29.8 | 11.0 | 49.0 | 588 |
| | | Light | 52.7 | 22.6 | 70.5 | 259 |
| | | Heavy | 59.6 | 37.0 | 76.6 | 47 |
| | Male | Abstain | 17.4 | 6.2 | 32.3 | 599 |
| | | Light | 36.2 | 15.2 | 51.9 | 243 |
| | | Heavy | 51.1 | 27.7 | 74.5 | 47 |
| 10 | Female | Abstain | 33.5 | 12.3 | 60.0 | 441 |
| | | Light | 52.0 | 21.4 | 70.7 | 352 |
| | | Heavy | 63.1 | 38.8 | 83.5 | 103 |
| | Male | Abstain | 22.7 | 5.9 | 43.4 | 389 |
| | | Light | 28.1 | 10.9 | 51.7 | 331 |
| | | Heavy | 38.4 | 21.9 | 84.8 | 139 |

Although attempted suicides constitute direct lethal threats, other nonsuicidal behaviors contribute to accidental deaths and, thus, increase adolescent mortality. However, rather than contemplating immediately lethal actions, adolescents may place themselves at increased risk for fatal or serious injury accidents by engaging in a variety of reckless or otherwise imprudent behaviors. We performed two-way analyses of variance (ANOVAs; Sex × Alcohol Group) separately for 8th and 10th graders on a continuous, composite risk score (summed across all nine risk behavior items) as the dependent variable.[1] The ANOVA models were statistically significant for both 8th, $F(2, 1,773) = 9.03$, $p < .001$, and 10th graders, $F(2, 1,745) = 15.13$, $p < .001$. The Sex × Alcohol Group interaction was statistically significant across grade levels, and a graphical plot of the interactions is illustrated in Figure 1. It appears that a slightly steeper slope for boys than girls at each grade level may account for the significant interaction effects. However, these interaction effects do not appear to be salient with regard to the substantive findings which indicate that sex and alcohol group are both predictive of higher levels of risk-taking behaviors.

In order to investigate the combined influence of alcohol use and risk taking by adolescents, we specified four logistic-regression models. The dependent variables for the models were suicidal ideation and attempts for each grade level, and the predictor variables were sex, alcohol use, and number of risky activities. Second-order interaction terms (e.g., Sex × Alcohol Use) were also entered in the logistic-regression models and were typically nonsignificant or trivial with respect to their association with the dependent variables.[2] The most parsimonious and significantly consistent model across grade levels and across the two dependent variables was the "main effects" model. The results of the main effects logistic-regression models are presented in Table 2. The logistic-regression models indicate that all three predictors were statistically significant ($p < .001$) across grade levels and dependent variables; the magnitude of effects were generally in the low-to-moderate range.

So as to provide clarity regarding the expected probabilities of having had suicidal thoughts or having attempted suicide, we used a categorical logit model predicting suicidal ideation and attempts by: Sex, drinking group (abstain, light, heavy), and risk category (low, moderate, or

---

[1]Analyses were conducted for each of the 9 risky behaviors and were consistent with the risk composite score findings in showing that a large proportion of adolescents in the high alcohol use group engaged more frequently in high-risk behaviors than those who consume little or no alcohol. A table summarizing these analyses is available upon request from the authors.

[2]Only one of six interaction terms was significant for 10th-graders (Drinking Group × Risk Category on Suicidal Ideation). The partial $r$ for this association was $-.05$.

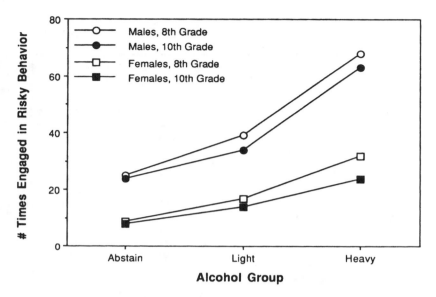

FIGURE 1    Graphical plot of statistically significant interactions (Alcohol Group ×
Risky Behaviors) for 8th- and 10th-grade adolescent males and females.

high).[3] As shown in Table 3, both suicidal ideation and attempts are
more probable among individuals in the heavy alcohol groups and
among high risk takers than among the other groups. The highest
likelihood of suicidal behaviors was among heavy drinkers who also
engaged in high levels of risky behaviors. Abstainers engaging in low
levels of risk taking were least likely to think about or attempt suicide.
Again, this pattern emerged for both boys and girls across both grade
levels.

## DISCUSSION

The alcohol use and suicidal behavior findings of this study with a
nationally representative sample of early and mid-adolescents are similar in several ways to prior research conducted with nonrepresentative
community and clinical samples (e.g., Brent et al., 1988; Garrison, 1989;
Smith & Crawford, 1986). First, the prevalence of suicidal ideation and
attempts was soberingly high for both early and mid-adolescents. These

---

[3]Consistent with the findings of the logistic-regression models, all parameters in the
categorical logit models were statistically significant ($p < .001$) and overall model fit was
indicated for each of the four specified models.

TABLE 2
Logistic-Regression Models Predicting Suicidal Behaviors by Sex, Alcohol Use, and
Risky Activities

| Models/Predictors | Coefficient | SE | Significance | R | Exp(B) |
|---|---|---|---|---|---|
| Model 1: Suicidal ideation (8th graders) | | | | | |
| Intercept | −2.24 | 0.14 | .000 | | |
| Sex (0 = M, 1 = F) | 0.87 | 0.12 | .000 | 0.15 | 2.39 |
| Alcohol use | 0.46 | 0.06 | .000 | 0.17 | 1.58 |
| Risky activities | 0.22 | 0.05 | .000 | 0.08 | 1.24 |
| Model 2: Suicidal attempts (8th graders) | | | | | |
| Intercept | −3.65 | 0.20 | .000 | | |
| Sex (0 = M, 1 = F) | 0.94 | 0.17 | .000 | 0.15 | 2.55 |
| Alcohol use | 0.41 | 0.06 | .000 | 0.17 | 1.50 |
| Risky activities | 0.39 | 0.07 | .000 | 0.14 | 1.48 |
| Model 3: Suicidal ideation (10th graders) | | | | | |
| Intercept | −1.81 | 0.14 | .000 | | |
| Sex (0 = M, 1 = F) | 1.03 | 0.12 | .000 | 0.18 | 2.80 |
| Alcohol use | 0.19 | 0.04 | .000 | 0.09 | 1.21 |
| Risky activities | 0.24 | 0.05 | .000 | 0.09 | 1.27 |
| Model 4: Suicidal attempts (10th graders) | | | | | |
| Intercept | −3.28 | 0.20 | .000 | | |
| Sex (0 = M, 1 = F) | 1.03 | 0.16 | .000 | 0.16 | 2.81 |
| Alcohol use | 0.31 | 0.05 | .000 | 0.15 | 1.36 |
| Risky activities | 0.21 | 0.07 | .000 | 0.07 | 1.23 |

Note: The R statistic corresponds to a partial correlation between the dependent variable and each of the independent variables. The Exp(B) reflects the odds of change for the dependent variable when the independent variable increases by one unit. Sample size for the 8th graders was 1,772 and for the 10th graders it was 1,746. M = male; F = female.

rates of suicidal ideation and attempts are consistent not only with prior adolescent suicide studies (e.g., Garrison, 1989), but also with findings regarding the prevalence of dysphoria and depression among children and adolescents (e.g., Kendall, Cantwell, & Kazdin, 1989). Both the childhood/adolescent suicide and depression literatures suggest that there are a number of children and adolescents who are experiencing disturbed affective states (e.g., helplessness, hopelessness, rejection, hostility, guilt) and engaging in self-destructive thought processes and behaviors. Second, the prevalence of suicidal ideation and attempts for both adolescent groups (i.e., 8th and 10th graders) increased with the level of alcohol use. Over 20% of heavy drinkers (regardless of sex or grade level) reported having attempted suicide. Third, the relation between suicidal behaviors and alcohol use paralleled the relation between exposure to suicide and level of alcohol use. That is, higher levels of alcohol use were associated with a higher probability of knowing someone who had attempted suicide. Brent et al. (1988)

TABLE 3
Expected Probabilities of Engaging in Suicidal Behaviors as a Function of Alcohol Use and
Risk Taking

| Grade | Sex | Alcohol Group | Probability of Suicidal Ideation | | | Probability of Attempted Suicide | | |
|---|---|---|---|---|---|---|---|---|
| | | | Low Risk Taking | Moderate Risk Taking | High Risk Taking | Low Risk Taking | Moderate Risk Taking | High Risk Taking |
| 8 | Female | Abstain | 0.26 | 0.33 | 0.41 | 0.08 | 0.13 | 0.23 |
| | | Light | 0.46 | 0.54 | 0.62 | 0.14 | 0.23 | 0.37 |
| | | Heavy | 0.55 | 0.63 | 0.70 | 0.24 | 0.35 | 0.52 |
| | Male | Abstain | 0.13 | 0.17 | 0.22 | 0.03 | 0.05 | 0.10 |
| | | Light | 0.26 | 0.33 | 0.40 | 0.06 | 0.10 | 0.19 |
| | | Heavy | 0.33 | 0.41 | 0.49 | 0.11 | 0.17 | 0.30 |
| 10 | Female | Abstain | 0.33 | 0.39 | 0.50 | 0.12 | 0.13 | 0.20 |
| | | Light | 0.44 | 0.51 | 0.62 | 0.19 | 0.21 | 0.30 |
| | | Heavy | 0.51 | 0.58 | 0.68 | 0.33 | 0.35 | 0.47 |
| | Male | Abstain | 0.15 | 0.19 | 0.26 | 0.04 | 0.05 | 0.08 |
| | | Light | 0.22 | 0.27 | 0.37 | 0.08 | 0.09 | 0.13 |
| | | Heavy | 0.27 | 0.33 | 0.43 | 0.15 | 0.16 | 0.24 |

*Note.* Table entries are based on the results of categorical logistic-regression analysis.

reported that the social networks of suicide attempters are more likely to contain individuals who have engaged in suicidal behaviors than individuals in social networks of nonsuicide attempters. Fourth, sex differences were found across grade levels for both suicidal ideation and attempts, with a larger percentage of girls reporting having engaged in suicidal thoughts and attempts. This finding is consistent with prior research on adolescent suicidal behaviors (e.g., Bettes & Walker, 1986), but must be tempered by findings indicating that boys complete more suicides than girls (e.g., Hawton & Goldacre, 1982).

In addition to the significant associations between alcohol use and suicidal behaviors, significant associations were found between alcohol use and risky behaviors. A high sensation-seeking predisposition has been found to be associated with alcohol use, illicit drug use, and driving while intoxicated arrests with adolescents and young adults (Johnson & White, 1989; Windle & Barnes, 1988; Zuckerman, 1972). The findings of this study are of importance because they generalize the range of risk-taking behaviors beyond strictly substance-related and delinquent or deviant activities discussed by R. Jessor and S. L. Jessor (1977) to include recreational activities. The association of these activities with alcohol use thus broadens the scope of problem behavior theory to include leisure, or recreational, activities that may increase the threat of injury, serious injury, or accidental death among adolescents. The alcohol–recreational activity association is important because it is possible that moderate to heavy alcohol use during some of these activities may impair motor performance, reduce judgmental capacities, and limit self-monitoring skills.

The logistic-regression analyses indicated that sex, alcohol use, and risky activities were significant predictors of suicidal ideation and attempts. Sex was the most potent of the three predictors, as the odds of suicidal ideation and attempts were between two and one half and three times greater for girls than boys for samples in both grade levels. Higher levels of alcohol use and risky activities also significantly increased the odds of suicidal ideation and attempts. Subgroup comparisons using the categorical logit model indicated that the associated estimated probability of attempted suicide among heavy alcohol-using girls who were high risk takers was relatively high. For the 8th graders, the probability of having attempted suicide for this subgroup was 0.52, and for the 10th grade subgroup was 0.47. Therefore approximately one half of heavy alcohol-using, high risk-taking female adolescents had attempted suicide. Subsequent research should be pursued to investigate the factors and processes involved in these interrelations between alcohol use, high risk-taking activities, and suicidal behaviors.

There are several limitations that merit consideration in interpreting these findings. First, the only method of measurement was self-report with no collateral informants or objective records (e.g., medical records). Therefore, reliability estimates could not be calculated and consensual validity could not be established. Second, the survey items regarding suicidal ideation and suicide attempts were limited to two response items (yes–no); thus the evaluation of a broader range of suicidal behavior (e.g., reason for attempting suicide, method of suicide attempt) was not possible. Third, although the risky activities tapped a range of recreational activities, there were several risky activities not included (e.g., parachute jumping, rock climbing). Fourth, although the sample was nationally representative and the participation rate was high, certain high-risk groups (e.g., school dropouts, chronic absentees) may not have been well represented and may engage in a range of unhealthy behaviors. Fifth, although sex, alcohol use, and risky activities were significant predictors of suicidal ideation and attempts, the magnitude of effects was limited and considerable variation remained unaccounted for. Sixth, the data were derived from a cross-sectional research design, and data analyses were limited to associations rather than plausible representations as would have been possible with longitudinal data. Nevertheless, the findings of this study did identify significant associations between alcohol use, suicidal behaviors, and risky activities in adolescence that merit increased attention from the professional health-care community.

## ACKNOWLEDGMENTS

This research was supported, in part, by Biomedical Research Support Grant R05938 and by NIAAA Grant AA07861 awarded to Michael Windle.

## REFERENCES

Albert, N., & Beck, A. T. (1975). Incidence of depression in early adolescence: A preliminary study. *Journal of Youth and Adolescence, 4*, 302–307.

Bettes, B. A., & Walker, E. (1986). Symptoms associated with suicidal behavior in childhood and adolescence. *Journal of Abnormal Child Psychology, 14*, 591–604.

Brent, D. A., Perper, J. A., Goldstein, C. E., Kolko, D. J., Allan, M. J., Allman, C. J., & Zelenak, J. P. (1988). Risk factors for adolescent suicide. *Archives of General Psychiatry, 45*, 581–588.

Centers for Disease Control. (1985). *Youth suicide surveillance 1985.* Atlanta, GA: Author.

Clark, D. C., Sommerfeldt, L., Schwarz, M., Hedeker, D., & Watel, L. (1990). Physical recklessness in adolescence: Trait or byproduct of depressive/suicidal states? *Journal of Nervous and Mental Disease, 178*, 423–433.

Garfinkel, B. D., Froese, A., & Hood, J. (1982). Suicide attempts in children and adolescents. *American Journal of Psychiatry, 139*, 1257–1261.

Garrison, C. Z. (1989). The study of suicidal behavior in the schools. *Suicide and Life-Threatening Behavior, 19*, 120–130.

Hawton, K. (1986). *Suicide and attempted suicide among children and adolescents.* Newbury Park, CA: Sage.

Hawton, K., & Goldacre, M. (1982). Hospital admissions for adverse effects of medicinal agents (mainly self-poisoning) among adolescents in the Oxford region. *British Journal of Psychiatry, 141*, 106–170.

Jessor, R., & Jessor, S. L. (1977). *Problem behavior and psychosocial development: A longitudinal study of youth.* New York: Academic.

Johnson, V., & White, H. R. (1989). An investigation of factors related to intoxicated driving behaviors among youth. *Journal Studies on Alcohol, 50*, 320–330.

Kendall, P. C., Cantwell, D. P., & Kazdin, A. E. (1989). Depression in children and adolescents: Assessment issues and recommendations. *Cognitive Therapy and Research, 13*, 109–146.

Kosky, R., Silburn, S., & Zubrick, S. R. (1990). Are children and adolescents who have suicidal thoughts different from those who attempt suicide? *Journal of Nervous and Mental Disease, 178*, 38–43.

National Adolescent Student Health Survey. (1989). *A report on the health of America's youth.* Oakland, CA: Third Party.

Rutter, M. (1986). The developmental psychopathology of depression: Issues and perspectives. In M. Rutter, C. E. Izard, & P. B. Read (Eds.), *Depression in young people* (pp. 3–30). New York: Guilford.

Shaffer, D. (1986). Developmental factors in child and adolescent suicide. In M. Rutter, C. E. Izard, & P. B. Read (Eds.), *Depression in young people* (pp. 383–396). New York: Guilford.

Smith, K., & Crawford, S. (1986). Suicidal behavior among "normal" high school students. *Suicide and Life-Threatening Behavior, 16*, 313–325.

Spirito, A., Brown, L., Overholser, J., & Fritz, G. (1989). Attempted suicide in adolescence: A review and critique of the literature. *Clinical Psychology Review, 9,* 335–363.

Windle, M., & Barnes, G. M. (1988). Similarities and differences in correlates of alcohol consumption and problem behaviors among male and female adolescents. *International Journal of the Addictions, 23,* 707–728.

Zuckerman, M. (1972). Drug usage as one manifestation of a "sensation seeking" trait. In W. Keup (Ed.), *Drug abuse: Current concepts and research* (pp. 154–163). Springfield, IL: Thomas.

Received September 19, 1990
Revision received September 12, 1991
Accepted January 23, 1992

JOURNAL OF RESEARCH ON ADOLESCENCE, 1(1), 93–106

# Family Structure, Family Processes, and Experimenting With Substances During Adolescence

Rebecca A. Turner, Charles E. Irwin, Jr., and
Susan G. Millstein
*Division of Adolescent Medicine*
*Department of Pediatrics*
*University of California, San Francisco*

Two family process variables posited to mediate the relationship between family structure and substance use were examined. Subjects were 124 middle school and high school volunteers from two types of family structure. Forty-one percent were from mother-only families while the rest were from two-biological-parent families. They were interviewed about their use of different substances, such as cigarettes, alcohol, marijuana, and other drugs, and completed an emotional detachment scale (Steinberg & Silverberg, 1986) and a parental limit-setting scale. No relationship was found between family structure and either emotional detachment from parents or parental limit setting. However, emotional detachment was predictive of adolescents' experimenting with substances beyond the effects of sociodemographic variables. Family structure also was predictive of experimentation even when sociodemographic and family process measures were controlled.

Recent studies have shown that adolescents from single-parent homes are at greater risk for truancy, school discipline problems, and arrests (Dornbusch et al., 1985); are more susceptible to antisocial peer pressure (Steinberg, 1986); and are more likely to initiate sexual intercourse (Newcomer & Udry, 1987) and substance use (Flewelling & Bauman,

Requests for reprints should be sent to Rebecca A. Turner, Department of Family and Community Medicine, AC–09, University of California, San Francisco, San Francisco, CA 94143.

229

1990; Stern, Northman, & Van Slyck, 1984). These findings have held up even when potentially confounding sociodemographic variables were controlled. However, the mechanisms by which adolescents of single parents are at greater risk for behavioral and health problems remain unclear. Only two studies have examined family processes which may mediate the effects of family structure. Dornbusch et al. (1985) found that even though family decision-making patterns were related to adolescent deviance (i.e., greater adolescent influence was associated with greater deviance), family structure had a stronger and independent effect on deviance. Similarly, Steinberg (1986) showed that variations in susceptibility to peer pressure among adolescents from different family structures were not entirely due to patterns of family decision making. There was risk associated with single parenting above and beyond the effects of family decision-making patterns.

It is important for researchers to understand the mechanisms producing the effects of family structure and to develop ways to intervene with families at risk. One family process variable that has been offered to explain why adolescents from single-parent families are more predisposed toward risky behaviors is parental limit setting. Dornbusch, Ritter, Chen, and Mont-Reynaud (1989) related that because single parenting is especially difficult and demanding, parents may be less able to set limits and may choose to grant early autonomy. Their data showed that single parents allowed adolescents to have more influence on decision making in four different areas: how to spend money, what clothes to wear, what friends to go out with, and how late to stay out. Also, other studies have linked self-care to susceptibility to peer pressure (Steinberg, 1987) and to substance use (Richardson et al., 1989). Richardson and her colleagues found that eighth graders who cared for themselves after school were much more likely to engage in tobacco, alcohol, and marijuana use, and that one mediator of this relationship was contact with peers. This finding held at all levels of sociodemographic factors and family structure.

Another possible cause for the observed relationship between family structure and adolescent deviance was noted by Steinberg (1986). He suggested that children from non-intact families are more emotionally detached from their parents and that this factor is related to susceptibility to peer pressure.

The construct of emotional detachment (originally referred to as emotional autonomy) was operationalized by Steinberg and Silverberg (1986), based on Blos's (1979) description of parent–child distancing that occurs during adolescence. Their emotional detachment measure contained items to measure four concepts: (a) individuation, perceiving that one is separate from parents and that parents do not know everything or understand everything about oneself; (b) parental deidealization, admitting disagreement with parents and perceiving that parents have faults; (c) perceiving parents as people, believing that parents behave differently when in the company of others; and (d) non-dependency (e.g., not depending on parents to solve problems). High emotional detachment was associated with susceptibility to peer pressure.

In three studies, Ryan and Lynch (1989) showed that the emotional detachment measure was also related to feelings of insecurity with parents, less utilization of parents, reported lack of parental acceptance, and less family cohesion. Ryan and Lynch also described emotional detachment as a psychological state associated with the adolescent's view of the parental context as rejecting and unsupportive. Detachment is experienced when "a relatively dependent person is severed from a source of guidance, affection or nurturance" (Ryan & Lynch, 1989, p. 340).

Ryan and Lynch also held that emotional detachment is a good index of failed attachments with parents either before and during adolescence, or of problems in negotiating the transition in parent–child relationships that necessarily occur with the adolescent's maturation. According to them, emotional detachment means that the adolescent is emotionally withdrawn from the family context; such distancing is not seen as a normal developmental process. Other reports in the literature underline the need for a balance between attachment to parents and autonomy from parents (a healthy form of separation) during the adolescent years (see Hill & Holmbeck, 1986, for a review).

In one of the Ryan and Lynch studies, an exploratory path model showed that parental divorce or separation was related to perceived lack of parental acceptance which in turn was related to emotional detachment. Hence, further studies are needed on emotional detachment and parents' marital status to determine whether a direct relationship exists, and whether these variables are related to substance use and other health-damaging behaviors. If adolescents from single-parent families are more detached from parents, it would explain why they are more susceptible to peer pressure. Peer relations, rather than family relations, may fill unmet dependency needs and be of greater importance to the emotionally detached adolescent.

The major objective of this study was to examine parental limit setting and the adolescent's emotional detachment from parents as mediators of the relationship between family structure and adolescent experimentation with substances. Although papers on family processes are available in the substance abuse literature, there is scant empirical work on family processes and substance use in nonclinical samples.

## METHOD

### Subjects

Subjects were 149 adolescents who had completed the second wave of data collection in a larger study on physical maturation and risk behavior. They were recruited by telephone from a group of urban, middle and high school students from public schools who were surveyed in their classrooms between 12 months and 25 months prior to the current effort. Of those contacted, 37% agreed to participate in the follow-up phase which required a visit to the university.

Of the 149 subjects on which this study was based, 10 were excluded because they were from step-parent families, 3 were excluded because they were not from mother-only households or the reason for the absence of one biological parent was due to death rather than separation or divorce, and 12 were excluded due to missing or insufficient data (i.e., they did not complete enough measures or critical items). Thus, 124 adolescents (63 males and 61 females) were included in this analysis.

The average age of subjects was 14.2 years for females ($SD = 1.4$) and 14.9 years ($SD = 1.4$) for males. The age ranged from 12 to 17 years in both sexes. Ethnic distribution was as follows: Asian, 15%; Black, 17%; Hispanic, 11%; mixed or other, 19%; and White, 38%. Fifty-one subjects (41%) were from mother-only families; all others were from homes with both biological parents. Because of the number of mother-only families, only the mother's educational level is reported for all subjects: less than high school, 6%; high school degree, 10%; some college, 35%; and college degree or greater, 49%. Information on parents' education was obtained via parent report on a sociodemographic questionnaire.

Because the earlier survey contained questions about ethnicity, parent's education, and other areas, we were able to determine how these subjects differed from the group of students from which they were drawn. There was almost no difference between the two groups in terms of ethnic distribution. However, these subjects tended to be from somewhat more educated families than the sample from which they were drawn (i.e., the distribution of mothers' education in the larger population was: less than high school, 11%; high school degree, 21%; some college, 23% and college degree or greater, 45%).

These subjects had higher scores on a vocabulary test and reported less failing grades. In addition, subjects indicated that they would be less likely to use marijuana within the next year than did other students. There was a nearly significant difference between subjects and other students in terms of "getting along with family, neighbors, or others," with subjects less likely to report having problems in these domains.

Subjects and other students did not differ in terms of their anticipated use of cigarettes, alcohol, or drugs other than marijuana. They did not differ on measures of self-esteem (Rosenberg, 1965) or career and life goals. And, they did not differ on a measure of life distress (e.g., bothered by feelings of anger and nervousness). In brief, we have evidence that the subjects in this study are not representative of the general population of students; they are academically better students, are from somewhat more educated families, and report that they are less likely to smoke marijuana than their peers.

### Procedure

Subjects were contacted by telephone or letter, when telephone numbers were unavailable, by a same-sex interviewer. They were told that they would participate in a study on teenagers and health behaviors, and that they would be asked about their thoughts and feelings about physical growth and changes and their health-related behaviors. Confidentiality was assured and written consent was obtained from both the parent and the adolescent following the telephone conversation. When subjects came in for their appointment, they completed paper-and-pencil measures and were then interviewed. They were given $10 and a university T-shirt as compensation for their time.

### Measures

In addition to the written, self-report instruments described next, measures of health-care utilization, egocentrism, physical maturation, body image, and cognitive functioning were obtained. Subjects were interviewed about their risk behaviors. Only the measures relevant to this study are described here.

*Substance use.* Subjects were asked whether they had ever tried and whether they were currently using cigarettes, chewing tobacco, alcohol, marijuana, cocaine, and psychedelics, or other drugs. Responses were coded in a yes–no format. A measure of experimental substance use was developed by summing the number of substances that a subject had ever tried. This score ranged from 0 to 7. Substances that the subject admitted to using currently were also summed, resulting in a score of 0 to 7 for this index as well. When subjects admitted to using substances, they were also queried about frequency and intensity of use.

*Parental limit setting.* The parental limit-setting measure, a self-report inventory, was developed for use in this research program (see

Appendix). Items were generated by interviewing a number of parents of adolescents who were affiliated with the university adolescent clinic (and not part of this study) to determine the behaviors that adolescents at different ages were allowed. Seventeen items were selected for the inventory. Subjects circled either yes or no, under two different columns, to indicate whether their mother and their father allowed them to engage in each behavior. Kuder-Richardson coefficients for internal consistency were .72 for mothers and .82 for fathers. The measure has high face validity and is significantly related to the initiation of adolescent risk behaviors including sexual behavior, substance use, and fighting (Turner & Irwin, 1990).

The measure of parental limit setting is obtained by summing, for each parent, the number of "yes" responses. Because this study focused on mother-only families, only the scores for mothers' limit setting were used in this analysis.

*Emotional detachment.*    The emotional detachment scale (Steinberg & Silverberg, 1986) indexes the extent to which adolescents are emotionally withdrawn from parents. It consists of 20 statements to which subjects respond on a 4-point scale, ranging from *strongly agree* (1) to *strongly disagree* (4). Representative items are: (a) Individuation: "I wish my parents would understand who I really am (+); (b) Nondependency: "If I were having a problem with one of my friends, I would discuss it with my mother or father before deciding what to do about it" (−); (c) Deidealization: "My parents hardly ever make mistakes" (−); and (d) Perceives parents as people: "I have often wondered how my parents act when I'm not around" (+).

## RESULTS

### Experimentation With Substances

The majority of subjects had tried alcohol (86.3%) and about half had tried cigarettes and marijuana. Cocaine and psychedelic drugs had been used by 8.1% of subjects. In terms of current use, 38.7% were still using alcohol while the rate of current usage for every other substance was less than 12% each (see Table 1). For boys, the mean number of substances ever used was 2.32 ($SD = 1.88$) and currently used was .82 ($SD = 1.02$). On the average, girls reported having used 1.84 ($SD = 1.13$) substances and currently using .43 ($SD = .64$). The variable, number of substances ever used, yielded a reasonable distribution of scores.

TABLE 1
Percentage of Subjects Who Reported Trying and Currently Using Substances

|  | Ever Tried[a] | Currently Use[a] |
|---|---|---|
| Alcohol | 86.3% | 38.7% |
| Cigarettes | 54.0% | 11.3% |
| Marijuana | 42.7% | 8.9% |
| Chewing Tobacco | 12.1% | 0 |
| Cocaine | 8.1% | 1.6% |
| Psychedelics | 8.1% | 2.4% |
| Other drugs | 5.8% | 2.4% |

[a]$n = 124$.

However, the distribution of scores for current substance use was highly skewed and was not used in subsequent analyses.

Among those who had tried substances, the responses on frequency and intensity measures were too invariant for a meaningful analysis of amount of substances used (e.g., how much marijuana) across family structures. For example, 54% of subjects who had used cigarettes reported smoking less than one per day. Of those having used alcohol, 57% had not had it in the last month. Forty-five percent of alcohol users said they typically drank two drinks or less in a given day ($M = 1.7$, $SD = 1.7$). The most consumed in a single day was 10 drinks, the amount reported by only four subjects. Eighty-five percent of subjects who had used alcohol rated themselves as light or experimental drinkers. Intensity of use of other drugs was also low in variability. Thus, it was clear that the majority of substance use was experimental in nature.

Hypothesis testing was conducted using hierarchical multiple regression with number of substances ever used as the dependent variable, an indication of the subject's willingness to experiment. All sociodemographic variables that we wished to control were entered into the equation first: age, gender, mother's education, and ethnicity. Second, family process variables (parental limit setting and emotional detachment from parents) were added in order to examine the degree of increase in variance accounted for by these factors. Then, family structure was added to the equation to examine whether living in a single-parent household was related to substance use, beyond the effects of sociodemographic and specific family process variables. Finally, the independent effect of two- and three-way interactions among age, gender, and family structure were considered.

For the first step, including sociodemographic variables, the overall model was significant, $F(6, 117) = 3.34$, $p < .005$, and accounted for 14.63% of the variance. Age and ethnic status accounted for the greatest amount of variance. Older adolescents experimented with more substances ($\beta = .2853$, $p < .014$), whereas Blacks ($\beta = -.2336$, $p < .011$) and Asians ($\beta = -.2011$) had tried fewer than had Whites (see Table 2).

In the second step, with sociodemographic variables controlled, emotional detachment contributed significantly to the variance ($\beta = .1828$, $p < .013$), whereas parental limit setting was only of borderline significance ($\beta = .1651$, $p < .079$). The greater the emotional detachment, the greater the number of substances tried by subjects. Overall, the addition of these family process variables significantly increased the variance accounted for by 5.01%, $F(2, 115) = 3.58$, $p < .05$.

When family structure was added, at the third step, there was an increase in $R^2$ of 3.06%, $F(1, 114) = 4.51$, $p < .05$. Adolescents from single-parent families had used 2.49 ($SD = 1.82$) substances whereas those in biologically intact families had used only 1.80 ($SD = 1.31$) substances. Although the addition of two-way interaction terms in the fourth step did not significantly increase the variance accounted for (change in $R^2 = 2.3\%$), the addition of a three-way interaction (Age $\times$ Family Structure $\times$ Gender) at Step 5 was significant, accounting for an additional 3.03% of the variance, $F(1, 110) = 4.63$, $p < .05$. Thus, the final model accounted for 27.97% of the variance in number of substances used.

Data are plotted in Figure 1 to describe the significant three-way interaction. From the graph, it is apparent that the effect of separation or divorce was especially significant for the behavior of males over the age of 15. Although it is generally found that risk behaviors increase with age during adolescence (Irwin & Millstein, 1987), in this sample, residing in a single-parent family was related to an accelerated trend in males. Because the current group of males in the highest age category

TABLE 2
Hierarchical Regression Analysis for Substance Use

|  | Experimental or Former Use Change in $R^2$ |
| --- | --- |
| Sociodemographic | |
| (age, sex, mother's education, ethnicity) | 14.63** |
| Family Processes | |
| (permissiveness, detachment) | 5.01* |
| Family Structure (FS) | |
| (mother only vs. intact) | 3.06* |
| Age $\times$ Sex, Age $\times$ FS, Sex $\times$ FS | 2.24 |
| Age $\times$ Sex $\times$ FS | 3.03* |
| Total | 27.97 |

[a]Change in $R^2$ at time of entry. [b]Black, Asian, and Hispanic were dummy coded. Comparison group was White.
*$p < .05$. **$p < .005$.

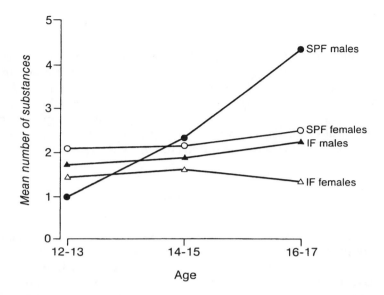

FIGURE 1    Number of substances ever tried by age, sex, and family structure. Each point represents between 5 and 18 subjects. SPF = single parent family; IF = intact family.

from single-parent families was small ($n = 9$), the three-way interaction should be interpreted with caution.

**Parental Limit Setting**

Scores on the parental limit-setting measure yielded a mean of 12.07 (*SD* = 2.99), and were normally distributed. The measure was not significantly correlated with emotional detachment ($r = -.09$); however, it was significantly related to subject age ($r = .30, p < .002$). A multiple regression analysis showed that age alone accounted for 8.6% of the variance in parental limit setting while gender accounted for less than 1% of additional variance. Ethnicity accounted for a large percentage of variance, 9.69%, above and beyond that accounted for by age and gender, $F(3, 115) = 19.53, p < .0009$. This difference is explained by the fact that Asian parents set more limits than Whites ($\beta = -.2990, p < .0009$. Hispanic parents also set more limits than Whites, but this only approached significance ($\beta = -.1467, p < .088$). Family structure did not significantly increase the explained variance in parental limit setting beyond that accounted for by age, gender, and ethnicity. That is, single parents did not set fewer limits for their adolescents than did parents in intact families.

## Emotional Detachment

Scores on emotional detachment were normally distributed with a mean of 2.75 ($SD$ = .33). Because of the predictive validity of the emotional detachment measure, we examined whether age, gender, ethnicity, or family structure would be significantly related to this variable. Using hierarchical regression, none of these were found to be significantly related. Even after all variables were entered into the equation, only 9.08% of the variance in emotional detachment was explained.

## DISCUSSION

This research has extended the empirical work on adolescent substance use, family processes, and family structure. Previous authors indicated that adolescents in mother-only homes may be more likely to engage in health risks because of fewer parental limits and greater emotional detachment from parents. In this study, when sociodemographic measures were controlled, the adolescents of mother-only families did not differ from those in biologically intact families on these two family process measures. However, the parents of White adolescents were reportedly less restrictive than Asian parents, and White adolescents were more likely than Asian adolescents to experiment with different substances.

After controlling for several possibly confounding factors as well as family processes, the adolescents of single parents were still more likely to engage in experimentation with substances than were those from intact families. Older males (age 16 to 17) from single-parent families were most likely to experiment with different substances; however, this finding was based on a small number of subjects. Nevertheless, other researchers have also found that boys tend to have a more difficult adjustment after divorce than do girls (Hetherington, Cox, & Cox, 1982; Tschann, Johnston, Kline, & Wallerstein, 1989).

These data suggest that adolescents from single-parent homes are more at risk because they are more willing to experiment, and/or because they have greater opportunities to override parental limits and thus, to experiment with different behaviors during adolescence. The dependent measure in this study is an index of willingness and ability to experiment with different substances; it is not a measure of problem behaviors per se. In fact, some researchers hold that experimentation with substances, and risk taking in general, during adolescence is normal and even associated with such positive attributes as competence and good adjustment (Baumrind, 1987; Shedler & Block, 1990). These notions are especially relevant in this study because our volunteer subjects might be considered "better than average" in terms of academic performance and adjustment. However, in our view, just because competent and well-adjusted adolescents experiment with risky behaviors does not mean that those behaviors are "healthy" (Irwin, 1987). Adolescent risk behaviors (e.g., driving while drinking, behaviors leading to sexually transmitted diseases and pregnancy) have very serious health consequences for a large number of young people.

Although adolescents have greater influence in family decision making in homes with single parents (Dornbusch et al., 1985), family structure appears unrelated to parental limit setting. The measure of limit setting used in this study was an index of adolescent behaviors allowed by parents (e.g., staying at home alone in the evening), not of parents' willingness or ability to monitor their adolescents and thus, attempt to maintain the limits that have been set. Furthermore, it was a unidimensional behavioral construct and was not intended to represent a general style or philosophy of parenting, such as permissiveness.

As stated, the relationships among constructs in this study were observed in a group of subjects who come from more educated families, who perform better in school, and who are less likely to use substances than their peers. In fact, there is some evidence that the relative impact of family structure may be greater in the population of subjects represented by these subjects. In a recent study conducted with a clinical population of adolescents (a more high-risk group), family structure was not a significant predictor for the majority of risk behaviors studied (Forman, Irwin, Turner, & Millstein, 1990).

There were limitations to this study. The sample was relatively heterogeneous with respect to age. And, we utilized a single informant to give information both on substance use and family relations, a factor which may have enhanced the observed relationships. On the other hand, it should be noted that these relationships held even though the data were based on interviews about substance use, a factor which could decrease the likelihood of self-disclosure and thus, the likelihood of significant findings.

An interesting outcome was that emotional detachment from parents was associated with experimenting with different substances. In earlier studies, emotional detachment has been associated with inability to resist peer pressure, low family cohesion, feelings of insecurity with parents, and less utilization of parents. Additional work has shown that emotional detachment is associated with the initiation of substance use and fighting in early adolescents (Turner, Irwin, Tschann, & Millstein, 1990). Thus, we conclude that a greater understanding of adolescents' health risk behaviors may be developed through further study of the emotional detachment concept.

239

## ACKNOWLEDGMENTS

Portions of this article were presented at the Society for Adolescent Medicine in San Francisco, March 1989. The research was supported in part by grants from the William T. Grant Foundation, the Bureau of Maternal and Child Health and Resources Development Grants MCJ 000978 and MCJ 060564.

We thank Aaron Ebata for his comments on a previous draft of this article, and Bruce Stegner and Jeanne Tschann for their guidance on the statistical analysis. We are indebted to Peggy Dolcini, Jeff Kamler, Todd Jacobs, Seth Ammermann, Sheryl Ryan, Leslie Babinski, Susan Kools, and Raquel Garcia for their help in data collection and data management. We also thank Marna Cohen for her assistance in developing the Parental Limiting-Setting Scale.

## REFERENCES

Baumrind, D. (1987). A developmental perspective on adolescent risk taking in contemporary America. In C. E. Irwin, Jr. (Ed.), *New directions for child development: Vol. 37. Adolescent social behavior and health* (pp. 93–125). San Francisco: Jossey-Bass.

Blos, P. (1979). *The adolescent passage*. New York: International Universities Press.

Dornbusch, S. M., Carlsmith, J. M., Bushwall, S. J., Ritter, P. L., Leiderman, H., Hastorf, A. H., & Gross, R. T. (1985). Single parents, extended households, and the control of adolescents. *Child Development, 56*, 326–341.

Dornbusch, S. M., Ritter, P. L., Chen, Z., & Mont-Reynaud, R. (1989, April). *Ethnic differences in family decision-making among adolescents*. Paper presented at the biannual meeting of the Society for Research in Child Development, Kansas City, MO.

Flewelling, R. L., & Bauman, K. E. (1990). Family structure as a predictor of initial substance use and sexual intercourse in early adolescence. *Journal of Marriage and the Family, 52*, 171–181.

Forman, S., Irwin, C. E., Jr., Turner, R. A., & Millstein, S. G. (1990, May). *Family structure, emotional distancing and risk-taking behavior in adolescents*. Paper presented at the annual meeting of the Society for Pediatric Research, Anaheim, CA.

Hetherington, E. M., Cox, M., & Cox, R. (1982). Effects of divorce on parents and children. In M. Lamb (Ed.), *Non-traditional families* (pp. 233–288). Hillsdale, NJ: Lawrence Erlbaum Associates, Inc.

Hill, J. P., & Holmbeck, G. (1986). Attachment and autonomy during adolescence. In G. J. Whitehurst (Ed.), *Annals of child development* (Vol. 3, pp. 145–189). Greenwich, CT: JAI Press.

Irwin, C. E., Jr. (1987). Editor's notes. In C. E. Irwin, Jr. (Ed.), *New directions for child development: Vol. 37. Adolescent social behavior and health* (pp. 1–12). San Francisco: Jossey-Bass.

Irwin, C. E., Jr., & Millstein, S. G. (1987). Biopsychosocial correlates of risk taking behavior in adolescence: Can the physician intervene? *Journal of Adolescent Health Care, 7*, 82S–96S.

Newcomer, S., & Udry, J. R. (1987). Parental marital status effects on adolescent sexual behavior. *Journal of Marriage and the Family, 49*, 235–240.

Richardson, J. L., Dwyer, K., McGuigan, K., Hansen, W. B., Dent, C., Johnson, A., Sussman, S. Y., Brannie, B., & Flay, B. (1989). Substance use among eighth-grade students who take care of themselves after school. *Pediatrics, 84*, 556–566.

Rosenberg, M. (1965). *Society and the adolescent self-image*. Princeton, NJ: Princeton University Press.

Ryan, R., & Lynch, J. H. (1989). Emotional autonomy versus detachment: Revisiting the vicissitudes of adolescence and young adulthood. *Child Development, 60,* 340–356.

Shedler, J., & Block, J. (1990). Adolescent drug use and psychological health: A longitudinal inquiry. *American Psychologist, 45,* 612–630.

Steinberg, L. (1986). Single parents, stepparents, and the susceptibility of adolescents to antisocial peer pressure. *Child Development, 58,* 269–275.

Steinberg, L. (1987). Latchkey children and susceptibility to peer pressure: An ecological analysis. *Developmental Psychology, 22,* 433–439.

Steinberg, L., & Silverberg, S. (1986). The vicissitudes of autonomy in early adolescence. *Child Development, 57,* 841–851.

Stern, M., Northman, J. E., & Van Slyck, M. N. R. (1984). Father absence and adolescent problem behaviors: Alcohol consumption, drug use and sexual activity. *Adolescence, 18,* 403–411.

Tschann, J. M., Johnston, J. R., Kline, M., & Wallerstein, J. S. (1989). Family process and children's functioning during divorce. *Journal of Marriage and the Family, 51,* 431–444.

Turner, R. A., & Irwin, C. E., Jr. (1990, March). *Attachment, autonomy and health risk behaviors*. Paper presented at the biennial meeting of the Society for Research on Adolescence, Atlanta, GA.

Turner, R. A., Irwin, C. E., Jr., Tschann, J. M., & Millstein, S. G. (1990). *Autonomy, connectedness and the initiation of health risk behaviors in early adolescence*. Manuscript submitted for publication.

Received March 9, 1990
Revision received October 11, 1990
Accepted October 17, 1990

## APPENDIX

About Your Privileges
Listed below are different activities. Which of these activities do your
parents or guardians allow you to do?

|  | Your Mother or Female Guardian | Your Father or Male Guardian |
|---|---|---|
| Do Your Parents/Guardians Allow You To: | | |
| Stay out with friends until midnight . . . . . . . . . . . . . . . . . . . . . | Yes  No | Yes  No |
| Make your own decisions about how to spend free time . . . . . . . | Yes  No | Yes  No |
| Have same-sex friends to your house without adults there . . . . . | Yes  No | Yes  No |
| Go out on dates without adults present . . . . . . . . . . . . . . . . . . | Yes  No | Yes  No |
| Be left at home alone during the afternoon. . . . . . . . . . . . . . . . | Yes  No | Yes  No |
| Be left at home along during the evening. . . . . . . . . . . . . . . . . . | Yes  No | Yes  No |
| Sleep over at a friends house. . . . . . . . . . . . . . . . . . . . . . . . . . . | Yes  No | Yes  No |
| Decide on your own bedtime. . . . . . . . . . . . . . . . . . . . . . . . . . . | Yes  No | Yes  No |
| Decide on the type of clothes to wear . . . . . . . . . . . . . . . . . . . . | Yes  No | Yes  No |
| Have a part-time job. . . . . . . . . . . . . . . . . . . . . . . . . . . . . . . . . | Yes  No | Yes  No |
| Travel out of town without an adult present. . . . . . . . . . . . . . . . | Yes  No | Yes  No |
| Decide how to spend your money . . . . . . . . . . . . . . . . . . . . . . . | Yes  No | Yes  No |
| Ride in a car with your friends . . . . . . . . . . . . . . . . . . . . . . . . . | Yes  No | Yes  No |
| Date members of the opposite sex . . . . . . . . . . . . . . . . . . . . . . . | Yes  No | Yes  No |
| Go steady with a boy/girl friend . . . . . . . . . . . . . . . . . . . . . . . . | Yes  No | Yes  No |
| Drive the family car for your own recreation . . . . . . . . . . . . . . . | Yes  No | Yes  No |
| Drive a car . . . . . . . . . . . . . . . . . . . . . . . . . . . . . . . . . . . . . . . . | Yes  No | Yes  No |

JOURNAL OF RESEARCH ON ADOLESCENCE, 5(2), 225–252

# The Contributions of Mothers and Fathers to the Intergenerational Transmission of Cigarette Smoking in Adolescence

Denise B. Kandel

*Department of Psychiatry and School of Public Health*
*Columbia University*
*and*
*New York State Psychiatric Institute*


Ping Wu

*Department of Psychiatry*
*Columbia University*
*and*
*New York State Psychiatric Institute*

Similarity on cigarette smoking among mothers, fathers, and young adolescents (mean age = 12.6 years) and the differential relevance of sociopsychological processes underlying similarity between parent and child were examined in a sample of 201 triads, in which each respondent was interviewed independently. There is a significant and dose-related association between maternal smoking and children's smoking, especially among daughters. Both maternal role modeling and socialization affect lifetime smoking by the child, but only role modeling affects current smoking. The maternal role modeling effect is stronger for daughters than for sons and persists with the inclusion of perceived smoking by the adolescent's close friends in the model. The observed familial concordance on smoking between parent and child cannot disentangle environmental from genetic effects.

---

Requests for reprints should be sent to Denise B. Kandel, Department of Psychiatry, Columbia University, 722 West 168th Street, Box 20, New York, NY 10032.

Smoking by young adolescents constitutes a serious public health problem. Tobacco cigarettes and alcoholic beverages represent the first drugs of entry into the developmental sequence of involvement in the use of marijuana and other illicit drugs (Kandel & Yamaguchi, 1993; Kandel, Yamaguchi, & Chen, 1992). The earlier the age of onset into the use of cigarettes or alcohol, the greater the risk of progression to a higher-stage drug. For instance, in a statewide survey of New York State high school students, we found that seniors who had used crack had started using cigarettes 2 years earlier, on the average, than seniors who had not used any other drugs besides cigarettes (Kandel & Yamaguchi, 1993). Furthermore, much evidence has accumulated regarding the numerous long-term negative health consequences of smoking, including cancer and cardiovascular and lung diseases (U.S. Department of Health and Human Services, 1983, 1984, 1989). Because adolescence constitutes the period of major risk for initiation to cigarette smoking (Johnston, O'Malley, & Bachman, 1992; Kandel & Logan, 1984), it is important to understand the factors that are related to early initiation of cigarette smoking.

In this article, we focus on the intergenerational transmission of smoking behavior as reflected in similarity of cigarette smoking between parents and children. We are interested in determining the relative influence of mothers and fathers on young adolescents and the processes that could account for these influences.

## PROCESSES OF INTERGENERATIONAL TRANSMISSION

Intergenerational transmission, as manifested by similarity between parent and child, can be accounted for by three processes. These processes are not mutually exclusive. Similarity can be due to (a) modeling and imitation of the parent by the child; (b) socialization of the child by the parent, including the quality of interactions between parent and child and social reinforcement (reflected in the explicit prescription of norms and standards); and (c) a genetic predisposition. With the data at our disposal, the third genetic hypothesis cannot be assessed and differentiated from modeling. We may conclude that a familial effect is present if the effect of parental behavior persists with statistical controls for other factors.

### Child Smoking and Modeling of Parents

An association between parental and child smoking has previously been reported. However, the majority of studies are based on the child's report of parental behaviors rather than on the parent's self-reports. Out of 54 studies that examined the influences of parental smoking on children's smoking, 12 collected independent data from parents. Six studies obtained data from a single parent only (Bewley & Bland, 1977; Brook, Gordon, & Brook, 1986; Foshee & Bauman, 1992; Gfroerer, 1987; Green, Macintyre, West, & Ecob, 1990; Pulkkinen, 1983); six studies obtained independent data from both parents. The studies used different analytical techniques, did not always collect data for both boys and girls, and did not always report results for each sex separately. Overall, two studies found mother's smoking to have a stronger influence on the child's smoking than father's smoking (Melby, Conger, Conger, & Lorenz, 1993; Rossow, 1992); one study found fathers to be more important than mothers (Hops, Tildesley, Lichtenstein, Ary, & Sherman, 1990); two studiess found sex-specific effects, with mothers more important for daughters and fathers more important for sons (Banks, Bewley, Bland, Dean, & Pollard, 1978; Murray, Kiryluk, & Swan, 1985); and one found no parental effect (Annis, 1974). The highest odds—either ratios odds, calculated by us from data presented by the authors (Banks et al., 1978; Bewley & Bland, 1977; Murray et al., 1985), or adjusted odds, reported by the author (Rossow, 1992)—are observed for mother–daughter pairs and range from 3 to 4. Of the 23 studies that examined each parent's influence on the basis of children's reports of parental behaviors, seven found mothers to be more influential than fathers (Bauman, Botvin, Botvin, & Baker, 1992; Bothwell, 1959; Hover & Gaffney, 1988; Hundleby & Mercer, 1987; Krosnick & Judd, 1982; Lanese, Banks, & Keller, 1972; Neukirch & Cooreman, 1983). One study (Chassin et al., 1981) found fathers to be more influential than mothers. Several studies report a same-sex parental effect, with father's perceived smoking associated with son's smoking and mother's perceived smoking associated with daughter's (Beaglehole, Eyles, & Harding, 1978; Burchfiel, Higgins, Keller, Butler, & Donoghue, 1989; Levitt & Edwards, 1970). Thus, inconsistent findings have been reported regarding the relative influence of mothers and fathers, whether the data are based on parental self-reports or the children's perceptions. On balance, a larger number of investigations support a more influential role for mothers than for fathers.

The role modeling hypothesis suggests that the parental effect would be stronger when both parents smoke than when only one parent does so. The only studies that have examined this issue are based on children's reports of parental smoking. Most find that parental influence is indeed strongest in those families where both mothers and fathers are reported to be smoking than when only one parent does so (e.g., Bewley, Bland, & Harris, 1974; Horn et al., 1959; Lemin, 1967;

Morison, Medovy, & MacDonnell, 1964; Nolte, Smith, & O'Rourke, 1983; Palmer, 1970; Rawbone, Keeling, Jenkins, & Guz, 1979; Salber & MacMahon, 1961; Williams, 1973).

### Child Smoking and Parental Socialization Practices

Besides imitation of the parent by the child, similarity between parent and child on smoking could be due to parental attributes such as personality traits or child-rearing practices, which would be related to the parents' own smoking and would favor smoking by the child. These child-rearing practices include two different domains: the quality of the interactions between parent and child and social reinforcement, that is, the setting of norms that define the appropriate behaviors and values concerning specific arenas.

A substantial body of research has documented the role of parental socialization practices on children's drug involvement. These practices are similar to those predictive of acting-out and delinquent behavior. Drug use by children and adolescents has been found to be related to lack of parental affection; conflictual mutual detachment; poor child identification with the parent; and inappropriate child management techniques, in particular, explosive discipline, weak or excessive parental controls, poor monitoring, lack of supervision of the child's activities, and inconsistent parenting (Barnes, 1990; Barnes & Farrell, 1992; Baumrind, 1985; Block, Keyes, & Block, 1986; Brook, Brook, Gordon, Whiteman, & Cohen, 1990; Brook, Whiteman, et al., 1986; Brook, Whiteman, Nomura, Gordon, & Cohen, 1988; Coombs & Landsverk, 1988; Dishion & Loeber, 1985; Dishion, Patterson, & Reid, 1988; Dishion, Ray, & Capaldi, 1992; Elliott, Huizinga, & Ageton, 1985; Hawkins, Lishner, & Catalano, 1985; Heath & Martin, 1988; Huba & Bentler, 1980; Hundleby & Mercer, 1987; Jacob & Leonard, 1991; Jessor & Jessor, 1977; Kandel, Kessler, & Margulies, 1978; Kellam, Simon, & Ensminger, 1983; Leonard, 1990; Needle et al., 1986; Pandina & Schuele, 1983; Simcha-Fagan, Gersten, & Langner, 1986; Simons, Conger, & Whitbeck, 1988; Vicary & Lerner, 1986; Zucker & Noll, 1987.)

However, relatively little research has been conducted on parental socialization practices as they relate specifically to child smoking. As for other forms of substance use, parental affection, involvement, and monitoring have been found to be negatively related to child smoking; poor discipline has been found to be positively related (Brook, Gordon et al., 1986; Brook, Whiteman, Gordon, & Brook, 1983; Dishion et al., 1988; Hundleby & Mercer, 1987; Melby et al., 1993; Mercer & Kohn, 1980; Skinner, Massey, Krohn, & Lauer, 1985). Whereas Krohn, Skinner,

Massey, and Akers (1985) reported no direct impact of perceived parental attitudes regarding smoking either on the initiation or maintenance of the child smoking, a number of other studies (most based on the child's perception of parental attitudes) do report an effect (Brook et al., 1983; Brook, Gordon et al., 1986; Chassin et al., 1981; Krosnick & Judd, 1982; Murray et al., 1985; Neukirch & Cooreman, 1983; Palmer, 1970). Nolte et al. (1983) found that parental attitudes exerted a greater impact than parental behaviors.

Although our emphasis is on potential parental influences, we recognize the important role that peers play in adolescents' drug involvement, especially in the early stages of initiation (e.g., Brook et al., 1990; Dishion et al., 1988; Huba & Bentler, 1980; Kandel et al., 1978).

In addressing the issue of the intergenerational transmission of smoking behavior, we are interested in two issues: (a) What is the impact of parents on their child smoking and is there a differential impact of mothers and fathers? (b) What processes account for the transmission of behaviors from parent to child? We test two basic hypotheses: (a) Parental smoking determines the child's smoking. The relative influence of mothers and fathers remains to be determined. (b) Both modeling of parental behaviors and socialization practices underlie parent–child similarity in smoking. Again, the relative importance of each process remains to be determined.

## METHODS

### Sample and Data

The analyses were based on a sample of 201 mother–father–child triads, in which the child, ranging in age from 9 to 17 years, was the first born in the family. One parent was the focal member of a longitudinal cohort that has been followed for 19 years, since the subject was aged 15 to 16 (the New York State follow-up cohort; NYS). The cohort constitutes a representative sample of former adolescents enrolled in Grades 10 and 11 in New York State public high schools in 1971–1972, and it was selected from a stratified sample of 18 high schools throughout New York State (Kandel, Single, & Kessler, 1976). The target population for the adult follow-up was drawn from the enrollment list of half the homerooms from Grades 10 and 11 and included students who were absent from school at the time of the initial study. The inclusion of these former absentees assures the representativeness of the sample and the inclusion of the most deviant youths (Kandel, Raveis, &

Kandel, 1984). Respondents were first contacted in 1971 and reinterviewed in 1980, 1984, and 1990. The 1,160 young adults reinterviewed in 1990 represent 72.0% of the original target adolescents enrolled in the sample schools.

In 1990, personal interviews were also conducted with spouses and partners if there was a child aged 6 to 17 years in the household, with the first-born child aged 9 to 17 years (if there was one), and with the second born child aged 9 to 17 years (if there was one); 58.9% of households contained only one eligible child. The completion rates for spouses/partners and first-born children were 82.3% and 90.5%, respectively. Data from all respondents were obtained through structured personal interviews, which took, on the average, 1½ hr to complete for the adults and 1 hr for the children.

Analyses reported in this article are based on the sample of 201 triads in which both parents and the first-born child were interviewed. To carry out the analyses for mothers and fathers, male and female parents among those in the focal sample and spouses/partners were combined across each sample. Because women marry at an earlier age than men, 63.7% of mothers in the triads were from the focal sample and 36.3% were from the spouse/partner sample. The converse distribution characterizes fathers in the triads. The mean age of mothers is 34.4 years ($SD = 2.1$); fathers, 35.8 years ($SD = 4.3$); and children, 12.6 years ($SD = 2.5$). The mothers were relatively young at the birth of their child.

The analytical sample includes 66.1% of all the first-born children in that age group; the remaining children either lived in a single-parent family (13.2%), in a family with two lesbian parents (.7%), or represented cases in which either a parent or the child was not interviewed (20.1%). Comparison on selected variables of mothers included and excluded from the analyses reveals no differences between the two groups. Because no interviewed father was single, the comparison between parents included and excluded from the analyses was carried out only among mothers. Married mothers included in the triads did not differ from married mothers not included or from single mothers on extent of smoking within the last year, highest year of schooling completed, age at interview, previously divorced, number of years married (for those married), and four selected patterns of interaction with the child, including closeness, consistency of discipline, extent of monitoring, and rules about smoking (data not presented). Because our sample was selected from high school students, its educational attainment is slightly higher than that of a somewhat comparable group residing in the Northeast of the United States drawn from a national sample.[1]

It should be noted that the relatively small size of the sample, especially when the analyses are carried out for boys and girls separately, affects our ability to detect statistically significant effects.

## Measures of Parental and Child Smoking

*Parental smoking.* Parents were classified into four categories that took into account lifetime and last year self-reported cigarette smoking as well as the quantity of cigarettes consumed in the last month the parent smoked within the last year. The categories were: never smoked, smoked but not within the last year, smoked less than a pack a day within the last year, and smoked at least a pack a day within the last year. In addition to classifying each parent individually, two classifications of joint mother–father smoking patterns were developed for smoking lifetime and for smoking at least a pack a day within the last 12 months. The four categories included: neither smoked, father only, mother only, and both.

---

[1]Because of the particular demographic characteristics of the sample—for example, restricted age of respondents and their children, married status, and New York State origin—it is not possible to assess its generalizability from published census data. However, we had available to us the 1990 data tape from the National Household Survey on Drug Abuse (NHSDA), an annual household survey of a national probability sample of individuals of ages 12 and older, and we were able to compare our sample on educational level and on smoking rates with a subgroup drawn from the national sample. From the 1990 survey, we identified a subsample of men ($N = 111$) and women ($N = 177$) matched as closely as possible to the NYS subsample: Northeast resident, currently married with a first-born child aged 9 to 17, and within the age range represented in our sample (i.e., 24 to 57 for men and 22 to 48 for women). The age and race distributions in the NHSDA subsample were then standardized on the distributions observed in the NYS cohort. The samples differ somewhat on educational level and on father's rate of current smoking. As expected, because our sample was initially selected from high school students in Grades 10 and 11, the educational level of our sample is higher than that observed in the corresponding national subsample. The mean number of years of education completed by fathers is 13.2 ($SD = 2.0$) in the NYS cohort and 12.4 ($SD = 2.2$) in the NHSDA; for mothers, it is 12.9 ($SD = 1.7$) and 12.4 ($SD = 2.1$), respectively. Although lifetime rates of smoking are identical, the rates of self-reported current smoking are higher for fathers in our sample than in the NHSDA. The proportion of fathers who reported ever smoking is 79.5% in our sample compared with 77.1% in the NHSDA, but 44.0% and 31.3%, respectively, for smoking within the last year. The difference is statistically significant. The comparable proportions for mothers are 79.6% versus 82.3% for lifetime smoking and 42.8% versus 37.5% for last year smoking. Methodological work on the validity of self-reported drug use indicates that underreporting varies with the degree of confidentiality experienced by respondents in the interview situation and increases for recent comparisons with lifetime reports (Turner, Lessler, & Gfroerer, 1992). The higher rates of self-reported current smoking observed among fathers in our sample compared with the NHSDA may reflect differential rapport developed by interviewers with respondents in the two studies.

*Child smoking.*    The children were asked whether they had ever smoked and how many times they had smoked in their lifetime and within the last year. The precoded response categories ranged from 1 to 2 times to 40 or more times.

## Measures of Parental Socialization Practices

The socialization measures cover the quality of parenting and of norm setting identified in prior research as important correlates and predictors of child's conduct problems and involvement in drugs. Identical questions were included in the interview schedules for focal respondents, spouses, and children. For most items, the children were asked separately about their father and their mother. The measures were developed on the basis of psychometric analyses carried out separately for children, fathers, and mothers. As discussed in greater detail later, the final measures included in the analyses are based on reports from two informants: each parent's report about his or her parenting practices and the child's report about that parent.

*Measures of quality of parenting.*    Three broad parenting dimensions were measured: (a) warmth, (b) discipline, and (c) monitoring. Specific factors for discipline included rewards for positive behaviors, discipline for negative behaviors, and consistency of discipline. Each respondent was asked how frequently the parent engaged in specific interactions with the child relevant to each dimension.

*Measures of parental norm setting.*    To obtain information about parental norms, we asked respondents what rules parents had for the child. One of the 12 items specifically pertained to rules against smoking cigarettes.

Factor analyses of the parenting items were conducted for eight multiitem scales that measured closeness, rewards for positive behaviors, discipline for negative behaviors, and monitoring. In addition, consistency of discipline consists of the mean value on two four-category items. Rule against smoking includes a single dichotomous item. With rare exceptions, the resulting factor structures were identical in the different samples. Based on the results of the factor analyses and the reliabilities, 10 parent–child relationships scales were retained for our analyses. Parent-specific scales were created, which aggregated the parent and child report for that parent. Alpha values, calculated over the total range of items included in the multiinformant scales (mother and child, father and child), ranged from .40 to .82. These reliabilities are comparable to those reported by other investigators (e.g., Brook et al., 1990; Melby et al., 1993); discipline-related scales consistently have lower reliabilities than closeness or monitoring scales. The reliabilities of the scales based on single informants are all consistently lower than the joint mother–child scales and lower or equal in size in 7 of the 10 scales for the joint father–child scales. In two cases, the differences were extremely small, less than .10. Because of individual response bias, multiple informant measures for parenting are preferred over measures from a single respondent and lead to less distorted parameter estimates (Dishion et al., 1988; Melby et al., 1993). Details about the scales, including items included and reliabilities, appear in the Appendix.

Similar to others who have obtained independent reports from family members (e.g., Gecas & Schwalbe, 1986; Krohn, Stern, Thornberry, & Jang, 1992; Lorenz, Conger, Simon, & Whitbeck, 1991), we find that parents' and children's perceptions of parenting domains are not highly correlated and range from .21 to .47 for mothers and .13 to .38 for fathers. Each person perceives the interactions in terms of his or her personality characteristics, social roles, and position in the family (Gecas & Schwalbe, 1986; Jessop, 1981). Only two informants, one parent and the child, were purposefully included in the scales. Because we were interested in testing the role of socialization practices in moderating parental influences, parental behaviors and practices needed to be parent-specific. These combined measures were included in the analyses reported in this article, although we also carried out analyses in which each respondent-specific measure was substituted for the aggregated measures.

### Other Variables

All the models included three other variables found in prior research to be related to adult or to child smoking: highest years of education completed by either parent (responses ranged from 11 to 20 years) and child's age and sex (0 = boy, 1 = girl).

Selected models also included a dichotomous measure of the child's perceived use of smoking by close friends. The original five response categories were reduced to two categories of lifetime smoking (*none* or *one* close friend vs. *some, most,* or *all* close friends).

### Statistical Strategies

Logistic regressions were estimated to predict the child's smoking behavior for the lifetime and during the last year. In a first step, we included the demographic variables and each parent's smoking pattern to determine the overall effect of parental behaviors on the child.

In a second step, we added the multiinformant parental socialization measures to assess the extent to which parental smoking retained an effect after controlling for quality of parent–child interactions, norm setting, and other variables that may be related to these smoking behaviors. In a third step, we included the peer-related smoking variable. If the parental smoking effect remained in the second and third models, we concluded that parental influence was consonant with a role modeling (as well as a genetic) effect. The full model was estimated for boys and girls separately.

## RESULTS

### Distribution of Parental and Child Smoking

Parental smoking in the families follows the sex-specific patterns characteristic of young men and women in the population. The prevalence of lifetime and former smoking is identical among fathers and mothers, although fathers are heavier smokers than mothers. Eighty percent of each sex (79.5% of fathers, 79.6% of mothers) have ever smoked; 44.0% of fathers and 42.8% of mothers smoked within the last year; 72.7% of fathers who smoked within the last year smoked at least a pack of cigarettes a day compared with 58.1% of mothers. With regard to the children, similar proportions of boys and girls report having ever smoked, 25.7% and 29.7%, respectively, and having smoked within the last year, 16.5% and 20.9%, respectively.

### Similarity Between Parents and Children

First, we examined the distribution of the children's smoking as a function of each parent's smoking, as reported by each parent independently. Children whose parents smoke are more likely to be smokers themselves (Table 1).

Maternal and paternal influences differ, however. The influence of mothers is stronger than the influence of fathers and is dose-related. Similarity between child and mother appears only when mothers are currently smoking at least a pack of cigarettes a day, whereas for fathers, the same pattern appears whether he is currently smoking or not and irrespective of the amount he smokes. Almost four times as many children have ever smoked or are currently smoking when their mothers currently smoke a pack or more of cigarettes a day, compared with children whose mothers have never smoked. Only twice as many smoke when their fathers have ever smoked, irrespective of their current smoking status.

## TABLE 1
### Child Cigarette Smoking by Parental Lifetime/Past Year/Quantity Cigarette Smoking, by Child's Sex (201 Triads)

| Percentage of Children Who Smoked | Mother Smoking | | | | Father Smoking | | | |
|---|---|---|---|---|---|---|---|---|
| | Never Smoked (%) | Smoked, Not Past Year (%) | Smoked Past Year, < Pack (%) | Smoked, Past Year, ≥ Pack (%) | Never Smoked (%) | Smoked, Not Past Year (%) | Smoked Past Year, < Pack (%) | Smoked Past Year, ≥ Pack (%) |
| Lifetime | | | | | | | | |
| Total | 15.0 | 17.6 | 22.2 | 56.0*** | 14.6 | 28.6 | 29.2 | 34.4 |
| n | 40 | 74 | 36 | 50 | 41 | 70 | 24 | 64 |
| Boys | 17.4 | 17.0 | 29.4 | 50.0* | 12.5 | 23.4 | 38.5 | 30.3 |
| n | 23 | 47 | 17 | 22 | 16 | 47 | 13 | 33 |
| Girls | 11.8 | 18.5 | 15.8 | 60.7*** | 16.0 | 39.1 | 18.2 | 38.7 |
| n | 17 | 27 | 19 | 28 | 25 | 23 | 11 | 31 |
| Past year | | | | | | | | |
| Total | 10.0 | 9.5 | 11.1 | 44.0*** | 9.8 | 21.4 | 25.0 | 18.8 |
| n | 40 | 74 | 36 | 50 | 41 | 70 | 24 | 64 |
| Boys | 13.0 | 8.5 | 11.8 | 40.9** | 0.0 | 14.9 | 38.5 | 18.2* |
| n | 23 | 47 | 17 | 22 | 16 | 47 | 13 | 33 |
| Girls | 5.9 | 11.1 | 10.5 | 46.4*** | 16.0 | 34.8 | 9.1 | 19.4 |
| n | 17 | 27 | 19 | 28 | 25 | 23 | 11 | 31 |

*$p \le .05$. **$p \le .01$. ***$p \le .001$ (chi-square test).

Not only is maternal influence stronger than paternal influence, but it is somewhat stronger on daughters than on sons. Compared with children of mothers who never smoked, when mothers currently smoke a pack or more a day, daughters are almost eight times as likely to be current cigarette smokers, whereas sons are only three times as likely. Paternal influence is the same on sons and daughters.

We expected parental influence to be strongest in those families in which both parents are currently smoking. We developed two classifications of joint mother–father smoking patterns, one for smoking for lifetime and another for smoking within the last 12 months. Because the highest rates of child smoking were observed in families where mothers smoked at least a pack of cigarettes a day, the joint parental cigarette smoking variable for the last year was defined on the basis of the use of a pack or more of cigarettes a day (Table 2). Our expectation is confirmed only with respect to lifetime parental use: The proportion of children having ever smoked cigarettes is higher in families in which both parents report having ever smoked compared with those in which only one parent or no parent has done so. With respect to current (last year) parental use, however, the highest rates of child smoking are observed in families in which only the mother currently smokes at least a pack of cigarettes a day. This is a curious result, which may be a chance finding due to the small sample size.

*Is the effect of parental smoking spurious?*    Further analyses document that the parental effect is specific to smoking and is not spurious.

Because individuals who are heavy users of a particular class of drugs are also more likely to be using other classes of drugs, the effect of parental smoking could be masking the effect of other drugs or

TABLE 2

Child Cigarette Smoking by Joint Parental Lifetime and Past Year Cigarette Smoking
(201 Triads)

| Percentage of Children Who Smoked | Parental Joint Cigarette Smoking | | | | | | | |
|---|---|---|---|---|---|---|---|---|
| | Lifetime | | | | ≥ 1 Pack/Day in Last Year | | | |
| | Neither (%) | Father Only (%) | Mother Only (%) | Both (%) | Neither (%) | Father Only (%) | Mother Only (%) | Both (%) |
| Lifetime | 0.0 | 19.4 | 18.8 | 33.6* | 15.5 | 25.6 | 64.0 | 48.0*** |
| Past year | 0.0 | 12.9 | 12.5 | 22.7 | 9.1 | 12.8 | 60.0 | 28.0*** |
| Total N | 9 | 31 | 32 | 128 | 110 | 39 | 25 | 25 |

*p ≤ .05. ***p ≤ .001 (chi-square test).

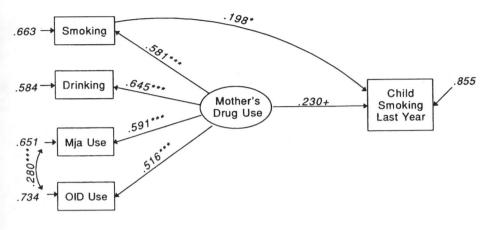

+ p < .10; * p < .05; *** p < .001    Chi-Square = 1.99   df = 3   p = .575

FIGURE 1 General effect of mother's drug use and specific effect of mother's smoking on child smoking in last year (standardized coefficients).

could result from a general tendency to use drugs. To test this hypothesis, we examined the impact of parental smoking within the context of a measurement model in which we estimated simultaneously the effect of a latent tendency to use drugs and the specific effect of parental smoking, controlling for this latent tendency to use drugs.

We present the results of an analysis for maternal influence on the child frequency of smoking within the last year, implemented through LISREL (Jöreskog & Sörbom, 1989). We assumed that the latent tendency to use drugs was reflected in manifest indicators of the use of four different drug classes. In addition to the measure of cigarette smoking, we included quantity/frequency measures of drinking, marijuana use, and the use of illicit drugs other than marijuana. (To improve the fit of the model, the correlation between the error terms for marijuana and other illicit drugs variables needed to be freed.) Because it was not possible to estimate simultaneously a model with the paths from the latent construct and all four manifest indicators, separate estimations were carried out with each manifest indicator of drug use. Both the paths from maternal smoking and from the general tendency to use drugs are almost equal in size (Figure 1), although the former reaches higher statistical significance than the latter. Thus, in the presence of a general tendency to use drugs, maternal smoking is still specifically relevant for the child smoking. By contrast, none of the other three drug classes had a statistically significant impact on the child smoking over and beyond the effect of the latent drug use construct.

## Parental Smoking, Child Smoking, and Socialization Practices

To determine whether the parental smoking effect is truly a modeling effect or whether it reflects factors other than drug use that are related to parental smoking, we explored the relevance of the transmission mechanisms outlined earlier.

As we noted, intergenerational similarity can be due to imitation (or genetic susceptibility) as well as to the social environment created by the parent for the child. Parents who smoke may exhibit particular parenting styles, which may favor negative development in the child, including smoking. In particular, closeness between parent and child, nonexplosive forms of discipline, and parental monitoring of the child reduce deviant participation by the child and may also, therefore, reduce smoking. We assessed the robustness of the parental smoking effect controlling for other familial covariates that may be related to parental smoking and that may constitute either intervening processes or confounding factors. Our analysis proceeded in two steps. First, we examined the relations between parental socialization and smoking by each member of the triad. In a second step, we estimated multivariate models that included parental socialization practices and smoking behaviors.

*Parental smoking and parental socialization practices.* Because parents' relationships with their children are partially dependent upon the child's age and because the child's smoking increases with age, the correlations were estimated controlling for the child's age.

As expected, parental smoking is related to specific parenting styles. The correlations are relatively low, with the exception of rules against smoking. Parents who smoke exhibit less positive parenting than those who do not smoke. Both mothers and fathers who smoke are characterized by inconsistent discipline (Table 3). In addition, maternal smoking is related to decreased feelings of closeness toward the child and the absence of rules against smoking; paternal smoking is related to decreased use of physical discipline.

*Child smoking and parental socialization practices.* The relations between parental socialization practices and smoking among children, controlling for the child's age, are identical for mothers and fathers

(Table 3). The relevant dimensions of parenting for the child smoking overlap partially with the significant dimensions observed for parental smoking. Reduced closeness, lack of monitoring, and absence of rules against smoking are the important maternal and paternal socialization practices. High scores on these dimensions are associated with reduced rates of smoking by the children. Children who smoke have parents who are less close to them, exert lower levels of monitoring, and are less likely to have explicit parental rules against smoking than children who do not smoke.

Thus, lowered closeness and absence of rules against smoking characterize the socialization practices related both to maternal and to child smoking. Reduced monitoring either by mothers or fathers is related to the child smoking, whereas inconsistent discipline is related both to mother's and father's smoking. Reduced physical discipline relates only to smoking by fathers.

These correlations were reestimated, using each person's report of parental socialization practices rather than the aggregated measures.

TABLE 3
Partial Correlations of Parental and Child Self-Reported Smoking With Parental
Socialization Practices, Controlling for Child's Age (201 Triads)

| Socialization Practices[b] | Parental Life/ Last Year Quantity Cigarette Smoking[a] | | Child Frequency Last Year Cigarette Smoking | |
|---|---|---|---|---|
| | Mother Socialization[c] | Father Socialization[d] | Mother Socialization[e] | Father Socialization[d] |
| Quality of parenting | | | | |
| Warmth | | | | |
| Closeness | −.14* | .02 | −.22** | −.18** |
| Rewards | | | | |
| Emotional rewards | .09 | −.02 | .02 | −.10 |
| Material rewards | −.10 | .08 | −.01 | −.10 |
| Discipline | | | | |
| Punitive discipline | −.01 | −.03 | .07 | −.01 |
| Physical discipline | −.08 | −.17* | −.05 | −.05 |
| Love withdrawal | −.02 | .04 | .04 | .09 |
| Cognitive discipline | −.03 | .08 | −.04 | −.09 |
| Consistency of discipline | −.14* | −.14* | −.10 | −.10 |
| Monitoring | −.06 | .02 | −.16* | −.22** |
| Norm setting | | | | |
| Rules against cigarette smoking | −.17** | −.06 | −.36*** | −.36*** |

[a]The four categories were: Never smoked cigarettes; Yes, but not last year; Last year, less than a pack; Last year, a pack or more. [b]Measures were based on combined parent and child reports. [c]$n = 196$. [d]$n = 198$. [e]$n = 195$.
*$p ≤ .05$. **$p ≤ .01$. ***$p ≤ .001$.

With two exceptions involving children's smoking, the results are al-most identical. By and large, the same factors that are significant in the combined measure are significant in the respondent-specific percep-tual reports. However, the negative correlations between child's smok-ing within the last year and parental rules against smoking increase from −.36 ($p \leq .001$) to −.45 ($p \leq .001$) when the child's measure is substituted for the aggregated measure; both with respect to mothers and fathers, the negative correlation of child smoking with parental smoking rule is much stronger for the child's perception (−.45, $p \leq .001$) than the correlation with father's report (−.19, $p \leq .01$) or espe-cially mother's report (−.13, $p \leq .10$). The negative correlation between maternal closeness and child smoking, which was −.22 ($p \leq .01$) for the aggregated measure of closeness, is −.20 ($p \leq .01$) for the child's percep-tion of closeness and −.14 ($p \leq .05$) for the mother's perception. For fathers, these negative correlations are −.18 ($p \leq .01$) for the aggregated measure and −.21 ($p \leq .01$) for the child's perception but −.08 for the father's perception. Thus, we do not find, as others have reported, that the correlations between a child outcome and the child's report of the quality of parenting are necessarily stronger than with the parent's independent report (Felson, 1990; Gecas & Schwalbe, 1986; Krohn et al., 1992).

**Modeling or Socialization: A Test of a Hypothesis**

A test of the modeling versus socialization hypothesis was conducted by estimating the unique effect of parental smoking in multivariate analyses that included measures of each parent's smoking and parental socialization practices. In a first step, parent-specific regressions were run. To reduce the number of covariates in the models, we included in the logistic regressions three sociodemographic variables known from prior work to be related to children's smoking (age and sex) and to adult smoking (parental years of education) and the four parental socialization practices that had shown significant relations with paren-tal and children's smoking across at least two of the four sets of associ-ations we examined (see Table 3). The socialization measures covered both quality of parenting and norm setting: closeness, consistency of discipline, monitoring, and rule against smoking; and were based on the combined reports of each parent and the child. None of the social-ization practices were significant in the father-specific model. In a second step, to specify the impact of smoking by one parent controlling for smoking by the other parent and to identify the contribution social-ization practices as potential explanatory factors in the relations be-tween parent and child smoking, two hierarchical models were run for

TABLE 4

Adjusted Odds[a] From Logistic Regressions Predicting Child's Smoking Lifetime and Last Year From Demographic Covariates, Maternal Smoking, Paternal Smoking, and Maternal Socialization Practices

| | Smoking Lifetime | | Smoking Last Year | |
|---|---|---|---|---|
| Variable | Model 1[c] | Model 2[d] | Model 1[c] | Model 2[d] |
| Child's age | 2.1*** | 2.0*** | 1.7*** | 1.6*** |
| Child's sex (= girl) | 1.9 | 2.0 | 2.0 | 2.3 |
| Parent years of education | 1.0 | 1.0 | .8[†] | .8[†] |
| Maternal smoking (vs. never) | | | | |
|   Not last year | 1.6 | 1.5 | 1.0 | .9 |
|   Last year, < pack a day | 1.0 | 1.0 | .8 | .8 |
|   Last year, ≥ pack a day | 4.7* | 3.3[†] | 4.4* | 3.3[†] |
| Paternal smoking (vs. never) | | | | |
|   Not last year | 3.2[†] | 1.9 | 3.3 | 2.4 |
|   Last year, < pack a day | 2.4 | 1.4 | 2.4 | 1.6 |
|   Last year, ≥ pack a day | 2.6 | 1.7 | 1.1 | 1.0 |
| Maternal closeness[b] | — | .4[†] | — | .7 |
| Maternal consistency of discipline[b] | — | .5[†] | — | .9 |
| Maternal monitoring[b] | — | 2.0 | — | .6 |
| Maternal rules against smoking[b] | — | .4[†] | — | .6 |
| Constant | −11.64*** | −6.75 | −5.81 | −.44 |
| Chi-square | 94.40*** | 98.63*** | 65.73*** | 64.50*** |
| df | 9 | 13 | 9 | 13 |

[a]Exponentiated unstandardized coefficients. [b]Maternal socialization practices based on combined mother and child reports. [c]$n = 198$. [d]$n = 192$.
[†]$p \le .01$. *$p \le .05$. ***$p \le .001$.

each measure of child smoking. The first model included the demographic and the two parental smoking variables; the second added the multiinformant maternal socialization variables. The mother-specific socialization measures were included, because, in the parent-specific models, maternal smoking and maternal socialization practices had statistically significant effects on the child smoking, whereas father's smoking did not. (We considered and rejected the inclusion of a combined measure of socialization practices based on mother–father–child reports of mother and father, because it would obscure the parent-specific relations between parental smoking and parental socialization practices.) A variant of the second model, in which the separate measures of mother's and father's smoking were replaced by a joint parental smoking variable, was run on the total sample of children. The adjusted odds predicting the child's lifetime and last year smoking, based on the regression coefficients, are displayed in Table 4 for all children, and odds for smoking in the last year for boys and girls are displayed separately in Table 5. Because there are both continuous and

TABLE 5

Adjusted Odds[a] From Logistic Regressions Predicting Girls' and Boys' Smoking in Last Year From Maternal Smoking, Paternal Smoking, Demographic Covariates, Maternal Socialization Practices, and Perceived Friend Smoking

| Variable | Boys | | | Girls | | |
|---|---|---|---|---|---|---|
| | Model 1[d] | Model 2[e] | Model 3[f] | Model 1[g] | Model 2[h] | Model 3[h] |
| Child's age | 1.7*** | 1.5* | 1.1 | 1.8** | 1.7** | 1.2 |
| Parent years of education | .7 | .7 | .7 | .8 | .8 | .8 |
| Maternal smoking (vs. never or not last year)[b] | | | | | | |
|   Last year, < pack a day | 1.3 | 1.1 | .8 | .9 | .6 | 1.0 |
|   Last year, ≥ pack a day | 2.9 | 2.0 | 2.5 | 10.5* | 8.7* | 8.6* |
| Paternal smoking (vs. never or not last year)[b] | | | | | | |
|   Last year, < pack a day | 4.2 | 5.0 | 6.0 | .1 | .1 | .2 |
|   Last year, ≥ pack a day | 1.6 | 1.8 | 2.1 | .1* | .1* | .1* |
| Maternal closeness[c] | — | 1.2 | — | — | .4 | — |
| Maternal consistency of discipline[c] | — | .6 | — | — | 1.1 | — |
| Maternal monitoring[c] | — | 1.1 | — | — | .2 | — |
| Maternal rules against smoking[c] | — | .4 | — | — | .7 | — |
| Having some friends ever smoked (vs. no or only one friend ever smoked) | — | — | 39.8** | — | — | 21.5** |
| Constant | −3.615 | −.225 | .305 | −6.260 | 3.298 | −2.484 |
| Chi-square | 33.24*** | 32.54*** | 47.67*** | 37.92*** | 42.37*** | 47.76*** |
| df | 6 | 10 | 7 | 6 | 10 | 7 |

[a]Exponentiated unstandardized coefficient. [b]*Never* and *Not last year* categories combined because of zero cases in one cell for boys. [c]Maternal socialization practices based on combined mother and child reports. [d]$n = 109$. [e]$n = 104$. [f]$n = 107$. [g]$n = 89$. [h]$n = 88$.
*$p \leq .05$. **$p \leq .01$. ***$p \leq .001$.

categorical variables in the equations, the comparison of coefficients must be made cautiously.

Both for smoking lifetime and smoking in the last year, the most important predictor of the children's smoking is age (Table 4, Model 1). Not surprisingly, smoking increases with age. The higher odds for girls than for boys in rates of smoking do not reach statistical significance. Heavy maternal smoking increases the odds of the child smoking; high parental education decreases the odds. Father's smoking prior to the last year has a stronger effect on the child's lifetime smoking than any other paternal behavior, but the effect is weaker than the effect of maternal smoking.

The socialization variables do not lead to a significant increase in the overall chi-square value of the model; coefficients for individual parenting variables are stronger for lifetime than last year smoking. Controlling for parents' smoking patterns, closeness between parent and child, consistency of parental discipline, and rule against smoking reduce the child's experimentation with cigarette smoking. The introduction of these variables reduces the effect of maternal smoking by about 25% (Table 4, Model 2). The odds are still higher than three, but the effect is only significant at $p < .10$, probably because of the relatively small sample size. Controlling for socialization practices, children whose mothers smoke a pack or more a day are three times more likely to have ever smoked or to be currently smoking than children whose mothers smoke less than a pack a day or do not smoke at all. We tested the interaction between parental smoking and rule against smoking under the assumption that norm setting would be more effective when it was consonant with parental behaviors. The interaction was not significant.

The third model substituted the joint mother–father smoking classification for the separate parental smoking variables (data not presented). Confirming the univariate findings highlighted earlier, when the mother is the only parent who smokes at least one pack a day in the household, her smoking has creates higher odds for the child smoking, especially for smoking within the last year, than when both she and her husband also smoke heavily: The odds for the child smoking in the last year are 5.0 ($p < .05$) compared with 1.7 when both parents smoke or .9 when only the father smokes.

Because it is important on theoretical and policy grounds to consider sex-specific family processes, analyses were carried out separately for boys and girls. Data for smoking in the last year are presented in Table 5. Although the odds for specific variables are much larger for one sex than the other, because of small sample sizes, most of the sex interactions do not reach statistical significance. However, the data suggest new hypotheses to be tested in larger samples.

The effect of maternal smoking is sex- and behavior-specific: It appears among daughters but not among sons, and, for daughters, smoking within the last year but not lifetime. Because of small sample sizes when the sample is disaggregated by sex of the child and because the paternal cell for being a nonsmoker had no cases of boys smoking in the past year, the parental smoking categories were reduced from four to three. Never users and former users were grouped into one category. In the absence of the socialization variables, the odds of a daughter's smoking when the mother smoked heavily within the last year are higher than 10. By contrast, a heavy-smoking father appears to discourage smoking by daughters. The opposite effects of smoking by mothers and fathers reflect the fact, discussed earlier, that mothers have a particularly strong influence on their daughters when they are the only parent to smoke heavily in the household. However, the interaction between sex and maternal smoking is not statistically significant (data not presented). The introduction of the socialization variables reduces slightly the odds of maternal smoking on daughters' smoking.

An attempt was made to account for the greater influence of mothers than fathers on the child smoking. Indeed, a plausible explanation underlying a role modeling interpretation is that mothers spend more time with their children than fathers and therefore are more influential. Because smoking is a highly visible behavior, amount of time spent with the child may be an important explanatory factor. Because we had no information about the amount of time each parent spent with the child, we used as a proxy the mother's labor force participation. We hypothesized that working mothers would spend less time with their children and, therefore, would have less influence on the child's smoking than nonworking mothers. We differentiated mothers into three groups according to their labor force participation: do not work, work part-time, and work full-time. Working mothers have older children than mothers who do not work. The results were the opposite of what we expected. Even after controlling for the child's age, the highest rates of children's smoking are observed among the children of working mothers (data not presented).

### Parental and Peer Influences

Given the known importance of peers on adolescents' drug behavior, we also estimated a model in which we considered the role of parents in the presence of perceived peer cigarette smoking (Table 5, Model 3). Because of the small sample size, the peer variable was included without the socialization variables. Perceived peer smoking has by far the highest odds of any variable in the model; the odds are almost twice as high for boys as for girls (39.8 vs. 21.5). However, with the inclusion of the peer variable, the odds of maternal smoking on daughter's smoking are reduced only slightly and by the same amount as by the inclusion of the socialization variables. This result is all the more important when we keep in mind that the perceived peer effects we estimated inflate to a significant (but unknown) degree the actual influence of peers and their influence relative to that of parents. This inflation is due to two different processes. One process is attribution, whereby perceptions are determined, in part, by the person's own behaviors and values (Davies & Kandel, 1981). In addition, cross-sectional associations between friends reflect not only socialization and interpersonal influence but also selection and assortative pairing on the basis of prior similarity (Kandel, 1978). The latter process leads to an overestimation of the cross-sectional peer effects by about 100% (Kandel, 1978). The extent to which attribution distorts the estimates of influence has not been quantified. The odds reflecting the effect of peer smoking are inflated by a factor of two at a minimum and exaggerate the difference in influence between mothers and peers, especially because parental behaviors are based upon self-reports. In this context, the maternal effect on girls' smoking is all the more remarkable, because the odds are only half as high as those of peer smoking. Interestingly, the inclusion of the peer variable reduces the effect of child age to nonsignificance. The effect of age probably reflects the increased association of older children with smoking peers.

## DISCUSSION AND CONCLUSION

As most previous investigators, we have found that children whose parents smoke are more likely to be smokers themselves than children whose parents do not smoke. Maternal smoking has a stronger effect than paternal smoking on smoking by young adolescents; it has a stronger effect on daughters than on sons—especially current smoking—and appears when mothers are current and heavy smokers. At this time, the reasons mothers are more influential than fathers are not well understood. However, the findings provide important evidence in support of the intergenerational transmission of smoking, especially because they are based on independent reports from parents. The translation of effects into attributable population risks (Fleiss, 1981) highlights the importance of parental, and especially maternal, smoking on the child smoking. About a third of lifetime smokers among boys and 60% among girls could be attributed to lifetime smoking by mothers. Almost a quarter of lifetime smokers among boys and close to half among girls could be attributed to heavy-smoking mothers (data not presented). The attributable risks are sizeable.

The intergenerational transmission of smoking from mother to daughter is also independent in a large part of smoking in the peer group. However, perceived peer smoking is the most important determinant of the child smoking, especially for boys, and explains, in part, the observed effect of child's age. As we had hypothesized, certain parental socialization practices, such as closeness, consistency of discipline, monitoring, and rule setting, are correlated with both parental and child smoking. In the multivariate models, these factors predict lower levels of child's smoking, especially for lifetime. For both lifetime and last year smoking by the child, socialization practices reduce only slightly the effect of maternal smoking. The persistence of the maternal effect with controls for parental socialization practices indicates that the effect of maternal smoking is mostly independent of these practices.

Smoking by children clearly has a familial component. With our data, imitation and role modeling effects cannot be clearly differentiated from a genetic effect. Within the limitations of the inferences that we can make, we conclude that parental effects reflect mainly role modeling of mothers by daughters, especially with respect to current smoking by the child. Furthermore, the generalizability of the findings is subject to the specific characteristics of our sample. The families we have studied are intact, the mothers were relatively young at the birth of their child, the children are first born and at the early-adolescent stage. The extent to which these results would generalize to single-mother households, to children irrespective of birth order, and to older adolescents remains to be established.

Intervention and prevention practices targeted toward reducing or preventing cigarette smoking among children tend to target the child's life skills, knowledge, attitudes about smoking, and resistance skills toward peer pressure. Our investigation points to another important and neglected focus of intervention, namely, the smoking behavior of the youths' parents in early adolescence.

## ACKNOWLEDGMENTS

An earlier version of this article was presented at the meeting of the Society for Research on Adolescence, Washington, DC, March 1992.

Work on this article was partially supported by research grants DA03196, DA04866, and DA02867 to Denise Kandel and research scientist award DA00081 to Denise Kandel from the National Institute on Drug Abuse. Partial support for computer costs was provided by Mental Health Clinical Research Center Grant MH30906 from the National Institute of Mental Health to the New York State Psychiatric Institute.

We gratefully acknowledge the research assistance of Christine Schaffran.

## REFERENCES

Annis, H. M. (1974). Patterns of intra-familial drug use. *British Journal of Addiction, 69,* 361–369.

Banks, M. H., Bewley, B. R., Bland, J. R., Dean, S., & Pollard, V. (1978). Long-term study of smoking by secondary schoolchildren. *Archives of Disease in Childhood, 83,* 12–19.

Barnes, G. M. (1990). Impact of the family on adolescent drinking patterns. In Collins, R.

L., Leonard, K. E., & Searles, J. S. (Eds.), *Alcohol and the family: Research and clinical perspectives* (pp. 137–161). New York: Guilford.

Barnes, G. M., & Farrell, M. P. (1992). Parental support and control as predictors of adolescent drinking, delinquency, and related problem behaviors. *Journal of Marriage and the Family, 54*, 763–776.

Bauman, K. E., Botvin, G. J., Botvin, E. M., & Baker, E. (1992). Normative expectations and the behavior of significant others: An integration of traditions in research on adolescents' cigarette smoking. *Psychological Reports, 71*, 568–570.

Baumrind, D. (1985). Familial antecedents of adolescent drug use: A developmental perspective. In C. L. Jones & R. J. Battjes (Eds.), *Etiology of drug abuse: Implications for prevention* (Research Monograph 56; pp. 13–44). Rockville, MD: National Institute on Drug Abuse.

Beaglehole, R., Eyles, E., & Harding, W. (1978). Cigarette smoking habits, attitudes, and associated factors in adolescents. *New Zealand Medical Journal, 87*, 239–242.

Bewley, B. R., & Bland, J. M. (1977). Academic performance and social factors related to cigarette smoking by schoolchildren. *British Journal of Preventive and Social Medicine, 31*, 18–24.

Bewley, B. R., Bland, J., & Harris, R. (1974). Factors associated with the starting of cigarette smoking by schoolchildren. *British Journal of Social and Preventative Medicine, 28*, 37–44.

Block, J., Keyes, S., & Block, J. H. (1986, March). *Childhood personality and environmental antecedents of drug use: A prospective longitudinal study*. Paper presented at the meeting of the Society for Life History Research in Psychopathology, Palm Springs, CA.

Bothwell, P. (1959). The epidemiology of cigarette smoking in rural school children. *Medical Officer, 102*, 125–132.

Brook, J. S., Brook, D. W., Gordon, H. S., Whiteman, M., & Cohen, P. (1990). The psychosocial etiology of adolescent drug use: A family interactional approach. *Genetic, Social and General Psychology Monograph, 116*, 111–267.

Brook, J. S., Gordon, A. S., & Brook, D. W. (1986). Fathers and daughters: Their relationship and personality characteristics associated with the daughter's smoking behavior. *Journal of Genetic Psychology, 148*, 31–44.

Brook, J. S., Whiteman, M., Gordon, A. S., Brook, D. W. (1983). Fathers and sons: Their relationship and personality characteristics associated with the son's smoking behavior. *The Journal of Genetic Psychology, 142*, 271–281.

Brook, J. S., Whiteman, M., Gordon, A. S., & Cohen, P. (1986). Some models and mechanisms for explaining the impact of maternal and adolescent characteristics on adolescent stage of drug use. *Developmental Psychology, 22*, 460–467.

Brook, J. S., Whiteman, M., Nomura, C., Gordon, A. S., & Cohen, P. (1988). Personality, family, and ecological influences on adolescent drug use: A developmental analysis. In H. Coombs (Ed.), *The family context of adolescent drug use* (pp. 123–160). New York: Haworth.

Burchfiel, C. M., Higgins, M. W., Keller, J. B., Butler, W. J., & Donahue, R. P. (1989). Initiation of cigarette smoking in children and adolescents of Tecumseh, Michigan. *American Journal of Epidemiology 130*, 410–415.

Chassin, L., Presson, C. C., Bensenberg, M., Corty, E., Olshavsky, R. W., & Sherman, S. J. (1981). Predicting adolescents' intentions to smoke cigarettes. *Journal of Health and Social Behavior, 22*, 445–455.

Coombs, R. H., & Landsverk, J. (1988). Parenting styles and substance use during childhood and adolescence. *Journal of Marriage and the Family, 50*, 473–482.

Davies, M., & Kandel, D. B. (1981). Parental and peer influences on adolescents' educational plans: Some further evidence. *American Journal of Sociology, 87,* 363–387.

Dishion, T. J., & Loeber, R. (1985). Male adolescent marijuana and alcohol use: The role of parents and peers revisited. *Journal of Alcohol and Substance Abuse, 11*(1,2), 11–25.

Dishion, T. J., Patterson, G. R., & Reid, J. R. (1988). Parent and peer factors associated with drug sampling in early adolescence: Implications for treatment. In E. R. Rahdert & J. Grabowski (Eds.), *Adolescent drug abuse: Analyses of treatment research* (pp. 69–93). Rockville, MD: National Institute on Drug Abuse.

Dishion, T. J., Ray, J., & Capaldi, D. (1992, March). *Parenting precursors to male adolescent substance use.* Paper presented at symposium on Family Processes and Adolescent Substance Use at the meeting of the Society of Research in Adolescence, Washington, DC.

Elliott, D. S., Huizinga, D., & Ageton, S. S. (1985). *Explaining delinquency and drug use.* Beverly Hills, CA: Sage.

Felson, R. B. (1990). Comparison processes in parents' and children's appraisals of academic performance. *Social Psychology Quarterly, 53,* 264–273.

Fleiss, J. L. (1981). *Statistical methods for rates and proportions* (2nd ed.). New York: Wiley.

Foshee, V., & Bauman, K. E. (1992). Parental and peer characteristics as modifiers of the bond–behavior relationship: An elaboration of control theory. *Journal of Health and Social Behavior, 33,* 66–76.

Gecas, V., & Schwalbe, M. L. (1986). Parental behavior and adolescent self-esteem. *Journal of Marriage and the Family, 48,* 37–46.

Gfroerer, J. (1987). Correlation between drug use by teenagers and drug use by older family members. *American Journal of Drug and Alcohol Abuse, 13,* 95–108.

Green, G., Macintyre, S., West, P., & Ecob, R. (1990). Do children of lone parents smoke more because their mothers do? *British Journal of Addiction, 85,* 1497–1500.

Hawkins, J. D., Lishner, D. M., & Catalano, R. F., Jr. (1985). Childhood predictors and the prevention of adolescent substance abuse. In C. L. Jones & R. J. Battjes (Eds.), *Etiology of drug abuse: Implications for prevention* (pp. 75–126). Washington, DC: Superintendent of Documents, U.S. Government Printing Office.

Heath, A. C., & Martin, N. G. (1988). Teenage alcohol use in the Australian twin register: Genetic and social determinants of starting to drink. *Alcoholism: Clinical and Experimental Research, 12,* 735–741.

Hops, H., Tildesley, E., Lichtenstein, E., Ary, D., & Sherman, L. (1990). Parent–adolescent problem-solving interactions and drug use. *American Journal of Drug and Alcohol Abuse, 16,* 239–258.

Horn, D., Courts, F., Taylor, R., & Solomon, E. (1959). Cigarette smoking among high school students. *American Journal of Public Health, 49,* 1497–1511.

Hover, S. J., & Gaffney, L. R. (1988). Factors associated with smoking behavior in adolescent girls. *Addictive Behaviors, 13,* 139–145.

Huba, G. J., & Bentler, P. M. (1980). The role of peer and adult models for drug taking at different stages in adolescence. *Journal of Youth and Adolescence, 9,* 449–465.

Hundleby, J. D., & Mercer, G. W. (1987). Family and friends as social environments and their relationship to young adolescent's use of alcohol, tobacco, and marijuana. *Journal of Marriage and the Family, 49,* 151–164.

Jacob, T., & Leonard, K. (1991, November). *Family and peer influences in the development of adolescent alcohol abuse.* Paper prepared for National Institute on Alcohol Abuse and Alcoholism-supported conference, Working Group on the Development of Alcohol-Related Problems in High-Risk Youth: Establishing Linkages Across Biogenetic and Psychosocial Domains, Washington, DC.

Jessop, D. J. (1981). Family relationships as viewed by parents and adolescents: A specification. *Journal of Marriage and the Family, 43,* 95–107.

Jessor, R., & Jessor, S. L. (1977). *Problem behavior and psychosocial development: A longitudinal study of youth.* New York: Academic.

Johnston, L. D., O'Malley, P. M., & Bachman, J. G. (1992). *Smoking, drinking, and illicit drug use among American secondary school students, college students, and young adults, 1975–1991.* Rockville, MD: National Institute on Drug Abuse.

Jöreskog, K. G., & Sörbom, D. (1989). *LISREL 7 users' reference guide.* Mooresville, IN: Scientific Software, Inc.

Kandel, D. B. (1978). Homophily, selection and socialization in adolescent friendships. *American Journal of Sociology, 84,* 427–436.

Kandel, D. B., Kessler, R., & Margulies, R. (1978). Adolescent initiation into stages of drug use: A developmental analysis. In D. B. Kandel (Ed.), *Longitudinal research on drug use: Empirical findings and methodological issues* (pp. 73–99). Washington, DC: Hemisphere–Wiley.

Kandel, D. B., & Logan, J. A. (1984). Patterns of drug use from adolescence to young adulthood: I. Periods of risk for initiation, continued use, and discontinuation. *American Journal of Public Health, 74,* 660–666.

Kandel, D. B., Raveis, V. H., & Kandel, P. I. (1984). Continuity in discontinuities: Adjustment in young adulthood of former school absentees and school dropouts. *Youth and Society, 13,* 325–352.

Kandel, D. B., Single, E., & Kessler, R. (1976). The epidemiology of drug use among New York State high school students: Distribution, trends and change in rates of use. *American Journal of Public Health, 66,* 43–53.

Kandel, D. B., & Yamaguchi, K. (1993). From beer to crack: Developmental patterns of involvement in drugs. *American Journal of Public Health, 83,* 851–855.

Kandel, D. B., Yamaguchi, K., & Chen, K. (1992). Stages of progression in drug involvement from adolescence to adulthood: Further evidence for the Gateway Theory. *Journal of Studies on Alcohol, 53,* 447–457.

Kellam, S. G., Simon, M., & Ensminger, M. E. (1983). Antecedents in first grade of teenage drug use and psychological well-being: A ten-year community-wide prospective study. In D. Ricks & B. Dohrenwend (Eds.), *Origins of psychopathology: Research and public policy* (pp. 17–42). New York: Cambridge University Press.

Krohn, M. D., Skinner, W. F., Massey, J. L., & Akers, R. L. (1985). Social learning theory and adolescent cigarette smoking: A longitudinal study. *Social Problems, 32,* 455–473.

Krohn, M. D., Stern, S. B., Thornberry, T. P., & Jang, S. J. (1992). The measurement of family process variables: The effect of adolescent and parent perceptions of family life on delinquent behavior. *Journal of Quantitative Criminology, 8,* 287–315.

Krosnick, J., & Judd, C. (1982). Transitions in social influence at adolescence: Who induces cigarette smoking? *Developmental Psychology, 18,* 359–368.

Lanese, R. R., Banks, F. R., & Keller, M. D. (1972). Smoking behavior in a teenage population: A multivariate conceptual approach. *American Journal of Public Health, 62,* 807–813.

Lemin, B. (1967). Smoking in 14-year-old school children. *International Journal of Nursing Studies, 4,* 301–307.

Leonard, K. E. (1990). Summary: Family processes and alcoholism. In R. L. Collins, K. E. Leonard, & J. S. Searles (Eds.), *Alcohol and the family: Research and clinical perspectives* (pp. 272–281). New York: Guilford.

Levitt, E., & Edwards, J. (1970). A multivariate study of correlative factors in youthful cigarette smoking. *Developmental Psychology, 2,* 5–11.

Lorenz, F. O., Conger, R. D., Simon, R. L., & Whitbeck, L. B. (1991). Economic pressure and marital quality: An illustration of the method variance problem in the causal modeling of family process. *Journal of Marriage and the Family, 53,* 375–388.

Melby, J. N., Conger, R. D., Conger, K. J., & Lorenz, F. O. (1993). Effects of parental behavior on tobacco use by young male adolescents. *Journal of Marriage and the Family, 55,* 439–454.

Mercer, G. W., Kohn, P. M. (1980). Child-rearing factors, authoritarianism, drug use attitudes, and adolescent drug use: A model. *The Journal of Genetic Psychology, 136,* 159–171.

Morison, J., Medovy, H., & MacDonnell, G. (1964). Health education and cigarette smoking. *Canadian Medical Association Journal, 91,* 49–56.

Murray, M., Kiryluk, S., & Swan, A. V. (1985). Relation between parents' and children's smoking behavior and attitudes. *Journal of Epidemiology and Community Health, 39,* 169–174.

Needle, R., McCubbin, H., Wilson, M., Reinect, R., Lazar, A., & Mederer, H. (1986). Interpersonal influences in adolescent drug use: The role of older siblings, parents, and peers. *International Journal of the Addictions, 21,* 739–766.

Neukirch, F., & Cooreman, J. (1983). Influence des parents sur le tabagisme de leurs enfants [The influence of parents on the smoking of their children]. *Social Science Medicine, 17,* 763–769.

Nolte, A. E., Smith, B. J., & O'Rourke, T. (1983). The relative importance of parental attitudes and behavior upon youth smoking behavior. *Journal of School Health, 53,* 264–271.

Palmer, A. B. (1970). Some variables contributing to the onset of cigarette smoking among junior high school students. *Social Science and Medicine, 4,* 359–366.

Pandina, R. J., & Schuele, J. A. (1983). Psychosocial correlates of alcohol and drug use of adolescent students and adolescents in treatment. *Journal of Studies on Alcohol, 44,* 950–973.

Pulkkinen, L. (1983). Youthful smoking and drinking in a longitudinal perspective. *Journal of Youth and Adolescence, 12,* 253–283.

Rawbone, R. G., Keeling, C. A., Jenkins, A., & Guz, A. (1979). Cigarette smoking among secondary school children in 1975: Its prevalence and some of the factors that promote smoking. *Journal of Epidemiology and Community Health, 32,* 53–58.

Rossow, I. (1992, April). *Additive and interactional effects of parental health behaviors in adolescence: An empirical study of smoking and alcohol consumption in Norwegian families.* Paper presented at the Youth and Drugs Conference, Larkollen, Norway.

Salber, E., & MacMahon, B. (1961). Cigarette smoking among high school students related to social class and parental smoking habits. *American Journal of Public Health, 51,* 1780–1789.

Simcha-Fagan, O., Gersten, J. C., & Langner, T. S. (1986). Early precursors and concurrent correlates of patterns of illicit drug use in adolescence. *Journal of Drug Issues, 16,* 7–28.

Simons, R. L., Conger, R. D., & Whitbeck, L. B. (1988). A multistage social learning model of the influences of family and peers upon adolescent substance abuse. *The Journal of Drug Issues, 18,* 293–315.

Skinner, W. F., Massey, J. L., Krohn, M. D., & Lauer, R. M. (1985). Social influences and constraints on the initiation and cessation of adolescent tobacco use. *Journal of Behavioral Medicine, 8,* 353–376.

U.S. Department of Health and Human Services. (1983). *The health consequences of smoking: Cardiovascular disease. A report of the Surgeon General.* (DHHS Publication No. PHS 84–50204). Rockville, MD: U.S. Department of Health and Human Services, Public Health Service, Office on Smoking and Health.

U.S. Department of Health and Human Services. (1984). *The health consequences of smoking: Chronic obstructive lung disease. A report of the Surgeon General.* (DHHS Publication No. PHS 84–50205). Rockville, MD: U.S. Department of Health and Human Services, Public Health Service, Office on Smoking and Health.

U.S. Department of Health and Human Services. (1989). *Reducing the health consequences of smoking: 25 years of progress. A report of the Surgeon General.* (DHHS Publication No. CDC 89–8411). Rockville, MD: U.S. Department of Health and Human Services, Public Health Service, Centers for Disease Control.

Vicary, J. R., & Lerner, J. V. (1986). Parental attributes and adolescent drug use. *Journal of Adolescence, 9,* 115–122.

Williams, A. F. (1973). Personality and other characteristics associated with cigarette smoking among young teenagers. *Journal of Health and Social Behavior, 14,* 374–380.

Zucker, R. A., & Noll, R. A. (1987). The interaction of child and environment in the early development of drug involvement: A far ranging review and a planned very early intervention. *Drugs and Society, 1,* 57–97.

Received May 24, 1993
Revision received November 30, 1993
Accepted January 3, 1994

JOURNAL OF RESEARCH ON ADOLESCENCE, 4(2), 249–269
Copyright © 1994, Lawrence Erlbaum Associates, Inc.

# The Path to Alcohol Problems Through Conduct Problems: A Family-Based Approach to Very Early Intervention With Risk

Eugene Maguin
*Western Psychiatric Institute and Clinic*
*University of Pittsburgh*

Robert A. Zucker and Hiram E. Fitzgerald
*Michigan State University*

A program to prevent the development of conduct problems among preschool sons of alcoholic fathers was established as a way to interrupt what is likely to be one of the major mediating factors in the development of risk for alcoholism in later years. A community sample of 104 alcoholic men who: (a) had been convicted for driving while impaired with high blood alcohol concentrations (BACs), (b) were living in an intact relationship, (c) were the fathers of 3- to 5-year-old sons, and (d) lived within a 30-mile radius of the treatment facility was recruited from all district courts in a four-county area. Subjects were randomly assigned to one of two intervention formats, both parents or mothers only, or to a control group. The intervention combined a parent-training model with a marital issues component, and it spanned a 10-month interval. Evaluations were conducted at preintervention, midtreatment, termination, and 6-month follow-up. Overall, the intervention program had significant effects on negative, prosocial, and affectionate behavior at termination, but only the prosocial behavior effect persisted at follow-up. Some format differences were also observed, however; the both-parents format had greater impact on prosocial behavior than the mothers-only

Requests for reprints should be sent to Eugene Maguin, Life History Studies, Western Psychiatric Institute and Clinic, 3811 O'Hara Street, Pittsburgh, PA 15213.

format at both termination and follow-up. Ongoing difficulties and resolutions of conducting outreach-based early intervention programming with this population are discussed.

According to national epidemiologic data, substance abuse can be expected to affect approximately 17% of the adult population sometime during their lives (Regier et al., 1990); if one narrows the problem solely to alcohol abuse/dependence among males, the lifetime prevalence figure runs to approximately one fourth of the U.S. population (Helzer, Burnam, & McEvoy, 1991). How might one intervene very early on in a preventive way with what ultimately grows into such a large clinical problem? The program of work reported here began with the epidemiologic fact just noted, added several pieces of evidence pertaining to the development of risk, considered what interventions might likely alleviate such risk, and then crafted a population-based intervention regimen to address these issues quite early in the life course. The risk marker selected for access to the population was also derived from the previously mentioned data; it involved selecting male children from households in which the father was already alcoholic.

Such children are a compelling target group for preventive activity for a variety of reasons. Not only does substantial trouble already exist in the parental generation, but the children are at significantly greater risk to become alcohol or drug abusers themselves. (Current estimates put this figure at four to six times the likelihood in the general population; Russell, 1990.) In addition, elevated risk is present for a wide variety of other difficulties that begin even earlier in the life cycle than substance abuse. Such difficulties include hyperactivity, oppositional behavior and conduct problems, and their developmentally more advanced manifestations—including delinquency and the development of antisocial patterns of adaptation in adulthood (Sher, 1991; Zucker, 1989). Moreover, much recent work links the causal paths into adolescent alcohol and other drug abuse to those very same factors that are identified as more prevalent in early childhood among male children of alcoholics (COAs; cf. Kellam, Ensminger, & Simon, 1980; Pihl & Peterson, 1991; Zucker, 1989). Finally, as commonly noted in reviews of this area (Patterson, DeBaryshe, & Ramsey, 1989; Zucker & Fitzgerald, 1991), this risk envelope is very similar to the one known to be related to the emergence and continued development of antisociality even into adulthood (Olweus, 1979). In addition, continuity of process appears most likely to take place when the earlier nonalcohol specific risks are of greater severity (Loeber & LeBlanc, 1990; Tartar & Vanukov, in press).

Thus, the promise is offered that by addressing risk for conduct-related difficulty in early childhood and using preventive intervention techniques originally designed to alleviate it, one may be able to intervene, and arrest risk development, in the highest risk environments out of which alcohol and other forms of substance abuse are known to emerge. The program described here, the Michigan State University Multiple Risk Child Outreach Program (Zucker, Maguin, Noll, Fitzgerald, & Klinger, 1990),[1] was formulated with these goals in mind. Its first goal, therefore, was the arrest of conduct problems in young children. The long-term hypothesis is that such work would serve dual functions: (a) It would be useful in its own right and (b) it would intervene on processes that are believed to be causal to later alcohol abuse and alcoholism (Zucker & Gomberg, 1986; Zucker & Noll, 1987). The specific program we put in place represents an effort that focuses on a considerably earlier developmental period than the vast majority of preventive intervention programming currently being done (Hawkins, Catalano, & J. Y. Miller, 1992). It incorporates a broadly based, systemic model that includes a focus on family factors as well as individual child factors (G. E. Miller & Prinz, 1990), and its recruitment methodology is based on a primary prevention/outreach model that used a population net to access children at risk.

More concretely, in the present study, a group of families with preschool-age sons were accessed using a population screening procedure. Once identified, families were randomly assigned to either of two service delivery formats of an intervention program that has been found to be effective in producing significant and long-lasting decreases in aggression and noncompliance in both clinic- and self-referred families (Patterson, Chamberlain, & Reid, 1982; Webster-Stratton, 1981, 1982). Two delivery formats were used. In the first, only mothers were involved; in the second, both parents were involved.

On the basis of the success of parent-training programs with both clinic- and self-referred populations, it was expected that irrespective of delivery format, compared to families not participating in the program, intervention group families would report (a) significantly lower levels of such negative child behaviors as aggression and noncompliance, (b) significantly higher levels of such prosocial child behavior as minding and cooperative play, and (c) significantly higher levels of affectionate behavior toward the parents at the midtreatment, program termination, and follow-up assessments.

---

[1]The original name for this program was the Michigan State University Prevention of Conduct Disorders Project (Zucker & Noll, 1987).

The both-parents format was added on the basis of both the family therapy (Minuchin, 1974) and the marital discord literatures (Gottman & Katz, 1989), which suggest that addressing family issues with both parents present should lead to more effective long-term outcomes; the empirical literature is currently equivocal on this point (Budd & O'Brien, 1982; Horton, 1984; Webster-Stratton, 1985). Nonetheless, from Webster-Stratton (1985), it was anticipated that the both-parents format, compared to the mother-only format, would show significantly lower levels of negative behavior and higher levels of prosocial and affectionate behavior at the midtreatment, termination, and follow-up assessments.

## METHOD

### Subjects

Program participants were the first 104 families recruited from district courts in four mid-Michigan counties who, as part of the program protocol, were initially asked to take part in "a study of child health and family development." At that point, only casual mention was made of the possibility of later child-focused work. The initial assessment of child and family functioning involved a substantial (10-session) protocol. Families had to meet the following inclusion criteria: conviction of the father for driving while impaired (DWI) or driving under the influence of liquor (DUIL), with a blood alcohol concentration (BAC) of at least 15 mg per 100 ml (0.15%) when arrested and no prior DWI or DUIL arrests or a BAC of at least 0.12% and multiple arrests; subsequently, the father had to pass a protocol screen ensuring that he also met Feighner diagnostic criteria (Feighner et al., 1972) for probable or definite alcoholism (approximately 90% met the *definite* level); and, in addition, a biological son, ages 3.0 to 6.0 years, as well as the child's biological mother had to be living with the father at the time of first contact.

Although all fathers met the criteria for alcoholism, almost none of them identified themselves as alcoholic. In addition, the fact that these men were convicted drunk drivers indicates that their alcoholism was more heavily combined with antisociality than is true of other types of alcoholics (Babor & Dolinsky, 1988). Other analyses we conducted show that 60% are classified as Type 2 alcoholics according to Cloninger's (1987) typology, 25% are classified as Type 1 (nonantisocial, later onset), and 14% are classified as indeterminate (Zucker, Ellis, & Fitzgerald, in press). Thus, the present group is most representative of the subset of alcoholics known as the most damaged, as having the most antisocial comorbidity and earliest onset, and as the group most likely to have substance abuse manifested among their offspring (Zucker & Fitzgerald, 1991).

Demographic characteristics of the sample are as follows: mean age of the parents at first assessment contact was 29.3 years for the mothers and 31.4 years for the fathers. Although 16% of the mothers and 21% of the fathers had not finished high school, 42% of mothers and 38% of fathers had some post-high-school education. The biological parents in 99 of the families were married to each other and had been for a mean of 7.3 years.

At the time of the initial evaluation, families were randomly assigned to either of the two intervention formats or to a control group. At the conclusion of the evaluation, those families that were still intact and lived within 30 miles of the university were invited to participate in a sustained follow-up program on the basis of their earlier protocol designation. The treatment assignments involved two different intervention alternatives, both of which were described as "a program to improve parent–child communication patterns." Families whose random assignment was to the control condition were asked to take part in three follow-up assessments spaced at approximately 6-month intervals.

Of the 104 families initially recruited, 81 families met intervention protocol eligibility criteria and 23 families did not (12 had separated, 5 had moved from the intervention area, and 6 had failed to complete the initial evaluation). Comparisons between eligible and ineligible families revealed no significant demographic differences. On the Child Behavior Checklist (CBCL; Achenbach & Edelbrock, 1983), more, though not significantly, ineligible than eligible boys (36.8% versus 23.5%, respectively) scored in the clinical range ($T > 63$) of the externalizing behavior scale. Although the families that were not eligible for the intervention protocol are not relevant to the issue of treatment success, they are relevant to the issue of outreach generalizability and the likely implementation success of population-based programs. The reader is referred to Maguin (1991) and Zucker et al. (1990) for detailed information about recruitment and retention of subjects as well as about procedural details.

### Intervention Regimen

The intervention regimen (Zucker, 1991; Zucker, Noll, Kriegler, & Cruise, 1986) employed was a modification and extension of social learning therapy, a behavior modification strategy developed for the treatment of older aggressive/antisocial children at the Oregon Social

Learning Center (OSLC; Patterson, Reid, Jones, & Conger, 1975). Although the OSLC parent-training protocol formed the core of the child intervention, the Michigan State University protocol had some significant differences in both clientele and implementation. First, the average age of the target child was about 4.4 years at the first contact, compared to the average of about 12 years reported by Patterson (1974). Second, the protocol involved outreach to an already designated high-risk population, but the offering of help was not made within the context of offering treatment. Thus, families were neither self-selected nor court referred, and some needed to be convinced of the usefulness of the program. Third, the program was offered as an educational package rather than as treatment; it was described as one that would enhance parent–child communication and improve parent–child relationships. Thus, the families were volunteers rather than clients. Fourth, fathers typically were initially much less convinced of the need for the program. Because of this not-uncommon reluctance, much of the early work involved finding some common ground around which the intervention could legitimately proceed. Last, family conflict and marital dissatisfaction were frequently encountered. A common source of dissatisfaction among wives was spouse's drinking and related difficulties. Thus, any effort to work with the children—even in the early sessions—had to also confront this problem, which included the wife's anger at her husband's drinking and the husband's dissatisfaction with his spouse's nagging. As a result, although not a part of the framework for recruitment, special attention was routinely paid to the parents' alcohol and drug problems and marital functioning as part of the intervention program. Where indicated, referrals to Alcoholics Anonymous, as well as community treatment agencies, were made for focused work on these difficulties, and the extent of compliance with these referrals was then monitored as part of the intervention work.

The study design is diagrammed in Figure 1. The overall length of the intervention was 28 sessions, spanning approximately 1 year, and it was divided into two phases. During Phase 1, intervention staff taught child management skills (i.e., tracking, contracting, and time-out) through weekly sessions with families and twice-weekly telephone contacts. Phase 1 ended when the family had either (a) satisfactorily acquired the child management skills or (b) had completed between 12 and 16 sessions. In this latter instance, the exact Phase 2 transition was determined by staff decision. During Phase 2, interveners conducted 12 biweekly face-to-face sessions, along with at least weekly telephone contacts, to support and reinforce child management skills and address significant marital issues and individual substance abuse issues.

Although the nominal physical setting for the intervention was the Clinical Center at Michigan State University, about 45% of the families received some or all of the intervention program in their homes. The

INTERVENTION DESIGN

BOTH PARENTS AND MOTHER ONLY CONDITIONS

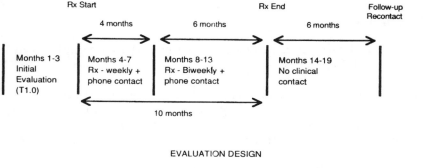

EVALUATION DESIGN

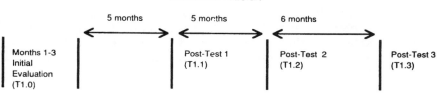

FIGURE 1  Schedule of initial assessment, intervention program, and posttest assessments for the intervention and control groups.

treatment staff were primarily post-masters-level doctoral students in clinical psychology who additionally received approximately 20 hours of training in the treatment paradigm and 4 hours of group supervision each week from one of two licensed clinical psychologists.

## Procedure

Both parents in all families, irrespective of the family's eligibility or intervention status, were asked to take part in all three posttest assessments, for which they received compensation. Posttest 1 (PT 1) was conducted between the first and second sessions of Phase 2 for the intervention families and at a nominal 26-week interval after initial assessment completion for all other families. Posttest 2 (PT 2) was conducted at the conclusion of the intervention program for intervention families and at a nominal 26 weeks after Posttest 1 completion for all other families. Posttest 3 was conducted at a nominal 26 weeks after completion of Posttest 2 for all families (see also Figure 1). Although the nominal 26-week interval was dictated by the study design, the actual interval between posttests was monitored regularly and adjustments were made in posttest scheduling for control and ineligible intervention group families so as to maintain an approximately equal interval between posttests for both intervention and other families.

**Evaluation Instruments**

Each of the following four evaluation instruments was completed by both of the child's parents.

*Child Behavior Checklist–Revised (CBCL–R).*   The CBCL–R (Achenbach & Edelbrock, 1983) is perhaps the most commonly used parent rating scale in clinical use. It was used here to provide a standardized index of the level of symptomatic functioning of the study children.

*Conners Parent Questionnaire–Modified (CPQ–M).*   CPQ–M is a 51-item shortened and slightly modified version of the original Conners Parent Questionnaire and the Revised Conners Parent Questionnaire (Conners, 1973; Goyette, Conners, & Ulrich, 1978); it uses the same 4-point response format.

*Child Behavior Rating Scale–Preschool Version (CBRS–P).*   The CBRS–P (Noll & Zucker, 1985a) is an 84-item child behavior questionnaire consisting of 49 desirable child behavior items (e.g., minds, shows affection, appropriately expresses anger) and 35 undesirable child behavior items (e.g., pushes or hits, inappropriately expresses anger), which are rated on a 7-point scale ranging from *never* (1) to *always* (7).

*Parent Daily Report–Modified (PDR–M).*   The PDR–M (Noll & Zucker, 1985b) uses 22 items taken verbatim from the CBRS–P to which parents respond by reporting whether each of the behaviors had occurred in the previous 24 hours. At each assessment, each parent was interviewed by telephone on alternate days for 3 days each.

**Outcome Measures**

Outcome measures were built in a three-step process, originally involving a content analysis of the four outcome instruments administered, followed by confirmatory factor analysis on data pooled over parents and assessments to evaluate the provisionally identified clusters (see Hunter & Gerbing, 1982), and concluding with a second-order confirmatory factor analysis to evaluate the possible existence of higher order constructs. From this work three outcome measures were developed that (a) met necessary construct development criteria of internal consistency, along with parallelism with other variables, and (b) were judged suitable in content to evaluate intervention effects. These measures were *negative behavior composite, prosocial behavior composite,* and *affectionate behavior.*

The negative behavior composite comprised four more specific negative behavior constructs (anger arousal, aggression, hyper, and defiant). The behaviors included in these scales describe children who, in the negative extreme, are seen as being aggressive, rude, defiant, oppositional, restless and overactive, and given to sharp and dramatic explosions of anger. The prosocial behavior composite consisted of three more specific prosocial behavior constructs (compliant, polite, and plays well). The behaviors included in these scales describe children who, in the positive extreme, are seen as being compliant to parent requests, respectful of the rights of other children and adults, and able to play easily with other children. The affectionate behavior measure consisted of a single construct that is a measure of the parent's perception of the target child's expressed affection toward the parent.

Under a model that treated parents as equal raters or observers of their child's behavior, the construct score was the mean of each parent's score on the construct, and the reliability of that score was the between-parent correlation corrected by the Spearman-Brown formula for two measurements. The resulting reliability estimate was .70 for the negative behavior composite, .55 for the prosocial behavior composite, and .58 for affectionate behavior.

## Analysis of Change

The impact of the intervention was computed by the change score (i.e., the difference in the averaged within-parent construct scores) for each pair of time points. The resulting change scores were then correlated with intervention group membership (Yes–No) to yield a point biserial correlation as an index of whether significant change took place.

## RESULTS

### Initial Symptomatic Status

Although none of the study children had clinical contact, the CBCL–R was used to provide an index of the extent to which clinically significant problems were present. On the basis of a T score of more than 63 on the externalizing scale, 23.5% of the eligible boys were in the clinical range, which was not significantly different than the ineligible boys' scores.

## Final Intervention Status

At the conclusion of the intervention program, a review showed that 17 of the 23 families (74%) offered the mother-only protocol and 12 of the 28 families offered the both-parents protocol (43%) had completed the entire intervention sequence. Over the course of the intervention, an additional 4 families (3 in the mother-only group and 1 in the both-parents group) had separated and thus became ineligible. Of the families that did not complete the intervention protocol, 4 mother-only families and 3 both-parents families received partial treatment because they completed at least five sessions before withdrawing, and 12 both-parents families and 3 mother-only families either refused the intervention or failed to complete five sessions. Significantly more families in the both-parents condition than in the mother-only condition either refused the intervention offer or withdrew before completing five sessions, $\chi^2(1, N = 15) = 4.27, p < .05$. Overall, the attrition rate for the intervention group was 43%, which is certainly comparable to intervention outreach studies (e.g., 25% to 50%, from Andrews et al., 1982; or 28%, from Garber, 1988) but is somewhat high compared to self- or clinic-referred parent-training programs ($M = 28\%$, range: 0% to 50%; Forehand, Middlebrook, Rogers, & Stiffle, 1983).

We also compared families that refused treatment with those completing treatment on a variety of demographic, parent-functioning, and child-behavior variables, but we found no differences (Maguin, 1991). Because of the small sample size, however, the power of the tests was quite low. Of the 26 eligible families assigned to the control group, 3 families refused to complete all three scheduled posttests and were counted as dropouts from the control group.

Intervention effects were examined using the subset of 52 families that either completed the intervention or—in the case of the controls—continued to remain eligible for it (i.e., the families were still intact and living in the immediate geographic area of the program).

## Overall Intervention Effects

It was expected that the group receiving the intervention would show a significant decrease in negative behavior and a significant increase in prosocial behavior relative to the control group. Table 1 presents the means and standard deviations of the composite construct measures for the intervention and control groups at the four measurement points. A higher score indicates that a child has "more" of the construct. Table 2 presents the measures of change of the intervention group relative to the control group, as assessed by point biserial

TABLE 1
Across-Time Means and Standard Deviations for Intervention and Control Groups
on the Composite Intervention Measures

| Scale | Pretest | Midtreatment | Termination | Follow-Up |
|---|---|---|---|---|
| Negative composite | | | | |
| Intervention | | | | |
| M | 3.08 | 2.98 | 2.90 | 2.92 |
| SD | 0.56 | 0.58 | 0.60 | 0.65 |
| n | 29 | 29 | 28 | 29 |
| Control | | | | |
| M | 2.94 | 3.01 | 2.96 | 2.82 |
| SD | 0.56 | 0.61 | 0.61 | 0.58 |
| n | 23 | 23 | 23 | 22 |
| Prosocial composite | | | | |
| Intervention | | | | |
| M | 2.70 | 3.12 | 3.17 | 3.11 |
| SD | 0.57 | 0.53 | 0.60 | 0.60 |
| n | 29 | 29 | 28 | 29 |
| Control | | | | |
| M | 2.86 | 2.77 | 2.98 | 2.98 |
| SD | 0.49 | 0.64 | 0.69 | 0.56 |
| n | 23 | 23 | 23 | 22 |
| Affectionate | | | | |
| Intervention | | | | |
| M | 3.11 | 3.06 | 3.03 | 2.89 |
| SD | 0.75 | 0.94 | 0.88 | 0.76 |
| n | 29 | 29 | 28 | 29 |
| Control | | | | |
| M | 3.21 | 3.11 | 2.80 | 2.82 |
| SD | 0.60 | 0.86 | 0.69 | 1.05 |
| n | 23 | 23 | 23 | 22 |

TABLE 2
Relationship of Group Membership (Intervention Vs. Control) to Across-Time Change
on the Composite Intervention Measures (Point Biserial Correlations)

| | Time Period | | |
|---|---|---|---|
| Scale | Pretest to Midtreatment[a] | Pretest to Termination[b] | Pretest to Follow-Up[c] |
| Negative composite | | | |
| r | −.23* | −.30* | −.04 |
| Prosocial composite | | | |
| r | .42** | .26* | .26* |
| Affectionate | | | |
| r | .04 | .24* | .13 |

Note. A positive correlation indicates that the intervention group increased more than
did the control group.

[a]$n = 52$. [b]$n = 51$. [c]$n = 51$.

*$p < .05$. **$p < .01$. (Both are one-tailed.)

correlations. Correlations were computed to assess change (a) at mid-treatment, (b) over the whole of the intervention period, and (c) over the whole of the intervention as well as the follow-up period. A significant positive correlation here indicates that the intervention group increased more than the control group between the two time points, and a significant negative correlation means that the intervention group decreased more than the control group.

As predicted, the correlations for negative behavior composite (Table 2) show negative behavior decreased more in the intervention group compared to the control group at both the midtreatment probe ($r = -.23$) and at treatment termination ($r = -.30$) relative to the initial assessment. Change in the level of negative behavior over the period from initial assessment to follow-up, however, did not favor the intervention group over the control group. Table 1 shows that the means for the intervention group decreased steadily from pretest to termination, with no change thereafter. In addition, as one would anticipate, the means for the control group vary over this interval. This variation included a substantial decrease in negative behavior from termination to follow-up. Unfortunately, on these grounds, a clear interpretation of the follow-up effects is not possible.

As predicted, correlations for the prosocial behavior composite indicate that the level of prosocial behavior increased significantly more in the intervention group compared to the control group over the period from initial assessment to midtreatment probe ($r = .42$), from initial assessment to treatment termination ($r = .26$), and from initial assessment to follow-up ($r = .26$). Thus, increases in prosocial behavior remained after the intervention had ceased.

Correlations for affectionate behavior toward parents show an advantage for the intervention group only at the conclusion of the intervention (i.e., the initial assessment to posttest correlation, $r = .24$, is positive and significant). The data do not show an advantage for the intervention group at either the midtreatment probe or at the posttreatment, 6-month follow-up. Thus, the benefits of increased affection from child to parents were not lasting.

## Comparison of Intervention Formats

The second hypothesis predicted that the both-parents intervention would be more effective than the mother-only format. Table 3 presents the means and standard deviations of the three outcome measures for the two intervention protocols, and Table 4 compares their relative success by means of point biserial correlations between format and change score. A positive coefficient indicates the both-parents format

TABLE 3
Across-Time Means and Standard Deviations for Mother-Only and Both-Parents
Formats on the Composite Intervention Measures

| Scale | Pretest | Midtreatment | Termination | Follow-Up |
|---|---|---|---|---|
| Negative composite | | | | |
| Mother only | | | | |
| M | 3.09 | 2.96 | 2.94 | 2.95 |
| SD | 0.54 | 0.63 | 0.56 | 0.63 |
| n | 17 | 17 | 16 | 17 |
| Both parents | | | | |
| M | 3.05 | 3.01 | 2.84 | 2.86 |
| SD | 0.61 | 0.54 | 0.67 | 0.69 |
| n | 12 | 12 | 12 | 12 |
| Prosocial composite | | | | |
| Mother only | | | | |
| M | 2.81 | 3.13 | 3.08 | 3.10 |
| SD | 0.39 | 0.39 | 0.45 | 0.53 |
| n | 17 | 17 | 16 | 17 |
| Both parents | | | | |
| M | 2.54 | 3.10 | 3.28 | 3.13 |
| SD | 0.75 | 0.71 | 0.77 | 0.72 |
| n | 12 | 12 | 12 | 12 |
| Affectionate | | | | |
| Mother only | | | | |
| M | 3.27 | 3.27 | 3.08 | 3.02 |
| SD | 0.56 | 0.67 | 0.67 | 0.66 |
| n | 17 | 17 | 16 | 17 |
| Both parents | | | | |
| M | 2.87 | 2.76 | 2.96 | 2.71 |
| SD | 0.93 | 1.19 | 1.12 | 0.88 |
| n | 12 | 12 | 12 | 12 |

TABLE 4
Intervention Format Contrasts (Both Parents Vs. Mother Only)
as Related to Across-Time Change on the Composite Intervention Measures
(Point Biserial Correlations)

| | Time Period | | |
|---|---|---|---|
| | Pretest to Midtreatment[a] | Pretest to Termination[b] | Pretest to Follow-Up[c] |
| Negative composite | | | |
| r | .14 | −.03 | −.06 |
| Prosocial composite | | | |
| r | .22 | .36* | .27[+] |
| Affectionate | | | |
| r | −.10 | .21 | .07 |

Note. A positive correlation indicates that the both-parents protocol was more effective
in producing change in the expected direction than was the mother-only protocol.
[a]$n = 29$. [b]$n = 28$. [c]$n = 29$.
*$p < .05$. [+]$p < .10$. (Both are one-tailed.)

showed an advantage relative to the mother-only format, and a negative coefficient indicates the converse.

The effect correlations for the negative behavior composite show an overall pattern of small effects at each time period with no advantage to either intervention format. In contrast, the results for the prosocial behavior composite show a consistent pattern of advantage for the both-parents format. Although the effect correlation is not significant at the midtreatment probe, it is in the same direction as the significant effects at posttest ($r = .36$) and also at follow-up ($r = .27$). The results for affectionate behavior show no clear evidence favoring one format over the other.

## DISCUSSION

The predicted increases in prosocial child behavior for intervention families were found at midtreatment, termination, and follow-up. Predicted decreases in negative child behavior for intervention group families were found at midtreatment and termination but not at follow-up. A significant increase in affectionate behavior among intervention families was found only at termination. Thus, the intervention program was successful in not only increasing prosocial behavior at the conclusion of the program but the increase also persisted after the program had ended. Although the program succeeded in decreasing negative behavior during treatment and at termination, differences between the intervention children and controls did not persist at follow-up. Similarly, although a positive impact on affectionate behavior was observed at termination, this effect did not persist. Finally, comparison of the two intervention formats showed the anticipated advantage for the both-parents format over the mother-only format only for prosocial behavior; both delivery formats were equally effective in reducing negative behavior.

The effect for negative behavior noted at midtreatment (i.e., the conclusion of the child management skills teaching) is most comparable to termination data for those programs that ended with time-out and contracting or included an assessment near the end of the child-focused program (e.g., Forehand & King, 1977; Patterson & Reid, 1973; Webster-Stratton, Kolpacoff, & Hollinsworth, 1988). Although reports of prosocial behavior change have been less frequently examined, two studies (Fleischman & Szykula, 1981; Webster-Stratton, Kolpacoff, & Hollinsworth, 1988) included a measure that combined prosocial and affectionate behaviors. The Webster-Stratton, Kolpacoff, & Hollinsworth study, which is the most directly comparable because it was a pre–post design, also found a significant improvement in prosocial behavior.

The significant decrease in negative behavior found at termination is quite comparable to that reported in the literature. A comparison of the effect correlation at midtreatment ($r = -.23$) with that at termination ($r = -.30$) suggests that a further reduction in negative behavior did not occur during the latter, parent-focused portion of the intervention. An analysis of the Patterson (1974) data by Maguin (1991) showed the same result. The increase in prosocial behavior at termination found here is similar to that found by Fleischman and Szykula (1981). Comparison of the correlations at midtreatment and termination, however, indicates that some attenuation of the prosocial effect occurred.

Almost all parent-training studies (e.g., Fleischman, 1981; Fleischman & Sykula, 1981; Forehand, Griest, & Wells, 1979; Forehand & King, 1977; Patterson & Reid, 1973) have found a significant decrease in negative behavior from pretest to follow-up. Although, in this study, we did not find such a decrease, an inspection of the across-time means for both intervention and control groups shows that this is more attributable to the variability of the control group than to an increase in negative behavior by the intervention group. By contrast, the finding of a significant increase in prosocial behavior at the follow-up is also reported by Fleischman and Szykula (1981).

Finally, the weak intervention format difference effects are generally consistent with the small literature on father involvement in parent training. Horton's (1984) review of father involvement consisted of just three studies and found no evidence of a convincing advantage for the both-parents format relative to the mother-only format for negative behavior. The differences in prosocial behavior that we observed here cannot be contrasted against this earlier work because none of those studies included measures of prosocial behavior.

Nonetheless, the question of the benefits of one- versus two-parent involvement may, to some extent, be miscast. In very recent analyses of our study data, Nye, Zucker, and Fitzgerald (1993) examined the dimension of a family's involvement in the work of the program. They found that families did not uniformly benefit from the intervention and that the level of involvement rather than whether one or two parents participated mediated the response to the program.

More generally, an examination of how the participating families in this program differed from families in other programs and how the present intervention program met the unique circumstances of the participating families is useful in understanding the mixed, and partially discrepant, results observed here. All families in this program were characterized by the presence of severe alcohol problems and in many cases by significant drug and marital problems as well. Because previous parent-training studies have selected samples solely on the basis of child behavior, they have, to some degree, also sampled other family characteristics that are associated with conduct problems. The degree to which these other factors may have played a role in enhancing or detracting from outcome is, however, indeterminate, because parent characteristics have typically not been well-specified. In contrast, the use of a clearly identifiable familial risk factor, paternal alcoholism, the use of an outreach model, and the absence of an avowedly clinical focus all set this study apart in significant ways.

To elaborate on these points, the father's drunk-driving conviction and the severity of the alcohol-impairment selection criteria meant that his alcoholism frequently was a prominent factor in the life of the family. For example, some of these men were not able to drive legally because their licenses had been suspended and, when some of them did, that created even more of a problem. Concomitantly, successful implementation of the program required sustained attention to the child management regimen to ensure its effective implementation. Last, and perhaps most important, despite the father's frequently visible alcoholism (and sometimes also the mother's), the intervention only gradually was able to move in on these issues given that families were recruited on the basis of child difficulty. Although this orientation may provide initial entre to a population that seeks assistance only reluctantly and tentatively, it also means that the motivational impetus to seek help is different from that of self-referred or court-referred parents. In addition, although virtually all mothers in the program acknowledged that their child was a problem at times, this was not as common among the fathers.

Thus, intervention staff were required to address both child and parent problems from a disadvantaged status, and they needed to walk a line that balanced issues of holding the families in the protocol against the need to confront and take risks about addressing ongoing alcohol and other family-related difficulty. In retrospect, the outreach, population-based, rather than problem-focused, nature of the original contract was seen as hobbling the intervention team's efforts, and it also likely contributed to the weak treatment effects.

This study illustrates the significant accomplishments, as well as difficulties, related to the implementation of a community-based, substance abuse risk prevention activity (see also Lorion & Ross, 1992). When family problems are severe, such work tests the envelope of applicability of coping/behavioral enhancement intervention efforts. Within this framework, the long-term question of how early to intervene, and for how long, to produce lasting change, cannot yet be answered. Our work indicates that efforts lasting as long as even a year have demonstrable, but only modest, impact. Nonetheless, a chronic-disease framework for such work, which would specify the need for periodic "inoculations" to maintain control of the disorder (as in diabetes), would suggest that over fairly long spans of developmental time, the problematic behavior can be brought under full control. A similar perspective has been advocated, beginning during early childhood, for the reduction and prevention of juvenile delinquency (Zigler, Taussig, & Black, 1992), and it is consistent with some of the evidence amassed during our study. Within this context, the work of O'Farrell (1989), relating to the issue of relapses in family work with alcoholics, is particularly relevant. O'Farrell made the point that relapses are a common occurrence during the initial stages of drinking cessation and that booster sessions at later intervals are needed to address relapses. In a parallel vein, families might benefit from booster sessions—such as were used by Patterson (1974)—after completing the intervention program (see also Lochman, 1992).

Finally, it may be that additional external pressure needs to be brought to bear on those families that are most deeply troubled and also of highest risk. Such pressure could be applied if a public-health model were used by the courts in working with this subset of alcoholic families. Within this framework, a more clearly pressured approach (e.g., by way of court order) would be required to bring the family into the treatment net in a manner that would allow immediate and direct attention to the substance abuse issues that are so central to the maintenance and embellishment of child risk. Our group is currently engaging in pilot work that will evaluate the workability of such an alternative approach (Zucker & Bermann, 1992), with the hope that such work will allow us to more carefully specify a menu of alternative preventive interventions, that can be differentially applied to families with different risk profiles and that may thereafter be evaluated in a long-term way.

## ACKNOWLEDGMENTS

This work was primarily supported by grants to Robert A. Zucker, Robert B. Noll, and Hiram E. Fitzgerald from the Michigan Department of Mental Health, Prevention Services Unit, and from the Governor's Initiative Against Alcohol and Drug Abuse Grant Program of the Office of Substance Abuse Services, Michigan Department of Public Health.

We are indebted to Robert B. Noll for his substantial involvement in earlier phases of this project, including supervision of a part of the intervention protocol. We also especially thank Susan K. Refior, Patricia Wehner, and Susan Lotus, who served as field coordinators and initial recruiters of the study families. Susan K. Refior, in particular, deserves a special note of thanks for the substantial work that permitted effective follow-up.

Robert A. Zucker is now at the Departments of Psychiatry and University of Michigan Alcohol Research Center, University of Michigan.

## REFERENCES

Achenbach, T. M., & Edelbrock, C. (1983). *Manual for the Child Behavior Checklist.* Burlington: University of Vermont.

Andrews, S. R., Blumenthal, J. B., Johnson, D. L., Kahn, A. J., Ferguson, C. J., Lasater, T. M., Malone, P. E., & Wallace, D. B. (1982). The skills of mothering: A study of parent–child development centers. Monographs of the Society for Research in Child Development, 47(6, Serial No. 198).

Babor, T. F., & Dolinsky, Z. S. (1988). Alcoholic typologies: Historical evolution and empirical evaluation of some common classification schemes. In R. M. Rose & J. Barret (Eds.), *Alcoholism: Origins and outcome* (pp. 245–266). New York: Raven.

Budd, K. G., & O'Brien, T. P. (1982). Father involvement in parent training: An area in need of research. *Behavior Therapist, 5(3),* 85–89.

Cloninger, R. (1987). Neurogenetic adaptive mechanisms in alcoholism. *Science, 236,* 410–416.

Conners, C. K (1973). Rating scales for use in drug studies with children [Special issue: Pharmacotherapy of children]. *Psychopharmacology Bulletin,* 24–29.

Feighner, J. P., Robins, E., Guze, S., Woodruff, R. A., Winokur, G., & Munoz, R. (1972). Diagnostic criterion for use in psychiatric research. *Archives of General Psychiatry, 26,* 57–63.

Fleischman, M. J. (1981). A replication of Patterson's *Intervention for boys with conduct problems. Journal of Consulting and Clinical Psychology, 2,* 342–351.

Fleischman, M. J., & Szykula, S. A. (1981). A community setting replication of a social learning treatment for aggressive children. *Behavior Therapy, 12,* 115–122.

Forehand, R., Griest, D. L., & Wells, K. C. (1979). Parent behavioral training: An analysis of the relationship between multiple outcome measures. *Journal of Abnormal Child Psychology, 7,* 229–242.

Forehand, R., & King, H. E. (1977). Noncompliant children: Effects of parent training on behavior and attitude change. *Behavior Modification, 1,* 93–108.

Forehand, R., Middlebrook, J., Rogers, T., & Stiffle, M. (1983). Dropping out of parent training. *Behavior Research and Therapy, 21,* 663–668.

Garber, H. L. (1988). *The Milwaukee Project: Preventing mental retardation in children at risk.* Washington, DC: American Association of Mental Retardation.

Gottman, J. M., & Katz, L. F. (1989). Effects of marital discord on young children's peer interaction and health. *Developmental Psychology, 25,* 373–381.

Goyette, C. H., Conners, C. K., & Ulrich, R. F. (1978). Normative data on Revised Conners Parent and Teacher Rating Scales. *Journal of Abnormal Child Psychology, 6,* 221–236.

Hawkins, J. D., Catalano, R. F., & Miller, J. Y. (1992). Risk and protective factors for alcohol and other drug problems in adolescence and early adulthood: Implications for substance abuse prevention. *American Journal of Orthopsychiatry, 54,* 415–425.

Helzer, J. E., Burnam, A., & McEvoy, L. T. (1991). Alcohol abuse and dependence. In L. N. Robins & D. A. Regier (Eds.), *Psychiatric disorders in America: The epidemiologic catchment area study* (pp. 81–115). New York: Free Press.

Horton, L. (1984). The father's role in behavioral parent training: A review. *Journal of Clinical Child Psychology, 13,* 274–279.

Hunter, J. E., & Gerbing, D. W. (1982). Unidimensional measurement, second order factor analysis, and causal models. In B. Staw (Ed.), *Research in organizational behavior* (Vol. 4, pp. 267–320). Greenwich, CT: JAI.

Kellam, S. G., Ensminger, M. E., & Simon, M. B. (1980). Mental health in first grade and teenage drug, alcohol, and cigarette use. *Drug and Alcohol Dependency, 5,* 273–304.

Lochman, J. E. (1992). Cognitive-behavioral intervention with aggressive boys: Three-year follow-up and preventive effects. *Journal of Consulting and Clinical Psychology, 60,* 426–432.

Loeber, R., & LeBlanc, M. (1990). Toward a developmental criminology. In M. Tonry & N. Morris (Eds.), *Crime and justice: A review of the research* (Vol. 12, pp. 375–473). Chicago: University of Chicago Press.

Lorion, R., & Ross, J. G. (1992). Programs for change: a realistic look at the nation's potential for preventing substance abuse among high risk youth [Special issue: Programs for change: Office for Substance Abuse Prevention models]. *Journal of Community Psychology,* 3–9.

Maguin, E. (1991). *Evaluation of a community program for the prevention of conduct problems among preschool sons of alcoholic fathers.* Unpublished doctoral dissertation, Michigan State University, East Lansing.

Miller, G. E., & Prinz, R. J. (1990). Enhancement of social learning family interventions for childhood conduct disorder. *Psychological Bulletin, 108,* 291–307.

Minuchin, S. (1974). *Family and family therapy.* Cambridge, MA: Harvard University Press.

Noll, R. B., & Zucker, R. A. (1985a). *Child Behavior Rating Scale.* Unpublished manuscript, Michigan State University, East Lansing.

Noll, R. B., & Zucker, R. A. (1985b). *Parent Daily Report–Modified.* Unpublished manuscript, Michigan State University, East Lansing.

Nye, C. L., Zucker, R. A., & Fitzgerald, H. E. (1993, August). *Treatment predictors of child outcome in a early intervention program.* Paper presented at the meeting of the American Psychological Association, Toronto, Canada.

O'Farrell, T. J. (1989). Marital and family therapy in alcoholism treatment. *Journal of Substance Abuse Treatment, 6,* 23–29.

Olweus, D. (1979). Stability of aggressive reaction patterns in males: A review. *Psychological Bulletin, 86,* 852–857.

Patterson, G. R. (1974). Retraining of aggressive boys by their parents: Review of recent literature and a followup evaluation. *Canadian Psychiatric Association Journal, 19*, 142–161.

Patterson, G. R., Chamberlain, P., & Reid, J. B. (1982). A comparative evaluation of a parent training program. *Behavior Therapy, 13*, 638–650.

Patterson, G. R., DeBaryshe, B. D., & Ramsey, E. (1989). A developmental perspective on antisocial behavior. *American Psychologist, 44*, 329–335.

Patterson, G. R., & Reid, J. B. (1973). Intervention for families of aggressive boys: A replication study. *Behavior Research and Therapy, 11*, 383–394.

Patterson, G. R., Reid, J. B., Jones, R. R., & Conger, R. E. (1975). *A social learning approach to family intervention: Vol. 1. Families with aggressive boys.* Eugene, OR: Castalia.

Pihl, R. O., & Peterson, J. B. (1991). Attention-deficit hyperactivity disorder, childhood conduct disorder, and alcoholism: Is there an association? *Alcohol Health and Research World, 15*, 25–31.

Regier, D. A., Farmer, M. E., Rae, D. S., Locke, B. Z., Keith, S. J., Judd, L. L., & Goodwin, F. K (1990). Comorbidity of mental disorders with alcohol and other drug abuse. *Journal of the American Medical Association, 264*, 2511–2518.

Russell, M. (1990). Prevalence of alcoholism among children of alcoholics. In M. Windle & J. S. Searles (Eds.), *Children of alcoholics: Critical perspectives* (pp. 9–38). New York: Guilford.

Sher, K. J. (1991). *Children of alcoholics.* Chicago: University of Chicago Press.

Tartar, R. E., & Vanukov, M. M. (in press). Stepwise developmental models of alcoholism etiology. In R. A. Zucker, J. Howard, & G. M. Boyd (Eds.), *The development of alcohol problems: Exploring the biopsychosocial matrix of risk .* Rockville, MD: National Institute of Alcohol Abuse and Alcoholism.

Webster-Stratton, C. (1981). Modification of mothers' attitudes and behaviors through a videotape modeling group discussion program. *Behavior Therapy, 12*, 634–642.

Webster-Stratton, C. (1982). The long-term effects of a videotape modeling parent-training program: Comparison of immediate and 1-year follow-up results. *Behavior Therapy, 13*, 702–714.

Webster-Stratton, C. (1985). The effects of father involvement in parent training for conduct problem children. *Journal of Child Psychology and Psychiatry and Allied Disciplines, 26*, 801–810.

Webster-Stratton, C., Kolpacoff, M., & Hollinsworth, T. (1988). Self-administered videotape therapy for families with conduct problem children: Comparison with two cost-effective treatments and a control group. *Journal of Consulting and Clinical Psychology, 56*, 558–566.

Zigler, E., Taussig, C., & Black, K (1992). Early childhood intervention: A promising preventative for juvenile delinquency. *American Psychologist, 47*, 997–1006.

Zucker, R. A. (1989). Is risk for alcoholism predictable? A probabilistic approach to a developmental problem. *Drugs & Society, 4*, 69–93.

Zucker, R. A. (1991). *Protocol details of the Michigan State University Multiple Risk Child Outreach Program.* (Available from R. A. Zucker, Departments of Psychiatry and University of Michigan Alcohol Research Center, University of Michigan, Ann Arbor, MI, 48109.)

Zucker, R. A., & Bermann, E. (1992). *Michigan State University–University of Michigan pilot project on family intervention with substance abusive families.* Unpublished manuscript, Michigan State University, Department of Psychology and Longitudinal Studies Program, East Lansing.

Zucker, R. A., Ellis, D. A., & Fitzgerald, H. E. (in press). Developmental evidence for at least two alcoholisms: Vol. 1. Biopsychosocial variation among pathways into symptomatic difficulty. *Annals of the New York Academy of Science.*

Zucker, R. A., & Fitzgerald, H. E. (1991). Early developmental factors and risk for alcohol problems. *Alcohol Health and Research World, 15,* 1–24.

Zucker, R. A., & Gomberg, E. S. L. (1986). Etiology of alcoholism reconsidered: The case for a biopsychosocial process. *American Psychologist, 41,* 783–793.

Zucker, R. A., Maguin, E. T., Noll, R. B., Fitzgerald, H. E., & Klinger, M. T. (1990, August). *A prevention program for preschool C.O.A.s: Design and early effects.* Paper presented at the meeting of the American Psychological Association, Boston.

Zucker, R. A., & Noll, R. B. (1987). The interaction of child and environment in the early development of drug involvement: A far ranging review and a planned very early intervention. *Drugs & Society, 2,* 57–97.

Zucker, R. A., Noll, R. B., Kriegler, J., & Cruise, K A. (1986). *A program for the prevention of conduct disorders: Intervention manual.* Unpublished manual, Michigan State University, Department of Psychology, East Lansing.

Received August 8, 1992
Accepted September 24, 1993

Developmental Psychology
1993. Vol. 29, No. 1, 19–30

# Unraveling Girls' Delinquency: Biological, Dispositional, and Contextual Contributions to Adolescent Misbehavior

Avshalom Caspi, Donald Lynam, Terrie E. Moffitt, and Phil A. Silva

We examined processes linking biological and behavioral changes in different contexts during adolescence by studying an unselected cohort of New Zealand girls from childhood through adolescence when they entered either mixed-sex or all-girl secondary schools. The impact of menarcheal timing on female delinquency was moderated by the sex composition of schools; early-maturing girls in mixed-sex settings were at greatest risk for delinquency. Individual differences in delinquency were also significantly more stable among girls in mixed-sex schools than among those in all-girl schools. These contextual variations are interpreted in terms of the differential distribution of reinforcements and opportunities for delinquency.

The life course is punctuated by numerous biological and social events that require individuals to organize their behavior around newly defined tasks. Puberty is among the most profound of these biosocial transitions. Thus, the onset of menarche in the adolescent girl not only signals her approaching reproductive capacity, but it also elicits new expectations from others, alters her reference group, and reorganizes her body image and sexual identity (Brooks-Gunn & Petersen, 1983; Koff, Rierdan, & Silverstone, 1978). Menarcheal onset is also associated with increases in the prevalence of norm-breaking behaviors and social deviance during the adolescent years (Stattin & Magnusson, 1990).

In an effort to contribute to our understanding of the etiology of female delinquency, this article examines the processes linking biological and behavioral changes in different contexts during adolescence. Our work represents an effort to integrate an ecological approach to the study of human development, sociological perspectives on delinquency causation, and recent advances in our understanding of the role of biological maturation in adolescent social behavior. Biosocial models of adolescence highlight the hormonal and social-stimulus effects of pubertal changes on behavior (Petersen & Taylor, 1980; Udry, 1988). Sociological perspectives on delinquency causation focus our attention on the role of social norms in the initiation and maintenance of deviant behavior (Matza, 1969). And an ecological approach to human development alerts us to the possibility that developmental processes, not only behavioral outcomes, vary across different environmental settings (Bronfenbrenner, 1979).

Integrating these conceptual frameworks, this article reports a longitudinal analysis of juvenile delinquency in an unselected birth cohort of girls from New Zealand. There, we have followed a group of girls as they passed from childhood through adolescence and tracked their biological changes as they entered either mixed-sex or all-girl secondary schools. We examined whether and how processes linking biological and behavioral changes (a) vary in different school contexts and (b) differ as a function of the behavioral predispositions of the developing girls.

Before turning to the longitudinal study, we briefly survey previous research on the timing of pubertal development and consider the role of school contexts in shaping the personal and social significance of biological changes in adolescence. We then elaborate our rationale for focusing on the sex composition of schools in our effort to unravel the roots of female delinquency.

Avshalom Caspi, Donald Lynam, and Terrie E. Moffitt, Department of Psychology, University of Wisconsin—Madison; Phil A. Silva, Dunedin Multidisciplinary Health and Development Research Unit, Dunedin, New Zealand.

This work was supported by United States Public Health Service Grants MH-43746 and MH-45070 from the Antisocial and Violent Behavior Branch of the National Institute of Mental Health (NIMH) to Terrie E. Moffitt. Avshalom Caspi was supported by a grant from NIMH (MH-41827) and by a Spencer Fellowship from the National Academy of Education. The Dunedin Multidisciplinary Health and Development Research Unit is supported by the Medical Research Council and Health Research Council of New Zealand. We express our appreciation to the interviewers who collected the data and to the young New Zealanders who are members of the sample. Ericka Overgard edited the manuscript and designed the graphics. The comments of anonymous reviewers were very helpful to us.

Correspondence concerning this article should be addressed to Avshalom Caspi or Terrie E. Moffitt, Department of Psychology, 1202 West Johnson Street, University of Wisconsin, Madison, Wisconsin 53706.

## Psychosocial Implications of Pubertal Timing

Differences in the timing of puberty have important implications for girls' development. In particular, previous research suggests that the menarcheal experience of early-maturing girls differs from that of later maturing girls (Brooks-Gunn, Petersen, & Eichorn, 1985; Grief & Ulman, 1982; Ruble & Brooks-Gunn, 1982). Especially noteworthy is the recent convergence of findings from three longitudinal studies conducted in three different countries. Simmons and Blyth (1987) found several problems among early-maturing girls in their American study, including body image disturbances, lower academic success, and conduct problems in school. Stattin and Magnusson (1990) reported more norm violations, as well as sexually precocious behavior, among early-maturing girls in Sweden. Caspi and

Moffitt (1991) showed that the early onset of menarche was associated with disruptive psychosocial reactions among New Zealand teens.

Early maturation may have negative consequences for the adolescent girl because she risks negotiating the demands of her new status without the benefit of those social and institutional structures that support and smooth the way for later maturing girls. Moreover, precocious puberty may trigger an invidious nexus of social comparisons at a developmental period that is already characterized by heightened vulnerability. In addition, early-maturing girls may be vulnerable to peer pressures, because others attribute greater social maturity to them than is warranted by their chronological age (Eichorn, 1975). Whatever the explanation, early-maturing girls experience difficulties in adolescence. The early onset of menarche disrupts previously existing social equilibria and presents the adolescent girl with an ambiguous, novel, and uncertain event to which she must now respond.

## Social Context of Pubertal Development

Responses to the social and biological changes of puberty depend on the social context in which they occur (Petersen & Taylor, 1980). Perhaps the most relevant context is school. Schools not only instruct but also provide youths with opportunities for social interaction. Indeed, what matters most about schools are their characteristics as cultural and social organizations, in particular, the values and norms to which they expose their pupils (Rutter, Maughan, Mortimore, & Ouston, 1979).

The cultural and social organization of schools may also shape girls' responses to puberty. Simmons and Blyth (1987) examined the transition to early adolescence among youths in two educational contexts: a K-6 and a K-8 elementary school. Girls who matured early and who began to date early suffered more self-image problems if their transition to seventh grade involved a shift from a K-6 elementary school into a junior high school than if they remained in a K-8 system. Simmons and Blyth suggested that the girls' vulnerability in seventh grade may stem from the social and sexual pressures exerted by older boys in their new peer culture.

A study of pubertal development among dancers and nondancers also revealed important contextual effects on behavior. Brooks-Gunn and Warren (1985; Gargiulo, Attie, Brooks-Gunn, & Warren, 1987) compared the psychological effects of on-time versus late physical maturation among girls enrolled in national ballet company schools with girls enrolled in nondance private schools. There were few psychological effects attributable to differences in maturational timing among the nondancers. Among the dancers, however, on-time maturing girls experienced significantly more self-image disturbances than did later maturing girls. In combination, these studies suggest that contextual factors shape the personal and social significance of pubertal timing.

## Pubertal Development and the Sex Composition of Schools

Although previous studies have not examined the implications of variable sex composition in the school environment for girls' reactions to pubertal changes, we have reason to suppose that early-maturing girls in mixed-sex schools will encounter more difficulties than girls in single-sex schools. Part of the reason may have to do with the differential nature of social opportunities that operate in the two types of schools. In comparison with all-girl schools, the social composition of mixed-sex schools offers girls more opportunities to become involved in delinquent acts while, at the same time, subjecting them to a variety of social and sexual pressures from peers. Indeed, previous research has shown that delinquent behavior is more normative in schools with an equal mix of boys and girls than in all-girl schools (Rutter et al., 1979). After all, boys are much more likely than girls to engage in norm-breaking and delinquent activities (Hindelang, Hirschi, & Weis, 1981). In such settings, then, girls are more likely to encounter delinquent role models and to be reinforced by peers for participating in delinquent activities (Giordano, 1978). Differential association theory (Cressey, 1964) would thus lead us to predict that early-maturing girls in mixed-sex schools are more likely to engage in delinquency than girls in same-sex schools because opportunities for delinquent peer affiliations are differentially distributed across the two contexts. Moreover, once they begin to engage in delinquency, girls in mixed-sex schools may be more likely to persist in such behavior because there may be more social reinforcements for delinquency in mixed-sex schools than in all-girl schools.

The early-maturing girl in a mixed-sex school finds herself at the confluence of biological, psychological, and social changes. She is physically developed, psychologically immature, and socially vulnerable. Although the physically mature girl is more likely to be attractive to boys and to affiliate with older youths, it is not clear whether she possesses the requisite cognitive skills with which to confront situations that are likely to tax her ability to resist social pressures from peers (Eichorn, 1975). Indeed, research has shown that the relation between early maturation and a variety of "norm-breaking" behaviors is mediated by the tendency of early-maturing girls to associate with older peers (Stattin & Magnusson, 1990).

In addition to affiliating with older peers, the nature and context of children's friendships undergo important changes in the transition from preadolescence to adolescence. In preadolescence, the salient developmental task is achieving intimate relationships with youths of the same sex (Gottman & Mettetal, 1986). The onset of puberty adds pressures for achieving relationships with persons of the opposite sex. These pressures may be especially severe for early-maturing girls who are increasingly exposed to the predatory behavior of males. In his studies of adolescent sexuality, Udry (1988) found that androgenic hormones predicted sexual interest and noncoital sexual behaviors among girls, independent of levels of physical development, but the social-stimulus value associated with advanced physical development was required for the transition to sexual intercourse among girls, independent of their hormone levels (Udry, 1990). These results indicate that boys are responsive to the physical development of girls, and, along with other studies of peer influences on girls' delinquency (e.g., Giordano, 1978), suggest that early-maturing girls may encounter different opportunities, pressures, and reinforcements in mixed-sex schools than in single-sex schools.

In summary, we set out to study three related issues in this article. First, we examine whether the impact of menarcheal timing on female delinquency depends on the sex composition of the school environment. Second, we examine whether early-maturing girls, once initiated, will be significantly more likely to persist engaging in antisocial behavior if they are in mixed-sex schools than in all-girl schools. Third, we examine individual differences in processes that mediate the relation between menarcheal timing and delinquency.

## Method

### Subjects

Subjects were adolescent girls involved in the Dunedin (New Zealand) Multidisciplinary Health and Development Study. The cohort's history has been described by Silva (1990). Briefly, the study is a longitudinal investigation of the health, development, and behavior of a complete cohort of consecutive births between April 1, 1972, and March 31, 1973, in Dunedin, New Zealand. Perinatal data were obtained and, when the children were traced for follow-up at 3 years of age, 1,139 children were deemed eligible for inclusion in the longitudinal study by residence in the province. Of these, 1,037 (91%) were assessed. The children's fathers are representative of the social class distribution in the general population of similar age. Members of the sample are predominantly of European ancestry.

Girls constituted 501 of the 3-year-olds who were enrolled in the longitudinal study. Psychological, medical, and sociological measures were collected at age 5; 462 at age 7; 460 at age 9; 447 at age 11; 415 at age 13; and 474 at age 15. The present study required data about girls' schools. Three quarters of the girls participating at age 13 still lived in the province of Otago, and we were later able to obtain information about the gender composition of their schools. These 297 girls constituted the subjects described here. Comparisons between girls studied and those not studied are reported later in this section.

### Measures

*Menarche.* Because of the practical difficulties in assessing body hair and breast growth in young girls, behavioral scientists have commonly used self-reports of menarche to measure pubertal development (Brooks-Gunn, Warren, Rosso, & Gargiulo, 1987). Age at menarche is an indicator of the more advanced stages of pubertal development; in most healthy girls, menarche follows 6 to 12 months after the height spurt and after breasts and pubic hair have developed to Tanner's fourth stage (Tanner, 1978).

We obtained self-reports of age at menarche from the girls when they were 15 years old. We were able to supplement missing menarche data for 13 girls by substituting their mothers' reports. Reliability and validity of these data have been reported elsewhere (Caspi & Moffitt, 1991; Moffitt, Caspi, Belsky, & Silva, 1992). The reported age at menarche (in months) ranged from 102 to 180 ($M = 155.28$, $SD = 12.12$, $Mdn = 156$, or 13.0 years of age).[1] This distribution is consistent with data reported by Tanner (1978) for seven western nations. For a portion of our analyses, girls were assigned by their age at menarche to one of three menarcheal groups: *early* (12 years and 5 months or younger; $n = 122$), *on time* (12 years and 6 months to 13 years and 6 months; $n = 173$), and *late* (13 years and 7 months or older; $n = 121$). The early and late groups constituted the extreme 30% tails of the distribution in menarcheal age.[2]

*School context.* New Zealand youths enter secondary schools at age 13. Of the 297 girls living in the province of Otago for whom we could secure information about school characteristics, 132 attended mixed-sex secondary schools and 165 attended all-girl secondary schools.

Any examination of the effects of secondary schools as developmental contexts requires that we also consider possible variations in school intake: Are there any systematic differences between students who enroll in mixed-sex and those who enroll in all-girl secondary schools that could jeopardize our ability to interpret our findings? We examined three critical variables: parental values, social class, and childhood behavior problems.

1. *Parental values:* It is possible that parents who enroll their daughters in all-girl secondary schools share a distinct value system. For example, if such parents profess religious beliefs, expect achievement, or exercise close supervision over their children, such values may serve to deter delinquency in their daughters. To evaluate this possibility, we turned to evidence from the Moos Family Environment Scales (Moos & Moos, 1981; Parnicky, Williams, & Silva, 1985), completed by the mothers of our subjects when the girls were 7 years old. This instrument comprises 10 subscales: Cohesion, Expressiveness, Conflict, Independence, Achievement Orientation, Intellectual–Cultural Orientation, Active–Recreational Orientation, Moral–Religious, Organization, and Control. Using two-tailed $t$ tests, we compared the parents of girls in coed and girls' schools on all 10 family climate subscales. No differences were statistically significant ($p > .05$). We used multiple regression analysis to determine whether a linear combination of these values predicted school choice. It did not; parental values accounted for only 3% of the variance in school choice ($p > .2$).

Although these parental values were not systematically linked to school choice, New Zealand parents do give careful thought to the selection of a school for their children. According to a recent survey, the main reasons New Zealand parents gave for choosing their children's school were (a) the school's "reputation" (53% mentioned), (b) locality or closest to home (53% mentioned), and (c) that previous family members had attended the same school (33% mentioned), a reason perhaps unique to this tradition-conscious country (Silva, 1987).

2. *Social class:* The parents' occupations were rated on a 6-point scale that is used to assign social class in New Zealand (Elley & Irving, 1972). A comparison of girls attending mixed-sex versus all-girl secondary schools revealed a statistically significant difference between them in terms of their family socioeconomic status (SES; 3.14 vs. 3.49), $t(279) = 2.28$, $p < .05$; higher SES families were more likely to enroll their daughters in girls' schools. The SES will be controlled in subsequent analyses.

3. *Childhood behavior problems:* Because of our interest in juvenile delinquency in early and middle adolescence, it is especially critical to establish whether girls with behavior problems earlier in childhood were more likely to be enrolled in mixed-sex rather than all-girl secondary schools.

The Rutter Child Scale (RCS; Rutter, Tizard, & Whitmore, 1970) was filled out by parents and teachers when the girls were 9 years old. The 42 items inquired about antisocial, inattentive, impulsive, hyperactive, and anxious-withdrawn behavior and were rated as follows: $0 = does not apply$, $1 = applies somewhat$, and $2 = certainly applies$ (see McGee, Williams, & Silva, 1985). The RCS items regarding antisocial, inattentive, impulsive, and hyperactive behaviors were summed to provide a rating scale of "externalizing" behavior problems at age 9. We

---

[1] Nineteen girls had not yet menstruated by the age-15 assessment; their age of onset was thus coded as 16 years (192 months). All analyses described here were repeated excluding these 19 girls. Excluding them did not change the results in any way, so their data were used for this report.

[2] In an earlier report, we used a more extreme trichotomy: 20%-60%-20% (Caspi & Moffitt, 1991). Because the present report is limited to girls attending schools in the province of Otago, we have adopted a more liberal 30%-40%-30% split to increase our cell sizes. These designations are similar to those used by Simmons and Blyth (1987).

standardized and combined the parent and teacher ratings into a single score to improve the reliability and validity of this measure; multi-agent reports of behavior problems are more reliable than single-agent reports, and parents and teachers provide complementary information in their role as informants (Loeber, Green, Lahey, & Stouthamer-Loeber, 1990). A comparison of girls attending mixed-sex and all-girl secondary schools revealed no significant difference between them in terms of childhood behavior problems ($t < 1$).

*Norm-breaking behaviors (age 13).* The Self-Reported Early Delinquency instrument (SRED; described fully in Moffitt, 1989; Moffitt & Silva, 1988) was designed specifically for use in New Zealand. The SRED contains 29 items tapping norm-violating behaviors and 29 items tapping more serious illegal behaviors. The norm-violating scale, which is weighted for the seriousness of each item, was used in this study as the measure of norm breaking at age 13.[3] It includes items such as stealing money from milk bottles, breaking windows, stealing from pupils at school, getting drunk, going to R-rated films, swearing loudly in public, and making prank telephone calls. One-month test-retest reliability ($r = .85$), internal consistency (Kuder Richardson Formula 20, $r = .90$), concurrent validity (with parental reports of antisocial behaviors, $r = .43$, $p < .001$), and criterion validity (with police records, $p < .01$) were good.

*Self-reported delinquency (age 15).* At age 15, only the 29-item scale of illegal behaviors from the SRED was administered to the girls. They were asked to report whether they had done each act "never," "once or twice," or "three or more times" during the past year. Items included behaviors such as shoplifting, automobile theft, breaking and entering, smoking marijuana, using harder drugs, buying alcohol, fighting, and using weapons. As at age 13, the items on this scale were weighted for seriousness, using New Zealand norms.

*Familiarity with delinquent peers (age 13).* This measure assesses familiarity with delinquent patterns of behavior among peers. Before reporting on their own delinquent behavior, the girls were first presented with items from the SRED and were asked, "Do your friends, or other kids your age that you know, do these things?" The girls sorted each of the 58 norm-violation and delinquent items into three piles: $0 =$ "I don't know anyone who has done this," $1 =$ "Only one or two kids do it," and $2 =$ "Lots of kids I know do it." Scores were summed to create an index of familiarity with peer delinquency. Although our measure relies entirely on the subjects for reports about their peers' delinquency, we believe that the girls' subjective perceptions of group norms about delinquent behavior are important for their own behavior.

The three measures of delinquency do not include any items that refer to sexual behavior. In New Zealand, minors cannot be asked about their sexual experiences for research purposes.

## Procedure

The subjects were seen within approximately 1 month of their 9th, 13th, and 15th birthdays for a full day of testing at the Dunedin Multidisciplinary Health and Development Research Unit. The menarche and delinquency measures used in the present study (which was only one of several studies being conducted) were administered in the morning, in separate sessions that were counterbalanced in order and separated by 10-min breaks. Each interviewer was carefully trained and was unaware of the subjects' data on the other measures. The parent and teacher rating scales were mailed out before the laboratory assessments.

## Are the Girls We Studied Representative of the Full Sample?

For this study, data were needed for menarche, school characteristics, social class, childhood behavior problems, and delinquency. Of the 501 girls in the cohort, 416 had information about the onset of menarche, but only 297 had school data. Information about SES was missing for 14 girls; behavior ratings at age 9 were missing for 31 girls; and delinquency assessments at both ages 13 and 15 were missing for 82 and 6 girls, respectively. In sum, 265 girls had data on every measure.

Because most girls with missing data for one measure did have present data on the other measures, it was possible to test statistically for attrition effects. Multiple regression analysis was used to determine whether a linear combination of the central measures in this study was affected by girls' *present* versus *missing* status. Predictor variables were age at menarche in months, externalizing behaviors in late childhood, norm violations and peer delinquency at age 13, self-reported delinquency at age 15, school type, and social class. A pairwise correlation matrix of these variables was analyzed. The outcome variable was a dichotomous dummy variable representing the studied girls versus the remainder. Missing status accounted for 6% of the variance in study measures ($p < .05$). Externalizing disorders in late childhood contributed almost all of this $R^2$ ($\beta = .20$), indicating that girls with a childhood history of conduct difficulties were less likely to have all of the data needed to be included in our multivariate tests. This bias should have the practical effect of attenuating associations between childhood conduct problems and delinquency outcomes.

## Results

The results are presented in three sections. First, we examine whether early-maturing girls in mixed-sex schools are at greatest risk for familiarity with delinquent peers and for involvement in delinquent behavior. Second, we examine whether early-maturing girls are more likely to persist engaging in antisocial behavior if they are in mixed-sex schools than in all-girl schools. Third, we examine the processes that mediate the association between menarcheal timing and delinquency among girls in mixed-sex schools.

### Impact of Menarcheal Timing on Girls' Behavior in Different School Contexts

*Familiarity with delinquent peers at age 13.* Our analysis begins with an examination of the hypothesis that early-maturing girls in mixed-sex schools are more likely to be familiar with delinquent peers than are their counterparts in all-girl schools.

We carried out a 3 (time of menarche) × 2 (school type) analysis of covariance (ANCOVA) using the summary index of familiarity with peer delinquency at age 13 as the outcome variable. The overall tests were followed by planned comparisons to test the effects of menarcheal timing in different school contexts. To facilitate interpretation of the outcomes, we introduced two covariates to our analyses: social class and externalizing behaviors in late childhood. Neither covariate was significantly associated with familiarity with delinquent peers, $F(1, 263) = 0.33$, *ns*, and $F(1, 263) = 0.99$, *ns*, respectively.[4]

---

[3] The illegal scale was not used in this study because over half of the girls reported no illegal behaviors at age 13. The norm-violation and illegal behavior scales at age 13 were correlated .98.

[4] The correlation between age-9 externalizing behaviors and age-13 norm violations was .14 ($p < .01$) among all girls who participated at age 13. This association is stronger than that observed in the subsample of girls analyzed here because, as we have already noted, girls with relatively extreme conduct problems were selectively missing the complete complement of age-13 data needed for our present analysis.

The group means from this preliminary analysis are shown in Figure 1. There was a significant main effect for time of menarche, $F(2, 263) = 3.15$, $p < .05$. The main effect for school type was statistically significant, $F(1, 263) = 6.73$, $p < .01$. The interaction effect was not significant, $F(2, 263) = 0.48$, ns.

This analysis should be regarded as preliminary, because the omnibus $F$ tests did not address our focused questions; that is, it did not allow us to compare our specific predictions about the differential effects of menarcheal timing with the obtained data. To examine our hypothesis that the effects of early maturation on familiarity with delinquent peers were more pronounced in mixed-sex schools, we derived a set of predictions to be tested in a series of planned contrasts (see Rosenthal & Rosnow, 1985). Consistent with our prediction, early-maturing girls in mixed-sex settings had more familiarity with delinquent peers than did their early-maturing peers who were attending all-girl schools (19.23 vs. 14.17), $t(263) = 2.12$, $p < .05$. Between-school comparisons among the other two menarcheal groups yielded equivocal support for our predictions. At age 13, on-time maturers in mixed-sex settings had slightly more familiarity with delinquent peers than their counterparts in all-girl schools (16.79 vs. 13.77), $t(263) = 1.66$, $p < .10$, and late-maturing girls in mixed-sex settings did not differ from their all-girl school counterparts (13.60 vs. 12.00), $t < 1$. In summary, the results suggest that girls in mixed-sex schools were more familiar with delinquent peers than their counterparts in all-girl schools, and this difference was especially pronounced among early-maturing girls.

*Norm-violating behaviors at age 13.* Do early-maturing girls in mixed-sex schools also engage in more delinquent patterns of behavior? To explore this question, we repeated the aforementioned ANCOVA followed by planned comparisons to test the hypothesized effects by using the index of norm-violating behaviors at age 13 as the outcome variable. Once again, neither of the covariates was significantly associated with the outcome variable, $F(1, 262) = 0.85$, ns, and $F(1, 262) = 0.24$ ns, respectively.

The group means from this analysis are shown in Figure 2. The results revealed a significant main effect for time of menarche, $F(2, 262) = 4.63$, $p < .01$. The main effect for school type was not statistically significant, $F(1, 262) = 0.92$, ns.[5] The interaction effect, which should be regarded as preliminary, was statistically significant, $F(2, 262) = 3.15$, $p < .05$.

To compare our predictions to the obtained data, we turned again to the set of planned contrasts. Consistent with our prediction, the results showed that early-maturing girls in mixed-sex schools engaged in significantly more norm-violating activities at age 13 than did their early-maturing counterparts in all-girl schools (4.25 vs. 2.08), $t(262) = 2.98$, $p < .01$. In addition, we carried out between-school comparisons separately for on-time and late-maturing girls. On-time maturing girls attending mixed-sex schools did not engage in significantly more norm-violating behaviors than their counterparts in all-girl schools (2.25 vs. 2.46), $t < 1$. Nor did late-maturing girls in mixed-sex schools differ in terms of delinquent activities from their counterparts in all-girl schools (1.26 vs. 1.36), $t < 1$. In summary, the results suggest that early-maturing girls were more likely to engage in norm-violating behaviors, and this effect was especially pronounced among early maturers in mixed-sex schools.

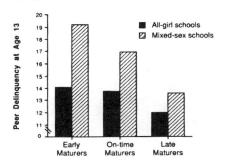

*Figure 1.* Familiarity with delinquent peers in early adolescence as a function of age at menarche and school type.

*Self-reported delinquency at age 15.* What about middle adolescence 2 years later? With biennial data, we can address several questions about the impact of pubertal development on girls' development across adolescence.

First, do the effects of early maturation persist or do they fade away by age 15? If the impact of early menarche on delinquency is merely immediate and short-lived, early-maturing girls might reduce their involvement in delinquent activities by the time they reach middle adolescence.

Second, do girls who begin menstruating in the intervening years catch-up with their early-maturing peers in delinquent behavior? If there is a catch-up effect by middle adolescence, girls who mature on time should not differ from their early-maturing counterparts in terms of delinquent behavior at age 15. However, we would still expect late-maturing girls to engage in significantly fewer delinquent activities than both their early- and on-time peers.

Finally, if there is a catch-up effect, is the impact of pubertal development on adolescent problem behavior confined to girls who attend mixed-sex schools? Our previous results, as well as differential association theory, suggest yes. In fact, on-time maturers in mixed-sex schools were slightly more familiar with delinquent peers than on-time maturers in all-girl schools. It is thus likely that the incidence of "drift" into delinquency at age 15 will be more pronounced among girls in mixed-sex settings.

[5] An observant colleague noted that our measure of peer delinquency is problematic because it measures *perceptions* of delinquent behavior among peers. It may be that perceptions reflect the respondents' own behavior rather than their peers' actual behavior. We do not believe, however, that our subjects' reports about peer delinquency are entirely projection. This interpretation is not consistent with our finding a significant effect of school type on reports of peer delinquency but no such effect on self-reports of norm violations; that is, although girls in mixed-sex schools did not report that they engage in more norm-violating behaviors, they did report more knowledge about delinquent patterns of peer behavior, a finding consistent with other research on the sex composition of schools (Rutter et al., 1979).

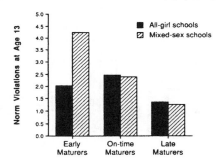

*Figure 2.* Norm violations in early adolescence as a function of age at menarche and school type.

To explore these questions, we carried out a $3 \times 2$ ANCOVA followed by planned comparisons to test the hypothesized effects by using self-reported illegal delinquency at age 15 as the outcome variable. Once again, we introduced social class and externalizing behaviors in late childhood as covariates into the analysis. Neither variable was significantly associated with illicit activities, $F(1, 261) = 0.05$, *ns,* and $F(1, 261) = 1.16$, *ns,* respectively.

The group means from this analysis are shown in Figure 3. The results revealed a significant main effect for time of menarche, $F(2, 261) = 3.81$, $p < .05$. As can be gleaned from Figure 3, early and on-time maturers did not differ from each other in terms of self-reported delinquency at age 15, but both groups differed significantly from later maturing girls. The main effect for school type was not significant, $F(1, 261) = 1.88$, *ns.* The interaction effect in this preliminary analysis was not significant, $F(2, 261) = 1.06$, *ns.*

As before, we used a set of planned contrasts to compare our specific predictions with the obtained data. The first prediction was supported: At age 15, just as they had at age 13, early-maturing girls in mixed-sex schools engaged in significantly more delinquent activities than did their counterparts in all-girl schools (3.16 vs. 1.78), $t(261) = 2.02$, $p < .05$. The second prediction received marginal support: At age 15, in contrast to the assessment 2 years earlier, on-time maturers in mixed-sex schools engaged in slightly more delinquent activities than their all-girl school counterparts (3.49 vs. 2.45), $t(261) = 1.78$, $p < .10$. The third prediction was confirmed: Late-maturing girls in mixed-sex schools did not differ significantly in terms of their self-reported delinquency from their counterparts in all-girl schools (1.26 vs. 1.51), $t < 1$.

In summary, the effect of early maturation did not simply fade away; early-developing girls engaged in antisocial behavior at least through age 15. In addition, they were joined by a new group of girls; at age 15, on-time maturers caught up with their biologically older predecessors. As at age 13, however, the effect of menarcheal timing at age 15 was moderated by school con-

text, and the impact of earlier menarche on delinquency continued to be pronounced among girls who were attending mixed-sex schools.

Thus far, we have treated the age-13 and age-15 data as distinct cross-sections. Left unaddressed is the connection between girls' behavior over time. Are those girls who engage in a variety of norm-breaking activities in early adolescence likely to engage in increasingly deviant activities in middle adolescence? We turn now to examine the persistence of delinquent behavior as it unfolds in different school settings.

### Predictability and Stability of Female Delinquency

In the introduction we suggested that different environmental settings may play an important role in regulating behavioral consistencies among adolescents to the extent that these settings offer different opportunities and reinforcements for delinquent behavior. In a mixed-sex school setting, delinquent girls are likely to find reinforcements and opportunities for their activities. Thus, if the peer group serves as a convoy throughout development—providing guides for norm formation and the consolidation of behavior patterns over time (Cairns, Perrin, & Cairns, 1985)—we should find that individual differences in delinquent activities are very stable and predictable throughout adolescence among girls who attend mixed-sex schools. In contrast, delinquent girls in all-girl school settings are more likely to be viewed as deviant; deviant individuals are often disliked and are thus more likely to be coerced into more modal patterns—what Cattell (1982) has called "coercion to the biosocial mean" (p. 353). If this is the case, we should find relatively little individual-difference stability in the delinquent activities of girls attending same-sex schools.

To examine these issues, we estimated path analyses that model individual differences in delinquent activities separately by school type. The results are shown in Figure 4.

Consistent with the results presented earlier, the path analy-

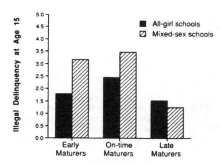

*Figure 3.* Self-reported delinquency in middle adolescence as a function of age at menarche and school type.

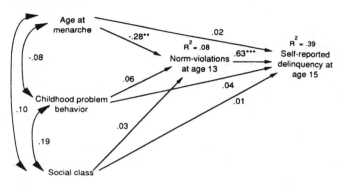

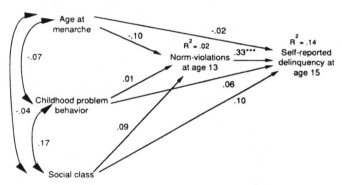

*Figure 4.* The predictability and stability of female delinquency in different school contexts. (*$p < .05$; **$p < .01$; ***$p < .001$.)

sis revealed differences in the effects of menarcheal timing on norm-violating behaviors. Among girls in mixed-sex schools, there was a significant relation between the onset of menarche and norm-violating behaviors at age 13 ($\beta = -.28$, $p < .01$). Among students in all-girl schools, menarcheal timing had no significant effect on norm-violating behaviors ($\beta = -.10$, *ns*).

The results also showed that the delinquent behaviors of girls in mixed-sex schools were more stable across time than the delinquent behaviors of girls in same-sex schools. In mixed-sex schools, there was a strong tendency for girls who engaged in norm-violating behaviors at age 13 to progress to illicit activities at age 15 ($\beta = .63$, $p < .001$). The stability of individual differences was still significant, but considerably lower, among girls in same-sex schools ($\beta = .33$, $p < .001$). A *t* test for the difference

between the relation of norm-violating behavior at age 13 and illicit activities at age 15, based on a comparison of regression coefficients (Cohen & Cohen, 1975), showed that the stability and persistence of antisocial behavior was significantly greater among girls in mixed-sex schools, $t(261) = 4.09$, $p < .001$.

### Toward an Understanding of Developmental Processes: A Role for Individual Differences

Thus far, our results have suggested that the effect of menarcheal timing on delinquent behavior is potentiated in mixed-sex school settings. In addition, individual differences in delinquent behavior are also more stable in mixed-sex schools. Although these findings have pointed to the importance of familiarity with delinquent peers, the question remains: Does familiarity with delinquent peers mediate the relation between menarcheal timing and delinquency among girls in mixed-sex schools?

To address this question, we confined the following analysis to girls in mixed-sex schools because early maturation and norm violation were related only in this group of girls. In addition, we stratified the girls in mixed-sex schools into two groups on the basis of their childhood history of externalizing behavior problems. The first group of girls scored above the median on the age-9 parent and teacher ratings of externalizing problems. The second group scored below the median on these scales. We divided the girls into these two groups because developmental criminologists have pointed to two distinct groups of delinquents: those with an early history of behavior problems who tend to persist in their deviant behavior through adolescence to adulthood and those with a later onset who tend to desist at the end of adolescence (Farrington et al., 1990; Loeber & LeBlanc, 1990; Moffitt, 1990; White, Moffitt, Robins, Earls, & Silva, 1990). Recent research thus suggests that inquiries about the etiology of crime should attend to the childhood histories and attributes that distinguish between different adolescent offenders (Moffitt, 1992).

With childhood behavior histories in mind, we tested the hypothesis that familiarity with delinquent peers mediates the association between menarcheal timing and delinquent behavior. The results are shown in Figure 5.

The zero-order correlation between timing of menarche and norm violations was about the same for girls without ($r = -.23$) and with ($r = -.25$) a childhood history of externalizing problems. Although the correlation was of similar magnitude in both groups, the path analyses in Figure 5 suggest that the mediational process governing this association differed in each of the two groups.

1. Among girls without a childhood history of externalizing problems (Panel A), the effect of menarcheal timing on norm violations was *indirect;* the effect was almost entirely mediated by familiarity with delinquent peers. Early maturers were significantly more likely to know delinquent peers ($\beta = -.27$, $p < .05$); in turn, familiarity with delinquent peers was related to norm-violating behaviors ($\beta = .68$, $p < .001$). It appears that among girls without a previous history of behavior problems, the influence of menarcheal timing on juvenile delinquency was socially mediated by their familiarity with delinquent peers.

2. Among girls with a childhood history of externalizing problems (Panel B), the effects of menarcheal timing and peer delinquency on norm-breaking behaviors were *additive;* both exerted an independent influence on norm-violating behaviors ($\beta$s = $-.28$ and $.62$, respectively). The absence of an indirect effect of menarcheal timing through familiarity with delinquent peers is attributable, in part, to the fact that, among girls with a history of behavior problems, early menarche did not increase their likelihood of knowing delinquent peers beyond the risk already incurred from their externalizing behavior problems. Girls with a history of behavior problems were significantly more likely to know delinquent peers than girls without this childhood history (18.57 vs. 14.39), $t(127) = 2.16$, $p < .05$, but menarcheal timing within this subgroup was not associated

with knowing delinquent peers ($\beta = -.01$, *ns*). In short, girls with a history of childhood behavior problems were likely to know delinquent peers regardless of timing differences in menarche.

## Discussion

The prevalence of offending and a variety of clinical disorders tend to increase during and after puberty (McGee et al., 1990; Moffitt, 1990). This epidemiological fact poses a unique challenge to life-course analysis: How are biological events and changing developmental contexts linked to behavioral changes in adolescence?

We tackled this question as part of our ongoing effort to understand the roots of delinquency. Specifically, we set out to study three related issues. First, we examined whether the impact of menarcheal timing on female delinquency depends on the sex composition of the school environment. Second, we examined whether early-maturing girls, once initiated, are significantly more likely to persist engaging in delinquent activities if they are in mixed-sex school settings. Third, we examined individual differences in the processes that mediate the relation between menarcheal timing and delinquency among adolescent girls.

Previous research has shown that early puberty is associated with behavior problems in girls, and this association has been observed in our sample as well. However, the present study shows that this association is confined to girls who were enrolled in mixed-sex educational settings. Early menarche did not seem especially troublesome for 13-year-olds who attended all-girl schools. When we observed our sample again 2 years later, the girls who had experienced menarche in the meantime had caught up with their early-maturing peers in terms of delinquency, but only if they too attended mixed-sex schools. Thus, the impact of menarcheal timing on female delinquency varied considerably across school contexts. The effects of menarcheal timing were most pronounced in mixed-sex settings, whereas they were nullified in same-sex schools. These contextual differences were not explained by differential selection into schools.

In addition, the results showed that, from early to middle adolescence, individual differences in delinquent behavior were significantly more stable among girls in mixed-sex schools than among girls in same-sex schools. Mixed-sex settings seemed to offer favorable conditions for the continuity of deviant behaviors, whereas the normative controls in same-sex settings may have suppressed these tendencies. More generally, it appears that deviant activities may need the support of the peer group not only for their initiation, but apparently for their maintenance as well. Collectively, these findings suggest that at least two factors are necessary for the initiation and maintenance of female delinquency: puberty and boys.

*Puberty.* Our emphasis on puberty differs fundamentally from earlier discussions of sexuality and female crime (e.g., Cowie, Cowie, & Slater, 1968; Konopka, 1966; Thomas, 1923). We believe that the onset of puberty operates as a releaser or sign stimulus to others in the social environment (e.g., male and

A. Girls without a childhood history of externalizing problems (N=66)

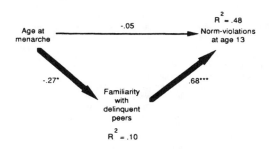

B. Girls with a childhood history of externalizing problems (N=55)

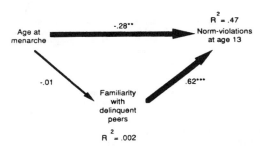

*Figure 5.* Menarcheal timing, familiarity with delinquent peers, and norm-violating behaviors: Individual differences in developmental processes. (Social class was included as an exogenous variable in estimating these models. $*p < .05; **p < .01; ***p < .001$.)

female peers as well as some adults).[6] Puberty thus creates a "press" for new, adultlike ways of behaving among adolescent girls. These functions, however, may be complicated by the uncertain status of the adolescent in our age-graded society.

In olden times, biological maturity was attained at an older age while social status came at an earlier age. However, improved nutrition and health care have lowered the age of biological maturity while forces of modernization have increased the age at which adult status is ascribed to teens. The result is a 5- to 10-year period in which adolescents are biologically mature, yet they are asked to delay assuming adult responsibilities and privileges. Pubertal changes make the remoteness of social maturity painfully apparent to teens. They remain financially and socially dependent on their families of origin and are allowed few

decisions of real import. Yet, they want desperately to establish intimate bonds with the opposite sex, to make their own decisions, and to accrue their own material belongings, as adults do.

This emergent phenomenology of the pubertal girl coincides with her entry into a high school society dominated by older peers. From her perspective, older delinquents do not appear to

---

[6] We have treated pubertal development only in terms of its social-stimulus value. It is also possible that the early onset of menarche may be accompanied by unique hormonal profiles that may have independent contributions to social behavior. Although we cannot disentangle social-stimulus effects from direct hormonal effects in our data, any explanation would have to contend with the modification of maturational effects in different school contexts.

suffer from the "maturity gap" (Moffitt, 1992). They are able to obtain possessions (e.g., cars, clothes, or drugs) by theft or vice that are otherwise inaccessible to teens who have no independent incomes; they are often free of their family of origin, and they seem to go their own way, making their own rules; and they seem more sexually experienced and self-confident with the opposite sex. In short, delinquency appears to offer an effective means of knifing off childhood apron strings, and older delinquent peers demonstrate the technique. Thus, delinquency is modeled for young girls by peers, and many of its consequences are powerfully reinforced, at least from a teen perspective. As a result, girls may begin to engage in a variety of norm-breaking behaviors in an adaptive effort to secure adult privileges (Jessor & Jessor, 1977; Silbereisen & Noack, 1988).

*Boys.* Importantly, the significance and implications of norm-breaking behaviors will be shaped by the social composition of developmental contexts such as schools. In particular, the present study suggests that the presence of boys in mixed-sex educational settings may serve to dilute school norms for tolerable conduct. Our findings showed that girls in mixed-sex schools were more familiar with delinquent peers and may have thus had more opportunities for participating in delinquent behavior. Indeed, the temporal sequence of our findings provides a clue about the process by which pubertal maturation may influence delinquent behavior.

1. Early-maturing girls in mixed-sex schools, in comparison with their peers in all-girl schools, had significantly more familiarity with delinquent peers at age 13 and had already, at age 13, engaged in significantly more antisocial activities than their peers in all-girl schools.

2. On-time maturing girls in mixed-sex schools, in comparison with their peers in all-girl schools, had slightly more familiarity with delinquent peers at age 13, but they had not yet themselves participated in significantly more antisocial activities than their peers in all-girl schools. However, by age 15, after the onset of menarche, these girls engaged in slightly more antisocial behavior than their peers in all-girl schools.

3. Late-maturing girls in mixed-sex schools, in comparison with their peers in all-girl schools, neither had more familiarity with delinquent peers nor engaged in significantly more antisocial activities than their peers in all-girl schools.

This pattern of results suggests that pubertal development first brings girls into contact with delinquent patterns of behavior, after which they may begin to sample from some of these activities. However, the last analysis in the present study suggested that to understand this process more thoroughly we must also consider the role of earlier predispositions in shaping contemporary behavior.

Familiarity with delinquent peers is often thought to produce delinquent behaviors through the principles of social learning (Cressey, 1964; Matza, 1969). Left unaddressed is the question, Where does the familiarity with delinquent peers come from? The answer appears to depend on the type of person. Individual girls differ widely in their predisposition to antisocial behavior, and our findings suggest that there are distinct pathways to delinquency among girls enrolled in coed schools.

For girls who had little predisposition to behave antisocially (as evidenced by a childhood with few or no behavior problems), early menarche worked its influence on delinquency

through the medium of peers. These girls' awareness of peer delinquency depended on their having attained menarche. And once they became aware of peer delinquency, they began to engage in it themselves. Physical maturation was thus their ticket of entry into the delinquent world of boys. In contrast, girls who had a record of behavior problems in childhood, long before the onset of menarche, were familiar with delinquent peers regardless of their menarcheal status. One possibility is that girls with a childhood history of externalizing problems, regardless of when they reach menarche, seek out peers who will reinforce their behaviors (cf. Caspi & Herbener, 1990; Kandel, 1978).

But why does early menarche exert such a powerful effect on the delinquent behavior of girls with this childhood history? One explanation draws on the hypothesis that dispositional effects on behavior are most pronounced when individuals experience profound discontinuities in their lives, especially during unpredictable and off-time transition events in the life course (Caspi & Bem, 1990; Caspi & Moffitt, in press). Thus, Caspi and Moffitt (in press) have proposed that salient individual differences are likely to be magnified and accentuated during periods of discontinuity as each individual, in an effort to regain control over the changing situation, attempts to assimilate discrepant events into existing cognitive and action structures. In short, a transition event that is characterized by ambiguity, novelty, and uncertainty (the early onset of menarche) is likely to accentuate the effects of preexisting attributes (behavior problems) on behavior (delinquency). Not surprisingly, then, girls with childhood behavior problems responded to the stress of early maturation by engaging in their most familiar pattern of behavior: antisocial behavior.

In summary, it appears that girls in our sample came to delinquency by means of two different pathways. This observation is consistent with other research showing that although there are multiple "causes" of delinquency, the processes that link these causes may differ across individuals. In fact, Moffitt (1990, 1992) has recently suggested that there are different subtypes of adolescent delinquents. The delinquent presentations of these subtypes are indistinguishable in adolescence (when delinquent behavior is at its demographic peak), making subtypes difficult to detect during adolescence. Theoretically, this uniform behavioral presentation conceals at least two distinct chains of etiological events that can only be identified by their unique developmental courses (Moffitt, 1990, 1992). Research that fails to acknowledge the possibility of different natural histories for different groups of delinquent individuals may overlook important findings about the origins of antisocial behavior.

In general, our study has benefited from an auspicious combination of factors. The design was prospective and longitudinal, the data included markers of biological age in a single age cohort, and the New Zealand setting allowed us to study adolescent development in mixed- versus single-sex school contexts. Each feature lends itself to a brief lesson for the study of delinquency.

1. Longitudinal designs are indispensable. Cross-sectional studies are not designed to discover developmental pathways. Our longitudinal design allowed us to discover that familiarity with delinquent peers had different implications for girls with different behavioral histories. In addition, we learned that con-

textual factors play an important role in the maintenance of delinquency over time, not just in its initiation. Longitudinal approaches are essential for social scientists seeking to understand the processes by which people become delinquent, persist, and desist.

2. Biological age may be more relevant for understanding (adolescent) crime than chronological age. The meaning of the relation between age and crime is of central concern to criminologists (Farrington, 1986; Hirschi & Gottfredson, 1983). However, the discussion has been limited to chronological age. Adolescence is a crucial developmental stage for criminology for two reasons: It is the age of onset of illegal behavior for most offenders, and the peak prevalence and incidence of property crimes occurs during the teen years. Although individual differences in biological age vary widely among adolescents of the same chronological age, these differences have been all but ignored by theoretical criminologists. In fact, chronological age is not necessarily the best scale for development, and our research suggests that biological age may matter more than chronological age for girls' delinquency. Magnusson (1988, p. 70) has thus suggested that "adding. . . biological age to the data space will improve explanations of variance in developmental data." The influence of biological maturation on boys' delinquency clearly merits parallel investigation.

3. Cross-national research can teach us about our own nation. American readers may question the relevance of a study of school contexts in New Zealand for youths in America. Few American students attend single-sex secondary schools, and those who do comprise a select group (e.g., expensive private schools or military academies). As we have seen, such selection factors are not very pronounced in New Zealand. As such, we view the New Zealand project as having offered a unique opportunity to capitalize on a "natural" experiment. Specifically, we have been able to examine how the impact of a universal biological event on behavior is controlled by the social context.

## Conclusion

Research on crime and human nature has been fraught with disciplinary tensions, many of which stem from the unwarranted fear that "an emphasis upon the causative role of a biological–universal event [may serve] to downgrade the importance of other internal and contextual factors" (Cairns, personal communication, June 23, 1990; see also Denno, 1985; Wilson & Herrnstein, 1985). We trust that our study has allayed such fears, because, as we have shown, biological, dispositional, and contextual factors are all clearly implicated in the genesis of female delinquency. Indeed, adolescent social behavior represents a joint articulation of an evolutionary past and a social present, and its analysis can only proceed with insights gleaned from multiple disciplines.

## References

Bronfenbrenner, U. (1979). *The ecology of human development*. Cambridge, MA: Harvard University Press.

Brooks-Gunn, J., & Petersen, A. C. (Eds.). (1983). *Girls at puberty: Biological and psychosocial perspectives*. New York: Plenum Press.

Brooks-Gunn, J., Petersen, A. C., & Eichorn, E. (1985). The study of maturational timing effects in adolescence. *Journal of Youth and Adolescence, 14,* 149–189.

Brooks-Gunn, J., & Warren, M. P. (1985). The effects of delayed menarche in different contexts: Dance and non-dance students. *Journal of Youth and Adolescence, 14,* 285–300.

Brooks-Gunn, J., Warren, M. P., Rosso, J., & Gargiulo, J. (1987). Validity of self-report measures of girls' pubertal status. *Child Development, 58,* 829–841.

Cairns, R. B., Perrin, J. E., & Cairns, B. D. (1985). Structure and social cognition in early adolescence: Affiliative patterns. *Journal of Early Adolescence, 5,* 339–355.

Caspi, A., & Bem, D. J. (1990). Personality continuity and change across the life course. In L. Pervin (Ed.), *Handbook of personality theory and research* (pp. 549–575). New York: Guilford Press.

Caspi, A., & Herbener, E. S. (1990). Continuity and change: Assortative marriage and the consistency of personality in adulthood. *Journal of Personality and Social Psychology, 58,* 250–258.

Caspi, A., & Moffitt, T. E. (1991). Individual differences are accentuated during periods of social change: The sample case of girls at puberty. *Journal of Personality and Social Psychology, 61,* 157–168.

Caspi, A., & Moffitt, T. E. (in press). When do individual differences matter? A paradoxical theory of personality coherence. *Psychological Inquiry.*

Cattell, R. B. (1982). *The inheritance of personality and ability.* San Diego, CA: Academic Press.

Cohen, J., & Cohen, P. (1975). *Applied multiple regression/correlation analysis for the behavioral sciences.* Hillsdale, NJ: Erlbaum.

Cowie, J., Cowie, V., & Slater, E. (1968). *Delinquency in girls.* New York: Humanities Press.

Cressey, D. R. (1964). *Delinquency, crime, and differential association.* Dordrecht, The Netherlands: Martinus Nijhoff.

Denno, D. W. (1985). Sociological and human developmental explanations of crime: Conflict of consensus? *Criminology, 23,* 711–741.

Eichorn, D. E. (1975). Asynchronizations in adolescent development. In S. Dragastin & G. H. Elder, Jr. (Eds.), *Adolescence in the life cycle: Psychological change and the social context* (pp. 80–95). New York: Wiley.

Elley, W. B., & Irving, J. C. (1972). A socio-economic index for New Zealand based on levels of education and income from the 1966 Census. *New Zealand Journal of Educational Studies, 7,* 153–167.

Farrington, D. (1986). Age and crime. In M. Tonry & N. Morris (Eds), *Crime and justice: A review of research* (Vol. 7, pp. 189–250). Chicago: University of Chicago Press.

Farrington, D., Loeber, R., Elliott, D. S., Hawkins, D. J., Kandel, D. B., Klein, M. W., McCord, J., Rowe, D., & Tremblay, R. (1990). Advancing knowledge about the onset of delinquency and crime. In B. Lahey & A. Kazdin (Eds), *Advances in clinical child psychology* (Vol. 13, pp. 283–342). New York: Plenum Press.

Gargiulo, J., Attie, I., Brooks-Gunn, J., & Warren, M. P. (1987). Girls' dating behavior as a function of social context and maturation. *Developmental Psychology, 23,* 730–737.

Giordano, P. C. (1978). Girls, guys, and gangs: The changing social context of female delinquency. *Journal of Criminal Law and Criminology, 69,* 126–132.

Gottman, J., & Mettetal, G. (1986). Speculations about social and affective development: Friendship and acquaintanceship through adolescence. In J. M. Gottman & J. G. Parker (Eds.), *Conversations of friends* (pp. 192–235). New York: Cambridge University Press.

Grief, E. B., & Ulman, K. J. (1982). Psychological impact of menarche on early adolescent females: A review of the literature. *Child Development, 53,* 1413–1430.

Hindelang, M. J., Hirschi, T., & Weis, J. G. (1981). *Measuring delinquency.* Beverly Hills, CA: Sage.

303

Hirschi, T., & Gottfredson, M. (1983). Age and the explanation of crime. *American Journal of Sociology, 89*, 552–584.

Jessor, R., & Jessor, S. (1977). *Problem behavior and psychosocial development.* San Diego, CA: Academic Press.

Kandel, D. B. (1978). Homophily, selection and socialization in adolescent friendships. *American Journal of Sociology, 84*, 427–436.

Koff, E., Rierdan, J., & Silverstone, E. (1978). Changes of representation of body image as a function of menarcheal status. *Developmental Psychology, 14*, 635–642.

Konopka, G. (1966). *The adolescent girl in conflict.* Englewood Cliffs, NJ: Prentice-Hall.

Loeber, R., Green, S. B., Lahey, B. B., & Stouthamer-Loeber, M. (1990). Optimal informants on childhood disruptive behaviors. *Development and Psychopathology, 1*, 317–337.

Loeber, R., & LeBlanc, M. (1990). Toward a developmental criminology. In M. Tonry & N. Morris (Eds), *Crime and justice* (Vol. 12, pp. 375–473). Chicago: University of Chicago Press.

Magnusson, D. (1988). *Individual development from an interactional perspective.* Hillsdale, NJ: Erlbaum.

Matza, D. (1969). *Becoming deviant.* Englewood Cliffs, NJ: Prentice-Hall.

McGee, R., Feehan, M., Williams, S., Partridge, F., Silva, P., & Kelly, J. (1990). DSM-III disorders in adolescence. *Journal of the American Academy of Child and Adolescent Psychiatry, 29*, 611–619.

McGee, R., Williams, S., & Silva, P. A. (1985). Factor structure and correlates of ratings of inattention, hyperactivity, and antisocial behavior in a large sample of 9-year-old children from the general population. *Journal of Consulting and Clinical Psychology, 53*, 480–490.

Moffitt, T. E. (1989). Accommodating self-report methods to a low-delinquency culture: A longitudinal study from New Zealand. In M. W. Klein (Ed.), *Cross-national research in self-reported crime and delinquency* (pp. 43–66). Norwell, MA: Kluwer Academic.

Moffitt, T. E. (1990). Juvenile delinquency and attention deficit disorder: Boys' developmental trajectories from age 3 to age 15. *Child Development, 61*, 893–910.

Moffitt, T. E. (1992). *Adolescence-limited and life-course persistent antisocial behavior: A developmental taxonomy.* Unpublished manuscript, University of Wisconsin, Madison.

Moffitt, T. E., Caspi, A., Belsky, J., & Silva, P. A. (1992). Childhood experience and the onset of menarche. *Child Development, 63*, 47–58.

Moffitt, T. E., & Silva, P. A. (1988). Self-reported delinquency: Results from an instrument for New Zealand. *Australian and New Zealand Journal of Criminology, 21*, 227–240.

Moos, R., & Moos, B. (1981). *Family environment scale manual.* Palo Alto, CA: Consulting Psychologists Press.

Parnicky, J. J., Williams, S., & Silva, P. A. (1985). Family environment scale: A Dunedin (New Zealand) pilot study. *Australian Psychologist, 20*, 195–204.

Petersen, A. C., & Taylor, B. (1980). The biological approach to adolescence. In J. Adelson (Ed.), *Handbook of adolescent psychology* (pp. 117–155). New York: Wiley.

Rosenthal, R., & Rosnow, R. L. (1985). *Contrast analysis: Focused comparison in the analysis of variance.* Cambridge, England: Cambridge University Press.

Ruble, D. N., & Brooks-Gunn, J. (1982). The experience of menarche. *Child Development, 53*, 1557–1566.

Rutter, M., Maughan, B., Mortimore, P., & Ouston, J. (1979). *Fifteen thousand hours: Secondary schools and their effects on children.* Cambridge, MA: Harvard University Press.

Rutter, M., Tizard, J., & Whitmore, K. (1970). *Education, health and behavior.* London: Longman.

Silbereisen, R., & Noack, P. (1988). The constructive role of problem behaviors in adolescence. In N. Bolger, A. Caspi, G. Downey, & M. Moorehouse (Eds.), *Persons in context: Developmental processes* (pp. 152–180). New York: Cambridge University Press.

Silva, P. A. (1987). *4,000 Otago teenagers: A preliminary report from the Pathways to Employment Project.* Dunedin Multidisciplinary Health and Development Research Unit, University of Otago Medical School, New Zealand.

Silva, P. A. (1990). The Dunedin Multidisciplinary Health and Development Study: A 15-year longitudinal study. *Pediatric and Perinatal Epidemiology, 4*, 96–127.

Simmons, R. G., & Blyth, D. (1987). *Moving into adolescence: The impact of pubertal change and school context.* New York: Aldine De Gruyter.

Stattin, H., & Magnusson, D. (1990). *Pubertal maturation in female development.* Hillsdale, NJ: Erlbaum.

Tanner, J. M. (1978). *Fetus into man.* Cambridge, MA: Harvard University Press.

Thomas, W. I. (1923). *The unadjusted girl.* Boston: Little, Brown.

Udry, J. R. (1988). Biological predispositions and social control in adolescent sexual behavior. *American Sociological Review, 53*, 709–722.

Udry, J. R. (1990). Hormonal and social determinants of adolescent sexual initiation. In J. Bancroft (Ed.), *Adolescence and puberty: The 3rd Kinsey Symposium* (pp. 70–87). New York: Oxford University Press.

White, J., Moffitt, T. E., Robins, L., Earls, F., & Silva, P. A. (1990). How early can we tell? Preschool predictors of boys' conduct disorder and delinquency. *Criminology, 28*, 323–350.

Wilson, J. Q., & Herrnstein, R. J. (1985). *Crime and human nature.* New York: Simon & Schuster.

Received July 2, 1991
Revision received October 23, 1991
Accepted April 2, 1992  ∎

Developmental Psychology
1992, Vol. 28, No. 4, 731–740

# Attributional and Emotional Determinants of Aggression Among African-American and Latino Young Adolescents

Sandra Graham, Cynthia Hudley, and Estella Williams
Graduate School of Education, University of California, Los Angeles

Attribution theorists propose that negative actions of others perceived as intended elicit anger, and anger then functions as a motivator of hostile behavior. We examined the understanding of these attribution-affect-action linkages among young ethnic minority adolescents. Forty-four Latino and African-American middle-school children labeled as aggressive and a matched group of nonaggressives read causally ambiguous scenarios describing negative outcomes initiated by a hypothetical peer. They then made judgments about the peer's intentions, their own feelings of anger, and the likelihood that they would behave aggressively toward that peer. Concerning the relations between these variables, the data supported a mediational model of emotion as postulated by attribution theory. The implications of these findings for attributional change were discussed.

Studies of childhood aggression reveal a social phenomenon rapidly emerging as a serious contemporary problem. A large empirical literature has documented the stability of aggression from childhood to young adulthood (Loeber, 1982; Olweus, 1979) as well as its relation to a host of negative outcomes, including school dropout in adolescence (Cairns, Cairns, & Neckerman, 1989), rejection among peers (Coie, Dodge, & Kupersmidt, 1990), juvenile delinquency (Loeber & Stouthamer-Loeber, 1987), and even adult criminality and psychopathology (Kohlberg, Ricks, & Snarey, 1984; Robins, 1978; Wilson & Herrnstein, 1985). The societal ramifications of this problem have become even more compelling with the growing realization that many of the known correlates of childhood aggression listed previously are disproportionately prevalent among ethnic minorities, particularly African-American males. It is well documented, for example, that Black male youths are less likely than their White counterparts to complete high school (Jaynes & Williams, 1989; Reed, 1988), more likely to have been arrested as juveniles (Farrington, 1987), and more likely to have been imprisoned for criminal behavior as young adults (Wilson & Herrnstein, 1985). It is, therefore, not surprising that the last decade has produced a burgeoning psychological literature concerned with the antecedents of antisocial behavior among children and adolescents.

One particularly fruitful approach to this topic has been provided by psychologists working within a social cognitive perspective. These researchers investigated how children's infer-

ences about others in social situations are related to subsequent aggressive behavior. For example, guided largely by the work of Dodge and his colleagues, a number of studies reported that aggressive children display a marked attributional bias to infer hostile intent following a peer-instigated negative event (e.g., being pushed while waiting in line), particularly when the cause of the event is portrayed as ambiguous (see review in Dodge & Crick, 1990). Such biased intentionality attributions are then hypothesized to lead to retaliatory behavior. Even among nonaggressive populations, the child who believes that another acted with malicious intent can feel justified in the endorsement of aggressive behavior. The problem with aggressive children, however, is that, either through some process of social cue distortion or selective recall of available information, they often inappropriately assume hostile peer intent in situations of attributional ambiguity.

Although this research capitalizes on an implicit attribution-behavior linkage, the processes relating intentionality judgments to aggressive responding in children have yet to be fully explored. Why, for example, does perceiving a peer as responsible for a negative event lead to aggression? That is, what mediating processes and mechanisms account for the proposed cognition-to-action sequence documented by Dodge and others?

To address this question, we turn to attribution theory as conceptualized by Weiner (1985, 1986), which deals extensively with the construct of causal responsibility and the related concept of causal intentionality (also see Weiner, 1991). According to this formulation, responsibility attributions are linked to behavior through the mediating influence of emotion. To illustrate, consider the evidence supporting these linkages that has been gathered in the domain of helping behavior. When people are perceived as not responsible for negative outcomes, this tends to elicit pity and prosocial behavior such as help (imagine a normal child's reaction to a mentally handicapped peer who continually experiences academic difficulty). In contrast, individuals judged as responsible for negative events often elicit anger, and help tends to be withheld (consider the same child's reaction to the gifted peer who never completes assignments).

This article was written while Sandra Graham was a Fellow at the Center for Advanced Study in the Behavioral Sciences, Stanford, California, with support from the Spencer Foundation and the Ford Foundation Postdoctoral Fellowship for Minorities. We thank Ms. Willis Charles and the students of Washington Middle School for their patience and cooperation. Appreciation also is extended to Kaori Karasawa for her help with data analysis and to Bernard Weiner for his comments on an earlier version of this article.

Correspondence concerning this article should be addressed to Sandra Graham, Graduate School of Education, University of California, Los Angeles, California 90024.

305

Anger is, therefore, a moral emotion often associated with judgments of "ought," "should have," or "could have" (see Averill, 1982). Furthermore, a very reliable finding in this attribution literature is that emotions of pity and anger, more so than responsibility attributions, directly influence helping behavior (see Graham & Weiner, 1991; Schmidt & Weiner, 1988). Thus, attribution theorists propose a thought-emotion-action sequence in which thoughts determine feelings and feelings, in turn, function as guides to behavior. This sequence is consistent with other emotion theories that view emotions as responses to cognitive appraisal (e.g., Roseman, 1984) as well as precursors to action (Tompkins, 1970).

As intimated previously here, much of the empirical support for the proposed motivational role of emotion has come from research in the helping domain. However, we view aggression and helping behavior as theoretically complementary motivational domains. Although phenotypically different behaviors, both helping and aggression are partly the consequence of perceived responsibility in others; thus, the same attribution principles relating responsibility inferences to emotions and action should be applicable to both. Applying these principles to the study of peer aggression, imagine a situation in which a child experiences a negative outcome, such as damage to a favorite video game, at the hands of a peer. Among socially competent children, to the degree that the peer provocation is perceived as intentional (i.e., the provocateur is responsible for the damage), we expect feelings of anger to be evoked and anger, in turn, to be directly related to retaliation. In contrast, to the degree that the damage is perceived as unintended, anger should be mitigated and hostile behavior less likely to be endorsed.

The attributional conception of affects as motivators of both prosocial and antisocial behavior is consistent with current developmental approaches to emotion that focus less on the disorganizing function of emotions and more on their capacity to organize and regulate adaptive behavior (see Thompson, 1990). Thus, from an attributional perspective, the thinking-feeling-acting linkages hypothesized here represent rational sequences in response to social dilemmas, and they are also part of competent social information processing. Individuals process social cues to infer intentionality in others, and from these inferences certain emotional reactions and behaviors toward others logically follow. Yet much of the current literature indicates that aggressive children are less competent social information processors than their nonaggressive counterparts, particularly when the context requires accurate inferences about intent (see Dodge & Crick, 1990). This raises the question of whether aggressive children's thoughts, feelings, and actions following peer provocation are consistent with the sequence outlined previously.

Figure 1 graphically depicts this sequence, beginning with the antecedent cues, such as the recency of the provocation or the distinctiveness of the provocateur's behavior, that elicit intentionality inferences. We already know that aggressive children often use such cues in a manner that biases them toward perceiving peer provocations as intentional (Linkage 1). However, are feelings of anger systemtically related to these attributional inferences? An alternative model might predict that socially deviant children experience intense anger following peer provocation somewhat independently of perceived intent; both feelings of anger (Linkage 3) and inferences about intentionality (Linkage 4) then influence aggressive behavior. Thus, the breakdown in the temporal sequence proposed by attribution theory occurs with the thought-to-emotion path (Linkage 2). This is consistent with the portrayal of aggressive children as having low thresholds for emotional arousal following negative social encounters (see Parke & Slaby, 1983).

Yet another temporal sequence could be hypothesized in which the initial response to peer provocation is anger arousal. Perhaps aggressive children first respond with anger toward the peer provocateur, and anger, in turn, influences judgments about intent. Pertinent to this model, Dodge and Somberg (1987) reported that aggressive boys who were exposed to a condition of interpersonal threat (which heightened feelings of being "upset") showed more biased intentionality attributions than when they were in an affectively neutral condition. In the emotion literature, moreover, a number of researchers documented the effects of feeling states on subsequent cognitive processing (e.g., Bower & Cohen, 1982), so there are both theoretical and empirical precedents for hypothesizing an emotion-to-attribution linkage.

We pursued these questions regarding the role of emotion in peer aggression in the study reported here. Because our interest in peer aggression grows out of our concern with the psychological functioning of ethnic minority youth, our research participants were aggressive and nonaggressive African-American and Latino adolescents. These children were given a set of scenarios describing negative outcomes initiated by a hypothetical peer, with the cause of the outcome manipulated to be either prosocial, accidental, ambiguous, or hostile. They then made judgments about the intentions of the peer provocateur, their own feelings of anger, and the likelihood that they would respond aggressively toward that peer.

This methodology allowed us to examine two basic research questions. First we asked, "Are there mean differences between aggressives and nonaggressives in reported inferences about intentionality, anger, and hostile behavior across a range of negative outcomes varying in the causal intent of a peer provocateur?" On the basis of previous research, we predicted that, in ambiguous situations, aggressive children would infer greater peer intentionality and endorse more hostile behavioral options than would their nonaggressive counterparts. We also expected aggressives to report experiencing more intense anger. Second, we asked, "Does the social information processing of the young adolescents sampled here reveal systematic relations among thinking, feeling, and aggressive action tendencies as postulated by attribution theory?" Causal modeling procedures were used to test the mediational model of emotion and to compare it with the alternative models suggested previously. We anticipated that reported anger would mediate the relation between perceived intentionality and behavior among nonaggressive adolescents. With aggressive subjects, we were uncertain as to how thought, feeling, and action would be interrelated and considered this an important question to be addressed in the present research.

## Method

### Selection of Subjects

Participants were selected from a junior high school located in an economically depressed community of metropolitan Los Angeles. Its

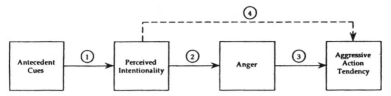

*Figure 1.* An attribution-emotion-action temporal sequence in the domain of aggression.

ethnic composition was almost exclusively African-American and La-tino. The school was a recipient of Chapter One compensatory educa-tion funds and about 30% of its students qualified for the district free-lunch program. Participation in this program requires a family income below the poverty level. Thus, by all available indicators, the popula-tion from which our sample was drawn was of low socioeconomic status.

Approximately 300 seventh and eighth graders, distributed across nine classrooms and from whom parental permission was obtained, initially were screened as possible subjects. We used a combination of both teacher ratings of aggression and peer nominations as a criterion for subject selection.

*Teacher ratings.* The nine participating teachers completed an eight-item aggression scale for each child in their homeroom. Adapted from Coie and Dodge (1988), the items on the scale described common types of childhood aggression (e.g., "This child threatens or bullies others to get his or her own way") to which teachers responded in 5-point scales (1 = *not at all;* 5 = *very much*). Scores therefore ranged from 5 to 40; high numbers indicated more perceived aggressiveness.

*Peer nominations.* Students were administered groupwide sociome-tric interviews by one of three African-American female experi-menters. With the aid of a classroom roster, children were asked to write down the names of the three students in their homeroom whom they liked most, the three whom they liked least, and the three who best fit each of five behavioral descriptions. Three of these descriptors portrayed aggressive behavior (e.g., starts fights, disrupts the group, has a very short temper), whereas the remaining two described proso-cial behavior (e.g., works well with others, is helpful to other students). Children were encouraged to be honest in their nominations and they were assured of response confidentiality. To alleviate any discomfort that may have been elicited by negative evaluations of others, the socio-metric procedure concluded with a competitive game, complete with the awarding of prizes, that most children appeared to find very en-gaging.

Seven individual scores for each child were first calculated by sum-ming the number of nominations received in each of the seven catego-ries. From these totals, we then derived a social preference score for each child, calculated as the number of "liked most" minus "liked least" nominations, an aggression score, which was the sum of the nominations on the three aggressive behavioral descriptions, and a prosocial score, computed as the sum of the nominations for the two prosocial categories.[1]

To be classified as aggressive, a child had to (a) score above the teacher median on perceived aggressiveness; (b) have a social prefer-ence score less than 0; and (c) have at least twice as many aggressive as prosocial nominations. Our goal in the selection procedures was to unambiguously identify an aggressive sample by choosing children who were not only perceived as aggressive but who were also disliked by peers and not viewed as behaving prosocially. More specifically, then, the sample consisted of aggressive-rejected young adolescents. Our methods were similar, although not identical, to the classification

schemes based on teacher ratings and peer nominations used in other studies of aggressive children (e.g., Dodge & Somberg, 1987; Sancilio, Plumert, & Hartup, 1989).

From the initial pool, 44 children met all of these criteria. As is typically the case in research of this type, boys in our sample were overrepresented among those perceived as aggressive (37 boys vs. 7 girls). However, inasmuch as girls are often not investigated in social cognitive studies of aggression, the decision was made to include both genders in this study. In terms of ethnic composition, there were 15 Latino and 22 African-American boys in addition to 1 Latina and 6 African-American girls. On the selection criteria, the aggressive group (*M* age = 13.55 years) had the following characteristics: teacher rating *M* = 30.32, *SD* = 7.89; social preference *M* = −2.55, *SD* = 4.52; peer-nominated aggression *M* = 21.21, *SD* = 15.31; and peer-nominated prosocial behavior *M* = 1.23, *SD* = 1.49.

To create a nonaggressive socially accepted group, we selected 44 subjects matched by gender and ethnicity with the experimental group but who (a) scored below the teacher median on perceived aggression; (b) had a social preference score greater than 0; and (c) had received at least twice as many prosocial as aggressive peer nominations. It should be noted that these adolescents were not an extreme nonaggressive group inasmuch as girls by far were perceived as least aggressive in the entire sample. However, the 37 boys and 7 girls who comprised the nonaggressive sample (*M* age = 13.48 years) differed significantly from the aggressive sample on all of the selection criteria: teacher rating *M* = 12.02, *SD* = 5.58; social preference *M* = 1.77, *SD* = 2.66; peer-nomi-nated aggression *M* = 1.66, *SD* = 2.39; and peer-nominated prosocial *M* = 7.71, *SD* = 5.71 (all *ps* < .001).

### Attributional Questionnaire

We created eight story themes that described a negative outcome occurring to the respondent, initiated by a hypothetical peer provoca-teur, with the intent of the provocation manipulated to be either proso-cial, accidental, ambiguous, or hostile. The negative outcomes de-scribed either damage to one's property (e.g., a homework paper that gets ruined); physical harm (e.g., getting pushed by someone playing ball during recess); goal obstruction (e.g., losing one's place to someone who cuts in line); or social rejection (e.g., making plans with someone who fails to show up). Four versions of each story were created to match the four intentionality conditions. For example, in the homework paper theme subjects first read the following:

> Imagine that you are on your way to school one morning. You are walking onto the school grounds. At that moment, you happen to look down and notice that your shoelace is untied. You put the notebook that you are carrying down on the ground to tie your

---

[1] We used raw preference scores rather than standardized scores be-cause class sizes across the nine selected classrooms were very similar, ranging from 29 to 31 students.

shoelace. An important homework paper that you worked on for a long time falls out of your notebook. Just then, another kid you know walks by and steps on the paper, leaving a muddy footprint right across the middle.

The scenario was then completed with one of the four intent manipulations:

1. This other kid turns to you and says, "I could see that your paper was going to blow in the gutter. I'll help you copy it over." (prosocial)
2. The other kid stops and says, "Excuse me. I didn't see your paper lying there." (accidental)
3. The other kid looks down at your homework paper and then up at you. (ambiguous)
4. The other kid laughs at you, says, "That's your tough luck" and then turns and runs into the school. (hostile)

### Dependent Variables

For each scenario, children made 11 judgments, all reported on 7-point rating scales. Two questions assessed attributions of intentionality. Participants were reminded of the negative outcome and were then asked whether the hypothetical peer provocateur "meant to do that to you" and whether he or she did it "on purpose." The rating scales were anchored with *for sure no* and *for sure yes* and at the midpoint with *maybe*.

The next set of questions dealt with children's affective reactions to the outcome. Although many emotions are likely to be elicited by the scenarios used here, we focused only on that subset theoretically linked to perceived responsibility in others. Participants were, therefore, asked how mad, angry, and grateful (thankful) they would feel toward the peer provocateur if the negative outcome actually occurred. We included the positive emotion of gratitude inasmuch as one scenario was manipulated to be of prosocial intent. Children reported their affective intensities on scales anchored with *not at all mad* (angry and so on) and *very mad*.

Following the intentionality and affect questions, subjects were presented with six behavioral alternatives, partially adapted from Dodge, Murphy, and Buchsbaum (1984). The behaviors varied along a continuum and could be categorized as prosocial ("do something nice for this other kid"), neutral ("do nothing, just forget it"), instrumental ("ask the other kid why they did that"), appealing to authority ("tell an adult"), indirectly hostile ("do something to get even"), or directly and immediately hostile ("have it out right then and there"). Only the last two behavioral alternatives were considered to be full-blown aggressive responses. The six behavioral options were presented as "some things other kids say they would do right away if this happened to them." Children were requested to think about what they probably would do first if the negative outcome described actually happened to them. They then rated each behavioral alternative on a scale anchored with *definitely would not do this* and *definitely would do this.*

Ratings of intentionality, emotion, and behavioral choice were elicited in that order for all eight stories, although within a category of dependent variables the order of specific questions was varied. Maintaining a constant order was judged necessary to avoid confusing subjects across repeated presentation of the same questions and to help sustain their attention, given the necessity of administering the questionnaire in groups.[2]

### Design and Procedure

Approximately 1 month following completion of the sociometric interviews, the same three female experimenters returned to the school to administer the attributional questionnaire. To avoid singling out the target sample, all students with parent permission who were present on the testing days were administered the questionnaire in groups of 8 to 12 either in their regular classroom or in a resource room made available for the research.

The attributional questionnaire consisted of the eight story themes, each paired with one type of intent manipulation. There was one prosocial-intent scenario, one hostile-intent scenario, two scenarios that were manipulated to be accidental, and four scenarios of ambiguous intent. We balanced the intent conditions in this manner because we wanted to oversample ambiguous situations (the context of much previous research) but at the same time have a range of causal conditions represented. The order of presenting the intent manipulations was the same for all subjects, with ambiguous stories presented first and last and then alternating with the other intent manipulations in the second through seventh scenarios. What varied between subjects were the eight stimulus orders created by pairing the story themes with the causal manipulations.

The questionnaire was assembled in booklet form and distributed to the participants. The experimenter read all of the scenarios and dependent measures out loud while subjects followed along and responded independently. Each subject made 88 judgments: 8 scenarios with 11 dependent variables. The entire procedure lasted about 25 min.

## Results

Preliminary analyses showed no effect of subject ethnicity, gender, or stimulus order. These variables are, therefore, ignored in subsequent analyses. Because ratings on the two measures of causal inference were highly correlated (average $r = .84$), these judgments were combined into a single intentionality index. Ratings of "mad" and "angry" were similarly interrelated (average $r = .66$) and were also averaged to create a single anger index. These averaged variables were then analyzed in separate 2 × 8 (Status Group × Causal Condition) analyses of variance with repeated measures on the second factor.

### Intentionality

Table 1 shows the ratings on intentionality as a function of status group and causal condition. The analysis revealed a main effect of causal condition, $F(7, 602) = 31.57$, $p < .001$. All subjects inferred that the negative outcome was least intended by the peer provocateur in the two accidental causal conditions ($M = 3.74$) and the prosocial condition ($M = 3.76$) and most intended in the hostile condition ($M = 6.46$), with the four ambiguous attributional conditions ($M = 4.70$) falling between these two extremes. Post hoc analyses using Fisher's least significant difference test indicated that the means for the accidental

---

[2] Initially, we had planned to test subjects individually and vary the order of presenting attribution, emotion, and behavior questions. However, unanticipated time constraints imposed by the school administrators required that children be tested in groups of 8 to 12 rather than individually. After pilot work in the group setting, we became convinced that, with this population, it was considerably easier to proceed through the questionnaire with a constant ordering of the dependent variables. We acknowledge that this particular ordering may have biased the results in favor of the attribution-emotion-behavior sequence that we hypothesize. On the other hand, in similar such judgments studies in the helping domain (albeit with college students), the order of asking the questions has not been shown to influence subjects' judgments (Schmidt & Weiner, 1988; B. Weiner, personal communication, March 20, 1991).

Table 1

*Mean Ratings on Intentionality, Emotions, and Aggressive Action as a Function of Status Group and Causal Condition*

| Variable | Causal condition | | | | | | | | |
|---|---|---|---|---|---|---|---|---|---|
| | Pro | Acc 1 | Acc 2 | Amb 1 | Amb 2 | Amb 3 | Amb 4 | Hos | M |
| Intentionality | | | | | | | | | |
| Nonaggressive | 3.6 | 3.7 | 3.5 | 3.6 | 4.1 | 4.8 | 4.4 | 6.4 | 4.3 |
| Aggressive | 3.9 | 3.8 | 4.0 | 4.1 | 4.9 | 5.8 | 5.8 | 6.5 | 4.9 |
| Anger | | | | | | | | | |
| Nonaggressive | 3.9 | 4.3 | 4.5 | 5.0 | 5.2 | 5.8 | 5.7 | 6.6 | 5.1 |
| Aggressive | 3.8 | 5.1 | 5.1 | 5.5 | 5.6 | 5.7 | 6.0 | 6.6 | 5.4 |
| Gratitude | | | | | | | | | |
| Nonaggressive | 3.5 | 1.7 | 1.7 | 1.3 | 1.2 | 1.1 | 1.3 | 1.1 | 1.6 |
| Aggressive | 3.1 | 1.7 | 1.4 | 1.8 | 1.7 | 1.5 | 1.3 | 1.3 | 1.7 |
| Get even | | | | | | | | | |
| Nonaggressive | 2.6 | 3.4 | 3.7 | 4.4 | 4.5 | 4.9 | 4.8 | 6.2 | 4.3 |
| Aggressive | 3.6 | 4.3 | 4.6 | 5.0 | 4.8 | 5.3 | 5.4 | 6.1 | 4.9 |
| Have it out | | | | | | | | | |
| Nonaggressive | 2.5 | 2.9 | 3.4 | 4.1 | 3.8 | 4.6 | 4.3 | 5.8 | 3.9 |
| Aggressive | 3.2 | 3.9 | 3.8 | 4.7 | 4.7 | 5.5 | 4.8 | 6.0 | 4.6 |

*Note.* Rating scales range from 1 to 7. *n* = 44 in both the aggressive and nonaggressive groups. High numbers indicate greater perceived intentionality, reported emotion, and likelihood of aggressive action. Pro = prosocial; Acc = accidental; Amb = ambiguous; and Hos = hostile.

and prosocial conditions did not differ ($ps > .10$), whereas all other comparisons between marginal means were significant ($ps < .05$).

There also was a main effect of status group, $F(1, 86) = 13.82$, $p < .001$. Across all causal conditions, aggressive adolescents perceived the peer-instigated negative outcomes as more intended ($M = 4.85$) than did their nonaggressive counterparts ($M = 4.28$). Although the Status Group × Causal Condition interaction was not significant ($p > .15$), planned contrasts between group means using the Bonferroni statistic (Kirk, 1968) indicated that the differences between aggressives and nonaggressives were not significant in the prosocial, accidental, and hostile intent conditions. However, when the cause of the provocation was portrayed as ambiguous, the intent attributions of aggressive subjects were significantly higher in three of the four scenarios ($ps < .05$).

### Emotion

Turning next to reported affective intensity, the anger ANOVA yielded a main effect of cause, $F(7, 602) = 33.22$, $p < .001$. Similar to intentionality judgments, subjects reported that they would feel least angry in the prosocial condition ($M = 3.61$) and most angry in the hostile condition ($M = 6.61$). Independent of manipulated intent, however, aggressive youths reported feeling more angry than did nonaggressives: For the status group main effect, $F(1, 86) = 3.83$, $p = .05$.

For the positive emotion of gratitude, only the cause main effect was significant, $F(7, 602) = 35.63$, $p < .001$. In both status groups, Table 1 shows that reported feelings of gratitude were predictably very low in all scenarios except the one manipulated to be prosocial. Ratings of gratitude in the prosocial condition were significantly higher ($ps < .01$) than in each of

the other causal conditions, which did not differ from one another.

### Action Tendencies

The six behavioral ratings were analyzed in a 2 × 8 (Status Group × Causal Condition) multivariate ANOVA with repeated measures on the second factor. The analysis revealed a multivariate main effect of cause, $F(42, 602) = 5.44$, $p < .001$, that also was documented in each univariate ANOVA ($ps < .05$). Children's endorsement of response options varied by manipulated intent although not in a systematic manner. More important, the analysis also yielded a multivariate main effect of status group, $F(6, 81) = 2.52$, $p < .05$. Univariate analyses revealed that aggressive and nonaggressive respondents differed only in their endorsement of the two most hostile behavioral alternatives: "get even," $F(1, 86) = 5.11$, $p < .05$, and "have it out right then and there," $F(2, 86) = 7.19$, $p < .01$. As Table 1 shows, aggressive children were more likely to prefer these behavioral alternatives. The multivariate Status Group × Causal Condition interaction was not significant ($F < 1$), indicating that the differences between aggressives and nonaggressives on action tendencies were not more evident given particular kinds of attributional cues.

In sum, the strongest finding in the analyses of mean differences between status groups was the tendency among aggressive adolescents to infer greater intentionality in situations of ambiguous peer provocation. Relative to their nonaggressive counterparts, aggressive subjects were also more likely to report feeling angry at the peer provocateur and to endorse hostile retaliatory behavior. Unlike the attributional judgments, however, these group differences in emotion and behavioral choice were more evenly distributed across all eight causal conditions.

## Relations Between Variables

In the next set of analyses, we examined correlations among ratings of intentionality, anger, and hostile action tendencies across the range of causal conditions and social dilemmas considered (Table 2). For ease of presentation, in this and all subsequent analyses, ratings on the two aggressive action tendencies ("get even" and "have it out") were averaged to create a single behavioral variable. Furthermore, to ensure response independence in this repeated measures design, the data for the correlational analyses were based on one set of scenario ratings from each subject randomly selected from among the eight scenarios to which all participants had responded. With 88 subjects, this selection procedure allowed for each causal condition to be represented 11 times, approximately equally distributed among aggressive and nonaggressive children.[3]

For nonaggressive subjects, Table 2 shows strong positive correlations among intentionality, anger, and likelihood of behaving aggressively. The more individuals perceive a peer as intentionally causing them harm, the more anger they feel and the greater the likelihood of their behaving aggressively. All of these relations are in accord with attributional predictions. The same pattern of findings is also true for aggressive children, although Table 2 reveals that the magnitude of the correlations is not as great among this group.

## Model Testing

Next we examined the temporal relations between these variables. We have proposed that thoughts guide feelings and feelings, in turn, determine behavior. Are the data for aggressive and nonaggressive adolescents in the present study consistent with this mediational model of emotion?

To address this question, we used structural equation modeling (SEM) using the multisample analysis of the EQS statistical program (Bentler, 1989). As in other SEM approaches such as LISREL, EQS calculates parameter estimates (path coefficients) of the structural model as well as a goodness-of-fit chi-square statistic that evaluates whether or not a tested model reproduces the sample data (i.e., the covariance matrix). A non-significant chi-square indicates that the proposed model is consistent with the data and, therefore, represents an adequate fit. Because the chi-square statistic is sensitive to both large and small samples, EQS also reports a measure of practical fit that is independent of sample size: the Bentler-Bonett Normed Fit Index (NFI). The values of this index can range from 0 (no fit) to 1 (perfect fit), with values greater than .90 indicating an acceptable fit (Bentler & Bonett, 1980). Finally, the multisample EQS procedure generates a goodness-of-fit chi-square that simultaneously tests the fit of a hypothesized model in more than one group. Thus, we were able to test whether a particular model was the same in both nonaggressive and aggressive subjects.

Using EQS, we tested the model in which perceived intent was hypothesized to influence anger and anger then exerted a direct influence on aggressive action tendency (Linkages 2 and 3 in Figure 1). The influence of intent on action was assumed to be indirect, that is, mediated by anger. We examined this model in relation to one that included the path from intent to action

Table 2

*Means, Standard Deviations, and Correlations Among Intentionality, Anger, and Aggressive Action Tendency by Status Group*

| | Status group | |
|---|---|---|
| Measure | Nonaggressive | Aggressive |
| Intent | | |
| M | 4.23 | 4.44 |
| SD | 1.844 | 1.872 |
| Anger | | |
| M | 5.26 | 5.24 |
| SD | 1.619 | 1.486 |
| Action | | |
| M | 8.64 | 9.26 |
| SD | 4.035 | 3.837 |
| Intent × Anger correlation | .70*** | .51*** |
| Intent × Action correlation | .61*** | .33* |
| Anger × Action correlation | .66*** | .41** |

$* p < .05.$  $** p < .01.$  $*** p < .001.$

(Linkage 4), and we compared it with two alternative models suggesting different relations between the variables. With these relatively simple three-variable models, the small sample size analyzed here does not pose serious interpretive problems.

Table 3 shows the parameter estimates of each model, expressed as standardized path coefficients, their associated test statistics ($z$ tests), and, where applicable, the chi-square and Bentler-Bonett NFI generated to evaluate the fit of the model. Because the multisample procedures revealed differences between status groups in all but one analysis (Model 1 presented later), the data are reported separately for nonaggressive and aggressive subjects.

The first set of parameters in Table 3 (Model 0) estimates the coefficients for the model that included direct paths from intent and anger to action as well as the influence of intent on action that is mediated by anger (Linkages 2, 3, and 4 in Figure 1). Because Model 0 is completely saturated (i.e., all of the variables are interconnected), it cannot be tested with chi-square procedures. However, Model 0 is of interest for comparative purposes because it estimates the strength of the direct path from intent to action and, therefore, sheds light on whether this linkage is necessary to adequately represent the data. Whereas the paths from intent to anger ($B_1$) and anger to action ($B_2$) are significant in Model 0 of both status groups, Table 3 shows that

---

[3] Even with this representation of all causal conditions, using only one set of ratings per subject might not adequately represent the general pattern of data. We, therefore, repeated the selection procedure seven times, each time selecting a different set of ratings from each subject. Correlations between intent–anger, intent–action, and anger–action were calculated for each set of ratings separately by status group. We then tested the difference between these correlations using $r$-to-$z$ transformations (Hedges & Olkin, 1985). None of these sample $r$s was significantly different in either status group (all $p$s > .05). Thus, the correlations presented in Table 2 are believed to capture the relationships between variables that are based on subjects' data in all eight scenarios.

Table 3

*Parameter Estimates and Goodness of Fit of Four Structural Models by Status Group*

| | Status group | | | | | | | | | |
| --- | --- | --- | --- | --- | --- | --- | --- | --- | --- | --- |
| | Nonaggressive | | | | | Aggressive | | | | |
| Parameter | Path | $z$ | $\chi^2$ | $p$ | NFI | Path | $z$ | $\chi^2$ | $p$ | NFI |
| Model 0 (saturated model) | | | | | | | | | | |
| $B_1$: Path from intent to anger | .702 | 6.46 | | | | .513 | 3.92 | | | |
| $B_2$: Path from anger to action | .459 | 2.97 | | | | .332 | 2.08 | | | |
| $B_3$: Path from intent to action | .288 | 1.86 | | | | .162 | 1.01 | | | |
| Model 1 (mediational model) | | | 3.330 | ns | .942 | | | 1.016 | ns | .954 |
| $B_1$: Path from intent to anger | .702 | 6.46 | | | | .513 | 3.92 | | | |
| $B_2$: Path from anger to action | .661 | 5.77 | | | | .415 | 2.99 | | | |
| Model 2 (independent effects) | | | 29.181 | < .001 | .490 | | | 13.110 | < .001 | .411 |
| $B_1$: Path from intent to anger | .320 | 2.62 | | | | .167 | 1.18 | | | |
| $B_2$: Path from anger to action | .508 | 4.16 | | | | .341 | 2.42 | | | |
| Model 3 (mediational model) | | | 8.016 | < .01 | .860 | | | 4.115 | < .05 | .815 |
| $B_1$: Path from intent to intent | .702 | 6.46 | | | | .513 | 3.92 | | | |
| $B_2$: Path from intent to action | .610 | 5.05 | | | | .332 | 2.31 | | | |

*Note.* A $z$ score greater than 1.96 indicates a significant path. For all chi-square tests, $df = 1$, $N = 44$. NFI = Bentler-Bonett Normed Fit Index.

the direct path from intent to action ($B_3$) is relatively weak and fails to reach conventional levels of significance. This suggests that freeing the path from intent to action (i.e., $B_3 = 0$) might be a more parsimonious model to account for the data of both aggressive and nonaggressive children.

This model, which evaluates the hypothesized mediational role of emotion, is tested in Model 1. The multisample analysis yielded $\chi^2(2, N = 88) = 4.346$, $p > .10$, NFI = .945. This indicates a good fit of the model in each status group. For nonaggressives, Table 3 reveals that Model 1 generated a nonsignificant $\chi^2(1, N = 44) = 3.330$, NFI = .942. Similarly, for aggressives, Model 1 yielded $\chi^2(1, N = 44) = 1.016$, NFI = .954.

Next we tested two alternative models that might also be plausible. Earlier we raised the possibility of independent effects of cognition and emotion. Among aggressive children, for example, it may be that attributions to intent instigate hostile behavior without the mediating (and regulating) influence of affect or that feelings of anger precipitate aggression even in the absence of perceived hostile intent. Thus, Model 2 evaluates whether perceived intentionality and reported anger independently determine aggressive action tendency without any mediational effects. The significant chi-squares and low NFI values suggest that this model should be rejected in both status groups.

Finally, Model 3 tested a mediational model that reversed the causal relations between cognition and emotion. Feelings of anger toward the peer provocateur were hypothesized to influence perceived intent, and intent, in turn, directly influenced hostile action tendencies. This model also revealed an unacceptable fit among both groups of children. In sum, for this data set at least, the model proposing a mediational role for emotion remains the most parsimonious one for both nonaggressive and aggressive children.[4]

### Relations Within Ambiguous Contexts

These analyses considered the full range of causal conditions to which children responded. However, because previous re-

search on attributional bias among aggressive children has mainly examined this phenomenon in ambiguous contexts, we conducted the same causal modeling procedures using only the data from the four ambiguous causal conditions. One set of ratings in an ambiguous condition was randomly selected from each subject and used as input for the analyses (see Table 4).

Because of the restrictions in the range of causal conditions, it was expected that the magnitude of the correlations would be reduced when only the data from ambiguous conditions were analyzed. Comparing the zero-order correlations in Table 2 to those in Table 4, it is evident that this proved to be the case. Nonetheless, Table 4 reveals that the correlations among intent, anger, and aggressive action tendency remained significant for both status groups and that, as before, the relations were stronger for nonaggressive adolescents.

The EQS results for each status group are displayed in Table 5. For nonaggressives, the findings are consistent with the overall analyses and again document the mediational role of emotion. That is, the nonsignificant chi-square generated for Model 1 indicated a good fit of the model. This was supported by the nonsignificant path from intent to action in the saturated model ($B_3 = .234$). In addition, the significant chi-squares gen-

---

[4] In a replication, we ran the same EQS analyses on another randomly selected set of correlations. The pattern of results was quite similar to that reported in Table 3. Specifically, Models 2 and 3 were rejected in both status groups. For nonaggressives, Model 2 $\chi^2(1, N = 44) = 37.413$, $p < .001$, NFI = .530; and Model 3 $\chi^2(1, N = 44) = 11.744$, $p < .001$, NFI = .639. For aggressives, Model 2 $\chi^2(1, N = 44) = 11.969$, $p < .001$, NFI = .853. For aggressives, Model 2 $\chi^2(1, N = 44) = 11.969$, $p < .001$, NFI = .639; and Model 3 $\chi^2(1, N = 44) = 10.667$, $p < .01$, NFI = .617. Model 1 yielded an acceptable fit among aggressives, $\chi^2(1, N = 44) = 3.226$, $p > .05$, NFI = .903. The one deviation from the pattern in Table 3 was the fit of Model 1 among nonaggressives. Model 1 yielded $\chi^2(1, N = 44) = 4.351$, $p < .05$, suggesting questionable fit. However, the measure of practical fit (NFI = .945) indicated an acceptable model.

Table 4

*Means, Standard Deviations, and Correlations Among the Variables in the Ambiguous Causal Conditions by Status Group*

| | Status group | |
|---|---|---|
| Measure | Nonaggressive | Aggressive |
| Intent | | |
| M | 4.280 | 4.900 |
| SD | 1.942 | 1.580 |
| Anger | | |
| M | 5.440 | 5.450 |
| SD | 1.356 | 1.281 |
| Action | | |
| M | 8.800 | 9.610 |
| SD | 3.468 | 3.289 |
| Intent × Anger correlation | .47** | .36* |
| Intent × Action correlation | .44** | .36* |
| Anger × Action correlation | .56** | .34* |

\* $p < .05$.    \*\* $p < .001$.

erated by Models 2 and 3 indicated that neither of these alternative conceptualizations was acceptable.

With the aggressive sample, on the other hand, the pattern of findings is not consistent with the overall analysis. Even though Model 1 was acceptable, $\chi^2(1, N = 44) = 3.387$, $p > .05$, an NFI of .767 suggested questionable fit. Furthermore, there was evidence that Model 3, which reversed the sequence between intent and anger, also was tenable, $\chi^2(1, N = 44) = 2.600$, $p > .09$, NFI = .821. It was not possible to directly compare these models with chi-square difference tests because they are not hierarchically nested. The model that tested independent effects, however, was again rejected.

## Discussion

In 1983, Parke and Slaby concluded their critique of the social cognitive literature on childhood aggression by observing that "the extent to which cognitive models of aggression incor-

porate other dimensions such as affect will determine their ultimate usefulness; it is unlikely that simple cognitive models alone will suffice" (p. 573). In the present article, we have taken up the challenge implied in Parke and Slaby's remarks. Our goal has been to document the usefulness of an attributional approach to childhood aggression that also incorporates emotion.

In so doing, we set out to answer two basic questions. The first asked whether there were differences between aggressives and nonaggressives in their perceptions of peer intent, their feelings of anger, and the likelihood that they would behave aggressively toward that peer. Concerning attributions to intent, we replicated the well-documented finding of biased intentionality inferences among aggressives, in this case with a population of ethnic minority adolescents. Although many of the previous studies include ethnic minority children in their samples, few have been concerned with adolescent populations (see Coie et al., 1990). Aggressive youths were also more likely to state that they would feel angry toward the peer and to endorse hostile behavioral alternatives.

The differences between aggressives and nonaggressives on these individual variables admittedly were not great. For example, all of the adolescents in this sample reported relatively high anger and at least moderate endorsement of aggressive behavior. Nonetheless, in agreement with Dodge and Crick (1990), we argue that the cumulative effects of multiple measures are likely to be substantial and, therefore, capture meaningful differences between aggressive adolescents and their nonaggressive counterparts.

The second question guiding our research asked how perceived intent, anger, and hostile behavior were interrelated among the populations studied. Here we tested a particular set of relations postulated by attribution theory. Specifically, we examined a temporal sequence whereby perceived intentionality elicits anger, and anger then functions as a guide to aggressive behavior.

When considering the full range of causal conditions examined here, the causal modeling analyses supported the pro-

Table 5

*Parameter Estimates and Goodness of Fit of Four Structural Models in the Ambiguous Causal Conditions by Status Group*

| | Status group | | | | | | | | | |
|---|---|---|---|---|---|---|---|---|---|---|
| | Nonaggressive | | | | | Aggressive | | | | |
| Parameter | Path | z | $\chi^2$ | p | NFI | Path | z | $\chi^2$ | p | NFI |
| Model 0 (saturated model) | | | | | | | | | | |
| $B_1$: Path from intent to anger | .470 | 3.49 | | | | .356 | 2.50 | | | |
| $B_2$: Path from anger to action | .446 | 3.21 | | | | .242 | 1.64 | | | |
| $B_3$: Path from intent to action | .234 | 1.69 | | | | .277 | 1.88 | | | |
| Model 1 (mediational model) | | | 2.751 | ns | .906 | | | 3.387 | ns | .767 |
| $B_1$: Path from intent to anger | .470 | 3.49 | | | | .356 | 2.50 | | | |
| $B_2$: Path from anger to action | .556 | 4.39 | | | | .340 | 2.37 | | | |
| Model 2 (independent effects) | | | 10.714 | < .001 | .635 | | | 5.814 | < .05 | .598 |
| $B_1$: Path from intent to action | .248 | 1.92 | | | | .284 | 2.01 | | | |
| $B_2$: Path from anger to action | .470 | 3.63 | | | | .247 | 1.75 | | | |
| Model 3 (mediational model) | | | 9.227 | < .01 | .686 | | | 2.600 | ns | .821 |
| $B_1$: Path from anger to intent | .470 | 3.49 | | | | .356 | 2.50 | | | |
| $B_2$: Path from intent to action | .444 | 3.25 | | | | .363 | 2.56 | | | |

*Note.* A z score greater than 1.96 indicates a significant path. For all chi-square tests, $df = 1$, $N = 44$. NFI = Bentler-Bonett Normed Fit Index.

posed mediational role of emotion with both aggressive and nonaggressive children. Substantively, we interpret this to mean the following: When socially deviant and normal adolescents reason about, for example, social rejection or some other interpersonal dilemma with negative consequences, much of the relationship between what they think (e.g., "He did it on purpose") and the way they intend to behave (e.g., "Let's have it out right here and now") can be accounted for by how they feel (e.g., "I'm really angry about this"). As previously indicated, we view the use of these thinking-feeling-action linkages as both a rational response to social dilemmas and as part of competent social information processing.

Aggressive adolescents appear to display less of this competence in situations of attributional ambiguity. A model that tested the influence of feelings on attributions described aggressive subjects' data in the ambiguous conditions just as well as the attributional conception in which emotions are consequences of cognitions. At present, then, we are uncertain as to how thought, feeling, and action are interrelated when aggressive children are confronted with ambiguously caused peer provocation. If the alternative model is plausible, then emotions may play a greater role on the antecedent side of biased intentionality attributions than the more cognitively oriented approaches suggest. Most of the research on attributional antecedents in the peer-aggression literature has been guided by cognitive information-processing paradigms. Understanding how children integrate various informational cues to arrive at accurate interpretations of intent has been the goal of such work (Dodge & Crick, 1990). Yet there is growing interest in the role that emotions like fear, distress, and even anger play in the initial response to provocation (Dodge, in press). We believe our methods and our approach are useful for researchers concerned with both the determinants of intentionality inferences among aggressive children, be they cognitive or emotional, as well as their consequences and relation to subsequent behavior.

## Implications for Intervention

A natural outgrowth of the burgeoning literature on social cognitive determinants of aggression has been an increased interest in the development of intervention programs for aggressive children based on social cognitive skill training (see Coie & Koeppl, 1990). Along these lines, some empirically based programs that include an attributional component have reported promising results (e.g., Guerra & Slaby, 1990; Lochman, Burch, Curry, & Lampron, 1984).

The present findings also have implications for intervention research, particularly when conceptualized in terms of a thinking-feeling-acting temporal sequence. Referring back to this sequence as outlined in Figure 1, it is clear that a reasonable starting point for intervention can be at the level of attributional change, that is, training aggressive-prone children to perceive peer provocations as less intentional (Linkage 1 in Figure 1). It then follows logically that feelings of anger should be mitigated (Linkage 2). Yet most interventions that focus on the anger component of aggression have been fashioned after cognitive behavior modification programs of Michenbaum and others in which aggressive children are taught to control their anger by various self-talk strategies (e.g., Camp, 1977; Michenbaum, 1985). Few, if any, such programs relate feelings of anger back to their attributional antecedents.

As our data indicate, among aggressive children in ambiguous situations, perceived intent and feelings of anger were less systematically related. Thus, an important dimension in interventions that focus on the anger component of aggression might not so much be training in anger reduction as training children to realize that anger is an appropriate emotional response only when a peer's negative actions are clearly (unambiguously) guided by hostile intent. If the attributional change agent can help strengthen the relationship between the emotion and its eliciting antecedent thoughts in aggressive children, then it is reasonable to expect that anger can take on the more adaptive role of regulator rather than instigator of negative other-directed behavior.

Of course, caution must be exercised when drawing implications from our findings, given the hypothetical nature of the stimuli used here as well as the invariant order of eliciting judgments about causal thoughts, feelings, and behavior. Nonetheless, we do not wish to understate what we see as the theoretical richness and heuristic value of our conceptual analysis as a model for intervention based on attributional change.

## Implications for the Study of Aggression Among African-Americans

Because African-American boys are overrepresented among school-aged children labeled as *aggressive*, it is common practice for studies of childhood aggression to include large numbers of Black males in their samples. Often this is acknowledged almost parenthetically as part of sample description. Rarely do such studies attempt to relate their findings back to issues that may be particularly relevant to the sampled population.

The sample in this study was exclusively ethnic minority, predominantly African-American. This makes sense inasmuch as peer aggression and its correlates are such serious problems among African-American males. At a more theoretical level, however, we chose to study African-Americans in this context because we believe that attributional approaches to the topic of aggression are particularly relevant for this group. The central constructs of attribution theory—perceived responsibility (in self as well as others), emotional reactions to success and failure (both academic and social), and expectations for the future—are the variables that have proved most durable in research concerned with social cognitive functioning of African-Americans (see Graham, 1988).

That a biased attributional tendency was documented in our ethnically diverse adolescent population certainly adds to our belief in the robustness of that phenomenon. Moreover, the presence of systematic thinking-feeling-action relations among nonaggressive ethnic minority youth supports the generality of some basic attribution principles relating emotion to thought and behavior. Whether these relations would be the same or different among populations other than ethnic minorities is less central to our concern. For rather than engage in comparative racial analyses, we study general psychological principles that apply to a great range of subject populations. African-American and nonethnic children may just fall at different points along a basic dimension, in this case, for example, amount of exposure to peer aggression.

On the other hand, we also must acknowledge that causal

thinking and reported emotion accounted for only a modest amount of variance in action tendencies of the aggressive adolescents who participated in this study (about 19% in multiple regression analyses). This was in contrast to 48% of the variance in the analysis that sampled all causal conditions. At the least, these data remind us of the complex array of nonattributional (and nonsocial cognitive) factors that are known determinants of aggression in ethnic minority youths, such as low intelligence quotient, poor school performance, economic deprivation, and family instability to name but a few. Furthermore, given the sociocultural environment from which our sample of young adolescents was drawn, it is unclear to what extent being quick to assign blame or having a low threshhold for retaliatory behavior might operate as genuine survival strategies for coping with the vagaries of daily life that have come to be characteristic of the urban minority underclass. In sum, as psychologists who study a social phenomenon that seems to be particularly prevalent in African-Americans, we acknowledge the need to place our findings (including prescriptions and proscriptions) within our subjects' broader sociocultural context.

## References

Averill, J. R. (1982). *Anger and aggression: An essay on emotion*. New York: Springer-Verlag.

Bentler, P. M. (1989). *EQS structural equations program manual*. Los Angeles: BMDP Statistical Software.

Bentler, P. M., & Bonett, D. G. (1980). Significance tests and goodness of fit in the analysis of covariance structures. *Psychological Bulletin, 88*, 588–606.

Bower, G. G., & Cohen, P. (1982). Emotional influences in memory and thinking: Data and theory. In M. S. Clarke & S. T. Fiske (Eds.), *Affect and cognition: The 17th annual Carnegie symposium on cognition* (pp. 291–332). Hillsdale, NJ: Erlbaum.

Cairns, R., Cairns, B., & Neckerman, H. (1989). Early school dropout: Configurations and determinants. *Child Development, 60*, 1437–1452.

Camp, B. (1977). Verbal mediation in young aggressive boys. *Journal of Abnormal Psychology, 86*, 145–153.

Coie, J., & Dodge, K. A. (1988). Multiple sources of data on social behavior and social status in the school: A cross-age comparison. *Child Development, 59*, 815–829.

Coie, J., Dodge, K. A., & Kupersmidt, J. (1990). Peer group behavior and social status. In S. Asher & J. Coie (Eds.), *Peer rejection in childhood* (pp. 17–59). New York: Cambridge University Press.

Coie, J., & Koeppl, G. (1990). Adapting intervention to the problems of aggressive and disruptive children. In S. Asher & J. Coie (Eds.), *Peer rejection in childhood* (pp. 309–337). New York: Cambridge University Press.

Dodge, K. A. (in press). Emotion and social information processing. In J. Garber & K. A. Dodge (Eds.), *The development of emotion regulation and deregulation*. New York: Cambridge University Press.

Dodge, K. A., & Crick, N. R. (1990). Social information-processing bases of aggressive behavior in children. *Personality and Social Psychology Bulletin, 16*, 8–22.

Dodge, K. A., Murphy, R., & Buchsbaum, K. (1984). The assessment of intention-cue detection skills in children: Implications for developmental psychopathology. *Child Development, 55*, 163–173.

Dodge, K. A., & Somberg, D. R. (1987). Hostile attributional biases among aggressive boys are exacerbated under conditions of threat. *Child Development, 58*, 213–224.

Farrington, D. P. (1987). Epidemiology. In H. C. Quay (Ed.), *Handbook of juvenile delinquency* (pp. 62–105). New York: Wiley.

Graham, S. (1988). Can attribution theory tell us something about motivation in blacks? *Educational Psychologist, 23*, 2–21.

Graham, S., & Weiner, B. (1991). Testing judgments about attribution-emotion-action linkages: A lifespan approach. *Social Cognition, 9*, 221–243.

Guerra, N., & Slaby, R. (1990). Cognitive mediators of aggression in adolescent offenders: 2. Intervention. *Developmental Psychology, 26*, 269–277.

Hedges, L. V., & Olkin, I. (1985). *Statistical methods for meta-analysis*. New York: Academic Press.

Jaynes, G. D., & Williams, R. (Eds.). (1989). *A common destiny: Blacks and American society*. Washington, DC: National Academy Press.

Kirk, R. (1968). *Experimental design: Procedures for the behavioral sciences*. Belmont, CA: Brooks/Cole.

Kohlberg, L., Ricks, D., & Snarey, J. (1984). Childhood development as a predictor adaptation in adulthood. *Genetic Psychology Monographs, 110*, 91–172.

Lochman, J., Burch, L., Curry, J., & Lampron, L. (1984). Treatment and generalization effects of cognitive behavioral and goal setting interventions with aggressive boys. *Journal of Consulting and Clinical Psychology, 52*, 915–916.

Loeber, R. (1982). The stability of antisocial and delinquent child behavior. *Child Development, 53*, 1431–1446.

Loeber, R., & Stouthamer-Loeber, M. (1987). Prediction. In H. C. Quay (Ed.), *Handbook of juvenile delinquency* (pp. 325–382). New York: Wiley.

Michenbaum, D. H. (1985). *Stress innoculation training*. New York: Pergamon Press.

Olweus, D. (1979). Stability of aggressive reaction patterns in males: A review. *Psychological Bulletin, 86*, 852–857.

Parke, R. D., & Slaby, R. G. (1983). The development of aggression. In E. H. Hetherington (Ed.), *Carmichael's manual of child psychology* (Vol. 4, pp. 641–647). New York: Wiley.

Reed, R. (1988). Education and achievement of young black males. In J. T. Gibbs (Ed.), *Young, black, and male in America: An endangered species* (pp. 37–96). Dover, MA: Auburn House.

Robins, L. N. (1978). Studies of childhood predictors of adult antisocial behavior: Replications from longitudinal studies. *Psychological Medicine, 8*, 611–622.

Roseman, I. J. (1984). Cognitive determinants of emotion: A structural theory. In P. Shaver (Ed.), *Review of personality and social psychology* (Vol. 5, pp. 11–36). Newbury Park, CA: Sage.

Sancilio, M., Plumert, J., & Hartup, W. (1989). Friendship and aggressiveness as determinants of conflict outcomes in middle childhood. *Developmental Psychology, 25*, 812–819.

Schmidt, G., & Weiner, B. (1988). An attribution-affect-action theory of motivated behavior: Replications examining help giving. *Personality and Social Psychology Bulletin, 14*, 610–621.

Thompson, R. (1990). Emotion and self-regulation. In R. Thompson (Ed.), *Nebraska symposium on motivation* (Vol. 36, pp. 367–348). Lincoln: University of Nebraska Press.

Tompkins, S. (1970). Affect as the primary motivational system. In M. B. Arnold (Ed.), *Feelings and emotions* (pp. 101–110). New York: Academic Press.

Weiner, B. (1985). An attributional theory of achievement motivation and emotion. *Psychological Review, 92*, 548–573.

Weiner, B. (1986). *An attributional theory of motivation and emotion*. New York: Springer-Verlag.

Weiner, B. (1991). On perceiving the other as responsible. In R. Dientsbier (Ed.), *Nebraska symposium on motivation* (Vol. 38, pp. 165–198). Lincoln: University of Nebraska Press.

Wilson, J. O., & Herrnstein, R. J. (1985). *Crime and human nature*. New York: Simon & Schuster.

Received October 30, 1990
Revision received October 18, 1991
Accepted October 28, 1991 ∎

# HOMELESS ADOLESCENTS: A DESCRIPTIVE STUDY OF SIMILARITIES AND DIFFERENCES BETWEEN RUNAWAYS AND THROWAWAYS

**Gerald R. Adams, Thomas Gullotta and Mary Anne Clancy**

ABSTRACT

A sample of 43 homeless adolescents was categorized as being either runaways, throwaways, or societal rejects. Comparisons of these categories of homeless youths were completed to assess the descriptive utility of internal social control, strain, and psychopathological theory in making distinctions between various homeless adolescents. Descriptive data support the view that control and psychopathology perspectives provide some promise for understanding differing types of runaway adolescents. Sex differences between runaway and throwaway youths were explored. However, few sex × type of homeless adolescent interactions were observed. Implications for secondary prevention, based upon these data, are offered.

Nationally, more than one-half million adolescents leave home yearly. Typically these youths are referred to as runaways. Recent reviews of the available research indicate multiple causes for runaway behavior (Adams, 1980; Adams & Munro, 1979; Gullotta, 1978; Opinion Research Corporation, 1976; Young, Godfrey, Mathews, & Adams, 1983). Runaways report poor parent-child relationships (Van Houten & Golembiewski, 1978; Libertoff, 1976), extreme family conflict (Blood & D'Angelo, 1974; English, 1973; Gottlieb & Chafetz, 1977; Hildebrand, 1963), alienation from parents (D'Angelo, 1972), interpersonal tension (Community Health and Welfare Council, 1972), and poor communication with parents (Opinion Research Corporation, 1976) as primary factors behind running away from home. Some evidence suggests that runaways are more likely to come from either single-parent or very large families (Johnson & Peck, 1978; Opinion Research Corporation, 1976), although there is some contradictory evidence for such an assumption (Mathews & Ilon, 1980). Johnson and Peck (1978) also have reported that a larger than expected number of runaways come from families where all the siblings are of the opposite-sex. Collectively, a large body of research suggests that poor parent-child relations contributes to runaway behavior (Wolk & Brandon, 1977) with runa-

Support for this project was provided by the Youth Emergency Service, YMCA of Metropolitan Hartford and the Division of Research, Utah State University. Reprint requests to Gerald R. Adams, Ph.D., Family and Human Development, Utah State University, Logan, Utah 84322.

*ADOLESCENCE, Vol. XX No. 79, Fall 1985*
*Libra Publishers, Inc., 4901 Morena Blvd., Suite 207, San Diego, CA 92117*

ways having parents who provide limited or poor supervision and who express much unhappiness with their adolescents.

In addition to parent-child conflict, Brennan, Huizinga, and Elliott (1978) maintain that poor teacher-student relations and school problems are causal factors behind adolescents leaving home. Other proposed causes of runaway behavior include high incidences of physical abuse and neglect (Lourie, Campiglia, James, & DeWitt, 1979; Gullotta, 1978), incestuous relations with a family member (Robey, Rosenwald, Snell, & Lee, 1964) and delinquency (Brennan et al., 1978).

While running away may be a logical reaction to a stressful situation, departing from home for an extended period of time, when one is not prepared to care for oneself, can result in several negative consequences (Young et al., 1983).

A survey of the literature on homeless children indicates that most social scientists and family service investigators have focused their attention on making distinctions between runaways and nonrunaways. However, important distinctions need to be made between various types of runaway youths (Adams, 1980; Brennan et al., 1978). For example, as Gullotta (1978) has noted, many runaways are more than youths on the run—youths who can and are likely to return home after a brief runaway experience. Some youths are actually castaways or adolescents who are thrown out of their homes and told not to return.

In the present study three types of homeless youths were identified through interviews: (a) *runaways* who left home because of perceived family conflict, alienation, and poor social relations; (b) *throwaways* who have been encouraged or asked to leave home, and (c) *societal rejects*—youths who appear to have been rejected by peers, family, and teachers and are provided no immediate long-term services by public social service agencies. Unfortunately, only two societal rejects were identified in our sample; therefore, most of the data address differences between runaways and throwaways.

Several theoretical perspectives have been advanced as to the causes of leaving home. From the psychoanalytic perspective, children are thought to leave home due to interpersonal strife and an overly close relationship with the opposite-sex parent. In contrast, internal social control theory (Hirschi, 1969) suggests that adolescents leave because they are not emotionally attached and care little how their behavior impacts upon their parents. Strain theory proposes that deviant behavior, such as running away, is the product of socially induced pressures toward deviance. For example, peer pressure problems or delinquent friends pressure youths to leave home. From the psychopathological perspective, runaway behavior is thought to be an expression of undercontrolled impulsive personality characteristics. Given

716

the distinctions between runaways and throwaways, it was hypothesized that while both types of homeless adolescents would report family problems, throwaways would report the least evidence of emotional bonding with family members and the highest degree of family conflict. Conversely, we hypothesized that runaways, in comparison to throwaways, would express more impulsivity and peer-relations problems. Finally, we expected both groups to report a generally poor self-image. Thus, we anticipated that internal social control theory would best describe the conditions of throwaways, while strain and psychopathological theory, in various combining elements, would best describe the reported history of runaways.

METHOD

A sample of 43 homeless adolescents who volunteered to participate at the Youth Emergency Service of the YMCA of Metropolitan Hartford, Connecticut, completed a comprehensive interview constructed from items originally devised for the *National Statistical Survey of Runaway Youth* (Opinion Research Corporation, 1976). The sample included 9 male and 13 female runaways, 11 male and 8 female throwaways and 2 male societal rejects. The majority of runaways were between 11 and 15 years of age (72%) with a range between 11 and 17. Throwaways were somewhat older on the average, with the majority being between 15 and 17 years of age (79%). The two societal reject youths were 16 and 17 years of age. Assuming one can view the distinction between the three types of youths as progressively more complex as one moves from runaways to throwaways to societal rejects, the data suggest that age is correlated with greater seriousness associated with leaving home. Previous research suggests that runaways come from all social classes. However, comparatively few of the runaways (10%) or throwaways (11%) in this sample came from middle-class homes (professional and managerial), using father's occupational status as the criterion of SES. Interestingly, all of the societal rejects came from lower-lower social-class homes.

Further demographic information on the sample indicates that consistent with data reported by the *National Statistical Survey of Runaway Youth*, the majority of runaways (85%) and throwaways (67%) had left home more than once prior to the current run. Indeed, in the national survey it was reported that primarily multiple-time runners use shelters such as that provided by the YMCA in Hartford. Our data would confirm this finding. For both runaways and throwaways the range of previous runaway incidents was between one and seven times.

When asked how long the adolescent had thought about running away prior to leaving, on average the runaway reported approximately 6 months, while the throwaway reported less than one week.

The major results of this study are reported here. For related findings the authors will supply an extended technical report on request.

*Primary reason for running away.* Reported reasons for leaving home in previous studies have varied from "seeking adventure" to "sexual abuse." The 43 homeless youths in our study likewise offered numerous reasons. However, 74% of the runaways reported leaving home because they were not getting along with their parents. Others reported such reasons as physical abuse (5%), delinquency (5%), wanting independence (5%), or mental illness (5%). Throwaways (84%) also reported difficulty with parents as the primary reason for leaving. Further, some 22% of the throwaways not only indicated parent-child conflict but that their parents openly wanted them to leave home. Collectively, these data indicate that the family is perceived in the majority of cases to be the primary reason adolescents leave home.

Further questioning about perceived parental relations revealed little evidence of physical abuse between parents; however, throwaways (47%) were more likely than runaways (22%) to report that their parents did not get along well with each other. Adolescents were also asked about their perceptions of their parents' behavior toward them. A wide range of reponses were reported. On a series of questions with a response format of always, pretty often, once in a while, almost never, or no opinion, each youth was asked to respond to several questions regarding their mother's and father's behavior.[1] On the positive side, a majority of runaways perceived their mothers as frequently talking about things with them (68%) and infrequently drinking too much (76%). However, runaways perceived their mothers as frequently calling them names (55%) and providing too much restrictive supervision (77%). For throwaways, mothers were perceived as saying unpleasant things about them (61%) and also providing too restrictive supervision (72%). The remaining perceptions of mothers were generally positive.

Perceptions of fathers were more varied and less positive. For runaways, fathers were seen as seldom satisfied with their son or daughter (50%), infrequently helpful with hobbies (42%), seldom talking to them

[1]Percentages reflect the collapsed distinction between always and pretty often versus once in a while and almost never.

718

(37%), and restrictive in their supervision (55%). Fathers were infrequently seen as saying unpleasant things about them or calling them names, were seldom viewed as punishing or beating them, and perceived as infrequently drinking too much. In contrast, throwaways perceived their fathers as frequently saying unpleasant things about them (58%), commonly calling them names (82%), while frequently punishing (64%) and beating (70%) them. Fathers were also perceived as not being satisfied with them (73%), infrequently helping with hobbies (82%) or talking to them (80%). Once again, highly restrictive supervision was perceived by throwaways (80%).

*Sibship, single-parent homes, and birth order.* Past research has indicated that a higher than chance proportion of youths who run away come from single-parent homes, large families, or families with all opposite-sex siblings. Further, some data suggests that first-borns may be more likely to run than later borns. No support for differences between runaways and throwaways for any of these hypotheses were found with this sample.

*Peer relations.* Many past studies also have indicated that runaways experience severe peer-relations problems. Those in this sample appear to be no different. When asked if other students in school included them in their activities, both runaways (69%) and throwaways (63%) reported that they were infrequently invited to join them. Further, when questioned on how often they would like to be included, both runaways (82%) and throwaways (63%) indicated that they would like to be included more often.

Only 13% of the runaways and 11% of the throwaways reported that difficulties with peers created problems which instigated running away. Further data suggest that neither runaways nor throwaways blindly follow their peers. When asked whether they always do what their friends want, the primary response of both runaways and throwaways was only once in a while. When asked if they argued for their own point of view, the majority of runaways (65%) and throwaways (53%) reported that they did so.

*Teacher-student relations.* Past research has indicated that runaways experience problems with their teachers and are likely to be viewed as impulsive youths. Using a seven-point scale with a series of contrasting characteristics (troublesome/cooperative, good/bad, breaks rules/obeys rules, rude/polite, bright/stupid, a friend/an enemy, easily frustrated/difficult to frustrate, strong willed/weak willed, secure/insecure, loses temper/never loses temper, acts without thinking/thinks before acting), the youths responded as to how they thought their teachers perceived them. Collapsing the scores for descriptive purposes into three general levels of response (low, medium, and high) the following

719

general profile emerged (see Table 1). It was found that both runaways and throwaways believe they are perceived as cooperative, good, rule-complying, polite, bright and friendly by their teachers. However, runaways thought their teachers perceived them as easily frustrated,

Table 1:  Youth's View of Teacher's Perception

| Characteristics | Low | | Medium | | High | |
|---|---|---|---|---|---|---|
| | n | % | n | % | n | % |
| Cooperative | [a]4 | (17.4) | 5 | (21.7) | 14 | (60.9) |
| | [b]1 | (5.2) | 6 | (31.6) | 12 | (63.2) |
| Good | 3 | (13.0) | 6 | (26.1) | 14 | (60.9) |
| | 4 | (21.1) | 4 | (21.1) | 11 | (57.8) |
| Obeys Rules | 8 | (34.7) | 5 | (21.7) | 10 | (43.6) |
| | 4 | (21.1) | 6 | (31.6) | 9 | (47.3) |
| Polite | 2 | (8.7) | 6 | (26.1) | 15 | (65.2) |
| | 1 | (5.2) | 4 | (21.1) | 14 | (73.7) |
| Bright | 3 | (13.1) | 5 | (21.7) | 15 | (65.2) |
| | 1 | (5.2) | 6 | (26.3) | 13 | (68.5) |
| Friend | 2 | (10.0) | 3 | (15.0) | 15 | (75.0) |
| | 2 | (11.1) | 1 | (5.6) | 15 | (83.3) |
| Easily Frustrated | 2 | (9.1) | 5 | (22.7) | 15 | (68.2) |
| | 7 | (36.8) | 5 | (26.4) | 7 | (36.8) |
| Strong Willed | 3 | (13.6) | 5 | (22.8) | 14 | (63.6) |
| | 2 | (10.5) | 4 | (21.1) | 13 | (68.4) |
| Secure | 4 | (18.2) | 8 | (36.4) | 10 | (45.5) |
| | 9 | (47.4) | 3 | (15.8) | 7 | (36.8) |
| Loses Temper | 4 | (17.4) | 7 | (30.4) | 12 | (52.2) |
| | 10 | (52.6) | 3 | (15.8) | 6 | (31.6) |
| Acts Without Thinking | 6 | (26.1) | 8 | (34.8) | 9 | (39.1) |
| | 5 | (26.3) | 4 | (21.1) | 10 | (52.6) |

Note: [a] = runaways; [b] = throwaways

720

strong willed, impulsive and quick tempered. Throwaways thought their teachers saw them as strong willed and quick tempered.

*Self-image.* Prior research has suggested that homeless youths maintain a poor self-image. Applying a measure originally utilized by the Opinion Research Corporation (1976), the youths responded to items designed to measure self-perceptions of personal worth, failure, pride, satisfaction with self, and sensations of uselessness on a five-point scale (response format: highly disagree, disagree, uncertain, agree, and highly agree). Collapsed scores for uncertain, agree, and highly agree indicate that both runaways (78%) and throwaways (89%) believed they were persons of worth. As to satisfaction with self, 78% of the runaways and 73% of the throwaways were to some degree satisfied. However, 82% of the runaways and 79% of the throwaways saw themselves as being a failure, while 64% of the runaways and 63% of the throwaways were not proud of themselves. Finally, 69% of the runaways and 53% of the throwaways also reported feeling useless.

## Significant Sex and Category Differences

Very little research has attempted to determine whether there are significant sex differences between categories of runaways and/or non-runaways. However, there are reasons to suspect certain differences. For example, some evidence suggests that males leave home primarily because of parent-child conflict (Wattenberg, 1956), while females are inclined to run because of lack of perceived warmth and affection, perceived problems with parental marriages, and pressure by parents for their daughters to assume rigidly defined family roles (Robey et al., 1964; Wolk & Brandon, 1977). Therefore, a series of sex × homeless youth categories (runaways versus throwaways) were computed on several composite scales derived from the descriptive data summarized earlier.

Analyses were computed on seven summated scales. Internal consistency of these scales reached an acceptable level: self-image items (alpha = .64), positive teacher-perception items (alpha = .63), negative teacher-perception items (alpha = .61), negative maternal (alpha = .43) and paternal items (alpha = .89), and positive maternal (alpha = .52) and paternal (alpha = .86) items. On the positive teacher-perception scale, throwaways ($M = 27.14$) believed that their teachers would see them in more positive ways than did runaways ($M = 19.22$), $F(1,39) = 5.70, p < .02$. A significant sex × homeless adolescent category interaction, $F(1,39) = 3.50, p < .05$, revealed male runaways ($M = 19.22$) held less positive perceptions than female runaways ($M = 25.08$), while male ($M = 27.85$) and female ($M = 26.00$) throwaways did not differ from each other but were more positive than their runaway counterparts. On the negative teacher-perception scale, no main

721

effect for sex or runaway category was observed; however, a significant interaction effect was noted, $F(1,39) = 7.56$, $p < .009$. Male ($M = 19.67$) and female ($M = 12.31$) runaways differed from each other, with male runaways believing that teachers would judge them less favorably. For male ($M = 12.46$) and female ($M = 19.00$) throwaways, the converse was observed. No other significant differences were observed on the remaining scales.

### DISCUSSION

Consistent with prior research, both runaways and throwaways perceived extensive parent-child conflict in their homes. Further, throwaways were more inclined than runaways to perceive their parents as wanting them to leave home. Similarly, the interpersonal relationship between parents was perceived to be more stressed by throwaways. Collectively, the psychodynamics of the family were filled with communication problems, conflict, and stress. A common theme for both categories of homeless adolescents was the perceived restrictive supervision by both parents. Such findings support earlier work by the Opinion Research Corporation (1976) and Wolk and Brandon (1977) which suggests that homeless youths may come from overly controlled homes where parents provide little room for autonomy and independence to grow. Further, the homeless youths in our sample perceived their fathers as being seldom satisfied or helpful with their adolescents. Also, throwaways were inclined to see their fathers as highly punitive. These data provide support for the assumptions advanced in internal social control theory—that limited emotional bonding is correlated with leaving home. Thus, runaways and throwaways experience apparent parent-child conflict; however, some descriptive data suggest that throwaways may come from more detached and conflicting homes.

Our homeless adolescent sample showed no evidence of being overly conforming to peer pressure effects. However, they did show signs of being socially isolated. If this occurred during a period of high peer involvement, it could result in less peer pressure strain than further diminished bonding with significant others. Thus, minimal bonding with family members and peers is likely to result in less internalization of normative social norms and create a broadened sense of social isolation and alienation. Alienated from home and peers, the adolescent may leave home to find warmth, love, or a caring other on the streets. As Young et al. (1983) have shown, however, very little of a positive nature is likely to occur as a result of leaving home prematurely and being on the streets.

722

Some support for the psychopathological perspective can be found on the measures of teachers perceptions and self-image. While both runaways and throwaways perceive themselves as being worthwhile, they also show signs of doubt and insecurity. Similarly, on the teacher-perception evaluations, homeless adolescents reported that teachers would see them as being undercontrolled and impulsive. They do not report high alienation and problems with teachers. Some sex differences were noted, but overall, sex differences were notably absent.

The findings of this study have strong implications for secondary prevention. Most youths return home at some point following a runaway incident (Opinion Research Corporation, 1976). Given that family problems are the crux of homeless adolescents' problems, social service personnel need to work with the total family to reduce communication problems, parent-child conflict, and stress. Training programs for working with "difficult" adolescents are much needed. Further, many runaway and throwaway adolescents could profit from being introduced to positive peer counseling, and social competence and friendship initiation training. Reduced peer problems could help ease some of the stress that is apparent in the home. Finally, individual counseling efforts could be initiated to help the easily frustrated and more impulsive adolescents to control their impulses. Though these actions may prevent future runaway incidents, they cannot be effective in totally resolving the potential negative consequences of the initial runaway incident.

## REFERENCES

Adams, G. R. Runaway youth projects: Comments on care programs for runaways and throwaways. *Adolescence*, 1980, *3*, 321–334.

Adams, G. R., & Munro, G. Portrait of the North American runaway: A critical review. *Journal of Youth and Adolescence*, 1979, *8*, 359–373.

Blood, L., & D'Angelo, R. A progress report on values issues in conflict between runaways and their parents. *Journal of Marriage and the Family*, 1974, *36*, 486–491.

Brennan, T., Huizinga, D., & Elliott, D. S. *The social psychology of runaways.* Boston, MA: D.C. Heath and Co., 1978.

Community Health and Welfare Council of Hennipin County, Minneapolis, Minnesota. *Follow-up study of runaway youth served by the bridge.* U.S. Department of Health, Education and Welfare, Washington, D.C., 1972.

D'Angelo, R. *Families of sand: A report concerning the flight of adolescents from their families.* National Directory of Runaway Centers, 1830 Connecticut Avenue, N.W., Washington, D.C., 1972.

English, C. Leaving home: A typology of runaways. *Society*, 1973, *10*, 22–24.

Gottlieb, D., & Chafetz, J. S. Dynamics of families' generational conflict and reconciliation. *Youth and Society*, 1977, *9*, 213–224.

723

Gullotta, T. P. Runaway: Reality or myth. *Adolescence*, 1978, *13*, 543–550.

Hildebrand, J. A. Why runaways leave home. *Journal of Criminal Law, Criminology and Police Science*, 1963, *54*, 211–216.

Hirschi, T. *Causes of delinquency*. Los Angeles, CA: University of California Press, 1969.

Johnson, N. S., & Peck, R. Sibship composition and the adolescent runaway phenomenon. *Journal of Youth and Adolescence*, 1978, *7*, 301–306.

Libertoff, R. *Runaway children and social network interaction*. Paper presented at the American Psychological Association, Washington, D.C., 1976.

Lourie, I. S., Campiglia, P., James, L. R., & DeWitt, J. Adolescent abuse and neglect: The role of runaway youth programs. *Children Today*, November 1979, 27–29.

Mathews, L. J., & Ilon, L. Becoming a chronic runaway: The effects of race and family in Hawaii. *Family Relations*, 1980, *29*, 404–409.

Opinion Research Corporation. *National statistical survey on runaway youth*. North Harrison Street, Princeton, NJ, 1976.

Robey, A., Rosenwald, R. J., Snell, J. E., & Lee, R. E. The runaway girl: A reaction to family stress. *American Journal of Orthopsychiatry*, 1964, *34*, 762–767.

Van Houten, T., & Golembiewski, G. *Adolescent life stress as a predictor of alcohol abuse and/or runaway behavior*. Washington, D.C.: Youth Alternatives Project, 1346 Connecticut Avenue, N.W., 1978.

Wattenberg, W. Boys who run away from home. *Journal of Educational Psychology*, 1956, *47*, 335–343.

Wolk, S., & Brandon, J. Runaway adolescents' perceptions of parents and self. *Adolescence*, 1977, *12*, 175–188.

Young, R. L., Godfrey, W., Mathews, B., & Adams, G. R. Runaways: A review of negative consequences and diminishing choices. *Family Relations*, 1983.

724

JOURNAL OF RESEARCH ON ADOLESCENCE, 3(3), 271–294
Copyright © 1993, Lawrence Erlbaum Associates, Inc.

# Who Drops Out of and Who Continues Beyond High School? A 20-Year Follow-Up of Black Urban Youth

Jeanne Brooks-Gunn
*Teachers College*
*Columbia University*

Guang Guo
*University of North Carolina*

Frank F. Furstenberg, Jr.
*University of Pennsylvania*

The antecedents of dropping out of high school and continuing beyond high school are explored in a 20-year follow-up of the first-born children of about 250 Black teenage mothers who gave birth in the late 1960s in Baltimore. In 1988, the first-born children of the teenage mothers were making the transition to young adulthood (*M* age = 19 years). Thirty-seven percent had dropped out of school, 46% had completed high school, and 17% had gone on for postsecondary school education. Predictors of completing high school versus not completing high school were estimated as well as antecedents of continuing beyond high school versus completing high school. Events and characteristics occurring during the mothers' pregnancy in the first year of life, young childhood, middle childhood, and young adolescence were examined. Family circumstances (welfare use, presence of father or grandmother), maternal commitment to education, child's elementary grade school failure, child's preschool cognitive ability, and young adolescent behaviors such as pregnancy were potential antecedents. Number of years the father was present, high maternal educational aspirations in the child's first year of life, being prepared for school, and not repeating a grade during elementary school were predictive of completing high school. Few years on welfare, high

Requests for reprints should be sent to Jeanne Brooks-Gunn, Center for Young Children and Families, Teachers College, Columbia University, New York, NY 10027.

preschool cognitive ability, attendance in preschool, and no grade failure in elementary school were predictive of continuing beyond high school. Policy implications of these findings are considered.

Educational attainment is one of the most potent predictors of life-course trajectories in adulthood (Featherman & Hauser, 1978; Haveman & Wolfe, 1984; Jencks et al., 1979; Sewell & Hauser, 1975). Decisions about whether to complete high school and, if so, whether to obtain postsecondary school education are made typically during the transition to young adulthood (Hogan & Astone, 1986). These decisions themselves may be seen as the culmination of individual proclivities as well as a series of events and choices made during the childhood and young adolescent years. Whatever the process by which they are made, decisions about dropping out of or continuing beyond high school, in and of themselves, constitute some of the most important made by youth in Western society.[1]

The antecedents of educational attainment have been studied using a variety of disciplines and conceptual models, with intergenerational effects always considered to be a major determinant (Hauser & Featherman, 1977; Haveman, Wolfe, & Spaulding, 1991; Hill & Duncan, 1987; Rumberger, 1987). Sets of antecedents include family factors, contexts other than the family, and individual characteristics. Family factors include economic situation, socialization practices, and relationships. Economic situation encompasses actual income as well as the ways in which resources are allocated in the family (Becker, 1981; Becker & Tomes, 1986).[2] Family socialization includes such processes as specific parenting behaviors and beliefs about parenting that influence children, observations made by children, and modeling of parental behavior (Maccoby & Martin, 1983). Relationships are usually not considered, even though intergenerational transmission of educational attainment

---

[1]It is important to note that these decisions, although they have vast ramifications, are subject to change. For example, national rates of high-school completion are about 10% higher for 20- to 24-year-olds than for 18- to 19-year-olds. Education continues for some individuals who are even older: In the Baltimore study of teenage mothers, one half spent at least 1 year in school between the times that their first born were 5 to 15, and one third of those who had not graduated from high school earlier did so during this period (Furstenberg, Brooks-Gunn, & Morgan, 1987a; see also Stroup & Robins, 1972).

[2]Income and time resources may interact in complex ways (i.e., working mothers have less time to spend with children but more economic resources to purchase high-quality child care than do nonworking mothers). These economic factors probably influence psychological factors (i.e., having less income may result in more psychological distress, which may influence the ways in which mothers treat their children).

may depend on how close children feel to their parents, or the impact of the mother–father relationship on children directly or indirectly. Specific familial events may influence children's education via a number of processes subsumed under these three sets of potential antecedents.[3]

Educational attainment is influenced also by larger contexts such as the peer group, the neighborhood, and the school (Bryk & Thum, 1989; Natriello, 1987; Wehlage & Rutter, 1986). Affiliating with peers who have already dropped out and exhibiting behavior not conducive to doing well in school are associated with lowered educational attainment (Cairns, Cairns, Neckerman, Ferguson, & Gariepy, 1989; Stattin & Magnusson, 1990). Opportunities to interact with peers with low attachment to education are probably greater in certain neighborhoods, specifically those characterized by high rates of unemployment, single parenthood, and poverty, as well as low numbers of professional workers. Several investigators have considered these to be "contagion" effects, that probably operate for youth behavior such as teenage childbearing and school drop out (Brooks-Gunn, Duncan, Klebanov, & Sealand, in press; Crane, 1991; Steinberg, 1987). School effects have been studied extensively, with most studies showing smaller effects of school composition and quality variables compared to familial sociodemographic variables (Mayer & Jencks, 1989). It is difficult to separate intergenerational from school contextual effects, given that more poor families tend to live in neighborhoods with poorer quality schools (Mayer & Jencks, 1989).

Individual differences exist in general cognitive ability and motivation, each of which is associated with school performance. Additionally, these characteristics themselves are associated with familial, school, and peer factors (Rumberger, 1983; Willett & Singer, 1991).

Most prospective studies of educational attainment begin when the child is in middle or senior high school, allowing for an examination of intergenerational factors such as parental education and occupation as well as school factors and individual characteristics during the adolescent years (Rumberger, 1987). By design, this research is unable to examine school and individual characteristics during the preschool or elementary school years, except through retrospective reports. A longer time frame is necessary to examine early antecedents of educational attainment (Brooks-Gunn, Phelps, & Elder, 1991).

---

[3]For example, father absence, which has been shown to influence educational attainment (McLanahan, 1985), may have its effect via a drop in income, less time spent with any parental figure, or lower quality child care being purchased (economic); less optimal socialization by the mother or fewer socialization opportunities due to the presence of only one mother (socialization); or loss of a parental attachment figure (relationship).

With the notable exception of recent analyses of the Panel Study of Income Dynamics (PSID; Haveman et al., 1991) and the National Longitudinal Survey of Youth (NLSY; Sandefur, McLanahan, & Wojtkiewicz, 1992), the *timing* of or *changes* in specific family, school, and peer events during the childhood and adolescent years has not been examined vis-à-vis educational attainment. Generally, it is believed that family events occurring during two transitional periods—young childhood or the transition from preschool to elementary school and young adolescence or the transition from elementary school to middle school— have more impact on behavior than events from other age periods (Brooks-Gunn, 1988; Lerner, 1984; Lerner & Foch, 1987; Wachs & Gruen, 1982). However, few studies are able to compare the impact of events occurring at different ages because they are not long-term prospective studies (Brooks-Gunn et al., 1991). Exceptions include several small-scale longitudinal studies spanning from birth or the first years of life through the transition to adulthood (cf. Furstenberg, Brooks-Gunn, & Morgan, 1987b; Gjerde & Block, 1991; Werner & Smith, 1982) as well as the nationally representative long-term follow-up studies such as the PSID, the National Survey of Children, and the Children of the NLSY (Brooks-Gunn et al., 1991; Chase-Lansdale, Mott, Brooks-Gunn, & Phillips, 1991). Our study uses 20 years worth of data to look at events occurring prior to the birth of the child, during young childhood, middle to late childhood, and young adolescence as they relate to educational attainment at age 19.

This article focuses on two educational outcomes—completing high school and continuing beyond high school. These transitions must be modeled separately because their antecedents may differ (Mare, 1980; Mare & Chen, 1986; Willett & Singer, 1991). The data come from a 20-year follow-up of Black urban teenage mothers and their first-born children (Furstenberg et al., 1987b). We focus on the educational attainment of the first-born children as they make the transition into adulthood.

## METHOD

### Sample

The sample is based on the Baltimore study, which is a long-term, multigenerational study of teenage mothers, their mothers, and their first-born children. In 1966 to 1968, teenagers younger than 18 who were pregnant with their first child and who came to a hospital in Baltimore for prenatal care were interviewed as part of an evaluation of a prenatal-care program for adolescent mothers. At that time, 404 teenagers and their mothers were interviewed. The teenage mothers were reinterviewed five times over the next 20 years—1, 3, 5, 17, and 20 years after the initial interview. The first-born children were assessed at the 5-year contact point (1972, when they were preschoolers), the 17-year point (1984, when they were in the middle of adolescence), and the 20-year point (1988, when they were making the transition into adulthood).

At the 20-year follow-up, 254 first-born children were seen; they were on average a little older than 19 years.[4] For the three pairs of twins, one case was selected for analytic purposes ($n = 251$; 125 males and 126 females). Attrition occurred primarily in the first years of the study, because of giving up the child for adoption and leaving the Baltimore area. Most of the small sample of White mothers were also lost to follow-up. Of those children who were seen at the 5-year point, 82% were seen 15 years later at the 20-year follow-up (Furstenberg, Levine, & Brooks-Gunn, 1990; see Furstenberg et al., 1987b, for analyses of respondents and nonrespondents at the 17-year follow-up).

The original group of teenage mothers, although not selected to be a representative sample, was similar to Black youths who became mothers in Baltimore in the late 1960s (Furstenberg, 1976). The young mothers came from relatively disadvantaged backgrounds; one fourth of their families were on welfare, half of them came from single parent homes, half had four or more siblings, half of their mothers had a 10th grade education or less, and most of their mothers were teenage parents themselves.

At the 17-year follow-up, a little more than two thirds of the original Black teenage mothers had received a high school education, one fourth were receiving welfare, and three fifths had work continuously the past 5 years. These mothers had, on average, 2.3 children. Examination of family incomes indicates that one fourth were enjoying a relatively high income (more than $25,000 a year), with another one fourth earning more than $15,000 but less than $25,000. The rest would be classified as poor or near poor. Comparisons with three national samples of Black mothers of the same age residing in metropolitan areas indicate that the Baltimore study families are similar to representative samples of teenage childbearers, and more disadvantaged than older childbearers (Furstenberg et al., 1987b; p. 144).

Although one third of the mothers were married at the 1984 follow-

---

[4]We realize that school attainment is underestimated in our sample, given the age range. Many of the Baltimore study first-borns had failed a grade in school, resulting in high-school graduation occurring later for some youths. Indeed, 24 youths were still in high school in 1988.

up, only one half of these mothers were married to the father of the first-born child. Consequently, only 16% of the offspring had resided with their biological fathers throughout their childhood and young adolescence. Only one fifth of the youths not living with their fathers saw them on a weekly basis during their young adolescent years, with the figure being similar during the young childhood years. Although in almost all cases the teenage mothers were the primary parents, many of the children lived with their grandmothers, especially when they were young. One fourth of the offspring had spent at least 3 months apart from their mothers at some point in their lives, and one tenth had lived with someone else for 2 years or more. Indeed, one third of the offspring reported in 1984 that someone other than their mothers was also "like a mother to them," suggesting that co-parenting occurred in many families (Brooks-Gunn & Chase-Lansdale, 1991; Brooks-Gunn & Fursten-berg, 1987).

## Measures

*Educational attainment.* In 1988, the youths were asked what the highest grade was that they had completed. They were also asked about dropping out of and returning to high school.

*Maternal and familial characteristics.* Maternal and familial charac-teristics were examined by the time of their occurrence. Four develop-mental stages were defined, based on the age of the first-born children — pregnancy of mother/first year of child's life, young childhood, middle childhood, and young adolescence. Characteristics of the family envi-ronment in the second half of adolescence were not examined because they were measured at the same time as the dependent measures.

The following family characteristics of the teenage mothers' family of origin were measured prior to the birth of the target child: number of children in the family (three or more coded as *high*), employment of the head of household, education of the parents (high school completion coded as *high*), and welfare receipt during the teenage mother's child-hood and adolescence. The following maternal characteristics were included for the childhood and adolescent stages because they have been shown to be associated with educational attainment: maternal education, welfare use, presence of father, presence of grandmother, and changes of head of household.

Three measures of maternal commitment to education were con-structed: having failed a grade in school prior to the time of the preg-nancy, having high eduational aspirations for the child when the child was 1 year of age (going beyond high school), and having completed high school during the young childhood and young adolescent period. These measures tap somewhat different aspects of educational commitment: actual attainment (and timing of attainment), aspirations, and ability (i.e., having failed a grade in school being used as a very rough proxy for ability and motivation).

Welfare use was measured each year of the mother's life since the birth of the child through a life-event calendar. Such calendars yield quite accurate data (see Furstenberg et al., 1987b, for a discussion of the reliability of these data). The number of years on welfare was calculated for three developmental stages: young childhood (birth through 4 years), childhood (5 through 10 years), and young adolescence (11 through 15 years).

The life-event calendars were used to determine the presence of the biological father, presence of the grandmother, and single head of household for each year of the child's life and for all developmental stages.[5]

*Child gender.* Sex of the child was entered at all periods except pregnancy.

*Child's cognitive ability.* In the young childhood period, the verbal and general ability of the child were measured using the Peabody Picture Vocabulary Test (PPVT; Dunn & Dunn, 1981), which assesses verbal ability by asking children to point to one of four pictures that depicts a word read to them (the mean in this sample was 86; the national norm is 100) and the Caldwell Cooperative Child Behavior Inventory (Cooperative Tests & Services, 1970), which assesses a range of skills including concept recognition, associative vocabulary, and social responsiveness (mean was 63; national norm is 100). Scores were transformed into age-standardized $z$ scores based on the standard deviations of the sample by age. From the information gathered in 1984, grade failure during elementary school was ascertained. During adolescence, youths were asked also about their aspirations for higher education (dummy coded as *desire for postsecondary school education*).

*Child's schooling history.* Unfortunately, little information is available on the quality of schools attended by the youths. Two available measures are whether the child was attending preschool in 1972 (often

---

[5]Single-parent head of household could not be entered into equations with father and grandmother presence. Substituting single-parent head of household for presence of father of the child resulted in no significant effects on dropping out of school or continuing education past high school.

Head Start or another community program for disadvantaged young-sters). In middle and senior high school, the racial composition of the school was reported; this represents a very rough proxy for what has been termed *social isolation* (Wilson, 1991), and is associated directly with poverty and indirectly with school quality measures such as amount spent per pupil (Orfield & Ashkinaze, 1991). The measure used here was the number of Black students out of every 10, averaged across grades and schools.

*Adolescent behavior.*   Three other measures were collected when the child was 14 to 16; these were number of times having run away from home, having imbided alcohol, having been pregnant (or gotten a girl pregnant). These reflect problem behaviors generally associated with lower educational attainment (Jessor & Jessor, 1977; Mensch & Kandel, 1988). Additionally, pregnancy, childbearing, and marriage are the most common reasons for girls' dropping out of high school (Ekstrom, Goertz, Pollack, & Rock, 1986).

## RESULTS

### Educational Attainment

Of those who were not still in high school (230), 17% had completed at least 1 year of, or were currently in their first year of, post-high school education, 46% had graduated from high school and had not gone on for further education, and 37% had left high school prior to completing the 12th grade (at this point). Youths who had a high school equivalency degree were considered to have graduated from high school ($N = 15$). The dependent variables in the following logistic regressions are based on these three groups: dropouts, graduates, and continuers.

The overall dropout rate for the sample is 34%, with more boys than girls having dropped out at least once (40% vs. 29%). More than four fifths of those who reported dropping out left school only once. The vast majority of dropouts occurred in the 9th, 10th, and 11th grades. Virtually no dropouts were reported in 7th and 8th grades. Figure 1 presents the survival curves by grade and gender for those individuals who did not drop out (Willett & Singer, 1991). By 10th grade, the number of boys having dropped out was higher than the number of girls, a difference that continues through high school.

Slightly more than two fifths of the sample had repeated a grade in school (49% of the boys and 36% of the girls). Grade repetition was associated with eventual school dropout, as is seen in Figure 2.

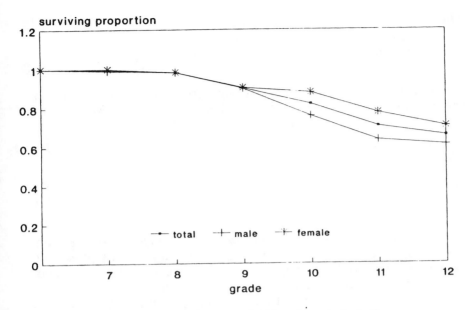

FIGURE 1 Surviving the hazard of dropping out of school.

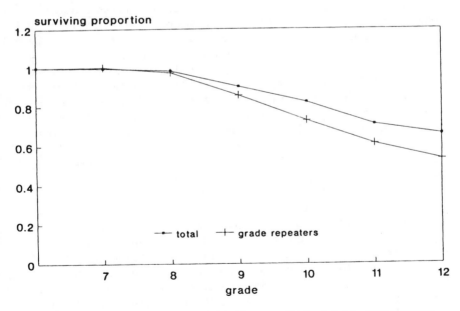

FIGURE 2 Surviving the hazard of dropping out of school, total versus repeaters (those who have ever repeated in grades 1-6).

## Regression Analyses

The statistical model used here is the continuation ratio model, a variation of the logistic regression (Fienberg, 1980; Mare, 1980):

$$\frac{p_2^{+3}}{p_1} = \exp{(XB_1)} \qquad (1)$$

$$\frac{p_3}{p_2} = \exp{(XB_2)} \qquad (2)$$

where $p_1$, $p_2$, and $p_3$ stand for the probabilities of being in the ordered categories of dropouts, high-school graduate, and post-high-school education, respectively; $X$ stands for a vector of covariates; and $B_1$ and $B_2$ stand for two sets of coefficients for the two odds ratios. The sum of $p_1$, $p_2$, and $p_3$ is unity. The first odds ratio (Equation 1) represents the probability of being a high-school graduate or having received at least some post-high-school education rather than dropping out of high school ($N = 230$). The second odds ratio (Equation 2) is the probability of receiving some post-high-school education rather than being a high-school graduate. The second odds ratio is constructed on the condition that every respondent has graduated from high school ($N = 146$). We estimated these models using S–PLUS, a statistical package (StatSci, 1991). Two sets of regression models for the two odds ratios were estimated for each of the four developmental stages. A model including factors from pregnancy and childhood-developmental stages was also constructed. In Tables 1 through 3, coefficients rather than exponentiated coefficients are presented. For instance, in Table 1, the coefficient $-0.67$ for male in the young childhood period is interpreted as male being more likely to drop out of school. The exponent (0.67) is 1.95, which is interpreted as a male being two times more likely than a female to drop out of school.

Additionally, a set of analyses was conducted in order to see whether the predictors have different effects for the two contrasts—graduates versus dropouts and postsecondary attenders versus graduates (test of the null of equal effects). Two models are estimated during one single data set that combines the two contrasts. In the more restrictive model, the predictors are constrained to have the same effects for the two contrasts. In the less restrictive model, the predictors are allowed to have different effects for the two contrasts. Because the two models are nested, a likelihood ratio test is conducted to see whether the less restrictive model (which has more parameters) improves over the more

TABLE 1
Antecedents of High-School Completion[a]: Logistic Regressions by Age of Child

| Antecedents | Prebirth/ Infancy[b] | Young Childhood[c] | Middle Childhood | Young Adolescence |
|---|---|---|---|---|
| Family Circumstances | | | | |
| Number of years father was present | — | 0.17 | 0.32*** | 0.44** |
| Number of years grandmother was present | — | 0.04 | 0.15 | −0.07 |
| Number of years on welfare | — | −0.08 | −0.07 | −0.05 |
| Educational Commitment | | | | |
| Grandmother's education | — | — | — | — |
| Aspirations of mother[d] | 0.63** | — | — | — |
| Educational attainment of mother[e] | — | 0.29 | — | 0.31 |
| Off grade level | −0.45 | — | — | — |
| Child's scholastic performance | | | | |
| Preschool general ability[f] | — | 0.35** | — | — |
| Grade failure[g] | — | — | −1.34*** | — |
| Educational aspirations[d] | — | — | — | 1.68*** |
| Child's schooling history | | | | |
| Preschool attendance | — | 0.37 | — | — |
| Racial composition of middle school | — | — | — | −0.21*** |
| Child's gender (Male) | — | −0.67*** | −0.71*** | −1.16*** |
| Adolescent behavior | | | | |
| Number of times run away | — | — | — | −0.34* |
| Drink | — | — | — | −0.79** |
| Number of pregnancies | — | — | — | −1.73*** |

Note. Dashes represent coefficients not measured in the time/age period.

[a]The reference category is high-school dropout. [b]The logistic regressions for the prebirth period also included the following socioeconomic characteristics of the family of origin: number of children in the family, and receipt of welfare. These variables did not predict high-school completion in the grandchildren. [c]The number of years for young childhood were birth to 4; for middle childhood, 5 to 10; and for adolescence, 11 to 15. [d]Educational aspirations was dummy coded as aspiring to postsecondary education. [e]Educational attainment was dummy coded as high-school graduate. [f]Caldwell Child Behavior Inventory, age standardized. [g]Grade failure in elementary school.

*$p < .10$. **$p < .05$. ***$p < .01$. (All $p$ values two-tailed.)

restrictive model. For each age period, the added explanatory power in the less restrictive model is highly statistically significant, suggesting that the predictors for the two contrasts are different.

## Antecedents of Completing High School by Age of the Child

Table 1 presents the coefficients for the independent variables for each developmental stage separately. The models for each of the stages are

TABLE 2

Antecedents of Continuing Beyond High School[a]: Logistic Regressions by Age of Child

| Antecedents | Prebirth/ Infancy[b] | Young Childhood[c] | Middle Childhood | Young Adolescence |
|---|---|---|---|---|
| Family Circumstances[c] | | | | |
| Number of years father was present | — | −0.24 | −0.17** | −0.18* |
| Number of years grandmother was present | — | 0.19 | 0.13 | 0.14 |
| Number of years on welfare | — | −0.35 | −0.35*** | −0.30* |
| Educational Commitment | | | | |
| Grandmothers' education | — | — | — | — |
| Aspirations of mother[d] | 0.33 | — | — | — |
| Educational attainment of mother[e] | — | 0.14 | — | 0.68 |
| Off grade level | −0.48* | — | — | — |
| Child's scholastic performance | | | | |
| Preschool general ability[f] | — | 0.57* | — | — |
| Grade failure[g] | — | — | −1.95** | — |
| Educational aspirations[d] | — | — | — | 1.33** |
| Child's schooling history | | | | |
| Preschool attendance | — | 0.78* | — | — |
| Racial composition of middle school | — | — | — | −0.03 |
| Child's gender (Male) | — | −0.10 | 0.13 | −0.15 |
| Adolescent behavior | | | | |
| Number of times run away | — | — | — | −0.53 |
| Drink | — | — | — | 0.42 |
| Number of pregnancies | — | — | — | −1.03 |

Note. Dashes represent coefficients not measured in the time/age period.

[a]The reference category is high-school graduation. [b]The logistic regressions for the prebirth period also included the following socioeconomic characteristics of the family of origin: number of children in the family, receipt of welfare. These variables did not predict postsecondary education. [c]The number of years for young childhood were birth to 4; for middle childhood, 5 to 10; and for adolescence, 11 to 15. [d]Educational aspirations was dummy coded as aspiring to postsecondary education. [e]Educational attainment was dummy coded as high-school graduate. [f]Caldwell Child Behavior Inventory, age standardized. [g]Grade failure in elementary school.

*$p < .10$. **$p < .05$. ***$p < .01$. (All $p$ values two-tailed.)

significantly different from the null model, $p < .01$ for the prebirth period, and $p < .001$ for the other three periods.

The prebirth/infancy age model (column 1) includes family of origin background variables and teenage mother education variables. Only the latter contribute to the likelihood of school dropout 20 years later. When the teenage mother had aspirations to go beyond high school, the likelihood of her child's dropping out of school 20 years later is reduced.

The young childhood age model (column 2) includes both maternal characteristics and child characteristics that contribute to the odds of

TABLE 3
Childhood Antecedents of High-School Completion and Postsecondary Schooling[a]

| Antecedents | High-School Completion[a] | Postsecondary Schooling[b] |
|---|---|---|
| Family circumstances[c] | | |
| Number of years father was present (0–4) | −0.09 | −0.29 |
| Number of years father was present (5–10) | 0.34*** | −0.07 |
| Number of years of welfare (0–4) | −0.02 | −0.28* |
| Number of years of welfare (5–10) | 0.00 | −0.11 |
| Educational commitment | | |
| Aspirations of mother[d] | 0.54* | −0.00 |
| Educational attainment[e] | 0.09 | 0.23 |
| Off grade level[d] | −0.28 | −0.22 |
| Child's scholastic performance | | |
| Preschool general ability[e] | 0.20 | 0.53* |
| Grade failure[f] | −1.22*** | −1.75*** |
| Child's preschool attendance[e] | 0.50 | 0.79 |
| Child's gender (Male) | −0.65*** | 0.08 |

[a]Reference category is school dropout. [b]Reference category is high-school graduation. [c]1st to 10th year. [d]Measured prior to the child's birth. [e]Measured in the young childhood period. [f]Grade failure during elementary school.
*$p < .10$. **$p < .05$. ***$p < .01$. (All $p$ values two-tailed.)

dropping out of high school 15 years later. Only child characteristics contribute, with general ability and preschool attendance reducing the likelihood of dropping out of school.

The middle childhood age model (column 3) indicates that the presence of the father of the child exerts a positive influence on graduating from high school. The largest effect is seen for having repeated a grade during elementary school.

In the young-adolescence age model (column 4), the presence of the father of the child is still a protective factor for preventing dropout. Racial composition of the high school is associated with dropout, with less racially integrated school environments being a risk factor for dropout. The youth's aspirations for postsecondary-school education are associated with staying in school (reducing dropout by about 80%), whereas pregnancy, drinking, and running away increase the likelihood of dropping out.

Table 3 presents an overall logistic regression model predicting school dropout, summarizing across the first three developmental stages. Here, three maternal education variables are entered: aspirations for post-high-school education in the child's first year of life, being off grade level at the time of the pregnancy, and maternal education in the child's first years of life. Family characteristics include number of years of father presence and welfare use in early childhood (birth to 4 years) and childhood (5 to 10 years).[6] Child characteristics include sex, general ability score, and grade repeat in elementary school. Characteristics from the first half of adolescence were not entered because they may co-occur with the decision to drop out. High maternal aspirations for one's own education around the time of the birth of the child reduce the likelihood of dropping out of school 15 to 20 years later, not of educational attainment, and all other variables. Maternal educational attainment in the early years and being on grade level are not protective factors. Father presence in middle childhood contributes to high-school graduation. Repeating a grade in elementary school and being a boy increase the odds of dropping out of high school dramatically.

## Antecedents of Postsecondary Education by Age of the Child

Table 2 presents the logistic regressions for each of the four ages; the comparison is continuing postsecondary education versus not going beyond high-school graduation. Each model is significantly different from the null model.

Being off grade level at the time of the pregnancy reduced the odds of continuing past high school for the offspring 20 years later. Attending preschool and high general ability in preschool were significantly associated with postsecondary-school education. Sex of the child did not contribute to the model.

Father presence and welfare use during middle childhood reduce the likelihood of attending postsecondary schools. Repeating a grade during elementary school lowers the likelihood of continuing school by about 85%.

The effects of welfare and father presence are similar during the young-adolescent period. Aspirations for additional education raise the likelihood of obtaining postsecondary schooling by age 19.

In the overall model (Table 3), the negative effects of welfare use persist. The high general ability raises the odds of postsecondary schooling, whereas the repetition of a grade in elementary school lowers the odds.

## DISCUSSION

The findings from the analyses of childhood and adolescent antecedents of two school transitions—completing high school and obtaining

---

[6]Regressions were also constructed entering welfare use and father presence for the two developmental stages together. Results indicate father presence was associated with completing high school, and number of years of welfare with not going on to college.

postsecondary education—have several policy implications. First and most generally, the Baltimore study focuses on a group at great risk for low education at all points in the school career. To some, it may be surprising that given their risk status, two thirds of the Baltimore sample had completed high school, and one sixth were obtaining postsecondary schooling. Nevertheless, about one third of these Black urban youths had dropped out of school. Many of these youths had difficulties early on. About 50% had preschool cognitive test scores equal to or under 85; low scores on preschool assessments such as the ones used in the Baltimore study indicate that the children were not well prepared for elementary school,[7] and not being prepared has consequences 15 years later. More than one third had failed a grade during elementary school, perhaps the strongest harbinger of school disengagement later on. By the time the children were making the transition to adulthood, one third had dropped out of high school and only 17% were obtaining post-secondary schooling. Although a fraction of the dropouts will go on the get GEDs (perhaps 10%; Willet & Singer, 1991) and a number of high-school graduates will enter college, it is unlikely that a large proportion of this sample will become college graduates, based on their mothers' experiences in the last two decades as well as on national projections (Furstenberg et al., 1990). This study mirrors others in documenting the disengagement of a large number, but not the majority, of poor Black urban youths today (Fine, 1986).[8]

---

[7]Although preschool assessments, like cognitive tests at all age points, exhibit some biases against disadvantaged and minority children, they are modestly associated with achievement in elementary school, as seen in the Baltimore study (correlations between Caldwell Preschool Inventory and the PPVT with grade failure are $-.20$ and $-.16$). This is in part due to the fact that teachers, and the school setting in general, value the behaviors—cognitive, motivational, and emotional—measured in preschool tests (Alexander & Entwhisle, 1988; Lee et al., 1990).

[8]To address the issue of representativeness, comparisons with the National Survey of Children (NSC) were made (Furstenberg, Hughes, & Brooks-Gunn, 1992). The NSC is a longitudinal study of a nationally representative sample of 2,279 children born between 1964 and 1969 who were interviewed when they were ages 7 to 11. A subsample of a little more than a thousand children was seen again in 1981 and in 1987–1988. The youths were between 17 and 21 years of age at the last interview, comparable in age and cohort to the Baltimore sample (Furstenberg, Nord, Peterson, & Zill, 1983; Peterson & Zill, 1986). Compared with the NSC Black sample in 1988, who were ages 18 to 21, the Baltimore Black youths were more likely to experience grade failure (42% vs. 26%) and school dropout (34% vs. 17%), and less likely to have graduated from high school (63% vs. 86%). These differences are no doubt influenced by the fact that the Baltimore sample is composed entirely of youths whose mothers were teenage childbearers. The youths in the NSC sample whose mothers were age 17 or younger at the birth of the first child were more likely to have dropped out and to have repeated a grade than those whose mothers were age 20 or older at the time of the birth of the first child. However, the Baltimore youths' educational history was still lower than that of the NSC Black youths of teenage

Second, and perhaps more important from a policy view, this 20-year follow-up documents the familial factors over the childhood and adolescent years most likely to predict success (keeping in mind that a limited, albeit an important, set of family factors was measured in this study on a yearly basis). Experiences in the family of origin of the mother constitute the basis on which mothers develop their commitment to education as well as influence the mother's life-course trajectory. Here, maternal aspirations for education beyond high school at the time of birth exert an influence on high-school dropout 20 years later, controlling for maternal educational ability very roughly (via whether the mother was off grade level at the time of the pregnancy) and family-of-origin characteristics. In contrast, being on grade level, rather than aspiring to post-high-school education, contributed somewhat to their children's postsecondary educational attainment. It is possible that grade repetition is capturing both general ability and educational commitment, and that ability is more important for continuing education than for not dropping out of school.[9] These findings speak to the importance of keeping teenage mothers engaged in schooling. Not only is the mother's school and work trajectory altered (Furstenberg, Brooks-Gunn, & Morgan, 1987a; Upchurch & McCarthy, 1989, 1990), but so is the child's. Programs that help the teenage mother stay in school, provide the young child with high-quality care, and provide the mother with parenting skills are particularly promising interventions (Clewell, Brooks-Gunn, & Benasich, 1989; Furstenberg, Brooks-Gunn, & Chase-Lansdale, 1989; Polit, 1989). In an earlier phase of the Baltimore study that focused on the mothers of the youths in this analysis, one half of the original teenage mothers who participated were randomly assigned to a

---

childbearers (Furstenberg et al., 1992). This difference might be due to the urban composition of the Baltimore sample (the NSC sample is not large enough to conduct separate analyses for metropolitan area youths), given regional and community variations in dropout rates (Ekstrom et al., 1986) as well as slight age variations across samples. A partial answer to this speculation is offered by analyses conducted comparing the Baltimore sample to the sample of 3,618 youths assessed in the National Assessment of Educational Progress (NAEP) Young Adult Literacy Survey in 1985 (Kirsch & Jungeblut, 1986). The Baltimore sample was similar to the NAEP subsample of metropolitan Black youths in terms of literacy scores (with 19% of the Baltimore and 17% of the NAEP subsample being functionally illiterate; Baydar et al., 1993). High-school graduation rates were also similar (30% in the Baltimore and 25% in the NAEP samples of youths 19 years of age or older). Consequently, we believe that our results are relevant for Black youths in metropolitan areas. However, given that dropout rates, and their predictors, differ for Whites, Hispanics, and Blacks in some studies (e.g., Ekstrom et al., 1986; but see Haveman et al., 1991), our results should not be generalized to other ethnic groups (Coombs & Cooley, 1968; Rumberger, 1987).

[9]At the same time, decisions regarding dropping out or staying in school may be of some consequence to eventual cognitive ability (Shavit & Featherman, 1988).

special prenatal clinic, and more than one half (nonrandom assignment) went to a special high school for pregnant teenagers. Participation in the special high school was associated with higher aspirations following the birth of the child, higher educational attainment, and decreased welfare use. These factors incluenced the educational attainments of the young mothers' offspring (Furstenberg et al., 1987b). These findings speak to the influence of teenage mothers' schooling on their own, as well as their children's, well-being.

As expected, family circumstances over the child's life played a significant role in educational attainment (Featherman, Spenner, & Tsunematsu, 1988). Welfare use exerts a risk factor for not continuing past high school but does not influence dropout rates in this relatively disadvantaged sample. Previous research, including both Black and White families and a greater number of families at the higher end of the socioeconomic scale, is mixed as to the influence of welfare receipt on high-school attainment (Stafford, 1986). In the analyses most comparable to ours, welfare receipt is negatively associated with high school graduation in the PSID sample of Blacks and Whites; the PSID does not include measures of preschool ability or grade failure, which could account for the differences between the results of the PSID in the Baltimore study (see also Sandefur et al., 1992). Moving families off welfare, which could influence the school histories of children, is a goal of many programs. The Family Support Act of 1988 is a national programmatic approach to shortening welfare stays. Whether this act will alter the proportion of families receiving public assistance is not known yet; it also is unclear whether any indirect benefits accrue to children (Chase-Lansdale & Brooks-Gunn, in press). By providing child care and health-insurance vouchers, programs initiated under the Family Support Act have the potential of influencing young children directly, via higher quality care and better health (Hayes, Palmer, & Zaslow, 1990; Hofferth & Phillips, 1987; Lobach, in press; McCormick & Brooks-Gunn, 1989).

The presence of the father in the middle childhood and young adolescent years of the child's life significantly lowers the rate of school dropout. Whether this effect is due to a positive father–child relationship, the indirect effects of the presence of the father on the mother–child relationship, income, or unmeasured differences associated with familial stability is not known. However, in a set of analyses not reported here, stability of male presence was measured by the number of changes in males residing in the household over the child's life; a high number of transitions was associated with dropout, over and above the presence of the biological father, suggesting an adverse influence of marital disruptions or familial transitions more generally on

341

educational attainment. Others have reported a similar finding (Hetherington & Arestek, 1988; Lee, Brooks-Gunn, Schnur, & Liaw, 1990; McLanahan & Garfinkel, 1990; see also Duncan, Brooks-Gunn, & Klebanov, in press, for a similar finding for age 5 behavior problems and IQ). We cannot determine whether the father presence and male-stability effects are in part due to overall income or changes in income, as some have hypothesized (although we do not expect income to account for the entire effect; Astone & McLanahan, 1991; Garfinkel & McLanahan, 1986; Sandefur et al., 1992). A paradoxical effect of father presence was found for continuing beyond high school, because those youth whose fathers were present were less likely to be continuers (in the separate developmental-stage models, but not in the overall model). Exploratory analyses including only the youth who completed high school indicate that those with fathers present were more likely to be working than those whose fathers were absent. We speculate that father presence may encourage entrance into the work force, rather than discontinuation of education, given the relatively high unemployment rates of Black urban youths (Wilson, 1987).

General ability in young childhood and attending preschool were associated with continuing education past high school. In an analysis of the predictors of literacy in young adulthood, preschool ability was also associated with high literacy levels in young adulthood (Baydar, Brooks-Gunn, & Furstenberg, in press). The mean literacy levels of youth going on were higher than those for youth who graduated from high school or dropped out. General ability was highly associated with grade failure in 1984 (Furstenberg et al., 1987b). Taken together, these findings suggest that preschool ability influences school dropout indirectly via its impact on grade failure, whereas it has direct effects on continuing post-secondary-school education. General preschool ability is itself influenced by familial characteristics in the first years of life, suggesting one of the possible paths by which family conditions influence life-course trajectories. A set of regressions was run omitting grade failure in the childhood-age models. Father presence still predicted completing high school, and years on welfare was associated with not going beyond high school. These findings support our speculation that effects of family circumstances in middle childhood are not based solely on grade failure, but that each makes a contribution to school success.

Attendance in preschool also had beneficial effects on continuing in school, a finding that is consonant with the efficacy of preschool programs on the cognitive and scholastic functioning of disadvantaged children (Brooks-Gunn, 1990; Clarke-Stewart & Fein, 1983; Haskins, 1989; Ramey, Bryant, & Suarez, 1985). Interestingly, the majority of evaluations of preschool interventions indicate that gains made on cognitive and achievement tests are reduced during the elementary school years, to be replaced by reductions in grade-failure rates (Lazar, Darlington, Murray, Royce, & Snipper, 1982). As seen in these analyses, grade failure is a potent predictor of educational attainment (see also Cairns et al., 1989). Grade failure is not solely a measure of cognitive ability, but probably taps behavior problems, motivation, and school engagement. These less cognitive factors may explain why intelligence and achievement test-score differences between children who received preschool intervention and those who did not are reduced in the elementary school years, whereas grade-failure rates differentiate the two groups.

In addition to grade failure, the racial composition of the school made a difference, with greater proportions of Black students being associated with lower rates of high school completion. We suspect this measure is a rough proxy for a number of factors: poverty status of other students, expenditures per pupil, residence in poorer neighborhoods, higher dropout rates, and possibly social isolation from employment opportunities and role models (Coleman, 1966; Edelman & Howe, 1984; Mayer & Jencks, 1989; Wehlage, 1989; Wilson, 1991). In schools with high dropout rates and high levels of poverty, youths may have more opportunities to associate with individuals contemplating dropout (Cairns et al., 1989).

During the young adolescence period, as expected, several child characteristics were highly associated with educational attainment. The youths' own aspirations for postsecondary schooling in 1984 predicted dropping out and continuing in 1988. Of course, these aspirations themselves are a consequence of past educational history and family circumstances. As expected, becoming pregnant was a risk factor for dropping out (Ekstrom, Goertz, Pollack, & Rock, 1986; Upchurch & McCarthy, 1989). Drinking and running away from home were also associated with dropping out 4 years later. Dropping out of school may be the culmination of previous school failure, low-quality education, perceived limited opportunities, and encouragement in behaviors not conducive to school performance.

Pregnancy did not reduce the odds of obtaining postsecondary education; Black teenage mothers are more likely to go on for postsecondary schooling than are White or Hispanic young mothers (Upchurch, 1992). Although we did not look at parenthood (given that few adolescents were parents at the 17-point follow-up), Upchurch found that young mothers who graduate from high school were more likely to obtain postsecondary schooling than young women who did not become mothers but who received a graduate equivalency diploma (GED) rather than finishing regular high school. (Unfortunately, not enough of the Baltimore youth had GEDs for us to examine this issue.)

As a final note, dropout rates differ substantially for boys and girls. Part of the discrepancy is accounted for by boys' much higher rates of grade failure.[10] If boys do not drop out of high school, they are equally likely as girls to pursue higher education.

In conclusion, the childhood experiences of young adults who drop out of high school are different from those who do not. These findings speak to the importance of providing services to families of teenage mothers in the preschool years, both to the child and to the mother (Chase-Lansdale, Brooks-Gunn, & Paikoff, 1991; Clewell et al., 1989; Smith, in press). Such two-generational approaches are likely to increase education and income of mothers as well as provide school readiness skills for preschoolers (Chase-Lansdale & Brooks-Gunn, in press).

## ACKNOWLEDGMENTS

Portions of this article were presented at a conference, "Outcomes of Early Childbearing: An Appraisal of Recent Evidence," sponsored by NICHD (May, 1992, Bethesda, MD). The research reported here was supported by the Robert Wood Johnson Foundation and the Ford Foundation. The National Institute of Child Health and Human Development and the Commonwealth Fund also contributed to earlier phases of the study. Their generosity is appreciated. The research was conducted while Jeanne Brooks-Gunn was at Educational Testing Service and Guang Guo was at Princeton University. We thank Rosemary Deibler for her assistance in article preparation.

## REFERENCES

Alexander, K. L., & Entwhisle, D. R. (1988). Achievement in the first 2 years of school: Patterns and processes. *Monographs of the Society for Research in Child Development, 53* (2, Serial No. 218).

Astone, N. M., & McLanahan, S. S. (1991). Family structure, parental practices and high school completion. *American Sociological Review, 51,* 403–412.

Bane, M. J., & Ellwood, D. T. (1986). Slipping into and out of poverty: The dynamics of spells. *Journal of Human Resources, 21,* 1–23.

---

[10]These analyses do not speak to the possibility of differential predictors of educational attainment for boys and girls. Several interaction terms were entered in a set of regressions to see if differential effects of grade failure, low preschool scores, welfare receipt, and presence of father were found for boys and girls. No interaction terms were significant. However, given that the reasons for dropping out have been described as somewhat gender specific (Ekstrom et al., 1986; Upchurch & McCarthy, 1990), investigators with larger samples are urged to consider gender more explicitly.

Baydar, N., Brooks-Gunn, J., & Furstenberg, F. F., Jr. (in press). Antecedents of literacy in disadvantaged youth. *Child Development*.

Becker, G. S. (1981). *A treatise on the family*. Cambridge, MA: Harvard University Press.

Becker, G. S., & Tomes, N. (1986). Human capital and the rise and fall of families. *Journal of Labor Economics, 4*, S1–S39.

Brooks-Gunn, J. (1988). Transition to adolescence. In M. Gunnar & W. A. Collins (Eds.), *Development during transition to adolescence: Minnesota symposia on child psychology* (Vol. 21, pp. 189–208). Hillsdale, NJ: Lawrence Erlbaum Associates, Inc.

Brooks-Gunn, J. (1990). Promoting healthy development in young children: What educational interventions work? In D. E. Rogers & E. Ginzberg (Eds.), *Improving the life chances of children at risk* (pp. 125–145). Boulder, CO: Westview.

Brooks-Gunn, J., & Chase-Lansdale, P. L. (1991). Children having children: Effects on the family system. *Pediatric Annals, 20*, 467–481.

Brooks-Gunn, J., Duncan, G. J., Klebanov, P., & Sealand, N. (in press). Do neighborhoods influence child and adolescent behavior? *American Journal of Sociology*.

Brooks-Gunn, J., & Furstenberg, F. F., Jr. (1987). Continuity and change in the context of poverty: Adolescent mothers and their children. In J. J. Gallagher & C. T. Ramey (Eds.), *The malleability of children* (pp. 171–188). Baltimore: Brookes.

Brooks-Gunn, J., Phelps, E., & Elder, G. H. (1991). Studying lives through time: Secondary data analyses in developmental psychology. *Developmental Psychology, 27*, 899–910.

Bryk, A. S., & Thum, Y. M. (1989). The effects of high school organization on dropping out: An exploratory investigation. *American Educational Research Journal, 26*, 353–383.

Cairns, R. B., Cairns, B. D., Neckerman, H. J., Ferguson, L. L., & Gariepy, J.-L. (1989). Growth and aggression: I. Childhood to early adolescence. *Developmental Psychology, 25*, 320–330.

Chase-Landsale, P. L., Brooks-Gunn, J., & Paikoff, R. L. (1991). Research and programs for adolescent mothers: Missing links and future promises. *Family Relations, 40*, 396–404.

Chase-Lansdale, P. L., & Brooks-Gunn, J. (Eds.). (in press). *Escape from poverty: What makes a difference for poor children?* New York: Cambridge University Press.

Chase-Lansdale, P. L., Mott, F. L., Brooks-Gunn, J., & Phillips, D. (1991). Children of the NLSY: A unique research opportunity. *Developmental Psychology, 27*, 918–931.

Clarke-Stewart, K. A., & Fein, G. G. (1983). Early childhood programs. In P. H. Mussen & E. M. Hetherington (Eds.), *Handbook of child psychology: Vol. 4. Socialization, personality, and social development* (4th ed., pp. 918–999). New York: Wiley.

Clewell, B. C., Brooks-Gunn, J., & Benasich, A. A. (1989). Evaluating child-related outcomes of teenage parenting programs. *Family Relations, 38*, 201–209.

Coleman, J. S. (1966). *Equality of educational opportunity*. Washington, DC: U.S. Government Printing Office.

Coombs, J., & Cooley, W. W. (1968). Dropouts in high school and after high school. *American Educational Research Journal, 5*, 343–364.

Cooperative Tests and Services. (1970). *The preschool inventory: 1970 handbook* (rev. ed.). Princeton, NJ: Educational Testing Service.

Crane, J. (1991). The epidemic theory of ghettos and neighborhood effects on dropping out and teenage childbearing. *American Journal of Sociology, 69*, 1126–1159.

Duncan, G. J., Brooks-Gunn, J., & Klebanov, P. K. (in press). Economic deprivation and early-childhood development. *Child Development*.

Duncan, G. J., & Rogers, W. L. (1988). Longitudinal aspects of poverty. *Journal of Marriage and the Family, 50*, 1007–1021.

Dunn, L. M., & Dunn, L. M. (1981). *Peabody Picture Vocabulary Test* (rev. ed.). Circle Pines, MN: American Guidance Service.

Edelman, M. W., & Howe, H. (1984). *Barriers to excellence: Our children at risk*. Boston: National Coalition of Advocates for Students.

Ekdstrom, R. B., Goertz, M. E., Pollack, J. M., & Rock, D. A. (1986). Who drops out of high school and why? Findings from a national study. *Teachers College Record, 87,* 356–373.

Featherman, D. L., & Hauser, R. M. (1978). *Opportunity and change*. New York: Academic.

Featherman, D. L., Spenner, K. I., & Tsunematsu, N. (1988). Class and the socialization of children: Constancy, change, or irrelevance? In R. M. Lerner & M. Perlmutter (Eds.), *Child development in life-span perspective* (pp. 67–90). Hillsdale, NJ: Lawrence Erlbaum Associates, Inc.

Fienberg, S. E. (1980). *The analysis of cross-classified data* (2nd ed.). Cambridge, MA: MIT Press.

Fine, M. (1986). Why urban adolescents drop into and out of public high school. *Teachers College Record, 87,* 393–409.

Furstenberg, F. F., Jr. (1976). *Unplanned parenthood: The social consequences of teenage childbearing*. New York: Free Press.

Furstenberg, F. F., Jr., Brooks-Gunn, J., & Chase-Lansdale, L. (1989). Adolescent fertility and public policy. *American Psychologist, 44,* 313–320.

Furstenberg, F. F., Jr., Brooks-Gunn, J., & Morgan, S. P. (1987a). Adolescent mothers in later life. *Family Planning Perspectives, 19,* 142–151.

Furstenberg, F. F., Jr., Brooks-Gunn, J., & Morgan, S. P. (1987b). *Adolescent mothers in later life*. New York: Cambridge University Press.

Furstenberg, F. F., Jr., Hughes, M. E., & Brooks-Gunn, J. (1992). The next generation: Children of teenage mothers grow up. In M. K. Rosenheim & M. F. Testa (Eds.), *Early parenthood* (pp. 113–135). New Brunswick, NJ: Rutgers University Press.

Furstenberg, F. F., Jr., Levine, J. A., & Brooks-Gunn, J. (1990). The daughters of teenage mothers: Patterns of early childbearing in two generations. *Family Planning Perspectives, 22,* 54–61.

Furstenberg, F. F., Jr., Nord, C. W., Peterson, J. L., & Zill, N. (1983). The life course of children of divorce: Marital disruption and parental conflict. *American Sociological Review, 48,* 656–668.

Gjerde, P. F., & Block, J. (1991). Preadolescent antecedents of depressive symptomatology at age 18: A prospective study. *Journal of Youth and Adolescence, 20,* 217–232.

Haskins, R. (1989). Beyond metaphor: Efficacy of early childhood education. *American Psychologist, 44,* 274–282.

Hauser, R. M., & Featherman, D. L. (1977). *The process of stratification: Trends and analyses*. New York: Academic.

Haveman, R., & Wolfe, B. (1984). Schooling and economic well-being: The role of nonmarket effects. *Journal of Human Resources, 19,* 377–407.

Haveman, R., Wolfe, B., & Spaulding, J. (1991). Childhood events and circumstances influencing high school completion. *Demography, 28,* 133–157.

Hayes, C. D., Palmer, J. L., & Zaslow, M. E. (1990). *Who cares for America's children: Child care policy for the 1990s*. Washington, DC: National Academy Press.

Hetherington, E. M., & Arastek, J. (1988). *The impact of divorce, single parenting, and step-parenting on children*. Hillsdale, NJ: Lawrence Erlbaum Associates, Inc.

Hill, M. S., & Duncan, G. (1987). Parental family income and the socioeconomic attainment of children. *Social Science Research, 16,* 39–73.

Hofferth, S. L., & Phillips, D. A. (1987). Child care in the United States, 1970 to 1995. *Journal of Marriage and the Family, 49,* 559–571.

Hogan, D. P., & Astone, N. M. (1986). The transition to adulthood. *Annual Review of Sociology, 12,* 109–130.

Jencks, C., Bartlett, S., Corcoran, M., Crouse, J., Eaglesfield, D., Jackson, G., McClelland,

K., Meuser, P., Olneck, M., Schwartz, J., Ward, S., & Williams, J. (1979). *Who gets ahead?. The determinants of economic success in America.* New York: Basic Books.

Jessor, R., & Jessor, S. L. (1977). *Problem behavior and psychosocial development.* New York: Academic.

Kirsch, I., & Jungeblut, A. (1986). *Literacy: Profiles of America's young adults.* Princeton, NJ: Educational Testing Service.

Lazar, I., Darlington, R., Murray, H., Royce, J., & Snipper, A. (1982). Lasting effects of early education: A report from the Consortium for Longitudinal Studies. *Monographs of the Society for Research in Child Development, 47*(2–3, Serial No. 195).

Lee, V., Brooks-Gunn, J., Schnur, E., & Liaw, T. (1990). Are Head Start effects sustained? A longitudinal comparison of disadvantaged children attending Head Start, no pre-school, and other preschool programs. *Child Development, 61,* 495–507.

Lerner, R. M. (1984). *On the nature of human plasticity.* New York: Cambridge University Press.

Lerner, R., & Foch, T. T. (1987). *Biological–psychological interactions in early adolescence: A life-span perspective.* Hillsdale, NJ: Lawrence Erlbaum Associates, Inc.

Lobach, K. S. (in press). Health policy in the Family Support Act: Implications for quality of health services to children. In P. L. Chase-Lansdale & J. Brooks-Gunn (Eds.), *Escape from poverty: What makes a difference for poor children?* New York: Cambridge University Press.

Maccoby, E. E., & Martin, J. A. (1983). Socialization in the context of the family: Parent–child interaction. In P. H. Mussen & E. M. Hetherington (Eds.), *Handbook of child psychology: Vol. 4. Socialization, personality, and social development* (4th ed., pp. 1–101). New York: Wiley.

Mare, R. D. (1980). Social background and school continuation decisions. *Journal of the American Statistical Association, 74,* 295–305.

Mare, R. D., & Chen, M. D. (1986). Further evidence on sibship size and educational stratification. *American Sociological Review, 51,* 403–412.

Mayer, S. E., & Jencks, C. C. (1989). Growing up in poor neighborhoods: How much does it matter? *Science, 243,* 1441–1446.

McCormick, M. C., & Brooks-Gunn, J. (1989). Health care for children and adolescents. In H. Freeman & S. Levine (Eds.), *Handbook of medical sociology* (pp. 347–380). Englewood Cliffs, NJ: Prentice-Hall.

McLanahan, S. (1985). Family structure and the reproduction of poverty. *American Journal of Sociology, 90,* 873–901.

McLanahan, S., & Garfinkel, I. (1990). Single mothers, the underclass, and social policy. *Annals of the American Academy of Political and Social Science, 501,* 92–105.

Mensch, B. S., & Kandel, D. B. (1988). Dropping out of high school and drug involvement. *Sociology of Education, 61,* 95–113.

Natriello, G. (Ed.). (1987). *School dropouts: Patterns and policies.* New York: Teachers College Press.

Orfield, G., & Ashkinaze, C. (1991). *The closing door: Conservative policy and Black opportunity.* Chicago: University of Chicago Press.

Peterson, J. L., & Zill, N. (1986). Marital disruption, parent–child relationships, and behavior problems in children. *Journal of Marriage and the Family, 48,* 295–307.

Polit, D. F. (1989). Effects of comprehensive programs for teenage parents: Five years after Project Redirection. *Family Planning Perspectives, 21,* 164–169.

Ramey, C. T., Bryant, D. M., & Suarez, T. M. (1985). Preschool compensatory education and the modifiability of intelligence: A critical review. In D. Detterman (Ed.), *Current topics in human intelligence.* Norwood, NJ: Ablex.

Rumberger, R. W. (1983). Dropping out of high school: The influence of race, sex, and family background. *American Educational Research Journal, 20,* 199–220.

Rumberger, R. W. (1987). High-school dropouts: A review of issues and evidence. *Review of Educational Research, 57*, 101–121.

Sandefur, G. D., McLanahan, S., & Wojtkiewicz, R. A. (1992). The effects of parental marital status during adolescence on high school graduation. *Social Forces, 71*, 103–121.

Sewell, W. H., & Hauser, R. M. (1975). *Education, occupation and earnings: Achievement in the early career.* New York: Academic.

Shavit, Y., & Featherman, D. L. (1988). Schooling, tracking, and teenage intelligence. *Sociology of Education, 61*, 42–51.

Smith, S. (in press). Two-generational program models: A new strategy and direction for future research. In P. L. Chase-Lansdale & J. Brooks-Gunn (Eds.), *Escape from poverty: What makes a difference for poor children?* New York: Cambridge University Press.

Stafford, F. P. (1986). Women's work, sibling competition, and children's school performance. *American Economic Review, 77*, 972–980.

StatSci. (1991). *S-PLUS for DOS, reference manual.* Seattle: Statistical Science.

Stattin, H., & Magnusson, D. (1990). *Pubertal maturation in female development.* Hillsdale, NJ: Lawrence Erlbaum Associates, Inc.

Steinberg, L. (1987). Single parents, step-parents, and susceptibility of adolescents to antisocial peer pressure. *Child Development, 58*, 269–275.

Stroup, A. L., & Robins, L. N. (1972). Elementary school predictors of high school dropout among black males. *Sociology of Education, 45*, 212–222.

Upchurch, D. M. (1992, May). *Early schooling and childbearing experience: Implications for post-secondary school attendance.* Paper presented at a National Institutes of Child Health and Human Development conference on Outcomes of Early Childbearing, Bethesda, MD.

Upchurch, D. M., & McCarthy, J. (1989). Adolescent childbearing and high school completion in the 1980s: Have things changed? *Family Planning Perspectives, 21*, 199–202.

Upchurch, D. M., & McCarthy, J. (1990). The timing of first birth and high school completion. *American Sociological Review, 55*, 224–234.

Wachs, T. D., & Gruen, G. E. (1982). *Early experience and human development.* New York: Plenum.

Wehlage, G. G. (1989). Dropping out: Can schools be expected to prevent it? In L. Weis, E. Farrar, & H. G. Petrie (Eds.), *Dropouts from school: Issues, dilemmas, and solutions* (pp. 1–19). Albany: State University of New York Press.

Wehlage, G. G., & Rutter, R. A. (1986). Dropping out: How much do schools contribute to the problem? *Teachers College Record, 87*, 374–392.

Werner, E. E., & Smith, R. S. (1982). *Vulnerable but not invincible: A longitudinal study of resilient children and youth.* New York: McGraw-Hill.

Willett, J. B., & Singer, J. D. (1991, Winter). From whether to when: New methods for studying student dropout and teacher attrition. *Review of Educational Research, 61*, 407–450.

Wilson, W. J. (1987). *The truly disadvantaged: The inner city, the underclass, and public policy.* Chicago: University of Chicago Press.

Wilson, W. J. (1991). Studying inner-city social dislocations: The challenge of public agenda research. *American Sociological Review, 56*, 1–14.

Received January 6, 1992
Revision received December 15, 1992
Accepted December 15, 1992

# Acknowledgments

Jessor, Richard. "Risk Behavior in Adolescence: A Psychological Framework for Understanding and Action." *Developmental Review* 12 (1992): 374–90. Reprinted with the permission of Academic Press, Inc.

Compas, Bruce E., David C. Howell, Vicky Phares, Rebecca A. Williams, and Normand Ledoux. "Parent and Child Stress and Symptoms: An Integrative Analysis." *Developmental Psychology* 25 (1989): 550–59. Copyright 1992 by the American Psychological Association. Reprinted by permission.

Fisher, Celia B., Ann Higgins-D'Alessandro, Jean-Marie B. Rau, Tara L. Kuther, and Susan Belanger. "Referring and Reporting Research Participants at Risk: Views from Urban Adolescents." *Child Development* 67 (1996): 2086–2100. Reprinted with the permission of the Society for Research in Child Development.

Levitt, Mira Zamansky, Robert L. Selman, and Julius B. Richmond. "The Psychosocial Foundations of Early Adolescents' High-Risk Behavior: Implications for Research and Practice." *Journal of Research on Adolescence* 1 (1991): 349–78. Reprinted with the permission of Lawrence Erlbaum Associates, Inc.

Werner, Emmy E. "High-Risk Children in Young Adulthood: A Longitudinal Study from Birth to 32 Years." *American Journal of Orthopsychiatry* 19 (1989): 72–81. Copyright 1989 by the American Orthopsychiatric Association, Inc. Reprinted by permission.

Noam, Gil G., Katherine Paget, Gayle Valiant, Sophie Borst, and John Bartok. "Conduct and Affective Disorders in Developmental Perspective: A Systematic Study of Adolescent Psychopathology." *Development and Psychopathology* 6 (1994): 519–32. Reprinted with the permission of Cambridge University Press.

Leadbeater, Bonnie J., Sidney J. Blatt, and Donald M. Quinlan. "Gender-Linked Vulnerabilities to Depressive Symptoms, Stress, and Problem Behaviors in Adolescents." *Journal of Research on Adolescence* 5 (1995): 1–29. Reprinted with the permission of Lawrence Erlbaum Associates, Inc.

Scott-Jones, Diane, and Anne B. White. "Correlates of Sexual Activity in Early Adolescence." *Journal of Early Adolescence* 10 (1990): 221–38. Reprinted with the permission of Sage Publications Inc.

Ensminger, Margaret E. "Sexual Activity and Problem Behaviors among Black, Urban Adolescents." *Child Development* 61 (1990): 2032–46. Reprinted with the permission of the Society for Research in Child Development.

Treboux, Dominique, and Nancy A. Busch-Rossnagel. "Age Differences in Parent and Peer Influences on Female Sexual Behavior." *Journal of Research on Adolescence* 5 (1995): 469–87. Reprinted with the permission of Lawrence Erlbaum Associates, Inc.

Rimberg, Helene M., and Robin J. Lewis. "Older Adolescents and AIDS: Correlates of Self-Reported Safer Sex Practices." *Journal of Research on Adolescence* 4 (1994): 453–64. Reprinted with the permission of Lawrence Erlbaum Associates, Inc.

Bachman, Jerald G., and John Schulenberg. "How Part-Time Work Intensity Relates to Drug Use, Problem Behavior, Time Use, and Satisfaction Among High School Seniors: Are These Consequences or Merely Correlates?" *Developmental Psychology* 29 (1993): 220–35. Copyright 1993 by the American Psychological Association. Reprinted by permission.

Windle, Michael, Carol Miller-Tutzauer, and Donna Domenico. "Alcohol Use, Suicidal Behavior, and Risky Activities Among Adolescents." *Journal of Research on Adolescence* 2 (1992): 317–30. Reprinted with the permission of Lawrence Erlbaum Associates, Inc.

Turner, Rebecca A., Charles E. Irwin, and Susan G. Millstein. "Family Structure, Family Processes, and Experimenting With Substances During Adolescence." *Journal of Research on Adolescence* 1 (1991): 93–106. Reprinted with the permission of Lawrence Erlbaum Associates, Inc.

Kandel, Denise B., and Ping Wu. "The Contributions of Mothers and Fathers to the Intergenerational Transmission of Cigarette Smoking in Adolescence." *Journal of Research on Adolescence* 5 (1995): 225–51. Reprinted with the permission of Lawrence Erlbaum Associates, Inc.

Maguin, Eugene, Robert A. Zucker, and Hiram E. Fitzgerald. "The Path to Alcohol Problems Through Conduct Problems: A Family-Based Approach to Very Early Intervention with Risk." *Journal of Research on Adolescence* 4 (1994): 249–69. Reprinted with the permission of Lawrence Erlbaum Associates, Inc.

Caspi, Avshalom, Donald Lynam, Terrie E. Moffitt, and Phil A. Silva. "Unraveling Girls' Delinquency: Biological, Dispositional, and Contextual Contributions to Adolescent Misbehavior." *Developmental Psychology* 29 (1993): 19–30. Copyright 1993 by the American Psychological Association. Reprinted by permission.

Graham, Sandra, Cynthia Hudley, and Estella Williams. "Attributional and Emotional Determinants of Aggression Among African-American and Latino Young Adolescents." *Developmental Psychology* 28 (1992): 731–40. Copyright 1992 by the American Psychological Association. Reprinted by permission.

Adams, Gerald R., Thomas Gullotta, and Mary Anne Clancy. "Homeless Adolescents: A Descriptive Study of Similarities and Differences Between Runaways and Throwaways." *Adolescence* 20 (1985): 715–24. Reprinted with permission of Libra Publishers, Inc.

Brooks-Gunn, Jeanne, Guang Guo, and Frank F. Furstenberg Jr. "Who Drops Out of and Who Continues Beyond High School? A 20-Year Follow-Up of Black Urban Youth." *Journal of Research on Adolescence* 3 (1993): 271–94. Reprinted with the permission of Lawrence Erlbaum Associates, Inc.